BRANDYWINE

A Military History of the Battle that Lost Philadelphia but
Saved America, September 11, 1777

Michael C. Harris

Savas Beatie
California

Library of Congress Cataloging-in-Publication Data

Harris, Michael C., 1978-

Brandywine: A Military History of the Battle That Lost Philadelphia but Saved America, September 11, 1777 / Michael C. Harris. —First edition.

pages cm

Includes bibliographical references and index.

ISBN 978-1-61121-162-7

1. Brandywine, Battle of, Pa., 1777. 2. Pennsylvania--History--Revolution, 1775-1783—Campaigns. I. Title.

E241.B8H37 2014

974.8'03—dc23

2013044299

SB

Published by

Savas Beatie LLC

989 Governor Drive, Suite 102

El Dorado Hills, CA 95762

Phone: 916-941-6896 / (E-mail) sales@savasbeatie.com

05 04 03 02 01   5 4 3 2 1

First edition, first printing

Savas Beatie titles are available at special discounts for bulk purchases in the United States by corporations, institutions, and other organizations. For more details, contact Special Sales, P.O. Box 4527, El Dorado Hills, CA 95762, or please e-mail us at sales@savasbeatie.com, or visit our website at www.savasbeatie.com for additional information.

Proudly published, printed, and warehoused in the United States of America.

To the men of both sides
who served along the Brandywine

Table of Contents

Table of Contents (continued)

Table of Contents (continued)

Table of Contents (continued)

*Maps have been placed throughout the book
for the convenience of the reader.*

Preface

An Oft-Overlooked Battle

Until recently, Americans have been preoccupied with victories on the battlefield, and have preferred not to be reminded about past mistakes. Much more time and effort has been spent, for example, studying American victories during the Revolution such as Trenton, Princeton, Saratoga, and Yorktown, than defeats. The lack of study or deep interest in the September 11, 1777, battle of Brandywine is perhaps a reflection of our interest in victories and "turnings points." The combat along the Brandywine was neither.

The Brandywine defeat has been relegated to a minor role in American historiography. This lack of attention is both wholly undeserved and rather shocking given that more troops fought along the Brandywine (nearly 30,000) than during any other battle of the entire American Revolution, its 11 hours of fighting make it the longest single-day battle of the war, and it covered more square miles (10) than any other engagement. Invariably people are surprised when they hear those three facts about Brandywine. And yet, it remains one of the least known or understood large-scale engagements of the Revolution.

The Early Context

Most early studies of the Brandywine were written by area residents who over-emphasized the local role in the battle, and in so doing developed a host of unsubstantiated "facts" that have assumed in some cases near-mythological proportions. Well-researched histories with the battle as the primary focus are few and far between.

The earliest accounts were written within days of the fighting by participants from both sides. British accounts are almost all recitations of battle-related events. Several important broader themes, however, run through the early American accounts. Some reflect the belief that a new form of government would come out of the battle and eventually the war. Others reflect the central role religion played in the lives of Americans in the late eighteenth century, with divine providence seen guiding all events. A general order published soon after the battle supported these notions when Washington proclaimed to his troops: "Altho' the event of that day . . . was not so favorable as could be wished, the General . . . has full confidence that in another Appeal to Heaven . . . we shall prove successful."[1] Some American officers, like Brig. Gen. George Weedon, retained their optimism despite having lost the battle. "Such another victory [for the British] would establish the Rights of America," announced Weedon, "and I wish them the honor of the Field again on the same terms."[2]

Over time, other accounts of the September 1777 battle clouded these contemporary recollections and helped shove Brandywine into the shadows. Later histories of the war focused on a few high-profile individuals whose reputations had the power to arouse their fellow citizens, and not research-based studies of the actual event. They presented the Revolution as an event of importance for all mankind due to the emergence of the new republic—a great human event thanks to God's guidance.[3]

For much of the nineteenth century, local and state history emphasized the region's role in shaping the national republic.[4] Works on the Revolution and the battle of Brandywine presented dramatic hero-centric epics during the period of idealization in American historiography. According to Ernst Breisach, these heroes became the manifestations of national character.[5] And with these dramatizations, myths of a different variety took form and root.

1 John D. Fitzpatrick, ed., *The Writings of George Washington from the Original Manuscript Sources 1745-1799* (Washington, D.C., 1933), Vol. 9, 211.

2 Brigadier General George Weedon to John Page, September 11, 1777, Chicago Historical Society.

3 Ernst Breisach, *Historiography: Ancient, Medieval and Modern* (Chicago, 2007), 229.

4 Ibid., 227.

5 Ibid., 256.

Mythologies

Jacob Neff's 1845 history of the American Revolution devoted part of a chapter to the battle of Brandywine. Neff's work was heavy on poetic prose but light on details, focusing instead on American gallantry and the defeat of the invaders. "With . . . great disadvantage on the part of the Americans (who were also much inferior in numbers and in arms)," proclaimed Neff, "the armies rushed together in fierce and desperate conflict."[6] In fact, the Americans were not outnumbered, and they were armed no worse than the men serving under William Howe. Neff's work also discussed the role of the Marquis de Lafayette and his "gallant" wounding, and heaped praise on Nathanael Greene:

> General Greene came up with the reserve, and, by a singularly skilful maneuver, opened his ranks for the fugitives, and after they had passed through, like a father protecting his children, closed his ranks behind them, checked the pursuit of the enemy by the fire of his artillery, and completely covered the retreat. This, with many other splendid achievements, invests the character of Greene with an air of romance, which will always be felt by the American people, and elicit unbounded praises from the unborn Homers of our country.[7]

George Bancroft's 1866 history of the United States includes a military study of the battle and campaign. Although a monumental achievement for its time, Bancroft's study was riddled with errors and continued the theme of hero worship: "As Washington rode up and down his lines the loud shouts of his men witnessed their love and confidence, and as he spoke to them in earnest and cheering words they clamored for battle."[8]

Bancroft's book also mentions the engagement of Hessian troops, and refers to "the vigorous charge of the Hessian and British grenadiers, who vied with each other in fury as they ran forward with the bayonet."[9] From the time of the Revolution through many generations thereafter, Americans

6 Jacob Neff, *The Army and Navy of America: Containing a View of the Heroic Adventures, Battles, Naval Engagements, Remarkable Incidents, and Glorious Achievements in the Cause of Freedom* (Philadelphia, 1845), 336.

7 Ibid., 337.

8 George Bancroft, *History of the United States, From the Discovery of the American Continent* (Boston, 1866), vol. 9, 396.

9 Ibid., 397. The actual role of the Hessians at Brandywine is discussed in detail elsewhere in this book.

remained genuinely angry that King George hired Germanic troops to fight against them. As a result, most histories of the Revolution and the battle overemphasized the role—real or imagined—of those troops.

An 1881 history of Chester County, Pennsylvania, includes another basic account of the battle that includes several incorrect and undocumented claims. The study perpetuates the notion, for example, that Americans went into the battle with subpar weaponry. This belief lived on for most of the next century even though there is no primary evidence to support this claim.[10] The Chester County history also made excuses for Washington's failure that day, and elevated a local citizen named Thomas Cheyney to hero status for "saving" the American army.[11]

The Country and Interpretations Evolve

By the end of the nineteenth century, America faced several changes that influenced how the story of the Revolution was told. The transformation from a collection of rural economies into an industrialized nation after the Civil War tarnished the idealistic view many Americans had about their nation. The earlier period had glorified war and emphasized the greatness of heroes such as Washington and Lafayette, but the carnage wrought by the Civil War went a long way toward eliminating that mindset. The postwar industrialization, coupled with the massive influx of European immigrants brought class struggles to the forefront of the American consciousness. The writing of history started to emphasize the role of the common man rather than heroes or the upper class.

A series of historical markers were placed on the Brandywine battlefield in 1915. The dedication ceremonies included a presentation on the history of the battle by a Professor Smith Burnham. The professor's speech continued to note certain heroes, though in a much subdued manner. For example, he emphasized the minor role played in the battle by the young John Marshall, future chief justice of the United States. The importance of the common man theme to the ultimate victory and formation of the country made a forceful appearance when he focused on a handful of local participants. Religion played no role in this account.

---

10 J. Smith Futhey and Gilbert Cope, *History of Chester County Pennsylvania* (Philadelphia, 1881), 72.

11 Ibid. Both Washington's lapses and Thomas Cheyney's contributions (or lack thereof) to the battle are discussed elsewhere at length.

Unfortunately, the address was not supported by documentation and misrepresented several basic details of the battle. One of the people chronicled included a local "old man" who, claimed Professor Burnham, guided Washington to the northern sector of the fighting.[12] Burnham's address also emphasized Thomas Cheyney's supposed role in notifying Washington of Howe's flank march, and in so doing, saved the Patriot army from annihilation. "One cannot help thinking that if there had been more men with the spirit of Squire Cheyney between Kennett Square and the forks of the Brandywine," said the professor, "the history of the battle might have read very differently."[13] Burnham continued the "commoners as heroes" theme when he concluded that "the eleven thousand ragged farmers who tried to hold this field against the flower of the British army were the men who made this republic possible."[14]

Up to this point in American historiography, the heroes of the American Revolution, men like Washington, Greene, and Lafayette, had been glorified as great men. But as the American Progressive movement gained prominence in the early- to mid-twentieth century, the emphasis shifted to social history. As the role of the common man gained ground and the emphasis on heroes faded, war was interpreted along socioeconomic rather than political or military themes. With less emphasis on military themes, nearly all the accounts about the Brandywine penned during this period were written by residents of the region. No scholarly histories of the battle were published during this period.

Robert Bruce produced a short self-published study of the region and battle in 1922, but like so many similar accounts it was largely undocumented, full of factual mistakes, and perpetuated myths.[15] The Continental Army's lack of training at this stage of the war was also a theme in Bruce's narrative.

The 150th anniversary of the battle in 1927 witnessed the publication of several short local histories of the battle. Like most works of this period, they were folksy unsubstantiated narratives. Most of these accounts, however, offered significant value for historians by identifying various property owners scattered about the Brandywine battlefield. As might be expected, the story of how Cheyney saved Washington's army was

---

12 Smith Burnham, "The Story of the Battle of Brandywine," *Second Report of the Pennsylvania Historical Commission* (Harrisburg, 1918), 41.

13 Ibid., 39-40.

14 Ibid., 42.

15 Robert Bruce, *Brandywine: The Battle at Chadds Ford and Birmingham Meeting House, in Adjoining Parts of Chester and Delaware Counties, Pennsylvania, September 11, 1777* (Clinton, NY, 1922), 27.

prominent in these narratives. "Many of the descendents of Old Squire Cheyney are living in this session today," claimed one author, "and proud may they be of him because through his information Washington's entire army was perhaps saved from capture."[16] Most also gave credit to the soldiers of the feeble American army despite their loss by stating, for example, that "[a]lthough a defeat for the Americans it showed courage when one considers the Americans lacked arms and equipment and discipline."[17]

Partial Correctives

Christopher Ward's well-received 1952 history of the American Revolution included a chapter on the battle of the Brandywine. Unlike nearly all prior accounts it was documented and included an excellent geographic description of the region. Given the battle's complexity it is not surprising that it was also not entirely accurate, and also persisted in retelling the Cheyney story. [18] In an effort to show the steadfast bravery displayed by the American soldiers, Ward emphasized the hubris and professionalism of the British troops: "They came on with the arrogant assurance that marked the disciplined troops of that period of formal, dress-parade warfare."[19] He also credited American fighting ability when he wrote (with some embellishment), "Though they had been as badly beaten as any army could be without being entirely destroyed, there had been no panic."[20]

As the middle of the twentieth century approached, less emphasis was placed on socioeconomic aspects of the war and more on the collective effort of the American people to overcome struggles through time. John Reed's 1965 study of the Philadelphia Campaign offers a single chapter on Brandywine that reflects this evolution. Reed's account is a straightforward, if rather dry military study based upon several primary accounts. It also constitutes one of the earliest reliable studies of the campaign. For example, Reed was the first to propose that the Hessians played little or no role in the

---

16 Wilmer W. MacElree, Charles W. Heathcote, and Christian C. Sanderson, "Battle of Brandywine," *150th Anniversary of the Battle of Brandywine* (the Brandywine Memorial Association, 1927), n.p.

17 Ibid.

18 Christopher Ward, *The War of the Revolution* (New York, 1952), Vol. 1, 346.

19 Ibid., 350.

20 Ibid., 354.

battle ("The Hessians . . . were only lightly engaged for the most part"[21]), contravening the long-held belief that the German troops were heavily involved in the fighting.

However, Reed's interpretation contains some fallacies, including the recurring Cheyney story, and paid little attention to the social aspects of the battle, such as the effects on the civilian population. Reed's treatment represents the overcoming oppression theme: "Though Brandywine was admittedly an American defeat, it had stunned Howe by its fierceness, and gave the Americans spirit."[22] Reed's book was the first in a series of studies over the next couple decades that focused almost exclusively on the military aspects of the campaign and the battle. The bicentennial of American independence in 1976 sparked a renewed interest in the American Revolution.

The first book-length treatment of the battle itself arrived in 1976 with the publication of Samuel S. Smith's *The Battle of Brandywine*. Smith's well-researched effort is based on numerous primary accounts. He was the first historian to analyze and interpret the various conflicting reports that poured into Washington's headquarters that day, and he was also one of the first to debunk many of the myths of the battle. In fact, Smith did not even mention the story of Cheyney warning Washington about Howe's approach. Unfortunately, Smith credited the Hessians with more battlefield success than they deserved when he wrote, "Stone's regiment had just passed the summit of the hill and was moving slightly down the front slope to align with the left of Stirling's division, when the Hessian grenadiers struck."[23] Despite these minor lapses, Smith's work is solid and deserved a wider audience. Unfortunately, it was self-published and not widely available, so few students of the war are even familiar with its existence. The unfortunate result is that most of the subsequent writing on the Brandywine battle continued to rely upon earlier, less well researched, accounts.

In 1977, one year after the appearance of Smith's solid study, John Pancake devoted part of a chapter to the Brandywine engagement in his book *1777: The Year of the Hangman*. Although supported by notes, Pancake's monograph is not well researched and contains more than its share of inaccuracies. It is also evident that Pancake was not familiar with the geography of the region when he penned his book. Pancake's *1777* includes

---

21 John F. Reed, *Campaign to Valley Forge: July 1, 1777-December 19, 1777* (Philadelphia, 1965), 140.

22 Ibid.

23 Samuel S. Smith, *The Battle of Brandywine* (Monmouth Beach, NJ, 1976), 17.

the tale of local farmer Cheyney, and the unsupported assertion that memories of Long Island haunted Washington.[24]

Little would be written about Brandywine again until 1990 and the appearance of W. J. Wood's *Battles of the Revolutionary War: 1775-1781*. Wood's account includes an undocumented chapter on the battle. While focusing heavily on its military aspects, Wood also found space to recount the tale of Thomas Cheyney.[25] The text contains numerous mistakes and questionable interpretations. For example, Wood incorrectly states that General de Borre's brigade (part of Sullivan's division) constituted the extreme right flank of the new American position on Birmingham Hill.[26] He also claimed Washington arrived on the far right in time to help save the American position on Birmingham Hill, even though there is no documentation of Washington ever doing so.[27] Unfortunately, Wood also assigns William Maxwell the role that Nathanael Greene's division played at the end of the battle.[28] Wood's easy enjoyable prose tends to cover up such inaccuracies.

A few years later in 1993, David Martin wrote a chapter on the Brandywine in his study *The Philadelphia Campaign: June 1777-July 1778*. Although his book is well written and generally accurate, it is also bereft of citations. Martin's account focuses heavily on the military aspects of the battle, but the Cheyney tale once again pops up.[29] Martin, too, incorrectly gives credit to the Hessian grenadiers for helping break up Sullivan's division.[30] It is unlikely Martin was overly familiar with the battlefield terrain for he asserts the British could see Nathanael Greene south of Dilworth, which would have been impossible.[31]

The Brandywine chapter found in Gregory Edgar's 1998 study *The Philadelphia Campaign: 1777-1778* incorporates several primary quotations, but does not include proper citations. Edgar included the Thomas Cheyney story yet again: "He was a patriot, lived in the area, and had been out on his own doing some scouting all morning. The . . . British flanking column had

---

24 John S. Pancake, *1777: The Year of the Hangman* (Tuscaloosa, AL, 1977), 170.

25 W. J. Wood, *Battles of the Revolutionary War 1775-1781* (Cambridge, MA, 1990), 100.

26 Ibid., 107.

27 Ibid., 109.

28 Ibid., 111.

29 David G. Martin, *The Philadelphia Campaign: June 1777-July 1778* (Conshohocken, PA, 1993), 60-1.

30 Ibid., 64-5.

31 Ibid., 69-70.

seen him and fired at him."[32] The account includes several "facts" that are misleading and undocumented. It also attributed the rout of Sullivan's division to one of the battalions of Hessian grenadiers, despite the fact that the Hessians were not engaged (the British Brigade of Guards accomplished the feat).[33] Edgar also claimed that Greene marched his division four miles to the right of the army, his final stand took place in Sandy Hollow, and that Hessians attacked that final American line; none of these claims are true.[34]

The most recent treatment of the battle (and only the second of book-length after Smith's self-published effort in 1976) is Bruce Mowday's 2002 book *September 11, 1777: Washington's Defeat at Brandywine Dooms Philadelphia*. A local newspaper reporter, Mowday's study offers no new interpretations and essentially consists of a recounting of all the myths, tales, and legends of the battle that had made an appearance over the previous two centuries. Mowday's version pushes the envelope on the Cheyney myth a step further by crediting the outcome of the entire battle to Cheyney's actions: "Over two centuries Squire Cheyney has emerged as a folk hero in the Brandywine Valley. Cheyney risked his life to warn the American army of the British movements."[35] Mowday's text also perpetuates the glorification of the Hessian role in the afternoon fighting: "Hazen's regiment was protecting Stirling's left but was driven off by the charge of the Hessian grenadiers."[36]

It was not until 2006 that a well-documented history of the battle replete with eyewitness accounts appeared in the form of Thomas McGuire's *Philadelphia Campaign: Brandywine and the Fall of Philadelphia*. Nearly one-third of the first installment of this two-volume study is devoted to combat along the Brandywine. McGuire is both a long-time resident of the region that includes the battlefield and a trained historian. He unfolds almost the entire story through the eyes of the participants, interjecting little of his own judgment or analysis. By using a primary account by a British officer and

32 Gregory T. Edgar, *The Philadelphia Campaign: 1777-1778* (Bowie, MD, 1998), 24.

33 Ibid., 30.

34 Ibid., 34-5.

35 Bruce E. Mowday, *September 11, 1777: Washington's Defeat at Brandywine Dooms Philadelphia* (Shippensburg, PA, 2002), 4.

36 Ibid., 125. In 2003, Stephen R. Taaffe published *The Philadelphia Campaign, 1777-1778* (University Press of Kansas, 2003). It is a well-researched overall primer on the campaign. Unfortunately, it has few useful maps and does not offer any new or thought-provoking analysis or interpretations. The entire Brandywine battle, which includes the Thomas Cheyney story and an error-filled accounting of Nathanael Greene's evening stand and the final British attack, is covered in just 14 pages.

official casualty data, McGuire demolished the myth of significant participation by the Hessian grenadiers.[37] His treatment of the Cheyney story was also tempered. After providing facts about the Pennsylvanian, he notes that Cheyney's role, real or imagined, remains one of the great mysteries of the battle: "Sometime in the middle of the day, having received specific information of the flank movement from someone credible, *possibly* [emphasis added] Squire Cheyney, Washington sent a terse and impatient note to Col. Theodorick Bland."[38]

A New Study

Given that more than two centuries have passed since the Battle of Brandywine, it is surprising that so little has been written about the engagement, and that so much of what has been written is wrong or myth-mongering. There are many factors at play that make it difficult to relate this part of the war accurately and well. The lead up to the battle, as well as the fighting that took place on both fronts was complex, and many of the records for both sides are either missing or were never compiled in the first place. This is especially true for the Continental army. The lack of attention by historians and writers from outside the region allowed locals through the centuries to develop and embellish stories that we now know are either but partially true or complete myths spun from whole cloth.

About nine years ago, I was hired to serve as the museum educator at Brandywine Battlefield State Historic Site. At the time, I was well versed in Civil War history but considered myself only an amateur student of the American Revolution. I was thus greatly disappointed when I discovered there was no reliable book on one of the most remarkable battles of the entire Revolution. This, in turn, led me to embark on the long voyage of research and writing that led to the book you are now reading.

Two things in particular drove me to prepare and publish my work. First, Thomas McGuire published the first volume of his monumental history of the Philadelphia campaign in 2006. McGuire is a meticulous researcher who spent time delving into repositories in Great Britain. His publication contained a considerable section on the battle of the Brandywine, and it was widely hoped it would become the quintessential

37 Thomas J. McGuire, *Philadelphia Campaign: Brandywine and the Fall of Philadelphia* (Mechanicsburg, PA, 2006), Vol. 1, 208.
38 Ibid., 189.

study on the battle. Unfortunately, it lacks detailed maps, which are essential for understanding military history (and especially something complex like Brandywine) and does not include an order of battle. McGuire's research is outstanding and has been very helpful in pointing me in the direction of quality sources. My own work is thus meant not to replace his fine book, but to enhance what he has done and then take it one step further.

I realized that same year that I could not advance my employment position at the park without a Master's degree. I decided to pursue an M.A. in military history at the American Military University, with a concentration in the American Revolution. Every paper I wrote for any course was related (somehow) to the Brandywine combat. This forced me to pursue aspects of the campaign and battle I would otherwise have not considered.

Since those heady days, I was furloughed from my park position, became a high school social studies teacher, and completed my Master's degree. Nevertheless, the battle of the Brandywine remained embedded in my thoughts. My Master's thesis deals with its military aspects. Length constraints forced me to leave out any analysis of the larger campaign, civilian accounts, historiographical discussions, and detailed terrain analysis. Thankfully, Savas Beatie has allowed a more full exploration of the campaign and the battle I always felt was lacking in the thesis.

Like every book, I am certain mistakes of fact and other errors have crept into mine, and any that have are of my own making. This work contains statements and interpretations that will not sit well with many in the Brandywine community. My treatment relies heavily upon primary source material, some of it unused in this manner until the publication of my book. If I could not corroborate a story with an eyewitness or contemporary account, I make that clear in a footnote and refuse to weave it into the story as gospel. Like anyone who wants only the truth, I welcome challenges to my interpretation, and any news about the unearthing of additional documentation that may otherwise alter the telling of the remarkable story of that one day along the Brandywine Creek in a September long ago.

Acknowledgments

An undertaking of this magnitude requires the assistance of many people. If I fail to include your name, please know I appreciate deeply your help in making this book a reality.

I would like to collectively thank the staffs at the following repositories: the Historical Society of Pennsylvania, the Chester County Historical Society, the Library of Congress, the National Archives, the Chicago Historical Society, the William Clements Library, the British Library, the

Historical Society of Delaware, Durham University in England, the Princeton University Library, the Canadian Archives, and Alnwick Castle.

I would like to personally thank one person in particular: Kathie Ludwig, the faithful librarian at the David Library of the American Revolution, assisted me in many ways over the years. More than once she helped me track down an elusive source, and she was the first to introduce me to Google Books.

The latter is an amazing source I recommend to all researchers. This use of technology allowed me to locate and download a large number of eighteenth-century sources (and other out of print books) that would have otherwise been difficult and expensive to obtain, as did www.archive.org. A more recent online source, www.fold3.com, managed by the National Archives, makes it possible to perform a keyword search in Revolutionary War pension files and the Pennsylvania archives. Lastly, the website www.wardepartmentpapers.org is also an excellent source for keyword searching those invaluable documents. As wonderful as technology can be, however, there is still something special about perusing the actual book, so I purchased many of these sources to have them handy on my shelf.

Two fellow historians took the time to debate the battle with me and show me locations associated with the campaign with which they were familiar. I met award-winning author and Revolutionary War historian Arthur Lefkowitz several years ago when he visited the Brandywine for a tour with some colleagues. Our friendship grew out of that meeting, and he took the time one Saturday several summers ago to show my wife and me around northern New Jersey where several actions took place early in the campaign. Arthur's knowledge of the war is broad and deep, and he is always willing to share what he knows. Thank you. The other man to whom I owe a great debt is Thomas McGuire. I met Tom before I worked at the Brandywine, but our friendship did not blossom until my employment there. In the early years, when I was still trying to figure out the complexities of Brandywine, an e-mail to Tom always resulted in an answer or a source that might provide the answer. On several occasions Tom took the time to drive me around southeastern Pennsylvania, following the routes of the armies during the campaign. Tom, I cannot thank you enough.

Several living historians from the eighteenth-century community assisted me along the way. Rick Keller and Ernie Cowan explained the inner workings of the Ferguson rifle and the struggles of Patrick Ferguson better than any book could hope to do. Joyful was the day they gave me the opportunity to fire one of their reproduction Fergusons.

Long-time friend Don Gallagher also warrants a thank you. Early in life, Don helped to instill in me the value of reading history. We have re-enacted together for years, but I will always value my friendship with Don more for our vigorous discussions of new books and theories on history.

Several people read chapters or the entire manuscript and provided constructive criticism that improved my work. They include Thomas McGuire, Mike Jessberger, Wayne Todd, Glenn Williams, Bill Welsch, and Arthur Lefkowitz.

I would also be remiss if I did not thank the talented staff at Savas Beatie. My developmental editor, Rob Ayer, immensely improved the manuscript and helped bring the project to fruition, as did Alexandra Maria Savas's copyediting. Sarah Keeney assisted in various ways throughout the project as well, as did Lee Merideth, who had the patience to read through the manuscript and create the book's index. Another man with a great deal of patience is Hal Jespersen, who created the wonderful maps that accompany the text. With the two of us being on opposite sides of the country and communicating through email, getting the maps the way I wanted them was quite an ordeal. Thank you for your perseverance, Hal. A big thank-you also goes to Managing Director Theodore P. Savas, who believed in my vision and saw that my dream became a reality. Ted's patience with the manuscript, thought-provoking discussions, and helpful suggestions materially improved the book.

Lastly, I would be remiss if I did not thank my wife. Over the years she has endured more than should be asked of a spouse. From volunteering on the re-enactment weekends at the Brandywine, to helping find sources in various repositories, to encouraging my horrible habit of buying more and more books for the shelves, to reading everything I have written and providing helpful comments, she has always been there. All the hours I have put into this over the years have been deducted from time I could and would have otherwise spent with her. Thank you, and I love you.

Note on Sources and Methods

This work relies heavily on primary source material. Spelling and grammar in the eighteenth century would not pass muster in any classroom today. However, to preserve and instill the flavor of the period, I have refrained from correcting sentence structure and misspellings when directly quoting them. I also have avoided the use of "sic," which interrupts the flow of the narrative. Though a united Germany did not exist in 1777, both "German" and "Hessian" are used interchangeably to identify the various Germanic troops who served with Howe's army.

Prelude to the Campaign of 1777

A World War and Imperial Angst

The American Revolution was the direct result of a global conflict that ended twelve years before the shots fired on Lexington green. The Seven Years' War (1754 – 1763), known in North America as the French and Indian War, was a continuation of the War of the Austrian Succession following a short peace among European nations. By 1756, Great Britain and France were making major military commitments in North America. Although Britain sent resources to aid Prussia and Hanover on the European mainland, partially to keep the French occupied there, the main British commitment was in North America and the West Indies. The war quickly escalated and soon involved all the great powers of Europe. It spread to distant lands, from the American frontier to Canada, Europe, the Caribbean, India, and beyond. The British government mobilized numerous regiments to send to the various fronts and dispatched its massive naval fleet to the different theaters of operation. Although the fighting in North America effectively ended in 1760, British forces, including American colonial troops, remained engaged in the West Indies until 1763.

The end of the Seven Years' War found Great Britain deeply in debt. In the British view, the war had largely been fought for the interests of the American colonists. Indeed, one of those colonists serving the British army named George Washington led the detachment that fired the first shots of the war. The British Parliament decided to reduce the national debt and that the colonists across the Atlantic should help bear the cost of imperial administration: the organizing, administering, policing, and defending of the newly acquired territories ceded by France and Spain in the Treaty of Paris.

This decision was not without reason. Many Americans had perceived the French as encroaching on British lands along the Ohio River. Washington was pursuing a mission to deliver an ultimatum to the French to vacate the Ohio country or be removed by force when the first shots of the war rang out. It was this dispute between the French and the colonists deep in the interior of America that rapidly developed into a world war that forced Great Britain to fight on multiple fronts and expend more money than anyone had originally envisioned.

The cost of supporting British regiments, especially in faraway North America, was high. Since the war had begun to protect the interests of American colonists, why shouldn't they foot a major portion of the bill? Parliament's answer was one of its few options: taxation. An option it did not have was the ability to correctly predict how the Americans would react to these new taxes. The colonists protested the new measures by arguing that the war had been fought more for imperial interests than colonial ones. Many Americans also believed they had already helped pay the price of the war in blood and treasure. Although some American colonists were rich in terms of land holdings, nearly everyone was cash poor, without the specie required to pay new taxes.

The Pot Simmers

Prior to 1764, American colonists had been left largely alone, had never been directly taxed by parliament, and rarely worried about the lack of representation in that body. The 1764 Sugar Act, which levied a tax on sugar and molasses, came first. This had the most impact on the New England colonies because they required sugar and its byproduct to produce the rum they traded for European goods. Outrage over the tax led to its repeal in 1765.

The colonists were not totally opposed to paying taxes. They had been paying taxes for years to the Crown, to their individual colonies, and to their counties. The slogan "taxation without representation" was the colonists' effort to claim what they saw as their traditional right as freeborn British subjects to be taxed only by their own consent, or by their elected representatives in the lower houses (assemblies) of the legislatures of their own colonies. The colonists opposed the imposition of "internal" taxes, with Parliament bypassing their assemblies to tax them directly, as it would do with the Stamp Act of 1765.

Colonists were outraged not just at the idea of new (and in their view illegal) taxes, but that the tax revenues were to be used in Great Britain and not in the colonies where the taxes were to be paid. Parliament argued that it needed revenue to both pay off the country's debts and provide for ongoing expenses. Maintaining a military presence in North America after the French and Indian War was an expensive proposition. The result was the passage of two more acts in 1765: the previously mentioned Stamp Act, and the Quartering Act (which required colonists to provide room and board for British soldiers on station in the colonies).

As upsetting as the quartering provision proved to be, the Stamp Act was even worse. The latter required colonists to purchase stamps to be affixed to most printed materials, from newspapers to legal documents. Outraged responses to the new tax ranged from throwing the stamps into American harbors when they were delivered from London, to attacking the homes of tax collectors and even assaulting the collectors themselves. The Stamp Act was rendered impotent through mass disobedience when many of the colonists refused to use the stamped paper required for business and legal documents. When ships full of raw materials could not be cleared to sail for England and Scotland, British factories slowed down and workers were laid off. Some colonial courts simply refused to use stamped documents or simply disregarded them.

Parliament was rapidly losing control of its colonies. American opposition and British industry protests translated into an act that cost more to enforce than the revenue it produced. Parliament repealed the Stamp Act in 1766.

In 1767 Parliament passed the Townshend Acts, which included taxes on such things as glass, lead, paper, paint, and tea. Although these taxes remained in place for the next few years, tempers continued to simmer across the Atlantic. Colonists opposed the Townshend Acts because they were an attempt by Parliament to disguise an "internal tax" as an "external tax." Most Americans did not strenuously object to external taxes, such as import and export duties paid to the royal treasury. The Townshend duties, however, were an import tax designed to raise revenue so that the royal and proprietary governments could spend money independent of the colonial assemblies—thereby lessening the only check the colonists could exert on their governors.

Colonists once again turned to nonimportation and nonexportation to render the Townshend Acts counterproductive. Britain responded by dispatching additional troops to North America to help enforce the levies. These red-coated symbols of perceived British aggression became the objects of ridicule for many Americans. Tempers boiled over late one night in Boston in 1770 when a mob of colonists pelted a small detachment of British guards with snowballs and other objects. The soldiers opened fire, killing and wounding several Bostonians in what is known as the Boston Massacre. In an effort to calm tempers and prevent an open rebellion, Parliament repealed all the taxes except the one on tea. Ironically, the repeal came the same day the shots were fired in Boston.

With the exception of Massachusetts, a relative calm settled over the colonies until June 1774. When a group of Massachusetts colonists dressed as Indians stormed a British tea ship and threw chests of the precious cargo into Boston harbor in 1773 (an act that was repeated in many North American harbors, though with less notoriety), Parliament reached its tipping point. In 1774, the body voted to shut down the port of Boston, decreed that all colonial government officials would thenceforward have to be appointed by Parliament, and required that all legal trials be conducted in London. In essence, the colonists would no longer be permitted to run their own affairs. Americans responded by sending representatives to meet in Philadelphia in what would be known as the First Continental Congress. The delegates agreed to boycott all imports from Great Britain.

A column of British troops marched out of Boston toward Lexington on the night of April 18, 1775, in an effort to confiscate colonial arms and gunpowder. The skirmishes the next day at Lexington and Concord, followed by guerilla style fighting most of the way back to Boston left hundreds dead, wounded, and missing. The unrest in the colonies was now armed rebellion. George Washington was appointed commander in chief. The American Revolution was underway.

Escalating War

The war that followed lasted longer than anyone on either side imagined and would eventually bring in many of Europe's great powers including France, Spain, and Holland. The war continued just as inauspiciously for the British when they suffered disproportionately high casualties on June 17 attacking Bunker's (Breed's) Hill near Boston. A months-long siege followed that eventually drove the British out of that important port city to Halifax in Nova Scotia, where they regrouped during the spring of 1776. When the British left Boston, the Continental Army represented the sole military force within the boundaries of the future United States. That fall and winter, an American force marched into Canada in an attempt to make it the fourteenth colony, but bad weather, disease, and the bloody failure at Quebec defeated the effort.

Whatever gains were achieved by the Americans in 1775 vanished in 1776. After the Declaration of Independence was signed in July, and while many colonists were still hoping for reconciliation, American armies suffered repeated defeats. The skeleton force left in Canada was driven back to Lake

Champlain in New York. The rejuvenated and reinforced British in Nova Scotia under Gen. William Howe launched an amphibious operation against New York City, defeated the Continental Army on Long Island, at White Plains, and again at Fort Washington. By December, the decimated Continentals were in head-long retreat across central New Jersey with the British in hot pursuit. The rebellion teetered on the edge of collapse. Winter convinced Howe to end pursuit and finish off Washington the next spring.

Unfortunately for the British army, Washington had other ideas. The second calendar year of war ended with Washington leading the ragged and demoralized remnants of the Continental Army across the Delaware River in a daring Christmas night operation leading to an assault against a Hessian outpost at Trenton, New Jersey. The stunning and lopsided American victory was followed up in early January of 1777 when Washington recrossed the Delaware River, repulsed a column led by Gen. Charles Cornwallis, and then conducted a night flank march around the surprised British general to engage an enemy detachment in Cornwallis's rear at Princeton, New Jersey, on January 3. Washington's pair of victories infused the patriot cause with fresh vigor while simultaneously forcing General Howe, the senior British officer in North America, to withdraw many of his New Jersey outposts into the New York City area for the winter.

Following his only sizeable battle victories of the war until Yorktown in 1781, Washington quickly moved his remnant of an army into winter quarters in the Watchung Mountains in and around Morristown, New Jersey. Washington's primary tasks that winter and spring of 1777 were to rebuild, reorganize, and reequip his army. The British, meanwhile, maintained their general headquarters in New York, with their field headquarters in New Brunswick, New Jersey, a provincial trading town on the Raritan River. Additional outposts under the command of Lord Cornwallis dotted the landscape between the Raritan and Perth Amboy, the capital of East Jersey.

Washington's Strategy

The appointment by the Continental Congress of George Washington as commander in chief of the fledgling American army proved wise in the long run. It was also risky. The Virginian had never commanded large bodies of men in combat, and had exercised but limited departmental command during the French and Indian War. He had never served as a British Regular, nor had he attended any European military schools.

Following the 1776 loss of New York City, Washington adopted a strategy of avoiding major pitched battles except if it was possible to receive an attack while defending a strong position. This, he believed, would keep the Continental Army intact and in the field. Another option proposed by Charles Lee, one of Washington's generals and a former British officer, was to wage an "irregular" war with smaller forces to drain away British strength. In many ways, this idea would be incorporated into Washington's larger strategy. Many members of Congress, however, favored a perimeter defense—the defense of every colony and every major city. This was a political favorite, but would have spread out Continental forces and guaranteed defeat everywhere.[1]

Washington would become best known for conducting essentially a Fabian-style of warfare. After his losses in New York, Washington realized that his inexperienced troops were no match for European professionals. Although he repeatedly told Congress he needed a larger professional army of his own, he also realized his smaller army was easier to supply and could move more quickly than the British. By attacking with speed and retreating even more rapidly, Washington could avoid suffering substantial casualties, preserve his command, and live to fight another day. In other words, Washington would use the forests and interior of North America to avoid major battles and eventually frustrate and make it too expensive for England to suppress the colonists. He thus sought to preserve the Continental Army while stalling the British until he was in a better condition to fight on terms of his own choosing. Washington described his strategy as "time, caution, and worrying the enemy until we could be better provided with arms and other means, and had better disciplined troops to carry on."[2]

The war grew more unpopular in London with each passing month as the financial cost of waging it rose with the losses in manpower and assets. The British leaders needed to find a way to bring the war to a speedy conclusion. As one of his biographers noted, despite the need to preserve his army, Washington "nursed fantasies throughout the war about fighting a grand climactic battle that would end the conflict with a single stroke."[3] The usually disciplined Virginian, however, refused to do so and instead fought a war of attrition in keeping with the general Fabian strategy he favored. He believed that once the leaders of the British government got tired of losing men and

---

1 David Hackett Fischer, *Washington's Crossing* (Oxford, 2004), 79-80.

2 Ibid., 40; Fischer, *Washington's Crossing*, 79. This Fabian strategy was named for Fabius Cunctator, a Roman general who had fought a delaying campaign against the Carthaginians; John Ferling, *A Leap in the Dark: The Struggle to Create the American Republic* (Oxford, 2003), 190; Charles Royster, *A Revolutionary People at War: The Continental Army & American Character, 1775-1783* (Chapel Hill, 1979), 116; Ron Chernow, *Washington: A Life* (New York, 2010), 208; James Thomas Flexner, *Washington: The Indispensable Man* (Boston, 1969), 131.

3 Chernow, *Washington*, 208.

equipment, of spending a great deal of money, and of dealing with the resultant criticism at home, they would quit.

As noted, when the battles around New York demonstrated that Washington's army was not ready to win head-to-head fights against the British, he resorted to unconventional warfare like daybreak assaults, sneak attacks, and trickery, with Trenton and Princeton providing two good examples. Guerilla warfare, known at that time as partisan warfare or *petite guerre*, would also become a major component of American strategy. However, by 1777 the British had also made great strides in the same direction, and supplemented their light infantry, dragoons, and Highlanders with German jaegers (elite light infantry suitable for many purposes).

When the 1777 campaign season opened, the Continental Army was still a long way from being able to match British capabilities.

William Alexander (Lord Stirling), one of Washington's most senior division commanders, was born in 1726 in New York. An accomplished mathematician and astronomer, Alexander served during the French and Indian War as an aide-de-camp to Governor Shirley of Massachusetts. Later, while in London, he attempted to claim the vacant title of Earl of Stirling. Although only partially successful in his effort, he would nonetheless be known to most thereafter as Lord Stirling. Once back in the colonies, he became the surveyor-general for East Jersey and helped found Columbia University.

Prior to the war, he ran an iron works in Morris County, New Jersey, and lived in a stone mansion in Basking Ridge.

He began the war as a colonel in the New Jersey militia, and in 1776 was appointed brigadier general and captured in the fighting on Long Island. Once an exchange was worked out for Montfort Browne, the governor of Nassau in the Bahamas captured in a naval action, Stirling rejoined the colonial effort and served with Washington at Trenton. Hessian von Heeringen, who set eyes on Alexander after his capture in 1776, seemed unimpressed with the man: "My Lord Stirling himself is only an *echappe de famille*, and does not pass for a lord in England. He looks as much like my Lord Granby as one egg does like another."[1] Despite outward appearances, Lord Stirling, wrote one historian of the campaign year of 1777, "emerged as one of the hardest fighters in the army. He had also earned a reputation as one of its hardest drinkers, but no one ever accused him of being drunk in combat."[2]

John Armstrong, born in 1717 in Ireland, was educated as a civil engineer and immigrated to Pennsylvania to serve as a surveyor for the Penn family. In this role, he laid out the town of Carlisle and became the surveyor of Cumberland County. During the French and Indian War, he commanded the Pennsylvania contingent on the 1758 Forbes Expedition to capture Fort Duquesne in western Pennsylvania, and knew Washington at the time. When the Revolution broke out, he was initially sent to Charleston to help lay out the defensive works there. However, he returned home to take command of the Pennsylvania militia, a rough job he would learn anew along the banks of the Brandywine.

A native of Lancashire, **John Burgoyne** was born in 1722 and received his education at Westminster School. His military career began in the dragoons, but he was best known as a commander of light cavalry in North America. Burgoyne saw service in Portugal, became a member of Parliament in 1761, and made colonel with a command in the 16th Light Dragoons two years later. By the eve of the Revolution he was a major general—with a literary and acting career to boot. In 1775, the ambitious soldier got his first taste of warfare in America under Thomas Gage in Boston, and found himself a subordinate to Guy Carleton in Canada the following year. Burgoyne would eventually scheme and charm his way into command of the British column that would move south from Canada into upstate New York in 1777 to its fate at Saratoga.

---

1 Edward J. Lowell, *The Hessians and the Other German Auxiliaries of Great Britain in the Revolutionary War* (Gansevoort, NY, 1997), 67.

2 John S. Pancake, *1777: The Year of the Hangman* (Tuscaloosa, AL, 1977), 165.

Henry Clinton, the only son of Admiral George Clinton and former governor of New York, was raised in that colony and spent time as a captain-lieutenant in the New York militia before joining the British Coldstream Guards in 1751. He fought with distinction at Bunker Hill before being promoted to lieutenant general, and would serve as William Howe's second-in-command for the next two years.[3]

Lord Charles Cornwallis would also play a major part in the Brandywine campaign. He was born in London in 1738 and educated at Eton and Cambridge University. He joined the military in 1756 and attended the military academy at Turin, Italy. Cornwallis served in Germany during the Seven Years' War and later became a member of the House of Lords, like William Howe as a member of the Whig party. He took part in the battle of Long Island, the second battle of Trenton, and the battle of Princeton. In his late thirties, Cornwallis was a strong, imposing man with a full face, large nose, and heavy-lidded eyes, one of which had a cast from a hockey accident earlier in life. Pennsylvania Quaker Joseph Townsend described that when Cornwallis was "on horseback, [he] appeared very tall and sat very erect. His rich scarlet clothing, loaded with gold lace, epaulets, etc., occasioned him to make a fine martial appearance."[4]

Carl von Donop was born to nobility in 1732 and thus blessed with valuable connections in the European courts. He was the personal adjutant to the Landgraf of Hesse-Kassel and served during the Seven Years' War. When the British government hired Hessian troops for the American Revolution, von Donop was made commander of the grenadiers dispatched to fight in the rebellious colonies. His men fought throughout the New York campaign (Long Island, Kip's Bay, and Harlem Heights). Von Donop was the senior officer in southern New Jersey in late 1776. His warnings of

3 John F. Luzader, *Saratoga: A Military History of the Decisive Campaign of the American Revolution* (New York, 2008), xxii.

4 Joseph Townsend, *Some Account of the British Army, Under the Command of General Howe, and of The Battle of Brandywine, on The Memorable September 11th, 1777, And the Adventure of that Day, Which Came to the Knowledge and Observation of Joseph Townsend* (Philadelphia, 1846), 22.

a pending American attack were brushed aside by his superior, Gen. James Grant. He would fight at and survive Brandywine, only to be fatally injured the following month at the much smaller affair at Red Bank.

Johann Ewald was a jaeger captain destined to play a major role at Brandywine. Born in 1744 in the Hessian city of Cassel, Johann was the son of a postal employee and

a merchant's daughter. He entered the military at age 16 during the Seven Years' War and fought across modern-day Germany and was wounded in the leg in 1761. Eight years later he was assigned to the Leib Regiment. A drunken argument in 1770 led to a duel with a friend and the loss of his left eye, after which he sported a glass eye and an eye patch. Ewald was promoted to captain in 1774 in the Hessian Jaeger Corps and arrived in America during late summer in 1776, where he quickly established himself as a good and dependable officer. His jaeger company had been engaged in the fighting around New York over the previous year. He was a 33-year-old bachelor of medium height, slender build, and erect carriage. That May he was injured in a skirmish near Bound Brook, and for the ensuing six months forced to perform his duty from the back of a horse.

Patrick Ferguson was born in Aberdeenshire, Scotland, on June 4, 1744, and spent the majority of his life in the army. A commission as coronet was purchased for him in 1756, after which he spent two years studying at the Royal Military Academy in Woolwich. He saw military service with the 2nd Royal North Britain Dragoons in Germany and Flanders during the Seven Years' War. When he fell seriously ill in 1762, Ferguson was sent home to Scotland to recuperate. Six years later he became a captain in the 70th Regiment of Foot and served in the West Indies in Grenada and on the island of Tobago, where he suffered ill health yet again, this time from an arthritis flare-up, and was invalided home in the fall of 1772. The next year he was sent to Halifax, Nova Scotia. When he returned to Scotland in 1774, he was made captain of the 70th's light company, and that same year attended General Howe's Light Infantry School. The 33-year-old Scottish officer served under Gen. Wilhelm von Knyphausen at the Brandywine, and again in the Carolinas Campaign of 1780, during which he would meet his end (and achieve a certain level of infamy) at King's Mountain.

The widely disliked British **Gen. James Grant** was an interesting character. The veteran of the Seven Years' War in North America and former governor of Florida was born in 1720 in northern Scotland and began his military career by purchasing a commission in 1744 in the Royal Scots, with whom he fought at the 1745 battle of Fontenoy in present-day Belgium. He botched the 1758 assault on Fort Duquesne and was captured. Grant was quite familiar with the politics of the American colonies. After serving in the colonies before the Revolution, he rose to command the 55th Regiment of Foot. In 1776, he served General Howe as a division commander during the New York campaign and played a key role in the Long Island fighting. Grant was in his late forties in 1777, and ardently anti-American. "Grant" wrote one historian, "was, depending upon one's perspective, a canny political operator and generous host or a braying buffoon with little idea of generalship." One account describes Grant as "grown fat and gouty from overindulgence, savoring the delicacies prepared by Baptiste, his black cook."[5]

Nathanael Greene, who was born in 1742 into a Rhode Island Quaker family, suffered a childhood accident that left him with a life-long limp. He also suffered from asthma, and endured a painful spot in his right eye from a smallpox inoculation. Greene sold toys to earn money to buy books, and was the owner of an iron fabrication business before the war. After serving briefly with a Rhode Island militia company, he was commissioned a brigadier general in 1775 and given command of all of Rhode Island's troops. Even though he had no real military expertise and no battle experience, George Washington immediately liked Greene, and was convinced he was the best among his many generals.

Greene's first field test was the successful defensive action at Harlem Heights in September 1776, one of the very few bright spots of the New York Campaign. Greene offered bad advice and was responsible for the disaster at Fort Washington, but he redeemed himself by leading a wing of the army well at both Trenton and Princeton.

---

5   Mark Urban, *Fusiliers: The Saga of a British Redcoat Regiment in the American Revolution* (New York, 2007), 80-81.

Two historians characterized him thusly: "He was a thoughtful strategist, rather than an inspiring leader. He knew how to make the most of limited resources. He seldom showed brilliance, but he had much of Washington's capacity for enduring."[6]

A native of Haverhill, Massachusetts, **Moses Hazen** had a great deal of combat experience by the time his regiment deployed west of Philadelphia. He had fought in the French and Indian War as the commander of a ranger company at Crown Point, Louisburg, Quebec, and Sillery, before settling in Canada. From 1771 to 1773, Hazen served as a lieutenant in the British 44th Regiment of Foot and married a Catholic woman. He was a prominent Canadian landowner when the Revolution broke out in 1775, and the British seized his land and imprisoned him. Hazen joined Richard Montgomery's advance into Canada in 1775 and was commissioned a colonel in January 1776 to raise a regiment of Canadians. The regiment, which became known as "Congress's Own," was involved in the retreat from Montreal in the spring of 1776. It later joined Washington on Long Island and wintered at Morristown with the rest of the army.

Admiral **Richard Howe** was Gen. William Howe's older brother and in command of the British fleet in North America. Howe joined the navy at the age of 13 and served throughout the War of the Austrian Succession and the Seven Years' War, where he fought in the important naval victory at Quiberon Bay in 1759. He was 50 in 1777 and stood five feet, nine inches tall, with (in the words of his biographer), a "large nose and mildly protruding lips [that] detracted from his impressive brown eyes."[7] Like his brother, the admiral was sympathetic to the American cause, which may have influenced how he employed his naval power. His naval blockade of the American cosat proved ineffective.

Washington's antagonist for the 1777 Campaign, **William Howe**, was born in England in 1729 and entered the army in 1746 as an officer in a dragoon regiment. He fought in the War of the Austrian Succession, commanded the light infantry under James Wolfe during his Canadian operations during the Seven Years' War, and served in Havana. In 1761, Howe was elected to Parliament, and later trained the army's light infantry companies. In June of 1775, Howe commanded the assaults at Bunker (Breed's) Hill near Boston, and that October was elevated to overall command in North America. His 1776 New York Campaign nearly (and likely could have) destroyed the Continentals.

---

6   George F. Scheer and Hugh F. Rankin, *Rebels & Redcoats: The American Revolution Through the Eyes of Those Who Fought and Lived It* (New York, 1957), 422.

7   Ira D. Gruber, *The Howe Brothers & the American Revolution* (New York, 1972), 45.

Like many of the American officers, Howe was a Whig, and also like many on both sides of the Atlantic, he believed the Revolution was a war between brothers that could be settled over a bottle of wine and a good meal. The six-footer was tall for his day with a swarthy complexion and dark hair. This is how a Pennsylvania Quaker named Joseph Townsend described Howe in September of 1777: "He was mounted on a large English horse much reduced in flesh, I suppose from their being so long confined on board the fleet. . . . The general was a large, portly man, of coarse features. He appeared to have lost his teeth, as his mouth had fallin in." One historian left this description of the general: "He was a large man, still soldierly and handsome in a dark, overbearing way, though softened by years of peace and coarsened by the indulgence of an insatiable appetite for high living."[8]

William Maxwell was allegedly born in Ireland about 1733 but was living with his family in New Jersey by 1747. He served as a militia officer during the French and Indian War, and took command of the 2nd New Jersey Battalion when the Revolution erupted. Maxwell served as a member of the New Jersey Provisional Congress in 1775-1776, and in the Canadian Expedition in 1776. In October of that year he was appointed brigadier general and took part in Washington's successful late December campaign. Maxwell was the senior brigadier in Washington's New Jersey-based army. Within a few months he would be assigned to a prominent command and play a key part in the battle along the Brandywine.

Francis Nash was born in Virginia in 1742, moved at an early age to North Carolina, and quickly rose to local prominence there as a merchant and as an attorney. In 1763, Nash became clerk of the court of pleas and quarter sessions. At various times he was a representative to the House of Commons and a member of the Royal militia. When war broke out in 1775, he was elected lieutenant colonel of the 1st North Carolina Regiment. He became a colonel in 1776, and a brigadier general by February 1777. Nash was sent to raise troops in western North Carolina and then join

8 Townsend, *Some Account*, 25; Scheer and Rankin, *Rebels & Redcoats*, 54.

Washington in the Philadelphia area. His ability on the battlefield was yet to be determined.

Born in Boston in 1750, **Henry Knox** lost two fingers in a musket accident early in life. He eventually opened up a bookstore and became well-read on military issues in general, and ordnance in particular. During the winter of 1775-1776, he orchestrated a daring removal of artillery from Fort Ticonderoga and its transfer to Boston. This feat earned him a promotion to head the Continental artillery. He helped improve the defenses of Connecticut and Rhode Island, and after Trenton was promoted to brigadier general. During the winter of 1776-1777, Knox was commissioned to raise a brigade of artillery. He was also ordered to create an arsenal at Springfield, Massachusetts. By 1777, he had been in command of the Continental artillery for more than a year. One historian described the former bookstore owner this way: "Knox was a huge man; at six foot two, he was as tall as the commander-in-chief. But unlike the muscular Washington, Knox weighed 280 pounds, with little muscle. His body was

distinguished by his huge belly, fat hands, and tree trunk-sized thighs. The stout Knox was an unforgettable figure with a round and cheerful face, sharp gray eyes, and a sunny disposition."[9]

Baron Wilhelm Reichsfreiherr zu Inn-und Knyphausen was born in 1716 in Luxembourg. He became a general in Hesse, but traditionally served the Prussian kings.[10] In 1776, he was sent to North America as second in command of the hired German troops; in 1777, at the age of 61, he became their overall commander. The previous year, he had been

---

9 Chadwick, *George Washington's War*, 13.

10 The provinces of Hesse and Prussia were two different kingdoms. The princes of Hesse often "rented" their troops to other kingdoms, much as they rented them to the British.

instrumental during the assault on Fort Washington on upper Manhattan Island (near the site of the George Washington Bridge today). A Philadelphian described him as "a noble specimen of a German baron, of the ordinary height & strong frame; there was a sabre mark on one of his cheeks extending from the eye to the chin."[11]

Although baptized **Marie Joseph Paul Yves Roch Gilbert du Motier**, and was hereditarily Marquis du Lafayette, Baron de Vissac, and Seigneur de St. Romain, he was better known as simply, the **Marquis de Lafayette.** The native of Chavaniac Auvergne, France, who was born on September 6, 1757, grew to more than six feet tall, a height which at that time was nearly as imposing as his name. Lafayette's father died two years later at the battle of Minden in 1759 during the Seven Years' War. In 1768,

Lafayette moved to Paris with his mother to enter the College du Plessis. Two years later, when his mother and grandmother died during the same week, the young man inherited a great deal of wealth and joined the royal army as a sous-lieutenant in the Kimip Musketeers. Four years later at 16, he entered a pre-arranged marriage with the 14-year-old Marie Adrienne Francoise de Noalles, a member of one of the most powerful families in France, and became a member of the Free Masons.

Lafayette became a captain in the Noailles Dragoons in 1775, and later that same year his wife bore him Henriette, their first child. Fascinated by the upheaval on the other side of the Atlantic, on December 7, 1776, Lafayette signed an agreement with Silas Deane, the American army commissioner in Paris, to serve as a major general in the Continental Army. The next year, Lafayette bought his own ship and sailed for America, accompanied by Baron Johann de Kalb and a dozen other French officers. At some point during the summer of 1777, his second child Anastasie was born; Henriette died the same year.

---

11 Jacob Mordecai, "Addenda to Watson's Annals of Philadelphia," in *Pennsylvania Magazine of History and Biography* (Philadelphia, 1974), vol. 98, 165.

John Laurens was born in 1754 in Charleston, South Carolina. Laurens was the son of Henry Laurens, who became president of the Continental Congress later in the war, and had the moneyed privilege of a private tutor as a child. Educated in Geneva, Switzerland, Laurens then spent six years in England as a law student, entering that profession in London. Laurens was also an opponent of slavery throughout his life. He married in 1776 and, after visiting with Benjamin Franklin in Paris, he returned to Charleston, South Carolina, in April 1777. After serving briefly in the south, he came north and offered to serve as a volunteer without pay. In August, Washington invited him to join his staff as a volunteer aide. Laurens proved quite useful to Washington. He was fluent in French, had traveled in central Europe, and had attended higher institutions of learning. Upon his return to the colonies, Laurens was anxious to serve the infant nation. He wrote, "You ask me, my Dear Father what bounds I have set to my desire of serving my Country in the Military Line—I answer glorious Death, or the Triumph of the Cause in which I am engaged."[12]

Thomas Mifflin was a Quaker born in Philadelphia on January 10, 1744, and was 33 during the Philadelphia campaign. He graduated from the College of Philadelphia in 1760 and seven years later married his cousin, Sarah Morris. Prior to the war, Mifflin was a respected Philadelphia merchant, a trustee of the College of Philadelphia, and a member of the Governor's Council. Washington was a frequent dinner guest at the Mifflin home during visits to Philadelphia. After he became city warden in 1771, Mifflin began speaking out against British taxation policies, which led to his appointment as a delegate to the Continental Congress. A militia major when the war erupted, he spent six weeks as one of Washington's aide-de-camps and accompanied the general to Cambridge, Massachusetts, to assume command of the army.

Mifflin's elevation to quartermaster general of the army on August 14, 1775, when Joseph Trumbull resigned, resulted in his excommunication by the Quaker church. Questions of corruption would later be raised regarding Mifflin's tenure in that difficult department. In July 1777, Mifflin abandoned his duties and returned to his country home in Reading, Pennsylvania. His department was left in the charge of assistant quartermasters for the rest of the campaign.

Captain John Montresor was born in 1736 on Gibraltar and spent his early life there and on Minorca. During the late 1740s, Montresor attended Westminster School in England and learned the principles of engineering from his father, who was also a military engineer. During the French and Indian War, he came to North America with his father and served as an ensign in the 48th Regiment of Foot. He was wounded

---

12 Chesnutt, David R., and C. James Taylor, eds. *The Papers of Henry Laurens*, vol. 12 (Columbia, SC 1990), 330.

during that war, promoted to lieutenant, and became a member of the Corps of Engineers. After the war, Montresor helped prepare maps of Acadia (a region that today includes parts of Quebec and Maine), the St. Lawrence River, and the Kennebec River in northern New England. He also designed and built Fort Niagara and Fort Erie. He was in Boston when the Revolution erupted, and took part in the New York campaign before accompanying Howe on the 1777 campaign.

Timothy Pickering was the senior staff officer traveling with Washington's Continental Army. Born in Massachusetts in 1745 and graduated from Harvard in 1763, he was employed in Salem in the office of the registrar of deeds until the eve of the war. Pickering studied law and was admitted to the bar in 1768 before joining the militia. He rose to the rank of colonel in 1774. Pickering's "Plan of Discipline" was widely used in the army until it adopted Baron von Steuben's manual in 1778. Pickering took part in the Lexington alert in 1775 and in the New York and New Jersey campaigns through early 1777. His service brought the 32-year-old to the attention of Washington, who appointed Pickering to his top staff position, adjutant general, on June 18, 1777. Pickering's postwar writings provide valuable insight into the events at headquarters and the ensuing confusion that unfolded during the battle of the Brandywine.

Casimir Pulaski was born on March 6, 1745, on a family estate near Warsaw, Poland, and later received formal schooling. In the late 1760s, he led a partisan force against the Russian army during a series of revolts in his native land. At age 23, he took command of the military arm of the Confederation of Bar, a patriotic movement that sought to evict the Russians from Poland and restore sovereignty to the country, and was eventually captured by the Russians in that capacity. In 1771, he was implicated in a plot to abduct the king, and was sentenced to death as a result. He fled Poland, and after briefly aiding the Turks against Russia and spending time in a French debtors' prison, he came to America. Pulaski landed at Marblehead, Massachusetts, on July 23, 1777, and caught up with Washington's army on August 21. Likely, Pulaski was wearing the uniform of a Polish hussar when he arrived.

Benjamin Rush was born outside of Philadelphia in 1745, and attended West Nottingham Academy, the College of Philadelphia, and Edinburgh University. He returned to the colonies in 1769, opened a medical practice, and published several medical books. The doctor signed the Declaration of Independence. In 1777, he was appointed surgeon general of the middle department of the Continental Army, and would play a prominent role in the aftermath of the battle along the Brandywine.

Lord George Sackville, better known as Lord Germain, served as the Secretary of State for the American Department. Born in 1716, he was known as Lord George

Sackville from 1720 until 1770, and thereafter Lord Germain. He served in the army in Europe in the 1740s and 1750s in the War of the Austrian Succession and the Seven Years' War, but his service at the 1759 Battle of Minden hung like a cloud over the rest of his life. General Sackville led the British section of the Allied army and failed to execute an order for a cavalry charge issued by the Allied commander. Sackville (who would be dismissed from the army) demanded a court-martial to clear his name. The guilty verdict claimed he "disobeyed the orders of Prince Ferdinand of Brunswick, whom he was by his commission bound to obey as commander-in-chief, according to the rules of war . . . is hereby adjudged to be, unfit to serve His Majesty in any military capacity whatever." Just three members fewer than the two-thirds majority needed to execute the punishment voted to sentence him to death.

His periodic time in Parliament since the early 1740s served to launch a political career. He was made Secretary of State for the American Department in November 1775, which made him responsible for colonial administration and military operations, and thus responsible for the conduct of the war.[13] His efforts to dictate actions from London, and the manner in which he handled communications, would play a significant role in the eventual British defeat.

The well educated **Adam Stephen** was born in Scotland around 1718. He graduated from King's College in Aberdeen, studied medicine in Edinburgh, and became surgeon in the Royal Navy. Stephen moved to Virginia, practiced medicine in Fredericksburg, joined the militia in 1754, and served as an officer in George Washington's Virginia regiment. He served in the French and Indian War in the Battle of Fort Necessity and was involved in the disastrous 1755 Braddock Expedition. When the war ended in 1763, Stephen assume command of the regiment and fought in Pontiac's Rebellion.

Stephen was obviously on good terms with Washington, but his ability to command a division in battle was suspect. He would eventually go before a court-martial and be found guilty of being drunk during combat at Germantown—and kicked

---

13 Luzader, *Saratoga*, xxiii-xxiv. Lord Germain became Viscount Sackville in 1782.

out of the army. One historian wrote this about him: "Like [Lord] Stirling, Stephen was fond of liquor but, unlike the Irishman, there was growing evidence that the Virginian was beginning to rely on the bottle to stiffen his resolution in battle. Washington tolerated him because they had fought together in the Seven Years' War, and because there were simply not enough major generals available."[14]

The son of Irish indentured servants, **John Sullivan** was born in 1740 in Berwick in what is now the state of Maine, but when the war broke out was living in New Hampshire. He studied law, was described as an "able, if somewhat litigious," lawyer, and served as a major of militia before the war. In June of 1775 he was

appointed brigadier general in the army, took part in the Canadian operations, and was promoted to major general in August of 1776. During part of the New York campaign, Sullivan commanded Nathanael Greene's division when Greene fell ill.

Sullivan was captured during the battle of Long Island, and General Howe used him as a pawn in the contemplated peace negotiation by sending him as an errand boy under parole to speak with Congress on the topic. Sullivan was exchanged in September for Brig. Gen. Richard Prescott, who had been captured in November 1775. When Gen. Charles Lee was taken prisoner in northern New Jersey, Sullivan was put in command of Lee's division and performed well at Trenton.

Colonel H. von Heeringen of the Hessian Fusilier Regiment von Lossburg described Sullivan following his capture in 1776: "John Sullivan was a lawyer, and previously a domestic servant, but a man of genius, whom the rebels will much regret." A historian has described Sullivan as "overly optimistic, always sure of success, seldom achieving it." Bruce Chadwick has left this description of Sullivan: "Fellow officers and many of his men disliked him because of his argumentative

14 Pancake, *1777*, 165-166.

personality and hot temper. And, they said, he was always complaining about something."[15]

George Washington was born on February 22, 1732, in Virginia. In 1749, he was appointed the official surveyor for Culpepper County, and in that capacity helped lay out the town of Alexandria. He was afflicted with smallpox in 1751 and his face remained scarred for the rest of his life.

In 1752 Washington was commissioned a major in the Virginia militia, and the following year the governor, under orders from the king, sent him to deliver an ultimatum to the French in the Ohio Valley. It was Washington who ordered the shots fired that opened the global Seven Years' War. He was promoted to lieutenant colonel, fought in the battle at Fort Necessity in the Pennsylvania back country in July 1754, and was an aide-de-camp to Gen. Edward Braddock during the disastrous expedition to the forks of the Ohio River. Washington was elected to the Virginia House of Burgesses in 1758, and married widow Martha Custis the following year.

After Lexington and Concord, Washington was named commander in chief of the Continental Army and rode to Boston to assume command. His limited military experience did not prepare him for maneuvering large armies or the use of massed artillery, nor had it exposed him to cavalry. He was 45 during the 1777 campaign. Modern perception imagines Washington as a grey-haired old man leading troops into battle, when in fact he pulled his dark red hair (he never wore a wig) pulled back into a queue and powdered it white during the Revolution. He was considered a formidable man, strong and robust. Joseph Townsend, the young Quaker who witnessed the battle of the Brandywine, recalled General Washington as "a stately, well-proportioned, fine-looking man, of great ability, active, firm and resolute,

15 Lowell, *Hessians*, 66; Scheer and Rankin, *Rebels & Redcoats*, 129; Chadwick, *George Washington's War*, 73.

of a social disposition, and . . . considered to be a good man."[16] Earlier in the war, a Hessian officer described the Virginian as one who "does not show in his face the greatness with which he is generally credited. His eyes have no fire, but the smiling character of his expression when he speaks inspires affection and respect." Another German officer who was captured at Trenton in late 1776 described him thusly: "Washington is a courteous and elegant man, but seems to be very polite and reserved, speaks little, and has a sly physiognomy. He is not very tall and also not short, but of medium height, and has a good figure."[17] In 1777, Washington was a general in desperate need of a battlefield victory.

The bombastic **Anthony Wayne** was born in Chester County, Pennsylvania, in 1745. He attended an academy for two years, became a prosperous tanner, and spent a year as a surveyor. In 1774, Wayne was elected to the Pennsylvania legislature. He later became a colonel of the 4th Pennsylvania Battalion, which he commanded at Fort Washington during the New York-area campaign of 1776. Wayne took part in the Canadian expedition and was put in command of Fort Ticonderoga in upper New York. In February 1777, he was promoted to brigadier general while commanding a

portion of the Pennsylvania Line at Fort Ticonderoga before joining the army at Morristown, where he was placed in command of the First Pennsylvania Brigade of Benjamin Lincoln's division. When Lincoln was detached to serve under Horatio Gates during the Saratoga campaign, the 32-year-old Wayne took over temporary command of the division. Wayne, writes one historian, "commanded the Pennsylvania Line and had impressed the commander in chief as an able administrator, but he had not had combat experience as a division commander." Wayne, he added, was "belligerent and pugnacious in battle, but not mad."[18]

---

16 Townsend, *Some Account*, 23.
17 Lowell, *The Hessians*, 101-102.
18 Pancake, *1777*, 166.

Ludwig von Wurmb was born into nobility in May 1736. First serving in the military during the Seven Years' War, von Wurmb rose to the rank of captain by age 23. Prior to transferring to the Jaeger Corps, he fought with the Regiment von Ysenburg at Hastenbeck, Sandersburg, and Lutterberg. He then fought with the jaegers and was wounded at Lubeck in 1760. He was captured with his detachment at Ullrichstein Castle two years later. Coming to North America during the American Revolution, he commanded the Hessian jaeger corps throughout the war. During the Philadelphia campaign, his battalion of Hessian jaegers included a single company of Anspach-Bayreuth jaegers.

BRANDYWINE

A Military History of the Battle that Lost Philadelphia but
Saved America, September 11, 1777

Chapter 1

The 1777 Campaign Takes Shape

"I observed to him there was no letter to Howe to acquaint him with the plan
or what was expected of him in consequence of it."[1]

— Undersecretary William Knox, March 1777

The Pieces in Place

As the spring of 1777 dawned, George Washington was unsure of
William Howe's intentions for the fighting season. From New
York City, Howe could move north along the Hudson River to form a junction
with the Canadian army, he could move directly overland toward the American
capital at Philadelphia, or he could board a portion of his army onto ships to sail
to any number of American ports.

Lacking any significant naval force to monitor British movements,
Washington was forced into a reactive strategy during the spring and summer
months. If Howe pushed north, he would follow him and harass his rear. If the
British used their ships, he would need to wait and see where they turned up
along the lengthy American coastline. Washington's defensive positions around
Morristown, New Jersey, already placed him in a position to protect the
overland route to Philadelphia.

---

1 Luzader, *Saratoga*, 354-355. Luzader cites the original source as the William Knox Papers,
which were published in the British Historical Commission Publications.

During the maneuvering that led Washington to the banks of the Brandywine, he attempted to hinder British movements with militia and other troops while the main army (which was being reconstituted that spring) waited for the opportune moment to make a stand.[2] Washington would later decide the favorable terrain along the Brandywine presented that opportunity.

The year 1777 was a major turning point in the American Revolution. While Washington remained on the defensive, the British high command formulated plans to take the initiative. Two British armies in North America were available to carry out the King's strategy—one led by William Howe and the other by John Burgoyne. Although the latter's army would not be directly involved at Brandywine, his campaign would have far-reaching repercussions on Howe's efforts, and Howe's on Burgoyne's.

The previous year, until the middle of December, had gone dramatically well for the British forces in North America. Prior to withdrawing for the winter, the northern army had driven south to Fort Ticonderoga in what would become upper New York state, pushing the Americans from its path. William Howe's army had captured New York City, mauled George Washington's army, and pursued it across New Jersey by mid-December.

These victories made capturing Philadelphia an attractive and attainable goal. In the traditional European mindset, taking the colonial capital should end the war. However, doing so was not part of the original British strategic plan.

Strategic Thinking

The British strategy for the opening years of the war had revolved around the New England colonies, targeting them as the core of the rebellion. The prevailing opinion was that New England should be isolated from the other colonies by seizing control of the Hudson River-Lake Champlain corridor. In the minds of the British leadership, dividing the colonies would mean victory. As early as late 1775, Howe had advocated the Hudson River plan. Using his main force at New York City, Howe would ascend the Hudson from the south to link up with Guy Carleton's forces moving down from Canada, and together strike into Massachusetts from the west.

2 Edward G. Lengel, *General George Washington: A Military Life* (New York, 2005), 223.

Lord George Germain, the powerful if largely ineffective Secretary of State for the American Department, backed Howe's Hudson River plan.[3] Germain, together with Lord North and others in the British government, wrongly assumed American troops could not defeat British troops, that the colonial war would unfold like the conflicts on the European continent, and that victory would re-establish allegiance. Because of the extraordinary distances involved, combined with his false assumptions and manner of handling things, Germain refused to dictate specific and clear orders. A memorandum later found in his papers outlined British thoughts on war strategy:

> By our having the entire Command of the Communication between Canada and New York, which is both convenient and easy, being almost altogether by Water, the Troops from both these Provinces will have it in their power to act in Conjunction, as occasion or necessity may require. In consequence whereof, the Provinces of New England will be surrounded on all Sides, whether by His Majesty's Troops or Navy, and liable to be attacked from every Quarter, which will oblige them to divide their Force for the protection of their frontier settlements, while at the same time all intercourse between them and the Colonies to the southward of the Hudson's River will be entirely cut off.[4]

Following the British capture of New York City and the surrounding area in the fall of 1776, Howe proposed to direct the impetus of the main part of his forces north along the Hudson. Such a proposal was in line with the Hudson River plan. Howe wrote to Germain on November 30 outlining his thoughts. Based upon the difficulties Guy Carleton had encountered in 1776, Howe assumed that the column out of Canada could not reach Albany before September 1777. Therefore, Howe proposed a three-part plan to bring the war to a close by the end of the following year:

> A 10,000-man army would operate out of Rhode Island, penetrate north into Massachusetts, and capture Boston. Lieutenant General Henry Clinton would command this force.

---

3   Luzader, *Saratoga*, xxiii-xxiv. Lord Germain became Viscount Sackville in 1782.

4   Piers Mackesy, *The War for America: 1775-1783* (Lincoln, NE, 1964), 59-60; "Observations on the War in America [1776]," Germain Papers, William Clements Library, Ann Arbor, MI. This memorandum was probably not written by Germain.

"A description of the situation, harbour &c of the city and port of Philadelphia." This British engraving (on both facing pages) was published in London in 1768. It depicts the colonial capital from across the Delaware River and includes the "Battery" and the "State house," as well as a street plan between the Schuylkill and Delaware rivers. *Library of Congress*

Another 10,000-man army would push north along the Hudson River to reach Albany and form a junction with the army coming south from Canada. Presumably, this force would fall under Howe's personal command.

Lastly, another 8,000-man column in New Jersey would block Washington's main army and threaten Philadelphia. Howe proposed to attack Philadelphia and Virginia in the autumn, "provided the success of other operations will admit of an adequate force to be sent against that province."[5]

In summation, Howe's idea was to use a force to hold George Washington's Continental Army in New Jersey while sending two columns north for the New England campaign, one along the Hudson and the other out of Rhode Island. It was an ambitious, daring plan; however, at the time—with Washington reeling across New Jersey, desertion depleting his army, expiring enlistments further diminishing it as an effective force, and Carleton

5 John Stockdale, ed., *The Parliamentary Register; or, History of the Proceedings and Debates of the House of Commons: Containing an Account of the most interesting Speeches and Motions; accurate Copies of the most remarkable Letters and Papers; of the most material Evidence, Petitions, &c laid before and offered to the House, During the Fifth Session of the Fourteenth Parliament of Great Britain* (London, 1802), vol. 10, 362.

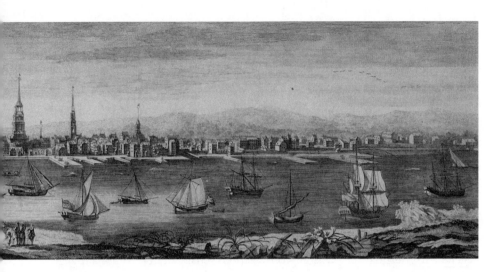

demonstrating that the American force along Lake Champlain was conquerable—the undertaking seemed doable.

To fulfill it, Howe requested 15,000 reinforcements, which he boldly proposed could be acquired from either Hanover or Russia. But while the British government had negotiated contracts for the use of regiments from the Germanic duchies the previous year, the skyrocketing costs of the war made the acquisition of additional Germanic troops, let alone Russian ones, unlikely. Recruitment for the British regiments of the line proceeded slowly, at best. Overall, the chances of Howe receiving anything close to 15,000 additional men were slim. Perhaps sensing Parliamentary resistance, Howe informed Germain that if "the force I have mentioned [were] sent out, it would strike such terror through the country, that little resistance would be made to the progress of his Majesty's arms in the provinces of New England, New York, the Jerseys, and Pennsylvania, after the junction of the northern and southern armies." Hinting at concerns over available horseflesh, Howe also requested additional mounts be sent across the Atlantic for the two regiments of light dragoons.[6]

Unlike other politicians and military men, men such as Lord Germain and Gen. Charles Cornwallis, General Howe believed the primary key to victory was the occupation of colonial territory rather than the destruction of the Continental Army. The more area the British forces occupied, so went this line of thinking, the more opportunity there would be for Loyalists to wrestle back control of their own affairs and enroll in provincial organizations. Rather than rely on costly battles, Howe intended to achieve victory by moving with "impressive strength through centers of rebellion, relying upon overawing the disaffected, animating the loyal, and demonstrating to the wavering the futility of resistance."[7] Howe conceptualized the war quite differently than did Washington, who throughout the conflict proved more willing to lose territory and key cities in return for the preservation of his principal field army.

Howe's plan, however, was formulated before Washington fled west across New Jersey instead of north into the Hudson Highlands, and before Howe drove west across the Raritan River in pursuit of the American leader. Germain did not receive the dispatch proposing Howe's plan until after the British disaster at Trenton on the day after Christmas, 1776. Before the letter even reached its destination, Washington's actions changed the entire strategic landscape.

Germain's response almost two months later was crafted without knowledge of the Trenton debacle. Germain thought Howe's proposal a "well digested plan," but went on to observe that the northern army would likely reach Albany sooner than Howe had calculated. The request for heavy reinforcements "really alarmed" Germain, who promised Howe 4,000 troops in the form of 800 additional Hessian jaegers, 1,800 British, and 1,200 Hessians. With these additions, Germain calculated Howe would have 35,000 troops with which to begin his spring campaign.[8]

Germain's math, however, did not add up. Howe calculated that he had only 20,000 effectives. Even if detached men and the sick and wounded attached to the army were counted, few of them in an active campaign would be pulling a trigger. As a result, Germain's 4,000 reinforcements would only give Howe about 24,000 men for the spring campaign. Howe's strategy of reoccupying territory throughout the colonies as he advanced, however, would require troops to garrison areas in his rear.

It was Germain's hope that, after the successes of 1776, the costs of the war could be trimmed back. He was unwilling to return to the Germanic duchies for more troops, let alone make a request to the Russians for troops to swell Howe's ranks. As for the requested horses, Howe could expect only 100 because the expense of "sending to so great a distance is enormous, and the

7   Luzader, *Saratoga*, xxii, 2-3.

8   Stockdale, *Parliamentary Register*, vol. 10, 382.

hazard of their arriving safe very great." As far as Germain was concerned, Howe could acquire the horses he might need from the American countryside. How much Howe would have to alter his ambitious 1777 campaign remained to be seen.[9]

The distance and time required to coordinate colonial strategy with the authorities in England was on full display even before Germain's letter reached Howe's headquarters on March 9, 1777. By that time, Howe had changed his operational plans and had once again written Germain as much. On December 20, 1776, after Washington fled across the Delaware River, Howe abandoned the plan to move up the Hudson River and wrote to Germain that the next effort should be to capture Philadelphia. It was there, he explained, the principal American army was now gathered for its protection. Thus, Howe's plan had already changed before his November 30 dispatch reached Germain, whose reply Howe would not receive until the following March.[10]

Howe's new strategy was reinforced by the ease with which Washington was driven out of New Jersey and across the Delaware River. Convinced that American sentiment had changed, Howe decided that a quick strike into the middle colonies would bring about a decisive victory and perhaps end the war. British leadership remained convinced throughout the Revolution that, if given the opportunity, Loyalists in North America would rise in large numbers to support the British—and Philadelphia was thought to be a hotbed of Loyalism. Howe also believed that the preservation of Philadelphia was in many ways symbolic for Washington and his army and he was correct: One of Washington's hopes in 1777 was to protect and hold the city. If Howe was going to bring Washington to battle, the easiest way to do so was to threaten Philadelphia.

The Setting

As the largest American port and colonial seat of government (not to mention the third-largest city in the entire British Empire), Philadelphia was an attractive objective. Although it was established less than a century earlier, the city grew more rapidly than the older cities of Boston and New York. The

---

9 Luzader, *Saratoga*, 4.

10 *Stockdale, Parliamentary Register*, vol. 10, 382-383; *Report on the Manuscripts of Mrs. Stopford-Sackville, of Drayton House, Northhampshire* (Hereford, 1910), vol. 2, 52-53.

founding Penn family's offers of lucrative land deals, coupled with the province's Quaker tolerance of all faiths, contributed to the heavy and steady influx of immigrants to both the city and the surrounding countryside. These new inhabitants included religious dissenters and settlers from the British home islands and central Europe, including a large number of German immigrants. In fact, so many Germans arrived that the village of Germantown was founded on the periphery of Philadelphia in 1683.[11]

Philadelphia was laid out in a grid pattern, with the north-south streets running parallel to the Delaware River (and for the most part numbered) and the east-west streets named mostly after trees and other plants. The streets were fifty feet wide, paved with cobblestone, and lined with sidewalks of brick or flagstone. An exception was High Street, a 100-foot wide thoroughfare with a market shed running down the middle of three blocks from the old courthouse at Second Street. Other than a scattering of church steeples and other cupolas, no building stood above four stories. By 1777, the city with between 30,000 and 40,000 citizens boasted more than 5,000 houses and some 3,000 other buildings including warehouses, merchant facilities, and small workshops. Nearly all of these mostly red brick structures were erected within one square mile.

Flour and lumber exports made the region quite wealthy. The flour industry alone demanded the production of thousands of barrels annually, which in turn required sawmills to make the barrel staves, forges to produce iron straps for the hoops, and coopers to assemble them all. Barrels were also shipped to the West Indies for the transportation of sugar, molasses, and rum. These same lumber and iron businesses were also capable of producing war materials for the American army. During the war, most of the trade goods entering the colonies through Philadelphia came from the West Indies in the form of booty captured by privateers.[12]

Being the largest port in British North America, Philadelphia had a large working-class population of rough dockworkers and laborers, as well as hundreds of small, independent craftsmen such as leatherworkers, shoemakers, printers, carpenters, and smiths of all kinds. Transportation of goods into and out of the city required porters, carters, draymen, and teamsters—tough, able-bodied characters who quenched their thirst at the more than 150 licensed

---

11 McGuire, *Philadelphia Campaign*, vol. 1, 124.

12 Ibid., 125.

taverns in the city. Others were more comfortable patronizing illegal taprooms populating back alleys and waterfront areas.

Politics firmly divided the population. The Scotch-Irish, Presbyterian protestants who had been driven from Northern Ireland by heavy taxes, were strongly in favor of American independence. Members of the Church of England, or Anglicans, were divided between loyalty to the Crown and their support for American independence. Half of Philadelphia was composed of Germans who were either neutral for religious reasons or supported the war effort. The members of the large Quaker contingent preferred neutrality, but were often "passively loyal to the crown." The small number of Jews and Irish and German Catholics in the city kept a low profile.[13]

The lower Delaware valley and the farmlands to the south and west were rich centers of agricultural output and manufacturing that made a major contribution to the American war effort. The mid-Atlantic region supplied grain, horses, cattle, sheep, forage, cloth, lumber, and flour for the Continental Army. There were more than two dozen flour mills in the area. Five gunpowder mills in the area produced most of the army's ammunition. Uncounted local iron forges and furnaces supported the war by manufacturing cannon, cannonballs, horseshoes, wagon parts, shovels, and swords. German artisans farther inland produced the coveted Pennsylvania rifle. Salt, a precious commodity in any age without refrigeration, together with other sundries such as soap, candles, medicines, and blankets were all produced in the Philadelphia region. The area had long been renowned for its paper mills, whose products were necessary for Continental money, regimental books, writing paper, and small arms cartridges.

The port was both a shipbuilding facility and a major hub for the importation of goods key to American military success. What little foreign trade Americans were able to nurture during the war was principally channeled through Philadelphia. Large quantities of French weapons and gunpowder were smuggled in from the Caribbean, while rice and other foodstuffs, together with liquor, tobacco, and indigo, arrived from the Chesapeake region. Philadelphia's shipyards turned out small and large vessels for military purposes. The entire Pennsylvania militia navy, which answered to the province, was created in Philadelphia's shipyards. In March of 1777, a foundry opened on the waterfront

13 McGuire, *Philadelphia Campaign*, vol. 1, 126.

opposite Old Swedes Church to produce brass cannon. Even the yard of the State House (today's Independence Hall) doubled as a muddy artillery park.

By 1777, the signs of war were visible everywhere in and around Philadelphia. Howe had good reason to want to wrest it from Washington's grasp.

Sentiment

The young United States was rich in some goods, but hard currency was in short supply. Congress resorted to the printing of paper money, which almost immediately began to lose its value. Inflation set in quickly, and by 1777 the price of nearly everything had skyrocketed. A shortage of precious metals hampered colonial efforts, as did a critical shortage in lead. Congress tried to remedy the situation by ordering that lead down spouts be removed from buildings to make ammunition for the army.[14]

Unfortunately for the colonial cause, the spirit and enthusiasm within the city for the Revolution was waning. Alexander Graydon, a Philadelphia captain captured at Fort Washington and home on parole, described the mood. "I soon discovered that a material change had taken place during my absence from Pennsylvania," he wrote, "and that the pulses of many that, at the time of my leaving it, had beaten high in the cause of Whiggism and liberty, were considerably lowered." While this was true among urbanites, the majority of the people in the surrounding countryside remained enthusiastic about the war.[15]

Philadelphia's disenchantment with the Revolution offered the British an opportunity to take advantage of their uncertainty. Pennsylvania's people remained less militant than the New Englanders to the north or the Virginians to the south. Much of this was because of their diversified economy, which was less affected by Parliament's taxation policies than other regions. Many felt they profited from the imperial connection. As far as these citizens were concerned, they already enjoyed the "kind of society that other Americans aspired to, and it had become a reality without needing a revolution."[16]

---

14 McGuire, *Philadelphia Campaign*, vol. 1, 127-128.

15 Alexander Graydon, *Memoirs of a Life, Chiefly Passed in Pennsylvania, within the Last Sixty Years* (Edinburgh, 1822), 299.

16 Luzader, *Saratoga*, 5.

Joseph Galloway, former speaker of the Pennsylvania Assembly, had led General Howe to believe that the Loyalists there would rise up to assist him. Galloway claimed that up to ninety percent of Pennsylvania's citizens were loyal to the Crown, and informed Howe that they would reaffirm their allegiance to the King should a British army march upon Philadelphia.[17] Howe was convinced. The people in the middle colonies, he argued, were "disposed to peace, in which sentiment they would be confirmed, by our getting possession of Philadelphia, I am, from this consideration, fully persuaded, the principal army should act offensively on that side, where the enemy's chief strength will certainly be collected."[18]

Strategic Re-Thinking

By the time Howe wrote his December 20, 1776, letter to Germain, he no longer intended to wait for the reinforcements he had requested in his previous letter. Instead, he would drive toward Philadelphia in the spring of 1777. A threat to Philadelphia would force Washington to stand and fight a pitched battle, and Howe intended to beat him decisively in the field. Such a victory, he believed would accelerate the war's end.

In order to march into Pennsylvania, Howe's earlier proposal would have to be stripped down considerably. The Rhode Island column originally slated to move north would have to be eliminated unless reinforcements were sent to him; a mere 2,000 men would remain behind to garrison Rhode Island. The proposed garrison for New York City would be reduced to 4,000 men, and only 3,000 troops would stay behind on the Lower Hudson to potentially assist the column marching south from Canada into upstate New York. After deducting these garrisons, Howe concluded he would have about 10,000 men for the advance into Pennsylvania.

Howe's December 1776 proposal also reiterated his earlier thoughts about the northern army. It could not be expected in Albany before the middle of September. As far as Howe was concerned, the New England plan that had been in place since 1775 was no longer applicable due to changing strategic circumstances in North America. Thus, advancing up the Hudson River was no

17 John W. Jackson, *With the British Army in Philadelphia* (San Rafael, CA, 1979), 3.

18 Stockdale, *Parliamentary Register*, vol. 10, 371.

longer necessary, nor part of Howe's strategic thinking. Howe projected that by the time Burgoyne arrived in Albany, he would be done with his operations in Pennsylvania or reinforcements from Europe would be available to move up the Hudson to assist Burgoyne. Howe's dispatch to Germain basically tossed out the long-planned New England campaign, but it did not completely eliminate hope that a column of troops would be available to assist the northern army by September.

Understanding that Lord Germain might have other ideas, Howe asked him "to point out any general plans that may be thought most advisable, both with respect to the present strength of the army, and on the event of reinforcements, remarking the periods of times in which these troops may be expected."[19]

Unfortunately for Howe and the rest of the British, this latest dispatch to London was constructed before the British disaster at Trenton, and as previously noted, Germain did not receive it until two months later. It was also based on an incorrect understanding of the situation. Historian Richard Ketchum wrote that Howe's strategy showed an "unwillingness to recognize that the capture of Philadelphia, beyond its potential psychological impact on rebels and loyalists, could not in itself determine the outcome of the war." Such a capture, Ketchum continued, "in strategic as well as geographic terms . . . led nowhere." For Howe to win in 1777, he "must destroy Washington's army, and seizing a piece of real estate—no matter how valuable—was no way to achieve that." Washington, inspired by his victories at Trenton and Princeton, was emboldened to defend the city as long as it remained in American hands, but always knew it was more important to fight another day rather than be destroyed.[20]

A month later, following the double defeats at Trenton and Princeton, a dejected Howe again wrote to Germain. In his dispatch of January 20, 1777, Howe reported the setback and declared that the only way to achieve victory in 1777 was to bring Washington to a general engagement. Howe knew this would be difficult because the Americans move "with so much more celerity than we possibly can." Needing to replace the losses incurred during the last week of December, Howe now increased his reinforcement request to 20,000 and—

19 Stockdale, *Parliamentary Register*, vol. 10, 371-372.

20 Richard M. Ketchum, *Saratoga: Turning Point of America's Revolutionary War* (New York, 1997), 59.

setting the stage for Burgoyne's disaster in upstate New York—hinted for the first time of a desire to use the fleet to move some troops closer to the American capital. However, at this point Howe intended this movement to be an auxiliary one, and not the principal thrust. Nevertheless, if more men were sent, Howe hoped he could send a column north out of Rhode Island. This newest dispatch arrived in London a month and a half after it was written.[21]

Howe later explained his reasoning before Parliament:

> The . . . suggestion is, that I ought to have gone up Hudson's-River, in order to facilitate the approach of the northern army to Albany. What would have been the consequences of such an expedition? Before the object of it would have been attained, the forts in the Highlands must have been carried, which would probably have cost a considerable number of men, defended, as they would have been, by Washington's whole force. But these forts being carried, how would the enemy have acted? In one of these two ways: He would either have put himself between me and New-York, or between me and the northern army. In either case I am of opinion, that the success of our efforts upon Hudson's-River, could not, from the many difficulties in penetrating through so very strong a country, have been accomplished in time to have possession of Philadelphia that campaign.
>
> But admitting I had at length reached Albany, what should I have gained, after having expended the campaign upon that object alone, that I had not a right to expect by drawing off General Washington, with the principal American army, from any operations on that side? When it is considered how invidious and how minute a scrutiny has been made into my conduct, and into the motives of my conduct, I shall not be thought to speak absurdly if I say, that had I adopted the plan of going up Hudson's-River, it would have been alleged, that I had wasted the campaign with a considerable army under my command, merely to ensure the progress of the northern army which could have taken care of itself, provided I had made a diversion in its favour, by drawing off to the southward the main army under General Washington.[22]

Howe's testimony hints at one of the greatest fears of eighteenth-century British commanders in North America. Although the British had troops all over the world, the recruitment and training of replacements for the British line

---

21 Stockdale, *Parliamentary Register*, vol. 10, 377-378.

22 *The Narrative of Lieut. Gen. Sir William Howe, in a Committee of the House of Commons, on the 29th of April, 1779, Relative to His Conduct, During His Late Command of the King's Troops in North America: to Which are Added, Some Observations Upon a Pamphlet, Entitled, Letters to a Nobleman* (London, 1780), 19-20.

regiments was an expensive and time-consuming process. Most commanders during the Revolution worried about engaging in assault tactics that would result in high casualties to soldiers who were difficult to replace. Howe had witnessed the appalling casualties suffered while attacking Breed's Hill during the battle of Bunker Hill. Throughout his time in command, he resorted to flanking maneuvers to reduce the risk of casualties to his own army. In Howe's mind, assaulting the fortifications in the rugged terrain of the Hudson Highlands, presumably with Washington's entire army defending them, was out of the question. Instead, with Philadelphia in his sights, Howe continued to make his own plans.

Complicating British decision-making, and unbeknownst to Howe, John Burgoyne returned to London from the Canadian front early in December 1776. Once back in London on leave, Burgoyne attended the winter sessions of Parliament and conducted some family business. Of prime importance were his orders from Carleton, who charged Burgoyne with fulfilling the needs of the northern army. Carleton had jotted down some strategic ideas for the 1777 campaign, but allowed Burgoyne substantial discretion in its execution. Carleton expected to conduct the northern campaign without any assistance from Howe's army at New York City.[23]

As the next several months passed, Burgoyne seemed to have forgotten that fact. During his voyage across the Atlantic, Burgoyne elaborated and expanded upon the thoughts Carleton had outlined for the spring campaign. When he met with both Germain and King George III, he presented his thoughts based upon the supposition that he would eventually make the Canadian army available for Howe's use. The primary objective of his army would be to capture Fort Ticonderoga. Thereafter, argued Burgoyne, the "sole purpose of the Canada army [was] to effect a junction with General Howe, or after co-operating so far as to get possession of Albany and open

---

23 Luzader, *Saratoga*, xx-xxi. Guy Carleton played only a minor role in the Philadelphia Campaign but is worth a short biography. He was born in 1724 to an Anglo-Irish family and was a professional soldier. By the time of the Revolution, he had already spent a number of years in North America. He led the invasion of New York from Canada in 1776 and served as governor general of Quebec and commander in chief of His Majesty's forces in Canada. Carleton's efforts prevented the Americans from making Canada the fourteenth colony. Like many of his peers, Carleton had hopes for political and military advancement. Neither Carleton nor the army under his command answered to William Howe. Carleton's hopes, however, were hampered by Lord George Germain, who soon ordered Burgoyne to take command of Carleton's field army for the move south into New York.

communication to New York, to remain upon the Hudson's river, and thereby enable that general to act with his whole force to the southward."[24]

Burgoyne also presented an alternative. He proposed taking the Canadian army by ship to form a junction with Howe's main army, bypassing the Lake Champlain-Hudson River plan altogether. While this proposal was rejected, Burgoyne throughout the planning process assumed an eventual junction with Howe. King George III reviewed Burgoyne's proposals and for the most part agreed, at least in principle. Most importantly, he noted that Burgoyne's "force [should move] down to Albany & Join at that place [with Howe's army]."[25]

On March 26, 1777, Burgoyne received orders to lead the British army in Canada south along the Lake Champlain-Hudson River corridor to form a junction with William Howe's army near Albany. Unbeknownst to Howe and Carleton, Burgoyne had been lobbying Germain, the King, and Parliament to supplant Carleton as the field commander in Canada and lead that army in 1777. The ambitious Burgoyne's proposals for the campaign were in line with the longstanding plan to split New England away from the other colonies.

The orders to Burgoyne contained very important details. Once Burgoyne secured Lake Champlain, he was to proceed to Albany and "put himself under the command of Sir William Howe." The orders made it clear that no matter what operations or contingencies arose during the campaign, Burgoyne was to never lose sight of the "intended junction with Sir William Howe as their [Burgoyne's army] principal objective." To ease his mind about Howe's intentions, Germain told Burgoyne that he would "write to Sir William Howe" informing him of the campaign plans.[26]

Burgoyne assumed the Canadian army should advance in the general direction of Howe's army, per the Hudson River plan, even though he seems to have been aware of Howe's change of strategy. According to Piers Mackesy, Howe "must first clear the lower Hudson and help Burgoyne to establish himself at Albany. . . . Howe intended to favour Burgoyne's advance in some degree with a detachment." Therefore, Burgoyne formulated his plans based on the New England concept. He would drive down the Lake Champlain corridor

24 Ibid., 8-9; Stockdale, *Parliamentary Register*, vol. 10, 207.

25 John Fortescue, ed., *The Correspondence of King George The Third: From 1760 to December 1783: Printed from the Original Papers in the Royal Archives at Windsor Castle* (London, 1928), vol. 3, 443-444.

26 Stockdale, *Parliamentary Register*, vol. 10, 212.

while a diversionary column operated in the Mohawk River Valley. He assumed, despite the prize of Philadelphia, that Howe would somehow still aid him in the lower Hudson Valley.[27]

Although Germain had promised to inform Howe of the plans, in none of his letters to Howe in the spring of 1777 did he detail Burgoyne's expedition and explain what Howe was expected to do in support of the operation. Germain's oversight has been attributed to inconvenience. Germain had given instructions for the preparation of a letter to Howe detailing the approved Canadian operations, to be sent with a copy of Burgoyne's instructions. On the way to his country retreat, Germain stopped at his office to sign the letter. "I observed to him there was no letter to Howe to acquaint him with the plan or what was expected of him in consequence of it. His lordship [Germain] stared and D'Oyley [deputy secretary] stared but said he would in a moment write a few lines. 'So,' says Lord Sackville, 'My poor horses must stand in the street all the time, and I shan't be to my time anywhere.' D'Oyley then said he had better go, and he would write for himself to Howe and include copies of Burgoyne's Instructions which would tell him all that he would want to know, and with that his Lordship was satisfied as it enabled him to keep his time, for he would never bear delay or disappointment."[28]

The proposed letter was in fact completed, but unsigned and unsent in a pile of government paperwork. After all, since Howe was familiar with the longstanding New England plan, there seemed to be no pressing reason for Germain to outline it again. "It is clear that Lord George expected the armies to join, that he assumed Howe understood the general plan, and that he believed Howe could take Philadelphia and join Burgoyne in a single campaign." Such an assumption was not unreasonable. The plan for conquering the Hudson Valley had been in place for a year and a half, and it was no mystery to Howe.[29]

Germain has received a great deal of blame for the confusing or absent orders issued in the spring of 1777. In an age before satellite images, GPS, Internet, email, telephones, or telegraphs, Germain was forced to rely upon face-to-face contact with his generals or dispatches sent across the Atlantic for vital intelligence. Sending dispatches to their destinations overseas via sailing

---

27 Mackesy, *War for America*, 115.

28 Luzader, *Saratoga*, 354-355, cites the original source as the William Knox Papers, which were published in the British Historical Commission Publications, but this could not be confirmed.

29 Gruber, *The Howe Brothers*, 187-188.

ships took several weeks, and they were usually outdated when they arrived. Germain had no personal contact with Howe during this period, and was forced to rely on his letters for information. While both Burgoyne and Henry Clinton (a subordinate from Howe's army) did sail to London during the winter, Germain had to take these self-serving officers and their information and opinions with a sizeable grain of salt.

When King George III approved Burgoyne's Hudson River plan and at the same time approved Howe's Philadelphia thrust, it was Germain's duty to point out the contradictory orders to the King, or at least inform the two principal generals of the 1777 campaign of the difference between their orders. However, Germain had allowed Howe a great deal of latitude in the campaign of 1776, and "saw no cause to interfere with his plans for the next."[30]

In March 1777, Germain informed Howe that the King felt that his changed plans were "solid and decisive."[31] Even though Howe would not receive this news until two months later, he had already decided that Philadelphia was more important than anything that might be happening on the northern front. Therefore, the advance from Canada was made with the full understanding that Howe would eventually support Burgoyne, but that he would not do so until the latter reached Albany.

Neither Germain nor King George III had ever commanded armies in the field, so they were unfamiliar with the logistics of moving an eighteenth-century army through a hostile countryside. What little knowledge they did possess related to recent warfare in Europe, where roads and farms could support large moving armies. In contrast, the North American wilderness lacked an extensive road network, and much of the countryside, especially on the northern front, was relatively wild. Also, even the more professional British officers rarely considered the American militia's ability to harass, delay, and capture moving columns and supply trains. Lack of knowledge of the American front led Germain and the King to naively believe that Howe could, within a few months, capture Philadelphia and then return to the New York City area to assist Burgoyne along the Hudson. Unfortunately for the British, it would take Howe a few months just to get close to Philadelphia, let alone capture, fortify, and garrison the American capital.

---

30 Stockdale, *Parliamentary Register*, vol. 10, 394.

31 Ibid.

Howe's decision to risk everything on taking Philadelphia played a large part in the disaster that would engulf Burgoyne in upstate New York. However, at least one historian has argued, "it would be entirely mistaken to assume that Howe sacrificed Burgoyne either through indifference or stupidity." Yet, it is clear Howe lacked enthusiasm for the Hudson River/New England plan. And "a lack of enthusiasm for it . . . leaves the impression that the failure of the government to send Howe reinforcements as numerous as he wished put him in a mood prejudicial to a sympathetic handling of the problem presented by Burgoyne's advance."[32] Even if Germain had been more forthright in his dispatches to Howe, it is doubtful the general would have abandoned his Philadelphia operation. "As it was," observed one writer, "Howe ignored Clinton's pleas for a thrust up the Hudson as well as Germain's instructions to Carleton."[33]

Howe's obsession with Philadelphia did not lead to quick and decisive action on that front. He spent two weeks sparring with Washington in northern New Jersey; another three weeks loading his army onto transport ships; more than a month moving the army to the upper reaches of the Chesapeake Bay; and finally, almost three weeks bringing Washington to battle along the banks of the Brandywine River.

Not until May 18 did Germain send a dispatch to Howe approving his plan to capture Philadelphia. Although the King would have preferred Howe take some action to affect New England, Germain endorsed Howe's plan of operations. The letter also implied that Howe would return to New York in time to assist Burgoyne in the fall: Howe's movement to Philadelphia was to be "executed in time for you to cooperate with the army ordered to proceed from Canada and put itself under your command."[34] A recent interpretation of the campaign leaves the impression that Germain never intended for Burgoyne to link up with Howe's army. John Luzader believes Germain's intention for 1777 was for Burgoyne to clear the Hudson River valley of rebels as far south as Albany. Once he reached Albany, he was to wait there for orders from Howe.[35] In any case, Howe did not receive this latest directive until August 18. By that

---

32 Troyer Steele Anderson, *The Command of the Howe Brothers During the American Revolution* (New York and London, 1936), 272-273.

33 Gruber, *Howe Brothers*, 266.

34 *Report on the Manuscripts*, vol. 2, 66-67.

35 Luzader, *Saratoga*, 26.

point, the bulk of his army had boarded ships, left New York, and traveled well up the Chesapeake Bay en route to Philadelphia.

Should Howe have assisted Burgoyne? Howe probably should have moved north, in keeping with the longstanding British strategy. Both the King and Germain were fully aware of Howe's thinking by the spring of 1777: Howe was going after Philadelphia, and he might not return to New York in time to assist Burgoyne. At no time, however, did they send a direct order to Howe to assist Burgoyne. In a lengthy letter to Germain, Howe explained that he expected Washington to follow him south to defend Philadelphia. If he was mistaken, and Washington went north into the Hudson River Valley, Howe would be hard on his heels.[36]

Time would prove Howe correct. Washington would in fact move south to defend Philadelphia, negating the need for Howe to move north in pursuit toward Albany. Also, if Luzader's interpretation is correct, Germain never intended Howe to do anything for Burgoyne before that officer reached Albany. Considering the amount of time it would take Burgoyne to reach Albany, Howe could perhaps have returned from Philadelphia with sufficient time to move north. Even if Burgoyne had been victorious at Saratoga, he could not have reached Albany before the end of October. By that time Howe had captured Philadelphia and perhaps could have been on his way back north, as intended in Germain's dispatches.

The result of all this strategic thinking and re-thinking, political maneuvering, and bureaucratic communication errors was that William Howe determined to strike out for Philadelphia without anyone else in the British high command fully understanding his intentions, or what his actions—even his success—would mean for the overall fate of the British war effort in North America.

36 Stockdale, *Parliamentary Register*, vol. 10, 414-415.

Chapter 2

Northern New Jersey: Preliminaries
January - June 1777

"It is highly probable, nay almost certain, they mean to make a push; their object is a secret, only known to them, tho' I have my conjectures."[1]

— George Washington, February 23, 1777

Initial Disposition of Forces

The maneuvers that initiated the Philadelphia campaign and ultimately led the armies to the banks of the Brandywine River did not begin until June of 1777, six months after Trenton and Princeton. Because there was neither a single major battle fought nor much maneuvering during those six months, this time period is often overlooked.

In fact, both Washington and Howe were active during this relative lull, but in very different ways. Washington spent these months rebuilding an army that was on the brink of collapse in December 1776. Even though it was an army-under-construction, Washington did not let it sit idle. Instead, he harassed and pestered British outposts in northern New Jersey in a series of skirmishes and raids. These activities not only kept the men alert and active, but also sharpened their skills in the field against a real enemy. Howe, meanwhile, spent this time sending dispatches to London that altered his plans for the spring,

---

1 Fitzpatrick, ed., *The Writings of George Washington*, vol. 7, 196.

while those in authority in London continued to conjure up a strategy sure to win the war in 1777, notwithstanding Howe's letters.

Washington's main army remained in the hills around Morristown, New Jersey, about 25 miles west of New York City throughout this period. A series of ridges known as the Watchung Mountains shields Morristown to the east. The formation rises from 450 to 879 feet above sea level, with cliff-like approaches in some places. Washington used this high ground to observe the countryside all the way to Sandy Hook, New Jersey, and keep an eye on the roads between New York City and Philadelphia. Morristown contained about 70 houses clustered around an eight-acre village green and was home to around 350 people. Several thousand more lived in the villages of Madison, Westfield, Chatham, Whippany, Boonton, Rockaway, Bound Brook, Parsippany, and Basking Ridge around Morristown. By the end of the winter, Continental troops were camping in all of those towns.

Morristown provided a number of advantages to the Continental Army. As noted, the town sat in the midst of hilly terrain that could be easily defended, even by an American army that was regrouping following the disasters of 1776. The town was home to numerous patriots and several of New Jersey's leaders. Just a few months previously, Charles Lee's division had camped there and found the population to be friendly. Scattered around the village were a number of ironworks which produced ammunition and perhaps cannon for the army. The town also had an organized body of militia, one of the few in the state. The town appeared very religious, which Washington deemed important. Morristown was also roughly the midway point between New York and Philadelphia, and close to the main road connecting the two ports. Finally, the town was within supporting distance of Washington's other bodies of troops in New York, Connecticut, and Rhode Island. In an emergency, his Continental Army could quickly shift to any of those areas.[2]

New York City hosted the general headquarters for the British, who also maintained a large field force at New Brunswick, New Jersey, a provincial trading town on the Raritan River. There were additional British outposts between the Raritan and Perth Amboy, the capital of East Jersey.[3]

2   Chadwick, *Washington's War*, 73-75.

3   West Jersey and East Jersey had been two distinct parts of the Province of New Jersey. This political division existed for 28 years, from 1674 to 1702. Although New Jersey was unified by 1777, many still referred to the area as "The Jerseys."

New Brunswick was composed of about 400 houses, many of which had been partly deserted or destroyed. The commercial village was a shadow of its former self. Before war came to the region the previous summer, New Brunswick had been a thriving port town with a mix of Dutch and English colonial architecture. The town served as a rendezvous point in 1776 when thousands of American troops moved north from the more southern colonies to defend New York.[4] When the Americans suffered repeated defeats attempting to hold New York and retreated across northern New Jersey, the town was evacuated and many of the residents fled. The British promptly occupied the town, which both sides pillaged.

After the British were defeated at Trenton and Princeton, the headquarters for New Jersey was established in New Brunswick. Fortifications were constructed, and several elite British and Hessian units garrisoned the town. These troops included British and Hessian grenadiers and Hessian jaegers, with Maj. Gen. Charles Cornwallis in command.[5]

While the British forces dug in and patrolled along the Raritan River, George Washington, just to the west in the mountains surrounding Morristown, evaluated and reorganized what was left of his Continental Army. What he discovered could only have been dismaying. Still with him were some militia from New Jersey and Pennsylvania, and small numbers of loyal Continental Regulars who had remained even after their enlistments ran out on December 31. Congress had approved the creation of a Continental Army in 1776 for just one year's duration. Those who had enlisted at that time fulfilled their commitment on the last day of the year; many left the army the next day. Thousands more had been killed, wounded, or captured. The force at Morristown was about 90 percent (roughly 20,000 men) smaller than the army Washington had led around New York City just a few months earlier. Congress and Washington faced a Herculean task in rebuilding the colonial force that spring of 1777.

---

4 One of the great stories taught to schoolchildren to this day occurred in the village that September of 1776. Future president John Adams and statesman and inventor Benjamin Franklin shared a bed in a small tavern room on the way to a peace conference with William Howe and his brother Admiral Lord Richard Howe. The two patriots spent the evening arguing over the value of fresh air, trading turns opening and closing the window. McGuire, *Philadelphia Campaign*, vol. 1, 8-9.

5 Ibid.

Mode of Warfare: Plundering and Petite Guerre

To buy time to rebuild the army, Washington authorized a series of ambushes and raids on the British outposts, but no large-scale engagements. Many of the opposing troops caught in these ambushes and raids tended to be Hessian. While Howe had issued orders forbidding the plundering of the countryside, the German troops contracted to assist the British war effort were not subject to British military discipline. There was little Howe could do to stop them from raiding the local inhabitants. Unfortunately for Howe, his British regulars saw the Hessian troops pillaging and decided they too should be allowed to reap the bounty around them. Discipline within Howe's army deteriorated as both Hessian and British soldiers roamed the area indiscriminately. While they were out seeking plunder, they were vulnerable to Washington's raids and ambushes.

Unfortunately for the fledgling American army, an outbreak of smallpox erupted as soon as it arrived at Morristown, sickening soldiers and civilians alike. Washington quickly decided to inoculate his entire army rather than run the risk of losing a number of the few troops he still had with him:

> Finding the small pox to be spreading much and fearing that no precaution can prevent it from running thro' the whole of our Army, I have determined that the Troops shall be inoculated. This Expedient may be attended with some inconveniences and some disadvantages, but yet I trust, in its consequences will have the most happy effects. Necessity not only authorizes but seems to require the measure, for should the disorder infect the Army, in the natural way, and rage with its usual Virulence, we should have more to dread from it, than from the Sword of the Enemy.[6]

While smallpox itself and the inoculations against it disabled many American soldiers, not all were knocked out of circulation. Notwithstanding the many popular histories of the American Revolution, British and Hessian troops were not the only soldiers stealing, plundering, and destroying private property in New Jersey that spring—American troops were just as guilty. Most of the thieving colonials were members of the New Jersey militia. Militiamen were notoriously undisciplined, and Washington had little control over them. As far

---

6   Fitzpatrick, ed., *The Writings of George Washington*, vol. 6, 473.

as these Jerseymen were concerned, it was their right to plunder from New Jersey Loyalists. Many of their neighbors had remained loyal to the Crown or had joined a British regular regiment or one of the many provincial regiments the British formed with American colonists. Much like Howe, Washington could do little to curb the plundering occurring along the periphery of his army.

Within weeks after the turn of the year, inflation combined with a lack of commerce and the difficulty in obtaining many goods further weakened Washington's army. Despair and apathy set in. Support from both locals and Congress plummeted, while desertion skyrocketed.[7] At the end of January, Washington informed the President of the Congress, John Hancock, that the army was "shamefully reduced by desertion and . . . [if] the people in the Country can be forced to give Information, when Deserters return to their old Neighbourhoods, we shall be obliged to detach one half of the Army to bring back the other." Washington also wanted the assemblies in the states providing militiamen to pass laws providing a severe penalty for hiding and protecting deserters.[8]

Despite these debilitating distractions, Washington managed some small-scale accomplishments. Captain Levin Friedrich Ernst von Muenchhausen of the Hessian Leib Regiment had been appointed Howe's aide-de-camp in November 1776, and served with him until Howe returned to England in May 1778.[9] According to von Muenchhausen, "Up to the 21st of January, nothing noteworthy happened except that our troops stationed in Jersey have been continuously harassed by Washington. Having a sizable army, he has forced us to abandon Elizabethtown, inflicting the loss of 80 Waldeckers, and now we are occupying only Brunswick and Amboy." The abandonment of Elizabethtown came about when the British sent out a reconnaissance party in the direction of Springfield composed of 13 members of the 17th Light Dragoons and a body of Waldeckers. When British

---

7   McGuire, *Philadelphia Campaign*, vol. 1, 17.

8   Fitzpatrick, ed. *Writings of Washington*, vol. 7, 81.

9   Captain von Muenchhausen proved invaluable to Howe as a multilingual aide. In an age of German-speaking officers, it was vital to have a staff member who spoke French—the language almost all professional European officers understood in the era. Von Muenchhausen was from Hanover. He arrived in North America in August of 1776 and served through the New York campaign before joining Howe's staff. Friedrich von Muenchhausen, *At General Howe's Side: 1776-1778: The Diary of General William Howe's aide de camp, Captain Friedrich von Muenchhausen,* trans. Ernst Kipping, ed. Samuel Steele Smith (Monmouth Beach, NJ, 1974), 4.

intelligence overestimated the number of troops Washington had at his disposal, they decided to abandon Elizabethtown.[10]

The conflict had devolved into what we today call guerilla warfare—ambushes and sniping punctuated by occasional atrocities. In the eighteenth century, this form of partisan warfare was known by the French term *la petite guerre*, or "small war." Late in February, Washington described what was occurring to his northern front commander, Maj. Gen. Philip Schuyler. "There have been and almost daily are, some small Skirmishes," he explained, "but without much loss on either side, they have generally been favourable to us."[11]

Washington did not expect this form of warfare to last. After noting the buildup of British forces at New Brunswick, he told Schuyler, "I do not apprehend, however, that this Petit Guerre will be continued long, I think matters will be transacted upon a larger Scale. The Troops at Brunswick have been considerably reinforced of late, and Genl. Howe and Piercy are said to have come over, their number there and the dependent posts, must be from 10 to 12,000; from these Circumstances," he concluded, "It is highly probable, nay almost certain, they mean to make a push; their object is a secret, only known to them, tho' I have my conjectures."[12] Luckily for Washington, whose army was in no state to wage a pitched battle, he was wrong: the bushwhacking continued for months, which in turn gave him time to rebuild the Continental Army.

Captain Sir James Murray of the British 57th Regiment of Foot also described the mode of fighting in a letter to his sister in Scotland. "We have a pretty amusement known by the name of foraging or fighting for our daily bread. As the rascals are skulking about the whole country, it is impossible to move with any degree of safety without a pretty large escort," he explained, "and even then you are exposed to a dirty kind of tiraillerie [random gunfire], which is more noisy indeed than dangerous." Notwithstanding Murray's light treatment of the matter, the stress and psychological toll of the constant harassment during these months eventually led to some of the savageness during the Philadelphia campaign—particularly at Paoli.[13]

---

10 Von Muenchhausen, *At General Howe's Side*, 9.

11 McGuire, *Philadelphia Campaign*, vol. 1, 17.

12 Fitzpatrick, ed., *The Writings of George Washington*, vol. 7, 196.

13 James Murray, *Letters from America 1773 to 1780: Being the Letters of a Scots Officer, Sir James Murray, to His Home during the War of American Independence*, Eric Robson, ed. (New York, 1950), 38.

Among the many skirmishes, one on February 23 escalated into a slightly larger engagement. A 2,000-man British foraging party departed Perth Amboy and headed in the direction of Woodbridge, New Jersey. As the men spread out to begin foraging, Continental troops under Brig. Gen. William Maxwell assaulted the grenadier company of the 42nd Royal Highlanders. Although the British fought well, they were heavily outnumbered and forced to withdraw, losing more than 70 casualties in the affair while the Americans lost only a few men. After visiting some of his wounded, Capt.-Lt. John Peebles of the 42nd Highlanders jotted down his thoughts on the previous day's action: "Several of them [were] in a very dangerous way poor fellows, what pity it is to throw away such men as these on such shabby ill managed occasions." A lack of support for the exposed Highlanders had doomed the operation.[14]

(Some) Escalation Begins

By March 1777, Washington was recruiting new soldiers, reorganizing his fragmented army, and determining his strategy for the year. On the 12th of the month, Washington sent a letter to Maj. Gen. Philip Schuyler, quoted here at some length for its exposition of Washington's thinking:

> It is of the greatest importance to the safety of a Country involved in a defensive War, to endeavour to draw their Troops together at some post at the opening of a Campaign, so central to the theatre of War that they may be sent to the support of any part of the Country, the Enemy may direct their motions against. It is a military observation, strongly supported by experience, that a superior Army may fall a sacrifice to an inferior, by an injudicious division. It is impossible, without knowing the Enemy's intentions, to guard against every sudden incursion, or give protection to all the Inhabitants; some principle object shou'd be had in view, in taking post to cover the most important part of the Country, instead of dividing our force, to give shelter to the whole, to attempt which, cannot fail to give the Enemy an Opportunity of beating us in Detachments, as we are under the necessity of guessing at the Enemy's intentions, and further operations; the great object of attention ought to be, where the most proper place is, to draw our force together, from the Eastward and Westward, to cover the Country, prevent the Enemy's penetration and annoy them in turn, shou'd our strength be equal to the attempt. There is not a State upon the Continent, but

---

14 John Peebles, *John Peebles' American War: The Diary of a Scottish Grenadier, 1776-1782*, ed. Ira D. Gruber (Mechanicsburg, PA, 1998), 98.

thinks itself in danger, and scarcely an Officer at any one post, but conceives a reinforcement necessary; to comply with the demands of the whole, is utterly impossible, and if attempted, would prove our inevitable ruin.[15]

Just two days later, Washington expressed his anxiety to Congress. Although the government was rapidly recruiting new soldiers to rebuild the army, they were not arriving fast enough for Washington. "I feel the most painful anxiety when I reflect on our Situation and that of the Enemy," he confessed. "Unless the Levies arrive soon, we must, before it be long, experience some interesting and melancholy event. I believe the Enemy have fixed their object, and the execution will surely be attempted, as soon as the roads are passable. The unprepared state in which we are," he concluded, "favors all their designs, and it is much to be wished they may not succeed to their warmest expectations."[16]

While troops from both sides skirmished in the countryside and Washington developed a strategy for the upcoming campaign, anyone who cared to notice might have paid attention to the Delaware River area in March, where a man named James Molesworth had just been apprehended. Molesworth, a Pennsylvania loyalist, had been introduced to Admiral Lord Richard Howe by Joseph Galloway, a man whose name will forever be connected with the fighting at Brandywine. The admiral commissioned Molesworth to hunt down Delaware River pilots familiar with the passage through the obstructions Americans had sunk in the channel. Molesworth managed to bribe a couple of pilots, but the three of them were captured before they could return to New York. Several patriot pilots had notified authorities about Molesworth's intentions. Molesworth confessed and was executed in late March. Elizabeth Drinker, a Philadelphia Quaker, noted the event in her diary: "A Young Man of the Name Molsworth was hang'd on the Commons by order of our present ruling Gentr'y."[17]

---

15 Fitzpatrick, *The Writings of George Washington*, vol. 7, 272-273.

16 Ibid., 287.

17 Samuel Hazard, ed., *Pennsylvania Archives: Selected and Arranged from Original Documents in the Office of the Secretary of the Commonwealth*, Series 1 (Philadelphia, 1853), vol. 5, 270-276; Steven Rosswurm, *Arms, Country, and Class: The Philadelphia Militia and the "Lower Sort" during the American Revolution* (New Brunswick, NJ, 1989), 156; Elizabeth Drinker, *The Diary of Elizabeth Drinker*, Elaine Forman Crane, ed. (Boston, 1991), vol. 1, 224.

Operations escalated in other ways as well. On April 12, Lord Cornwallis decided to ramp up the level of combat. A Continental outpost at Bound Brook, New Jersey, had been harassing British outposts for weeks and the British general had had enough. The Americans were under the command of Benjamin Lincoln, a Massachusetts native born in 1733 who had been elevated just two months earlier to the rank of major general. The next day, on April 13, Cornwallis led 4,000 British and Hessian troops along both sides of the Raritan River in an attempt to neutralize Lincoln's position. Although most of the Americans escaped, the British captured about 70 men and three artillery pieces. The British victory proved short-lived: when Cornwallis returned to New Brunswick that afternoon, American elements reoccupied Bound Brook. Historian Thomas McGuire succinctly summarized the day's events: "For all the fuss and bother, planning, marching, skirmishing, and recriminating, Cornwallis's goal was only partially realized and of short duration."[18]

The Bound Brook operation bothered Washington, and he made a prediction the next day. "If I am to judge from the present appearance of things the Campaign will be opened by General Howe before we shall be in any condition to oppose him." Washington was worried that the strong probe meant that Howe was close to beginning his campaign while the American army was still heavily outnumbered in men and weapons, was not as well-trained, and did not enjoy the same logistical support. Unbeknownst to Washington, however, British intelligence continued to overestimate the size of his army.[19]

Despite Washington's fears, the lethargic Howe was not yet ready to move. It would be several more weeks before he believed he was prepared to begin his important 1777 campaign. At the end of April, American division commander Nathanael Greene wrote his wife the latest news. "We learn the Enemy are to take the field the first of June," explained Greene. "Their delay is un[ac]countable already. What has kept them in their Quarters we cant immagin."[20]

---

18 McGuire, *Philadelphia Campaign*, vol. 1, 23. Although he commanded a division during the early stages of the Philadelphia Campaign, Lincoln was soon ordered north to organize the militia that would help stop Burgoyne's army moving south in upstate New York.

19 Dorothy Twohig and Philander D. Chase, eds., *The Papers of George Washington*, Revolutionary War Series (Charlottesville and London, 1999), vol. 9, 171.

20 Richard K. Showman, Robert M. McCarthy, and Margaret Cobb, eds., *The Papers of General Nathaniel Greene*, vol. 2, *1 January 1777-16 October 1778* (Chapel Hill, NC, 1980), 60.

One likely factor was the return on May 23 of a significant portion of the British garrison in Rhode Island to New York. After being informed that he could expect few reinforcements, Howe had abandoned all thoughts of his earlier plan of striking into Massachusetts from Rhode Island. He therefore brought back to his main army the men initially intended for that foray, which he intended to use to either increase the New York garrison or accompany him to Philadelphia.

Regardless of what else was or was not happening, skirmishing and partisan warfare continued along the Raritan River in New Jersey. On May 25—a blazing-hot day, according to Capt. von Muenchhausen—jaeger Capt. Johann Ewald found himself involved in a skirmish near Bound Brook. When the British received reports that the Americans had abandoned Bound Brook, they sent out a column on May 26 to secure the position. Major General James Grant, with the 1st Battalion of British Light Infantry along with a detachment of the 16th Light Dragoons, was tasked with the mission. The report of abandonment was untrue, and a lively skirmish took place. The British Brigade of Guards was sent out to support the operation when the firing broke out. Ensign Thomas Glyn, who marched with the Guards and was soon to return home with other Guards officers, recalled the scene: "The Enemy advanced with two pieces of Cannon & began to cannonade us, when we were ordered to lay down & being covered by the ground no loss ensued except Major General Grant having his Horse shot dead under him." Many were amused by the loss of Grant's horse, for he was not the most popular general officer in the British army. Indeed, several subordinates would not have been saddened to see the pompous Grant exit the army by any means. Lieutenant William Hale of the 45th Regiment of Foot, for example, wished "it had been the General instead of the horse, no man can be more detested."[21]

American Brig. Gen. Anthony Wayne, no slouch to pomposity himself, boasted about the action at Bound Brook to Doctor Benjamin Rush: "We Offered Gen'l Grant Battle six times the Other day he as often formed but always on our Approach his people broke and Ran after firing a few Volleys which we never Returned, being Determined to let them feel the force of our

---

21 Von Muenchhausen, *At General Howe's Side*, 12-13; McGuire, *Philadelphia Campaign*, vol. 1, 27; Thomas Glyn, *Journal of American Campaign: 1776-1777*, manuscript journal, 50a, Princeton University Library, Princeton, NJ; Walter Harold Wilkin, *Some British Soldiers in America* (London, 1914), 226.

fire and to give them the Bayonet under Cover of the Smoke." Wayne went on to say that Grant, "who was to March through America at the head of 5000 men had his Coat much Dirtied, his Horses head taken off, and himself badly Bruis'd for having the presumption at the head of 700 British Troops to face 500 Penns'as."[22]

The operation was a clear example of how poorly the British intelligence network performed that spring. The British consistently overestimated the strength of Washington's army, which was in a constant state of flux as the rebuilding continued. "The fact that a sizeable enemy corps can march away and be gone for two hours before we learn of it, shows that we are in a bad way in not having good spies among them," bemoaned von Muenchhausen.[23]

By May 28, Washington had shifted the majority of his army from its winter camp at Morristown to a forward position at Middlebrook. Washington, who always had more issues to manage than the time to do so, acquired about this time yet another headache in the form of a French officer. Sometime that May, Philippe Charles Trouson du Coudray arrived at Morristown with a document in his pocket authorizing him to assume command of all of the Continental Army artillery. The authorization to do so was signed by Silas Deane, one of the American commissioners sent by the Continental Congress to Paris. The problem for Washington, however, was that the position was held by the capable Henry Knox, a Boston native and former bookstore owner. The news infuriated American officers. With the Marquis de Lafayette about to join the army, many high-ranking officers were less than thrilled with the prospect of being outranked by young French officers. Nathanael Greene and John Sullivan submitted their resignations—operative if du Coudray's contract was honored. "A report is circulating here at Camp that Monsieur de Coudray a French Gentleman is appointed a Major General in the service of the United States, his rank to commence from the first of last August," was how Greene's letter of July 1 opened to John Hancock, the president of Continental Congress. "If the report be true it will lay me under the necessity of resigning my Commission as his appointment supercedes me in command." Washington was wise enough to

---

22 Letter to Dr. Benjamin Rush reproduced in Charles J. Stille, *Major-General Anthony Wayne and the Pennsylvania Line in the Continental Army* (Philadelphia, 1893), 71. Wayne's reference was in response to Grant's having once boasted in Parliament that he could easily ride through the American colonies at the head of 5,000 men.

23 Von Muenchhausen, *At General Howe's Side*, 13.

know that losing Knox, Greene, and Sullivan would be a blow the army could ill-afford, while refusing to honor the agreement threatened to alienate the French. The army commander wisely defused the situation by giving du Coudray a staff assignment as Inspector General of Ordnances and Military Manufactories. The Frenchman would later play a major role in the defense of the Delaware River. The artillery command remained with Henry Knox, and Greene and Sullivan remained with their infantry commands.[24]

While Washington was shifting his army to Middlebrook, a contingent of reinforcements for Howe's army arrived from Europe. A company of German riflemen from the principality of Anspach-Brandenburg was among them. Meant to be mounted, the men arrived heavily clothed and sporting knee-high boots. The horses and saddle gear these jaegers required, however, did not arrive with them. Throughout the upcoming campaign they would fight on foot while wearing the awkward uniforms of mounted troops. Along with the jaegers, a new contingent of officers from the three regiments of foot guards also arrived. Some of the officers who had come to America the previous year with the two battalions of Guards were now rotating home.[25]

The age of unpaved roads and horse-drawn transportation usually required good dry weather for active campaigning. May, however, slipped past without major British activity, and by the time June arrived in northern New Jersey, Howe had yet to make any positive movement. An expeditious campaign to capture Philadelphia would more likely than not have had a significant impact on Burgoyne's operation from Canada into upstate New York, while a delay served the opposite effect. Nicholas Cresswell, an Englishman who had been traveling through the American colonies since 1774, passed through Virginia and Pennsylvania before making his way to New York. After having been in the city nearly three weeks, he confessed, "I am as ignorant of the Motions or designs of our Army as if I had been in Virginia." The soldiers, thought Cresswell, "seem very healthy and long to be in action." Howe, he continued, was either "inactive, has no orders to act, or thinks that he has not force sufficient to oppose the Rebels, but which of these or whether any of them is the true reason I will not pretend to say." In fact, Cresswell held strong opinions as to why Howe remained inactive, one of which was the time he spent with his

---

24 Showman, McCarthy, and Cobb, eds. *Papers of Greene*, vol. 2, 109; John W. Jackson, *The Pennsylvania Navy, 1775-1781: The Defense of the Delaware* (New Brunswick, NJ, 1974), 97.

25 McGuire, *Philadelphia Campaign*, vol. 1, 33.

mistress, Mrs. Elizabeth Loring. The delay could only hurt the British cause, thought Cresswell: "But this I am very certain of, if General Howe does nothing, the Rebels will avail themselves of his inactivity by collecting a very numerous Army to oppose him, whenever he shall think it proper to leave Mrs. Lorain [Loring] and face them." Howe, of course, did have orders to begin the campaign. He was supposed to capture Philadelphia and return to the Hudson River area in time to assist Burgoyne coming down from Canada. Cresswell, however, was correct about one thing: Washington was using the extra time very judiciously by rebuilding his Continental Army.[26]

On June 4—King George III's birthday—General Howe hosted a large reception and the forts and ships in the harbor celebrated with each firing 21 gun salutes. Wrote one eyewitness, "You can imagine what thunderous noise it was, there being over 400 ships at anchor here. In the evening most of the houses were illuminated."

When the pomp and ceremony and favors of the flesh would end, and the campaign begin, remained anyone's guess.[27]

False Start

Just before major campaigning began, Hessian Captain von Muenchhausen prepared a helpful breakdown of the British army in and around New York:

In Rhode Island, under the recently exchanged Maj. Gen. Richard Prescott, were four Hessian regiments and three British regiments, totaling 2,750 men.

In New York City proper, under Hessian Gen. Wilhelm von Knyphausen, were five Hessian regiments, two British regiments, and three battalions of Provincials, totaling 4,100 men.

The 250 men of the 57th Regiment of Foot, under Lt. Col. John Campbell, were at Paulus Hook in New Jersey.

There were 1,000 provincials on Long Island.

---

26 Nicholas Cresswell, *The Journal of Nicholas Cresswell 1774-1777* (New York, 1928), 229.

27 Von Muenchhausen, *At General Howe's Side*, 13.

In Amboy, New Jersey, under Gen. John Vaughn, were 13 British regiments, four Hessian regiments, the 17th Light Dragoons, and 400 provincials, for a total of 6,150 men.

Colonel James Webster at Bonhamtown, New Jersey, commanded three English regiments and the 71st Highlanders, a total of 1,700 men.

In and around Piscataway, New Jersey, Brig. Gen. Alexander Leslie commanded the Hessian jaegers, the 42nd Highlanders, four British regiments, the Brigade of Guards, and some provincials, totaling 3,300 men.

Lord Charles Cornwallis at New Brunswick, New Jersey, oversaw two battalions of British grenadiers, two battalions of British light infantry, the 16th Light Dragoons, and four Hessian grenadier battalions, a total of 3,500 men.

Lastly, on Staten Island there were three British regiments and the Anspachers, totaling 1,950 men.

As set forth above in von Muenchhausen's accounting, the grand total available to General Howe was about 24,700 men.[28]

The question now confronting Howe was how best to get all these forces moving in a coordinated endeavor. He decided to begin with an expedition to Middlebush. This move constituted Howe's initial attempt to use an overland march directly toward Philadelphia in an effort to maneuver Washington out of the mountains. If he could draw the colonials into a battle on the plains of northern New Jersey and defeat them there, the remainder of the march to Philadelphia would be relatively simple. A quick victory and expeditious march would also bode well for Burgoyne's column from Canada, and prevent Washington from sending troops north.

Even though Howe had finally begun moving early that June, there was dissatisfaction within the ranks of his officer corps over the delay in doing so. According to Howe, he was forced to wait for the arrival of camp equipment and for grass to grow to feed his horses. At the beginning of 1777, Howe was indeed significantly hampered by a lack of provisions. The British government refused to supply him to any great extent with hay and oats, and thus required he obtain them in America. That logistical decision forced Howe to wait until

---

28 Von Muenchhausen, *At General Howe's Side*, 14.

green forage was available. Still, once the grass was high enough to eat he continued to drag his heels for weeks on end. Had he found a way to begin his campaign earlier that year, he might have had time to crush Washington's army prior to the onset of winter, and then possibly have enough time to aid Burgoyne. Finally, on the night of June 13, Howe marched the bulk of his army in two divisions from New Brunswick to Middlebrook, New Jersey, and went into camp. With some 17,000 men involved in the move, it was the largest British operation since the capture of Fort Lee, New Jersey, the previous November.[29]

Howe's intentions were unknown even to his own commanders. During the previous six months, boats that could be carried on wagons had been prepared in New York, leading many in the army to believe Howe intended to cross the Delaware River. "All the Long-Bottomed Boats were put into Waggons, and everything got in readiness," wrote one member of Howe's command. Others were less sure of what this meant and speculated the entire effort was nothing more than a diversion.[30]

Captain Archibald Robertson of the Royal Engineers, who served on Howe's staff during the campaign, noted that the army's destination was about five miles from New Brunswick and three miles from Hillsborough. According to Robertson, Washington's army was strongly encamped about four miles north of Bound Brook in the mountains. Many assumed Washington would fall back when Howe was seen to be on the move. Unfortunately for the weary British troops, he did not. "I believe it was generally imagined upon our Armys making the Aforesaid Move, He [Washington] would have quitted his stronghold and retreated towards the Delaware," the captain wrote in his journal. "However it proved otherwise, He stood Firm. No Certain Intelligence brought in of the Situation."[31]

Another of Howe's aides, von Muenchhausen, believed Howe had "planned a forced march at dawn in order to cut off and to throw back General Sullivan, who is at Princeton with 2000 men." The Hessian's conclusion was

---

29 Edward E. Curtis, *The British Army in the American Revolution* (Gansevoort, NY, 1998), 102; McGuire, *Philadelphia Campaign*, vol. 1, 36.

30 Thomas Sullivan, *From Redcoat to Rebel: The Thomas Sullivan Journal*, Joseph Lee Boyle, ed. (Bowie, MD, 1997), 116.

31 Archibald Robertson, *Archibald Robertson, Lieutenant General Royal Engineers: His Diaries and Sketches in America, 1762-1780*, ed. Harry Miller Lydenberg (New York, 1930), 137.

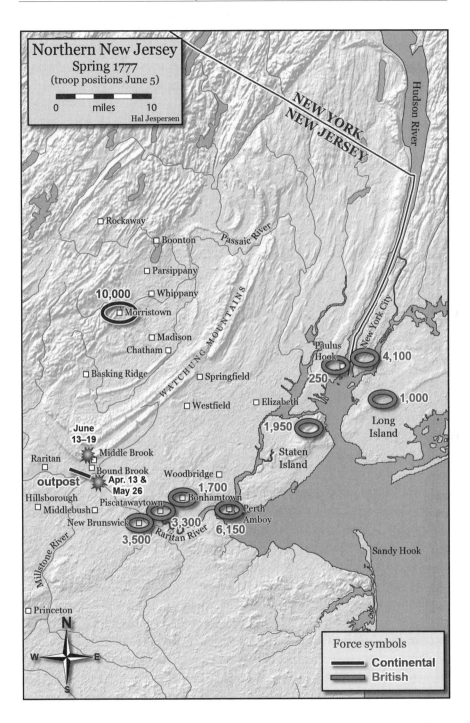

Northern New Jersey
Spring 1777
(troop positions June 5)

0   miles   10
Hal Jespersen

NEW YORK
NEW JERSEY

Hudson River

☐ Rockaway

☐ Boonton   Passaic River

☐ Parsippany

10,000   ☐ Whippany

☐ Morristown

☐ Madison
Chatham ☐

☐ Basking Ridge   ☐ Springfield

New York City

Paulus
Hook   4,100

250

1,000

☐ Westfield   ☐ Elizabeth

Long
Island

1,950

WATCHUNG MOUNTAINS

June
13–19
Middle Brook   Staten
Island

Raritan
☐   ☐ Bound Brook   Woodbridge ☐

outpost   Apr. 13 &
May 26   1,700

Hillsborough   Piscatawaytown   ☐ Bonhamtown

☐ Middlebush ☐   3,300   ☐   Perth
Amboy
New Brunswick ☐   6,150
3,500   Raritan River

Millstone River   Sandy Hook

☐ Princeton

N

W   E

S

Force symbols
━━━━━ Continental
━━━━━ British

easy to reach, for all the tents and heavy baggage had been left behind and the men ordered to carry provisions for three days—certain signs of a campaign march.[32] In addition, such a move was good strategy, for a sweep on Princeton could isolate and destroy Sullivan's Continental division. To the Hessian aide, the move to Middlebush signaled the beginning of Howe's long-awaited campaign. But Robertson, von Muenchausen, and many other British and Hessian officers would soon be disappointed.

*   *   *

Washington observed Howe's movement from his mountain stronghold. Among the many new units raised during the restructuring of the army was a regiment of riflemen under Col. Daniel Morgan of Virginia. Born in 1736, Morgan left home as a teenager to live in the Shenandoah Valley and later served on the American frontier in the French and Indian War and Lord Dunmore War of 1754-1763 and 1774, respectively. When the Revolution erupted in 1775, Morgan took command of two Virginia rifle companies as a captain and marched to Boston. He played a critical role in the invasion of Canada later that year, but was captured at Quebec. After his exchange, he was promoted to colonel of the 11th Virginia Regiment. Morgan was a man Washington could depend upon, and he was about to call for his services in the face of Howe's advance.

All the experienced riflemen throughout the army were detached from their parent regiments for service under Morgan. This reorganization grouped together about 500 frontiersmen, primarily from the mountains of Pennsylvania, Virginia, and Maryland, all armed with Pennsylvania long rifles. Washington issued Morgan orders to use his men as light infantry. "In case of any Movement of the Enemy you are Instantly to fall upon their Flanks and gall them as much as possible," instructed Washington, "taking especial care not to be surrounded, or have your retreat to the Army cut off."

Pennsylvania Rifles were accurate up to about 300 yards, but they were slower and harder to load. The standard smoothbore firearms carried by the two armies could be loaded two and even three times a minute under combat conditions, but a man carrying the Pennsylvania Rifle was lucky to get off one shot every minute under the same circumstances. The other deficiency with the

---

32 Von Muenchhausen, *At General Howe's Side*, 16.

weapon was that it was not constructed to hold a bayonet. Since the primary tactic of the British army was to close with the enemy and use the bayonet freely, riflemen facing such an assault were at a severe disadvantage.

Washington thus believed surprise was the best tactic for Morgan's men. "It occurs to me that if you were to dress a Company or two of true Woods Men in the right Indian Style and let them make the Attack accompanied with screaming and yelling as the Indians do, it would have very good consequences especially if as little as possible was said, or known of the matter beforehand."[33] Morgan would be lining the roads to greet Howe's advance.

The day after reaching Middle Brook, however, the unexpected took place. To the disbelief of officers on both sides, the British Army halted and established a camp. Light skirmishing broke out between the opposing sides near Hillsborough along the Millstone River. On June 15 Howe's chief engineer, Capt. John Montresor, oversaw the construction of three earthen redoubts. The halt, coupled with the erection of defensive fortifications, made it clear that Howe—at least for the moment—did not intend to go any farther.[34] The stop confused and maddened many of Howe's officers and men. Captain von Muenchhausen jotted down in his diary that many blamed "General Howe for not having followed Washington immediately." Howe's aide, however, went on to defend the decision. "Nobody in the world could be more careful than he is. This is absolutely necessary in this cursed hilly country."

American artillery chief Henry Knox thought the short movement and complete halt utterly perplexing. "It was unaccountable that people who the day before gave out in very gasconading terms that they would be in Philadelphia in six days should stop short when they had gone only nine miles," wrote Knox in a letter. "What his next manoeuvres may be I can't say, but we suppose the North River. . . . The motive for belief that the North River will be the scene of his operations is that intelligence is received that Mr. Burgoyne is about crossing the lakes to [Fort] Ticonderoga, and General Howe must make an attempt to push for a junction."[35]

---

33 Fitzpatrick, ed., *The Writings of George Washington*, vol. 8, 236-237.

34 McGuire, *Philadelphia Campaign*, vol. 1, 39-40.

35 Von Muenchhausen, *At General Howe's Side*, 16; Letter reproduced in Francis S. Drake, *Life and Correspondence of Henry Knox, Major-General in the American Revolutionary Army* (Boston, 1873), 43-46. The "North River" to which several officers on both sides refer is synonymous with the Hudson River.

After several days of standstill, Howe's intention became clear: Draw the Continental Army down from the mountains onto the open plain. If Howe's purpose was to entice his enemy to attack him, he was sorely disappointed. Washington had no intention of coming down out of the mountains to play on Howe's terms. "Washington is a devil of a fellow, he is back again, right in his old position, in the high fortified hills," wrote one of Howe's aides. "By retreating he supposedly intended to lure us into the hills and beat us there." British Maj. Charles Stuart was not surprised by Howe's attempt, but he did not believe it would work. Having recently lost his command of a grenadier battalion and been denied permission to return to England, Stuart was without a command that summer, and so accompanied Howe's army from New Brunswick.[36]

As far as Stuart was concerned, the "idea of offering these people battle is ridiculous; they have too much caution to risk everything on one action, or rather too much sense to engage an army double their numbers, superior in discipline, and who never make a show of fighting but upon the most advantageous ground. If we wish to conquer them," he concluded, "we must attack them." Stuart knew that the British could not be afraid to draw Washington into a pitched battle or even outright assault his lines. "If we wish to conquer them we must attack him, or if his posts are too strong, by a ruse de guerre place ourselves in that situation that he may expect to attack us to advantage."[37]

Civilians were baffled as well. A loyalist back in New York was simply disgusted by Howe's lethargy. "Hints from head-quarters, that his Excellency, ever attentive to the sparing of his Gallant Troops, could not bear the idea of risking two or three thousand brave men to be sacrificed by 'base scum, and dunghill villains' . . . . Rebellion, which a twelvemonth ago was really a contemptible Pigmy, is now in appearance become a Giant."

It was true that British field commanders, including Howe, were reluctant to unnecessarily bloody their regiments, especially in frontal assaults, because replacing veteran soldiers was a long and tedious process. But Howe had also become far too comfortable in New York. "All this time General Howe was at New York in the lap of Ease," wrote one eyewitness, "or rather, amusing

---

36 Von Muenchhausen, *At General Howe's Side*, 16; McGuire, *Philadelphia Campaign*, vol. 1, 39.

37 Mrs. E. Stuart Wortley, ed., *A Prime Minister and His Son: From the Correspondence of the Third Earl of Bute and Lt. General The Honourable Sir Charles Stuart, K.B.* (London, 1925), 112.

himself in the lap of a Mrs L[orin]g, who is the very Cleopatra to this Anthony of ours."[38]

Howe's army, composed of some of the finest troops in the world, was confronted by a motley hodge-podge of militia, frontiersmen, and Continental Regulars. No legitimate European officer considered Washington's force—determined though its men might have been—"real soldiers" or a "real army" compared with the professional grenadiers, light infantrymen, guardsmen, light horse, royal artillerymen, and Hessian jaegers fielded by Howe. Yet, as at least one historian has pointed out, this ragtag bunch assembled by Washington constituted the true origin of the United States Army: "Within the year, it would be baptized by fire at Brandywine, grow through hard experience at Germantown, and come to maturity at Valley Forge. If Washington can be described as the army's father, Howe might aptly be described as its nanny."[39] These experiences were giving birth to a nation that had the capacity and the willingness to defend itself.

Late on June 14, reports of the British advance arrived in Philadelphia. John Adams was not overly concerned by the news, writing to his wife that if the British were bold enough to capture the city, "they will hang a Mill stone about their Necks." The opinionated Adams believed the seizure of the city would seriously hamper the British war effort and that its capture would force the evacuation of New Jersey. "The Jersey Militia have turned out, with great Spirit. Magistrates and Subjects, Clergy and Laity, have all marched, like so many Yankees." Despite the hope he placed in the militia, Adams was also realistic. If Howe managed to cross the Delaware River and Washington was not there to stop him, Congress would need to leave Philadelphia and move "fifty or sixty Miles into the Country. But they will not move hastily."[40]

Another four days passed, during which Howe did nothing more than skirmish, plunder the countryside, and build some earthworks. He had moved fewer than 10 miles. If Howe had any hope of capturing Philadelphia and returning to the lower Hudson River by September to assist Burgoyne, his

---

38 *Historical Anecdotes, Civil and Military: in a Series of Letters, Written from America, in the Years 1777 and 1778, to Different Persons in England; Containing Observations on the General Management of the War, and on the Conduct of our Principal Commanders, in the Revolted Colonies, During that Period* (London, 1779), 40-42.

39 McGuire, *Philadelphia Campaign*, vol. 1, 43.

40 Paul H. Smith et. al., eds., *Letters of Delegates to Congress* (Washington, 1981), vol. 7, 195.

actions did not reflect these intentions. The slow pace suited Adams, who seems not to have cared whether the city was taken or not: "We are under no more Apprehensions here than if the British Army was in the Crimea." By sitting still during good campaign weather, Howe was essentially removing his army from the war effort. Confident in Washington's abilities, Adams added, "Our Fabius will be slow, but sure." Benjamin Rush, soon to be with Washington's army as a surgeon, wrote to Anthony Wayne that the "Accts we receive daily of the Strength, discipline, and Spirit of our Army give us great pleasure."[41]

When Washington failed to come down out of the mountains to offer battle, a disappointed Howe decided to give up on this approach and returned to New Brunswick on June 19. Howe quietly withdrew until he was far enough from Washington's outposts to feel secure. They marched, wrote an American eyewitness, "without beat of drum or sound of fife. When his army had gotten beyond the reach of pursuit, they began to burn, plunder and waste all before them. The desolation they committed was horrid, and served to show the malice which marks their conduct." Captain Johann Ewald confirmed this description when he wrote, "On this march all the plantations of the disloyal inhabitants, numbering perhaps some fifty persons, were sacrificed to fire and devastation."[42]

Once the Americans realized what was occurring, Nathanael Greene's division and Anthony Wayne's Pennsylvania brigade initiated a pursuit that triggered some minor skirmishes. It also revealed more of the depredations being committed against innocent civilians. Colonel Persifor Frazer of the Pennsylvania Line later described what they found: "They have in many instances behav'd very cruel to the Inhabitants where they pass'd. A respectable woman they Hung by the Heels so long that when they took her down she liv'd but a few Minutes. Plunder and Cruelty Mark their steps where there is scarce a soul but Tories."[43]

41 Smith, et. al., eds., *Letters of Delegates*, vol. 7, 207; Benjamin Rush to Anthony Wayne, June 18, 1777, Wayne Papers, Historical Society of Pennsylvania,vol. 3.

42 Drake, *Correspondence of Knox*, 45; Johann Ewald, *Diary of the American War: A Hessian Journal: Captain Johann Ewald*, ed. and trans. Joseph P. Tustin (New Haven, CT, 1979), 65.

43 Persifor Frazer, *General Frazer A Memoir Compiled Principally from his Own Papers by his Great-Grandson* (Philadelphia, 1907), 140.

Confusion in the Aftermath

Howe's sudden withdrawal perplexed many British officers, including Major Stuart. "We traced out 4 redoubts at Middebrook, and one to cover the Bridge at Hilsborough," the officer wrote in a letter home to his father, "most of which were nearly finish'd, when, to our astonishment, we received orders to retire to Brunswick." Stuart continued, "I am convinced that, from the redoubts built . . . and the pontoon bridge we incumbered ourselves with, we intended to establish a magazine there, and pursue our way to the Delaware . . . [but did not] for the fear of our escorts being attacked bringing provisions from Brunswick." However, Stuart was quick to point out that all armies face this sort of danger. "The risk which all armies are liable to was our hindrance here, and had absolutely prevented us this whole war from going 15 miles from a navigable river." Stuart concluded by commenting on Howe's tactics: "These retrograde movements appear just as incomprehensible to us as they can possibly do to you, for both in a military and a political sense it seems highly injudicious to have maintained posts." Howe abandoned posts that had cost the army nearly 2,000 men over the previous few months, including loyalist inhabitants of the region. Stuart was angry that those locals were left "unprotected and exposed to a cruel and implacable enemy . . . who have sought your protection and served you."[44]

Howe's intentions during this week in northern New Jersey are difficult to fathom. He moved thousands of troops and tons of equipment 10 miles and built three earthworks—only to return to where he started. Washington's army was certainly no threat to Howe. Perhaps he really believed his move would draw the Continental Army down from the mountains to fight a traditional European battle. At no previous time during the war, however, had Washington obliged Howe in such a manner; Washington rarely fought a battle without defensive works on ground of his own choosing. Howe's operation offered a good example of a professional British army conducting a half-hearted effort.

The tepid thrust into the countryside is more evidence Howe never meant to assault Philadelphia through New Jersey. The British fleet would carry his army into Pennsylvania, and that had always been his plan. At least some of Howe's officers understood that crossing the Delaware by marching through New Jersey was never Howe's purpose. One of his brigade leaders, Gen. James

44 Wortley, ed. *A Prime Minister and His Son*, 110-113.

Grant, wrote to Gen. Edward Harvey, adjutant general of the British Army in England, "As Washington had it still in his power to cross the Delawar at Easton or Alexandria, it became evident that moving to Flemington, Prince Town, Trenton or Penington would not have the desired Effect of drawing the Rebells from their fastnesses. Remaining longer in the Jerseys," Grant added, "could of course answer no good End, as we did not intend to pass the Delawar in Boats. It was therefore thought expedient to return the 19th to Brunswick & to proceed from thence on the more important operations of the Campaign."[45]

John Adams in Philadelphia, meanwhile, regarded Washington's seeming victory with glee. "The Tories in this Town seem to be in absolute Despair," he gloated, "and are Chopfallen, in a most remarkable Manner." Adams discussed the large Quaker population in the city: "The Quakers begin to say they are not Tories—that their Principle of passive Obedience will not allow them to be Whiggs, but that they are as far from being Tories as the Presbyterians." The future president was also excited about the growing Continental army, writing, "We have now got together a fine Army, and more are coming in every day."[46]

---

45 James Grant to Harvey July 10, 1777, in James Grant Papers, National Archives of Scotland, Edinburgh, microfilm copy in the David Library of the American Revolution, Washington Crossing, PA, microfilm 687, reel 28. One mystery of the planning and campaigning of 1777 centers on the construction of boats for a floating bridge. Why did Howe authorize these boats at such great labor and expense? Was it to throw off the many spies Washington had working in New York that spring? While there is no known writing by Howe on the subject, it is clear from the beginning Howe intended to use the fleet, and not these boats, to transfer his army.

46 Smith, et. al., eds. *Letters of Delegates*, vol. 7, 240. The principles of Quaker pacifism led many patriots to view Quakers as Loyalists for not supporting the American war effort.

Chapter 3

Northern New Jersey: To the Ships
June - July, 1777

"I propose going up the Delaware, In order to be nearer this place than I should be by taking The course of the Chesapeake which I once intended."[1]

— William Howe, July 16, 1777

British Withdrawal

On June 20, loyalist Nicholas Cresswell observed the fleet assembling to embark Howe's army. "When we got through the Narrows [the strait of water between Brooklyn and Staten Island] we were entertained with one of the most pleasing and delightful scenes I ever saw before," he wrote. "Four hundred sail of ships, brigs, schooners and sloops with five sail of the Line [large warships] all under-way and upon a Wind at once, in the compass of two miles. A gentle breeze and fine clear day added greatly to the beauty of this delightful view." He concluded, "They are all bound to Perth Amboy, it is said, to take the Troops on board."[2]

The rumors were accurate, for two days later Howe withdrew to Amboy, New Jersey, to begin loading the army onto transports for the voyage to the Delaware River. While the move puzzled many, Howe's adjutant general,

---

1 Stockdale, ed., *The Parliamentary Register,* vol. 10, 414-415.

2 Cresswell, *Journal,* 238.

Stephen Kemble, retained confidence in his superior. The native of New Jersey and brother-in-law (and former aide) to Gen. Thomas Gage possessed both field experience and background including service in the French and Indian War, to offer a valuable opinion. "[I] think his measures right, for few can know his Reasons and judge of the propriety of the Steps he has taken," Kemble scribbled into his journal. The army, he predicted, was headed by sea for the Delaware.[3]

While the British withdrew, Daniel Morgan's riflemen and a portion of Anthony Wayne's 1st Pennsylvania Brigade harassed their rear as they crossed the Raritan River. Troops under John Sullivan supported the operation. At times, the fighting was conducted at relatively close quarters. "By some late Accts.," explained British officer Capt. John Andre, "I fancy the British Grenadiers got a pretty severe peppering yesterday by Morgan's Rifle Corp; they fought, it seems, a considerable time within the distance of, from twenty, to forty yards; and from the concurring Acct. of several of the Officers, more than an hundred of them must have fallen." Andre speculated the fighting killed and wounded about 20 soldiers and a woman, a grenadier's wife. He was not far off the mark: British losses totaled about 30.[4]

A light infantryman at heart, Howe helped direct the rearguard during the withdrawal. "They skirmished with us for about half an hour," recalled von Muenchhausen, "and would probably have continued if General Howe had not brought up two cannon and fired several grape shot at the riflemen, whereupon they retreated." Once the patriots retreated, Howe "remained in this position for two more hours, showing the rebel gentlemen that he was waiting for them with this small corps. But since they showed no inclination to come and do battle, he proceeded with great caution and reached Amboy unmolested."[5]

Cresswell, the loyalist who had set eyes upon the massive British fleet, described the aftermath of the retreat and the fighting among the men of Howe's rearguard: "I never before saw such a shocking scene, some dead others dying, death in different shapes some of the wounded making the most pitiful

3 Stephen Kemble, *Journals of Lieut.-Col. Stephen Kemble, 1773-1789* (New York, 1883), 122. Kemble was promoted to major in 1772 and became deputy adjutant general of British forces in North America. He remained in that capacity under Howe through the Philadelphia Campaign.

4 John Andre, *Major Andre's Journal: Operations of the British Army under Lieutenant Generals Sir William Howe and Sir Henry Clinton June 1777 to November, 1778 Recorded by Major John Andre, Adjutant General* (Tarrytown, NY, 1930), 30.

5 Von Muenchhausen, *At General Howe's Side*, 18-19.

lamentations, others that were of different parties cursing each other as the author of their misfortunes. One old Veteran I observed (that was shot through both legs and not able to walk) very coolly and deliberately loading his piece and cleaning it from blood. I was surprised at the sight and asked him his reasons for it. He, with a look of contempt, said, 'To be ready in case any of the Yankees come that way again.'"[6]

Not only did Cresswell observe the wounded, but he also took the time to recall the devastation of the region. "All the Country houses were in flames as far as we could see. The Soldiers are so much enraged they will set them on fire, in spite of all the Officers can do to prevent it. They seem to leave the Jerseys with reluctance, the train of Artillery and Waggons extends about nine miles and is upwards of 1000 in number."[7]

Howe's withdrawal left Washington cautiously optimistic. "I cannot say that the move I am about to make towards Amboy accords altogether with my opinion," wrote the army commander, "not that I am under any other apprehension than that of being obliged to loose Ground again, which would indeed be no small misfortune as the Spirits of our Troops, and the Country, is greatly reviv'd (and I presume) the Enemys not a little depress'd, by their late retrograde motions."[8]

New Brunswick was not in good shape before the British occupation, but it was in much worse condition after the evacuation in June and the surrounding countryside was in a deplorable condition. The wear and tear of an occupying army contributed to the destruction of the town, as did purposeful vandalism. Lieutenant-Colonel William Palfrey, the paymaster general of Washington's army and a former member of Washington's staff, visited New Brunswick shortly after the British departure. "Never let the British troops upbraid the Americans with want of cleanliness, for such dog kennels as their huts were my eyes never beheld," explained a shocked Palfrey. "Mr. Burton's house, where Lord Cornwallis resided, stunk so I could not bear to enter it. The houses were torn to pieces, and the inhabitants as well as the soldiers have suffered greatly for want of provisions." Artist Charles Willson Peale, who traveled with Washington's army as a militia officer, recalled the destruction around New

---

6   Cresswell, *Journal*, 241-242.

7   Ibid. The same day Howe withdrew, Lt. Gen. Leopold Philip von Heister left for Europe, turning command of the Hessian troops in North America over to Wilhelm von Knyphausen.

8   Fitzpatrick, *Writings of Washington*, vol. 8, 295-296.

Brunswick: "How solitary it looked to see so many Farms without a single animal—many Houses Burnt & others Rendered unfit for use. The Fences all distroyed and many fields the wheat Reaped while quite Green."[9]

Action at Short Hills

During the move to the embarkation points, Howe continued to hope that his withdrawal would draw Washington down from the high ground. Elements of the Continental Army inched forward and occupied New Brunswick once Howe's forces withdrew. An American division under Maj. Gen. William Alexander (Lord Stirling), however, took up a position on Washington's left flank at Short Hills, several miles north of New Brunswick and east of Bound Brook. On June 24, other elements of the army moved about five miles closer to Howe's forces at Perth Amboy and encamped at Quibble Town.[10]

If Washington's move out of the mountains closer to the British lines did not provide Howe with the ideal opportunity he had been seeking, it at least offered possibilities worth exploring. In the middle of the night on June 25, Cornwallis led a column toward Short Hills by way of Woodbridge with the intention of cutting Stirling's division off from the mountain passes. Another column led by Gen. John Vaughan, with Howe in accompaniment, moved back toward New Brunswick before turning north toward Scotch Plains. Much like the strategy he had used on Long Island the previous August, Howe was trying to catch a portion of Washington's army in a pincer movement and destroy it.[11]

The front of Cornwallis's column engaged Stirling's pickets at sunrise. The fighting quickly escalated. By the end of the day, Stirling had been driven back after losing three artillery pieces in the process, and nearly being captured himself. Sergeant Thomas Sullivan of the 49th Regiment of Foot described the fighting and its outcome: "The Troops vying with each other upon this occasion attacked the Enemy so close, that, tho' they were inclined to resist,

---

9 McGuire, *Philadelphia Campaign*, vol. 1, 50-51; William Gordon, *The History of the Rise, Progress, and Establishment of the Independence of the United States of America: Including an Account of the Late War, and of the Thirteen Colonies, from Their Origin to that Period* (New York, 1801), vol. 2, 201; Lillian B. Miller, Sidney Hart, and Toby A. Appel, eds., *The Selected Papers of Charles Willson Peale and His Family*, vol. 1, *Charles Willson Peale: Artist in Revolutionary America, 1735-1791* (New Haven, CT, 1983), 233.

10 McGuire, *Philadelphia Campaign*, vol. 1, 52.

11 Ibid., 53.

could not long maintain their ground against so much Impetuosity, but were soon dispersed on all sides, leaving behind three Pieces of Brass Cannon."[12]

After driving away Stirling and his division, the British troops moved on the road to Westfield. The lack of drinkable water, coupled with a miserably hot and humid mid-Atlantic summer day, resulted in the death by sunstroke of several British soldiers. Just as they had done during their withdrawal from New Brunswick, the British committed depredations during the advance. The march carried them as far as Westfield, plundering and burning houses and driving off what little stock that remained along the way.[13]

That night, the Crown's forces camped at Westfield, where they desecrated the Westfield Presbyterian meeting house. "The Presbyterians and New England Congregationalists were Calvinist 'Dissenter' churches," explained one historian, "which were anti-Anglican and as such were regarded by many as the chief instigators of the Revolution, so their meetinghouses were often targeted by British forces." Washington's adjutant general, Col. Timothy Pickering, later described the disgraceful act the British committed on the meetinghouse. The British, he wrote, marked their war with "the most wanton devastation, burning some houses and plundering others, breaking in pieces and destroying what was not portable. Places of public worship seem everywhere marked as objects of their fury and bigoted rage. . . . [T]he meeting-house was converted into a slaughter-house, and the entrails of the cattle thrown into the pulpit."[14]

Pickering's observations proved that Washington's network of spies had failed him. It was inexcusable that the large British army, camped a mere eight miles away, could steal a march on the Continental Army. An opponent of Washington's sitting in the Continental Congress ranted, "Was it not shameful to be surprised when the Enemy were within 8 miles? Nothing but Severity will introduce Discipline into our Armies, and dear bought Experience only can convince our officers & Men of its Utility, nay of its absolute Necessity."

12 Ibid., 56; Sullivan, *From Redcoat to Rebel*, 122. Unbeknownst to Washington, the same day Stirling was fighting Cornwallis at Short Hills, Burgoyne's troops from Canada reoccupied the fortifications at Crown Point, New York, at the southern tip of Lake Champlain. Burgoyne's campaign was well underway; the same could not be said for Howe's operation.

13 McGuire, *Philadelphia Campaign*, vol. 1, 58; Fitzpatrick, *Writings of Washington*, vol. 8, 311.

14 McGuire, *Philadelphia Campaign*, vol. 1, 59; Octavius Pickering, *The Life of Timothy Pickering* (Boston, 1867), vol. 1, 145.

Pickering also took note of what transpired at headquarters that morning: "It was surprising to the General, that of so many parties he had ordered out to watch the enemy, none gave him earlier notice of the enemy's advancing." The failure of Washington's light troops, militia, and dragoons to inform him of an enemy movement would haunt Washington throughout the campaign, and its consequences along the Brandywine River would be sorely felt.[15]

After the mauling Stirling's men received, Washington refused to offer Howe battle on the open plains, choosing instead to pull his men back into the mountains. Howe's maneuver had almost worked. He inflicted serious damage upon an American division, and nearly lured Washington into an open-field fight. Scottish Gen. Grant was surprised by both of Washington's actions, his advance and his retreat. "We thought He might probably march small bodies from the Mountains to keep up an appearance of acting offensively, but did not imagine, that He would wantonly run a Risk of disgracing his Army by exposing Himself to the possible Necessity of a precipitate Retreat," wrote Grant, "which must have a bad effect upon his Troops, & discourage the Continent at large."[16]

Whatever the impact upon morale, Washington knew better than to waste his army in a pitched fight against the cream of the British army. Alexander Hamilton, a future U.S. secretary of the treasury and a member of Washington's staff, was in tune with his superior's thoughts and actions:

> We are continually strengthening our political springs in Europe, and may everyday look for more effectual aids than we have yet received. Our own army is continually growing stronger in men arms and discipline. We shall soon have an important addition of Artillery, now in its way to join us. We can maintain our present numbers good at least by inlistments, while the enemy must dwindle away; and at the end of the summer the disparity between us will be infinitely great, and facilitate any exertions that may be made to settle the business with them. Their affairs will be growing worse—our's better: so that delay will ruin them. It will serve to perplex and fret them, and precipitate them into measures, that we can turn to good account. Our business then is to avoid a General engagement and waste the enemy away by constantly goading their sides, in a desultory way.[17]

---

15 Smith, et. al., eds. *Letters of Delegates*, vol. 7, 280-281; Pickering, *Life of Pickering*, vol. 1, 144.

16 Grant to Harvey, July 10, 1777, Grant Papers.

17 Dennis P. Ryan, ed., *A Salute to Courage: The American Revolution as Seen through Wartime Writings of Officers of the Continental Army and Navy* (New York, 1979), 83.

Hamilton's perceptive observations would be borne out in time. The army was indeed steadily increasing through the recruitment of additional soldiers and the formation of new regiments; the necessary training and discipline had yet to be instilled in them; and, "more effectual aids" from Europe would eventually arrive in the form of an alliance with France and the assistance of naval and land forces. Several months of active campaigning, coupled with another winter, however, would be required before the fruits of Washington's strategy would bear significant fruit.[18]

The young and opinionated Alexander Hamilton gained Washington's attention at Trenton and joined his staff in 1777. Hamilton was born an illegitimate child, probably in 1755, on Nevis in the Caribbean. After his mother died in 1768, he moved to New York, and four years later attended Columbia University. For a time he worked for Caribbean merchants, and never finished college because of the onset of war. Early on he commanded a New York militia artillery battery on Long Island and fought at Trenton and Princeton in that capacity. His outstanding abilities catapulted Hamilton onto Washington's staff as an aide-de-camp in March 1777, where his fluency in French helped the army commander translate French documents. Hamilton and John Laurens also assisted Baron von Steuben in revising drill regulations the following year.

One of Hamilton's contemporaries described him as "under middle size, thin in person, but remarkably erect and dignified in his deportment. His hair was turned back from his forehead, powdered, and collected in a club behind. His complexion was exceedingly fair, and varying from this only by the almost feminine rosiness of his cheeks. He might be considered, as to figure and colour, an uncommonly handsome face," he contintued. "When at rest, it had rather a severe and thoughtful expression; but when engaged in conversation, it easily assumed an attractive smile. When he entered a room it was apparent, from the respectful attention of the company, that he was a distinguished person." One of Hamilton's many strengths was his initiative. "Washington tended to use him more for important military and political missions where superior intelligence, quick thinking, and aggressiveness were necessary," explained historian Arthur Lefkowitz. Hamilton was probably 21 years old when he reached the banks of the Brandywine.[19]

18 McGuire, *Philadelphia Campaign*, vol. 1, 57.

19 Graydon, *Graydon's Memoirs*, 149; Arthur S. Lefkowitz, *George Washington's Indispensable Men: The 32 Aides-de-Camp Who Helped Win American Independence* (Mechanicsburg, 2003), 100.

After fighting at Short Hills and ravaging the village of Westfield, Howe's men took a wide circuit the next day to Rahway, plundering along the way. According to a member of the New Jersey militia named William Clark, Howe used Clark's father's home in Westfield as his headquarters. When the British left, "the soldiers destroyed and took away all their movable property which damage was appraised at five hundred pounds." The British Army camped that night along the Rahway River, six miles from Amboy. As on the previous day, the intense heat claimed a few more British and Hessian lives. American light troops followed Howe throughout his withdrawal, but stopping the plundering proved impossible. "Along the road where they went," wrote one American officer, "[the British] stole sheep, cattle, and hogs, & robbed and plundered the houses as they went along, & committed such barbarities on the female sex as would make me blush to mention." With the Americans once again harassing their rear, Howe's columns on June 28 returned to their camps at Amboy. The short-lived jab at Washington was over.[20]

Washington tried to make sense of what had just happened. "Whether, finding themselves a little disgrac'd by their former move, they wanted to flourish off a little at quitting the Jerseys, or, whether by this sudden eruption they meant to possess themselves of as much fresh Provision as they could, plunder the Inhabitants; and spread desolation . . . I know not," he wrote, "but certain it is they have left nothing they could carry off, Robbing, Plundering, and burning Houses as they went." He may have been much closer to the truth than he realized. Obtaining sufficient provisions and forage for General Howe's army had been (and would continue to be) a constant and acute problem throughout the war. Considering that nearly everything the British in North America needed had to come from England—and was often spoiled by the long voyage across the Atlantic by the time it arrived—obtaining fresh supplies from the countryside was critical to the health and well-being of Howe's men.

Expecting the British to embark on their ships, Washington in the same letter expressed his concern about what came next. Where they would head with the fleet, he explained, "not I, can discover. By means of their Shipping

---

20 Revolutionary War Pension and Bounty-Land-Warrant Application Files (M804) [RWPF], Record Group 15, Records of the Veterans Administration, National Archives, Washington, D.C., file S973; McGuire, *Philadelphia Campaign*, vol. 1, 59; Samuel Hay to William Irvine, July 10, 1777, Irvine Papers within the Draper Manuscripts, the David Library of the American Revolution, Washington Crossing, PA, series AA, vol. 1, film 60, reel 70.

and the easy transportation that Shipping affords, they have it much in their power to lead us [in] a very disagreeable dance."[21]

Howe's thrust inland had proven one thing: His army could march about the countryside at pleasure, plundering and pillaging as it went, and it seemed as if Washington could do little to stop it. But how could the Crown subdue the rebellion if Washington would not offer pitched battle? "How the business is to be brought to a Conclusion I know not," expressed a frustrated British Gen. Grant. "We have no Friends & Lenity will not make our Enemys good Subjects—I have never varied from that opinion since I landed at Boston."[22]

After resting for a day, on June 30 the British army pulled in its outposts, evacuated New Jersey, and returned to Staten Island, New York. Howe was right back where he had been nearly a year before when he landed on Staten Island the previous July in preparation for his assault on New York City. After a year of maneuvering, fighting, slaughtering, plundering, and pillaging, all he could show for his efforts was control of New York City and its immediate surroundings, along with Newport, Rhode Island. Washington and the Continental Army were once again in complete control of New Jersey.

Loyalist Nicholas Cresswell had seen enough and decided to leave for England. His distaste for Howe was no less bitter upon his departure, denigrating both the British general and the Washington in the same sentence: "General Howe, a man brought up to War from his youth, to be puzzled and plagued for two years together, with a Virginia Tobacco planter. O! Britain, how thy Laurels tarnish in the hands of such a Lubber!" Major Stuart of the 43rd Regiment of Foot was also completely disgusted. "The consequence of this last unlucky retreat is that we have more clearly united those who were disaffected," explained Stuart. "[W]e have helped to increase and inspirit the rebel army, and we have begun a campaign, that well managed would settle the affairs of this country, with the stigma of a retreat."[23]

Howe's seeming failure dispirited some in his army and had failed to pull Washington out of the mountains, but as historian Matthew Spring concluded, "the Virginian declined to take the bait because he knew that Howe simply could not break contact with his bridgehead at New Brunswick. Indeed, over

---

21 Fitzpatrick, *The Writings of George Washington*, vol. 8, 315.

22 Grant to Harvey, July 10, 1777, Grant Papers.

23 Cresswell, *Journal*, 252; Wortley, ed., *A Prime Minister and His Son*, 113.

two months earlier, the British commander in chief had already committed himself to a seaborne invasion of Pennsylvania for the very same reason."[24]

While his actions frustrated his own men, they baffled Washington, who was trying to grasp Howe's overall intentions and deploy his command accordingly. The American leader began shifting small elements under his command. He ordered Brig. Gen. John Nixon's brigade north to help stop Burgoyne's invasion south into upstate New York. To replace Nixon's men, he sent Brig. Gen. Samuel Parsons' and Brig. Gen. James Varnum's brigades into the Hudson Highlands. Washington worried Howe's movement toward his fleet could be a feint "calculated to amuse and distract . . . to draw this Army to Peek's Kills and move to the Northward, that General Howe may, with more facility turn his Arms against Philadelphia. . . . Our situation is truly delicate and embarrassing," admitted the American leader.[25]

Washington was also becoming increasingly worried about a thrust across the Delaware and the agility of action Howe's navy offered British arms, and he shared his concern with Congress. "I doubt not but you will have the most vigilant look outs, kept along Delaware Bay and proper expresses and signals for communicating the earliest intelligence," he observed. "I think . . . some sensible, judicious men should be employed in that business, at this time, who would view things as they ought to be and from whose Accounts certain inferences and conclusions may be drawn, so as to form a proper line for our conduct. The most fatal consequences may flow from false information. . . . Things should be examined with all possible certainty. I shall not be surprised," he warned, "to hear of several Ships appearing in or off Delaware, tho Genl Howe's destination should be elsewhere. Their Fleet give them the most signal advantages, and opportunity of practicing a thousand feints."[26]

On July 3, Washington moved the bulk of the army back to Morristown. Washington felt Howe would take a "considerable time to remove his Baggage and Stores back again [to Amboy], that we could be in our old Camp at Middle Brook long before he could effect this." Morristown offered Washington the ability to shift his army north or south as needed. He had to be ready to block the Hudson or stop an invasion of New England, all the while with an eye on a

---

24 Matthew H. Spring, *With Zeal and With Bayonets Only: The British Army on Campaign in North America, 1775-1783* (Norman, OK, 2008), 34-35.

25 Reed, *Campaign to Valley Forge*, 23.

26 Fitzpatrick, *Writings of Washington*, vol. 8, 329-331.

heavy thrust by Howe to the south. On July 4, Washington moved John Sullivan's division to Pompton, New Jersey, to be better able to foil Howe.[27]

Celebrations

With their army once again in complete control of New Jersey, Americans celebrated their first year of independence on July 4, 1777. A local newspaper reported that the celebration was widely observed in Philadelphia:

> Last Friday the 4th of July, being the Anniversary of the Independence of the United States of America, was celebrated in this city with demonstrations of joy and festivity. About noon all the armed ships and gallies in the river were drawn up before the city, dressed in the gayest manner, with the colours of the United States and streamers displayed. At one o'clock the yards being properly manned, they began the celebration of the day by discharge of thirteen cannon from each of the ships, and one from each of the thirteen gallies, in honor of the Thirteen United States.[28]

John Adams also witnessed the celebration: "The wharves and shores, were lined with a vast concourse of people, all shouting and huzzaing, in a manner which gave great joy to every friend to this country, and the utmost terror and dismay to every lurking tory." Later in the day, members of Congress, Continental Army officers, and city officials gathered at City Tavern for an afternoon of feasting and drinking toasts. "The toasts," wrote one imbiber, "were in honour of our country, and the heroes who have fallen in their pious efforts to defend her." Perhaps Hugh Mercer was toasted that night. After the general was brutally killed at the battle of Princeton in early January, his body was carried to Philadelphia and laid in state at City Tavern. Partaking in the celebration by parading through town and firing volleys for the crowds was a brigade of North Carolina Continentals on its way to join Washington's Army in New Jersey.[29]

---

27 Philander D. Chase and Frank E. Grizzard, Jr., eds., *The Papers of George Washington*, Revolutionary War Series (Charlottesville and London, 2000), vol. 10, 195; Reed, *Campaign to Valley Forge*, 23.

28 *Pennsylvania Packet*, July 8, 1777, microfilm copy in the David Library of the American Revolution, Washington Crossing, PA, film 521, reel 1.

29 Smith, et al., eds., *Letters of Delegates*, vol. 7, 294; McGuire, *Philadelphia Campaign*, vol. 1, 64-65.

Outwardly, the city seemed fully behind independence. However, more than half the city's population was either disinterested or loyal to the King. The large population of Quakers in Pennsylvania made it unique among the thirteen colonies. Their belief in nonviolence kept them politically neutral regarding the war. While many agreed with the patriot cause, the vast majority refused to take up arms or support the war effort in any way. Likewise, Pennsylvania supported a sizable number of Loyalists within its borders. The combination of Quakers and Tories put the patriots of Pennsylvania in the minority.

When the city's patriots illuminated their homes and businesses during the independence celebration, many Loyalists found the dark windows of their homes shattered by the revelers. Unable to distinguish between the homes of Loyalists and those of the Society of Friends, many Quakers also had window panes shattered that night. Some Quaker shop windows were among those broken when the proprietors refused to close for the celebration. "The Town Illuminated," local Elizabeth Drinker remembered, "and a great number of Windows Broke on the Anniversary of Independence and Freedom."[30]

Circumstances on the northern front, however, were nothing to celebrate for the war there was not going well for the Americans. All indications suggested nothing was going to stop Burgoyne's march south to Albany. Although Washington's Army was unaware of it, the American garrison at Fort Ticonderoga in New York abandoned the position to Burgoyne on July 5. Two days later, the American rearguard fought a sharp and bloody holding engagement at Hubbardton (in what is now Vermont), but were outclassed by the elite troops Burgoyne sent against them.

The Reverend Henry Muhlenberg was the head of the Lutheran Church in North America, the father of Peter Muhlenberg, a brigade commander in Washington's Army, and a prodigious writer. After enjoying the celebrations that momentous day, he noted in his journal that the British had abandoned New Jersey and moved to Staten Island. "Where the storm will turn now," he scribbled, "no one knows as yet."[31]

---

30 McGuire, *Philadelphia Campaign*, vol. 1, 67-68; Drinker, *Diary*, vol. 1, 225.

31 The interesting Hubbardton fight was a British tactical victory, but a small-scale American strategic success. For more on this action, see Theodore P. Savas and J. David Dameron, *A Guide to the Battles of the American Revolution* (Savas Beatie, 2006), 99-103; Henry Melchior Muhlenberg, *The Journals of Henry Melchior Muhlenberg*, trans. Theodore G. Tappert and John W. Doberstein (Philadelphia, 1958), vol. 3, 56.

Embarkation

Howe had determined to his satisfaction that the overland route to Philadelphia was too well defended by Washington's forces. However, he had an option unavailable to his opponent: complete naval superiority. What he could not do by land, he would readily do by water. Howe began embarking his army off Sandy Hook, New Jersey, on July 8 at Decker's Ferry, Cole's Ferry (the terminus of the main ferry between New York City and Staten Island, located on the eastern shore of the latter), Simonsen's Ferry, and Reisen's Ferry on Staten Island. The laborious process was finished by the end of the following day.

The decision outraged loyalist Joseph Galloway, who complained that there had been nothing to stop Howe from gaining the Delaware River that spring: "Pontoons were built, and the flat-bottomed boats prepared and put on carriages to pass the Delaware." Howe justified his decision in a letter to Lord Germain on April 2, noting "the difficulties and delay that would attend the passage of the Delaware." Howe considered Washington's revitalized army too much of an obstacle in northern New Jersey, and claimed that going up the Delaware via the sea allowed him to stay as close as possible to the Hudson and to Burgoyne. Howe believed the movement by sea would force Washington to wait for further British developments before acting. Indeed, there were some who felt that the seemingly feckless beginning to the campaign had prevented Washington from sending troops to oppose Burgoyne's advance south, and from preparing defenses at Philadelphia.[32]

Howe wrote to Gen. Carleton in Canada warning of the change in plans and stating that Burgoyne and his southbound army were essentially on their own:

> Having but little expectation that I shall be able, from the want of sufficient strength in this army, to detach a corps in the beginning of the campaign to act up Hudson's River consistent with the operations already determined upon, the force your Excellency may deem expedient to advance beyond your frontiers after taking Ticonderoga will, I fear, have little assistance from hence to facilitate their approach, and as I shall probably be in Pennsylvania when that corps is ready to advance into this province, it

---

32 Joseph Galloway, *Letters to a Nobleman on the Conduct of the War in the Middle Colonies* (London, 1779), 46; *Manuscripts of Mrs. Stopford-Sackville,* vol. 2, 63.

will not be in my power to communicate with the officer commanding it [Burgoyne], as soon as I would wish; he must therefore pursue such measures as may from circumstances be judged most conducive to the advancement of his Majesty's service consistently with your Excellency's orders for his conduct.[33]

Even though Howe warned General Carleton that Burgoyne should not expect assistance from him, the difficulties in communication meant no one in authority in Canada would read his words for weeks. The once-confident Howe also advised Carleton that he would not be able to end the war in 1777. "Restricted as I am from entering upon more extensive operations by the want of force," explained the general, "my hopes of terminating the war this year are vanished."[34]

Washington was not the only one left guessing about Howe's intentions and purpose. While the Americans were celebrating the anniversary of their independence, discontent spread through the British ranks. Kemble, Howe's deputy adjutant general, was well aware of the grumbling. "[I] [f]ind from the general tenor of Officers Conversation that they are not well pleased with Affairs, but they often speak without thought," the staff officer wrote in his journal. "Asserted by severals that Guides offered to Conduct General Howe by a Road where he might Attack the Rebels in their Entrenchments to advantage, but that he took no Notice of it, this may be without foundation as well as the former, and the General is the best judge of his own Actions."[35]

Conjecture as to future operations coursed through the ranks. Some believed Howe would move them up the Hudson River to form a junction with the Canadian Army, while others argued in favor of mounting an expedition to any number of New England destinations. Another potential course of action involved a shift of the the war effort south to Savannah or Charleston, while a different approach to capturing Philadelphia also remained on the table.

Opposite Staten Island on the south side of Raritan Bay was a narrow strip of land called Sandy Hook. At the far end of Sandy Hook stood an octagonal lighthouse 100 feet tall topped with an iron beacon and a copper roof. The lighthouse was guarded by loyalist militiamen, while New Jersey militia

---

33 *Manuscripts of Mrs. Stopford-Sackville*, vol. 2, 65-66. Despite Howe's claim, the sea route made it more difficult to support Burgoyne.

34 Ibid.

35 Kemble, *Journals*, 124.

commanded by Gen. David Forman kept an eye on the lighthouse and its defenders. Forman's position also allowed him to monitor the comings and goings of the British fleet. "They have a Number of Brigs, Schooners, and Sloops, prepared for taking Horses on board," he passed on to higher command. "Their Stalls are all Cover'd and the Sides lined with Sheepskins with the Wool on to prevent the Horses Chafing—they would not make Use of Such precaution if they Intended up the North or East River." If the fleet was bound for somewhere other than up the Hudson, where was it going? A couple of British deserters gave him additional information: "The Common report Amongst the Sailors and Soldiers is that the Fleet is going to [the] Delaware."[36]

Washington gave Forman specific directions. "If the Fleet goes out to sea, I imagine they will stand off out of sight of land before they steer either Eastward or Southward, the better to hide their real intentions from us," explained Washington. "[I]f they do this, it will not be worth your while to send an express to this distance merely to acquaint me that they have gone to sea. But if they tack shortly after they leave the Hook," he continued, "and shape their Course either Eastward or Southward I shall be glad to know it."[37]

When all was said and done, Howe loaded more than 260 ships. Counting only enlisted personnel, his army was about 18,000 strong; officers, servants, staff, and camp followers probably added another 5,000. No one below the rank of colonel was permitted to take a horse on the expedition, and officers who had to rid themselves of their mounts were ordered to sell them to the artillery or to the mounted jaegers.[38]

The following units climbed aboard the troop transports: four jaeger companies (one of which was mounted), two battalions of British light infantry, two battalions of British grenadiers, the British Brigade of Guards, three Hessian grenadier battalions, the Queen's Rangers, Ferguson's British riflemen, four British brigades of infantry, one Hessian brigade of infantry that included the remnants of the brigade destroyed at Trenton the previous December, some heavy artillery, a light dragoon regiment, and the 71st Highlanders.

No one other than perhaps the Howe brothers knew when the fleet would depart. Like nearly everyone else participating in the massive military operation,

36 McGuire, *Philadelphia Campaign*, vol. 1, 70; Chase and Grizzard, eds., *Papers of Washington*, vol. 10, 207-209.

37 Fitzpatrick, *Writings of Washington*, vol. 8, 426.

38 McGuire, *Philadelphia Campaign*, vol. 1, 71; Ewald, *Diary*, 69-70.

Capt. William Dansey of the 33rd Regiment of Foot speculated on the destination: "Yesterday we emark'd but where we are going to Lord knows." Even Howe's aide von Muenchhausen was unsure: "Everyone surmises that we are going to Philadelphia."[39]

Meanwhile, those cooped up on the bobbing transports suffered from the intense summer heat. The conditions were nearly unbearable, and some regiments were gutted by sickness before they even departed the harbor. Those unlucky enough to be among the earliest to board spent three miserable weeks in that condition before the fleet departed. According to Maj. Carl Leopold von Baurmeister of Wilhelm von Knyphausen's staff, "All the Hessian troops who had participated in the Jersey expedition were, unfortunately, embarked too early and had to ride at anchor before Staten Island for two weeks. Consequently," he continued, "their store of fresh provisions diminished greatly, which was very unfortunate."[40]

British Inaction

The torpor that seemed to have overtaken General Howe continued to be perceived according to differing viewpoints—as had almost everything else since the colonists began their quest for independence. From the time fighting erupted around Lexington and Concord in 1775, it created vast differences of opinion among the American population. When the Continental Congress opted the following year to escalate the war effort to achieve complete independence, further divisions within the population occurred.

Prior to the war, Philadelphia aristocrat Joseph Galloway was one of the most powerful politicians in Pennsylvania and a member of the First Continental Congress. An unusual series of events, coupled with his political aspirations, turned him against the American cause. Galloway was the son of a prosperous merchant who married into a wealthy family. He pursued a career in law and opened his own practice at the age of eighteen. One historian described Galloway as "aloof, overbearing, even imperious, and sometimes hot-

---

39 William Dansey to Mrs. Dansey, letter dated July 10, 1777, original in the William Dansey Letters, the Delaware Historical Society, Wilmington, Delaware; Von Muenchhausen, *At General Howe's Side*, 20.

40 Carl von Baurmeister, "Letters of Major Baurmeister During the Philadelphia Campaign, 1777-1778," in *The Pennsylvania Magazine of History and Biography* (Philadelphia, 1935), vol. 59, 394.

tempered, a man [who] was esteemed for his talents, but never loved." During the years between the French and Indian War and the American Revolution, Galloway (along with Benjamin Franklin) was a prime mover in the creation of the Assembly Party in Pennsylvania. The movement's main platform was anti-proprietary. Proprietary party politicians wanted Pennsylvania to continue to be run by members of the proprietary family—the Penns. In contrast, men like Galloway and Franklin wanted Pennsylvanians to have more autonomy, were upset with how Indian relations had been handled by the proprietary family, and wanted the vast landholdings of the proprietors taxed and available for settlement. They also wanted the proprietary family's control replaced by a royal government. "Rumors circulated as well that the Assembly Party's leaders had a personal stake in royalization. Franklin, according to the buzz, was in line to become the colony's first royal governor and Galloway its chief justice."Galloway eventually rose to become the speaker of the Pennsylvania assembly, and the proprietary family soon lost majority control to the royalists.[41]

Tensions with Britain, meanwhile, continued to escalate. When Galloway took his seat in the First Continental Congress in 1775, most members held out hope for reconciliation. With exactly that thought in mind Galloway offered a "Plan of Union." The proposal was vetoed and stricken from the record, an embarrassment that did not sit well with a man of his ambition and standing. Galloway considered the delegates in Congress to be divided into two camps: "One ('men of property') standing for American rights, seeking a remedy of wrongs but intent on avoiding sedition and violence; the other ('Congregational and Presbyterian republicans, or men of bankrupt fortunes, overwhelmed in debt to British merchants') bent on independence."[42]

Once Congress pushed for independence, Galloway fled Philadelphia and retired to his country seat in Trevose, Bucks County, Pennsylvania. Harassed by threats of violence, he removed himself to New York City, where the main British Army was located at that time. Using his social standing, he worked

---

41 Ferling, *Leap in the Dark*, 47-48.

42 Benson Bobrick, *Angel in the Whirlwind* (New York, 1997), 104. Even though Galloway had participated in the First Continental Congress, he refused to sit in the Second Continental Congress as the war escalated against the mother country. In 1778, Galloway testified to Parliament regarding William Howe's campaign to capture Philadelphia in 1777. During the course of his testimony, Parliament, questioning his loyalty to the Crown, drilled him on his participation in the First Continental Congress.

through Ambrose Serle, secretary to Admiral Richard Howe, to gain an audience with General Howe. Galloway informed the general that 75 to 90 percent of Pennsylvanians were loyal and would form regiments and help provide garrison troops upon the appearance of the British Army. Galloway, explained one writer, "epitomized the lack of perception and the misunderstanding exhibited by Tory leadership." Simply put, intentionally or otherwise, he and others exaggerated loyalist sentiment in the colonies. Nevertheless, Howe consulted with Galloway during the planning stages of his campaign to capture Philadelphia. When the British troops began their campaign in the late spring of 1777, Galloway was with them.[43]

General Howe did not share his plan to sail up the Chesapeake Bay with his subordinates, Guy Carleton, John Burgoyne, or even George Germain. The one man wearing a British uniform who was aware of his ultimate plan was his brother the admiral. Galloway later claimed to have learned about the plan from the admiral. "I met on the road accidentally Lord Howe," he claimed. "From a conversation which passed between us, I suspected that Sir William was going with his fleet and army round to the Chesapeak." Galloway jotted down his objections to such a route—distance, weather, and terrain—and presented them to General Howe through the army's chief engineer, John Montresor. Howe summoned Galloway to his headquarters to question him. According to Galloway, Howe "asked me, How I knew he was going to the Chesapeak? I answered, I did not positively know it. He said, I did, from the paper in front of him, I replied, the paper was not positive, but conditional, supposing he intended to go there." Apparently satisfied, Howe asked Galloway an intelligence question about the region. "He then asked, whether my objections rested on the difficulties of the navigation of the Chesapeak? I replied, they did not."[44]

Although Admiral Howe knew where they were headed and Galloway had managed to figure it out for himself, everyone else accompanying the army seems to have remained in the dark. Virginia loyalist James Parker also traveled with the British Army, as a volunteer guide. "Formerly I had a very good spy of knowing things, 'tis not so now," Parker admitted, "every thing is Secret & mysterious." Knowing how brutal the hot and humid summer days of Virginia and Maryland could be, Parker hoped Howe was not heading south. "The Army

43 Jackson, *With the British Army*, 3; Jackson, *The Pennsylvania Navy*, 5.

44 "Mr. Joseph Galloway on the American War," *Scots Magazine*, 41 (October 1779), 526-527.

is in high health & Spirits now, I fear that will not long be the Case—if they go South in the dog days."[45]

Many of the experienced British officers also feared the approaching heat of summer. Colonel Carl von Donop, commander of the brigade of Hessian grenadiers, jotted down his thoughts in the middle of July: "God knows whether we shall go south or north, but the heat which is beginning to make itself felt with the approach of the dog-days makes one wish that the general would choose north rather than south." General Grant, who served in the French and Indian War and spent seven years as governor of East Florida, offered a different opinion. "The most intelligent are wide of the mark from a mistaken Idea of climate," he insisted, "which is the same all over America in the Months of July & August. During that time the Heats are as great at Boston as at St. Augustine." Grant firmly believed that the uncertainty of their destination had baffled Washington, who had "moved to Morris [County] to have it in his power to direct his course South or North."[46]

Sir Henry Clinton, soon to be left in command of the New York garrison, argued with Howe against the voyage to Philadelphia. Clinton feared that a rump force left behind at New York would be vulnerable to attack by Washington and too small to assist Burgoyne if Howe did not return in time. According to Clinton, it was "highly probable, the instant the fleet was decidedly gone to sea [that] Mr. Washington would move with everything that he could collect either against General Burgoyne or me and crush the one or the other, as neither would be very capable of withstanding such superior force unless timely intelligence should fortunately bring the fleet to our relief." Despite Clinton's arguments, Howe preferred his own plan, "which he told me [Clinton] could not with propriety be laid aside on account of its having been approved at home." Regardless of London's approval, Clinton explained the disadvantages Howe's army would face by heading south at that time of year. "I stated the probable risks and delays it would be exposed to from the sickness and southerly winds generally prevalent in that climate in the summer months," wrote Clinton, "and with all deference suggested the many great and superior

45 Letter/journal, James Parker to Charles Steuart, "New York, July 16, 1777," Parker Family Papers, originals in Liverpool, England, microfilm copies at the David Library of the American Revolution, Washington's Crossing, PA, film 45, reel 2.

46 Carl von Donop, "Letters from a Hessian Mercenary (Colonel von Donop to the Prince of Prussia)," ed. Hans Huth, in *Pennsylvania Magazine of History and Biography* (Philadelphia, 1938), vol. 62, 498; Grant to Harvey, July 10, 1777, Grant Papers.

advantages to be derived at the present moment from a cooperation of his whole force with General Burgoyne on the River Hudson."[47]

Having recently returned from London, Clinton knew that the King and Germain expected Howe to form a junction with Burgoyne. Although Howe argued that he had received no such order, Clinton assured him it was the intention of the British government. Germain had indeed approved the capture of Philadelphia, but he had not approved Howe doing so by going to sea, which promised to consume several more weeks of precious time. Both Galloway and Clinton offered persuasive reasons why Howe should reconsider his plan, to no avail; Howe was determined to reach Philadelphia by water.[48]

Clinton's command consisted of only some 7,400 men. These troops included the 17th Light Dragoons, Germanic and provincial troops, and the 7th, 22nd, 26th, 35th, 38th, 43rd, 52nd, 54th, 57th, and 63rd Regiments of Foot. Clinton warned Howe that he would be left with a command too weak for offensive operations once he garrisoned all the defensive works around New York. "My force being barely adequate to the garrisoning the numerous and extensive works raised and raising, and posts on Long, Staten, and York Islands and Paulus Hook which, comprehending a circuit of considerably more than 100 miles, would afterward leave no surplus whatsoever for offensive operations," complained Clinton. "And I had, moreover, but a scanty proportion of artillerymen, no chasseurs, and no cavalry which I was at liberty to use, the Seventeenth Dragoons being ordered to be held in constant readiness for embarkation."[49]

The waiting continued. On July 13, five days after Howe began loading his army aboard transports, one of his aides complained, "No one seems to be able to figure out why we are waiting here so long, considering the fact that everyone, except Howe and a few officers, are aboard ship." Von Muenchhausen was also concerned about the future of the campaign, and much of that concern centered around his lack of confidence in Howe's officer corps: "General Leslie who commands the Highland Scots, has broken his leg. It is a pity that we have to leave behind this very able and upright general, the like of

---

47 Henry Clinton, *The American Rebellion: Sir Henry Clinton's Narrative of His Campaigns, 1775-1782, With an Appendix of Original Documents*, ed. William B. Willcox (Hamden, CT, 1971), 61-62.

48 Pancake, *1777*, 101.

49 Clinton, *The American Rebellion*, 63.

which the English have only a few. . . . General Howe is in a difficult situation because he has but few capable generals under his command here." Spending so much time aboard ship gave men like von Muenchhausen time to speculate on the campaign and its possible outcomes. "It would have been better if we had not stayed here so long," he admitted, "but had gone to Philadelphia four weeks ago—these are my ideas. We could then be returning by land to support Burgoyne."[50]

The British fleet would remain anchored in the vicinity of Denys' Ferry until July 19.

The American Response

As Howe loaded his army onto ships and finalized his plans, the people of Pennsylvania remained confident that Philadelphia was safe. On July 11, however, confirmation of the abandonment and loss of Fort Ticonderoga reached Washington's headquarters. The news convinced him to position his men near the New Jersey-New York border until Howe's intentions became clear. The next day, Washington pushed much of the army north as he considered blocking Burgoyne. Washington had left New Jersey wide open for Howe to march overland to the Delaware, but the British general was determined to use his fleet and so had cast his eyes and intentions elsewhere.

Most of the Continental Army stopped near Pompton, New Jersey, where heavy rain brought marching to a halt for three days. General Sullivan was in the lead and arrived first in the area known as Smith's Clove. Few lived in this narrow valley just west of the point in the Hudson Valley where iron chains stretched across the river from near West Point to near New Windsor, New York. Smith's Clove was the most accessible route northwest of the river. Although it was still raining on July 14, the army moved eight miles north to Van Aulen's. The muddy road made the march difficult and fatigued Washington's men. The next day, the army moved another six miles into the Clove. Sullivan reached New Windsor with his division the same day.

Washington set up his headquarters at Suffern's Tavern in present-day Suffern, New York, and waited for Howe to show his hand. Each passing day increased his concern. He eased Sullivan and his division farther north across the Hudson to Fishkill, where his command would remain for several weeks,

50 Von Muenchhausen, *At General Howe's Side*, 21.

separated from the main army. If Burgoyne swept south too fast, Washington would have no choice but to move north to intercept him, which in turn would leave Philadelphia vulnerable to Howe.[51]

Much of Washington's increasing worry was the the result of his spy network's inability to discern Howe's intentions. John Adams offered a reason as to why: Howe, he insisted, did not have a firm plan. "It is impossible to discover the Designs of an Enemy who has no Design at all," proffered Adams. "An Intention that has no Existence, a Plan that is not laid, cannot be divined."[52]

While they had yet to uncover Howe's intentions, Washington's spies were bringing him information about the fleet. According to the reports coming into American headquarters, the British ships were being prepared for a longer voyage than a mere feint: "Small craft are constantly plying between New York and the [enemy] Fleet laden with Officers, Baggage and Stores put in packages and marked with their Names and Regiments, and that Transports are fitted up with Stalls over their main Decks for the Reception of Horses." Fearing that the destination might indeed be Philadelphia, Washington warned Congress, "the Works upon and obstructions in the Delaware should be carried on with Spirit and compleated as far as possible lest they should visit that quarter."[53]

Washington spread the Continental Army out to watch both the Hudson River and Howe's army, and to keep an eye on the Delaware. Francis Nash's North Carolina troops, the most recent unit to join the Continental Army, were ordered to Billingsport, New Jersey, along the Delaware on July 17. Lord Stirling's division marched into Peekskill, New York, on July 20. Two days earlier, Brig. Gen. James Potter's Pennsylvania militia brigade was ordered from Chester, on the other side of the Delaware, to Billingsport to join the New Jersey militia already present. These men would build an earthwork to strengthen the defenses along the Delaware, but at this point there was just a single row of *chevaux-de-frise* in the river.[54] These obstructions consisted of large log bins with additional iron-tipped logs jutting outward and facing down river. The bins were connected with heavy, wrought iron chains and filled with stones

---

51 Reed, *Campaign to Valley Forge*, 26-27.

52 Smith, et al., eds., *Letters of Delegates*, vol. 7, 334.

53 Fitzpatrick, *Writings of Washington*, vol. 8, 366.

54 Jackson, *The Pennsylvania Navy*, 102-103.

to sink them below the water line. These sorts of obstructions later proved effective against the British fleet.

Washington's shift of most of his army north from its winter encampments had brought it to an area known as Pompton Plains, a long valley that leads to the Hudson Highlands near West Point, New York. The army's purpose there was to observe British movements and remain in a position from which it could either block the Hudson River or rapidly move south to protect the capital. The raw and largely new Continental Army had benefited from the extra time Howe had allowed Washington to rebuild and train. "It wou'd surprise you to see the vast number of soldiers, Horses, Waggons, Drivers, Cattle and Provision, tents, etc., that are here; yet everything goes smoothly on," commented Col. Persifor Frazer.[55]

While the army was larger and at least partially supplied, it was still deficient in some areas. Colonel John Stone of the 1st Maryland Regiment noted some of the articles the army was lacking. Many soldiers, he observed, were without "Blankets or Tents, they must undoubtedly be lost. We are promised these necessary articles immediately. We have also suffered much for shoes, and I am afraid will suffer much more for that article this fall. We shall also be very bare of all kinds of Cloathing by the winter and unless we are furnished more than probable shall be in the same disagreeable situation we were last year. Much will depend upon having an army fit for the field this fall & winter."[56] The situation was so dire that civilians in the area were pressed to supply blankets for the army. Stone's comments notwithstanding, the condition of the army was far better than it had been in December. Rather than leading an army that was melting away and on the verge of disintegration, Washington was now overseeing a growing Continental Army with new recruits arriving every week.

Numerous problems still plagued the army, however, including its command structure. The problem that rankled so many and flared more than a few tempers was one of rank, which was based not on ability or competence but on seniority. Officers who served well in 1776, for example, often could not be elevated to higher positions of authority due to their lack of seniority. The system was already archaic by 1777, and would plague the United States for at least another 100 years. As John Adams put it, Continental Army officers

55 McGuire, *Philadelphia Campaign*, vol. 1, 77; Frazer, *General Frazer*, 149.

56 William H. Browne, *Archives of Maryland*, vol. 16, *Journal and Correspondence of Safety/State Council 1777-1778* (Baltimore, 1897), 319.

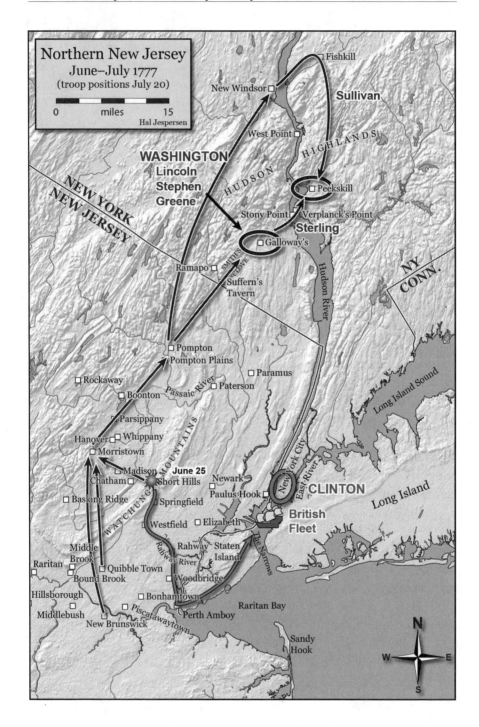

Northern New Jersey
June–July 1777
(troop positions July 20)

0   miles   15
Hal Jespersen

Fishkill

New Windsor

Sullivan

West Point

HUDSON HIGHLANDS

WASHINGTON
Lincoln
Stephen
Greene

Peekskill

Stony Point   Verplanck's Point

Sterling

Galloway's

NEW YORK
NEW JERSEY

HUDSON

Ramapo   SMITH'S CLOVE

Suffern's
Tavern

Hudson River

NY
CONN.

Pompton
Pompton Plains

Rockaway

Paramus

Boonton   Passaic River   Paterson

Parsippany

Hanover   Whippany

Morristown

WATCHUNG MOUNTAINS

Long Island Sound

Madison   June 25

Chatham   Short Hills

Basking Ridge   Springfield

Newark

Paulus Hook

New York City

East River

CLINTON

Long Island

Westfield   Elizabeth

British
Fleet

Middle
Brook

Rahway   Staten
Island

Raritan   Rahway River

Quibble Town

Bound Brook

Woodbridge

The Narrows

Hillsborough   Bonhamtown

Middlebush   Piscatawaytown

New Brunswick   Perth Amboy

Raritan Bay

Sandy
Hook

N
W   E
S

"[q]uarrell like Cats and Dogs. They worry one another like Mastiffs, Scrambling for Rank and Pay like Apes for Nutts." Not only did the officers from different states argue amongst themselves, but there was also a great deal of dissatisfaction regarding the many foreign officers who had offered their services to the new United States. Many American officers felt slighted when French and Polish officers were appointed to positions of authority ahead of them. Many difficult decisions awaited Washington in the months ahead, and assigning proper generals and other officers would prove especially thorny.[57]

Departure

While some sources on the campaign claim that the delayed departure had to do with adverse winds, the real reason for it was Howe himself. On July 15, he received word that Burgoyne had captured Fort Ticonderoga. The Americans did not put up much of a fight for the fort. After the British placed artillery on Mount Independence, which towered over the fortification (but had been left unguarded by the Americans), Gen. Arthur St. Clair withdrew his garrison in the middle of the night and began a long retreat southward.

The news was indeed welcome, but Howe drew the wrong conclusion from the victory. The moderate success made the British in general, and Howe in particular, overconfident. The ease of retaking Fort Ticonderoga convinced him that Burgoyne would have no trouble reaching Albany, New York. If he could so smoothly capture such an important bastion, what would prevent him from reaching his destination? Not that he needed much of an excuse, but the general now believed it was more than safe to order the fleet to sea.[58]

The British fleet began moving out to sea on Sunday, July 20. Engineer John Montresor's journal tells us that the fleet consisted of 266 transports and ships of war. Not only did the ships carry the troops with which Howe intended to assault Philadelphia, but also 300 rounds of ammunition for each cannon and provisions for each transport for three months.[59]

---

57 McGuire, *Philadelphia Campaign*, vol. 1, 78; Smith, et al., eds., *Letters of Delegates*, vol. 7, 103.

58 Reed, *Campaign to Valley Forge*, 21. To keep an eye on the Hudson River and distract the Americans, the British sent HMS *Vigilant* up the Hudson. The weak American defenses could do little to stop the ship from ascending the river, although she was unable to reach West Point.

59 John Montresor, "The Montresor Journals," ed. G. D. Delaplaine, in *Collections of the New York Historical Society for the Year 1881* (1882), 429.

The fleet was divided into six divisions, as follows:

First: the Brigade of Guards, the British light infantry, the Queen's Rangers, Ferguson's riflemen.
Second: the four British infantry brigades.
Third: the 71st Highlanders and the supply ships.
Fourth: the 16th Light Dragoons.
Fifth: the artillery, engineers, jaegers, and Hessian grenadiers.
Sixth: the Hessian infantry and more supply ships.[60]

Admiral Howe selected his flagship HMS *Eagle* to protect the front of the armada. Other warships, including HMS *Liverpool, Raisonable,* and *Augusta* joined the *Eagle* while the HMS *Isis, Somerset, Nonsuch, Swift,* and *Dispatch* brought up the rear. It was the largest armada ever assembled in American waters to that point, and would not be surpassed until the American Civil War.[61]

Just a few days before the ships departed, Howe wrote to Germain that he intended to ascend the Delaware River, not Chesapeake Bay. Howe began by explaining that Washington had moved his army toward the New Jersey-New York border. After noting that the farther north Washington moved, the harder it would be for the American general to return to protect Philadelphia, Howe assured Germain that he was leaving enough troops under Clinton to protect New York City. Taking a moment to consider Burgoyne's position, he added, "If General Washington should march with a determination to force General Burgoyne, the strength of General Burgoyne's army is such as to leave no room to dread the event." Having assured Germain that Burgoyne could take care of himself, Howe declared that, "under the circumstances I propose going up the Delaware, In order to be nearer this place than I should be by taking The course of the Chesapeake which I once intended, or preferred to that of the Delaware provided the enemy had discovered a disposition to defend Pennsylvania." It would be more than a month before Germain received Howe's dispatch of his latest deviation from the original plan. By the time the letter was dropped on Germain's desk, Howe and his fleet were just three days from landing in the upper reaches of Chesapeake Bay—nowhere near the Delaware River.[62]

60 Ewald, *Diary,* 72. It is not clear where in the fleet the British grenadiers would sail.

61 Reed, *Campaign to Valley Forge,* 21.

62 Stockdale, ed., *The Parliamentary Register,* vol. 10, 414-415.

As noted, Howe had sent a letter to Canada informing Carleton that the northern forces could expect little help along the Hudson from the direction of New York City. It took a long time for that message to arrive, but Burgoyne promptly responded when it did. The general leading the Canadian column southward stated that he intended to follow his orders—and that he hoped that Howe would do so as well. "I wrote a second letter to Sir William Howe, wherein I repeated that I was entrusted with the command of the army destined to march from Canada," explained Burgoyne, "and that my orders were to force a junction with his excellency."[63] Howe, as stated earlier, never received a direct order to cooperate with the Canadian army. Even if Burgoyne forced his way through as far south as New York City, Howe would not be there to greet him.

The same day the fleet went to sea, Washington once again became convinced that Howe was moving up the Hudson. Accordingly, he moved the army 11 miles farther north into New York to the vicinity of an old log house not far from the New York-New Jersey border and south of Peekskill owned by a man named Galloway. Lord Stirling's division moved slightly east to King's Ferry at Stony Point, crossed the river to Verplanck's Point, and moved on to Peekskill. Sullivan's division was brought south to link with Stirling's men at Peekskill. Unfortunately for Washington, Howe was not heading up the Hudson.[64] The intelligence needed to confirm that reality would eventually come as a result of Washington's earnest entreaty to American eyes and ears:

> I am to request, that they will have a sufficient number of proper Lookouts fixed, at the Capes of Delaware, to whose accounts implicit confidence may be given, to make the earliest reports of the arrival of any Fleet, which Congress will transmit me by the speediest conveyance. As the enemy will probably make many Feints and have it unhappily but too much in their power, from their Shipping, I would advise, that the Look outs should be cautioned, to be extremely accurate in their Observations and Reports, mentioning with as much precision as possible, the Number of Ships that may appear. Our situation is already [truly] critical and may be rendered still more so, by inaccurate and ill grounded intelligence.[65]

---

63 *State of the Expedition from Canada as laid before the House of Commons, by Lieutenant-General Burgoyne, and Verified by Evidence; with a Collection of Authentic Documents, and An Addition of Many Circumstances Which were Prevented from appearing Before the House by the Prorogation of Parliament* (London, 1780), 6.

64 Reed, *Campaign to Valley Forge*, 30-31.

65 Fitzpatrick, *The Writings of George Washington*, vol. 8, 453-454.

Chapter 4

To Sea and the Delaware
July 1777

"No one any longer knew where we were bound. Everyone said something different and everyone had to leave the decision to General Howe."[1]

— Lieutenant Heinrich von Feilitzsch, August 1, 1777

A Beginning

After nearly two weeks of waiting aboard the troop transports, William Howe's army finally felt a sense of relief when, on Sunday, July 20, the British fleet moved out of New York harbor. Even the dropping of anchors once more just off Sandy Hook, New Jersey, did little to dampen their enthusiasm. The ships were moving, and the campaign was underway. Ambrose Serle, secretary to Admiral Richard Howe, thought the scene majestic: "Sailed this morning from Staten Island, with all the Transports, to Sandy Hook, where we came to Anchor. . . . So many Ships at one Time under Sail . . . rendered the Scene very grand & picturesque."[2]

Washington's observer near Sandy Hook, Gen. David Forman of the New Jersey militia, reported the arrival of Howe's flotilla that same day. "The enemys

---

1   Bruce E. Burgoyne, ed., *Diaries of Two Ansbach Jaegers* (Westminster, MD, 2007), 12.

2   Ambrose Serle, *The American Journal of Ambrose Serle, Secretary to Lord Howe, 1776-1778*, ed. Edward H. Tatum, Jr. (San Marino, CA, 1940), 239-240.

Fleet appeared in New York Narrows on their way to Sandy-Hook," observed Forman. "This Evening at sundown there was under the point of the hook and coming down 160 sail as near as we can count; it is beyond doubt that some of them have Troops on board, but to what amount cannot pretend to say." More ships appeared the next day. "Fifteen transports & men of war joined them, & about 10 o'clock 80 small brigs, schooners & sloops came out of the Narrows & joined the grand fleet."[3]

British optimism washed away on the 22nd when rainy weather held up the fleet. Howe was smart enough not to risk his armada in the open sea during a major storm. The convoy that was heading to England carrying Nicholas Cresswell and Gen. Philip von Heister was caught by the same storm at the eastern end of Long Island. Cresswell was less than happy about the delay, but described the frustration in something approaching verse: "The sea a roaring, the ship a rolling, the rigging breaking, the masts a bending, the sails a rattling, the Captain swearing, the Sailors grumbling, the boys crying, the hogs grunting, the dogs barking, the pots and glasses breaking, the Colonel ill of the C—p in bed. All from the Top Gallant truck to the keel, from the jibb boom to the taffrail in the utmost confusion."[4]

The storm let up on July 23, when the fleet weighed anchor and moved out to sea. Militia general Forman, attentive to duty, sent a detailed report at 6:30 a.m. that Wednesday: "The signal gun for sailing was fired. . . . [A]t seven they began to get under way, & stood for sea; after they got clear of the hook, they steered a south-east course, under a very easy sail. . . . I attended their motion until sundown, & perceived very little difference in their course." Forman was sure the British were heading south. He also reported some intelligence garnered from a British deserter: "I am this morning informed that some part of Gen' Howe's army that crossed from this state to Staten Island, have been sent to New York. He can not say what number, but he think not exceeding 500. He also informs, that the remainder, except two Hessian regt's that are left guard on Staten Island, embarked on board this fleet."[5]

The nature of the winds during the summer months made the voyage a long and tedious one. In July and August, the wind generally comes from the

---

3 Hazard, ed., *Pennsylvania Archives*, Series 1, vol. 5, 435-436.

4 Cresswell, *Journal*, 273.

5 Hazard, *Pennsylvania Archives*, Series 1, vol. 5, 439-440. All references are to Series 1 unless otherwise indicated.

south and southwest, the exact opposite of what the fleet required for a smooth voyage south to reach the Chesapeake Bay. This difficulty, coupled with the scorching hot and humid days, made it that much more miserable for everyone aboard. To this day, the stifling humidity in that part of the Atlantic is usually followed by intense afternoon thunderstorms. As a result, each time a storm approached, the ships had to scatter to avoid collisions. Fog also posed a problem and caused further delays. So uncooperative were the winds and weather that it would take Howe's armada a week to reach Cape May, New Jersey, a distance of fewer than 150 miles.[6]

Washington welcomed Forman's reports, but once the ships were out of sight, their ultimate destination remained uncertain. Without a navy to follow and report, Washington had to rely upon scouts posted along various sections of the coastline to determine the direction of Howe's fleet. Until something more definitive was learned, Washington's Army was left to mark time in New Jersey, moving from one place to another in anticipation of events still unknown. One Delaware officer complained about "marching and counter-marching, and often not knowing which."[7]

Based upon the most recent information, however, Washington reached the conclusion that Howe's ultimate destination was Philadelphia. Rather than continue shifting elements north toward the Hudson Highlands, he pulled the army back to the area around Ramapo, New Jersey. Historian John Reed described the Continental commander's position succinctly: "Washington feared being caught in a position so remote from Philadelphia that he would have small chance of succoring it." Washington ordered Sullivan and Stirling to bring their divisions back to the west side of the Hudson and follow the main army as it withdrew to the south. Each division was given separate orders to use different routes to hasten the concentration of the army. By remaining in northern New Jersey, Reed continued, Washington remained "uncommitted either to the north or south, and maintained a better than even chance, if necessity demanded, of marching across New Jersey in time to defend the capital city."[8]

6   McGuire, *Philadelphia Campaign*, vol. 1, 85.

7   Enoch Anderson, *Personal Recollections of Captain Enoch Anderson, an officer of the Delaware Regiments in the Revolutionary War*, ed. Henry Hobart, in *Historical and Biographical Papers of the Historical Society of Delaware*, vol. 2, No.16 (1896), 34.

8   Reed, *Campaign to Valley Forge*, 31, 32-33.

Two Pennsylvania officers were detached from the main army to help arrange the defense of the province that housed Philadelphia. On July 24, Gen. Anthony Wayne was ordered to Chester County, where his home was located, to help organize the local militia. General Thomas Mifflin, a wealthy Quaker merchant from Philadelphia in peacetime, was sent to his city to help arrange its defenses. With Benjamin Lincoln off to help stop Burgoyne's invasion, and Wayne dispatched to Pennsylvania, Adam Stephen was temporarily placed in command of Lincoln's division.[9]

Politicians in Philadelphia began to worry as plans to defend the city unfolded. The Pennsylvania Supreme Executive Council, the governing body for Pennsylvania, selected a sea captain, a man in his early 30s named John Hunn to seek out the British fleet. Hunn, instructed the council, was "[to] make the best of your way to the Sea shore and observe what course the Enemys ships stear, & their numbers, and if they mean to attack, send off a person in whom all confidence can be put, to Gen. Washington. . . . Repeat to the General your intelligence by another Express or two, and as much oftener as you may think proper, lest by any accident the first should miscarry. . . . Keep the business you are going upon as much a secret as possible as you pass thro' New Jersey."[10]

Washington also sought more information. He asked that a survey be done of the Delaware River shorelines. Someone needed to reconnoiter "well that part of the country in which is likely to be the scene of action all the probable places of landing and all the grounds convenient for incamping that are well situated with respect to those places and for covering and securing the forts—gaining an accurate knowledge of all the roads and by-paths, on both sides of the Delaware (particularly from Wilmington and Chester to Philadelphia) and on the Jersey side where there is a likelihood of the enemy's operating."[11]

Despite these and other measures, Washington remained nearly as unfamiliar with the terrain around the capital city of Philadelphia as did the Howe brothers.[12]

---

9   McGuire, *Philadelphia Campaign*, vol. 1, 85; Reed, *Campaign to Valley Forge*, 33.

10 Hazard, *Pennsylvania Archives*, vol. 5, 450-451.

11 Chase and Grizzard, Jr., eds., *Papers of Washington*, vol. 10, 447-448.

12 Reed, *Campaign to Valley Forge*, 35.

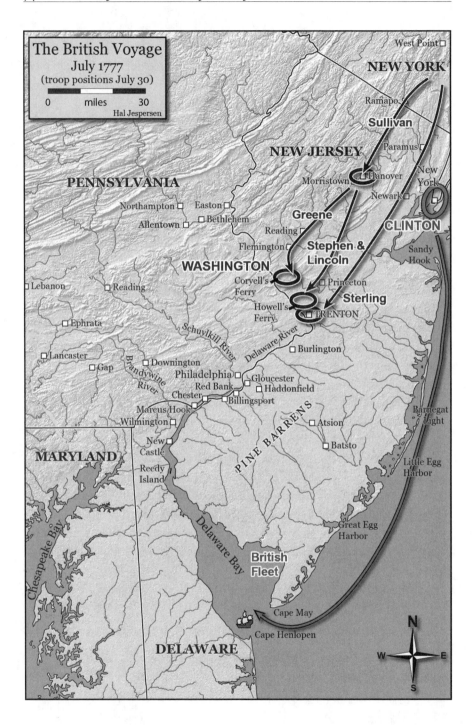

The British Voyage
July 1777
(troop positions July 30)

0   miles   30

Hal Jespersen

En Route

Captain Hunn, along with those who would send reports to the army, crossed the Delaware at Cooper's Ferry into Gloucester County, New Jersey. They had a 60-mile ride ahead of them to reach the New Jersey shoreline through an area that is not much more developed now than it was in the late eighteenth century. The men rode into Haddonfield, a village where the New Jersey legislature was then holding session, and of the many roads spiraling outward, took the Egg Harbor Road east. The riders reached a sparsely settled plain that frightened even the most seasoned travelers.

The Pine Barrens, described by one writer as "a strange primeval wilderness of gloomy forests, tangled cedar swamps, and mossy bogs interspersed with sandy plains of oddly dwarfed pines," boasted wolves, bears, and panthers in an area studded with thick stands of white Atlantic cedars and pitch pines, some of which were extremely tall. Some areas were covered with such thick canopies that at ground level it was as dark as night in midday. Among the thickets of laurel and holly, rattlesnakes lurked. Swarms of insects added to the misery of anyone riding through the region along a road little more than two sandy ruts created by heavy wagons transporting smuggled cargo, salt, timber, and iron goods including cannonballs. Not surprisingly, the Pine Barrens served as a popular hideout for smugglers and other criminals. "There is but few that Nowes the way through the Jerseys," admitted Hunn. The Hunn entourage emerged at the other end of the Barrens on July 25 at Little Egg Harbor. Home to a salt works and a hideout for American privateers, it was not much of a community. Hunn sent back his first report: no British ships were visible.[13]

There were no visible enemy ships because Admiral Howe was doing his best to keep his armada out of sight from the shoreline. Still, British engineer John Montresor, some 16 miles north of Little Egg Harbor in one of Howe's vessels, "saw the Jersey Shore . . . supposed to be Great Egg Harbour" the same afternoon Hunn was casting his anxious eyes seaward.[14]

---

13 McGuire, *Philadelphia Campaign*, vol. 1, 86-87; Arthur D. Pierce, *Smugglers' Woods: Jaunts and Journeys in Colonial and Revolutionary New Jersey* (New Brunswick, NJ, 1960), 240, 242; Hazard, *Pennsylvania Archives*, vol. 5, 467; Little Egg Harbor is today's Atlantic City.

14 Montresor, "Montresor Journals," 430. Montresor's ship was actually closer to Barnegat Light, north of Egg Harbor.

That same afternoon, Hunn and a few others rode south to Great Egg Harbor in Cape May County to the home of Capt. Nicholas Stillwell. Still unable to locate the fleet, the party visited their fellow sea captain, who was also a colonel with the local militia. At Stillwell's house, they came upon five prisoners from the British navy. The men were from the brig *Stanley*, and had been turned in by two deserters from HMS *Roebuck*. None, however, were associated with Howe's missing fleet, for the *Roebuck* was on blockading duty at the mouth of the Delaware and not part of the armada. Admiral Howe was following a wise course by keeping his fleet about 18 miles offshore, where his ships remained invisible to American spotters.[15]

While Hunn was interviewing the prisoners and hunting for the fleet, the Americans guarding the Hudson Highlands intercepted a message from Howe to Burgoyne, which Maj. Gen. Israel Putnam forwarded to Washington on July 25. According to the message, Howe was heading for New England. Washington remained unconvinced, believing instead that the message was simply disinformation. "To me, a stronger proof could not be given [that Howe] is not going to the Eastward [toward New England] than this Letter adduces," explained Washington. "It was evidently intended to fall into our hands, the complexion of it, the circumstances attending, it &cs., evinces this beyond a doubt in my Mind. . . . I am persuaded more than ever, that Philadelphia is the place of destination."[16]

The next morning, observers spotted a large portion of the fleet off Little Egg Harbor when adverse winds drove the British ships closer to shore. A doctor named John McGinnis sent a message to Thomas Mifflin in the American capital: "This morning halfe after Eight I Discovered Seventy Saile Beating to windard the wind at South making Short Tackes and keeping the Shore Close aboard."[17]

---

15 The men from the *Stanley* had been in search of a rum cargo from a schooner they had chased the previous day when their companions turned them in. Since 1775, HMS *Roebuck* had been gathering information from Loyalists, chasing smugglers, and interrupting the flow of continental commerce. Anyone familiar with the Delaware River region would have been familiar with the *Roebuck*. McGuire, *Philadelphia Campaign*, vol. 1, 87-88.

16 Fitzpatrick, ed., *The Writings of George Washington*, vol. 8, 468.

17 Reed, *Campaign to Valley Forge*, 40; John McGinnis to Colonel Bradford, July 26, 1777, Washington Papers online, Library of Congress, series 4, General Correspondence, July 1777, image 157, accessed March 4, 2013.

Washington's army, meanwhile, slowly moved south with Greene's, Stephen's, and Lincoln's divisions now within about five miles of Morristown. Stirling's division had much farther to travel, recrossing the Hudson and marching along a route via Paramus, Newark, and Elizabeth, New Jersey. Eventually, Stirling would swing west through New Brunswick and Bound Brook. Sullivan's division crossed the Hudson in the wake of Stirling's command, but its namesake remained behind recovering from an illness. Brigadier General Preudhomme de Borre, a French officer who would cause future problems for the army, led Sullivan's division in his stead. Washington sent orders for the division to proceed to Morristown instead of following Stirling's legions. The orders never reached the division, however, so its new commander followed Stirling all the way to Bound Brook. Washington would not realize the true location of Sullivan's men until August 2. Orders were also sent to the moving divisions to head for three separate crossings on the Delaware to speed passage over the river. Greene headed for Coryell's Ferry (near modern-day New Hope, Pennsylvania), while Stephen's and Lincoln's men headed a few miles north of Trenton to Howell's Ferry. Meanwhile, Stirling's men, followed by Sullivan's division, marched toward Trenton.[18]

When Dr. McGinnis's report about the fleet arrived in Philadelphia on July 27, Mifflin immediately passed the news on to Washington. "A Gentleman well known in this City is this Minute come to Town from little Egg Harbour. He declares he saw Seventy Sail of Vessels at 4 Oclock Yesterday Afternoon pass by little Egg Harbour toward Cape May. . . . The Destination of General Howe cannot now be mistaken as Egg Harbour is but a few Hours Sailing from our Capes." The fleet was 50 miles from Cape May. Washington, who was about 60 miles north of Philadelphia at Flemington, New Jersey, acknowledged Mifflin's message with cautious optimism. "The appearance of the enemy's fleet off Little Egg Harbour, if it does not amount to a certain proof that their design is against Philadelphia," he explained, "is at least a very strong argument of it." New orders would be issued to the army, he continued, "as soon as the movements of the Enemy makes it more evident that Philadelphia is their object. . . . It is far from impossible the Enemy may still turn about and make a stroke" for the Hudson River.[19]

18 Reed, *Campaign to Valley Forge*, 35-37.

19 Chase and Grizzard, eds., *Papers of Washington*, vol. 10, 439; Fitzpatrick, *The Writings of George Washington*, vol. 8, 492-493.

Then, to Washington's dismay, further reports of the British armada dried up. None of the spotters, including Hunn, could find the fleet along the Jersey shore. On July 27, the same day Mifflin opened Dr. McGinnis's report, a heavy storm scattered Howe's ships. Admiral Howe "fired Guns every half hour" to prevent collisions and keep contact with the various vessels. Despite his best efforts, scattered collisions were reported, though no major damage seems to have resulted. Beset by storms, high seas, and overcrowding on the old ships, some of the men and horses had been aboard so long that rations were now running dangerously low.[20]

While Howe's ships bobbed and heaved on a difficult sea, Washington reached Reading, New Jersey, accompanied by Nathanael Greene's division. Up to this point, the dusty roads had been conducive to rapid marching. In fact, Washington limited the pace of the march to preserve the health and stamina of the men. However, the same storm that hit the British fleet washed over Washington's Continentals. Greene and Washington finally reached Coryell's Ferry on July 28, but the rain turned the roads into deep mud that considerably slowed and exhausted the marchers.

Washington made his headquarters at the Oakham farm near the Coryell's Ferry crossing. The property was owned by Quakers, but Washington was apparently welcomed despite the owner's pacifist attitude. It was time to assemble additional militia. "[I]t will be as necessary for the Militia of Burlington, Gloucester, Salem and Cape May to be assembled, as those of Pennsylvania," Washington informed Governor Livingston of New Jersey. "[Have them] Assemble immediately at Gloucester." Although militia did not have to serve outside their state boundaries, Washington hoped the New Jersey militia would garrison the fortification at Billingsport and cross the river into Pennsylvania, if needed.[21]

Stirling's men eventually reached Trenton, and Stephen, with Lincoln's Pennsylvanians in tow, reached Howell's Ferry. Orders from Washington finally found Gen. de Borre with Sullivan's division at Bound Brook. The French general took the division to Morristown, decided he did not like the position, and moved east to Hanover. The result was an exhausting and wholly

---

20 Entry for July 28, Lord Cantelupe Diary, the Grey Papers, Durham University, England; Reed, *Campaign to Valley Forge*, 37.

21 Reed, *Campaign to Valley Forge*, 37; Fitzpatrick, *The Writings of George Washington*, vol. 8, 475-476. Gloucester is opposite Philadelphia.

unnecessary circuitous march that had, described one writer, "swung like a great fishhook down from the Highlands, then part way back again." The division's stay at Hanover would prove to be much longer than anyone intended.[22]

While Washington maneuvered his divisions pending definitive word of Howe's destination, and the storm thrashed the fleet and churned the roads of northern New Jersey, a notable arrival destined to play a remarkable role in the American Revolution rode into Philadelphia. Although he had been commissioned a major general by the American Congress, Lafayette entered the capital city that summer in 1777 without an active command. There was simply no suitable organization at that time for him to lead. The young indefatigable Frenchman vowed instead to serve as a volunteer at his own expense. He would serve Washington in whatever capacity he could.[23]

First Arrival

Even though it was just eight miles from Cape May on July 29, no one had yet reported sighting the British fleet. Unbeknownst to Howe, however, Washington had not been fooled into believing he was moving to help Burgoyne. For the first time in three days, Capt. Hunn sent a report to Philadelphia. "The Reasons you have had No Express," began the observer, "is the weather have Been So thick [foggy] this three days past that it has Been Impossible to Discover Wheather thear was a fleet off or Not, But the wind is Now as N.W. & the weather Verry Cleare & No fleet in sight. . . . [I]f the fleet is Bound to Delaware By the accounts of the wind & Weather they have had No Chance to arrive hear yet. I have sent No Express to General Washington as it is hard to get horses for so Long a Journey, But if theare should Be a fleet in sight Mr. Jones will go Express Immediately to head quarters."[24]

With but a slim indication that Howe's fleet was indeed heading south, Washington continued shifting elements of his army in that direction as well. By July 29 the lead elements reached Coryell's Ferry, not far north of where the general had famously crossed the Delaware the previous December. The steady movements, however, were exhausting the men, as Col. Persifor Frazer attested

---

22 Reed, *Campaign to Valley Forge*, 39.

23 Harlow Giles Unger, *Lafayette* (Hoboken, NJ, 2002), 37.

24 Reed, *Campaign to Valley Forge*, 40-41; Hazard, *Pennsylvania Archives*, vol. 5, 462-463.

in a letter to his wife: "We have March'd 2 Divisions consisting of 16 Rg/ts 90 Miles in four days, under several disadvantages. We cross'd the Delaware this morning with our Brigade. Orders arriv'd just then for the others to stand fast and for us to halt." The army was strung out all the way from Coryell's Ferry to the upper reaches of New Jersey near the New York border.[25]

Like Washington, John Adams was also frustrated at the lack of news regarding the enemy fleet. Tensions ran high in Philadelphia as rumors piled one upon another about Howe's destination. "They might as well imagine them gone round Cape Horn into the South Seas to land at California, and march across the Continent to attack our back settlements," grumbled Adams.[26]

Unbeknownst to Adams, however, the fleet was spotted off Cape May just as he was putting pen to paper that morning. Hunn could finally report the news everyone had been awaiting. "The fleet to the Number of 30 sail is Now in Sight. . . . I've not sent Mr. Jones off yet, but as soon as I am convinst they are bound up the Bay, I shall send the Express, but as there is but few that Nowes the way through the Jerseys, the Intilligence will go By Philadelphia as quick any way. . . . 45 sail in sight, & more of Cors will be in Sight. . . . [I]t appears to me they are bound up our Bay," concluded Hunn, who qualified his statement by adding, "but I may be dec'ved."[27]

The fleet was indeed entering Delaware Bay, into which the river bearing the same name emptied. The river, bay, and state were named for Thomas West, Baron de la Warr, who had succeeded Capt. John Smith as governor of Virginia in 1610. Cape May in New Jersey marked the northern extremity of the bay's mouth, while Cape Henlopen in Delaware marked the southern end. A lighthouse erected 10 years earlier by Philadelphia merchants was situated on a sand dune 50 feet above sea level at Cape Henlopen. Ironically, the 70-foot octagonal structure was built from Brandywine River granite, and in their journals and diaries, several British officers mentioned seeing the structure.

Two men, a ship pilot named Henry Fisher and David Hall, commander of the regiment of Continentals from Delaware, stood atop the lighthouse watching the fleet gather in the bay. Fisher reported that the "Fleet is in sight, and at this time about 4 Leagues from the Light House, there is 228 (two

---

25 Frazer, *General Frazer*, 151.

26 Smith, et al., eds., *Letters of Delegates*, vol. 7, 395.

27 Hazard, *Pennsylvania Archives*, vol. 5, 467-468.

hundred and twenty eight) sail. . . . [T]hey to all appearance will not be in till this afternoon." If Fisher's report was accurate and complete, Howe's fleet had been reduced by at least 30 ships during the week since it departed New York Harbor. Caesar Rodney, a signer of the Declaration of Independence and commander of Delaware militia, forwarded the news to Congress, scribbling on the message, "I have Sent a fresh man and Horse that this Inteligence may be sooner with you."[28]

Rodney's messenger galloped north through Delaware via sandy plains similar to the New Jersey Pine Barrens. The wooded territory was heavily interspersed with creeks and swamps. Since there was not much of a moon, the ride through the thick woods was especially gloomy and a bit dangerous. Once he emerged from the foreboding country, the rider climbed the hilly land around Wilmington. He pulled into Chester, Pennsylvania, in the early morning hours of July 31 after a long 10-hour ride of nearly 70 miles and handed Thomas Mifflin firm confirmation of the fleet's location.

After receiving confirmation from Mifflin, John Hancock immediately passed the news to Washington, who was 30 miles north of Philadelphia at Coryell's Ferry on the Delaware. The report reached him between 9:00 and 10:00 a.m., about 24 hours after Fisher and Hall began counting ships from the top of the lighthouse 160 miles away. It was the news Washington had been so eagerly awaiting. He immediately set his men in motion. The elements of his army gathered along the east bank of the Delaware above Trenton and crossed into Pennsylvania.[29]

When news of the approach of Howe's fleet spread, panic erupted in Philadelphia. The city magistrate ordered that all wagons within and near the city be prepared to remove stores, provisions, and other supplies that might aid the enemy. Congress passed a resolution recommending "to make prisoners such of the late crown & proprietary officers and other persons in and near this city as are disaffected or may be dangerous to the publick liberty and send them back into the country, there to be confined or enlarged upon parole as their characters & behavior may require." Among others, two prominent Pennsylvanians on the list to be arrested were Gov. John Penn, a grandson of

---

28 McGuire, *Philadelphia Campaign*, vol. 1, 92-93; Hazard, *Pennsylvania Archives*, vol. 5, 465; Caesar Rodney, *Letters to and from Caesar Rodney 1756-1784*, ed. George Herbert Ryden (New York, 1970), 201-202.

29 McGuire, *Philadelphia Campaign*, vol. 1, 94.

founder William Penn, and Chief Justice Benjamin Chew, a prominent Philadelphia lawyer.[30]

In the midst of the panic gripping the city, Washington rode into town about 10:00 p.m., escorted by 200 light dragoons. The Virginian was well ahead of his army. He spent the night at City Tavern, where he was introduced for the first time to Lafayette. The commander-in-chief impressed the Frenchman, who long recalled when he "beheld for the first time that great man." Although Washington "was surrounded by officers and citizens, it was impossible to mistake for a moment his majestic figure and deportment; nor was he less distinguished by the noble affability of his manner."[31]

If the British army meant to instill panic in the politicians and civilians in Philadelphia, the Howe brothers accomplished this goal. While panic and confusion would surely help their cause, their objective was the capture of the American capital. While patriot observers were busy counting ships and rushing reports to Philadelphia and Washington, William and Richard Howe faced a critical decision: Ascend the Delaware River with the fleet, or put back out to sea?

Decisions, Decisions

Captain Andrew Hamond was the commander of HMS *Roebuck*, which for months had been tasked with keeping a watchful eye on the Delaware and gathering intelligence. "This man," wrote one historian, "is a good example of the eighteenth-century naval officer who, by professional excellence, the support of powerful patrons and other good fortune, rose to positions of eminence in that highly competitive service." Hamond's father got him an appointment as a midshipman in 1753. Six years later his fine seamanship earned him a commission, and he served under Lord Richard Howe for the remainder of the Seven Years' War. In 1763, Hamond was noticed by the Earl of Sandwich for smuggling the earl's favorite wine into the basement of the Admiralty. He was given command of a frigate in 1771, and during the summer of 1775 he achieved command of the 44-gun *Roebuck*, with orders to blockade the Delaware and Chesapeake bays.

30 Jackson, *The Pennsylvania Navy*, 104; Hazard, *Pennsylvania Archives*, vol. 5, 469.

31 McGuire, *Philadelphia Campaign*, vol. 1, 94-95; Marquis de Lafayette, *Memoirs, Correspondence and Manuscripts of General Lafayette: Published by his Family* (New York, 1837), vol. 1, 18.

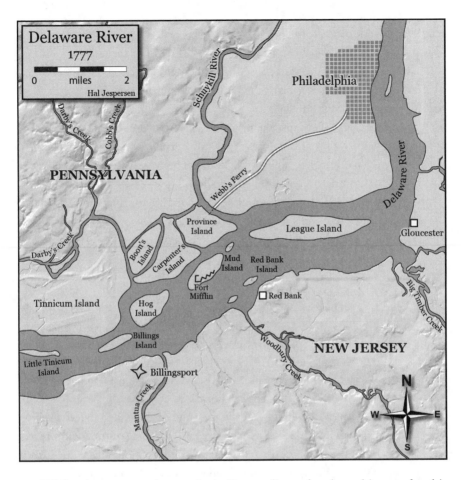

Delaware River 1777

0 miles 2

Hal Jespersen

PENNSYLVANIA

Philadelphia

Schuylkill River

Darby's Creek

Cobb's Creek

Webb's Ferry

Delaware River

Province Island

League Island

Gloucester

Darby's Creek

Boon's Island

Carpenter's Island

Mud Island

Red Bank Island

Big Timber Creek

Fort Mifflin

Red Bank

Tinnicum Island

Hog Island

Billings Island

Woodbury Creek

NEW JERSEY

Little Tinicum Island

Billingsport

Mantua Creek

N
W   E
S

While there were times when Hamond's and other ships under his command were absent from the region, he was the British officer most familiar with the American defenses. When he returned to Delaware Bay in April of 1777, Hamond was one of the few to be informed that Howe's army would soon head in his direction, and he was to make the necessary arrangements "to land it as high up the river as possible." Just a week before the fleet's arrival, he had flags placed around the bay to mark the shoals so the army transports could safely enter without having to use local pilots.[32]

Weather conditions were perfect when the fleet finally arrived. At 10:00 a.m. on July 30, Hamond reported to Admiral Howe's flagship HMS *Eagle* to

32 Denys Hay, "The Denouement of General Howe's Campaign of 1777," in *English Historical Review*, vol. 74 (1964), 500-501.

meet with the Howe brothers. Hamond was shocked to find the general still asleep. A short time later the two Howes and Hamond met in the admiral's cabin. One of the first questions posed was whether Hamond knew the location of Washington's army. The army, he replied, was across the Delaware heading for Wilmington. His intelligence source is not known, but Hamond's assessment was false. Perhaps one brigade was across the river, but the rest of Washington's army was strung out across northern New Jersey. Howe's most recent dispatch to Germain, however, stated that he would ascend the Delaware River only if Washington remained in northern New Jersey. If he had entered Pennsylvania instead, Howe was going to revert to the plan to ascend the Chesapeake Bay. Hamond's incorrect report made Howe's decision for him.[33]

Hamond summarized Howe's arguments against ascending the Delaware:

> As Washington, by the long passage of the Fleet from New York, had got his army over the Delaware before the fleet arrived, great opposition was expected to be given the Troops at landing at Newcastle or Wilmington the places intended. That the Enemy expecting the Fleet to come into the River had made uncommon preparations to annoy the Men of War & Transports with Fire Ships and fire rafts, and had besides a . . . number of Row Galleys, Xebecks, & Floating Batterys, in which the narrow navigation & rapid tides of the River might do great damage among the Transports.[34]

Hamond also updated the Howes on the state of American defenses along the Delaware, which he described as "strong," and the state of the Pennsylvania navy, which by June of 1777 consisted of 56 vessels of various sizes. The brown water colonial state navy had strategically placed its assets, with fire rafts stationed in Darby and Mantua creeks, in Pennsylvania and New Jersey, respectively, and in the Schuylkill River. The galleys and ships were positioned near the old fortification on Mud Island just below Philadelphia (soon to be called Fort Mifflin). A four-gun earthwork had been constructed near Darby Creek on Tinicum Island, and a two-gun battery on Bush Island. The latter was a small island located a few hundred yards from the New Jersey shoreline across from Mud Island (near the present site of Fort Mercer). Pennsylvania militia elements garrisoned these various posts.[35]

---

33 Hay, "The Denouement," 503.

34 Ibid., 504.

35 Jackson, *Pennsylvania Navy*, 90-92.

Notorious for its changing channels, shoals, sand bars, and appearing and disappearing islands, the Delaware offered a host of navigational problems. Two distinctly different situations were evident in the building of the *chevaux-de-frise*. The channel passage between Billingsport and Billings Island was narrow, but somewhat deeper than that at the second line of defense between Mud Island and the New Jersey shore. At the latter defense line the river was wider, but contained two prominent sand bars that created a main channel between Hog and Fort Islands on the west and the large shoal to the east. East of this shoal was a secondary channel with yet another sandbar near the New Jersey shore. The main river channel was sufficient to permit the passage of any eighteenth-century ship, but slightly shallower than the passage at Billingsport. The blocking *chevaux-de-frise*, composed of 30-foot-square boxes filled with stone and upward-pointing iron-tipped logs, were chained together about 60 feet apart, 24 more were placed in two irregular lines at Billingsport, and another 43 near Mud Island in four groupings. The redoubt at Darby Creek on Tinicum Island had limited effectiveness against small ships and cruisers, but a major thrust by the British fleet would have left the post isolated.[36]

As strong as these colonial defenses were, the powerful British armada could have forced a landing south of the first line of *chevaux-de-frise* in either Pennsylvania or New Jersey. The question confronting the Howe brothers was which option to follow. A landing in New Jersey would confront difficult terrain, including numerous creeks and marshes with few bridges the Colonials could easily destroy. Even if these natural obstacles could be overcome, the British would still find themselves on the east bank of the Delaware. Most Americans believed Marcus Hook, Pennsylvania, the logical landing site, which would provide the British army with an easy approach to Philadelphia and yet keep it within supporting distance of the British fleet. However, the river would still be barred to the fleet. The last viable option was to land the army at Wilmington or as high upriver as Chester, just a dozen miles from Philadelphia. A landing on the west side of the river could take the river defenses from the land side, where they were weakest.[37]

The defenses at all these places were essentially insignificant. Although protected by the Delaware River fortifications and the Pennsylvania navy

36 Jackson, *Pennsylvania Navy*, 353-61.

37 Ibid., 104; Reed, *Campaign to Valley Forge*, 42.

against a water assault from the south, Philadelphia had nothing to protect it from a land attack. The Schuylkill River and the Brandywine River were the only formidable natural barriers to the west, but they could be easily forded. Incredibly, despite the obvious risk to Philadelphia, not a single fortification or earthwork of any kind had been built to defend the largest and most important North American city from an overland invasion.

At least one historian of the Pennsylvania navy and this aspect of the war argued that it is false to assume the Howe brothers "were unfamiliar with the strength and weakness of the river defenses. Information not revealed by their reconnaissance or reported by spies would be furnished by . . . Tories like . . . Galloway." Except for the inland navy, other defenses were in a deplorable condition and garrisoned by only a handful of militia.[38]

General Howe, however, made the decision to sail farther south to the Chesapeake Bay. There, he argued, "The troops would be put ashore without any molestation, have time to recover the Horses after the fatigue of the Voyage before they entered Service, and where the Transports could remain in perfect security." After leaving Captain Hamond for a private conversation with his brother, Howe returned having reached the conclusion that Washington had learned their plans and they could no longer land on the Delaware. "Since there was no doubt that the Enemy was apprized of the plan of the Expedition . . . it confirmed him to his design of landing his army at the Head of Elk in the Chesapeake rather than the Delaware."[39]

The decision astonished Captain Hamond, who had only himself to blame. It was he, after all, who had informed the general that the Continental Army had crossed the Delaware when in fact it had not. Hamond later stated "that the general's wish and intention were first to destroy the magazines at York & Carlisle before he attacked the Rebel Army or looked towards Philadelphia; and therefore it was of course a great object to get to the westward of the Enemy." If Howe made an argument for destroying Continental magazines in the Pennsylvania back country, his intent was not reflected in his campaign; Howe would never march his army anywhere near York, Carlisle, or Lancaster.[40]

---

38 Jackson, *Pennsylvania Navy*, 101, 127.

39 Hay, "The Denouement," 504.

40 Ibid.

In addition to his men's exhaustion, perhaps the most significant factor contributing to Howe's decision was his belief that it would be too difficult and risky to land along the Delaware with Washington's Army operating in the area. Howe believed this even though Hamond told him the army could be safely landed 10 miles below New Castle, Delaware, at Reedy Island, where it would have been only 35 miles from Philadelphia. Trying to convince his superior without being insubordinate, Hamond pleaded against "the great length of time it would take to make such a detour with so large a fleet, contrasted with the immediate opportunity of getting the whole army ashore in 24 hours . . . but all to no purpose, the General seemed resolved, and the Admiral would not oppose him; and to the astonishment of both Fleet and Army, the signal was made to turn away, and steer for the Capes of Virginia."[41]

General Howe would later contend (with the benefit of hindsight) that the farther he drew Washington from the Hudson River, the more he was assisting Burgoyne's army. If Howe had approached Philadelphia via the Delaware River, however, he would have saved time, and the distance back to the Hudson River Valley would have been shorter, so there still would have been a chance he could have made himself directly available to aid Burgoyne. Once he opted to leave the Delaware and sail around the Delmarva Peninsula to the other bay, supporting Burgoyne would no longer be possible. Howe further explained his reasoning when he eventually testified before the English Parliament about his 1777 campaign:

> Several days must have been employed to surmount the difficulties of getting up the river [Delaware] and I inferred from thence, that I should not be able to land troops before General Washington would be in force at Wilmington. . . . There was besides no prospect of landing above the confluence of the Delaware and Christiana Creek [at Wilmington], at least the preparations the enemy had made for the defense of the river, by gallies, floating batteries, fireships, and fire rafts, would have made such an attempt extremely hazardous. I had also to consider that the country below, where the troops must have landed, and where only the transports could have laid in security, (I mean about Reedy-Island) was very marshy, and the roads upon narrow causeways intersected by creeks: I therefore agreed with the Admiral to go up Chesapeak Bay, a

41 Hay, "The Denouement," 505.

plan which had been preconcerted, in the event of a landing in the Delaware proving, upon our arrival there, ineligible.[42]

The decision that so shocked Captain Hamond marked yet another change in Howe's campaign plans. Had Howe known that Washington's army was not as close to Wilmington as Hamond alleged, would he still have shifted his destination to the Chesapeake? He had already hinted to Galloway, among others, that from the beginning he would make for the Chesapeake and not the Delaware.

In fact, it was not the decision to head for the Chesapeake, but his decision to enter Delaware Bay in the first place that was the great mystery. Perhaps the real reason the fleet stopped was to get an intelligence briefing from Hamond, which may account for Howe's late rise from bed that morning. Later, several officers blamed the unfortunate Hamond for the decision to steer for the Chesapeake. Captain Henry Duncan, adjutant to Admiral Howe, thought "our course had all along been for" the Delaware, but "from intelligence received from" the *Roebuck*, "the admiral and the general thought proper to steer to the southward."[43]

Despite Duncan's testimony placing the blame at Hamond's feet, one source lends credence to Hamond's version of events. According to The Earl of Carlisle, he met the Howes at the entrance to the bay, where he claims to have

informed them of the state of the river, and the chain, the cheveau de frize, &c. That they, on that, inquired into the state of Chesapeak, and the possibility of landing at the Head of Elk. It was urged to them that it would be better to land below the impediments, as they would by that means save the sea voyage, and be almost as near Philadelphia. To this was answered that the taking of the city was not the principal object; but as it afterwards appeared that all the magazines were then at York Town or Carlisle, and the taking of them would effectually crush Gen. Washinton, &c., therefore they pursued their intention of going up the Chespeak, as the destruction of the magazines was to be more easily effected by so doing.[44]

---

42 *Narrative of Howe*, 23-24. Christiana Creek is usually referred to today as Christiana River. I use the contemporary name throughout this book.

43 Henry Duncan, "The Journals of Henry Duncan," *Publications of the Navy Records Society*, ed. John Knox Laughton (London, 1902), vol. 20, 147-148.

44 *The Manuscripts of the Earl of Carlisle, Preserved at Castle Howard*, Historical Manuscripts Commission, 15th Report (London, 1897), Appendix, Part 6, 354.

Lord Germain would have been quite disturbed to learn that the colonial capital city of Philadelphia was not the principal object of the campaign. If this account is to be believed, Howe was not only abandoning General Burgoyne in distant upstate New York, but was also more concerned with a couple of back country American villages that would not affect the outcome of the war than he was with the American capital.

On the other hand, by landing southwest of Philadelphia, Howe's sizeable army would also threaten Lancaster, Pennsylvania, America's largest inland city. Lancaster was 60 miles west of the colonial capital, surrounded by rolling acres of rich farmland and dozens of mills, ironworks, and rifle shops. It had a thriving population of 5,000 and was a sizeable staging area for troops and supplies passing between New York, Virginia, and the western frontier at Fort Pitt. Lancaster also housed hundreds of British and Hessian prisoners of war. Other settlements in that part of the state included York, Carlisle, Lebanon, Downingtown, and Reading. The latter, just 30 miles north of Lancaster, was of primary importance because it did double duty as the Continental Army's main supply depot in the mid-Atlantic region. Lastly, both Lancaster and Reading contained general army hospitals.[45]

When the British fleet made the move back to sea on July 31, anger at General Howe's decision-making once again rippled through British and Hessian ranks. Admiral Howe's secretary, Ambrose Serle, was among those dumbfounded by the general's decision. "The Hearts of all Men were struck with this Business, every one apprehending the worst . . . without the Loss or Risque of a Battel—What will my dear Country think & say too, when this News is carried Home? . . . [W]e are bound to the Chesapeak; in which Situation, may GOD defend us from the Fatality of the worst Climate in America at this worst Season of the Year to experience it!—I can write no more," concluded the frustrated secretary, for "my Heart is full."[46]

Lieutenant Heinrich von Feilitzsch of the Anspach Jaegers agreed with Serle's sentiment and frustration. The 26-year old Hessian officer maintained a detailed journal for the years 1777-1780. He was less than impressed with the British leadership under which he served, but knew there was nothing anyone could effectively do about it. "No one any longer knew where we were bound,"

45 McGuire, *Philadelphia Campaign*, vol. 1, 123-124.

46 Tatum, Jr., ed., *Journal of Ambrose Serle*, 241.

he confessed. "Everyone said something different and everyone had to leave the decision to General Howe."[47]

Washington's capable division commander, Nathanael Greene, believed that the Hudson River was of much greater importance to the American cause and winning the war for the British than was the capture of the capital city. "The North [Hudson] River is the first object upon the continent. Philadelphia, the next, considering the temper and disposition of the people," thought Greene. "The Political principles of the Inhabitants of Pennsylvania, the lower Counties on the Delaware [the state of Delaware] and part of Maryland is a strong motive for General How to operate in that quarter. Philadelphia will influence almost all the Southern States," he concluded, "and the solicitude for its preservation in the army is beyond your conception."[48]

Like so many others on both sides, Loyalist Joseph Galloway was frustrated and furious with Howe's decision-making. He would later testify to a deeply interested Parliament investigating that general's war record that "there was no obstructions that I know of. There were no forts below the Chevaux-de-frize, nor any obstruction." Galloway would also later write that in early August, the "fort at Mud Island was garrisoned only by 130 militia and Billingsport with 90. The floating batteries were not manned, the lower Chevaux-de-frize were not placed in the river. The chain was not finished," he continued, and "the passage from the Capes to Philadelphia was open; Red Bank was not fortified or occupied in short, there was nothing to oppose the taking possession of Mud Island fort, the city of Philadelphia, and all the rebel water guard in the Delaware."[49]

General Howe's decision to commit a significant portion of the British forces in North America on an exhausting and circuitous voyage to assault Philadelphia meant that none of these men or guns would be available to assist General Burgoyne in upstate New York or the garrison under General Clinton manning New York City. Perhaps equally important, by consuming nearly another full month to sail the winding route up the Chesapeake to his destination, Howe guaranteed General Washington all the time he would

---

47 Burgoyne, trans. and ed., *Diaries of Two Jaegers*, 12.

48 Showman, McCarthy, and Cobb, eds., *Papers of Greene*, vol. 2, 126-127.

49 The Examination of Joseph Galloway, Esq; Late Speaker of the House of Assembly of *Pennsylvania. Before the House of Commons, In a Committee on the American Papers. With Explanatory Notes* (London, 1779), 28; Galloway, *Letters to a Nobleman*, 70.

require to concentrate his Continental army and position it to contest what, in the end, would have to be a direct land approach to reach and conquer Philadelphia.[50]

50 Reed, *Campaign to Valley Forge*, 32.

Chapter 5

To Sea and the Chesapeake
August 1-25, 1777

"This is a curious campaign: in the Spring we had the Enimy about our ears
every hour. . . . Now . . . we have lost [our enemy], compeld to wander
about the country like the Arabs in search of em."[1]

— Nathanael Greene, August 17, 1777

The Fleet Continues South

Despite the disappointment of loyalist Joseph
Galloway and numerous others, Howe's
fleet started moving down the Delaware coastline on the first day of August and
was just off Cape Henlopen by the end of that day. Hessian Johann Ewald
concluded that departing the Delaware was a "stratagem of the admiral to make
the enemy army uncertain of our landing."[2]

Indeed, with the fleet steering back out to sea, Washington was once again
forced to exercise caution since Howe could turn back at any moment. Still,
Washington decided to consolidate much of his army. Adam Stephen's two
American divisions crossed over Howell's Ferry and linked up with Nathanael
Greene on the York Road north of Philadelphia. The three divisions passed

---

1 Showman, McCarthy, and Cobb, eds., *Papers of Greene*, vol. 2, 142-3.

2 Ewald, *Diary*, 73.

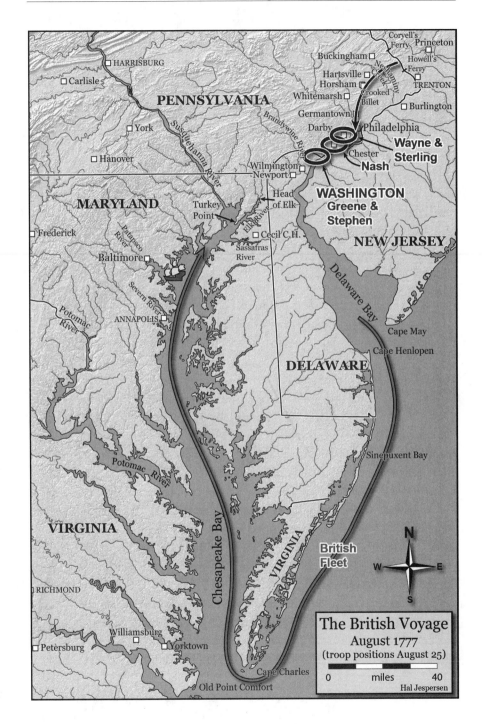

Coryell's Ferry
Princeton
Buckingham
Howell's Ferry
Hartsville
Horsham
TRENTON
Whitemarsh
Crooked Billet
Burlington
Neshaminy Creek
Germantown
HARRISBURG
Carlisle
PENNSYLVANIA
York
Darby
Philadelphia
Wayne & Sterling
Branchywine River
Hanover
Chester
Nash
Wilmington
Newport
WASHINGTON
Greene & Stephen
Susquehanna River
MARYLAND
Turkey Point
Head of Elk
Elk River
NEW JERSEY
Frederick
Patapsco River
Cecil C.H.
Sassafras River
Delaware Bay
Baltimore
Severn River
ANNAPOLIS
Cape May
Potomac River
Cape Henlopen
DELAWARE
Sinepuxent Bay
Potomac River
VIRGINIA
British Fleet
N
W   E
S
RICHMOND
Chesapeake Bay
VIRGINIA
Williamsburg
Yorktown
Petersburg
Cape Charles
Old Point Comfort

The British Voyage
August 1777
(troop positions August 25)

0   miles   40

Hal Jespersen

through Buckingham and reached Little Neshaminy Creek above Hartsville and camped for the night. Lord Stirling came over from Trenton and joined the other three divisions. The next morning, all four commands continued down the York Road, but before entering the capital, moved to the right and passed through the village of Germantown. The colonials camped on the high plateau east of the Schuylkill River on the property of Henry Hill.[3]

The men who arrived in Germantown had just marched more than 100 miles in a summer heat mixed with intermittent rain showers and needed rest. While they camped, other parts of the army prepared to take up the march. Washington ordered Israel Putnam to start stripping the Hudson Highlands to send more troops south. "I desire that you may keep two thousand Continental Troops and order the others to march Southward," he directed. "If any thing should induce me to think that the Enemy mean to send any part of their forces back again, I will immediately countermand the March of those Troops." The two New Jersey regiments in northern New Jersey under Elias Dayton were also ordered south. French officer de Borre was ordered to bring Sullivan's division south as well, but once again the message did not reach its destination.[4]

Washington spent the daylight hours far ahead of his army along the Delaware River, inspecting sites for various current and future fortifications as far south as Chester and Marcus Hook. Accompanying him for the first time as a member of his staff was the Marquis de Lafayette, who had traveled to America with a large number of French officers seeking American commissions. Most would be disappointed, but Lafayette kept the two youngest officers with him as aides. While Congress had made Lafayette a major general, it did not honor him with the command of any troops, so he would serve as an unattached general on Washington's staff during the ongoing campaign. Lafayette's presence posed a thorny problem for Washington. He could not give the foreigner a command without offending American-born generals, but neither could he ignore him without upsetting the delicate diplomatic negotiations with France.[5]

Washington consulted with several of his senior officers, especially those from Pennsylvania, about where to defend the capital. Three creeks were

---

3   Reed, *Campaign to Valley Forge*, 46.

4   Fitzpatrick, *Writings of Washington*, vol. 8, 503-4; Reed, *Campaign to Valley Forge*, 44.

5   Reed, *Campaign to Valley Forge*, 55-6.

suggested to him, all above Chester: Ridley, Crum, and Darby. Washington spent the night 15 miles below Philadelphia and even farther from the bulk of his army, which was still outside Germantown.[6]

At 9:00 p.m., a shock wave hit American headquarters when word arrived that the British fleet had left the bay. With the southwesterly winds, Howe's ships could quickly return to New York. A flurry of orders flew out of headquarters that either halted columns in place or ordered them to reverse their line of march. "This unexpected event makes it necessary to reverse our disposition and I have accordingly sent Orders to Sullivan's Division and the two other Brigades on the other Side of the Delaware, to return and recross the [Hudson River]," explained Washington.[7]

Over the next few days, questions about General Howe's puzzling strategy circulated throughout Philadelphia. "What this Man is after, no Wisdom can discover," exclaimed John Adams. Sarah Logan Fisher, who was as mystified as everyone else, put a poetic twist on the confusing situation: "But indeed the conduct of Howe may I think be justly said, in the words of the poet, 'to be dark and intricate, puzzled with mazes & perplexed with errors.' Strangely unaccountable is some of his conduct; perhaps time may unravel the mystery & justify his delays."[8]

Howe's disappearance put Washington in something of a quandary as to how to position his infantry divisions. Of one thing he was certain: he was loath to place a major river (the Delaware) between himself and the Hudson Highlands in New York. "If they had intended back to the [Sandy] Hook," Washington wrote to Israel Putnam, "we must have heard of their arrival there long before this time, as the Winds have been constantly fair. As the Sickly season has commenced to the Southward, and there is no capital object there, I cannot conceive that they are gone that way. I can therefore only conclude, that they intend to go round Long Island into the Sound, or still farther Eastward [New England]."[9]

6   Ibid., 46.

7   McGuire, *Philadelphia Campaign*, vol. 1, 98; Fitzpatrick, ed., *Writings of Washington*, vol. 9, 3-4.

8   Smith, et al., eds., *Letters of Delegates*, vol. 7, 403; Sarah Logan Fisher, "A Diary of Trifling Occurrences," ed. Nicholas B. Wainwright, *Pennsylvania Magazine of History and Biography* (Philadelphia, 1958), vol. 82, 440.

9   Fitzpatrick, ed., *Writings of Washington*, vol. 9, 34.

On the night of August 3, while Washington contemplated the new strategic situation, a severe storm assailed the British fleet. Engineer John Montresor recalled the horrifying experience: "At ½ past 6 P.M. smart lightening and appearing very stormy to the west. . . . At 7 this evening came on a violent storm . . . scarcely giving the Fleet time to take in their sails. . . . One ship laid for some time on her beam ends without righting. We Slipped our mizzen top sail without any other damage of any consequence—the lightning and thunder surpassed description and the heaviness of the rain. . . . A sloop likewise laid on her beam ends—7 men and a woman took to their boat, but kept her towed, but the painter breaking got adrift and was lost. The Sloop with four men on board, righted an hour after." The storms and adverse winds slowed the fleet considerably; by August 6, it was still 45 miles from the entrance to the Chesapeake Bay.[10]

The plague of indecision was once again forced upon the Continental Army. With its leaders unsure whether the British fleet was returning north, those divisions that had moved into Pennsylvania remained at Germantown for several days. While the army needed rest, remaining static for too long during the hot summer days made sanitation and the spread of disease a real concern. Throughout all wars of the eighteenth and nineteenth centuries, disease killed more men than battlefield wounds. Keeping encampments clean did not eliminate camp diseases such as dysentery and typhoid, but it reduced the spread and diminished their effect on an army. Several senior officers issued orders admonishing the men to constantly police their camps.

Because it was just a few miles from the capital, the Continental Army was visited by civilians, important and otherwise, during its stay at Germantown. Washington reviewed the army on August 8, with Lafayette in attendance. The young Frenchman left an insightful and helpful description of the army at this time:

> About eleven thousand men, ill armed, and still worse clothed, presented a strange spectacle. . . . [T]heir clothes were parti-coloured, and many of them were almost naked; the best clad wore hunting shirts, large grey linen coats which were much used in Carolina. . . . As to their military tactics, it will be sufficient to say that, for a regiment ranged in order of battle to move forward on the right of its line, it was necessary for the left to make a continued counter march. They were always arranged in two lines,

---

10 Montresor, "Montresor Journals," 432-3; Reed, *Campaign to Valley Forge*, 66.

the smallest men in the first line; no other distinction as to height was ever observed. In spite of these disadvantages, the soldiers were fine, and the officers zealous; virtue stood in place of science, and each day added both to experience and discipline.[11]

The days were passing and as of yet, no news of the fleet had reached Washington. Congressman Henry Laurens, whose son would soon serve on Washington's staff, thought the fleet "may now be in the Moon for aught we know, but he is probably gone to New England & will strive to join General Burgoine." In fact, Howe's missing armada was spotted off the coast of Maryland at Sinepuxent the day before on August 7, but it took a couple of days for the news to reach Washington.[12]

Unaware that the fleet had been spotted en route to the Chesapeake, Washington opted to position his army closer to the Delaware River in case it had to hasten back to the Hudson Highlands. On the same day he reviewed his army, Washington's troops moved about eight miles back to the Whitemarsh area and went into camp along Sandy Run. Part of the reason Washington began shifting back to the north was his growing belief that Howe may well head to the Deep South, perhaps to Charleston or even Savannah. If that was the case, the Americans would need to be in a position to move quickly to deal with Burgoyne in upper New York before doing anything to help the Carolinas or Virginia.[13]

Just after the army began the shift back to the Delaware River, news arrived that the fleet was off the coast of Maryland. "We have found Howe again. I thought he was lost in the Gulph stream," joked Congressman James Lovell. Washington received the news about 25 miles northeast of Philadelphia along Neshaminy Creek, where the army had moved on August 10. The new camp was ideally located at the intersection of the York and Bristol roads, about three miles east of the Crooked Billet (modern-day Hatboro), and was close to the southwest branch of Neshaminy Creek, whose banks in this location were fairly level and provided ready access to water for the troops. With news of Howe's

---

11 Lafayette, *Memoirs*, vol. 1, 19.

12 Smith, et al., eds., *Letters of Delegates*, vol. 7, 449; Reed, *Campaign to Valley Forge*, 52. Although the army and the politicians did not know it yet, another positive development for the Americans occurred on the northern front during their stay at Germantown. Barry St. Leger's British forces had been turned away from Fort Stanwix in New York. St. Leger's men comprised a cooperating column that would not be joining General Burgoyne near Albany.

13 Reed, *Campaign to Valley Forge*, 52.

location in hand, Washington opted to keep the army in this position until he obtained more concrete information. Earlier orders for Israel Putnam to send troops south resulted in the arrival of the North Carolina brigade under Francis Nash, which arrived about this time at Trenton.[14]

Howe's fleet reached the entrance to Chesapeake Bay on August 9, but it would be a few more days before his ships tacked into the bay proper. Under normal conditions, the voyage to the Chesapeake from New York should have taken only a few days. Instead, it took more than two weeks to reach its destination because of the stop in the Delaware and the terrible storms while at sea. The lengthy voyage weakened the entire British army. In addition to the damage suffered by the ships and the injured crew members, drinking water had to be rationed, horses died in large numbers, and the soldiers began to succumb to illness. Most had already been aboard ship for more than a month. According to Sir George Osborn, a British officer aboard one of Howe's ships, not all the men were suffering. "We shall probably land in three or four days and with the excessive heats of this month and the rains of September we must expect many agues and fevers," he wrote in a letter home. "At present the army is pretty healthy. I have three hundred on board this ship and not one sick man: I never have my own health better than at sea."[15]

Senior British leadership, however, had never planned for the army to be on ships for such an extended period of time. Fresh food and, more importantly, forage for the horses was nearly gone. "Since it was not forseen that we would be aboard ship so long, the horses were given very little space; this is the reason they are beginning to die." Engineer Montresor also commented on the state of the animals: "Master of the horse Sloop came on board to signifie the distress for want of forage. . . . Very sultry and close. . . .

14 Smith, et al., eds., *Letters of Delegates*, vol. 7, 459; Reed, *Campaign to Valley Forge*, 49, 52.

15 McGuire, *Philadelphia Campaign*, vol. 1,105. The Osborn letters are in a private family collection in England, and copies are inaccessible. These quotations of Osborn rely on McGuire's transcriptions. When horses died aboard ship, their carcasses were shoved overboard. "The fleet and army much distressed for the want of fresh water, having been for some time put to an allowance, but not so much so as the horse vessels, having been obliged to throw numbers of their horses overboard," wrote Montresor. Many carcasses washed up on the coast. Writing to his wife Abigail, John Adams noted, "[W]e are informed that many dead Horses have been driven on the Eastern shore of Maryland. Horses thrown overboard, from the fleet, no doubt." Montresor, "Montresor Journals," 440, Smith, et al., eds., *Letters of Delegates*, vol. 7, 567.

The Horse Vessels in general lying too for Food from the forage vessel, they being much distressed."[16]

When the soldiers' fresh food ran out, their diet was reduced to salt rations. The delay in leaving New York harbor was blamed for the distressing situation, "for that interval was taken up only in consuming our fresh Stock . . . [which] brought us to relish our Salt Pork." The officers, recalled Gen. James Grant, "were upon Salt Provisions for some Weeks before they came ashore, some of our Generals observed the same Regimen." Lieutenant William Hale, however, was experiencing at least some comfort. "Our fresh provisions were indeed exhausted for more than three weeks before our landing," he admitted, "[but] we drank claret all the way, every officer contributing so many days' pay made the expense very easy to the subalterns, and Col. Monckton supplied us with his own claret when ours was out."[17]

While some fared well at sea, most, like Jaeger Lt. von Feilitzsch, despised the enervating experience. "Anyone who has a desire to experience misery and misfortune should go aboard ship," he wrote. "Everyone can believe me that when I am again in Europe, should the opportunity arise for another such trip, I would certainly not go." The lieutenant set forth his reasons in vivid detail:

1) There is no bread except zwieback [hard biscuits] which is spoiled or full of worms.

2) Stinking water with all possible impurities mixed in, because on this trip, from the beginning until now, we have not one good drop.

3) The meat is miserable and frightfully salted so that it can hardly be eaten, and then one nearly dies of thirst.

4) The entire ship is full of lice, and when it storms no one can think of anything else. Anyone who has never gone to sea can not understand how miserable that can be. It is nearly impossible to take a step without risk of breaking your neck or a leg. Everything has to be securely fastened and still everything breaks and busts to pieces.[18]

---

16 Von Muenchhausen, *At General Howe's Side*, 23; Montresor, "Montresor Journals," 434-5.

17 Loftus Cliffe to brother Jack, October 24, 1777, Cliffe Papers, William Clements Library, Ann Arbor, Michigan; James Grant to Harvey, August 31, 1777, Grant Papers; Wilkin, *Some British Soldiers*, 227-9. Claret (a British name) was a reddish-purple wine grown in the Bordeaux region of France.

18 Burgoyne, *Diaries*, 12.

Meanwhile, Washington remained at a loss to explain the enemy's movements. Howe, he now opined, was headed for Charleston, South Carolina. "If his Intentions are such, as I have supposed them," wrote the American commander, "It appears to me, that an attempt to follow him, would not only be fruitless, but would be attended with ruinous consequences. . . . [W]e have no other alternative left, then to remain here idle and inactive, on the remote probability of his returning this way, or to proceed towards Hudson's River, with a view of opposing Genl Burgoyne [with the greater part of our force]."Until something changed, Howe would hold the initiative and Washington could do little more than await definitive news of the fleet's location.[19]

The Chesapeake Bay

To those on the ships, it was becoming apparent by August 12 that the fleet would soon enter the Chesapeake Bay. We "could smell the land, the fragrance of pines in particular. . . . The ships of war hoisted their Colours, supposed for seeing land," engineer Montresor jotted in his journal. When the conditions finally allowed, Admiral Howe guided his ships into the bay on August 14. Once past Cape Charles, Virginia, the British sailed north. The distant boom of signal guns washed over the ships, and a large cloud of smoke ashore was spotted: The Americans knew they were there.[20]

The armada spent the next ten days in a tedious and fitful move up the bay. Since the wind was often light, Howe usually sailed with the flood tide and anchored with the ebb tide. Captain Hamond was concerned about navigating the Chesapeake. Once the decision was made to ascend it, Hamond inquired whether any pilots familiar with the bay had been acquired to guide the fleet. "There were none that were much acquainted with the Navigation above Baltimore," he worried, "nor was there any particular plan found, that gave any directions more than what is laid down in the large chart of the Chesapeak."[21]

The surrounding majestic Maryland countryside impressed the British officers. "The Bay, the higher it is ascended, becomes more beautiful," wrote

19 Fitzpatrick, ed., *Writings of Washington*, vol. 9, 107-8.

20 Montresor, "Montresor Journals," 435-6; Reed, *Campaign to Valley Forge*, 67.

21 Ewald, *Diary*, 73; Hay, "The Denouement," 507.

one in his diary. Known to this day for its delicious crabs, the region offered up its welcome bounty to the fleet's passengers. "It's remarkable in this Bay the multitude of crabs that swim nearly to the surface of the water," penned an astonished but fully satisfied Montresor. "The Fleet caught thousands."[22]

Two days after entering the bay, yet another thunderstorm assailed the fleet. Lieutenant Heinrich von Feilitzsch described the storm as such "as has never been seen in Europe." A British sergeant left the most descriptive narrative of the storm's awesome power:

> A Thunder-Bolt killed 3 Horses in the Hold of a Transport, and split her Main-mast to Shivers; but by God's infinite mercy, there was not a man on board hurted. . . . A Woman's shift being burnt upon her body, lying in a Birth on a Transport, and she a Sleep, by a Flash of Lightning, without the least damage to her skin or Flesh, Also a Man's Coat and Shirt was burnt likewise on his Back, without his knowing of it till next morning: And the Arms [muskets] of three Companies of men were japanned [blackened] on Board the same ship by the same Flash.[23]

Once the storm blew out, the fleet anchored just off Old Point Comfort (where Fort Monroe sits today).

On August 17, the fleet anchored off the mouth of the Piankatunk River. After weathering yet another storm, the ships anchored two days later at the mouth of the Potomac River. HMS *Raisonable* stayed behind to patrol the mouth of the Potomac while the rest of the fleet moved north past the mouth of the river. The bay narrowed here, and both shorelines were now visible from the troop transports.[24]

The heat finally began to subside, but the British would long remember the intense temperatures. "Several of our People, who have been on the Coast of Guinea & in the West Indies, assured me, they never felt in either of those Countries such an intense suffocating heat, wch we have experienced for several Days and Nights together," journaled one soldier. "If possible, the Nights were more disagreeable than the Days." Von Muenchhausen was glad to

---

22 Tatum, Jr., ed., *Journal of Ambrose Serle*, 245; Montresor, "Montresor Journals," 440-1.

23 Burgoyne, trans. and ed., *Diaries*, 15; Sullivan, *From Redcoat to Rebel*, 125. More good news for the Americans arrived from the northern front when it was learned that on August 16, American militia defeated a Germanic force at Bennington, Vermont.

24 Reed, *Campaign to Valley Forge*, 68-9.

see the heat dissipate: "I am forced to complain about the intolerable heat we have been having to bear so far. If I could own the whole of America, I would refuse if I had to live in these hot regions."[25]

Two days later the ships slipped past the capital of Maryland at Annapolis, on the western shore of the bay at the mouth of the Severn River. Local militia demonstrated audacity by raising patriot flags over the earthworks there. "Two flags, which were to be seen just outside the city, showed that the commander-in-chief's warning of 18 July did not apply, but that the city's inhabitants, like most of the Americans, were rebels," explained one Hessian. "Through the telescope it could be seen that there were thirteen red and white stripes in these flags, which represented the thirteen provinces."[26]

Nobody in the provincial capital, however, was willing to fight a well-armed fleet. "A report that a British fleet was sailing up the Chesapeake Bay, has induced many people to quit Annapolis," the Reverend Francis Asbury, bishop of the Methodist Episcopal Church, noted in his journal: "Lord, give thy people faith and patience sufficient for their day of trial!" The reverend had little to fear, for Howe had no interest in Annapolis or her citizens. He did, however, care about navigating the bay. The farther up the Chesapeake his fleet sailed, the shallower and more treacherous the bay became. The fleet's larger ships had to be left behind.[27]

Continental Response

While Howe moved northward up the Chesapeake, Washington's main army remained deployed along the Neshaminy Creek, with headquarters in Warwick Township. Many elements of the Continental Army, however, were still quite a distance away. Francis Nash's North Carolina Brigade remained at Trenton, New Jersey, while John Sullivan's division and one-half of the New

---

25 Tatum, Jr., ed., *Journal of Ambrose Serle*, 244; Von Muenchhausen, *At General Howe's Side*, 24.

26 McGuire, *Philadelphia Campaign*, vol. 1, 111; Bruce Burgoyne, trans. and ed., *Enemy Views: The American Revolutionary War as Recorded by the Hessian Participants* (Bowie, MD, 1996), 168. These flags (not the stars and stripes made famous by Betsy Ross) consisted of thirteen stripes and were commonly flown above fortifications at this point in the Revolution. American troops did not carry the now-traditional stars and stripes in field combat until after the Federal period. See Appendix A for more on this subject.

27 Francis Asbury, *Journal of Rev. Francis Asbury, Bishop of the Methodist Episcopal Church*, vol. 1, *From August 7, 1771, to December 31, 1786* (New York, 1852), 254.

Jersey brigade were in northern New Jersey at Chatham. Israel Putnam was still holding the Hudson Highlands with Connecticut troops near Peekskill. Benjamin Lincoln's division, commanded by Anthony Wayne at this point, was at Graeme Park in Horsham on the outskirts of Philadelphia.[28]

Was Washington's army sufficient to repel Howe? Congress didn't think so, and the body passed a resolution recommending Maryland raise at least 2,000 militia and that Pennsylvania collect 4,000 of its militia to assist in repelling the threatened attack. Pennsylvania's troops were directed to report to Lancaster, Downingtown, and Chester, where they would be subject to Washington's orders. Other states also pitched in. Delaware was expected to have about 1,000 militia rendezvous at Christiana Bridge, and Virginia was asked to have some of her militia report to Frederick, Maryland.[29]

Many within the army tired of all the marching sought out definitive information about Howe's fleet, including Col. Walter Stewart, commander of the Pennsylvania State Regiment. "We expect however to change our situation very shortly, as it appears against the decrees of Fate our staying more than three or Four days at one place," Stewart complained to Gen. Horatio Gates. "For my part, I must say, I would not wish to move until we know with a certainty where the Enemy Intend operating, as we have Certainly for some time past been Marching and Counter Marching to very little purpose."[30]

The equally frustrated Nathanael Greene did his best to understand the Continental Army's strategic situation, which he considered "not a little awkward, buryed in the country out of hearing of the Enimy." The stress constantly weighed on them, especially Washington, whom the general decribed as "exceeding impatient; but it said, if Philadelphia is lost all is ruined." The ironic twists and turns of the "curious campaign" were not lost on Greene: "[I]n the Spring we had the Enimy about our ears every hour. The Northern Army could neither see nor hear of an Enemy. Now they have got the enimy about their heads and we have lost ours, compeld to wander about the country like the Arabs in search of em."[31]

---

28 McGuire, *Philadelphia Campaign*, vol. 1, 117-8.

29 Hazard, *Pennsylvania Archives*, vol. 5, 539-40.

30 Walter Stewart to Gates, "Camp at Cross Roads, Augt. 13th, 1777," Horatio Gates Papers, the David Library of the American Revolution, Washington Crossing, PA, film 23, reel 5, 62-3.

31 Showman, McCarthy, and Cobb, eds., *Papers of Greene*, vol. 2, 142-3.

Unfortunately, the men who would soon face Howe's Regulars would be without the services of Daniel Morgan's riflemen. The real threat of Indians traveling with Burgoyne's army necessitated the dispatch of Morgan's men to assist on the northern front. Washington would soon need to create a light infantry force to replace them.

Richard Henry Lee of Virginia, whose motion in the Second Continental Congress had called for independence from England, visited the army about this time and was impressed with what he found: "I think the Army is a gallant one, well disciplined, clothed, armed (for they all have bayonets now) and sound in every respect—The Soldiers in good health and spirits, and every thing looks *tout en Militaire.*" With the uncertainty and rumor mills boiling over about Howe and the fleet, some congressmen (perhaps Lee among them) urged Washington to push the army north to strike Burgoyne. Benjamin Harrison, another Virginian, wrote to Washington: "Can not a blow be given Burgoyne in his [Howe's] absence? If something can not be done in that quarter soon, N. York will certainly be lost."Until there was confirmed information that the fleet was actually in the Chesapeake, however, Washington was hamstrung. Speculation continued that Howe was heading south toward South Carolina.[32]

On August 21, however, Washington held a council of war (as he often did during his tenure) with his general officers. The lack of intelligence on Howe's whereabouts, coupled with a feeling of helplessness as the army marked time, convinced the council to unanimously agree to move the army north to either stop Burgoyne or attack New York City. The troops were to be in motion by 5:00 a.m. the next morning. Late that same day, however, news arrived from Congress confirming the presence of the British fleet in the Chesapeake. Unfortunately for Washington, the information was a week old. Orders changed quickly, and a flurry of messages went out to the various detachments of the army to pull together near the capital.[33]

On August 22, Howe's fleet sailed past the mouth of the Patapsco River, where it was able to secure some pilots for the ships.[34] Had the British chosen, they could have ascended that body of water to assault Baltimore. The city of 600 houses and several thousand citizens was rapidly growing into its destiny as

32 Smith, et. al., eds., *Letters of Delegates*, vol. 7, 513-4, 519.

33 McGuire, *Philadelphia Campaign*, vol. 1, 121-2.

34 Reed, *Campaign to Valley Forge*, 69.

a shipping port, but a small fort on Whetstone Point and some local militia were its only defenses; British men-of-war could have easily eliminated the threat. (Thirty-seven years later, the site would be bombarded by another British fleet during the War of 1812.) Despite the bravado displayed at Annapolis and proud boasting to the Maryland governor by the officers at Baltimore, the Maryland militia was in no condition to face British regulars backed by the Royal Navy. After passing the Patapsco River, the fleet anchored near Swan Point between the Elk and Sassafras Rivers.[35]

The Staten Island Operation

Back in July, Lord Stirling had proposed assaulting Staten Island on his way to join the main army. Washington initially gave him approval if his intelligence proved the British were maintaining a weak garrison there. Stirling had been led to believe there were only 1,000 provincial troops on the island, which, if true, would have warranted the assault. Luckily, before the Americans made the attack, they learned that the island contained British and Hessian regulars, so the operation was cancelled. Stirling, therefore, had continued his march to rejoin the main Continental Army.[36]

Nearly a month later, John Sullivan returned to command his division and again considered the possibility of an assault on Staten Island. Washington, trusting Sullivan's intelligence, approved the operation. On August 21, Sullivan's division and several New Jersey regiments departed Hanover, marched through Chatham and Springfield, and arrived on a point of land below Elizabeth that juts out toward Staten Island. In the middle of the night, the men were ferried over to Staten Island, achieving complete surprise. The next morning, Sullivan's division initially met only light resistance from some loyalist regiments. Throughout the morning hours, American regiments pushed across the island, capturing a great quantity of supplies. Henry Clinton feared a major attack on New York City in the absence of both Howe and most of the army. Sullivan again "effected an almost total surprise of two provincial battalions belonging to Skinner's Brigade, and after setting fire to the magazines at Decker's Ferry were on their march to Richmond; while another corps, that

35 McGuire, *Philadelphia Campaign*, vol. 1, 112-3; Reed, *Campaign to Valley Forge*, 69.

36 Reed, Campaign to Valley Forge, 36.

had landed on the west part of the island for the purpose of cutting off three other provincial battalions, had taken Lt. Col. Lawrence, with the great part of his battalion, prisoners." These elements of Sullivan's command that operated on the western part of the island landed near the Old Blazing Star Ferry.[37]

Clinton hurriedly sent the 52nd Regiment of Foot and some German Waldecker troops to Staten Island to stop the Americans. By early afternoon, they had pushed Sullivan's troops back to the southern end of island, so the Americans began ferrying back to New Jersey. About 200 men of Sulivan's rear guard were captured.[38]

Sullivan summed up the operation thusly: "In this Expedition we Landed on an Island possessed by the Enemy, put to Rout Six Regiments Killed wounded & made prisoners at Least four or five hundred of the Enemy vanquished every party that Collected against us Destroyed them Large Quantities of Stores took one vessel & Destroyed Six or Seven more took a Considerable number of Arms Blankets &c with many Cattle Horse &c marched victorious Through the Island."[39]

Despite its initial success, most viewed the operation as a failure since 200 men had been captured. Sullivan, thought many, had been involved in another American failure, for he was also linked to the disaster at the battle of Long Island the previous year. Timing also worked against him: the "failed" Staten Island operation came soon after other Continental forces lost Fort Ticonderoga. Personally disliked by several members of Congress, Sullivan's abilities again came into question and Congress demanded an inquiry into his conduct. On the day of the Staten Island operation, Washington received news of the Bennington victory. The inquiry into Sullivan's conduct would have to wait.[40]

The British Debark, the Americans Gird Up

The British fleet moved above Swan Point. Ships of this size had never been that far north in the Chesapeake Bay, and numerous British officers were

---

37 McGuire, *Philadelphia Campaign*, vol. 1, 141; Clinton, *The American Rebellion*, 68.

38 McGuire, *Philadelphia Campaign*, vol. 1, 141.

39 Otis G. Hammond, ed., *Letters and Papers of Major-General John Sullivan: Continental Army* (Concord, 1930), vol. 1, 461.

40 McGuire, *Philadelphia Campaign*, vol. 1, 142.

impressed with the skill of Admiral Howe. "Through the great abilities of our Naval officers it was happily effected as the bottom was muddy and the ships on it were cutting channels through it for each other." General Grant paid a high compliment to the admiral as well: "As the Navigation is extremely difficult, the Chanel in many places narrow and intricate—Lord Howe has great Merit in conducting the Fleet which he certainly did with Ability." Beginning on August 23, the Howe brothers began exploring the upper reaches of the Chesapeake Bay around the Susquehanna River, searching for landing places. Captain John Montresor of the Royal Engineers accompanied them. *The Annual Register* later reported that Admiral Howe had "performed the different parts of a commander, inferior officer, and pilot, with his · usual ability and perseverance" despite "a most intricate and dangerous navigation for such a multitude of vessels."[41]

The fleet anchored at the mouth of the Susquehanna. The British observed several armed Americans at Turkey Point. Maryland militiamen attempted to drive the cattle away from the coastal areas of the upper Chesapeake to keep them from falling into British hands, but were not entirely successful.[42]

On the same day, Washington's army moved back into the Germantown area, where Washington made his headquarters at the Stenton House. Stenton was the country seat of the Logan family. The estate was one of the largest and most valuable estates in the Philadelphia area, with 500 acres studded with many rare plants, trees, and other experimental cultivation. The large brick home was built in 1730 but was unoccupied by its owners in 1777. The original owner had passed away the previous year and the heir was studying medicine in Scotland.[43]

The Continental Army had left its camps along the Neshaminy Creek, marched down the York Road past Crooked Billet, and halted at Rising Sun Tavern (modern-day Nicetown). Washington's headquarters issued orders for guards to watch the roads leading from Philadelphia into the camps "to prevent an inundation of bad women from Philadelphia"—as if Washington didn't already have enough to worry about that night without "bad women."[44]

---

41 Montresor, "Montresor Journals," 442; Grant to Harvey, August 31, 1777, James Grant Papers; *The Annual Register: or, a View of the History, Politics, and Literature, for the year 1777*, 4th ed. (London, 1794), 126.

42 Ewald, *Diary*, 73-4; McGuire, *Philadelphia Campaign*, vol. 1, 115.

43 McGuire, *Philadelphia Campaign*, vol. 1, 100.

44 Reed, *Campaign to Valley Forge*, 78; Fitzpatrick, ed., *Writings of Washington*, vol. 9, 129-30.

After weeks of waiting for Howe's next move, the British commander was coming from the southwest—and no land defenses had been placed in that direction to protect Philadelphia. There were, however, several creeks and rivers that might be used to mount a defense: the Red and White Clay Creeks, the Brandywine, and the Schuylkill. Just as worrisome, Howe could march into the interior of Pennsylvania to threaten Lancaster or Reading. Washington also had to worry about storehouses at various locations west of Philadelphia.

After the operation on Staten Island, Sullivan's division withdrew to Springfield. Orders from Washington reached the division there, directing it to rendezvous with the main army in Pennsylvania. The next day, Washington paraded his army through Philadelphia. The troops marched five miles down the York Road, crossed the Cohoquonoque Creek at Pool's Bridge, then entered the city by way of Front Street, where most of the city's major shipping merchants had their businesses and warehouses. They continued south down Front Street and crossed over High Street (Market Street today), which was the main business thoroughfare running east-west. They made a right up Chestnut Street and marched the five blocks to the State House (modern-day Independence Hall) where Congress reviewed them.[45]

Washington wanted to make an impression on the people of Philadelphia. At the time, the Continental Army included around 11,000 men in just four divisions: Greene's, Stephen's, Wayne's, and Stirling's (in that marching order). Washington wanted proper spacing between all units, so he interspersed the field artillery between the divisions. The light dragoons were also properly spaced among the units, with Col. Theodorick Bland's regiment leading the way, right behind the commander in chief. The field musicians of the army were ordered to mass in the center of each brigade and play a quick step, "but with such moderation, that the men may step to it with ease; and without dancing along, or totally disregarding the music, as too often has been the case." Washington wrote to John Hancock, "I am induced to do this from the opinion of Several of my Officers and many Friends in Philadelphia, that it may have some influence on the minds of the disaffected there and those who are Dupes to their artifices and opinions."[46]

---

45 Reed, *Campaign to Valley Forge*, 62; McGuire, *Philadelphia Campaign*, vol. 1, 124.

46 Reed, *Campaign to Valley Forge*, 63-4; Pancake, *1777*, 166; Chase and Lengel, eds., *Papers of Washington*, vol. 11, 51-52.

To make the proper impression, Washington issued strict orders on some fronts. One concerned camp followers: "Not a woman belonging to the army is to be seen with the troops on their march thro' the city." The women attached to the army included the wives of soldiers, laundresses, and servants not all of good reputation, but who performed "a multitude of feminine tasks, good and bad, to ease the lives of the soldiers."[47] Men, like teamsters and drivers, and children, were also among them. Camp followers with the Continental Army added approximately 50 percent more people traveling with the armed personnel of the army.

These additional people traveled with the baggage wagons, which were directed to bypass the city and cross the Schuylkill River at the Middle Ferry bridge (site of the present Market Street bridge). The main army also crossed at this point. "The bridge, an unstable affair, was fashioned of pontoons roughly laid over with planking." After passing through Philadelphia, the army moved down the present Woodland Avenue and camped at Darby, about 10 miles south of the city.[48]

John Adams agreed with Washington's decision. "I like this Movement of the General, through the City, because, such a show of Artillery, Waggons, Light Horse and Infantry, which takes up a Line of 9 or 10 Miles upon their March and will not be less than 5 or 6 Hours passing through the Town, will make a good Impression upon the Minds of the timorous Whiggs for their Confirmation, upon the cunning Quakers for their Restraint and upon the rascally Tories for their Confusion." With the army stretched out for 10 miles, it took two hours to shuffle past the State House.[49]

An earlier chronicler of the American Revolution, Sydney George Fisher, left the following description of the army: "To give some uniformity to the motley hunting-shirts, bare feet, and rags, every man wore a green sprig in his hat. The best-clothed men were the Virginians, and the smartest-looking troops were Smallwood's Marylanders."[50]

John Adams's confidence was on the rise. "We have now an Army well appointed between Us and Mr. Howe, and this Army will be immediately joined

47 Chase and Lengel, eds., *Papers of Washington*, vol. 11, 50; Reed, *Campaign to Valley Forge*, 79-80.

48 Reed, *Campaign to Valley Forge*, 79-80.

49 Smith, et al., eds., *Letters of Delegates*, vol. 7, 533.

50 Sydney George Fisher, *The Struggle for American Independence* (Philadelphia, 1908), vol. 2, 20.

by ten Thousand Militia. So that I feel as secure here, as if I were at Braintree." The congressman was writing to his wife at their home in Braintree, Massachusetts, but was exaggerating the number of militiamen who were soon to join Washington's force. However, it was painfully clear to the sometimes fussy Adams that the army still lacked an ideal sense of professionalism. "The Army, upon an accurate Inspection of it, I find to be extremely well armed, pretty well cloathed, and tolerably disciplined. . . . Much remains yet to be done. Our soldiers have not yet, quite the Air of Soldiers. They don't step exactly in Time. They don't hold up their Heads, quite erect, nor turn out their Toes, so exactly as they ought. They dont all of them cock their Hats—and such as do, dont all wear them the same Way."[51]

As the Continental Army nonetheless basked in the glory of parading through its capital city, another violent thunderstorm struck the British fleet in the upper reaches of the Chesapeake Bay. General Grant recorded its effects on his ship. "The Isis was struck with Lightening, the night before we left her—the Main Mast damaged, & on Fire for a time. Lord Cornwallis and I were reading in the Cabin when it happened, which was filled in a Moment, with a Sulphureous Smell."[52]

With Howe's army soon to depart their ships, the Maryland and Delaware governments scrambled to meet the threat. The president of Delaware, John McKinley, issued orders to his militia commander, Caesar Rodney, to rally to the aid of Maryland. "You are therefore to array the Militia under your command as speedily as possible & have them well provided with Arms Accoutrements & Ammunition & as much Provisions as they can. . . . You are to march immediately with the Militia arrayed & provided as above & to such places as may be most necessary to annoy the Enemy & prevent them from effecting their purpose of plundering the Inhabitants & possessing themselves of any part of" Turkey Point.[53]

During the morning of August 25, Washington departed Darby and arrived along Naaman's Creek, just across the Delaware border, with Greene's and Stephen's divisions. According to Timothy Pickering's journal, "the army marched through Chester to Naaman's Creek, the General and family

---

51 Smith, et al., eds., *Letters of Delegates*, vol. 7, 538-9.

52 Grant to Harvey, August 31, 1777, James Grant Papers.

53 Rodney, *Letters*, 212-3.

advancing to Wilmington (a pretty town and pleasantly situated)." Pickering noted that Washington proceeded to Wilmington accompanied by some light cavalry. Wilmington was situated between Christiana Creek and the Brandywine River. The American headquarters was established on a hill west of town where the army would encamp as it arrived. The 500 Pennsylvania militiamen at Marcus Hook were ordered across the border and proceeded to Wilmington as well. Nash's North Carolinians pushed through Philadelphia and reached Chester during the day, headed toward the main army. Wayne's and Stirling's divisions remained at Darby for a day of rest.[54]

Washington was concerned about the public property at Head of Elk. "There are a quantity of public and private Stores at the Head of Elk, which I am afraid will fall into the Enemy's hands if they advance quickly, among others there is a considerable parcel of Salt. Every attempt will be made to save that." Hence, Washington sent a scouting party south to Newport.[55]

Around the same time that Washington's army was departing Darby, elements of the British fleet sailed up the Elk River and began off-loading the British army at Elk Ferry on Turkey Point in Maryland, just below Head of Elk and near Cecil Courthouse. Turkey Point was a thinly inhabited peninsula on the west side of the mouth of the Elk River. Johann Ewald described the region: "The whole peninsula, or headland, was a real wilderness. Just as we found the uncultivated vine, the sassafras tree, and wild melon in this region, so also was it full of different kinds of vermin. The woods, especially, were filled with snakes and toads. Each tree was full of big chaffers, which made such a noise during the night that two men could not speak to each other and understand what was said." Another jaeger officer was not impressed with the countryside. "Compared with other provinces where we have been, this region is not well-developed. A bare woods, here and there a small place with a house and a field, but where not a soul is to be seen. How desolate it is I will let another describe."[56]

In this location, Howe's army was about 60 miles from Philadelphia. This was just 20 miles closer than it had been in the spring skirmishes around New York City, and the Schuylkill and Brandywine Rivers were now in its way. More

---

54 Pickering, *Life of Pickering*, vol. 1, 152; Reed, *Campaign to Valley Forge*, 81-3.

55 Chase and Lengel, eds., *Papers of Washington*, vol. 11, 69; Reed, *Campaign to Valley Forge*, 83.

56 McGuire, *Philadelphia Campaign*, vol. 1, 133; Ewald, *Diary*, 75; Burgoyne, trans. and ed., *Diaries*, 16.

important to critics of the campaign, the army had spent nearly another month aboard ships just to arrive a bare 20 miles west of where Hamond had recommended they land on the eastern shore of Delaware at Reedy Island.[57]

The operation began around 6 a.m., with HMS *Vigilant* and HMS *Roebuck* leading the way followed by flat-bottomed troop transports. The heaviest warships—HMS *Augusta*, HMS *Isis*, HMS *Nonsuch*, and HMS *Somerset*—had been left behind near the Sassafras River.[58]

Lord Cornwallis commanded the vanguard, which included the Hessian jaegers, the British light infantry, and the British grenadiers. "The men were immediately formed by companies, without regard to seniority, in order to be prepared to resist the certainly nearby enemy, and to cover the landing of the entire army, but no enemy appeared." The vanguard pushed inland for three miles and spread out to cover the landing of the rest of the army. What little American militia was present was easily scattered by the professional European soldiers. Accompanying the lead elements of the British forces were the Howe brothers themselves. "At 10 the Adml and General went on Shore with the Army."[59]

Thus, Howe had been extremely lucky: his men were able to row ashore and press inland virtually unmolested. Had the Continental Army been present in significant force to oppose this vulnerable operation, the Crown's forces could well have suffered heavy losses or outright disaster. However, because the reports of the British fleet reached Washington long after the ships were in the Chesapeake, the American commander was only then marching into Delaware with his army.[60]

It took the British five trips in flatboats to unload the entire army. After the first load carrying Cornwallis with the British light infantry, British grenadiers, and jaegers, the balance unloaded in this order: *Second trip*: the Hessian grenadiers, the Queen's Rangers, the Brigade of Guards, and the 4th and 23rd Regiments of Foot; *Third trip*: the 5th, 10th, 15th, 27th, 28th, 40th, 42nd, 49th,

---

57 Pancake, *1777*, 164.

58 McGuire, *Philadelphia Campaign*, vol. 1, 133; Reed, *Campaign to Valley Forge*, 70.

59 Marie E. Burgoyne and Bruce E. Burgoyne, eds., *Journal of the Hesse-Cassel Jaeger Corps and Hans Konze's List of Jaeger Officers* (Westminster, MD, 2008), 6; Reed, *Campaign to Valley Forge*, 71; William James Morgan, ed., *Naval Documents of the American Revolution* (Washington D.C., 1986), vol. 9, 811.

60 Reed, *Campaign to Valley Forge*, 71.

and 55th Regiments of Foot; *Fourth trip*: the 17th, 33rd, 37th, 44th, 46th, 64th, and 71st Regiments of Foot; *Fifth trip*: the Hessian Brigade. The light dragoons and long-suffering wagon horses did not unload until the next day.[61]

As the British army landed, it began to rain, a rain that would last for 36 hours. The army's ammunition supply quickly became damaged: the cartridge boxes were drenched, and the Brigade of Guards alone lost 1,600 rounds of ammunition. The men were issued rum, biscuits, and cooked salt pork for five days.[62]

As Howe's men were landing at Turkey Point, panic set in among the people of Lancaster. Writing to his children from there, Christopher Marshall described the chaos caused in the backcountry settlement. "The Waggons are all engaged here in order to Carry our Stores and Some to take the Baggage of the Prisoners from this place to Reading &c as we were alarmed by Express the 23rd of Hows fleet having come up Chesapeak bay and intend to land about 35 miles from here. . . . The English, Scotch & Irish prisoners being 2 or 300 were sent off yesterday afternoon under a Strong guard for Reading. The Hessing [Hessian] Prisoners are Mustering for the same purpose and its said will be sent off this day, so that our place is in a great fermentation."[63]

A mixture of joy and confidence emanated from the pens of those writing from within the British Army. Despite the considerable distance to Philadelphia, James Parker noted the capital defenses that had been constructed along the Delaware—much damage could have been done to the fleet by the forts, fire rafts, and floating batteries. Ewald recalled landing "amid boisterous shouts of joy and in the best order." General Grant was happy to be on dry land after 49 days aboard ship. "You may believe every Body on Board was most heartily tired of their Situation, we have hardly recovered the Use of our Legs & the Horses are not very firm upon theirs." Captain Richard Fitzpatrick of the Brigade of Guards admired their new surroundings. "The inhabitants are almost all fled from their houses, and have driven their cattle with them; so we do not live luxuriously, though in a country that has every appearance of plenty, and is more beautiful than can be conceived, wherever the woods are at all

---

61 Ewald, *Diary*, 74.

62 McGuire, *Philadelphia Campaign*, vol. 1, 136.

63 Christopher Marshall to his children, August 25, 1777, Christopher Marshall Papers, vol. 14, "Christopher Marshall Letterbook, 1773-1778," the Historical Society of Pennsylvania, Philadelphia, PA.

cleared." As stated, amidst the beauty of the land, few inhabitants could be found. Lieutenant William Hale believed the "men [had been] called to strengthen Washington, the women fled to avoid barbarities, which they imagined must be the natural attendants of a British Army." A Hessian officer thought "we have not seen any females because they were told by the rebels that the Hessians would have misused them in an unpleasant manner, so they have all fled."[64]

The next phase of the campaign would need to answer whether the long voyage with all its costs had been worth it. In summary: Howe's army had spent over a month at sea, only to arrive in northeast Maryland just 20 miles closer to the American capital. Washington had used that time to recruit more soldiers and gel his army into a more effective fighting force. Meanwhile, the British had suffered through poor food and water during the last stretch of the trip. The greatest damage, that would have the greatest effect on the combat efficiency of the force, had been inflicted upon the army's horses.

The American Congress, finally aware of British intentions, called upon the patriots of the region to respond to the imminent threat.

---

64 Journal entry for August 29, Parker Family Papers; Ewald, *Diary*, 75; Grant to Harvey, August 31, 1777, James Grant Papers; Fitzpatrick to the Countess of Ossory, "Head of Elk, September 1, 1777," *Pennsylvania Magazine of History and Biography* (Philadelphia, 1877), vol. 1, 289; Wilkin, *Some British Soldiers*, 227; Burgoyne and Burgoyne, eds., *Enemy Views*, 171.

Chapter 6

To Pennsylvania & First Contact:
August 25 - September 2, 1777

"If there should be any Mills in the Neighborhood of the Enemy, and which may be
liable to fall into their hands, the Runners [the millstones]
should be removed and secured."[1]

— George Washington, August 31, 1777

Immediate Considerations

Once the all-day process of unloading the army from the troop
transports was complete, the camp grounds were secured
and prepared and Howe's soldiers set about building shelters. Since the army's
baggage and camp equipment were still on board ships and had not yet been
issued to the men, the troops resorted to building huts called wigwams. These
structures, explained one writer, "were lean-to shelters that were easily and
quickly constructed out of tree branches, fence rails, saplings, cornstalks, straw,
sod, and other such materials. They served well in lieu of tents to shelter the
men from the blazing sun and light rain, but did little in the case of heavy
downpours."[2] Just as the men finished constructing their shelters, yet another
"heavy storm of Rain, Lightning and Thunder" hit them. Howe's army spent

---

1   Chase and Lengel, eds., *Papers of Washington*, vol. 11, 100.

2   McGuire, *Philadelphia Campaign*, vol. 1, 135.

the next three nights in these conditions, "drenched to the skin by those torrents of rain common in the Southern climate."[3]

Howe was fortunate Washington's fresh army was not well positioned to greet him. His exhausted men had run out of fresh provisions well before they landed, and many of the horses needed to haul wagons, artillery, and serve as cavalry mounts had perished at sea. In addition, a significant percentage of the army's ammunition supply had been damaged when rain and sea water soaked the black powder during the fitful voyage. Howe's professionals were not ready to fight a battle.

The shortage of horses was the army's most severe problem. "The Horses look miserably emaciated by this long Voyage," explained Ambrose Serle, Admiral Howe's secretary. "Many of them will be but of little Use for some Time." During the army's first morning on land, Montresor observed and later commented upon a number of critical issues affecting the army: the "roads [were] heavy [muddy], and the horses mere Carrion, the soldiery not sufficiently refreshed, and great part of their ammunition damaged." While a number of horses died aboard the ships, quite a few more died immediately after the landing. The first night ashore, the unfortunate animals were .turned loose in a cornfield, where they "ate until they dropt dead in the field." According to Major Baurmeister, "During our passage twenty-seven men and one hundred and seventy horses died, and about one hundred fifty were disembarked totally unfit for duty—a natural consequence of spending more than five weeks on a voyage which in good weather can be made in six or eight days." A couple of weeks later, after the army had an opportunity to replace many of its missing mounts, Capt. von Muenchhausen wrote, "the 120 horses that the Knyphausen Corps had gathered on its march . . . cannot compensate for the 400 horses that perished on our unfortunately long voyage, or after landing here. I was more lucky than most officers since I did not lose a single horse at sea, but two of mine have died since we landed." The horses that survived the trip were simply too weak to be used for quite some time. "Neither baggage, supplies, cannon, nor ammunition could be transported without horses," observed historian Samuel Smith. "Even officers were reluctant to move without mounts."[4]

---

3   Montresor, "Montresor Journals," 442; Wilkin, *Some British Soldiers*, 227.

4   Serle, *Journal*, 246; Montresor, "Journals," 442; Edgar, *Philadelphia Campaign*, 12; Von Baurmeister, "Letters of Baurmeister," 398; Von Muenchhausen, *At Howe's Side*, 28; Smith, *Brandywine*, 5.

While the fodder for the horses had dwindled aboard ship, fresh food for the troops had also run out well before the army landed. Howe's opportunities for obtaining provisions for his army after landing were limited. The army was often encouraged to provide for the troops from the countryside, but Howe's commissary general, Daniel Wier, felt that depending upon North American supplies rather than shipments from England was proving an inadequate alternative. Wier, who had served as a commissary official in Germany during the Seven Years' War and in both the East and West Indies, was an experienced supply officer. His service taught him that armies could live reasonably well off the land in Europe, but America was an altogether different proposition. A large portion of the provisions he brought from New York for Howe's army was already spoiled. Of 2,000 bags of bread landed with the army, for example, "300 were condemned as unfit for Men to eat and of the 254 Bags carried on the March 50 or 60 were left on the way on the same Account." Much of the food had been damaged or destroyed by rats and other vermin, while other provisions had been damaged through careless storage aboard the victuallers.[5]

With the British army ashore, it was now imperative for Howe to make his way to a connection with the Delaware River. The British spent much of the war desperately short of land transportation, which forced them to remain as close as possible to navigable rivers. One assessment concluded that "[t]he insecurity of overland communications restricted an army's maximum operational range to about fifteen to twenty miles from navigable water." The need to travel by water had affected Howe's decisions in northern New Jersey, and it would affect his decisions now that he had landed in northeastern Maryland. He would never venture far from the fleet.[6]

Another factor affecting Howe's decisions was the need to preserve his army's fighting capacity. It was immensely difficult to replace troops lost in battle. The mechanism for creating replacements in England was archaic, and the 3,000-mile voyage across the Atlantic not only consumed time but lives as well. Howe had also witnessed the bloodshed wrought by frontal assaults against Breed's Hill. All of these factors played a large role in his repeated use of

5 Daniel Wier to John Robinson, October 25, 1777, "Copies of Letters from Danl. Wier, Esq., Commissary to the Army in America, to J. Robinson, Esq., Secretary to the Lords Commissioners of the Treasury; and from John Robinson, Esq., in Answer thereto in the Year 1777," Dreer Collection, Historical Society of Pennsylvania, Philadelphia, PA, case 36.

6 Spring, *With Zeal*, 35.

flanking movements thereafter. The difficulty in replacing well-trained troops in the eighteenth century, wrote one historian, "manifested itself in a concern not to lose troops unnecessarily to sickness and desertion by exposing them to hardships like short rations and inclement weather. In turn this curbed a field army's mobility by shackling it to magazines, bread ovens, and baggage trains." Howe would therefore spend the next several weeks maneuvering to avoid a major battle with Washington and create and maintain a connection with the Delaware River, from which he could be resupplied by the fleet.[7]

Of course, Howe could have been well ahead of schedule had he simply landed a month earlier in northern Delaware. He had believed in (or at least advocated for) the importance of capturing American stores in York and Lancaster, Pennsylvania, over the occupation of Philadelphia. However, his need to create a link with the Delaware River dictated that he move away from those back country settlements and closer to the colonial capital. Howe was barely back on land when he made the decision to disregard his stated reason for ascending the Chesapeake—York and Lancaster were no longer his goal.

After being cooped up on ships during the hottest weeks of the year desperately short of fresh food and water, Howe's men were more than ready to stretch their land legs and fill their bellies. The rampant pillaging they had so willingly inflicted upon northern New Jersey was about to be repeated in Maryland—despite Howe's warnings that his army must behave. The following general orders were issued the first morning on dry land: "Commanding Officers are to have the Rolls of their respective Corps immediately called, to examine the Men's Knapsacks and Haversacks, and Report to Head Quarters every Man in possession of Plunder of any kind." The directive did little good. "In spite of the strictest orders," recalled Major Baurmeister, "marauding could not at first be entirely prevented. Several men in the most advanced English troops were caught by General Howe. One of these marauders was hanged and six others were flogged within an inch of their lives." John Andre, a British officer who would finish his short life at the end of a rope in 1780 for helping Benedict Arnold betray his country, agreed, adding, "no method was as yet fixed upon for supplying the Troops with fresh provisions in a regular manner. The soldiers slaughtered a great deal of cattle clandestinely." The slaughter and waste of so much livestock, most of which simply rotted away, served to deny fresh meat to many of their comrades. "The houses in the immediate proximity

7 Ibid., 9.

of camp were plundered for more than simple necessities," explained one of Howe's men. "The criminal few were depriving a major part of the army sustenance for which it would have gladly paid."[8]

While the British Army recovered its landlegs and Howe issued orders to prevent plundering, General Washington set about trying to determine his opponent's intentions. Fully informed of Howe's whereabouts, he had by this time gathered an army of nearly equal size to oppose Howe's advance into northern Delaware. On August 26, all four divisions in the area (Greene, Stephen, Wayne, and Stirling) arrived at Wilmington. Washington was satisfied with his Continental Regulars, but the same could not be said for his militia, which was already sparring with Howe's advance elements. These men often came and went on their own, and how many would be in the ranks on a given day was unpredictable. There were other issues, like the rain that damaged the American Army's ammunition, much as it had ruined some of Howe's. Later that day, Sullivan's division reached Princeton, New Jersey, where the men quartered in the college buildings.[9]

On the same day his divisions gathered about Wilmington, Washington reconnoitered toward Head of Elk (modern-day Elkton) with Nathanael Greene, George Weedon, and Lafayette, accompanied by all his horse troops except Col. Elisha Sheldon's regiment. The party rode down the King's Highway to Newport and then on to Iron Hill near the Delaware-Maryland border, which the officers climbed to gain a view of the British Army. Iron Hill, which took its name from its blood-red soil, rose 200 feet above the sandy coastal plain of northern Delaware, but offered the Americans little in the way of visual advantage. The hill, explained Ewald, was "overgrown with woods, rising up like an amphitheater." The disappointed party descended, crossed the border into Maryland, and climbed Grey's Hill in another effort to observe the enemy. However, Washington and his lieutenants saw little else besides a few tents.[10]

Caught in a heavy rain near Head of Elk, the party ducked inside a farmhouse in the village. The decision worried Lafayette. "General Washington imprudently exposed himself to danger," worried the Frenchman. "After a long

---

8   Kemble, *Journals*, 477-8; Von Baurmeister, "Letters of Baurmeister," 399; Andre, *Journal*, 37.

9   Reed, *Campaign to Valley Forge*, 72.

10 Ibid., 84; Pickering, *Life of Pickering*, vol. 1, 152; McGuire, *Philadelphia Campaign*, vol. 1, 152; Ewald, *Diary*, 78.

reconnaissance, he was overtaken by a storm, on a very dark night. He took shelter in a farmhouse, very close to the enemy, and, because of his unwillingness to change his mind, he remained there with General Greene and M. de Lafayette. But when he departed at dawn, he admitted that a single traitor could have betrayed him." The home they chose was that of Robert Alexander, a Maryland loyalist. Ironically, when the British moved into town the next day, Howe established his headquarters in the same house.[11]

The next morning, under clearing skies, Washington returned to Wilmington and began setting up defensive positions and digging entrenchments. He sent part of the army four miles west behind White Clay Creek, and advance posts even farther west to Iron Hill. Francis Nash's nearly 1,000 North Carolinians arrived in Wilmington the same day. Meanwhile, Gen. William Smallwood, commander of the 1st Maryland Brigade, and Col. Mordecai Gist were sent into Maryland to organize the state's militia. The Maryland militiamen were to collect at the head of the Chesapeake, "to fall in upon the rear of the Enemy shou'd they move towards Philadelphia." Washington was also quick to point out that every able-bodied man was needed. "It is to be wished that every Man could bring a good Musket and Bayonet into the field, but in times like the present we must make the best shift we can, and I wou'd therefore advise you to exhort every man to bring the best he has. A good fowling piece will do execution in the hands of a marks man."[12]

Aware that his own army was still considerably spread out, Washington needed to delay and closely monitor Howe's advance. He dispatched elements of the Delaware militia under Cols. Evans, Daniel Hunter, and Daniel Undree to scout for the British advance to Christiana Bridge beyond the American positions behind White Clay Creek. The bridge was on the main road from Head of Elk to Wilmington. The move, hoped Washington, would also deny the British the ability to resupply their army from the immediate area. "The Enemy are in want of many necessaries," he explained, with which disaffected persons "would undoubtedly supply them if a watch is not kept over them."

11 Stanley J. Idzerda, et al., eds., *Lafayette in the Age of the American Revolution: Selected Letters and Papers, 1776-1790* (Ithaca, NY, 1977), vol. 1, 92; Reed, *Campaign to Valley Forge*, 84; McGuire, *Philadelphia Campaign*, vol. 1, 359.

12 Chase and Lengel, eds., *Papers of Washington*, vol. 11, 87.

Other militia elements gathered at Georgetown, near the mouth of the Sassafras River, to help move cattle and other livestock farther away.[13]

While at Turkey Point, Howe issued a proclamation to the people of Pennsylvania, Delaware, and the eastern shore of Maryland. The plundering by the British had become a public relations nightmare. In his proclamation, Howe apologized for the past treatment of the people, offered a general pardon to all who came forward, and promised to punish any of his soldiers who plundered property.[14]

However, the German troops were not subject to British military discipline, so Hessian foraging expeditions continued. "We found waist-high grass, oxen, sheep, turkeys, and all kinds of wild fowl," recalled a delighted Ewald. "Since we did not find any of the enemy, we skirmished with these animals, of which so many were killed that the entire Corps was provided with fresh provisions." A British artillery officer commented on the lack of effectiveness of Howe's strict orders: "General Howe has given strict orders against any kind of marauding, but it is not in anyone's power to prevent this where there is so large an army and such a mixture of troops. The Hessians are famous and infamous for their plundering." Nevertheless, at least two senior Hessian officers made an effort to curb the depredations of their troops. "Colonel von Donop and Lieutenant Colonel von Wurmb were praised in the orders . . . for maintaining the best discipline among their troops," he continued. "General von Knyphausen made ten men of Stirn's brigade run the gauntlet for some excesses. The best order and discipline have now been almost entirely restored."[15]

Movement Begins; Plundering Continues

Howe originally wanted to begin moving his army on August 27, but "[s]ince the heavy rain continues, and the roads are bottomless, and since the horses are still sick and stiff, we had to . . . countermand the order to march."[16] The next day, however, Howe decided otherwise and the British Army lurched

---

13 Reed, *Campaign to Valley Forge*, 86.

14 Ibid., 89.

15 McGuire, *Philadelphia Campaign*, vol. 1, 137; Ewald, *Diary*, 75; F. A. Whinyates, ed., *The Services of Lieut.-Colonel Francis Downman, R.A. in France, North America, and the West Indies, Between the Years 1758 and 1784* (Woolwich, 1898), 30.

16 Von Baurmeister, "Letters of Baurmeister," 30.

forward. Hessian Gen. von Knyphausen crossed the Elk River to Cecil Courthouse with about a third of the army to forage for cattle and horses. After driving away some American militia, Knyphausen easily occupied the place. Most of the detachment moved along the Newcastle Road to establish camps. However, Knyphausen did order a column to the south as far as the Bohemia River to capture cattle and horses and gather wagons. The remainder of the army, led by a jaeger patrol, stepped off early that morning northeast toward Head of Elk. Besides the detachment under Knyphausen, Howe left some 2,000 troops behind with the fleet.[17]

The *Jaeger Corps Journal* recorded just how little the British knew about this part of America and just how deeply in the dark Howe was about the location of Washington's command. "We had no reports about the enemy, and no maps of the interior of this land, and no one in the army was familiar with this area. After we had passed the city, no one knew which way to go." Troops were dispatched, continued the journal, "in all directions until finally a Negro was found, and the army had to march according to his directions. This Negro knew nothing about the enemy army, himself."[18]

Head of Elk was home to the Hollingsworth family, which controlled the local shipping businesses between Philadelphia and the Chesapeake region. The village, recorded an officer, contained "40 well built brick and stone houses." Any discerning eye would have seen a number of ships' masts at Elk Landing, a small commercial port. "Here was one of the key intermediary points of Chesapeake commerce, where goods traveling between Philadelphia and the Chesapeake region were transferred from land to water."[19]

British troops deployed and attacked the village, which was defended by the militia. According to American Jesse Hollingsworth, after a march of more than seven miles, the jaegers ran into some militia at a bridge about 9:00 a.m. "My Brother H[enr]y had a small Skirmish at Gilpins Bridge . . . & was slightly wounded in the Cheek," reported Hollingsworth. "We have several Deserters

---

17 Montresor, "Journals," 443; Reed, *Campaign to Valley Forge*, 98; Ewald, *Diary*, 75.

18 Burgoyne and Burgoyne, eds., *Journal of the Hesse-Cassel Jaeger Corps*, 6.

19 Ibid. McGuire, *Philadelphia Campaign*, vol. 1, 139-40. The army moved out in this order: foot jaegers and 21 mounted jaegers, the British light infantry, the Queen's Rangers, Ferguson's riflemen, the British grenadiers, an artillery brigade, the Hessian grenadiers, another artillery brigade, the British Brigade of Guards, the 1st and 2nd Brigades of British infantry with the army's baggage, the light dragoons (some of whom were dismounted due to the shortage of horses), the rest of the mounted jaegers, and the 71st Highlanders; Montresor, "Journals," 443.

& near 100 Prisoners taken by our light Horse in Scouting Parties." "According to Custom most of the Inhabitants have left their Houses & drove away their Cattle," wrote Scottish Gen. Grant, who went on to offer a favorable, if backhanded compliment of the local militia by writing, "The Militia in Arms, to pop at Straglers, & pick up Marauders in which they are too successful." Ewald recalled the American foot soldiers withdrawing "after an hour's skirmish." The militia destroyed the bridge they had been defending and fell back.[20]

Although the British army's engineers had to rebuild the bridge, a "great part of the Army forded the Creek in about 3 feet water on a gravelly bottom." Once across the creek, the jaegers fanned out south of the village. Once the bridge fell, the American militia hustled northeast from Head of Elk in the direction of Grey's Hill. When the British light troops moved forward and occupied Grey's Hill, the militia withdrew to Iron Hill. Captain Ewald, meanwhile, spotted merchant ships at anchor at Elk's Landing and reported their presence to Howe. The ships contained indigo, tobacco, sugar, and wine, all of which was quickly confiscated. "The greater part of their cargoes," wrote one eyewitness, "was distributed among the army, but the flour and corn were delivered to the English commissariat." Behind the British advance stretched a ten-mile long line of wagons, horses, and men. Very few of the latter enjoyed the newly found acquisitions. Francis Downman, a Royal artilleryman, recalled the fatiguing march, bad roads, weak horses, and intensely hot sun, just before complaining about having "nothing to eat or drink but apples and water."[21]

Once again, Howe settled down to forage. He was now about 50 miles from Philadelphia. Several streams and rivers stood before him and the capital, each of which he surely suspected Washington would use to defensive advantage. With both militia and Washington's Continental legions lurking in the area, relaxing was impossible.[22]

While the British were still occupying Head of Elk, Washington rode out a second time to reconnoiter Howe's army, just as the British commander was doing the same thing from his side of the field. From atop Iron Hill, Washington watched as the British took up positions on and around Grey's Hill

20 McGuire, *Philadelphia Campaign*, vol. 1, 139-40; Brown, ed., *Archives of Maryland*, vol. 16, 349; James Grant to Harvey, August 31, 1777, James Grant Papers; Ewald, *Diary*, 76.

21 Montresor, "Journals," 443; Von Baurmeister, "Letters of Baurmeister," 30, 399-400; McGuire, *Philadelphia Campaign*, vol. 1, 140; Whinyates, ed., *Services of Downman*, 30.

22 Reed, *Campaign to Valley Forge*, 74-5.

only a mile away. In a rather ironic twist, the two opposing commanders observed each other from the opposing hills. "We observed some officers on a wooded hill opposite us, all of them either in blue and white or blue and red, though one was dressed unobtrusively in a plain gray coat," wrote von Muenchhausen. "These gentlemen observed us with their glasses as carefully as we observed them. Those of our officers who know Washington well, maintained that the man in the plain coat was Washington."[23]

While the two most powerful men in North America eyed one another, the American Army was on the move. Nathanael Greene moved out from Wilmington and marched through Newport and Rising Sun to reach White Clay Creek, which sat in low ground that was not easily defended. Stirling's and Stephen's divisions joined Greene behind the creek. Wayne's division remained at Wilmington erecting defenses. Sullivan's errant division, meanwhile, passed through Trenton, crossed the Delaware River, and marched into Philadelphia during the day as it moved speedily to rejoin the main army.

In the midst of these chess-like maneuvers, Washington demonstrated some flexibility in command. He created the American light infantry brigade, consisting of "one Field Officer, two Captains, six Subalterns, eight Serjeants and 100 Rank & File from each brigade." Washington put New Jersey Gen. William Maxwell, the senior brigadier traveling with the portion of the army under his direct command, in charge of the new formation, and the unit took position at Iron Hill. Its mission was a tall one: Block the road to Wilmington via Cooch's Mill and Christiana. The absence of Daniel Morgan's riflemen necessitated the creation of this unit. (Morgan had been detached to assist in the northern campaign, leaving the army in need of a replacement to fill the valuable role of scouting and sniping.) The new organization was soon supplemented by about 1,000 Delaware and Pennsylvania militiamen. Maxwell's infantry unit had an immediate effect: One observer with Howe's army thought the Americans quite numerous in the area, "The hills from which they were viewing us seemed to be alive with troops."[24]

While Washington was moving into defensive positions and creating a new light infantry command, the British and German troops to their west were settling down for a few days of rest. "We will probably stay here today and

23 Von Muenchhausen, *At General Howe's Side*, 26.

24 Chase and Lengel, eds., *Papers of Washington*, vol. 11, 82; McGuire, *Philadelphia Campaign*, vol. 1, 144; Von Muenchhausen, *At General Howe's Side*, 26.

tomorrow to give our horses, which suffered exceedingly because of the unexpectedly long voyage, a chance to recover, and also to shoe them," came the explanation for the delay. The grenadier and light infantry battalions were posted at Grey's Hill to protect the British camps. Lieutenant William Hale described the new living conditions: "For this past week we have lived like beasts, no plates, no dishes, no table cloth, biscuits supply the place of the first but for the others no substitute can be found; my clothes have not been off since we landed. . . . I have had only two fresh meals since quitting the ship, but the Pork is so good as well for breakfast as dinner, that I feel no want of beef or mutton." Writing to his mother, Capt. William Dansey left a similar description of life on the road to Philadelphia: "We landed in this Country five Days ago with no other Conveniences than what we cou'd carry on our Backs. . . . I hope you will excuse, as also my present stile of Writing, as I am in an intire State of Illconveniency seated on the Ground at the Foot of a Tree, What a Savage Life ours is, I don't expect to have my Cloths off or see the inside of a House on this side of Christmas but thank God I keep my Health well."[25]

The complaining British officers at least had the help of servants to make life more bearable. The rank and file had no such conveniences, nor the freedom to find a shade tree outside of camp. They still discovered ways to deal with their plight, which despite the warnings and punishments implemented by Howe generally consisted of plundering the countryside. This pastime, however, was more dangerous now than ever before. "Several of our men very irregular in pursuit of fresh provisions, so as to fall into the Enemy's hands. . . . 23 of our Troops, 3 of which Hessians missing, supposed to be taken by the Enemy plundering," wrote one soldier. Ambrose Serle noted that "forty seven grenadiers, and several other Parties straggling for Plunder, were surprized and taken by the Rebels." The Hessians, he added, "are more infamous & cruel than any." John Peebles confirmed the harsh consequences for some of the unlucky wanderers when he told his journal, "2 men of the 71st. found in the wood with their throats cut, & 2 [Grenadiers] hang'd by the Rebels with their plunder on their backs."[26]

25 Von Muenchhausen, *At General Howe's Side*, 26; McGuire, *Philadelphia Campaign*, vol. 1, 145; Wilkin, *Some British Soldiers*, 228; William Dansey to Mrs. Dansey, August 30, 1777, the William Dansey Letters.

26 Montresor, "Journals," 443; Tatum, Jr., ed., *Journal of Ambrose Serle*, 246; Peebles, *Peebles' American War*, 129.

Losing irreplaceable troops due to unrestrained plundering infuriated Howe, who issued a flurry of orders from headquarters on August 29. The commanding general authorized the provost marshal of the army "to execute upon the Spot all Soldiers and followers of the Army, Straggling beyond the out posts, or detected in Plundering or devastation of any kind. . . . The Commanding Officers of Corps are immediately to send out Strong Patrols along their front and beyond their advance Sentries, to take up all Stragglers. . . . The present Irregularity of the Men makes it absolutely necessary for no Officer to leave Camp without permission of his Commanding Officer."[27]

Charles Stuart noted in a letter to his father that some 100 men had been lost while out plundering, and went on to describe the effect on the local populace. "A want of firmness in not enforcing orders," he wrote, coupled with "a total relaxation of discipline has been the cause of our beginning the Campaign by plundering and irregularity of every kind; most of the people either through disaffection or fear had left their houses, and those that remained had the melancholy prospect of seeing everything taken from them and the regret left of not having followed the stream."[28]

Unfortunately, the plundering problem would plague the army throughout the campaign. The seriousness of the problem is well-attested by the number of Howe's officers who wrote letters or commented in their diaries and journals about the rampant pillaging. "A soldier of ours was yesterday taken by the enemy beyond our lines, who had chopped off an unfortunate woman's fingers in order to plunder her rings," wrote one officer. "I really think the return of this army to England is to be dreaded by the peaceable inhabitants, and will occasion a prodigious increase of business for Sir J. Fielding and Jack Ketch. I am sure the office of the latter can never find more deserving objects for its exercise."[29]

Howe was attempting to curb the actions of his army and address these concerns when he learned of the disaster at Bennington, Vermont. This news was the first inkling that things were not going as well as they might on the northern front. Howe, however, was now in no position to assist Burgoyne in

---

27 Kemble, *Journals*, 480-1.

28 Wortley, ed., *A Prime Minister and His Son*, 116.

29 Fitzpatrick to the Countess of Ossory, "Head of Elk, September 1, 1777." Fielding was the founder of the London police and Ketch was a known executioner. McGuire, *Philadelphia Campaign*, vol. 1, 147.

any way. More depressing news arrived with the absence of Loyalists, who were not flocking to the king's standard as the British had believed they would. As noted, throughout the war the British overestimated the support of the local population. Howe had fully expected to raise several provincial regiments during his overland campaign to Philadelphia, and perhaps there was still time to do so. Unfortunately, the yield thus far had been much less than anticipated. "The prevailing disposition of the inhabitants, who, I am sorry to observe, seem to be, excepting a few individuals, strongly in enmity against us," Howe complained to Germain. "[M]any having taken up arms, and, by far the greater number, deserted their dwellings, driving off, at the same time, their stock of cattle and horses." While several British officers agreed that the decision to ascend the Chesapeake prohibited any support to the northern column, Howe later told Parliament that his inability to recruit these Loyalists was a reason for his failure to fulfill the king's orders to support Gen. Burgoyne.[30]

Three loyalist concerns worked against British recruitment efforts. One was their personality traits: Conservative, cautious, and anti-violence. This explained why the Quakers were viewed as Loyalists. However, a second reason the local people came forward reluctantly, if at all, was the British reception of loyalist volunteers elsewhere thus far in the war. Rather than being granted British Army commissions and the permanence that came with them, they were given temporary provincial commissions. As a result, even though such Americans remained loyal to the king, the British viewed all Americans as inferior to themselves. Accordingly, provincial troops were used not for the more rewarding combat roles, but rather less rewarding tasks like scouting, foraging, and garrisoning rear areas. Lastly, the British had an established track record of abandoning Loyalists after they came forward. Thousands flocked to the British banner after the occupation of New York City and northern New Jersey, for example, only to see their families and homes abandoned when Howe's army evacuated northern New Jersey. A related and just as serious issue was the treatment of loyalist property when the British Army was in an area. Despite Howe's efforts, his men plundered the countryside indiscriminately. The British, recalled a Pennsylvanian named John Miller, spared "neither friend nor foe, burning, robbing, stealing all the way they went."[31]

30 Gruber, *The Howe Brothers*, 239; Stockdale, ed., *The Parliamentary Register*, vol. 10, 418.

31 Edgar, *Philadelphia Campaign*, 13-14.

On August 29, while the British Army was recovering from the voyage and gathering supplies around Head of Elk, Washington's main army moved from behind White Clay Creek northeast to a position behind its tributary, Red Clay Creek. The army marched over the Lancaster (Newport Gap) Road to reach the higher and more defensible ground along Red Clay. Once there, the new American line extended from Newport, Delaware, on the southeast to near Marshallton to the northwest, with the small town of Stanton in the middle of the American positions. Sullivan's division passed through Darby and Chester and proceeded south to Wilmington, where it rejoined Washington's main army. Sullivan's unit had been separated from the army for a little more than seven weeks.[32]

While camped in northern Delaware keeping a watchful eye on the British legions to the west, Washington's own men proved that they, too, were not above plundering—a fact that caused great "astonishment" and vexed the leader to no end. A passionate plea in the form of a general order was issued in an effort to curb the foraging. "Notwithstanding all the cautions—the earnest requests, and the positive orders, of the Commander in Chief, to prevent our own army from plundering our own friends and fellow citizens," he wrote in the third person, "yet to his astonishment and grief, fresh complaints are made to him, that so wicked, infamous and cruel a practice is still continued—and that too in circumstances most distressing—where the wretched inhabitants, dreaded the enemy's vengeance for their adherence to our cause, have left all, and fled to us for refuge!" He continued: "We complain of the cruelty and barbarity of our enemies; but does it equal ours?" He continued in this philosophical vein before pointing out the obvious, that "If officers in the least connive at such practices, the licentiousness of some soldiers will soon be without bounds: In the most critical moments, instead of attending to their duty, they will be scattered abroad, indiscrim[in]ately plundering friends and foes; and if no worse consequences ensue, many of them must infallib[l]y fall a prey to the enemy."[33]

"We are doubtless a wicked generation, and our army too much abounds in profaneness and debauchery," Washington's adjutant general wrote his wife. "Nevertheless, our enemies do not fall behind us in vice, but rather, I believe, exceed us, and have besides none but the worst motives—the motives of

32 Reed, *Campaign to Valley Forge*, 62-3.

33 Chase and Lengel, eds., *Papers of Washington*, vol. 11, 141-2.

tyrants—to steel their hearts against us; whereas we have a just cause, on which the happiness, not of innocent Americans only, but of the thousands of poor, oppressed people in every kingdom in Europe, depends, to point our weapons and brace our arms, to urge them against the mercenary foe. Such a cause Providence, I hope, will favor and succeed."[34]

Taking Each Other's Measure

While plundering sapped the strength of both sides and terrorized the locals, several skirmishes during late August and early September set the tempo for the early days of the campaign. It was becoming increasingly clear to Howe's officers that Washington was not going to let them have Philadelphia easily. "They say that [Washington] threatens to fight rather than give up Philadelphia. If he risks an engagement in any accessible situation it will be a sign that he thinks his cause in a very desperate situation, or that he is very little acquainted with the nature of the troops that are to act for and against him," wrote Scotsman James Murray. "A month or two will enable us to judge with a little more certainty of the event, but I cannot help being still of opinion that the Cause of Liberty is in a very delicate situation: and I sincerely wish that it was over. It is a barbarous business and in a barbarous country. The novelty is worn off and I see no advantages to be reaped from it."[35]

On August 31, a skirmish between militia and elements of the British army erupted at Gilpin's Bridge, a crossing of the Big Elk. During its stay in the Head of Elk vicinity, the British Army's primary purpose was to replenish supplies used and lost on the voyage. After the skirmish at Gilpin's Bridge, however, Gen. Cornwallis pushed a detachment four miles beyond the camps, captured a mill village known as Iron Works, and destroyed a supply of stores and liquors.[36]

The terrain in northeast Maryland and northern Delaware was well suited to this type of warfare. An officer in Washington's army, Walter Stewart, described the region as one "formed by Nature for defence, having a great quantity of woods, large morasses they must pass through, and many

34 Pickering, *Life of Pickering*, vol. 1, 152-3.

35 Murray, *Letters from America*, 47-8.

36 Reed, *Campaign to Valley Forge*, 93, 97.

commanding hills, which the Militia may take post upon." With quality terrain to defend, the army was "in amazing high spirits, and very healthy."[37]

Washington wanted the militia to take advantage of these favorable conditions to continually harass British foragers "by alarming them frequently with light parties, beating up their Pickets, and intercepting as often as can be done, whatever parties they may send out to procure Supplies of forage, horses, cattle, provisions and necessaries of every kind." In addition to removing livestock from the path of the British Army, Washington added another task to the militia's duties. "If there should be any Mills in the Neighborhood of the Enemy, and which may be liable to fall into their hands, the Runners [the millstones] should be removed and secured," he ordered. This "will effectually prevent the Enemy from using the Mills. Grain, too, should be carried out of their way, as far as circumstances will admit."[38]

Beyond denying the British sustenance, Washington was starting to think ahead tactically. If he was forced to withdraw from Red Clay Creek, another position had to be prepared for defense. On August 31, Washington ordered elements of the Pennsylvania militia to Richling's and Gibson's Fords on the Brandywine River. As the army rearranged itself and prepared additional defenses, Washington announced to his men on September 1 that the siege of Fort Stanwix in New York state had been lifted.[39]

The British, meanwhile, were driving off stock and stores from Elk Forge, four miles north of Head of Elk, and reportedly heading toward Nottingham in southeastern Pennsylvania. It was also learned that Howe had sent his supply ships back around to the Delaware River. Knyphausen advanced to Carson's Tavern on September 2 under a nagging rain amid muggy conditions, with Grey's brigade farther ahead at Lum's Pond.[40]

---

37 Henry Steele Commager and Richard B. Morris, eds., *The Spirit of Seventy-six: The Story of the American Revolution as Told by its Participants* (Edison, NJ, 1967), 610.

38 Chase and Lengel, eds., *Papers of Washington*, vol. 11, 100. Removing the millstones from grist mills would have been a massive undertaking, as anyone who has visited one of the many surviving mills in the northeast can attest to the size and weight of these apparatuses, some weighing as much as two tons. That said, it may have been at least partially successful, for the British army and the civilians of Philadelphia would go through a very lean period later in the fall.

39 Reed, *Campaign to Valley Forge*, 94.

40 Showman, McCarthy, and Cobb, eds., *Papers of Greene*, vol. 2, 151-2; Reed, *Campaign to Valley Forge*, 99.

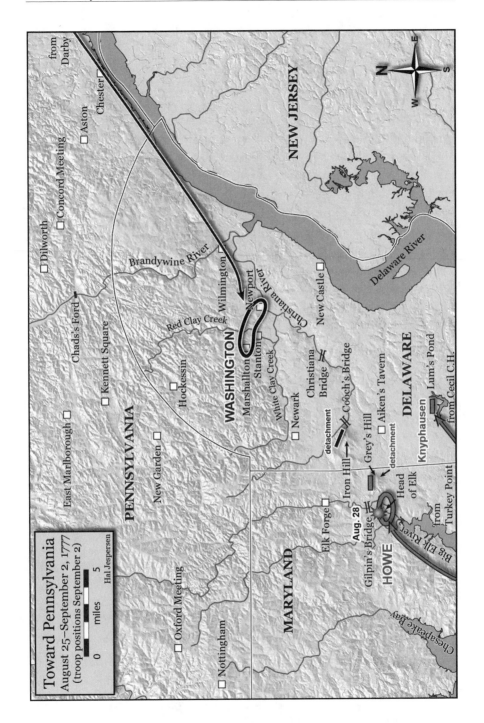

Toward Pennsylvania
August 25–September 2, 1777
(troop positions September 2)

0   miles   5

Hal Jespersen

NEW JERSEY

N
E
S
W

from Darby

Chester

Aston

Concord Meeting

Dilworth

Brandywine River

Chads's Ford

Kennett Square

East Marlborough

PENNSYLVANIA

New Garden

Hockessin

Red Clay Creek

Wilmington

Newport

Christiana River

Delaware River

New Castle

WASHINGTON

Marshallton

Stanton

White Clay Creek

Newark

Christiana Bridge

Cooch's Bridge

detachment

DELAWARE

Aiken's Tavern

Grey's Hill

detachment

Knyphausen

Lum's Pond

from Cecil C.H.

Iron Hill

Elk Forge

Aug. 28

Gilpin's Bridge

HOWE

Head of Elk

Big Elk River

from Turkey Point

Chesapeake Bay

MARYLAND

Oxford Meeting

Nottingham

Howe's lethargic, fitful movement was attributed to the continuing equine shortage, a problem of which Washington was well aware. "All accounts agree that [the enemy] are very much distressed for want of horses, numbers of which it is said died on the passage, and the rest are in exceeding bad order," wrote the American commander. "[T]his will probably occasion some delay and give time for the militia, who seem to be collecting pretty fast, to join us." Alexander Hamilton, a member of Washington's staff, also commented on Howe's "state of inactivity; in a great measure I believe from the want of horses, to transport his baggage and stores. It seems he sailed with only about three weeks provender and was six at sea. This has occasioned the death of a great number of his horses, and has made skeletons of the rest." He hypothesized that Howe would be "obliged to collect a supply from the neighbouring country before he can move, unless he should be disposed to make a more hazardous movement, than he would ever be able to justify, unless by a degree of success he has no right to expect." The upshot of the horse shortage was that Howe was willing to pay high prices for horses—any horses. This induced many American dragoons to desert to the enemy and sell their mounts to Howe.[41]

Despite many difficulties and vexations accompanied by much effort, the British Army was finally on the move.

---

41 Chase and Lengel, eds., *Papers of Washington*, vol. 11, 112; Harold C. Syrett, ed., *The Papers of Alexander Hamilton* (New York, 1961), vol. 1, 321.

Chapter 7

To the Brandywine
September 3-10, 1777

"Not just chusing to take the Bull by the horns we disappointed
Washington and turned his Right."[1]

— James Grant, October 20, 1777

First Engagement: Cooch's Bridge

The British rank and file were itching for battle. After being cooped up on ships for weeks and now having spent several days idling along the Elk River, they were ready to move. Would Washington risk his Continental Army in battle? Howe thought not. "I am of opinion," he wrote Lord Germain, "it will be a difficult matter to bring them to a general action, even though it should be in defense of Philadelphia."

In the same dispatch to Germain, Howe downplayed the recent American successes in the northern department against Burgoyne. "I cannot presume to say what credit is to be given to the successes of the rebels in that quarter," offered Howe, "but as their accounts of successes are in general much exaggerated, I am hopeful, even should theirs be true, that he [Burgoyne] will not be prevented from pursuing the advantages he has already gained with so much honour to himself." Unfortunately for Howe and the British cause in

---

1   James Grant to Harvey, October 20, 1777, James Grant Papers.

North America, the reports of American victories on the northern front were accurate, and Burgoyne's situation was rapidly deteriorating.[2]

Once on dry land Howe was ready to risk major combat. He had repeatedly avoided a pitch battle in northern New Jersey, but the campaign season was winding down and he had to bring Washington to battle. An American officer captured on September 1 would have agreed with Howe that Washington wanted to avoid a major battle. Admiral Howe's secretary, Ambrose Serle, overheard the man comment on the situation: "Washington, in his present Situation, cannot avoid Battle. He is a Fool, however, if he risques one."[3]

Knowing he would almost certainly have to fight, Washington was readying his defense for that possibility. Cooch's Bridge carried the main road to Wilmington across Christiana Creek just east of Iron Hill. Some of Washington's officers believed Christiana Creek offered a better defensive position than Red Clay Creek, but the only men Washington had there were Maxwell's light infantry and some militia. On the east side of the creek was a road system and open terrain, "by which an extended line might readily be supplied." On the west side around the base of Iron Hill were woods that offered excellent terrain for ambushes and skirmishing with the enemy. Lastly, the Christiana was a deeper and better defensive moat than the Red Clay.[4]

Although Nathanael Greene strongly recommended moving the entire army to the position, Washington disapproved. He did, however, direct Maxwell to be alert and "[watc]hfull and guarded on all the Roads. It will be well to place some of your [men] at the pass on the Road" continued Washington, "which has been represented to be so advantageous, attending at the same time to the rest. If the Enemy come on they will be well posted and may have an [opp]ortunity of annoying them greatly."[5]

When Maxwell moved into the area, his men not only occupied Iron Hill but also extended themselves about a mile south along the road leading to Aiken's Tavern. The terrain was studded with ambush positions. At the intersection of the King's Highway (the road to Wilmington) with the road to Aiken's Tavern, just west of Cooch's Bridge, stood the Cooch grist mill, and on

---

2   Stockdale, ed., *The Parliamentary Register*, vol. 10, 419-420.

3   Serle, *Journal*, 246.

4   Reed, *Campaign to Valley Forge*, 90.

5   Chase and Lengel, eds., *Papers of Washington*, vol. 11, 95.

a small rise nearby stood the family home of Thomas Cooch. The family, however, was long gone, having fled to Pennsylvania to escape the dangers of warfare.[6]

Howe's army began moving on the morning of September 3. The general decided to cut loose from the fleet, always a risky logistical move. However, the lethargic voyage meant that few supplies remained on the ships. General Howe informed his brother he would allow him 10 days to reach New Castle, Delaware, before initiating major action against Washington's army. The time would allow the army to continue gathering supplies and to outmaneuver Washington into Pennsylvania. Two infantry battalions under James Grant would remain at Head of Elk until the last of the British ships left the Elk River. As historian John Reed noted, "Howe could have easily crossed the Maryland-Delaware peninsula and there awaited the fleet, but this would have had the same effect as an original landing on the Delaware, and would have little explained to London the excessively long voyage into the Chesapeake."[7]

While enough horses had recovered or been procured to move the artillery and wagons, many of the light dragoons remained dismounted. Although Howe had enough of these cavalrymen for scouting the American positions, they could not "be used to perform the classic functions of screening and pursuit." This deficiency would plague Howe for weeks.[8]

In an effort to outflank the American positions on Iron Hill, the British moved to the south of that position and headed toward Aiken's Tavern. Crossing the Mason-Dixon line (surveyed between 1763 and 1767) into what originally had been the three lower counties of Pennsylvania, the British easily outflanked Maxwell's light infantry. The route Howe chose also allowed Gen. Knyphausen to rejoin the main army after foraging around Cecil Courthouse. The German's detached column returned with horses, cattle, and other livestock much needed by the army. When the army reached Aiken's Tavern, Howe made the structure his headquarters.[9]

---

6   Aiken's Tavern is modern-day Glasgow, Delaware. The modern road to Glasgow only follows part of the original roadbed; originally, the road followed a course much closer to Christiana Creek; Reed, *Campaign to Valley Forge*, 93, 103.

7   Pancake, *1777*, 167; Reed, *Campaign to Valley Forge*, 99.

8   Pancake, *1777*, 168. See Appendix H for a discussion of the functions of mounted troops.

9   McGuire, *Philadelphia Campaign*, vol. 1, 151-152. The British were settling into one of the first Welsh settlements in America, known as Pencader.

Johann Ewald was ordered to take six mounted jaegers and ride north toward Iron Hill to determine whether the Americans had reacted to the British movement. They had not gone far when an American detachment ambushed the seven men. A volley of gunfire rippled from behind a hedge, killing or wounding all six of Ewald's mounted jaegers. Ewald's normally calm horse was wounded in the belly and "reared so high several times that I expected it would throw me," recorded the Hessian officer, who had somehow escaped the hail of lead balls. Ewald called forward the foot jaegers still some distance behind him.[10]

A running two-mile fight developed as some 400 jaegers pushed north toward Cooch's Mill and the bridge spanning Christiana Creek. Foreshadowing what would occur eight days later along the Brandywine, Maxwell, through a series of small ambushes carried out by his novice light infantry, slowed the British advance. Iron Hill towered above the surrounding countryside as the jaegers approached the mill, the high ground studded with Maxwell's Continentals.[11]

Alerted to the fighting, Howe rode to the front to observe the unfolding situation. Once he understood what was transpiring, he ordered the jaegers to assault the hill. "The charge was sounded, and the enemy was attacked so severely and with such spirit by the jaegers," reported Ewald, "that we became masters of the mountain after a seven-hour engagement." The protracted combat included a two-front fight. While some of Maxwell's men were indeed upon Iron Hill, others had run across Cooch's Bridge and were fighting from the opposite side of Christiana Creek. Late in the engagement, Howe pushed forward additional element to support the exhausted jaegers. The 1st Light Infantry Battalion attempted to come up on the left flank, but was slowed by swampy ground. The inability of the light infantry to negotiate the swamp, explained Montresor, "prevented this little spirited affair from becoming so decisive." The 2nd Light Infantry Battalion arrived on the jaegers' right, followed by the British grenadiers. It was the arrival of these fresh troops that allowed the jaegers to dash across the bridge and drive the Americans away from Christiana Creek.[12]

---

10 Ewald, *Diary*, 77.

11 McGuire, *Philadelphia Campaign*, vol. 1, 152.

12 Ewald, *Diary*, 78; Montresor, "Journals," 446.

The two bodies of troops that faced each other that September day consisted of men who intended to take advantage of cover and pick off their opponents. The result was an unexpected and difficult slog for the Jaegers, who recorded the pesky opposition in their Corps Journal. "They were driven back into another woods with considerable effort," admitted the chronicler. "Here they defended themselves obstinately." Maxwell's light infantry had indeed fought "obstinately," but exhausted their ammunition doing so. Ludwig von Wurmb, commander of the jaegers, recalled that when the Americans ran out of powder and shot, "we went after them with the sword and made them flee." The withdrawal—or flight—of Maxwell's command toward Christiana Bridge was so disorganized "that great numbers threw down their arms and blankets" and left several dead and wounded behind on the ground. Despite its length, the combat resulted in fewer than 100 casualties combined for the two armies.[13]

Howe was overjoyed with the performance of the jaegers and light infantrymen. "They went on in ye most covered country you ever saw with more (I think) than their usual spirit," reported the general. "Their perfidity [fervor] was so great that ye Granadiers who were as willing to have had their share in ye business as could be wisht, could hardly keep up to support them in a run." Always fond of his light infantry, Howe may have seen some humor in the fact that the grenadiers had been unable to get into the fight. The view from the other side was also upbeat. Despite the fact that his men were eventually forced back, Washington was generally pleased with their performance, and told Congress as much. "This Morning the Enemy came out with considerable force and three pieces of Artillery, against our Light advanced Corps," he reported, "and after some pretty smart skirmishing obliged them to retreat, being far inferior in number and without Cannon." The engagement proved to Washington's satisfaction that Maxwell's light infantry could serve the same purpose Morgan's men had for the army.[14]

The engagement at Cooch's Bridge was not a major affair and had no effect on the outcome of the campaign or the war. However, by brushing aside the

---

13 Burgoyne and Burgoyne, eds., *Journal of the Jaeger Corps*, 8; Ludwig von Wurmb to Gen. Friedrich von Jungkenn, October 14, 1777, in *Journal of the Johannes Schwalm Historical Association*, vol. 6, no. 2 (1998), 10. Since the rifles the jaegers carried could not accommodate bayonets, the German light infantrymen carried large swords for hand-to-hand fighting; Andre, Journal, 43; McGuire, Philadelphia Campaign, vol. 1, 154.

14 William Howe to James Grant, September 3, 1777, James Grant Papers, microfilm 687, reel 37; Chase and Lengel, eds., *Papers of Washington*, vol. 11, 135.

Americans, Howe eliminated the threat against the new British camp at Aiken's Tavern and cleared Iron Hill of enemy troops.[15]

Despite a fairly solid performance, Maxwell and other officers attracted criticism. Lieutenant Colonel Louis Casimir and Baron de Holtzendorff scoffed at the performance. The baron, who had served on Frederick the Great's staff and authored a book on tactics, conversed with Congressman Henry Laurens, who claimed, "Baron Holzendorff this minute from Camp tells me one of our Generals misbehaved. The Enemy had Cannon, we had none, our Troops retreated. . . . The Baron whispers—'Your Soldiers my Dear Colonel are very good Mans, so good as any brave Mans in the World, but your Officers my Dear Colonel your Officers'—& then bursts his soft Laugh. I understand him and & believe he is pretty just in his meaning."[16]

Preparatory Lull

Following the engagement at Cooch's Bridge, Maxwell retreated to the main American position behind Red Clay Creek. Howe's army camped near the battlefield, with the Brigade of Guards settled on Iron Hill, the grenadiers and light infantry on the east bank of Christiana Creek, and everyone else spread between Iron Hill and Aiken's Tavern. Howe's left flank now rested on Iron Hill with his right flank just south of Aiken's Tavern. His army would remain in this position for the next five days.[17]

The British found themselves in an interesting position. The view from atop Iron Hill was as commanding as it was instructive. About seven miles to the east was the Delaware River—their immediate destination now within view. A turn in the opposite direction revealed the miles they had just traversed from Head of Elk and the upper reaches of the Chesapeake Bay. The optimistic among them saw their salvation in the Delaware. The pessimistic, when glancing back toward Turkey Point, noted the time wasted at sea. By September 4, the British fleet was no longer in the Chesapeake. The men knew they would be without tents and other "necessaries" until they reached Philadelphia.[18]

15 Small as it was, it was still the largest engagement ever fought on Delaware soil.

16 Smith, et al., eds., *Letters of Delegates*, vol. 7, 612.

17 Mowday, *September 11, 1777*, 46.

18 McGuire, *Philadelphia Campaign*, vol. 1, 157.

*   *   *

The news of the British advance, coupled with the defeat at Cooch's Bridge, spread panic once again throughout Philadelphia. Prominent patriots prepared to move to inland towns. Supplies and materials that might benefit the British were removed to Reading and other places in the backcountry. Congress and the state authorities, meanwhile, made arrangements to move to Baltimore and Lancaster, respectively.[19]

By September 5, Washington was busy stripping the Delaware River defenses of every available Continental soldier and militiaman to reinforce his main army confronting Howe. A muster of the river fortifications taken that day indicated the following troop strengths:

*   Billingsport: 30 Continental artillerymen, 50 Philadelphia militiamen with eight days to serve, and 50 laborers and carpenters;
*   Fort Mifflin: 30 Continental artillerymen, 15 militiamen, and 15 laborers;
*   Fort Mercer: no troops and only a few laborers;
*   Bush Island and Darby Creek redoubts: no garrisons.

Three rows of *chevaux-de-frise* jammed the river between Fort Mifflin and Fort Mercer. Congress's Navy Board recommended that Hog Island, Province Island, and Carpenters' Island all be flooded. The Board also suggested flatboats be used to bridge the channel between Fort Mifflin and Province Island. Washington requested that the Middle Ferry Bridge on the Schuylkill River be removed to the Delaware and that all boats be moved to prevent them from falling into enemy hands. At the same time, Washington ordered the banks of Darby Creek cut to overflow Province Island. Washington was doing all he could to see that, if the British fleet returned to the Delaware, its passage up to the American capital would not be an easy one.[20]

Realizing that a major engagement for the capital was now all but inevitable, Washington issued a general order dated September 5 in an effort to steel his men's nerves: "Should they [the British] push their design against Philadelphia, on this route, their all is at stake—they will put the contest on the event of a

19 Jackson, *Pennsylvania Navy*, 118.

20 Ibid., 118-119.

single battle: If they are overthrown, they are utterly undone—the war is at an end," he exhorted, though with some exaggeration. He continued: "Now then is the time for our most strenuous exertions. One bold stroke will free the land from rapine, devastations & burnings, and female innocence from brutal lust and violence.... If we behave like men this Third campaign will be our last."[21]

The next day Washington moved his headquarters from Wilmington to Newport and sent off the army's baggage in preparation for a possible fight. Joseph Clark, adjutant to Adam Stephen, commented on the day's events: "All the heavy Baggage was sent off to Brandywine, expecting next morning to make the attack, but the enemy did not come on, so nothing was done this day but fortifying; parapet walls were thrown up to a great extent, trees felled to secure the flanks & important passes." Washington also wanted the men to strip down and travel as lightly as possible. The officers, he ordered, "should only retain their blankets, great coats, and three or four shifts of under cloaths, and that the men should, besides what they have on, keep only a Blanket, and a shirt a piece, and such as have it, a great coat—All trunks, chests, boxes, other bedding and cloaths, than those mentioned, to be sent away."[22]

Convinced that Howe would drive straight toward Philadelphia using the King's Road through Wilmington from Cooch's Bridge, he deployed his troops in depth along Red Clay Creek from Newport toward Marshallton. John Sullivan's division anchored the American right, with Lord Stirling's division in place on Sullivan's left. Adam Stephen's division formed a second line behind Stirling's men, with Anthony Wayne's Pennsylvanians behind Stephen's troops forming a third and final line. Off to the right, behind Sullivan, Nathanael Greene moved his division into position. Scouting parties from the 2nd and 4th Continental Light Dragoons fanned out in front of the army to keep a watchful eye on the British camps, a move that triggered a series of skirmishes from September 3 to September 8.[23]

Washington was clearly bracing for major combat along Red Clay Creek, which begs the question of whether he gave serious consideration to Howe's

---

21 Chase and Lengel, eds., *Papers of Washington*, vol. 11, 147-148.

22 Joseph Clark, "Diary of Joseph Clark," *Proceedings of the New Jersey Historical Society* (1855), 97; Chase and Lengel, eds., *Papers of Washington*, vol. 11, 168.

23 Reed, *Campaign to Valley Forge*, 104; Stephen E. Haller, *William Washington: Cavalryman of the Revolution* (Bowie, MD, 2001), 32. With the exception of the militiamen who had been dispatched to the Brandywine, the Pennsylvania militia was quartered at Newport.

possible courses of action. Howe had never resorted to a frontal assault against Washington's Continental Army. At Long Island, White Plains, Short Hills, and most recently, Cooch's Bridge, Howe employed flanking movements to gain the ground he wanted without a bloody direct attack. And now, here along Red Clay Creek, that option was once again open to him. What convinced Washington that Howe would change his tactics from successful maneuvering and flanking remains something of a mystery. Nevertheless, the Continental Army constructed major entrenchments, including *abatis*—sharpened tree branches—to block the main roads and studded its lines with an impressive array of artillery. If Howe did choose to assault Philadelphia directly along this route, Washington and his army would be ready to meet him.[24]

Skirmishing between the two armies continued while the main British army remained largely idle at Aiken's Tavern. According to Friedrich von Muenchhausen, "the rebel patrols, which usually consist of 10 to 15 dragoons and 20 to 30 infantrymen, now appear more often, and they fire at our posts occasionally." American deserters also continued to ride their mounts into the British camps to sell them. "Many dragoons of the rebels have deserted. Undoubtedly the amount of money they get from us for their mounts is the reason," explained von Muenchhausen. With the last of the British ships having now sailed, James Grant marched with his two battalions on September 6 to rejoin the main British Army.[25]

The next day, September 7, orders coursed through the British Army to be prepared to march the following morning. The army would move in three divisions. The first, under Cornwallis, included the jaegers, the British light infantry, the British and Hessian grenadiers, and the Brigade of Guards. The second division, commanded by James Grant, included two troops of the 16th Light Dragoons, two brigades of artillery, the four British infantry brigades, a battalion of the 71st Highlanders, and the baggage train. The third and final division, under Knyphausen, comprised a brigade of artillery, the Hessian infantry brigade, the other two troops of the 16th Light Dragoons, the 40th Regiment of Foot, the other two battalions of the 71st Highlanders, the Queen's Rangers, and Ferguson's riflemen.[26]

---

24 McGuire, *Philadelphia Campaign*, vol. 1, 158-159.

25 Von Muenchhausen, *At General Howe's Side*, 28; Reed, *Campaign to Valley Forge*, 108.

26 Ewald, *Diary*, 79.

In anticipation of a British attack, Washington reiterated his previous directive to strip down and issued the following general orders: "The enemy have disencumbered themselves of all their baggage, even to their tents, reserving only their blankets, and such part of their clothing as is absolutely necessary—This indicates a speedy & rapid movement, and points out the necessity of following the example, and ridding ourselves for a few days of every thing we can possibly dispense with."[27]

The reports of orders to travel light, coupled with the departing British fleet convinced Washington that Howe was going over to the tactical offensive. With his men ready to fight, he issued another impassioned appeal to his army, this one referencing successes on the northern front opposite Burgoyne's army:

> Who can forbear to emulate their noble spirit? Who is there without ambition, to share with them, the applauses of their countrymen, and of all posterity, as the defenders of Liberty, and the procurers of peace and happiness to millions in the present and future generations? Two years we have maintained the war and struggled with difficulties innumerable. But the prospect has since brightened, and our affairs put on a better face—Now is the time to reap the fruits of all our toils and dangers! . . . The eyes of all America, and of Europe are turned upon us. . . . [G]lory awaits to crown the brave—and peace—freedom and happiness will be the rewards of victory.[28]

Washington's tireless efforts were paying off. The morale of the army had soared, their defensive position was strong, and the men were ready for a pitched battle with Howe's professional army. "Our troops will stand a very hot engagement," affirmed one man in the ranks. "I believe the General is determined to stand it to the last before he'll suffer the enemy to git Philadelphia."[29]

Into Pennsylvania

The major battle Washington expected did not occur. The British Army did indeed depart its camps between Cooch's Bridge and Aiken's Tavern on

---

27 Chase and Lengel, eds., *Papers of Washington*, vol. 11, 167-168.

28 Ibid., 148.

29 Reed, *Campaign to Valley Forge*, 106. Citation states the original document was in John Reed's personal collection.

September 8 before daylight—but Washington's entrenched army never saw it. Rather than head east against his position, as Washington anticipated, Howe marched north past Iron Hill, leaving the coastal plains of the Delmarva Peninsula to move into the hilly country beyond. Howe's order of march remained as previously noted, with General Cornwallis's division in the lead, followed by General Grant men. General Knyphausen's command, meanwhile, brought up the rear.[30]

The British army marched through Newark, Delaware, that afternoon. Ensign Carl Ruffer of the von Mirbach Regiment described the community as "a very pleasantly built city of about sixty houses, but completely uninhabited. Also, now and again, very pleasing country homes which previous to this time we had seldom encountered in this area because it is rather thinly settled." James Parker agreed. "The country is entirely deserted," he observed. "We pass the Village of Newark, remarkable for Sedition & Presbeterian sermons, the inhabitants had all left their houses." Captain Francis Downman of the Royal Artillery commented on similar matters, but went on to describe the difficulties of the march: "We went through Newark, a deserted and destroyed village. The front and centre of the army got to the heights of [Hockessin] in the afternoon after a very disagreeable march of 16 hours without anything to eat, and almost suffocated with dust, owing to the vast train of baggage wagons and cattle that were in front."[31]

After passing through Newark the army crossed well north of Washington's right flank at White Clay Creek, "which was surrounded on both sides by steep, rocky heights that formed a most frightful defile half an hour in length." Ewald, leading the column with the jaegers, was at a loss to understand why the Americans had not defended the position, "where a hundred riflemen could have held up the army a whole day and killed many men." As he moved through the area, Ewald remembered his "hair stood on end as we crammed into the defile, and I imagined nothing more certain than an unexpected attack at the moment when we would have barely stuck our nose out of the defile. For the precipitous rocks on both sides of the creek and along the defile were so steep that no one could scale them." But no one was there to shoot at the

---

30 McGuire, *Philadelphia Campaign*, vol. 1, 159; Reed, *Campaign to Valley Forge*, 109.

31 Burgoyne, trans. and ed., *Enemy Views*, 172; Journal entry, September 8, Parker Family Papers; Whinyates, ed., *Services of Downman*, 32.

jaegers. Three days later, during the battle of the Brandywine, Ewald and his jaegers would face a similar defile.[32]

After negotiating the difficult crossing of White Clay Creek, the army reached Hockessin, where Howe established his headquarters in the Nicholas house. If he continued on this course, the road Howe had chosen would take him to Lancaster via Gap, Pennsylvania.[33]

One of the most inexplicable occurrences of the campaign was the "day's" march—which is exactly the word artilleryman Downman used—conclusion at 10:00 a.m. For reasons that remain unclear, Howe halted after marching just 10 miles. He had organized and pulled off a difficult flanking march without a single American being the wiser for it. Had he chosen, he could have easily turned Washington's right flank and trapped the Continentals below Wilmington. Philadelphia would have fallen without a major engagement. His decision to stop provided Washington the time he needed to discover Howe was gone, learn the British Army's new location, and get his own army in motion toward the Pennsylvania border.[34]

While the British Army moved north, sliding past Washington's prepared positions, the Continental Army, for the most part, sat idle. John Armstrong, commander of the Pennsylvania militia, fully expected a battle, stating that "this morning we expected the approach of the Enemy & yet continue to look for their movemt. . . . The Army generally are in good Spirits & look for Action." Joseph Clark, the quartermaster for Stephen's division, believed the same thing: "By Monday morning everything was in readiness for an engagement; the Troops marched down and took post in the entrenchments and went through the exercise. The reserved corps took their station at a proper distance and performed several manoevers."[35]

Howe used a bit of deception by pushing elements of the British Army to within two miles of Washington's position as though to attack, but his intent was merely to cover the main army's passage through Newark toward the Pennsylvania border. Once Washington realized Howe was no longer in his front in strength, and was in fact moving to his right toward the Pennsylvania

---

32 Ewald, *Diary*, 79-80.

33 McGuire, *Philadelphia Campaign*, vol. 1, 160; Whinyates, ed., *Services of Downman*, 32.

34 Reed, *Campaign to Valley Forge*, 109.

35 Hazard, ed., *Pennsylvania Archives*, series 1, vol. 5, 598; Clark, *Diary*, 97-98.

border, he sent out Maxwell, along with George Weedon's brigade. Later in the day, explained Clark, "word came by a light horseman that the enemy were advancing very fast. Our troops were kept in readiness and a large scout sent out under the command of Gen'l Maxwell, who in their route fired several times upon the enemy." The exchange of fire never exceeded minor skirmishing, the bulk of which erupted near Hockessin late in the evening. Howe easily brushed aside the Americans with jaegers and light infantry.[36]

The unfolding of Howe's plans impressed many of his senior officers. "All marched in one column, and to our great surprise," wrote Howe's aide von Muenchhausen, "instead of taking the road by way of Christiana Bridge to Wilmington as expected, we went to our left by way of White Clay Creek and Newark. . . . [E]veryone is pleased with the good march and the fact that it was kept a secret, thus cutting off Washington from Lancaster." The British officers were as surprised by the march as Washington. Just a day before the movement, Howe's senior Hessian aide speculated that they were going to move straight toward the American position. "Everyone believes—and it is very plausible— that we shall take the main road by way of Christiana Bridge to Wilmington where we will meet our fleet in the Delaware," von Muenchhausen wrote at the time. "Washington who certainly suspects such a move, has put up some fortifications and *abatis* at Christiana Bridge." Francis Downman chimed in on the effect of the march. "We did not meet with the smallest interference in our march from the rebels," confirmed the Royal artilleryman, "for we took a different road to that which they expected, and where they had raised works and collected a force."

The vocal and always opinionated James Grant also recorded his observations on the rather clever maneuver. "Not just chusing to take the Bull by the horns we disappointed Washington and turned his Right the 8th by a forced march from Pencader by Newark to New Garden," the general boasted, "a handsome Move of 14 Miles which He did not think us equal to, knowing the state of our carriages & in fact was so much disconcerted upon finding that We might by a subsequent Move get possession of the Heights of Wilmington, that He quit his Camp in the night & fled with precipitation over the Brandy Wine."[37]

36 Clark, "Diary," 97-98; McGuire, *Philadelphia Campaign*, vol. 1, 160-161.

37 Von Muenchhausen, *At General Howe's Side*, 30; Whinyates, ed., *Services of Downman*, 32; Grant to Harvey, October 20, 1777, Grant Papers.

The British move left Washington scrambling to reestablish his position by moonlight, shifting his army to find new defensive ground to get his troops between Howe and Philadelphia. Joseph Clark recalled that the army had a good position, "such that the enemy could not pass that way to Philadelphia without meeting our army, and thereby bringing on a general engagement. . . . [T]hey, this night," Clark continued, "by a road, with good guides, got privately round our right wing of encampment and was advancing towards Philadelphia by the Lancaster road; we, however, got word of it in time, and the whole army moved at 1 or 2 o'clock at night." Fortunately for Clark, he was made aware of the early morning movement when another officer he was sharing a house with was notified that the army was moving. The brigade's major, wrote a relieved Clark, "woke me up and we came off in the night and joined the army before day."[38]

Washington did his best to couch the stolen march in a positive light. "The Enemy advanced towards us Yesterday with a seeming intention of attacking our post near New port," he explained in a letter to William Smallwood, who was organizing the Maryland militia. "We waited for them all day, but upon reconnoitering their situation in the Evening, we judged they only meant to amuse us in Front, while they marched by our right flank and gained the Heights of Brandiwine. Viewing things in this light, and the consequences that would necessarily follow if such an event took place," continued Washington, "It was thought advisable that we should change our ground and gain the Heights before 'em. This we are attempting, and I doubt [not] shall effect." Left with no choice, late on the night of September 8 and early the next morning, the Continental Army pulled out of its defensive position, marched north on a route closely parallel with Howe's, and crossed into Chester County, Pennsylvania.[39]

It is not clear why Washington assumed Howe was heading for Chads's Ford on the Brandywine River. Multiple American officers, in letters and diaries, acknowledged the same belief. That night the British forces were camped along a road leading to Lancaster, not Philadelphia. American storehouses at Lancaster, York, and Reading were a logical target, and targeting them was something Washington should have feared. Howe was now between Washington and those storehouses, and there was little the Americans could do

---

38 Clark, "Diary," 98. Lancaster Road is modern-day Route 41.

39 Chase and Lengel, eds., *Papers of Washington*, vol. 11, 179-180.

about it. Even if they could have gotten around Howe to protect the stores, such a move would have left the capital unprotected. Perhaps it was that knowledge that convinced Washington to protect the one thing he could still defend—Philadelphia.

Once outflanked from Red Clay Creek, the next defensible ground south of Philadelphia was at the Brandywine River. The main route across the Brandywine, the Great Post Road, used Chads's Ford. If Washington made the decision that night to get around Howe to protect Philadelphia, then Chads's Ford on the Brandywine was the logical place to take his army.[40]

The Local Area

By the time the sun rose on September 9, elements of both armies were moving into Chester County, one of the three original counties established in Pennsylvania by William Penn. The village of Chester (founded as Upland by the Swedes in the late 1630s) on the Delaware River was the site of the earliest European settlement in the state. The earliest settlement in the Brandywine Valley seems to have been established in the late 1600s. The name Brandywine probably derived from Andren Brainwinde, a Dutch settler who moved into the area around 1670. The valley's landscape closely resembles parts of England and Wales, making the location a natural choice for settlers. Quaker and Baptist meetinghouses were in place nearby as of 1718.

Chester County was mainly rural, with no towns of any significant size. Its rolling hills were covered with thick hardwood forests of chestnut, hickory, and oak, and the well-watered limestone topsoil was some of the best on the continent. "This region of Pennsylvania is extremely mountainous and traversed by thick forests; nevertheless it is very well cultivated and very fertile," observed Hessian Johann Ewald. The majority of the residents were farmers. According to James Lemon's *Best Poor Man's Country*, an average landholding in Birmingham Township, where most of the fighting would soon take place, was 110-133 acres.[41]

---

40 I use the 18th century spelling for Chads's Ford. At the time of the battle, fords were named after the home or property closest to the crossing point. In this case, that was the property of the widow of John Chads. The modern spelling—"Chadds Ford"—is a 19th century spelling.

41 Ewald, *Diary*, 80; James T. Lemon, *The Best Poor Man's Country: Early Southeastern Pennsylvania* (Baltimore, 1972), 91. The size was recorded in 1782.

Local families grew and made most of what they ate or used, supplementing remaining needs with trips to Wilmington or Philadelphia. Farm life was regulated by the seasons. During a typical September, the buckwheat fields, which would be harvested the following month, were in full bloom. Orchards dotted the region with apples and peaches ripe for the picking; cherry trees had recently yielded their fruit. Farm families plowed empty fields to plant winter wheat and rye, re-stuffed beds with straw, weeded gardens, hauled wood ash to the fields, brewed beer, and bagged and sorted seeds. A discerning eye would pick out smaller fields of flax, used for making linen. The tall corn needed for animal fodder was still green in September.[42]

Christopher Marshall, an elderly apothecary who had a shop in Philadelphia, had moved out to the country in the spring of 1777 to get away from the disease and political tensions pulsing through the capital city. The region impressed him. "Now the Indian Corn & Buckwheat makes a pleasing object, add to which the trees bending beneath the ripening Fruits, Herds of Cows, and Oxen keep fattening on luxuriant Pastures, yet my heart is heavy in the Contemplation of the distress that our once happy Land is now plunged in." The armies were drawing close. "Cast thy Eyes down into Chester County see the numbers there engaged in the Mutual Destruction of our friends and Country men, by a Banditi Sent by a monster headed by a villain, guided and directed by Rascalls and Trators to their Country," continued Marshall. "My heart recoils at the thought of such numbers of fine plantations pillaged laid wast and ruined."[43]

Except for iron manufacturing in the Schuylkill River valley, Chester County had no large-scale industry. Even after the Revolution, the Brandywine River valley never developed into an active trading or manufacturing center. However, there had always been a sprinkling of artisans or craftsmen to augment the self-sufficient husbandry men. It was not unusual for a farmer to also practice a trade, such as cabinetmaking or blacksmithing. Weaving was a cottage industry, and itinerant butchers, tailors, and cordwainers traveled the county.

Chester County boasted a population of 21,000 people when Washington and Howe brought war within its borders, about 500 of whom were slaves.

---

42 McGuire, *Philadelphia Campaign*, vol. 1, 166.

43 Christopher Marshall to "Respected Friend, letter dated 20 September 1777," Christopher Marshall Papers.

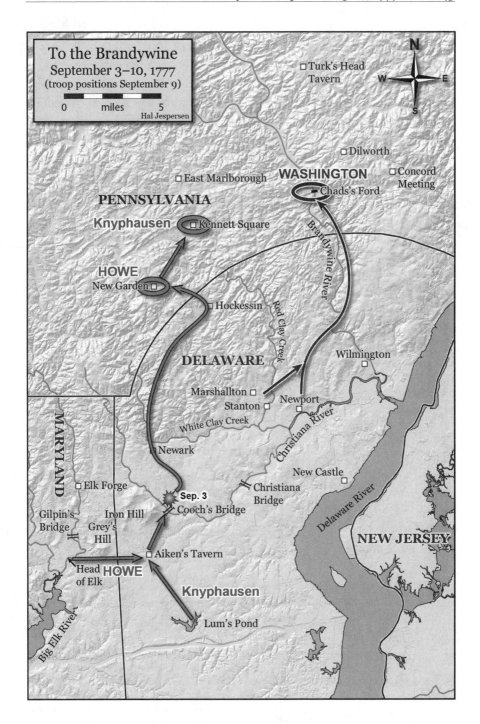

To the Brandywine
September 3–10, 1777
(troop positions September 9)

0   miles   5
Hal Jespersen

N
W   E
S

Turk's Head
Tavern

Dilworth

East Marlborough   WASHINGTON   Concord
Meeting
PENNSYLVANIA   Chads's Ford

Knyphausen   Kennett Square

HOWE
New Garden

Hockessin

Brandywine River

Red Clay Creek

DELAWARE   Wilmington

Marshallton
Stanton   Newport

White Clay Creek

Christiana River

Newark

MARYLAND   New Castle

Elk Forge

Christiana
Bridge

Gilpin's   Iron Hill
Bridge   Grey's
Hill

Sep. 3
Cooch's Bridge

Delaware River

Aiken's Tavern   NEW JERSEY

Head HOWE
of Elk   Knyphausen

Lum's Pond

Big Elk River

Only the county seat, Chester, had a population of 200 (by 1800). The rest of the "urban" population resided in tiny hamlets at crossroads centered on taverns, mills, and ferries. Blacksmith shops, other shops, and tanneries also provided natural meeting places. Shopkeepers or affluent farmers sometimes provided local banking services and distilled liquor for their neighbors. The most prosperous farmers usually operated grist mills, and by 1777 several were in place along the Brandywine and its tributaries. These included Butcher's textile mill, Fred's and Chads's grist mills, and Jones's and Brinton's Mills farther north. Milling persisted in the battlefield region well into the 20th century.[44]

Although almost exclusively rural, the major road linking Philadelphia with other cities farther south passed right through Chester County, and the American capital was within a day's journey of most of the county. Philadelphia drew the county's trade, its farmers exporting one-third to one-half of their wheat crop through the city, which also provided professional services and served as the county's religious, political, social, and cultural center. In addition to its farmers and millers, the region was home to a variety cabinetmakers, clockmakers, doctors, self-taught mathematicians, and scientists, with several members of the American Philosophical Society among them.

The intercourse between the county and Philadelphia kept the area in touch with the events of the day, but the region was far enough away from the commercial center to be self-reliant and able to live separately from Philadelphia, if necessary. The restrictive trade laws imposed by England that fueled the Revolution had little effect on the everyday life of the county's local residents.

New England soldier Elkannah Watson left perhaps the most descriptive contemporary narrative of the region, one that emphasized the contrast between freedom and slavery:

> Most of the slopes of the hill-sides are laid out into regular farms, and are under high cultivation. The verdure of the fields, and the neatness and superior tillage of the farms

---

44 McGuire, *Philadelphia Campaign*, vol. 1, 164; John B. Frantz and William Pencak, eds., *Beyond Philadelphia: The American Revolution in the Pennsylvania Hinterland* (University Park, PA, 1998), 1-2. Of two on the battlefield, Dilworth best retains its 18th century crossroads configuration. Present-day Chadds Ford seems to have taken on a more linear aspect about the time a covered bridge was erected a few hundred feet below the old ferry crossing in the 1830s; Frantz and Pencak, eds., *Beyond Philadelphia*, 2; McGuire, *Philadelphia Campaign*, vol. 1, 165.

in the rich vales, were so grateful to the eye, after being long accustomed to southern aspects. . . . The contrast, so obvious and so strong, in the appearance of these farms and of the southern plantations, will strike every observer, and can be imputed to but one cause. Here we witness the impulses and results of honest industry, where freemen labor for themselves. There we see the feeble efforts of coerced labor, performed by the enervated slave, uninspired by personal interest, and unimpelled by a worthy ambition. These distinctions are perceptible even between Maryland and Pennsylvania, separated only by an imaginary line."[45]

Indeed, the armies were shifting from an area distinctly southern in character to a region much more northern in sensibilities. Traditional southern culture was well known for its open hospitality and warmth. The same could not be said of Pennsylvania in general and rural regions in particular, where residents were much more aloof and resistant to displays of friendship and hospitality. One writer attributes this emotional distance, at least partly, to the "quietism" of the Quakers and many German sects, "who generally frowned upon outward display and, beyond commerce and marketing, mostly kept to themselves."[46]

Only a small proportion of the area's population supported the war. Most remained neutral for religious reasons or leaned toward the English side of the ledger. The eastern townships, where the battle of the Brandywine would be fought, had been settled largely by British Quakers for nearly a century, and Quakers comprised about 40 percent of Chester County's entire population. Their neutrality garnered contempt from the American soldiers, who viewed the Quakers as little more than Loyalists for not supporting the military effort to sever ties with England. "The villainous Quakers," complained Nathanael Greene in a letter to his wife, "are employd upon every quarter to serve the enemy. Some of them are confind and more deserve it." Joseph Townsend, a young man growing up along the Brandywine River and a Quaker, disagreed with Greene's characterization. "A majority of the inhabitants were of the Society of Friends, who could not consistently with their principles take any active part in the war," he explained, "and who generally believed it right to

45 Winslow C. Watson, ed., *Men and Times of the Revolution; or, Memoirs of Elkannah Watson, Including Journals of Travels in Europe and America, From 1777 to 1842, with his Correspondence with Public Men and Reminiscences and Incidents of the Revolution* (New York, 1856), 62.

46 McGuire, *Philadelphia Campaign*, vol. 1, 165.

remain at their dwellings, and patiently submit to whatever suffering might be their lot, and trust their all to a kind protecting Providence."[47]

The populace in southeastern Pennsylvania—neutral, loyalist, or otherwise—was consumed with fear that September. Reports from New Jersey of British burning and pillaging had filtered into the region. Civilians were especially worried about the Hessians, who had a well-earned reputation for looting and cruelty. "Here are some of the most distressing scenes imaginable," Gen. Greene wrote his wife. "The Inhabitants generally desert their houses, furniture moveing, Cattle driving and women and children traveling off on foot. The country all resounds with the cries of the people. The Enemy plunder most amazingly."[48]

The Brandywine, at Last

By the evening of September 9, Washington's army had marched a dozen miles from Red Clay Creek and crossed the Brandywine River at Pyle's Ford, about one mile south of Chads's Ford. Good marching and prompt decision-making regained the defensive advantage Washington had lost the previous day. His men were now behind yet another formidable body of water and between Howe and Philadelphia. According to a member of the 1st Continental Light Dragoons, the men had "set off with all the Baggage to Dilworths Tavern," which was about one mile northeast behind the new Continental defensive positions. Through at least September 9, Washington kept his baggage train close to the army.[49]

The march into Pennsylvania exhausted the men. One Pennsylvania officer remembered "being extremely fatigued for want of rest and severe marching." Well aware of both the good marching his men had just performed and their exhaustion, Washington included in his general orders for the day that, "such of

---

47 Frantz and Pencake, eds., *Beyond Philadelphia*, 4; Showman, McCarthy, and Cobb, eds., *Papers of Greene*, vol. 2, 163; Townsend, *Some Account*, 19. There were several ways for a Quaker to be disowned from their faith, not the least of which was supporting either army in any way. For Quakers, transgressions included joining the military; paying for a substitute to avoid military service; driving a team and wagon, collecting forage, or working as a smith for an army; paying taxes to support the war; and even becoming a tax collector. Mowday, *September 11, 1777*, 54.

48 Showman, McCarthy, and Cobb, eds., *Papers of Greene*, vol. 2, 154-156.

49 Reed, *Campaign to Valley Forge*, 110; Baylor Hill, *A Gentleman of Fortune: The Diary of Baylor Hill, First Continental Light Dragoons, 1777-1781*, ed. John T. Hayes (Ft. Lauderdale, FL, 1995), vol. 1, 69.

the troops as have not been served with Rum to day, are as soon as possible to be served with a gill a man." Providing the men with liquor after some special service or fatiguing march was common practice for both armies throughout the war, and the men appreciated the gesture nearly as much as they did the alcohol. Washington also ordered that the "Major and Brigadier Generals of the day, accompanied by the Quarter Mr General, will immediately reconnoiter the environs of the camp; and fix on the proper places for the posting of picquets, for its security."[50]

*   *   *

While the American Army was on the move, Howe's army was also heading north on a parallel course. In the middle of the day, the British crossed the Delaware state line into New Garden Township, Pennsylvania. As one German officer recalled, "the inhabitants of this region are generally Quakers, who since they did not want to participate in the war, did not flee, but arrived in crowds and asked for protection. Here, in this area, the army found an abundance of everything, through which the insatiable appetite of the soldier was satisfied to the greatest extent." Another jaeger officer also noted the differences between Pennsylvania and other places he had been. "I must note here in Pennsylvania, that the inhabitants are encountered everywhere. This province is more loyal to the King than all the others. Therefore," he concluded, "nothing is taken from the inhabitants." While the jaegers may not have been widely plundering private property during their move into Pennsylvania, pillaging by the British Army as a whole would soon plague the entire region.[51]

Howe's army moved along two roads in two columns. General Wilhelm von Knyphausen's column reached Kennett Square, approximately six miles west of Chads's Ford, late that night. Washington's men were positioned on the opposite side of the ford, and Wilmington was only a dozen miles distant. Howe originally intended for Knyphausen to stop at New Garden Meetinghouse, and sent von Muenchhausen forward with some dragoons to halt him. "The General [Howe] assumed that he would be able to catch up with

50 James McMichael, "Diary of Lieutenant James McMichael, of the Pennsylvania Line, 1776-1778," *The Pennsylvania Magazine of History and Biography*, William P. McMichael, ed. (Philadelphia, 1892), vol. 16, 129; Chase and Lengel, eds., *Papers of Washington*, vol. 11, 174.

51 McGuire, *Philadelphia Campaign*, vol. 1, 167; Ewald, *Diary*, 81; Burgoyne, trans. and ed., *Enemy Views*, 171.

General Knyphausen before he reached New Garden Meeting because his march would be slowed down by the large amount of baggage, cattle etc," explained von Muenchhausen. "We also were instructed to inform General Knyphausen that he should march early the next morning toward Kennett Square with the greatest precaution, because Washington's foreposts were already at Welch's Tavern." Welch's Tavern was just to the east of Kennett Square. By the time Howe's aide caught up with Knyphausen, however, he was already entering Kennett Square. "It was absolutely impossible for him to return to New Garden Meeting because of the loaded wagons and the ravined roads," von Muenchhausen continued. "Knyphausen permitted no fires, and was as quiet as possible, so that Washington who was nearby, would not discover his presence." Knyphausen's division camped on the eastern side of the village.[52]

Howe's second column marched into Kennett Square early the next morning under Gen. Charles Cornwallis and then another a good hour or so beyond to the right as far as East Marlborough, where it finally went into camp. For all intents and purposes, Howe's army was once again reunited.[53]

The roads the British Army took to reach Kennett Square were not of the highest quality. Many were quite narrow, and rain on the night of September 9 made moving the artillery and heavy baggage wagons even more difficult than usual. Engineer John Montresor described "[o]ur march this day about 6 miles through an amazingly strong country, being a succession of large hills, rather sudden with narrow vales, in short an entire defile." Since much of the movement occurred at night, brigades became separated from one another. Making sense of directions during the dark, wet night was often problematic, especially at the various crossroads along the way. "The line of baggage was produced, by the badness of the road and insufficiency of the horses, to a very great length," recorded Capt. Andre, "and the 4th Brigade, which was in front of it, had by quickening their pace to reach General Knyphausen, gained so much upon the carriages that there was a space of two or three miles between them. It was with some difficulty at a cross-road that it was ascertained which way the front of the column had passed."[54]

---

52 Von Muenchhausen, *At General Howe's Side*, 30; Reed, *Campaign to Valley Forge*, 111.

53 Ewald, *Diary*, 81.

54 McGuire, *Philadelphia Campaign*, vol. 1, 168; Montresor, "Journals," 449; Andre, *Journal*, 44.

Howe's move shifted his army into Pennsylvania to a point just west of the Brandywine River. The Americans, who were digging in behind the stream, were once again within reach for a general engagement. Eight days had passed since Howe cut loose from the fleet, and just two days remained until he was expected to meet up with his brother and the supply ships at New Castle.

Howe spent September 10 sending out scouting parties to learn all he could about the terrain from local Loyalists. Washington did much the same thing in an effort to glean knowledge about the roads and terrain along the Brandywine River. Knowledge—or lack thereof—of the roads and surrounding terrain would be play a large part in the battle about to be waged.

Chapter 8

The Continental Army
September 10, 1777

"I am exceedingly fatigued. I was on Horse back for upwards of
thirty hours and never closd my Eyes for near forty."[1]

— Nathanael Greene, September 10, 1777

The New Continental Army

Throughout September 9, 1777, the various
elements comprising Gen. George
Washington's Continental Army began arriving in the vicinity of Chads's Ford,
in southeastern Chester County, Pennsylvania. The patriot army included both
Continentals and militia, and not just Americans but Canadians and Europeans
as well. Even women and children marched with the army.

The army Washington marched into Chester County that September was
not yet the veteran, professional force it would become later in the war. These
regiments had not yet gone through the training and professional
transformation awaiting them at Valley Forge during the winter months to
follow. While many of the men and officers had invaded Canada, fought around
New York City, and taken part in the battles of Trenton and Princeton, just as
many others had seen virtually no action at all. Most of the first set of

enlistments had expired the previous year, and it had taken Washington the entire spring and much of the summer to rebuild his army. Many officers were thus new to their roles, and many of the regiments had not existed in their current form the previous year.

Desertion and the refusal to serve more than a single enlistment had been a constant problem for Washington since the day he assumed command of the army in 1775. Washington worried about losing troops throughout the summer of 1777. The bulk of the men, enlisted or otherwise, left the ranks for what they believed were legitimate reasons. They had farms to run, businesses to keep out of debt, and wives and children who had been left alone for months on end. More day-to-day, corporeal concerns also drove them from the ranks. They were cold, hungry, lacking proper clothing, unpaid, and often angry about missing promised bonuses. Others left because they hated having to report to French officers. Like in any army at any time in history, some simply hated officers. Many feared contracting smallpox and other diseases common to Washington's army. "One of the hallmarks of army culture was the filth in which enlisted men lived," explained one historian. "It also reflected common American resistance to European regular army-style discipline, as their British enemies maintained relatively more hygienic camps." It was not uncommon for troops to desert after just a few weeks of service.[2]

Washington realized the soldiers had "such an unconquerable desire of returning to their respective homes, that it not only produces shameful, and scandalous Desertions among themselves, but infuses a like spirit in others." "Again," he continued, "Men accustomed to unbounded freedom, and no control, cannot brook the Restraint which is indispensably necessary to the good order and Government of an Army; without which, licentiousness, and every kind of disorder triumphantly reign."[3]

Some units in the army had served across northern New Jersey and in northern Delaware earlier in the campaign. Most of the enlisted men who would fight at the Brandywine, however, had never faced veteran British and German troops. Thousands of these professionals were now camped just a few miles to their west.

---

2 Chadwick, *The First American Army*, 171; Gregory T. Knouff, *The Soldiers' Revolution: Pennsylvanians in Arms and the Forging of Early American Identity* (University Park, PA, 2004), 87. Pancake, *1777*, 74-5.

3 Fitzpatrick, ed., *Writings of Washington*, vol. 6, 110-11.

In the midst of the 1776 Trenton campaign, Congress authorized the recruitment of 88 regiments. Washington was also authorized to raise an additional 16 infantry regiments, three artillery regiments, 3,000 dragoons, and a corps of engineers. However, by the middle of May 1777, only 43 regiments had been assembled, averaging 200 men each. While the Continentals modeled their regiments after the British formations, they were not exact copies. For example, American regiments did not have grenadier and light infantry companies as part of their organization. While British colonels never commanded their regiments in the field, American colonels held the tactical command of their units until January 1778. In addition, noted historian John Luzader, "The number of companies and the strength of American regiments varied from state to state and from time to time."[4]

Despite these variables and circumstances, new recruits continued to arrive in number throughout the campaign, allowing Washington to field a respectable force at the Brandywine. Almost as important as the manpower were the supplies that had been stockpiled over the winter. These invaluable French imports enhanced Washington's army, and included 20,000 muskets, 1,000 barrels of gunpowder, 11,000 musket flints, and a wide assortment of clothing and blankets.[5]

The new recruits at the Brandywine were also different from those who had come earlier. Much of the patriotic ardor of the early months of the war had worn off, making recruitment much more difficult. The military setbacks of 1776 had a direct impact on the social status of recruits and the readiness of others to join. Military discipline, high mortality rates, and the rigors of camp life further served to discourage reenlistment. Paying a cash bounty to induce young men "of low social and economic status and those with few other options into the ranks of the army" became common.[6]

Although there were some factors that attracted recruits throughout the war (boredom, friendship, bounties, a desire to see the world or get away from parental supervision, and the political cause), as time passed, it became more difficult for recruiters to locate suitable replacements. After the Continental Congress introduced troop quotas for each state in 1777, wrote one historian,

4   Luzader, *Saratoga*, 226-7.

5   Pancake, *1777*, 78-9.

6   Caroline Cox, *A Proper Sense of Honor: Service and Sacrifice in George Washington's Army* (Chapel Hill, NC, 2004), 3.

"recruiters began to turn a blind eye to race in an effort to get men in the service." British deserters, Africans, and drifters were not accepted in 1775, but all that changed just two years later. "By 1777 a more realistic attitude dictated the acceptance of such undesirables, slaves and convicts. This was often the result of state laws which permitted men called to duty to furnish substitutes, and if the price was right recruiters accepted almost anyone."[7]

When Congress turned the responsibility for recruitment over to the individual states, each was, as noted, assigned a quota. Bounties and promises of land helped the states meet their requirements. "Such inducements make it clear that while some few of the troops may have joined the army because they felt an obligation to do their duty such high-minded motivation did not suffice for most." The simple fact was that most of the troops had stronger ties to their local townships and states than to any national cause. Regarding the manpower issue and motives, by the end of 1777 Washington would observe, "we may fairly infer that the country has been pretty well drained of that class of Men, whose tempers, attachments and circumstances disposed them to enter permanently, or for a length of time, into the army; and that the residue of such men, who from different motives, have kept out of the army, if collected, would not augment our general strength in any proportion to what we require."[8]

The upshot was that by the beginning of 1776, Washington had authorized the enlistment of free blacks, and the next year Rhode Island, New York, and Maryland approved enlisting slaves, who were promised their freedom in exchange for honorable service. By the fall of 1777, Africans could be found mixed in among the regiments positioned along the Brandywine. While a black soldier was often subjected to the same racial prejudices found elsewhere in eighteenth-century society, the army provided him with food, clothing, and shelter. His plight usually consisted of undesirable duties, such as orderly, cook, teamster, and other forms of laborious work. Despite this, there was little incentive for these men to desert, so they usually served out their full terms of enlistment.[9]

While Washington managed against long odds to rebuild the army during the winter of 1776-1777 at Morristown, his troops were still new to army life.

---

7   Cox, *A Proper Sense of Honor*, 12, 17.

8   Fitzpatrick, ed., *Writings of Washington*, vol. 10, 366.

9   Pancake, *1777*, 75-76.

Discipline was lacking within most of the units. "The men were by nature individually independent, and no officer at hand had the required time, experience and popularity to administer drill with needed severity," was how one historian put it. "It was only the dream of liberty, and love for the Commander-in-Chief that kept the army in any measure cohesive." Most of these men would have followed Washington into hell itself and were willing to endure any task he required.[10]

Just as Washington's troops often lacked discipline, so did his officers often lack maturity, which constituted a major discipline problem in its own way. Unfortunately for Washington, he was constantly working to settle petty problems within his officer corps. A dispute between officers over rank was a typical and occasionally thorny issue. Often, the aggrieved officers submitted requests for permission to resign, which obligated the commander in chief to smooth over hurt feelings to keep his men together. Many officers refused to lead by example, which in turn added to the lack of discipline among the troops. Officers were frequently guilty of the same offenses as the enlisted men, including desertion, drunkenness, and pillaging. Washington was forced to address the conduct of his officers time and again throughout the war. "It behooves every Man to exert himself. It will not do for the Commanding Officer of a Regiment to content himself, with barely giving Orders, he should see (at least know) that they are executed," directed Washington. "He should call his men out frequently and endeavor to impress them with a Just and true sense of their duty, and how much depends on subordination and discipline." Washington was also aware that the officers needed to set themselves apart from their men; otherwise their subordinates would treat them as equals and regard them "as no more than a broomstick, being mixed together as one common herd; no order, nor no discipline can prevail; nor will the Officer[s] ever meet with that respect which is essential to due subordination."[11]

The state of the army and the quality of its opposition would have discouraged almost anyone other than Washington. Luckily for Washington and the American cause, Gen. Howe's delays and halting approach to the 1777 campaign allowed what one observer called the "haphazard organization of the Continental Line [to] become more stabilized. Both the regiments and Washington's generals had acquired experience in troop movement and

10 Reed, *Campaign to Valley Forge*, 54.

11 Ibid.; Fitzpatrick, ed., *Writings of Washington*, vol. 6, 13, 110.

administration—but not combat. The army was now organized into divisions, and several major generals were beginning to emerge as competent commanders."[12]

One of the myths of the American Revolution is that the Continental Army that defeated the British Regulars was composed of Indian fighters, crack shots, and men who had spent their lives wielding their deadly long rifles. While certainly some of these types of men were sprinkled throughout the army, the truth is less exciting. The great majority of Washington's men, perhaps as many as nine in 10, were recruited from the cities and villages east of the Appalachian Mountains and were at least one generation removed from the frontier of today's imagination. Many had never seen an Indian nor fired a shot in anger in their lives. However, many hunted game or defended their livestock from predators, and so were at least familiar with firearms.

The majority of Washington's men were carrying not rifled weapons but smoothbores very similar to those carried by the British and Germans they were fighting. These weapons were accurate at about 50 yards or fewer, and took a good 20 to 30 seconds to reload. Even when fired at pointblank range (25 to 30 yards) the casualty rate was surprisingly low. As one historian observed, "Only when soldiers were organized into disciplined ranks so that their limited fire power could be concentrated and controlled could an army be effective."[13] Although Washington insisted that the Continental Army be trained according to the principles of European military science, such training would not take place to any degree until the coming winter at Valley Forge.

The questionable recruiting practices, the newness of the recruits, and the diminishing patriotism do not mean that these men were poor soldiers. Many would prove themselves, and they would become the backbone of the army that ultimately achieved victory at Yorktown. Although it had not yet undergone its complete transformation, the Continental Army was beginning to achieve some level of professionalism. At least some of the senior officers had fought in the French and Indian War, which made them familiar with British tactics and practices. Much of the organization and logistics that Washington attempted to instill in the patriot army were duplications of British precedents. Even many of the junior officers who had been too young to serve during the previous war

12 Pancake, *1777*, 165.

13 Ibid., 66.

had read British publications and English translations of various French and German studies of military science and tactics. It is also important to keep in mind that the army was not completely starting over: A number of the officers and noncommissioned officers now with the army—those who had stayed—had gained experience from the two years of service they had behind them in the current war.[14]

Joining these men along the banks of the Brandywine were camp followers in general, and women in particular. These hangers-on, who included sutlers, wives, and children, attached themselves to every army of nearly every time in history. Washington discouraged the practice and issued orders against their presence, but he also realized that these people helped hold his army together. "He came to accept the followers who helped root the men within the army," explains one historian. "Followers, in turn, further promoted that acceptance through their labor." The women were commonly used as washerwomen and nurses.[15]

Exactly how many troops Washington had in the field in September 1777 remains open to debate. Analyzing the number of troops serving with Revolutionary armies at any given time during the war is difficult, at best. According to the British *Annual Register* for 1776, "all calculations of this nature, though founded upon the best official information, will far exceed, even at a much nearer distance than America, the real effective number that can ever be brought into action." Few troop returns exist for Washington's army. A strength return dated May 20, 1777, survives in Washington's papers. The numbers used herein for Washington's army are therefore based on that return as well as a few additional sources. Most works on the battle of the Brandywine attribute 15,000 men or fewer to Washington during the Philadelphia campaign. However, my analysis gives the Continental Army at the time of the battle of the Brandywine approximately 17,000 men, divided into six divisions and four unattached brigades.[16]

The effectiveness—or lack thereof—of the army arrayed upon the banks of the Brandywine would soon be determined.

14 Luzader, *Saratoga*, 207.

15 John Resch and Walter Sargent, eds., *War & Society in the American Revolution: Mobilization and Home Fronts* (DeKalb, IL, 2007), 238.

16 *The Annual Register, or a View of the History, Politics, and Literature for the Year 1776* (London, 1788), 166.

Army Administration

An analysis of the inner workings of the Continental Army at the Brandywine begins with Washington's personal staff. The men responsible for managing the army's operations included many we will meet on the coming pages, including: Col. Timothy Pickering (adjutant general), Brig. Gen. Henry Knox (chief of artillery), Maj. Gen. Thomas Mifflin (quartermaster general), William Buchanan (commissary general), Dr. Benjamin Rush (head of the medical department), Maj. Gen. Marquis de Lafayette (unattached general), Casimir Pulaski (volunteer aide), Lt. Col. Robert Hanson Harrison (general military secretary), Lt. Col. Alexander Hamilton (aide-de-camp), Lt. Col. Tench Tilghman (aide-de-camp), Maj. John Fitzgerald (aide-de-camp), John Laurens (volunteer aide), Peter Thornton (volunteer aide), Lt. Col. Richard Kidder Meade (volunteer aide), and Capt. Caleb Gibbs (captain of the guard).

Soon after George Washington became commander in chief of the Continental Army in 1775, Congress authorized him to appoint a personal staff of one military secretary and three aides-de-camp. At various times throughout the war, Washington supplemented this authorization with voluntary, unpaid aides. Generals serving under Washington and commanding divisions or other detachments were authorized just two aides-de-camp each.

The general duties of an aide-de-camp were formally described two years later in the *Universal Military Dictionary*. An aide-de-camp was "an officer appointed to attend a general officer, in the field, in winter-quarters, and in garrison; he receives and carries their orders, as occasion requires. He is seldom under the degree of a captain, and all aids-de-camp have 10s. a day allowed for their duty. This employment is of greater importance than is generally believed: it is, however, often entrusted to young officers of little experience, and of as little capacity; but in most foreign services they give great attention to this article."[17]

"The military secretary's job was to compose letters and orders," explained Arthur Lefkowitz while describing the role as it applied to American Revolutionary service in general. "He was selected for his writing skills and discretion since he frequently had access to confidential information. He might be asked, for example, to attend councils of war and keep minutes." While the secretary was to maintain the general's paperwork, the several aides with

17 Smith, *Military Dictionary* (London, 1779), 3.

Washington served as "administrative assistant[s] and personal representative[s]" of the general. "Aides were generally entrusted to deliver important dispatches and other privileged information in camp, on the march, and in battle. During a battle, if there was no time to write a note or dispatch, a general would use one of his aides to deliver verbal orders."[18]

Washington was responsible for not only the army about to face Howe's professionals along the banks of the Brandywine, but also all other Continental units spread throughout the fledgling United States. Therefore, he did all he could to maintain contact with the units he had left in the Hudson Highlands, the army under Horatio Gates dealing with Burgoyne's invasion down the Hudson River valley, and other detached garrisons. He was also responsible for maintaining contact with Congress.

"[Washington] therefore relied on a small cadre of trusted subordinates— primarily his aides—to help him manage the affairs of the army," continued Lefkowitz, "and these men quickly found themselves enmeshed in a multitude of critical issues." Washington's orders had to be transcribed into written documents and copied several times. "Constantly with the commander, constantly in touch with the most important issues of the day, the aides were truly Washington's indispensable men," concluded Lefkowitz. "No one worked more closely with Washington than his aides; except for Martha, no one knew him better." As noted, Washington had no choice but to trust these men and rely upon their discretion. They were privy to sensitive documents "concerning strategy, troop location and movements, the supply situation, unrest in the army, and spy operations," and they often attended his councils of war as well.[19]

Martha Bland, the wife of Theodorick Bland, a senior dragoon officer with the American Army, left a description of Washington's aides in the spring of 1777. She was impressed with them all: "His aid de camps . . . are Col. Fitz Gerald an agreeable broad shouldered Irishman . . . Col. Hamilton a sensible Genteel polite young fellow a West Indian—Col. Meade—Col. Tillman a modest worthy man who from his attachment to the Genl voluntarily lives in his family and acts in any capacity that is uppermost without fee or reward— Col. Harrison Brother of Billy Harrison that kept store in Petersburg & as much like him as possible a worthy man—Capt. Gibbs of the Genls Guard a good

18 Lefkowitz, *Washington's Indispensable Men*, 5-6.

19 Ibid., xvi-xvii, 203.

natured Yankee who makes a thousand Blunders in the Yankee stile and keeps the Dinner table in constant Laugh—These are the Genls family all polite sociable gentlemen who make the day pass with a great deal of satisfaction to the Visitors."[20]

Servants

In addition to Washington's military family, his headquarters featured a staff of servants. After all, he was a wealthy man who was accustomed to certain comforts. He traveled throughout the war with his clothing, toiletries, bedding, tents, dinnerware, silverware, wine, liquor, and food. "This required," Lefkowitz noted in his award-winning book *Washington's Indispensable Men*, "a separate staff of cooks, cooks' helpers, and a steward [Caleb Gibbs] whose job it was to purchase everything consumed by the large household and to keep expense records. The steward was also in charge of all the male servants."[21] Washington's body servant was with him throughout the Revolution, and his aides may have had their own personal servants with them to take care of their clothes, horses, or other belongings. At any given time, some 12 to 15 servants worked in and out of Washington's headquarters.

Washington's housekeeper, a personable Irish woman named Elizabeth Thompson, was 73 at the time of the Brandywine. She supervised Isaac the cook and his assistants and made sure dinner was served promptly at three each afternoon, just as the commander wanted. She also took charge of the laundresses and the other household servants, and supervised the packing and unpacking of headquarters each time Washington shifted locations. However, she could not read or write. Because of this, Caleb Gibbs kept the accounts for Washington's household expenses during most of the Revolution.

Washington purchased a slave named Billy Lee in 1768. While personal servants did not appear in the expense account, it is known that Billy remained with the general throughout the war as his manservant. He addressed the general's personal needs, powdered his hair, laid out his clothes, shaved him, and assisted him in washing and dressing. Notes Lefkowitz: "Billy was an

---

20 Mrs. Bland's letter reproduced in Edward S. Rankin, ed., *Proceedings of the New Jersey Historical Society*, vol. 51, no. 3 (Newark, NJ, July 1933), 152.

21 Lefkowitz, *Indispensable Men*, 70.

excellent horseman and one of the few men capable of keeping up with his master."[22]

A negro by the name of Isaac worked as Washington's personal cook. The position of cook was both a skilled and responsible job, as all wartime foodstuffs were considered precious commodities too important to be wasted. Expensive imported spices and sugar were carefully doled out. Isaac prepared breakfast, a main meal set for 3:00 p.m., and a light meal in the evening. Margaret Thomas was the general's washerwoman. In addition to clothing, she was also responsible for cleaning household linens and tablecloths once a week. Thomas not only took care of Washington's personal clothing but also that of his staff members as well. Frank the hostler was responsible for the general's horses, saddlery, and equipment.[23]

While these personal servants certainly had been with Washington through the winter at Morristown and throughout the campaign across northern New Jersey and northern Delaware, most were not with the general at the Brandywine. Washington had issued orders requesting the officers of the army to travel with minimum extra clothing and directing that excess baggage be sent away from the army for the foreseeable future. Washington normally set the example, and it is unlikely he traveled with this family of servants to the Brandywine; it is more likely these people traveled with the baggage train when it departed the army.

Washington's Headquarters

Washington established the army's headquarters on September 9 at the home of Benjamin and Rachel Ring, about one mile east of Chads's Ford on the Great Post Road. The Ring family lived on the 150-acre farm Benjamin inherited from his father. Across the road from the house along a small creek was Ring's fulling mill and sawmill.

Benjamin was 48 and his wife Rachel was nine years younger (and four months into her ninth pregnancy) when Washington's army settled in along the

---

22 Ibid., 48.

23 These servants comprised the elite of the household staff. References to other servants in the accounts who were not listed by name probably indicate the presence of lower-paid support staff, including cook's helpers, housemaids, coachmen, hostlers, boys, and others to provide extra help with the cooking, washing, grooming, packing and unpacking, etc.

The Benjamin Ring House. Today, this structure is located within Brandywine Battlefield State Historic Site. Washington made his headquarters here during the battle. *Author*

Brandywine. The Rings had been married for 19 years, and had seven living children at the time of the battle: Elias (18), Samuel (16), Thomas (13), Nathaniel (10,) Lydia (8), Rachel (5), and Joshua (2). Another son, Benjamin, died in infancy six years earlier. The Rings had one indentured servant living with them. Although they were Quakers, Benjamin enrolled in the Chester County militia at various times during the war. He was likely not a reluctant host to Washington. If he served as a guide to the local terrain, however, he failed the general terribly.

Construction on the Ring house began around 1720, although details of its original construction are unclear. The structure was likely built in phases—a simple log structure followed by a two-story addition, with a kitchen added later. The house probably had a hipped roof at the time of the battle.

To what extent Washington and his staff used the house itself is open to debate. Washington may have stayed in the house or in a tent in the yard; the staff may have used the home. It may have also hosted war councils. There is evidence Washington and his generals ate at least one meal in the house. Based on Washington's practices in other campaigns, the house was likely the scene of preparations while the yard was filled with the tents of his staff.

During a battle or campaign, Washington tended to avoid housing his men and supplies in civilian households, especially if he did not plan staying long. He had two basic motivations for this. First, he worried about the possibility of boarding with a family still loyal to King George III. Second, he disliked intruding into a family's home and life. When he did use a home, Washington made it a habit to reimburse the owners for the use of the building and its furniture.

Washington and his staff almost certainly planned the Brandywine battle in the Ring house. In addition to the formulation of strategy, one would probably have found aides bent over their desks and tables drafting and copying letters and official orders for Washington to sign. As noted above, a meal was also likely served to the officers in the house following the day of planning.[24]

Nathanael Greene's Division

Major General Nathanael Greene's First Division consisted of approximately 2,500 men.[25] His two brigades were commanded by Brig. Gens. Peter Muhlenberg and George Weedon. Muhlenberg was the son of Henry Muhlenberg, the founder of Lutheranism in America. Peter, who was also a Lutheran clergyman, was educated in Germany and had served in the Prussian army. His brigade consisted of the 1st, 5th, 9th, and 13th Virginia regiments. Weedon was a native Virginian, a veteran of the French and Indian War, and an innkeeper in Fredericksburg before the war. He joined the Continental Army in the summer of 1775 and reached the rank of brigadier in February 1777. Weedon oversaw the 2nd, 6th, 10th, and 14th Virginia regiments, as well as the Pennsylvania State Regiment.

---

24 Just east of the Ring home along the Great Post Road sat the Gideon Gilpin home and farm. At the time of the battle, 38-year-old Gideon Gilpin lived here with his 34-year-old wife Sarah. They had four boys and two girls, all under the age of fourteen. There has been considerable debate whether the Marquis de Lafayette stayed at the Gilpin home prior to the battle or with Washington and his staff at the Ring home. It is possible Lafayette spent one night on each property, but the best primary evidence indicates he stayed at the Ring place with Washington on both nights. See Appendix B for a more detailed discussion.

25 Smith, *Brandywine*, 30; McGuire, *Philadelphia Campaign*, vol. 1, 170. On May 20, 1777, the strength return for six of the nine regiments was 1,338, or an average of 223 men per regiment. If we accept that average for the other three regiments, the division had 2,007 men in May. Since the army was still rebuilding at that point, McGuire's estimate for the division in September is a reasonable assumption.

Greene's division was not only the largest in the army but was also blessed with some of the best leadership. Greene was already considered the best tactician and strategist among the division commanders. His division was the best organized in the army, and Washington never hesitated giving Greene command on the hottest part of the field. Half of the army's Virginia troops were in Greene's division, and "by mid-1777, George Washington believed that the Virginia line of the Continental Army was full of convict servants." A number of indentured servants had been enlisted into Virginia regiments as substitutes for their masters. For many, the enlistment period in the army was likely shorter than the time remaining on their indentures. Also, it was easier to desert from the army than to escape from their "ever-watchful masters." In addition to indentured servants, many free blacks were now allowed into Virginia regiments, a decision that motivated escaped slaves to present themselves as free to recruiters. In addition, the slave masters often sent their slaves as substitutes for their own service. "By the middle years of the war, blacks constituted a significant minority in Virginia's Line in the Continental Army. Because middling and upper-class whites refused to fight for themselves, and because even lower-class whites only reluctantly joined the army, necessity forced white Virginians to rely on blacks for their defense."[26]

Given the responsibilities and stress that rested on his shoulders, it is not surprising that on the eve of the Brandywine battle, Greene wrote to his wife, "I am exceedingly fatigued. I was on Horse back for upwards of thirty hours and never closd my Eyes for near forty. Last night I was in hopes of a good nights rest, but a dusty bed gave me Astma and I had very little sleep the whole night, but little as it was I feel finely refreshd this morning."[27]

Benjamin Lincoln's (Anthony Wayne's) Division

With Benjamin Lincoln absent fighting with Horatio Gates in New York, his division at the Brandywine was under the command of Brig. Gen. Anthony Wayne. The 2,000 men were organized in two brigades commanded by Cols. Thomas Hartley and Richard Humpton. As the senior colonel, Hartley led the brigade in the absence of a general officer. He hailed from York, Pennsylvania,

26 Pancake, *1777*, 165; Resch and Sargent, eds., *War & Society*, 108, 109.

27 Showman, McCarthy, and Cobb, eds., *Papers of Greene*, vol. 2, 156.

and was 28 years old when the army deployed along the Brandywine. During the previous year, Hartley oversaw, along with Benedict Arnold, the evacuation of the post at Crown Point in New York. He commanded the 1st, 2nd, 7th, and 10th Pennsylvania regiments, along with Hartley's Additional Continental Regiment. A native of Yorkshire, England, Humpton was a 44-year-old former British officer who was also commanding his brigade in lieu of a general officer. The brigade contained the 4th, 5th, 8th, and 11th Pennsylvania regiments. Not only were both brigades commanded by colonels, but many of the regiments were led by lieutenant colonels and majors. In other words, a general lack of leadership and experience permeated the organization at all levels.[28]

John Sullivan's Division

The army's Third Division was under the command of Maj. Gen. John Sullivan and consisted of approximately 1,800 men from the states of Maryland and Delaware, and Canada.[29] Sullivan's two brigades fell under the command of the Frenchman Preudhomme de Borre, who could barely speak English, and, presumably, Col. John Stone. Brigadier General William Smallwood, who normally commanded the other brigade, was on detached service raising Maryland militia and would miss the Brandywine battle.

Since Stone was the senior officer, he probably oversaw the brigade during the battle. It contained the 1st, 3rd, 5th, and 6th Maryland regiments along with Hall's Delaware regiment. De Borre had served for 35 years in Europe before volunteering to fight with the Americans. He commanded the 2nd, 4th, and 7th Maryland regiments, the Pennsylvania German Regiment, and Hazen's French Canadians. The German Regiment, heavily recruited from German communities in Pennsylvania and Maryland, was created to counterbalance British efforts to use German soldiers from Europe against the colonies.[30]

---

28 Smith, *Brandywine*, 30-1; McGuire, *Philadelphia Campaign*, vol. 1, 170. The May 20, 1777, strength reports put the division at 1,845. McGuire's estimate of 2,000 represents a reasonable increase for this division from May to September. Wayne could not be made a major general at the time because Pennsylvania's quota was already taken up by Thomas Mifflin and Arthur St. Clair.

29 Smith, *Brandywine*, 30. The May 20, 1777, returns for this division give a strength of just over 1,800 men. Since the division had seen combat prior to Brandywine, any increases from recruiting likely would have been cancelled out.

30 Cox, *A Proper Sense of Honor*, 29-30.

William Maxwell's Light Infantry

Brigadier General William Maxwell was unfamiliar with the area along the Brandywine, so 200 men of the 8th Battalion of Chester County militia under the command of Col. Patterson Bell were attached to his light infantry force. Bell's men were equipped with their own guns and, more importantly were local residents who could provide Maxwell with critical information on local terrain conditions. Although these men had only organized themselves into a unit as recently as the 6th of the month in response to Howe's approach, they were not short on experience. Many had served under Bell in 1776 during the fateful battle of Long Island.[31]

Elements of the 2nd Battalion of Chester County militia under Capt. Allen Cunningham were also across the Brandywine working with Bell's men. The addition of Bell's troops meant that Maxwell's command now numbered about 1,000 light troops.[32]

The Reserve Divisions

Major General Adam Stephen's division of two brigades contained approximately 2,100 Virginia troops under Brig. Gens. William Woodford and Charles Scott.[33]

Woodford was a native Virginian and veteran of the French and Indian War. When the Revolution erupted, he was appointed colonel of the 2nd Virginia Regiment before rising to brigade command. His command included the 3rd, 7th, 11th, and 15th Virginia Regiments. Charles Scott began the war as lieutenant colonel of the 2nd Virginia before gaining command of the 5th Virginia in May 1776. He rose to brigade command in April 1777. Scott's brigade consisted of the 4th, 8th, and 12th Virginia Regiments as well as

31 Smith, *Brandywine*, 9.

32 McGuire, *Philadelphia Campaign*, vol. 1, 171, 172; Smith, *Brandywine*, 31. In early September, 100 men were ordered detached from each brigade in the army to serve in the light infantry. Smith states the militia regiment had 200 men. One thousand men is McGuire's reasonable estimate.

33 Smith, *Brandywine*, 30. The May 20, 1777, strength return for seven of the regiments was 1,711, an average of 244 men per regiment. Applying this average to the other two regiments yields a strength of 2,199, making 2,100 men a reasonable estimate for the division's strength in September.

Grayson's and Patton's Additional Continental Regiments. (Colonel Alexander Grayson had served Washington as an aide earlier in the war.) While the brigades enjoyed admirable leadership, rumors that Stephen was often drunk left a cloud over his division.

The division led by Maj. Gen. William Alexander (Lord Stirling) consisted of about 1,400 Pennsylvania and New Jersey troops. The division's two brigades were commanded by Brig. Gen. Thomas Conway and Col. Elias Dayton. Conway was born in Ireland and appointed brigadier general that May. He was disliked by many in the army for relentlessly drilling his brigade, which contained the 3rd, 6th, 9th, and 12th Pennsylvania Regiments and Spencer's New Jersey Regiment. Dayton became colonel of the 3rd New Jersey in January 1776 and commanded just two regiments at the Brandywine, the 1st and 3rd New Jersey. Just a few months before, Dayton and his regiment had been at Fort Stanwix along the Mohawk River in New York helping repel St. Leger's column moving to support General Burgoyne. The New Jersey brigade was understrength because two of its regiments had been left in northern New Jersey when the army shifted south. Lord Stirling was one of Washington's best division commanders, but he commanded one of the smallest units in the army.[34]

The recently arrived North Carolina brigade of about 1,000 men was commanded by Brig. Gen. Francis Nash. Nash's command was comprised of the 1st through 9th North Carolina regiments, many of which were short of their full complement of officers. Consequently, the brigade's combat ability was questionable.[35]

---

34 Smith, *Brandywine*, 31. The May 20, 1777, strength reports put the division at 1,451 men. Since this division had seen combat, 1,400 men is a reasonable estimate for the unit at the Brandywine. New Jersey soldiers averaged between 18 and 22 years of age and nearly half of them did not own any taxable property—more than twice the proportion of the general population. Twenty percent of New Jersey's soldiers were from another state or were foreign-born, with "no apparent connection to New Jersey society." Between 20 and 40 percent were serving as substitutes for others. As for New Jersey's officers, 84 percent came from the wealthiest one-third of society, and 32 percent from the richest tenth. Less than two percent of these officers had risen from the enlisted ranks. Cox, *A Proper Sense of Honor*, 12-3, 30 & 33.

35 McGuire, *Philadelphia Campaign*, vol. 1, 170. McGuire gives a 1,500-man estimate for this brigade. However, because this brigade was newly formed, it lacked many of its officers. And about two months later it had only 520 men. One thousand men is a more realistic strength for this brigade at the Brandywine.

The Dragoons and the Artillery

The other units in Washington's army consisted of the Light Dragoons Brigade and the Artillery Brigade. The Continental Congress did not authorize dragoon regiments until March 1, 1777—just a handful of months before the Battle of Brandywine. The legislation dictated that each of the four authorized regiments were to have six troops (companies), each consisting of a captain, lieutenant, cornet, and 41 enlisted men. Including regimental staff, each prescribed regiment officially numbered 280. However, due to supply shortages, expense, desertion, and occasional outright mutiny, these regiments rarely numbered more than 150 men. For example, the 4th Continental Light Dragoons was down to about 80 men by the middle of July of 1777. It is therefore reasonable to conclude that Washington had a dragoon brigade of four regiments, numbering no more than 150 men each, for a total of about 600 mounted personnel. Their commanders were Col. Theodorick Bland, Col. Elisha Sheldon, Lt. Col. Francis Byrd, and Lt. Col. Anthony White.[36]

Surprisingly little is known about the Artillery Brigade. Unfortunately, the primary records provide little information on the composition and number of guns with the army at the Brandywine. Commanded by Brig. Gen. Henry Knox, the brigade probably consisted of about 1,600 men in three regiments, plus seven independent companies. Each regiment was comprised of between eight and twelve companies.[37] Portions of the artillery brigade were held in reserve, but artillery was assigned to each division. It is unclear which specific units were so assigned, and which remained with the general artillery reserve.

The American Militia Problem

From the beginning of the Revolution, Washington believed the fledgling country needed a professional army to win the war, and that relying on militia was a losing proposition. Congress believed otherwise, with many of its members arguing that the maintenance of a standing army had been one of the

---

36 Haller, *William Washington*, 32.

37 Smith, *Brandywine*, 31. In January 1778, the artillery companies had about 74 men per unit after suffering heavy casualties throughout the campaign. So 1,600 men is a reasonable number at the time of the battle of the Brandywine. Unfortunately, strength returns do not indicate how many guns and what type.

chief American complaints against England, and that a militia was cheaper and easier to maintain.[38]

Washington's experience with militia dates back to the French and Indian War, when he was exposed to this form of military organization as a young provincial officer. At that time, Virginia law required that every white male over the age of 21 join the local militia. During the mid-eighteenth century, the primary role of militia was the defense of the frontier against Indian incursions. When the French and Indian War broke out, British officials hoped these militiamen could augment regular British troops, but they had been so long out of service that, by that time, the mechanism for raising militia no longer functioned properly. According to historian Edward Lengel, "eligible men ignored the call to enlist, and county officials, who for years had neglected elementary record-keeping, did not know who lived under their jurisdictions." Enforcement of the law was impossible. It was within this context that Washington was tasked with raising a force to defend the Virginia frontier. "Washington," continued Lengel, "sulked for two weeks . . . waiting futilely for men to answer his call, before giving up and returning . . . in humiliation."[39]

Washington's experience as the commander of the Virginia provincial regiment contributed to his belief in the necessity of an established, well-trained military force. Washington believed soldiers fought best within the European system of warfare: professional management, supply stockpiles, plentiful transportation, and high standards for training and discipline. Washington was wise enough to know that there were ways to use militia effectively, but that professional soldiers ruled the battlefield."[40]

After the American Revolution erupted and Washington was named commander in chief, he proceeded to the outskirts of Boston, where he once again had to deal with the militia issue. According to biographer James Flexner, Washington "quickly discovered that commonly no one gave or obeyed any orders. The militiamen, having elected their officers, expected due subservience to the sovereign voters." Washington's experience with the militia during and after the 1776 New York campaign did nothing to alter his negative opinion. On September 15, 1776, Gen. Howe launched his attack from Long Island to

---

38 Lefkowitz, *Indispensable Men*, 76-7.

39 Lengel, *General George Washington*, 30-1.

40 Ibid., 61-2.

Kip's Bay on Manhattan Island and the professional British soldiers easily dispersed the inexperienced American militia, who swept Continental Regulars away with them in their hasty flight to safety. The conduct disgusted Washington, whose desire for an army of professional soldiers only increased. In his eyes, depending upon one-year enlistments and militia was a recipe for failure.[41]

On September 25, 1776, Washington wrote a scathing letter about the militia to John Hancock, the president of the Continental Congress. "To place any dependence upon militia is assuredly, resting upon a broken staff," Washington argued, before moving on in an effort to justify his reasoning: "Men just dragged from the tender Scenes of domestick life, unaccustomed to the din of Arms; totally unacquainted with every kind of Military skill, which being followed by a want of confidence in themselves, when opposed to Troops regularly trained, disciplined, and appointed, superior in knowledge, and superior in Arms, make them timid, and ready to fly from their own Shadows." Washington wasn't finished. "The Jealousies of a standing Army, and the Evils to be apprehended from one, are remote," he insisted, "and in my judgment, situated and circumstanced as we are, not at all to be dreaded." Washington concluded, "If I was called upon to declare upon Oath, whether the Militia have been most serviceable or hurtful upon the whole, I should subscribe to the latter."[42]

One of the issues with militia regiments was the system of rotation practiced by most states. Only a portion of eligible men left for the front at a given time, and then rotated home after a few weeks or months and were replaced by others. What little discipline and training that had been instilled within these men was lost when they left the front for home. Since most of them had never seen combat before joining the army, whatever experience they gained during a campaign or battle was likewise lost when they rotated home. Ineffective militiamen who gained experience only to return to their farms and shops became a vicious cycle for the patriot army. As Washington ruefully acknowledged, "Men who have been free and subject to no controul, cannot be reduced to order in an Instant, and the Priviledges and exemptions they claim and will have, Influence the Conduct of others, and the aid derived from them is

41 Flexner, *Indispensable Man*, 68; Arthur S. Lefkowitz, *The Long Retreat: The Calamitous American Defense of New Jersey 1776* (New Brunswick, NJ, 1999), 11-12.

42 Chase and Grizzard, eds., *Papers of Washington*, vol. 6, 396-7.

nearly counterbalanced by the disorder, irregularity and confusion they Occasion."[43]

As Washington withdrew from New York and entered New Jersey in 1776, there was, according to a letter written to his brother John Augustine Washington, some hope of acquiring assistance from the New Jersey militia. Washington calculated he would be able to add at least 5,000 men to his defeated army.[44] However, according to historian Arthur Lefkowitz, New Jersey's militia were poorly organized and weak. In his history of the army's retreat across New Jersey, Lefkowitz noted that New Jersey militiamen were not quick to leave their homes and families unprotected, did not turn out in large numbers to support Washington, and utterly failed to defend their own state.[45]

The insufficiency of New Jersey's militia prompted Congress to vote in June 1776 to raise militia companies from Maryland, Delaware, and Pennsylvania. These companies were to form a mobile reserve called the Flying Camp. But as the New York campaign progressed, Washington began looking anywhere for reinforcements, and in desperation began drawing units away from the Flying Camp. "Washington," wrote one historian, "came to the grim realization that these poorly disciplined and dispirited troops represented a significant portion of the men still available to him. It was not a comforting prospect."[46]

In his study of the German troops who served in North America, Edward Lowell offered an apt description of the American militia. They were, he noted, "in some respects, more like the clans of Scotch Highlanders in the civil wars of the seventeenth and eighteenth centuries than like modern soldiers. They came or went, as patriotism or selfishness, enthusiasm or discouragement, succeeded each other in their breasts." Lowell thought that even though they were "often intrepid in battle, they were subject to panics, like all undisciplined troops, and were such uncomfortable customers to deal with that it was equally unsafe for their generals to trust them or for their enemies to despise them."[47]

43 Fitzpatrick, ed., *Writings of Washington*, vol. 6, 5-6.

44 Ibid., 397.

45 Lefkowitz, *Long Retreat*, 55-6.

46 Ibid., 38.

47 Lowell, *The Hessians*, 290-1.

Following the battle of Princeton, Washington continued to complain about the militia. The militiamen's lack of discipline and sense of independence infuriated him. Just as Lowell would later observe, Washington himself wrote, "They come and go when they please." He stressed again the importance of building a strong professional army that would be large enough to make the use of militia obsolete for the coming year.[48]

After Washington rebuilt his army during the spring of 1777 and found himself facing Howe's campaign to take Philadelphia, it became clear militia would once again have to be involved in the effort. Congress passed a resolution recommending Maryland call out at least 2,000 men. It also resolved that Pennsylvania collect 4,000 of its militia to assist in repelling the threatened attack, and Delaware another 1,000. Virginia militia, too, was to report.[49]

Pennsylvania's militia arrived without a good reputation. Due to the longstanding influence of Quakerism on the Pennsylvania Assembly, the colony had no official militia system until well into the Revolution. Militia were notoriously ill-trained and poorly disciplined, but the problem was compounded in Pennsylvania. Even compared to the failures of the New Jersey militia, the Pennsylvania militia was worse. "The militia of this country is not like the Jersey militia," observed American division commander Nathanael Greene. "Fighting is a new thing with these, and many seem to have a poor stomach for the business."[50]

Historian Gregory Knouff agreed in his analysis of Pennsylvania combatants. "Militiamen's election of officers and activism in the day-to-day activities of their units shaped their lives as soldiers," he explained. "Not surprisingly, relations between officers and enlisted men were far less authoritarian than those in the Continental army." In other words, because the soldiers elected most of their officers, prospective officers needed to gain popularity among the rank and file. Discipline, as a result, suffered accordingly. "Officers," Knouff continued, "could not afford to alienate their men by brutally punishing them."[51]

---

48 Frank E. Grizzard, ed., *The Papers of George Washington*, Revolutionary War Series (Charlottesville and London, 1998), vol. 8, 531-32.

49 Hazard, et al., eds., *Pennsylvania Archives*, Series 1, vol. 5, 539.

50 Showman, McCarthy, and Cobb, eds., *Papers of Greene*, vol. 2, 154-6.

51 Knouff, *The Soldiers' Revolution*, 82.

The Pennsylvania Militia Act, passed on March 17, 1777, called for obligatory military service for the first time since the French and Indian War. The legislation required service from all white males between the ages of 18 and 53 able to bear arms. However, the act exempted Congressional delegates, members of the Executive Council, judges of the Supreme Court, masters and faculty of colleges, ministers of the gospel, and servants. The basic unit for organizing the militia was the county, but the organizational focus was the company. Eight companies formed a battalion. Under the Act, militia units were to train regularly, and when absenteeism became a problem, members would be fined for missing their training period. The Act also included a provision that allowed the Executive Council to activate portions of the militia in the event of invasion. However, the period of active duty was limited to a mere 60 days.[52]

Prior to the adoption of the Pennsylvania militia system, an informal "association" of concerned citizens forming an ad hoc militia organization had been in place. The effectiveness of the "Associators" varied during each campaign. Although they despised authority, these men bore significant hardships during the winter campaign of 1776-1777. Nevertheless, they lived down to Washington's expectations and deserted in large numbers in 1777.[53]

The result of this checkered history was that by the time Washington's army arrived in southeastern Pennsylvania along the Brandywine, a powerful undercurrent of distrust existed toward John Armstrong's Pennsylvania militia. Armstrong, a native of Ireland and member of the Continental Congress, had the misfortune of commanding the least trusted organization attached to Washington's army. His Pennsylvania Militia Division numbered about 3,000 men.[54]

Good Enough?

And so the American force that mustered in Chester County, Pennsylvania, to meet William Howe's professional army constituted a mixed bag. There were

---

52 Samuel J. Newland, *The Pennsylvania Militia: The Early Years, 1669-1792* (Annville, PA, 1997), 146-7.

53 Rosswurm, *Arms, Country, and Class*, 111.

54 Hazard, *Pennsylvania Archives*, vol. 5, 539. Armstrong stated three days before the battle that he had just under 3,000 men present for duty.

many talented and experienced officers within its ranks. However, despite recent augmentation and improvements, the militia was shaky at best, as was their organization, leadership, and training. The men were dedicated to Washington as commander in chief, but their attachment to the national cause—in competition with state, local, and family concerns—was a thin reed indeed. They were easily swayed and distracted by the supply deficiencies they experienced and the poor examples they saw around them. The result was that no one had any idea how the army would perform when looking across the intervening distance into the barrels of enemy guns.

Chapter 9

The British Army
September 10, 1777

"[The light infantry was] the most dangerous and difficult Service of this War,
therefore you will rejoice with me in my good Fortune in being able to do my
Duty as a Soldier in a line that must be of infinite Service to me here after,
for the Preference in all Promotions is given to Light Infantry Officers."[1]

— William Dansey, March 15, 1777

The Component Parts

The professional European army approaching the Brandywine that
September was similar in some respects to Washington's
American command, but significantly different in others.

The regiment was the basic unit of the British Army. However, "regiment"
was an administrative rather than a "tactical" term. The administrative
commander of a regiment was its colonel, with whom the king contracted to
raise and equip the organization. With the exception of the various "Royal"
regiments, the colonels literally owned their commands and intended, as one
noted historian explained, to "profit financially and socially from that species of
property by selling commissions, receiving a bounty for each recruit,
negotiating lucrative contracts for uniforms, and retaining for each colonel the

---

1 William Dansey to Mrs. Dansey, March 15, 1777, original in the William Dansey Letters.

captaincy of one company." The financial logistics of running a regiment all but guaranteed some level of corruption. The government provided the colonel with an annual sum intended to be used to pay the soldiers, buy clothing for the regiment, and enlist replacements. Any money left unspent found its way into the colonel's pocket. Additionally, colonels often held the rank of general in the field. Generals, however, did not have a pay scale, so the salary of each such officer depended on his "being titular colonel of a regiment—that might or might not be part of his command as a general."[2]

While "regiment" was the administrative term for British Army units, tactically the unit was called a "battalion." For purposes of discussing eighteenth-century operations, however, the terms are synonymous since virtually every British regiment consisted of a single battalion. In the British army, colonels often functioned as generals in field armies and thus did not physically command their regiments (battalions) in the field. Because of this, the regiment's (battalion's) lieutenant colonel normally enjoyed that honor.[3]

Prior to the Revolution, the British army was composed of 70 regiments of foot (infantry regiments). However, the army was enlarged with the onset of war by creating new regiments and adding battalions to the existing regiments. In October 1775, the English government directed that every regiment in America, or slated for service there, be enlarged to provide stronger units for field service and to, as one historian put it, "enhance the recruiting and training infrastructure to accommodate wartime attrition." By the end of the war, 105 regiments were on the rolls.[4]

Every British regiment was composed of eight battalion companies and two flank companies. One flank company was composed of grenadiers, and the other light infantry. On paper, each full-strength regiment consisted of a colonel, a lieutenant colonel, a major, nine captains, 14 lieutenants, 10 ensigns, one chaplain, an adjutant, a quartermaster, a surgeon and his mate, 36 sergeants, 36 corporals, 24 drummers, two fifers, and 672 privates, for a total of 811 men. In reality, the regiments were smaller because of attrition, illness, and other factors. Every British regiment that fought at Brandywine was understrength.

---

2 Luzader, *Saratoga*, 226.

3 Ibid.. The exception at Brandywine was the 71st Highlanders, which went into action with multiple battalions.

4 Don N. Hagist, comp., *British Soldiers American War: Voices of the American Revolution* (Yardley, PA, 2012), 11.

The private soldiers wore plain black shoes with brass buckles, with heavy linen half or full gaiters over the top. Their breeches and waistcoat were of white linen or wool. Grenadiers were often specially trained for particular tasks, selected for their physical size, and were considered elite troops assigned unique headgear.

Battalion Companies

Within the battalion companies, privates were armed with the 15-pound flintlock known as the Brown Bess. This smoothbore musket was carried by most of the American and British soldiers. It fired a large .75 caliber lead ball. The musket's 14-inch bayonet made it a fearsome close-quarters weapon but diminished its already limited accuracy. A dozen separate motions were required to fire the Brown Bess, during which the soldier used his teeth to rip away one end of a paper cartridge so he could sprinkle a small amount into the priming pan before using his ramrod to seat the cartridge and ball down the muzzle. A well-trained soldier could get off up to three shots a minute under combat conditions. Since the bayonet, once mounted, made the loading process more difficult, only a single effective shot could be depended upon. The inaccuracy of the weapon made the volley the officers' preferred method of fire delivery; the difficulty in loading was one of the reasons the British made the bayonet charge their primary assault tactic.[5]

There is a common misconception that the British army fought in rigid lines of battle arrayed shoulder-to-shoulder. In reality, each line of battle consisted of two ranks (with a small interval between each), the men formed in open order about arms-length apart. However, even in open order the men were not spread out such that they operated independently. They still presented a solid mass (and thus a ready target), and delivered volleys at a similarly compact enemy formation at nearly point-blank range. The first two ranks were responsible for delivering the battalion's firepower. Six paces behind them stood a rank of file closers ready to step up and fill the gap created by the wounded and the dead.

Since it was desirable to withhold firing until within about 50 yards of an enemy line, maintaining fire discipline was essential. The prevailing professional opinion at that time espoused that it was better to receive, rather than deliver,

5 Luzader, *Saratoga*, 224.

the initial round of fire, and thus sustain some level of casualies so that when the fire was returned your own men were "close enough to the foe to ensure that every shot found a mark." The strict combat discipline of the British army was one of its greatest attributes.[6]

British soldiers rarely had the opportunity to pick their targets and fire at their own pace or will. Usually the men loaded and fired on command, with very little aiming at a particular person. Smoothbore muskets were very inaccurate, so there was little interest in target practice since the drain on lead and powder was not worth the expense and time. When a battalion delivered a volley fire, the "objective was to lay down a curtain of fire ahead of one's troops at the desired rate of one shot every fifteen or twenty seconds, assuring at least two volleys before closing with the enemy," explained the former historian of the Saratoga battlefield. "The men then resorted to clubbing with their muskets or stabbing with the bayonet, with which the British were famously effective."[7]

Accuracy may have been superfluous, but organized, controlled speed in both firing and movement was essential to success. The faster the defenders could load and fire, the more damage they could inflict upon the approaching attacking force. Contrarily, the faster the attackers could close with the enemy while simultaneously maintaining unit cohesion, the fewer casualties they would sustain and the stronger they would be when they reached their objective. Since the cartridge boxes were usually limited to 30 or fewer rounds, uncontrolled fire would quickly exhaust the ammunition supply. Once the firing began, thick black powder smoke enveloped the battlefield, which compounded the difficulties of officers trying to maintain effective control of their men. The field music of beating drums and tooting fifes, coupled with flags waving above the center of the battalion, could usually be heard and seen above the chaos and thus helped maintain control.[8]

The strict discipline and often harsh living conditions that made life difficult for the average British soldier also molded him into a well-trained and formidable opponent. The monotonous and repetitive drill to which he was subjected created a soldier who "moved when he was supposed to move with predictable precision and speed," wrote one historian of the era. The British

6 Luzader, *Saratoga*, 224.

7 Ibid., 224-225.

8 Ibid., 225.

generals lost several battles during the American Revolution, and eventually lost the war, but through no fault of the men in their ranks.

The officers who led these disciplined soldiers achieved their positions through either social rank or money. Commissions were purchased, and rising through the ranks from subaltern to colonel required either the death of an officer, an officer's retirement, or the sponsorship of a higher-ranking officer or government patron. In other words, many officers owed their position to someone else. This system created officers devoutly loyal to certain colonels or generals, but who would also undermine others within the same army.

There was no official schooling for British officers. Although well-read in military literature, they obtained the vital knowledge of their profession through hard experience. Young subalterns learning the ropes in their teenage years were ably supported by senior sergeants in their companies, proving the old adage that sergeants are the backbone of the army.[9]

Flank Companies and Additional Units

The eighteenth-century equivalent of elite soldiers were assigned to the flank companies of the various regiments. Throughout most of the Revolution, flank companies rarely served with their parent regiments, and were instead "brigaded" together to form battalions of light infantry or grenadiers.

The grenadier company was made up of the tallest and strongest men in the regiment. Originally, their function was to throw grenades into fortifications, but grenades were no longer in use by the time of the Revolution. The grenadier's uniform included a short sword and a tall bearskin cap instead of the cocked hats worn by the battalion men. The light infantry company consisted of fit men who often functioned as rangers or scouts. Their coats were cut short, they wore leather caps and red waistcoats, and carried small cartridge boxes and hatchets.

Both the grenadiers and light infantrymen were typically armed with muskets like the regular soldiers. However, at least some of the British light infantry were armed with British short rifles. Only a limited number of these weapons were sent to North America, and there is evidence that each light company received a small number, but not enough to arm the entire company. While only a limited number of British light troops were so armed, all the

---

9 Pancake, *1777*, 71-72.

German jaegers (the German equivalent of light infantry) were armed with a short jaeger rifle.

A corps of guides and pioneers under the command of Maj. Samuel Holland accompanied Howe's army on the Philadelphia campaign. This unit moved at the front of the marching army to clear obstructions. Holland's corps consisted of 172 men equipped with axes, saws, and shovels in addition to their muskets. They wore heavy leather aprons, gloves, and leather caps. They were permitted to wear beards, and a significant number of them were African.[10]

Artillery

The field artillery of the British army was organized into four battalions of eight companies each. Each company consisted of six officers, eight noncommissioned officers, nine bombardiers, 18 gunners, and 73 matrosses, or privates. The British artillery system was somewhat unique in that the gunners and matrosses were enlisted men, but the drivers were hired civilians.[11]

Artillerymen were usually armed with carbines, which were shorter and lighter versions of an infantryman's musket. Fusilier regiments, such as the 23rd of Foot (Royal Welsh Fusiliers), were originally formed to escort artillery, but served as infantry in North America.

Field guns ranged in size from the large 24-pounders to the small 3-pounders. Since 12-pounders required a large number of horses to haul them, and maintaining horses in North America was difficult, the British preferred using 6-pounders and 9-pounders. It was customary to allot two guns to each infantry regiment (known as battalion guns). However, some officers criticized this practice because it prevented a concentration of artillery fire.

Amidst the wide variety of artillery in the British service, the maximum range of the most powerful piece was about 2,000 yards, but no field gun was considered effective beyond 1,200 yards (and many of the smaller caliber much less than that). The guns were capable of firing solid shot, grape, or canister.[12]

---

10 McGuire, *Philadelphia Campaign*, vol. 1, 140.

11 Pancake, *1777*, 68; Curtis, *The British Army*, 6-7.

12 Artillerymen used solid shot against fortifications or opposing artillery. Grapeshot consisted of clusters of iron balls about two inches in diameter, which either devastated infantry or knocked down fence lines or hedges. Canister was literally a container filled with musket balls. These were the most effective anti-personnel weapons.

Most field pieces delivered their fire on a fairly flat trajectory. Howitzers, however, fired projectiles along a high arc. Exploding shells were set to detonate just above an enemy position, raining shrapnel down upon opposing combatants. The howitzer's shorter barrels, however, reduced their effective range of fire.[13]

Support

By regulation, the British army operating in North America was to be primarily provisioned via shipments from England. The most important provisions received in this manner included beef, pork, bread, flour, oatmeal, rice, peas, butter, and salt. Less important provisions, such as cheese, bacon, suet, fish, raisins, and molasses, also found their way to American shores. In addition, many types of vegetables, including potatoes, parsnips, carrots, turnips, cabbages, and onions, were dispatched by sea, although they were not always fresh or even edible by the time they reached the men in the field. For the most part, they were intended for those recovering in hospitals. Onions, sauerkraut, porter, claret, spruce beer, malt, vinegar, celery seed, and brown mustard seed were used as anti-scorbutics to help ward off scurvy.

Commissary generals constantly complained of moldy bread, biscuits teaming with insects, rancid butter, rotten flour, worm-eaten peas, and maggot-ridden beef. Not surprisingly, men frequently attempted to supplement their diet by foraging (looting) in the American countryside, which in turn led to depredations against civilians.[14]

While the British high command hoped in 1777 that the army would not need to depend on supplies from Great Britain, the army's commissary general often noted that North America could not be depended upon for supplies. The only alternative was the provision train. "No eighteenth-century commander raised in the European tradition would think of taking the field without such a train," explained one historian. "Armies of the period tended to be small and expensive to the point that even victories attended by considerable losses were unacceptable. Aware of the problems of health and morale that accompanied poor and short rations, few commanders willingly trusted the feeding of their

13 Pancake, *1777*, 68-69.

14 Curtis, *British Army*, 88-93.

armies to the chance that sufficient food could be obtained along the line of march." Long provision trains were simply a necessity.[15]

Provision trains, however, required healthy horses and lots of them. This, in turn, required tons of fodder, a precious commodity the British sought to obtain from the North American countryside, and even more horses to haul that fodder. During the planning for the summer campaign, Howe estimated he would need at least 3,662 horses—and all that went with them. Exactly how many horses Howe left with from New York is unknown, but we do know that many died and many more became ill during the voyage to the Chesapeake. While the exact number of horses Howe fielded along the Brandywine is also unknown, it was substantially fewer than the number that boarded his ships. The mobile workshops of blacksmiths, carpenters, harness-makers, and other tradesmen also required draft horses.[16]

As a result of all these needs, Howe's army sat idly several times during the campaign while foragers roamed the countryside seeking food and horses. Even though Washington issued several orders to clear supplies out of Howe's path, there was not enough time to completely achieve all that he desired. The result, observed R. Arthur Bowler, was that "in the first two months after the landings at Head of Elk, the [British] army fed almost every other day on fresh provisions from the well-developed farms of eastern Pennsylvania, long providers of food for the less well-endowed areas of the colonies."[17]

By the time of the American Revolution, England had long had a standing army, which had long recognized the need for an entirely different kind of support: women. Each company had an authorized quota. The return for the British army in New York for May 1777 showed one woman present for every eight men. The presence of women reduced desertions and they performed useful work like mending, cooking, nursing, and laundering. The women who accompanied the army to North America were supposed to be the wives of the enlisted soldiers (the wives of officers rarely accompanied them on campaign). The marital status of these women was often questionable, for proof of a legal marriage was not always required. The women traveled with the baggage wagons on the march, and so did not accompany the men directly.

15 Bowler, *Logistics*, 49, 55-56.

16 Ibid., 58.

17 Ibid., 58-59, 70.

German Auxiliaries

The German forces that served the British army were hired by King George III to support and aid the British war effort in North America. Great Britain was a global empire and so had military commitments throughout the world in Gibraltar, India, Canada, the Caribbean, the American colonies, and of course, the home islands of Great Britain. Military manpower was already stretched to its limits when the American Revolution began in 1775.

Despite popular belief, the German soldiers sent to North America were not mercenaries in the traditional sense, but rather armies from another country hired for use in the colonies. The individual soldiers were not paid by Great Britain directly, and received nothing more than their regular army pay and rations. Instead, England paid the various German princes for the use of their troops. The German soldiers were commanded by their own officers and often were not subject to British military discipline.

Six German rulers hired out their soldiers to Great Britain: Frederick II, Landgrave of Hesse-Cassel; William, his son, the independent Count of Hesse-Hanau; Charles I, Duke of Brunswick; Frederick, Prince of Waldeck; Charles Alexander, Margrave of Anspach-Bayreuth; and Frederick Augustus, Prince of Anhalt-Zerbst. Beceause the German troops sent to North America hailed from separate principalities, they were not all "Hessians," though they have traditionally been referred to by that name. Among those German troops who fought at the Brandywine, however, all but one company of jaegers were in fact true Hessians.

One of the reasons King George III was able to acquire these troops was because he was from the royal house of Hanover. Frederick II (not to be confused with his more famous namesake) of Hesse-Cassel was married to George III's sister. William, the oldest son of Frederick II, was not only the grandson of George II, but also the ruler of Hesse-Hanau. Duke Charles I of Brunswick had his son Prince Charles William Ferdinand marry a sister of George III. Beyond family obligations, Charles Alexander of Anspach-Bayreuth was so deeply in debt that he felt compelled to provide troops to England. The princes of Waldeck were known to raise men specifically for use by other countries, so providing men to England was merely an extension of an existing program. Frederick Augustus of Anhalt-Zerbst sent only a small number of men, and most of these had to be recruited from other provinces.

The British Parliament was not pleased about the hiring of auxiliary troops, and protests erupted in the House. The arguments expressed the supposed danger and disgrace of the foreign treaties involved, which acknowledged to all Europe that Great Britain was unable, either from want of men or their disinclination toward the intended service, to furnish a sufficient number of natural-born subjects for the campaign. Many argued that drawing off the national troops would leave Great Britain exposed to potential assaults and invasions of powerful neighboring and foreign nations, in general, and France and Spain in particular. "We have, moreover, just reason to apprehend that when the colonies come to understand that Great Britain is forming alliances, and hiring foreign troops for their destruction," came one Parliamentary protest, "they may think they are well justified by the example, in endeavoring to avail themselves of the like assistance; and that France, Spain, Prussia, or other powers of Europe may conceive that they have as good a right as Hesse, Brunswick, and Hanau to interfere in our domestic quarrels."[18]

Howe's Staff

Much like the staff Washington assembled to assist him in managing his army, a group of staff officers similarly served William Howe. Brigadier General James Paterson served as adjutant general, and Lt. Col. Stephen Kemble as deputy adjutant general. Brigadier General William Erskine was Howe's quartermaster general.[19] Captain Henry Bruen was his deputy quartermaster general, and Brig. Gen. Samuel Cleaveland was his chief of artillery. Daniel Wier served as commissary general, Capt. John Montresor his chief engineer, Capt. Archibald Robertson as engineer, and Capt. Robert McKenzie as military secretary. Howe had six aides serving him at the Brandywine battle: Majs. Cornelius Cuyler, Nesbitt Balfour, and William Gardiner, and Capts. Henry Fox, Henry Knight, and Friedrich von Muenchausen.[20]

---

18 Lowell, *The Hessians*, 30-31.

19 General Erskine was responsible for supplying the army's non-nutritional needs, from tents, camp kettles, and rope, to candles, shovels, and pickaxes. However, his most important duty was supplying wagons to transport the army's needs. Erskine's system included hired wagons and drivers fed from the quartermaster's funds. Howe dictated the wagon train be large enough to supply his army in the field for three weeks. By the third quarter of 1777, Erskine had 1,376 wagons and 3,111 horses. Erskine's responsibilities were daunting; his failure would have doomed any European army fighting in North America. Bowler, *Logistics*, 25.

20 Of Samuel Cleaveland, Howe's chief of artillery, virtually nothing is known. To date, no biographical information about this officer has been located. Before becoming the adjutant

Charles Cornwallis's Division

Cornwallis's division consisted of about 8,400 men in six brigades and various detachments. All of the troops under his command were veterans, and many of the organizations in which they served were considered the elite units of Howe's army. The division consisted of the following units (with their approximate strength in parentheses): Maj. Gen. Charles Grey's Third British Brigade (1,000); Brig. Gen. James Agnew's Fourth British Brigade (1,400); Brig. Gen. Edward Mathew's Brigade of Guards (1,000); the Light Infantry Brigade (1,300); the British Grenadier Brigade (1,400); Col. Carl von Donop's brigaded Hessian grenadiers (1,300); Lt. Col. Ludwig von Wurmb's Hessian Jaegers (500); Mounted jaegers (100); The 16th Light Dragoons, in two squadrons (200); and Royal artillerymen (200). Lieutenant Colonel Thomas Stirling's 42nd Royal Highlanders (600) were attached directly to Howe's headquarters, and therefore accompanied the column, bringing its total to about 9,000 men.[21]

Cornwallis and his officers would be called upon to play the leading role in the upcoming fight along the Brandywine, and his command was in good hands. Charles Grey, the commander of the Third Brigade, was born in 1729 in Northumberland, England. Since he was not the oldest son and could expect no inheritance, he pursued a military career. In 1744, he purchased a commission as ensign in the 6th Regiment and took part in suppressing the Jacobite rising. Grey spent time in Gibraltar and rose to captain, taking command of a company in the 20th Regiment of Foot. During the Seven Years' War, he was an adjutant on the staff of Duke Ferdinand of Brunswick and was wounded at Minden. Grey participated in a number of other engagements during that war, including Campen, the capture of Belle Ille, Havana, and the repulse of the invasion of

---

general in April 1776, Brig. Gen. Paterson had been the lieutenant colonel of the 63rd Regiment of Foot. Paterson was the officer sent to parlay with Washington for peace prior to the battle of Long Island; Robert McKenzie was a captain in the 43rd Regiment of Foot; Cornelius Cuyler was the major of the 55th Regiment of Foot; Henry Bruen was a captain in the 63rd Regiment of Foot; Nesbitt Balfour was the major of the 4th Regiment of Foot; Henry Fox was a captain in the 38th Regiment of Foot; William Gardiner was the major of the 45th Regiment of Foot; Henry Knight was a captain in the 43rd Regiment of Foot.

21 Smith, *Brandywine*, 29; McGuire, *Philadelphia Campaign*, vol. 1, 183. Strengths are based on commissary reports following the landing at Head of Elk a little over two weeks prior to the Brandywine fight. See "Copies of Letters from Danl. Wier, Esq., Commissary to the Army in America, to J. Robinson, Esq., Secretary to the Lords Commissioners of the Treasury; and from John Robinson, Esq., in Answer thereto in the Year 1777." Dreer Collection. The artillery consisted of four light 12-pounders and six 6-pounders as well as the battalion artillery.

Portugal. In 1772, he was promoted to colonel and served as aide-de-camp to King George III. Grey would become one of the more infamous British generals during the Revolution. His brigade included the 15th, 17th, and 44th Regiments of Foot and the 42nd Highlanders, which was detached to serve as Howe's headquarters guard on the day of the battle.

Brigadier General James Agnew, who led Cornwallis's Fourth Brigade, was born in 1719 in England. It is not clear when he entered the military; he was married before the Revolution. Agnew arrived in Boston in 1775 as a lieutenant colonel, fought on Long Island, and rose to brigade command. Early in 1777 he took part in the raid into Connecticut to seize patriot supplies. He commanded the 33rd, 37th, 46th, and 64th Regiments of Foot at the Brandywine.

Brigadier General Edward Mathew was born in 1729 and became an ensign in the Coldstream Guards in 1746. By 1775 he was a colonel and aide-de-camp to King George III. When the Revolution erupted, he was made commander of the Brigade of Guards, which fought throughout the 1776 New York campaign. The Brigade of Guards Mathew led in America was a special composite force made up of 1,000 men chosen by lottery from the three regiments of Foot Guards. Fifteen men from each of the Guard's 64 companies were selected to serve in America. During the eighteenth century, there were only three regiments of Foot Guards: the First Guards, also known as the Grenadier Guards; the Second, or Coldstream, Guards; and the Third Guards, or Scots Guards. Normally, these regiments were stationed in London or Westminster as bodyguards for the king. The unit was divided into two battalions of 500 men each and, unlike other British regiments, retained its own flank companies while on campaign. The Guards, who functioned much like a light infantry unit during the American campaigns, used common-sense, flexible tactics when faced with heavy gunfire. All of the Guards, officers and men alike, wore uniforms modified for campaign service, including shortened jackets without ornamentation and round hats, under which they wore cropped hair.[22]

The light infantry brigade was composed of the 1st and 2nd British Light Infantry Battalions. These battalions were formed by brigading together the various light infantry companies from regiments stationed in North America. The 1st Light Infantry Battalion, commanded by Col. Sir Robert Abercrombie of the 37th Regiment of Foot, was composed of the light companies of the following Regiments of Foot: 4th, 5th, 7th, 10th, 15th, 17th, 22nd, 23rd, 26th,

22 Curtis, *British Army*, 3.

27th, 28th, 33rd, 35th, 37th, and 38th. The 2nd Light Infantry Battalion, commanded by Maj. John Maitland of the Royal Marines, was composed of the light companies of the following Regiments of Foot: 40th, 42nd, 43rd, 44th, 45th, 46th, 49th, 52nd, 54th, 55th, 57th, 63rd, 64th, and two companies from the 71st.[23]

Flank battalions in general and light infantry battalions in particular were filled with battle-hardened veterans who had already seen severe and successful service in the army. Most British officers were proud to serve in the light companies. William Dansey thought the light infantry "the most dangerous and difficult Service of this War, therefore you will rejoice with me in my good Fortune in being able to do my Duty as a Soldier in a line that must be of infinite Service to me here after, for the Preference in all Promotions is given to Light Infantry Officers."[24]

The British Grenadier Brigade was composed of the 1st and 2nd British Grenadier Battalions. Much like the light infantry companies, the grenadier companies of the regiments stationed in North America had been consolidated into these battalions. The 1st British Grenadier Battalion was commanded by Lt. Col. William Medows of the 55th Regiment of Foot and was composed of the grenadier companies of the following Regiments of Foot: 4th, 5th, 7th, 10th, 15th, 17th, 22nd, 23rd, 26th, 27th, 28th, 33rd, 35th, 37th, 38th, and 40th. The 2nd Grenadier Battalion, commanded by Col. Henry Monckton of the 45th Regiment of Foot, consisted of the following grenadier companies: two Royal Marine companies, and those from the following Regiments of Foot: 42nd, 43rd, 44th, 45th, 46th, 49th, 52nd, 54th, 55th, 57th, 63rd, 64th, and 71st.[25]

Carl von Donop's men were elite Hessian soldiers, and his brigade contained three grenadier battalions at the Brandywine: the von Linsingen, von Minnigerode, and Lengerke. Even though, as noted, Hessian units were often

---

23 The Orderly Book of Captain Thomas Armstrong, 64th Light Company (in the George Washington Papers, available online at the Library of Congress), dates September 15 – October 3, 1777, confirms the composition of the 2nd Light Infantry Battalion. Ensign William, Lord Cantelupe of the Guards painted a chart into the flyleaf of his copy of the list of British officers, published in Philadelphia in February 1778, detailing the composition of the light infantry battalions. These charts are probably 90 percent accurate. Reconstructing the composition of these battalions was possible through the research of Thomas McGuire.

24 Spring, *With Zeal*, 62; William Dansey to Mrs. Dansey, letter dated 15 March 1777, original located in the William Dansey Letters.

25 This information on the composition of the grenadier battalions is based on a conversation with historian Thomas McGuire.

considered to be made up of elite soldiers, one British officer wrote the following, describing a commonly held belief about them: "They were led to believe before they left Hesse-Cassel, that they were to come to America to establish their private fortunes, and hitherto they have certainly acted with that principle."[26]

Wilhelm von Knyphausen's Division

Knyphausen's division contained approximately 6,800 men in three brigades and various detachments. The division consisted of the following units (with approximate strength in parentheses): the First British Brigade (1,400); Maj. Gen. James Grant's Second British Brigade (1,300); Maj. Gen. Johann von Stirn's Hessian brigade (2,200); the 71st Highlanders (1,200); the 16th Light Dragoons, in a single squadron (100); Capt. James Wemys's Queen's Rangers (300); Capt. Patrick Ferguson's rifles (90); and Royal artillerymen (200).[27]

General Knyphausen was also responsible for the army's extensive baggage train, which traveled with his column. Marching with the baggage were 75 New Jersey Volunteers. The three battalions of the 71st Highlanders guarded the baggage train, one battalion marching to the right of it, another to the left, and the third bringing up the rear. It required 131 wagons and 524 horses just to carry a two weeks' supply of hard bread and the other necessities of an army on campaign.[28]

The records are unclear about who led the two British infantry brigades with Knyphausen's column at the Brandywine. However, Gen. James Grant was probably in overall command of the two brigades, as he had commanded an independent division until just before the battle. The First Brigade contained the 4th, 23rd (Royal Welsh Fusiliers), 28th, and 49th Regiments of Foot. The Second Brigade contained the 5th, 10th, 27th, 40th, and 55th Regiments of Foot.

---

26 Lowell, *Hessians*, 86.

27 Smith, *Brandywine*, 29; McGuire, *Philadelphia Campaign*, vol. 1, 173. Strengths are based on a commissary report located in copies of Wier letters at the Historical Society of Pennsylvania. The artillery accompanying Knyphausen's column consisted of six medium 12-pounders, four howitzers, and the battalions' light artillery.

28 Spring, *With Zeal*, 38.

Major General Johann von Stirn, commander of the Hessian Brigade, was born in Borken in October 1712 and entered the Hessian service in 1728. Rising through the ranks of the Regiment Prinz Friedrich, von Stirn was a major by 1757. By the time the Revolution began he was the colonel of the Leib Regiment Infanterie and in command of a brigade in the Hessian army. Through the New York campaign, von Stirn commanded a Hessian brigade under Howe and continued in that capacity in 1777. His brigade consisted of the Leib Regiment, the von Mirbach Regiment, the von Donop Regiment, and the Combined Hessian Battalion. The Combined Hessian Battalion contained the survivors of the fighting around Trenton the previous December from the von Lossberg, von Knyphausen, and Rall regiments.

Little is known about James Wemys other than that he was a captain in the 40th Regiment of Foot and he was in command of the Queen's Rangers at the Brandywine. The Rangers were Americans recruited in 1776 from the loyalist population to serve the British army. British regiments of foot were clothed in the scarlet red coats for which they are famous, but the Queen's Rangers wore green jackets with white breeches. Other units with Howe's army were also dressed in shades other than red. All the Hessian regiments were clothed in blue coats with various levels of trim. The Jaeger Corps wore green jackets faced with red. At various times during the upcoming engagement, uniform colors would confuse men on both sides.

Ferguson's Rifles

Patrick Ferguson was a 33-year-old Scottish officer and captain in the 70th Regiment of Foot's light company. His rifle—the Ferguson Rifle—would play a pivotal role during the opening moments along the Brandywine. The Scotsman was serving with the 70th's light company when he began building and experimenting with a breech-loading weapon he believed the British sorely needed. He sought a way by which a ball and loose powder could easily and quickly be inserted at the breech end of the weapon. To achieve this, he fitted a screw plug that passed vertically through the barrel and was attached to the trigger guard. As the trigger guard was rotated, the plug, cut with a large thread, was withdrawn to expose the open end of the breech. One turn of the trigger guard was sufficient to lower the plug; the bullet was then placed in the hole and the powder poured in behind it. A quick turn of the trigger guard screwed the plug back up, and, apart from the necessary priming, the weapon was ready for firing. A well-trained rifleman could fire up to six times a minute.

Ferguson field-tested one of his rifles for the British military in April 1776. After a demonstration for the royal family later that year, the Master-General of Ordnance stopped producing jaeger rifles and began producing Ferguson rifles instead. The British Ordnance Department ordered 100 of the rifles from four different gunsmiths (25 apiece).

Ferguson was placed in command of a special company of 100 men, whom he recruited mostly from the 6th and 14th Regiments of Foot. After an intense training period, Ferguson and his riflemen arrived in New York in March 1777. His rifles were far more accurate than the standard smoothbores carried by most of the men in the battle and could be loaded and fired while kneeling or lying down. Much like the Queen's Rangers and jaegers, Ferguson's men wore green coats.[29]

British Tactics

British troops were trained to fight with line-of-battle discipline and skills. In Europe, whatever guerilla activities occurred had remained a peripheral nuisance with little or no effect upon the outcome of a war. While some authors wrote about partisan combat in the 1740s and early 1750s, the British military refused during this period to adopt any formal changes to their tactics. They remained convinced that experience and training in European warfare would always prove superior when fighting others following another tactical doctrine. All of that changed when the Seven Years' War reached North American shores.[30]

The Indians utilized small-scale or "guerilla" tactics and were not students of European warfare. Their war parties lived off the land, struck at vulnerable targets with extreme brutality, and then melted back into the woods before they could be attacked. The French, who had befriended many tribes through trade agreements, learned these tactics themselves. The rugged North American terrain lent itself to this style of warfare.

---

29 M. M. Gilchrist, *Patrick Ferguson: A Man of Some Genius* (Glasgow, 2003), 34. For additional information on Ferguson's Rifles, see Appendix E.

30 Peter E. Russell, "Redcoats in the Wilderness: British Officers and Irregular Warfare in Europe and America, 1740-1760," in *LW524: Student Reading Package, APUS Faculty, Fall 2009* (Charles Town, WV, 2009), 152-153; Ian K. Steele, *Warpaths: Invasions of North America* (New York, 1994), 196.

British overconfidence and an unwillingness to reassess their tactics led to disasters along the Monongahela and at Lake George during the French and Indian War. The Lake George combat in early September of 1755 proved that conventional warfare was not going to work well against an enemy determined to fight otherwise when a frontier trader recently appointed to be the British agent to the Iroquois attempted to fight his 1,500 troops like a Regular officer against a similar number of troops led by a European-trained French general who had adopted ambush techniques. The guerilla tactics adopted by the French caught British military leaders off guard, and although the fighting proved inconclusive, the lesson was there for anyone wise enough to see it: traditional European tactics were not effective against this new form of warfare in North America. These bloody experiences convinced the British to alter their routinized method of waging war to include irregular tactics.[31]

The army created new military organizations and developed frontier-style hit-and-run tactics (small mobile bands of backwoodsmen conducting surprise attacks) during and after the French and Indian War. The objective was to damage the enemy with the smallest force possible and retreat as necessary. Lord Loudon (John Campbell, the 4th Earl of Loudon), the overall commander of British armies during the French and Indian War, emphasized the importance of these units and took note that conventionally trained British Regulars were unsuited for such a task. Initially, the British relied on American frontiersmen distributed between Regular units in the hope they would acquire some discipline, and the Regulars some woodsmen skills. Many of the changes taking place during this period would impact the American Revolution.[32]

One of the first things the British did in their drive to adopt frontier tactics was authorize the creation of ranger units, the most famous of which was commanded by Robert Rogers. The Rangers' status fell somewhere between a Regular and a Provincial. These units were composed of some of the most rugged North American frontiersmen, who were unruly and, at times, unreliable. However, for a time these Rangers filled a void by gathering intelligence, disrupting the French supply system, capturing prisoners, ambushing enemy advance units, and conducting diversionary raids. Ranger duty was difficult, and death and capture were constant threats. These men

---

31 Steele, *Warpaths*, 193; John Ferling, *Struggle for a Continent: The Wars of Early America* (Arlington Heights, IL, 1993), 163.

32 Russell, "Redcoats in the Wilderness," 141-142; Ferling, *Struggle for a Continent*, 163.

knew the advantage of spreading out when advancing through heavy woods, were always alert to an ambush, and were not afraid to take cover when attacked. "Woods-wise Rangers," confirmed one historian, "had become widely recognized by regulars and provincials alike as among the most valuable of soldiers in the dangerous wilderness."[33]

Lord Loudon hoped the Rangers could "deal with the Indians in their own way," and while he understood the need for their services, he also began to doubt the capability of undisciplined units. The result was the creation of the Royal Americans, a corps of lightly armed mobile men who had learned unconventional tactics from Robert Rogers and others like him.[34]

Loudon also introduced light infantry units to Regular regiments. By the summer of 1758, all regiments had been trained to deal with ambushes, and the best marksmen had been issued rifles. The new Regular light infantry units were trained and able not only to do much of the scouting but also serve in regular lines of battle, where they were trained to impart their mobility to the line infantry around them. One British officer observed that the "art of War is much changed and improved here. . . . The Highlanders have put on breeches. . . . Swords and sashes are degraded, and many have taken up the Hatchet and wear Tomahawks."[35]

The British officer responsible for revolutionizing British light infantry was George Howe, who had trained under Rogers himself. Howe was the older brother of William and Richard Howe. Regulars assigned to light infantry units were more lightly clothed and armed than others. Howe ordered the tails cut off their coats and the queues (ponytails) removed from their heads. They left their heavy packs behind, and wore leggings for added protection in the brush. Lastly, they browned their musket barrels to reduce the glint of the sun.

British army officer Henry Bouquet took Howe's teachings a step further. Physical conditioning was implemented, including running long distances, leaping logs and ditches, and carrying heavy loads. Bouquet trained his light

---

33 John K. Mahon, "Anglo-American Methods of Indian Warfare, 1676-1794," in *LW524: Student Reading Package, APUS Faculty, Fall 2009* (Charles Town, WV, 2009), 130; Ferling, *Struggle for a Continent*, 163-164; Douglas Edward Leach, *Roots of Conflict: British Armed Forces and Colonial Americans, 1677-1763* (Chapel Hill, NC, 1986), 109, 123.

34 Russell, "Redcoats in the Wilderness," 157; Ferling, *Struggle for a Continent*, 164-165.

35 Steele, *Warpaths*, 209; Mahon, "Anglo-American Methods," 131; Daniel J. Beattie, "The Adaptation of the British Army to Wilderness Warfare, 1755-1763," in *Adapting to Conditions: War and Society in the Eighteenth Century*, ed. Maarten Ultee (Birmingham, AL, 1986), 73.

infantry to perform their drills on the run, and he made sure they could shoot while kneeling and lying down. Lastly, Bouquet taught them to disperse and rally in response to non-verbal signals.[36]

By the end of the French and Indian War, British infantry tactics had undergone a major transformation. British troops could no longer be stereotyped as fighting in rigid European lines of battle. The most important tactical lesson learned was the need for bushfighting, or skirmishing in heavy woods. This new tactic became the exclusive domain of specially equipped and trained regular light infantry. For the last three years of the French and Indian War, redcoats aimed their muskets at specific targets rather than merely leveling their weapons in the general direction of the enemy. "The army employed specialized units on a scale that would have been extraordinary in Europe," confessed one writer. Fewer grenadiers were used in North America and many more light infantrymen. In fact, whole battalions of light infantry had been created. These spry men could quickly move through the woods to secure the flanks of heavy marching columns on the roads. This innovative creation of light infantry would eventually reform the British Army.[37]

The British continued to improve upon their light infantry system during the years between the French and Indian War and the American Revolution. In 1772, Lt. Gen. George Townshend issued new instructions to his light infantrymen while commanding in Ireland. The purpose of these instructions was to enable the light companies to skirmish in woods either independently, with their parent regiments, or as part of a light battalion. Townshend took a significant step away from the 1764 Regulations by adopting the two-deep firing line at open intervals. He also taught his men to maneuver and form by files and enabled his officers to maintain control over loosely deployed light infantrymen. Lastly, firings were to occur in pairs rather than in volleys.[38]

Just before the beginning of the Revolution, William Howe in 1774 issued a new light infantry drill. Howe's drill focused on light battalions as opposed to Townshend's individual companies. Much like Townshend's, however, most of the maneuvers allowed the battalion to change its formations and facings with

---

36 Mahon, "Anglo-American Methods," 131.

37 Spring, *With Zeal*, 245; Fred Anderson, *Crucible of War: The Seven Years' War and the Fate of Empire in British North America, 1754-1766* (New York, 2000), 411; Howard H. Peckham, *The Colonial Wars: 1689-1762* (Chicago, 1964), 153.

38 Spring, *With Zeal*, 246-247.

men moving by files rather than by wheeling entire ranks. Howe not only expected individual companies to detach themselves from the battalion to act semi-independently during combat, but also that the battalion itself would maneuver more quickly than its opponent so it could outflank an enemy line. The soldiers themselves were trained to break ranks when under fire and seek cover where available instead of remaining vulnerable to enemy lead.[39]

Hessian officer Johann Ewald later summarized the characteristics of light infantry. First, he noted, they were self-reliant and independent and comfortable with becoming isolated because they believed they were tactically better than their opponent. Next, these men could appreciate and adapt to different terrains—jungle, mountains, forest, urban settings and environmental changes—night, rain, snow—and use them to their advantage. Lastly, light infantrymen had to be able to improvise; when necessary, such men must be willing to adapt to circumstances rather than sticking to doctrine.[40]

Even though these instructions of the early 1770s seem to demonstrate that the British had learned their lesson in the previous war, it is unclear whether Regular line infantry was being trained in these tactics. The opening actions of the American Revolution leads one to believe they were not. Regardless of what doctrine preached, the British were never able to bring themselves to fully apply the lessons of the French and Indian War. When hostilities erupted in 1775, the British failed to put their new theories into practice, and for the most part never adapted to conditions in the colonies even as the war progressed. (In contrast, American colonists effectively used a type of guerilla warfare to harass their enemy from the very beginning.) Instead, British light infantry battalions generally fought in line of battle, using the same linear formations and bayonet-oriented tactics as the rest of the infantry. British leaders entered the Revolution confident that European soldiers led by competent officers possessed the cohesion to dominate untrained American militiamen in open terrain.[41]

Many British officers in North America believed that bayonet shock tactics were just as effective in heavy woods as in open fields. However, events soon proved otherwise during the fighting around Lexington and Concord, where the Americans used varied terrain and cover to harass and slaughter their

39 Ibid., 247-248, 253.

40 Johann Ewald, *Treatise on Partisan Warfare* (Westport, CT, 1991), 32.

41 Spring, *With Zeal*, 260.

opponents all the way back to Boston. As one writer noted, the deadly withdrawal proved that, "[u]nder certain favorable conditions a small force of well-armed and woods-wise colonists could rout a much larger, more ponderous formation of professional European soldiers."[42] Despite witnessing this for themselves, the British held to their outdated theories.

Nevertheless, Howe did order all units, including grenadiers and Regular infantry battalions, to fight in loose order beginning in 1776. As noted earlier, the men were to fight in two ranks and at arm's length from each other, rather than shoulder-to-shoulder. Carl von Donop confirmed that Howe's orders were still in effect at the Brandywine when he wrote just nine days before the battle, "I hope . . . that we . . . may be a bit more closely drawn together for the attack. For unless we are, I cannot yet reassure myself that infantry with its files four feet apart can capture intrenchments by escalade." Von Donop, who had his doubts about the upcoming fighting, went on to state that the Americans were "drilled by French officers; and I am none too sure how our general is going to get himself out of this affair."[43]

While the British failed to practice what they had at least sometimes preached, the Americans continued to show their frontier skills during the war by developing light infantry units armed exclusively with rifles. Their task was to scout ahead to help advance the infantry lines. Most American units were incapable of maneuvering and fighting against the professional British formations in open-field combat, but fighting in thick woods neutralized the principal weakness of the Americans. "In short," concluded one historian, "all but the rebels' best troops were probably most effective when they operated in loosely directed swarms in broken terrain."[44]

British military development in North America during the eighteenth century is an interesting study in contradictions. Confronted with Indian-style warfare at the outbreak of the French and Indian War, British leadership realized the need for new tactics. Initially relying upon American frontiersmen to conduct guerilla operations, the British eventually created Regular units of light infantrymen to fight using these new partisan tactics. Following the peace treaty of 1763, the army continued to improve upon the light infantry system—

42 Ibid., 252; Leach, *Roots of Conflict*, 165.

43 McGuire, *Philadelphia Campaign*, vol. 1, 207; Von Donop, "Letters from a Hessian Mercenary," 499.

44 Spring, *With Zeal*, 259.

indeed, entire drill manuals were written to effect substantive change. However, when the American Revolution erupted, the British remained convinced that the colonists were incapable of successfully fighting their professional soldiers. While the Americans used the guerilla tactics they had employed for decades to achieve success, the British steered away from their light infantry doctrines and attempted to fight a conventional war against the unconventional Americans.

Despite the teachings of William Howe and the innovations of men such as Patrick Ferguson, the British were incapable of overcoming their own prejudices against the American fighting man. While the British would eventually excel at light infantry tactics in the nineteenth century, they would largely forget during the American Revolution the lessons learned during the French and Indian War.

Chapter 10

The Eve of Battle
September 10, 1777

"We are preparing to receive 'em & should they come on . . . we shall give 'em a repulse or . . . they will have to enjoy a painful & dear bought victory."[1]

— George Washington, September 10, 1777

The Theory of Operations

The 1775 carnage at Bunker Hill convinced many American officers they could inflict heavy casualties on the British by taking up a strong defensive position and forcing the enemy to attack it. Washington understood this principle and tried to replicate it, especially during his efforts to hold New York City and the surrounding terrain. With Howe's army approaching Philadelphia, he decided upon a similar strategy: He would make use of natural defensive barriers to keep the British out of the capital city.

Washington originally intended to make a stand along the Red Clay Creek in Delaware, but when Howe outflanked Washington, the American leader had no choice but to fall back. The next natural terrain feature upon which to fix a defense was the Brandywine River, which flowed mostly north and south roughly 25 miles west of Philadelphia. The stream was littered with crossings, the most prominent of which was Chads's Ford, the direct route between

---

1   Chase and Lengel, eds., *Papers of Washington*, vol. 11, 186.

Baltimore and Philadelphia. Washington intended to defend the various Brandywine crossings in an effort to get Howe to launch a direct attack into the strength of his army.[2]

The Brandywine stretches 60 miles before flowing into Christiana Creek south of Wilmington, Delaware. Many hills, most about 200 feet in elevation, dot the landscape on either side of the river along its entire length. Steep banks along much of its course, together with thick woods in many places, made crossing the stream in force difficult except across one of the several fords.[3]

The ease with which a modern-day hiker can step across the Brandywine anywhere along the portion Washington defended gives a false sense of the stream's defensive value in 1777. Historically, the Brandywine was five to six feet deep along much of its length. Even the fords were deep—at least chest-high for the average man. And that September, as the Americans deployed along the eastern side, the fords were deeper than normal because of the recent heavy rainfall.

Understanding the course and flow of the Brandywine was one thing, but Washington knew little about the rest of the terrain and the network of roads and paths that linked it all together. By the afternoon of September 10, his army was spread out over several miles, with numerous scouting parties and pickets ranging to the west to keep a watch on Howe's army encamped around Kennett Square. Despite having an entire day in the area, Washington remained completely ignorant of the surrounding terrain and roads. Reconnaissance patrols were lacking, and no one seems to have considered talking to some of the locals who were in the army. Two battalions of Chester County militia and two Pennsylvania Line regiments from the region were in the ranks. In addition, prominent officers like Gen. Anthony Wayne and Col. Persifor Frazer had homes in the region.

Most of the local inhabitants were Quakers, whose religious convictions left them opposed to the war and generally unwilling to volunteer as guides or informants concerning the geographical and topological aspects of the surrounding area. Those few who were pro-American had either left or were already on the army rolls. The result was an "American army even more

---

2   Spring, *With Zeal*, 7. The only other natural barrier between Howe and Philadelphia was the Schuylkill River, but that waterway was too close to Philadelphia for defense except as a last-ditch effort, and was easily fordable at many locations.

3   Edgar, *The Philadelphia Campaign*, 17-18.

uncertain of the immediate nature of the country than were the British," argued one writer. Washington knew the area was unfamiliar to him, and yet seems not to have taken the "precaution of having at hand someone who knew the countryside."[4]

An instruction sent to one of the many dragoon patrols, dispatched to scout Howe's approach, reflected this lack of knowledge:

> Since I wrote you a few hours ago another Horseman has come in, and says that the Enemy are moving up the Lancaster Road. . . . His Excellency therefore desires that you would . . . reconnoiter the Situation and destination of the Enemy as critically as possible. As you may not be acquainted with the Roads, and to what places they lead, try to get a Country man who can give you information. The General begs you to remember of how much importance it is to him to receive very particular information, & hopes you will exert yourself to obtain it.[5]

The scouting parties triggered some minor skirmishing and thievery. Lord Stirling, for example, sent a detachment from the 12th Pennsylvania Regiment across the river under Captains Alexander Patterson and Stephen Chambers, who managed to pilfer cattle and sheep from the enemy. "Shall detain a Milch Cow, for a few days if you have no objection," wrote back one of the officers, "as there is 10 of them amongst the 17 above mentioned."[6]

Major roads, as they always do, play a significant role in the development of battlefield strategy. Three main roads crossed the Brandywine in the 18th century: King's Highway (modern-day U.S. Route 13) at the head of the tidewater in Delaware's alluvial plain; the Lancaster Great Road (modern-day U.S. Route 30), which was too far inland to be useful to Howe; and the Great Post Road (modern-day U.S. Route 1), part of the road system connecting

---

4   Reed, *Campaign to Valley Forge*, 114; Pancake, *1777*, 169.

5   Smith, *Brandywine*, 30. Smith lists the following as his source of the quote: Captain Davis Hopkins correspondence, 4th Continental dragoons. L/R, Office, Chief of Ordnance, A-K, 1816, National Archives & Records Service, Washington, D.C. Upon inquiry, the National Archives referred to a subscription website that proved unhelpful.

6   Isaac W. Hammond, ed., *State of New Hampshire, Part 1, Rolls and Documents Relating to Soldiers in the Revolutionary War* (Manchester, NH, 1889), vol. 4, 197. During another of these skirmishes, Thomas Carragan of the 7th Battalion of Chester County Militia was wounded during the evening hours when he was surprised by a party of British light horse. He was thrown from his horse and badly bruised about the body. Thomas Lynch Montgomery, ed., *Pennsylvania Archives*, Series 5 (Harrisburg, PA, 1906), vol. 4, 557.

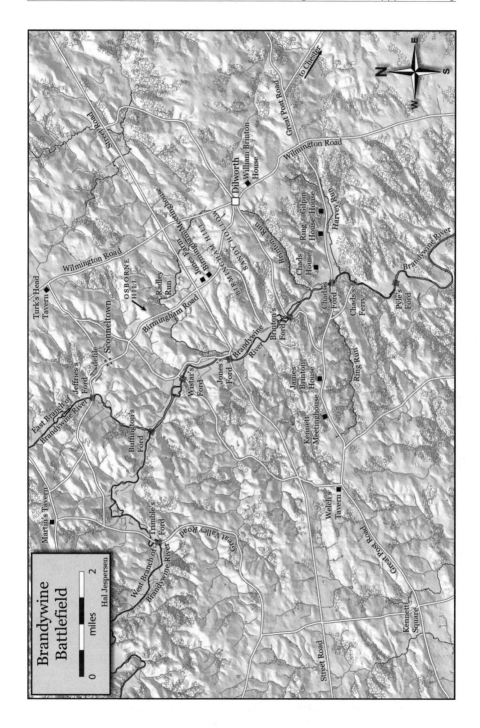

Brandywine
Battlefield

0   miles   2

Hal Jespersen

Boston to Savannah. The latter route (known as the Great Road to Nottingham because it led to the Nottingham family land tracts in northeastern Maryland) was the main artery in the area connecting the capital city of Philadelphia to Baltimore. Despite its extravagant-sounding name, in that era the Great Post Road was little more than one cart-width wide, with woods and farm clearings lining its course. Because Washington expected Howe to travel by the main route, he arranged his divisions behind the Brandywine to defend the crossings known to him.

American Dispositions

Washington posted Nathanael Greene's 2,500-man First Division several hundred yards south of the Great Post Road to guard a ferry crossing and be within supporting distance of Chads's Ford. The water was a little deeper along this stretch of the river, and a ferryman with a flatboat moved passengers and goods across by means of a rope stretched between the two banks. A four-gun battery on a hill off Greene's left flank covered the ferry crossing.[7]

On Greene's right were the 2,000 Pennsylvania troops comprising Anthony Wayne's Fourth Division. Wayne's primary responsibility was to defend Chads's Ford. The name is somewhat deceiving because it was actually a pair of fords: the Great Post Road crossed at one point about 300 feet above (north of) the modern-day U.S. Route 1 bridge, and another road (no longer in existence) crossed at the second ford about 150 feet below (south) the modern bridge. Wayne deployed his men along an elevation south of Harvey Run overlooking Chads's Ford. The right side of his line angled back away from the river toward Thomas Proctor's Pennsylvania artillery, which had unlimbered about 600 yards northeast of Chads's Ford. One of Proctor's artillerymen recalled an orchard behind his guns and wrote, "Across the road on the left was a buckwheat field opposite to a wood and the Brandewine between them."[8]

---

7 McGuire, *Philadelphia Campaign*, vol. 1, 170. Chads's Ford is in the vicinity of the modern-day Brandywine River Museum. The specific alignment of the individual units comprising Greene's division is not known. Unfortunately, the most reliable contemporary maps are from British and Hessian sources, and do not identify the initial American positions well.

8 Reed, *Campaign*, 113. The specific alignment of the individual units comprising Wayne's division is not known; McGuire, *Philadelphia Campaign*, vol. 1, 170; Jacob Nagle, *The Nagle Journal—A diary of the Life of Jacob Nagle, Sailor, from the year 1775 to 1841*, ed. John C. Dann (New York, 1988), 6.

A modern view of the John Chads House. An American artillery position was located on the hill to the right rear of the house. Washington came under British artillery fire while in the yard of the house with some of his staff. *Author*

Just above Wayne's position was a stone house owned by John Chads. The small community of Chads's Ford, first settled in 1687, was named after him, and the house, situated on a knoll above the ford, was built by 1704. Chads established the ferry in 1731 and maintained and supervised the operation until his death in 1760. Even as the armies gathered and Washington's soldiers stole her firewood and tore down her fences for more, Chads's widow Elizabeth remained in her home, as she would throughout the ensuing combat to follow. Lord Stirling would utilize the Chads house as his headquarters on the morning of battle.

John Sullivan's 1,800-man Third Division slid into place farther north about one-and one-half miles beyond Wayne's right flank. Sullivan's primary task was to guard Brinton's Ford, though his responsibility extended well north of that location. Indeed, his division anchored the right flank of Washington's army. There is some contemporary evidence that a temporary bridge made of wagons and fence rails spanned the Brandywine between Chads's and Brinton's fords, and a two-gun battery was positioned to cover this crossing. Sullivan also bore responsibility for guarding three additional fords above Brinton's as far north as Buffington's Ford.[9]

The first of these crossing points, Jones's Ford, is about one mile north of Brinton's Ford (where modern-day Route 926 crosses the Brandywine). Colonel David Hall's Delaware regiment was positioned there to guard it. Hall, who became a captain in the regiment in January 1776, rose to regimental command in April 1777. Colonel Moses Hazen's French Canadian regiment (Congress's Own Regiment) was divided to guard the next two fords to the north. The first, Wistar's (located at the modern-day Lenape Park), was about one and one-half miles north of Jones's, with the second, Buffington's, about five and one-half miles north of the Great Post Road, where the Brandywine divides into its east and west branches.[10]

As the right flank element of the army, Sullivan's division was vulnerable to a turning movement. Compounding this problem were issues concerning both its deployment and division- and brigade-level leadership. On the deployment front, the division was spread thin across several miles in an effort to monitor four separate fords. Maintaining tight control over such a wide disbursement would be difficult under the best of circumstances. Leadership issues added additional questions into the mix. Sullivan's combat ability was called into question after his performance on Long Island and during the recent operation on Staten Island. How he would perform if pressed remained to be seen. The leadership at the top of each of his two brigades was also an issue. One was led by a colonel, John Stone, because its general officer was on detached duty. The other was under the command of French-speaking Preudhomme de Borre, whom few American soldiers could understand. If Sullivan was separated from his division by way of wound, death, or capture, de Borre would assume divisional command by virtue of his rank.

The left flank of Washington's army appeared secure at first glance, albeit manned by the men in whom he had the least faith. Washington tasked Maj.

9 McGuire, *Philadelphia Campaign*, 171. The specific alignment of the individual units comprising Sullivan's division is not known; Smith, *Brandywine*, 30.

10 Smith, *Brandywine*, 30; McGuire, *Philadelphia Campaign*, vol. 1, 171. McGuire puts the Delaware regiment at 250 men, a significant increase from its May 20, 1777, return of 79 men, but that is in line with the increases that Greene's division saw; Smith, *Brandywine*, 30; McGuire, *Philadelphia Campaign*, vol. 1, 171. McGuire estimates Hazen's regiment at 400 men, which is very similar to its strength return of 393 men on May 20, 1777. It would have been difficult for this regiment to increase its numbers, considering it was recruited from French Canada and that region was under British control at the time.

Gen. John Armstrong's Pennsylvania Militia Division with guarding Gibson's and Pyle's fords about one mile south of the Great Post Road on Rocky Hill, a rugged cliff he deemed them easily capable of defending. Washington placed Armstrong's men here, far to the south, because he didn't trust them. He also was confident that they would not be directly tested because it was unlikely Howe would attempt to cross there. The Brandywine widened in front of Armstrong's position, the terrain was precipitous, and there was no direct route leading eastward to the fords in front of the militia. For all intents and purposes, Washington quarantined his militia force on the left flank of his army.[11]

While understandable, Washington's decision was not without its consequences. For reasons that remain obscure, Washington employed only small numbers of militia for intelligence and reconnaissance purposes. Those engaged in such endeavors were largely positioned west of Washington's main army beyond the Brandywine with Gen. Maxwell's light infantry, with the balance serving under Armstrong on the left flank. The result was that these potentially valuable assets were not fanned out farther north, where they could have scouted the various fords and roads on the army's more exposed flank. As local men, they would have had some knowledge of the fords along the Brandywine, and what they did not know they could have obtained from local residents to supplement their information. The positioning and misuse of his militia, coupled with the subsequent failure of his light horsemen, left Washington unfamiliar with the roads and fords beyond his exposed right flank when the battle began.

While most of his army was taking up key positions east of the river, Washington positioned Brig. Gen. William Maxwell's Light Infantry Brigade (about 1,000 men according to Lafayette) in front of Chads's Ford west of the Brandywine. Maxwell spread his men out in ambush positions spanning the Great Post Road between Kennett Meetinghouse, three miles from the river, and Chads's Ford. Just west of the ford, a log and earth battery and a breastwork of fence rails commanded the main approach to the river. General Washington, an unimpressed Lafayette would later write, "detached a thousand men under Maxwell, the senior but also the most inept brigadier general in the army." Like Sullivan, Maxwell's abilities had also been called into question.[12]

11 Hazard, *Pennsylvania Archives*, vol. 5, 539.

12 McGuire, *Philadelphia Campaign*, vol. 1, 171; Idzerda, et al., eds., *Lafayette Selected Letters and Papers*, vol. 1, 94.

The remaining elements of Washington's army were located in reserve behind the divisions guarding the Brandywine crossings. The Second Division under Maj. Gen. Adam Stephen was placed behind Wayne's position at Chads's Ford. Located on the right of Stephen's position about 800 to 1,000 yards behind Sullivan's division was the Fifth Division under Maj. Gen. William Alexander (Lord Stirling). The recently arrived North Carolina brigade under Brig. Gen. Francis Nash was also deployed behind Wayne. With the exception of small detachments to the various divisional headquarters, most of the approximately 600 dragoons with the army were stationed near Washington's headquarters one mile east of Chads's Ford.[13]

How and where Washington deployed his field artillery remains something of a mystery because the primary sources are woefully incomplete on this important issue. With the exception of Col. Thomas Proctor's Pennsylvania artillery regiment, most of the army's guns seem to have been held in reserve. Proctor's 250 gunners deployed their pieces on the heights running along the east side of the Brandywine north of the Great Post Road, where they threw up earthworks and redoubts for added protection, including a four-gun earth-and-log lunette on a knoll above the Chads House. Proctor's ordnance consisted of a Hessian 3-pounder re-bored to a 6-pounder after its capture at Trenton, two long range French 4-pounders, and an 8-inch howitzer capable of firing exploding shells made in Philadelphia. Opposite Brinton's Ford was another American battery that initially consisted of a pair of guns.[14]

Well beyond his right flank, however, Washington left three additional fords (Trimble's, Jeffries's, and Taylor's) completely uncovered. Trimble's was on the west branch of the Brandywine and Jeffries's on the east branch. Each of these fording points was more than one mile north of Moses Hazen's northern-most position at Buffington's Ford. Taylor's Ford was north of Jeffries's Ford, where the Old Lancaster Road (modern-day U.S. Route 30) crossed the east branch of the Brandywine. There is a possibility that Washington was unaware

---

13 McGuire, *Philadelphia Campaign*, vol. 1, 170; John B. B. Trussel, *The Pennsylvania Line* (Harrisburg, PA, 1993), 212.

14 Proctor's artillery regiment would be officially designated the 4th Continental Artillery Regiment later in the war. The regiment was offered for Continental service on June 6, 1777, but would not be accepted as such by Congress until September 3, 1778. There is some confusion surrounding the designation of Proctor's regiment because many believe the unit was formally part of the Continental organization as early as February 1777. Trussel, *Pennsylvania Line*, 193; Smith, *Brandywine*, 21. Other American batteries were assigned to other divisions in Washington's army, but the specifics remain elusive.

of these three fords, or that he knew of them but did not believe it necessary to guard them because they were so far removed from Chads's Ford. As he later explained it, "we were led to believe, by those whom we had reason to think well acquainted with the Country, that no ford above our picquets could be passed, without making a very circuitous march."[15]

The Eve of Battle

One of the most interesting stories about events the evening before the battle revolves around a sermon supposedly delivered by Rev. Jacob Trout to the Continental Army. Writer John Reed left a fanciful description of the event in his 1965 history of the campaign: "The camp appeared serene as the sun lipped the western hills of Chester County and readied to set. The serenity, however, was tense, as chaplains solaced the souls of the men who were about to enter battle. The Reverend Joab [Jacob] Trout gathered a number of the troops about him and led them in their devotions." A more recent study provides yet another description of the Trout sermon with some additional embellishments: "As the American army prepared for a night's rest, the Reverend Jacob Trout offered a sermon to the troops he gathered about him near Washington's headquarters, promising that the 'doom of the British is near.' The sermon was meant to ready the soldiers for the coming battle and possible death, to remind them of the atrocities of the British and their allies, and to remind them that their families were counting on their bravery. The new American flag was also used as inspiration for the troops."[16]

While these two accounts weave a heartwarming picture of the brave Continentals receiving spiritual guidance the night before one of the largest battles of the American Revolution, there is not a single contemporary soldier's account corroborating the event. More than 55 accounts of Americans who participated in Brandywine combat have come to light, and not one mentions the sermon. In fact, the earliest known account of the Trout sermon appeared more than a century after the battle in the *Magazine of American History* in 1885. One modern telling even claims Trout preached near Washington's headquarters. If that had been the case, it is reasonable to assume that at least

15 Fitzpatrick, ed., *Writings of Washington*, vol. 9, 426.

16 Reed, *Campaign*, 115; Mowday, *September 11, 1777*, 75.

one of the eight known accounts from Washington and members of his staff would have mentioned such an inspiring event.[17]

Other events of that evening, however, rest on a firmer foundation. Well aware that Howe's army was close by and that he would likely initiate battle the next day, Washington began issuing orders for men to prepare for an engagement. "No baggage is to be kept upon this ground that can possibly be dispensed with; and what cannot is to be loaded an hour before day and in readiness to remove," he instructed. "The men are to be provided with cooked provisions, for to morrow at least; for two days would be still better; if they can get such kinds that will keep." Washington went on to order that "[a] total stop is to be put to all loose, disorderly firing in camp, as otherwise it will be impossible to distinguish guns fired for an alarm." The importance of maintaining fire discipline to avoid confusion made itself evident just that morning when Hessian Gen. Wilhem von Knyphausen's division inched east of Kennett Square. "The alarm Guns were fir'd and the whole Army got Under Arms," recorded one officer in his journal. "However, the Enemy did not Approach."[18]

Even in the midst of preparations for a major battle, Washington evinced concern over the wanton destruction of personal property. "It being with much concern that the General hears the frequent complaints of the farmers, on account of the destruction of their fences &c. by which means their fields of grain and grass are exposed to devastation and ruin," chastised the frustrated army leader. "He wishes, that officers of every rank, for the sake of Justice and reputation of the American Arms, would exert themselves, to correct this species of abuse."[19]

Prior to bedding down for the night, Washington reported the situation to John Hancock, the president of Congress. "The Enemy are now lying near Kennets Square and in a tolerably compact body," he explained. "They have parties advanced on the Lancaster Road and on those leading over this [Chads's] Ford & to Wilmington. Manuvring appears to be their plan; I hope, notwithstanding, that we shall be able to find out their real—intended route &

17 Martha J. Lamb, ed., *Magazine of American History with Notes and Queries*, January-June 1885 (New York, 1885), vol. 13, 281; Mowday, *September 11, 1777*, 75.

18 Chase and Lengel, eds., *Papers of Washington*, vol. 11, 180-181; William Beatty, "Journal of Capt. William Beatty, 1776-1781," in *Maryland Historical Magazine* (Baltimore, 1906), vol. 3, 109.

19 Chase and Lengel, eds., *Papers of Washington*, vol. 11, 180.

to defeat their purposes. By Light Horsemen this instant come in," he concluded, "the Enemy are in motion, & appear to be advancing towards us."[20]

Washington learned a valuable lesson earlier in the war that "we should on all Occasions avoid a general Action, or put anything to the Risque, unless compelled by a necessity, into which we ought never to be drawn." In September 1777, however, Washington's Continental Army had been maneuvered into a position that necessitated a pitched battle. Leaving Philadelphia to fall to the British without a fight was unthinkable. Washington ended his long evening with a note to Gen. Israel Putnam, who was in command farther north in the Hudson Highlands. "We are preparing to receive 'em & should they come on, I trust under the smiles of providence & through our own conduct, that we shall give 'em a repulse or at the most, that they will have to enjoy a painful & dear bought victory."[21]

The British Pattern

While Washington deployed his army into defensive positions behind the Brandywine, William Howe's 15,200 men rested in and around Kennett Square three miles west. Howe made his headquarters in a tavern where he formulated his plans with the help of Joseph Galloway and a local Quaker named Parker. The British army commander spent most of September 10 studying the road network and terrain in the area to help him develop a plan of battle to engage and defeat Washington the next day. Howe's impatience had nearly gotten the better of him that morning. When he arrived at Kennett Square earlier in the day he wanted to immediately pitch into the Americans. Immediate battle, his staff officers informed him, was "impossible, since the men, and even more the horses, were completely exhausted. Counter orders, were therefore given, calling for a march [the following] morning." Howe prudently followed their advice.[22]

During the night of September 10, Howe developed his plan of attack. With his enemy posted on the far side of the river, Howe's options were limited. He could launch a direct attack in an effort to cross the fords and defeat or

---

20 Ibid., 182.

21 Fitzpatrick, ed., *Writings of Washington*, vol. 6, 28; Chase and Lengel, eds., *Papers of Washington*, vol. 11, 186.

22 Reed, *Campaign to Valley Forge*, 114; Von Muenchhausen, *At General Howe's Side*, 30-31.

dislodge them, find a way to turn one or both flanks, or some combination of attacking and flanking. As one historian observed, "because [British] commanders did not covet the ground beneath the rebels' feet, they usually proved reluctant to dash their forces obligingly against the enemy position when it appeared too strong to carry without heavy losses." Howe's own experiences confirmed this observation.[23]

The general now confronting Washington along the Brandywine assumed command of the British forces in North America in 1775 after London recalled Thomas Gage following the disastrous early efforts at Lexington, Concord, and Breed's (Bunker) Hill. It was Howe who had commanded the bloody British assault at Breed's Hill on June 17, 1775, where he witnessed what a well-entrenched ragtag patriot force could do to British Regulars. The experience shattered European military tradition. A bayonet charge by well-disciplined infantry had rarely failed European armies. Although the attack eventually succeeded at Breed's Hill, final victory only arrived after the entrenched patriots ran out of ammunition and lost the ability to fight back. Howe's June 17 plan of battle called for cutting off the redoubt by pinning down its defenders with a frontal attack while sending a flanking column up the shore of the Mystic River to gain the rear of the fort. However, the flanking column never fulfilled its mission because it was stopped by patriots sent to defend that exposed corridor. "Howe's memory of the slaughter on Breed's Hill had instilled in him a fatal caution which he carried with him for the rest of the war," argued one historian. Another historian agreed, writing that for Howe, Breed's Hill "left a deep impression and for the remainder of the war he shrank from frontal assaults whenever possible."[24]

For reasons discussed in previous chapters, but especially due to the difficulties of receiving reinforcements, it was not uncommon for British commanders in North America to avoid conducting frontal assaults. As a result, concentrating a strong force on the flank or flanks of an enemy position became the common tactic. One of the chief advantages of a flank attack was its psychological effect upon the troops being flanked, which "was vastly out of proportion to the physical force involved." Another advantage to a flank attack

---

23 Spring, *With Zeal*, 62-63.

24 Scheer and Rankin, *Rebels & Redcoats*, 60; Wood, *Battles of the Revolutionary War*, 9; Pancake, *1777*, 42; George Athan Billias, ed., *George Washington's Generals and Opponents: Their Exploits and Leadership* (New York, 1994), vol. 2, 47.

was that it gave a commander local superiority, even if he was outnumbered. Finally, and perhaps most importantly, flank attacks allowed the British to achieve conservation of force. The troops engaged to distract the enemy in front usually sustained light casualties because "they only pushed their attacks in earnest once the enemy army was already starting to crumble under the pressure of the flanking attack."[25]

The first opportunity for Howe to use his favorite tactic after Breed's Hill arrived on Long Island in the battle for Brooklyn Heights in the summer of 1776. There, Howe held Washington's army in place with a frontal diversionary attack and flanked it through the Jamaica Hills on its left with a powerful column. As Piers Mackesy phrased it, "Howe had begun the game like a skilled tactician. He had inflicted 2,000 casualties at the cost of 300, and driven the Americans back against the East River." Washington was barely able to retreat with what was left of his army across the East River to Manhattan Island, where he fortified Harlem Heights. Howe quickly outflanked this position as well, this time by conducting an amphibious landing to its rear. Following another retreat onto the mainland of southeastern New York, Washington settled into the White Plains area. The battle that unfolded there once again witnessed Howe conducting a flanking maneuver. There was an obvious pattern to the Birtish commander's victorious battlefield style.[26]

As the 1777 campaign season began in northern New Jersey, the engagement at Short Hills, New Jersey, once again witnessed the British using a flanking tactic. Charles Cornwallis led the flanking column intended to cut Lord Stirling's patriot division off from the mountain passes while another column under John Vaughan, along with Howe, moved directly against Stirling's position. As Thomas McGuire rightly believed, "The strategy was a replay of the Battle of Long Island, where Howe had masterfully outflanked and nearly annihilated Washington the previous year." Despite his success at Short Hills, Howe was unable to convince Washington to come out of the mountainous terrain in northern New Jersey. The disappointed British leader pulled his troops out of New Jersey, placed them on troop transports, and eventually landed in northeastern Maryland.[27]

25 Spring, *With Zeal*, 63, 65.

26 Mackesy, *War for America*, 88.

27 McGuire, *Philadelphia Campaign*, vol. 1, 53.

Once Howe began maneuvering in Maryland, flanking maneuvers again came into play. Rather than marching directly against Cooch's Bridge, he took a roundabout route through Aiken's Tavern to outflank Maxwell's American light infantry. Likewise, the British movement into Pennsylvania was a classic Howe flanking movement. Washington, despite what was now a pattern of previous moves by Howe, convinced himself that Howe would drive straight toward Philadelphia using the King's Road through Wilmington, Delaware, from Cooch's Bridge. Instead, a portion of the British Army marched to within two miles of Washington's position, supposedly to attack, but in reality to cover the movement of the main army through Newark toward Kennett Square, Pennsylvania. As he had done in the past, Howe's move was a diversionary one so he could slip around Washington's right flank.

Howe discussed his decision-making during his 1776 battles when he returned to London in 1779 and testified to a Committee of the House of Commons. "I do not hesitate to confess," he admitted, "that if I could by any maneuver remove an enemy from a very advantageous position, without hazarding the consequences of an attack, where the point to be carried was not adequate to the loss of men to be expected from the enterprise, I should certainly adopt that cautionary conduct, in the hopes of meeting my adversary upon more equal terms."[28]

Howe shied away from direct assaults and instead employed what would become his favorite battlefield maneuver: Push forward a diversionary force against the main enemy position while a strong column turned a flank. Despite Howe's repeated use of this combination, Washington seems not to have discerned this pattern from past encounters and was always unprepared for what had become a predictable offensive tactic.

Howe's Plan of Attack

Howe's operation to this point in the campaign positioned his army in Pennsylvania just west of the Brandywine River. Both armies were locked in place for a set-piece battle. Howe settled upon his plan of attack before the night of September 10 ended. There was nothing new in his tactical playbook. A diversionary force under Gen. Wilhelm von Knyphausen would march directly east along the Great Post Road against Washington's front, while Gen. Charles

---

28 Howe, *Narrative*, 7.

Cornwallis, whose column Howe would accompany, led the remainder of the army on a long northward flank march to cross the Brandywine River at an unguarded ford beyond the American right and then march into Washington's rear. Howe's simple but effective plan reflected his now-established preference for a strong demonstration against the center and a heavy attack on an enemy flank. John Reed, noted historian of the Philadelphia campaign, described the plan as "a holding action by Knyphausen . . . while Howe himself, with Cornwallis, made a grand flanking movement similar to . . . Long Island the year before, but in reverse."[29]

Unlike Washington, Howe was well-provided by area residents with information about the roads and terrain, so by the morning of the battle he was quite knowledgeable about the region. Prominent local Joseph Galloway had been with Howe since the army left New York, aided Howe before the battle, and eventually rode with him during the combat. Two other area residents who guided the British columns the next day were Curtis Lewis and John Jackson. Lewis lived in Chester County with his wife, joined Howe's army at Head of Elk, and had been acting as a guide ever since. John Jackson later recalled that the "day before Brandywine [he] was desired by [Joseph] Galloway to reconnoiter and offered 60 guineas for it." Jackson "would not do it for sake of Reward. Took one Curtis Lewis with him and reconnoitered the Enemy and brought back an account to General Howe a little before day. . . . Received 20 Guineas for this Service."[30]

If Howe had any doubt whether Washington would stand and fight, it vanished during September 10 when word arrived that Washington had "sent back his whole baggage to Chester." Unless something completely unforeseen intervened, the stage was set for one of the largest battles of the American Revolution. Nearly 30,000 troops were within a few miles of one another, prepared for action, and under orders to engage the enemy on the morrow. Howe ordered 20 empty wagons to accompany each battalion of grenadiers and light infantry for carrying the wounded.[31]

29 Benton Rain Patterson, *Washington & Cornwallis* (Lanham, MD, 2004), 123; Reed, *Campaign to Valley Forge*, 117.

30 Mowday, *September 11, 1777*, 50; Records of the American Loyalist Claims Commission 1776-1831, Great Britain, Audit Officer, AO 12/40/52, microfilm copy located at the David Library of the American Revolution, Washington Crossing, PA, film 263, reel 12, vol. 40.

31 Von Muenchhausen, *At General Howe's Side*, 31.

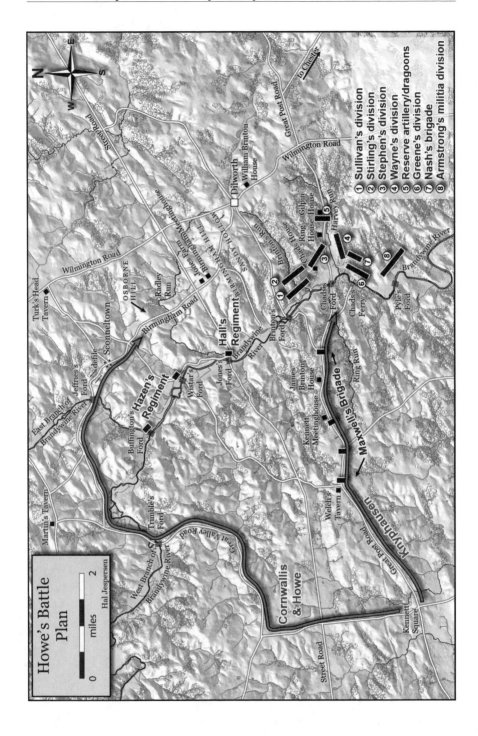

Howe's Battle Plan

0   miles   2

Hal Jespersen

① Sullivan's division
② Stirling's division
③ Stephen's division
④ Wayne's division
⑤ Reserve artillery/dragoons
⑥ Greene's division
⑦ Nash's brigade
⑧ Armstrong's militia division

The lack of mobility made it difficult for British armies to force a battle in North America advantageous to themselves. If Washington or any other American leader on the defensive believed the conditions under which he would fight were unfavorable, it was usually simply a matter of refusing battle by retreating out of range. Contrarily, if Howe or another British commander thought his enemy held the defensive advantage, he did not have to assume the offensive and oblige his opponent with a direct attack.

At the Brandywine, Washington not only believed he had to fight to hold Philadelphia, but that he held the advantage with the river in his front. Howe, however, had no intention of fighting the battle on Washington's terms. Dividing his army in the face of a large enemy force was a risk, but it was a risk Howe was more than willing to take. Washington had yet to prove his Continental Army was anything to be seriously feared. Although the ragtag American force had been lucky enough to score a pair of sharp successes at Trenton and Princeton, Howe had not been in direct command of those operations. Washington was confident he could win defending the important fords along the Brandywine. Howe, on the other hand, believed in his professional army and that his time-tested offensive tactics would win a potentially decisive victory and hand him the campaign's prize: Philadelphia.[32]

Only one of them could be right.

32 Spring, *With Zeal*, 9; Reed, *Campaign to Valley Forge*, 117.

Chapter 11

The Battle Begins: Morning
September 11, 1777

"[The Americans remained] planted like Cabbages whilst our parties divided, gaind their flanks, turned their breast works, and then after throwing away their fire, would run off."[1]

— Patrick Ferguson, January 31, 1778

The British Step Off

September 11 would be remembered as a hot and humid day, but it dawned cool, gray, and dreary, with the Brandywine valley shrouded in fog. A smoky haze drifting lazily from chimneys, bake ovens, and thousands of campfires added to the surreal ceiling hovering above the armies.[2]

The British were on the move early that morning. General Cornwallis's strong flanking column, with Lord Howe accompanying it, departed Kennett Square at 5:00 a.m., three-quarters of an hour before sunrise. Whether the northward march would be as effective as it would be long and arduous

---

1 Hugh F. Rankin, ed., "An Officer Out of his Time: Correspondence of Major Patrick Ferguson, 1779-1780," in *Sources of American Independence: Selected Manuscripts from the Collections of the William L. Clements Library,* ed. Howard H. Peckham (Chicago, 1978), vol. 2, 299.

2 McGuire, *Philadelphia Campaign,* vol. 1, 169.

remained to be seen. Local loyalist Joseph Galloway, who knew the area intimately, rode alongside Howe and Cornwallis while another local, Lewis Curtis, guided the advance guard. The marching order of Cornwallis's units remains obscure, as no primary source has surfaced with this information. Based upon how the column deployed on Birmingham Hill later that afternoon, a reasonable assumption would be as follows: Advanced Guard, British Grenadiers, British Light Infantry with the Hessian Jaegers, British Brigade of Guards, Hessian Grenadiers, 4th British Brigade, 3rd British Brigade, detachment of 16th Light Dragoons and 42nd Highlanders, and some combination of these two units guarding the wagons bringing up the rear.[3]

General Knyphausen's diversionary column also left Kennett Square about 5:00 a.m. "At daybreak the army marched in two columns," wrote Sgt. Thomas Sullivan of the 49th Regiment of Foot in his journal. "This Column took ye direct road towards Chad's-ford, 7 miles from Kennetts-square." At the head marched an officer and 15 men of the 16th Light Dragoons, Ferguson's Rifle Corps, and the Queen's Rangers, a total of about 400 men under the command of Capt. James Wemys. The order of march behind Wemys's detachment was the 1st and 2nd British Brigades under Maj. Gen. James Grant, Maj. Gen. Johann Stirn's Hessian brigade, the remainder of the squadron of 16th Light Dragoons, and the 1st and 2nd brigades of Royal Artillery, which Sullivan described as "six medium twelve pounders, four Howitzers, and the Light Artillery belonging to the brigades." The baggage and provision wagons, together with cattle for the entire army were escorted by two battalions of the 71st Highlanders, with the last battalion of the 71st bringing up the rear.[4]

The units leading the column, Ferguson's Riflemen and the Queen's Rangers, sported green uniforms. Both would be mistaken throughout the day (and in the later years) for Hessian jaegers. Ferguson and his men were going to have the pleasure of acting semi-independently: "Gen. Knyphausen, when I ask'd his orders was pleased to desire me to take my own way."[5]

The Great Post Road, down which the riflemen and rangers led Knyphausen's column, passed through a scenic terrain of rolling hills followed

---

3   Smith, *Brandywine*, 9; Wilhem von Knyphausen to George Germain, October 21, 1777, CO 5/94, pt. 2, 442, original in PRO/British National Archives, Kew, a copy located at Brandywine Battlefield State Historic Site.

4   Von Knyphausen to George Germain, October 21, 1777. Sullivan, *From Redcoat to Rebel*, 130.

5   DeWitt Bailey, *British Military Flintlock Rifles: 1740-1840* (Lincoln, RI, 2002), 49.

A 2013 view of the Kennett Meetinghouse. In addition to being the site of an American ambush on the morning of September 11, 1777, a Quaker meeting was taking place inside when the fighting opened around it. *Author*

by defiles and swales. Heavy woods lined the road in many places, with farms and other buildings populating the clearings along the way. Post-and-rail fences and stone retaining walls marked much of its course.

Deployed much as they had been at Cooch's Bridge a week earlier, Maxwell's light infantry assumed positions behind stone walls, fences, and on either side of the defiles with the intent of ambushing the advancing enemy. The three largest detachments were commanded by three field officers of the Virginia Line: Lt. Col. Richard Parker of the 10th Regiment, Lt. Col. William Heth of the 3rd Regiment, and Maj. Charles Simms of the 12th Regiment.

Captain Henry (Light Horse Harry) Lee, an officer in the Continental dragoons at the Brandywine who may have been positioned with a dragoon detachment west of the Brandywine that morning with Maxwell, left a description of this opening phase of the battle. Three detachments, Lee remembered, "were early in the morning separately and advantageously posted by the brigadier contiguous to the road, some distance in his front." The westernmost of these detachments, under Heth, began the morning in the vicinity of the stone Kennett Meetinghouse, where a number of Quakers were holed up that morning. Thursdays were not only baking day in the region but also mid-week meeting day for Quakers. A single company under Capt. Charles

Porterfield of the 11th Virginia Regiment, however, had pushed another mile or so west around Welch's Tavern. Porterfield's orders were straightforward: "deliver his fire as soon as he should meet the van of the enemy, and then fall back."[6]

Confusion at Welch's Tavern

The first shots of the battle of Brandywine broke the early morning silence about 6:00 a.m. when the leading elements of Knyphausen's column (Ferguson's Riflemen and the Queen's Rangers) approached Welch's Tavern, just short of three miles east of their jump-off point around Kennett Square."We were not above half a mile on the march, when Ferguson's Riflemen and the Queen's Rangers, commanded by Captain Weyms, of the 40th Regiments, attacked the advanced picquets of the enemys Light Infantry and Riflemen," remembered the Sergeant Sullivan. As is often the case with major historical events, myths and mistakes perpetuated through the years cloud the reality of what actually happened, and this was also true about the opening minutes of the Brandywine fighting.[7]

According to popular legend, American dragoons were drinking in the tavern when advance British elements under Capt. James Wemys stepped within shouting distance. Frightened, they ran out the back door, leaving their horses hitched to a post out front. A few Americans let loose a shot or two that mortally wounded a British horse, explained one popular writer, but "This casualty was more than compensated for when the British assumed control of the abandoned American mounts." The basic story was retold a few decades later, though with some embellishment, "with the Americans firing a volley out the door" before fleeing "through a rear window. One of the Hessians' horses was killed but its rider gladly replaced his mount with one of the healthier American ones left tied up in front of the tavern." A more recent study in 2002 perpetuates the tall tale and even claims the American dragoons were members

---

6 Henry Lee, *Memoirs of the War in the Southern Department of the United States* (Philadelphia, 1812), vol. 1, 15. "Light Horse Harry" Lee was the father of Robert E. Lee of Civil War fame. It is important for the reader to not confuse Kennett Square with the stone Kennett Meetinghouse. The former was about seven miles west of Chads's Ford, while the latter was about five miles west. In between was Welch's Tavern.

7 The entrance to modern-day Longwood Gardens is on the site where Welch's Tavern formerly stood. Sullivan, *From Redcoat to Rebel*, 130.

of Baylor's regiment: "Glancing out the window, one of the Americans saw the green uniforms of Knyphausen's lead units, and a rapid exodus followed after a wild exchange of shots. The British hit nothing, but the Americans hit one of their own horses left tied to the inn's hitching rail. The Battle of Brandywine had begun." The last author not only perpetuated the myth, but also has the Americans hitting one of their own horses rather than a British mount.[8]

While this story makes for an interesting (and in many ways comical) opening for the the bloodletting that was Brandywine, there is no evidence from any known eighteenth-century source to support it, and none of the books advocating its authenticity cite one. In fact, reports penned by those who were there that September morning in 1777 describe a much grimmer reality of what transpired around the tavern and its aftermath. Although the grounds of the establishment were not clear of Americans, there was no hasty exchange of lead that killed friendly horseflesh, or fleeing men stumbling out a window to escape.

Knyphausen's own lengthy report details the opening moments of the battle: "Advancing on the Road to Chads's Ford . . . I had hardly come up to Welch's Tavern when the advanced Corps viz. Captain Ferguson's Riflemen & the Queen's Rangers fell in with about 300 Riflemen of the Ennemy, who were posted in the Wood to the eastward of the Tavern." In other words, when the vanguard of Knyphausen's column moving east along the Great Post Road reached the vicinity of the tavern, elements of Maxwell's light infantry under Capt. Charles Porterfield opened fire on them—exactly as Porterfield had been ordered to do.[9] Porterfield's detachment almost certainly did not number 300 men, but the woods and fences they used as protection disguised their true strength from the approaching enemy.

Patrick Ferguson's memory was closer to reality, at least numbers-wise. "The first party we had to do with," reported the captain, "was an advanced Post of 150 men and some light horse, who threw away their fire and ran off, with the loss of three or four men and a horse whom we shot flying."

---

8   Reed, *Campaign to Valley Forge*, 118; Edgar, *The Philadelphia Campaign*, 20; Mowday, *September 11, 1777*, 84-85; Smith, *Brandywine*, 10. One of the better researched studies of the battle and campaign, *Brandywine* does not simply follow suit and repeat what others have written. Instead, the text makes it clear that no shots were fired at the tavern, and certainly not in the manner earlier perpetuated: "As Wemys's men reached Welch's Tavern . . . the balance of the Knyphausen column was formed in the road, waiting for word from Wemys that the way was clear to advance." Smith, *Brandywine*, 10.

9   Von Knyphausen to Germain, October 21, 1777.

Knyphausen's aide, Carl von Baurmeister, confirmed Ferguson's report: "our vanguard, i.e., the Riflemen and the Queen's Rangers arrived at Welch's Tavern, it encountered the first enemy troops. It drove them back and became master of the defile without delaying the march of the column." Sergeant Stephen Jarvis of the Queen's Rangers, who was also in the advance of Knyphausen's column that morning, recalled a warmer affair than did Ferguson and von Baurmeister. "[T]he first discharge of the enemy killed the horse of Major [John] Grymes, who was leading the column, and wounded two men in the Division directly in my front," penned the sergeant, "and in a few moments the Regiment became warmly engaged and several of our officers were badly wounded."[10]

Both Ferguson and von Baurmeister recalled the Americans being driven without any delay to the column, which is almost certainly correct. It is unlikely a prolonged engagement took place because neither Porterfield nor any of Maxwell's other men were supposed to do anything other than fire upon and harass Knyphausen's advance as they fell back to Chads's Ford.

Lieutenant Colonel Heth of the 3rd Virginia Regiment and Harry Lee praised the manner in which Porterfield opened the fighting. Writing to his friend Daniel Morgan, Heth described the morning combat: "I commanded as I mentioned before, a detachment of Light Infantry . . . part of which under our valuable Friend Porterfield began the action with day light—he killd (him self) the first men who fell that day." Indeed, Heth praised Porterfield for his entire body of work that day, writing, "His conduct through the whole day—was such, as had acquird him the greatest Honor—A great proportion of British Officers fell by a party under his command." Lee substantiated Heth's account, adding that Porterfield's "service was handsomely performed . . . and produced the desired effect."[11]

The battle of Brandywine had begun.

---

10 Bailey, *Flintlock Rifles*, 49. The "light horse" to which he referred belonged to either mounted militia assigned to Maxwell or the Continental dragoons, in whose company Capt. Henry "Light-Horse Harry" Lee may have spent the day; Von Baurmeister, "Letters of Major Baurmeister, 405; Stephen Jarvis, *Stephen Jarvis: The King's Loyal Horseman, His Narrative 1775-1783*, ed. John T. Hayes (Fort Lauderdale, FL, 1996), 97. I have been unable to determine whether Grymes was a major at the Brandywine, but it is unlikely. He was the second major of the Queen's Rangers in early November 1777. Since it is known that Capt. Wemys commanded the Rangers at the Brandywine, it is unlikely Grymes was a major at the time.

11 William Heth, "The Diary of Lieutenant William Heth while a Prisoner in Quebec, 1776," ed. B. Floyd Flickinger, in *Annual Papers of Winchester Virginia Historical Society* (1931), vol. 1, 33; Lee, *Memoirs of the War*, vol. 1, 15.

Toward Kennett Meetinghouse

Porterfield's withdrawal carried his men about three-quarters of a mile east down the Great Post Road to where Lt. Col. Heth was waiting with another 200 men.[12] Together, Heth's and Porterfield's men assumed a position on a slight elevation north of the road. There, where the road forked, the Americans waited under good cover for the approaching British. When the head of Knyphausen's column appeared, the American infantry fired a volley and once again withdrew east. To a sergeant in the 49th Regiment of Foot, however, the fitful march east from Kennett Square was not punctuated by brief moments of firing but "a running fire, mixed with regular vollies."[13]

Sometime between 7:00 and 7:30 a.m., the Queen's Rangers and Ferguson's Riflemen approached the vicinity of Kennett Meetinghouse, just more than one mile east of Welch's Tavern and about four-tenths of a mile beyond where the Americans had fired their last volley. Here, once again, Heth's and Porterfield's men formed on a wooded hill across the road from the meetinghouse.[14] The patriot light infantry fired a single volley that dropped a number of the Queen's Rangers.[15] Jacob Pierce, one of the Quakers at the meetingplace that morning, remembered "much noise and confusion" outside the building, but "all was quiet and peaceful within." Once again the tactic worked as planned, forcing the leading British elements to stop, form lines of battle, and set off after the Americans. All of this took time and effort, which was exactly the intent of the harassing gunfire.[16]

---

12 McGuire, *Philadelphia Campaign*, vol. 1, 175.

13 Smith, *Brandywine*, 10; Sullivan, *From Redcoat to Rebel*, 130. The fork is about where modern-day Route 52 intersects U.S. Route 1.

14 This hill was leveled in the creation of the modern roadway. In that era, the Great Post Road split and ran around both sides of the meetinghouse. Today, U.S. Route 1 passes several yards south of the building.

15 The Kennett Meetinghouse cemetery has a mass grave with between 50 and 100 battle casualties. On many days a German flag flies over the graves, which is unusual since Germany did not exist in 1777, and it is highly unlikely any of the Hessians with Knyphausen's column were killed near the meetinghouse. Unlike battlefields from America's later wars, the mass graves on the Revolutionary War fields likely contain a mix of American and British soldiers.

16 Sol Stember, *The Bicentennial Guide to the American Revolution* (New York: E. P. Dutton & Co., Inc., 1974), 91. While the source of this story is not the best, it is known that Quakers were within the meetinghouse during the battle, and the sentiment expressed in the quote at least captured the atmosphere Quakers would typically maintain even amid battle.

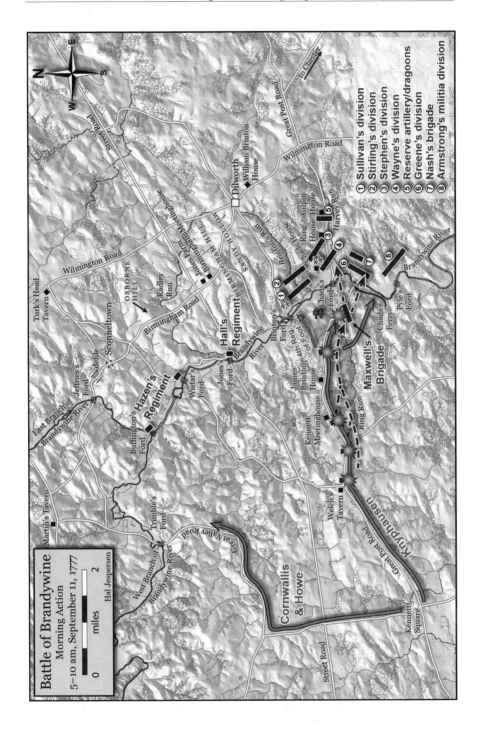

Battle of Brandywine
Morning Action
5–10 am, September 11, 1777

Hal Jespersen

0   miles   2

Once their volley was fired the Americans fell back down the Great Post Road to a position about 700 yards east of the meetinghouse. Waiting there was the detachment under Maj. Charles Simms of the 12th Virginia Regiment, another portion of Maxwell's command. The Virginians had taken up a good ambush position on a slight rise north of the road. The new arrivals formed behind a fence in a clearing.[17]

At this position, the Americans may have performed a ruse on the advancing enemy when some of them apparently turned their guns upside down in the universal sign of surrender. When the British moved forward, the Americans unleashed a point-blank killing volley into their ranks that dropped nearly 30 members of the Queen's Rangers. Thomas Sullivan, the observant sergeant fighting with the 49th Regiment of Foot, confirmed the story when he wrote that "the Queen's Rangers and the Rifle Corps, advancing to the foot of a hill, saw the enemy formed behind a fence, were deceived by the Rebel's telling them, that they would deliver up their Arms; but upon their advancing they fired a volley upon our men, and took to their Heels, killed and wounded about thirty of the Corps." While Sullivan's detailed contemporary journal entry strikes the right tone of veracity, there is no American account to substantiate whether the patriot fighters purposely deceived the Rangers. Light Horse Harry Lee, who wrote of this encounter, does not mention any trickery: "[The] British van pushed forward rapidly and incautiously until it lined the front of the detachment commanded by . . . [Major] Simms, who poured in a close and destructive fire, and then retreated. . . . The leading officer of the enemy was killed; and the detachment suffered severely."[18]

Ruse or otherwise, the Americans emptied their muskets and took off down the road. One of those Virginians scampering eastward was Capt. John Marshall, future Chief Justice of the United States.

---

17 Smith, *Brandywine*, 10.

18 McGuire, *Philadelphia Campaign*, vol. 1, 176-177; Sullivan, *From Redcoat to Rebel*, 130; Lee, *Memoirs of the War*, vol. 1, 15-16. As the fighting moved east along the Great Post Road, men of both armies would have passed the south side of the James Brinton home, known today as the Barns-Brinton House. The brick structure was built in the early 1700s, served as a tavern for a short time, and for most of its existence functioned as a family home. While modern U.S. Route 1 passes several hundred feet north of the building today, the eighteenth-century Great Post Road passed within a few feet of the southern elevation of the home. A low, stone retaining wall separated the yard from the roadway. John L. Cotter, Daniel G. Roberts, and Michael Parrington, *The Buried Past: An Archaeological History of Philadelphia* (Philadelphia, 1993), 442-443.

Simms's combined force (including Heth's and Porterfield's men) withdrew to a third position comprised of two separate locations, with the combined force now under Col. Josiah Parker of the 5th Virginia Regiment. The riflemen, with light artillery offering covering fire, were positioned to cover the junction of the roads leading to Chads's Ford and Chads's Ferry. Some of the men were on a small elevation within the fork of the roads, while the rest of the force was deployed to the rear along a ridge south of and overlooking the road to the ford.[19]

After having been ambushed three times, the troops marching at the head of Knyphausen's column were much more cautious during this stage of the advance. Part of the reason was because the type of hit-and-run fighting taking place along the Great Post Road was wearing down the advancing British troops. According to Ferguson's dismissive (and perhaps embellished) account of his advance, the Americans remained "planted like Cabbages whilst our parties divided, gaind their flanks, turned their breast works, and then after throwing away their fire, would run off leaving Arms, hats, blankets, &c." The loyalist officer, however, also admitted that "[m]y Lads were so fatigued with dashing after the Rebels over all surfaces that I found it necessary to leave one half by turns in the rear with the column of march and work my way with the other—which as my whole detachment was under 90 men was no great command." Nevertheless, Ferguson proudly claimed that "by avoiding the road, gaining their flanks, or keeping up a rattling fire from the ground or by bullying them we still got on."[20]

Ferguson's accounts must be used carefully because he often felt the need to defend the effectivness of his new rifle and how its use affected the advance that morning. For example, he exaggerated the aid his men provided to the Queen's Rangers during the eastward march toward Chads's Ford. "The Queen's Rangers Americans commanded by Rachel Wymess' husband," he reported, "seconded us with spirit and the line will do us the justice to allow that we kept them undisturbed and clear'd the way for them as fast as they could

---

19 Smith, *Brandywine*, 10. This new position was about 500 feet east of the present U.S. Route 1 crossing of Ring Run.

20 Rankin, ed., "An Officer Out of his Time," 299; Bailey, *Flintlock Rifles*, 49. Ferguson's report that he searched out the flanks, during which there would surely have been gunfire, together with the fact that he kept up a "rattling fire" explains Sgt. Thomas Sullivan's description of the advance as "a running fire, mixed with regular vollies for 5 miles and they still retreating to their main posts, until they got almost in gunshot of the Ford." Sullivan, *From Redcoat to Rebel*, 130.

A 2013 view of the James Brinton House. At the time of the Brandywine battle the Great Post Road passed by the front side of this home. Today, U.S. Route 1 passes behind the structure. *Author*

follow us." Ferguson's account is in fact disingenuous; the Rangers were ambushed on at least two occasions that morning, and lost a significant number of men while leading the column in its drive to catch and engage Maxwell's withdrawing light infantry.[21]

Thus far Maxwell's men had performed well, in a manner similar to their performance at Cooch's Bridge. The harassing American tactics, however, disgusted Ferguson, who had nothing but contempt for his opponents. "Such a set of base runaways never before presumed to disgrace a Gentlemans profession. . . . In the course of two hours my lads underwent the fire of 2000 men who were kind enough to fire in general in the air and run away." Ferguson's report doubled the size of Maxwell's command, which once again

21 Bailey, *Flintlock Rifles*, 49.

demonstrates how the woods and walls disguised his true strength. Ferguson's contempt was unfounded. Maxwell never intended to combat Knyphausen's column in an open-field fight. Whether or not Ferguson respected the American light infantry was irrelevant; Maxwell was performing his intended role.[22]

Knyphausen Approaches the Brandywine

General Knyphausen's diversionary column had by this time been engaged in stop-and-start marching for about three full hours, much of it punctuated by sharp ambush volleys and fitful skirmishing. It had yet to see or gain the important west bank of the Brandywine.

According to Major von Baurmeister of Knyphausen's staff, the front of the column "had arrived at a place where the road passes through some swampy land. On both sides of this lowland are hills and woods, and beyond it a road turns off to the left from the main road and runs through this lowland for about half a mile." The Great Post Road "was enfiladed by an enemy battery situated beyond the creek." Knyphausen's column had reached the defile where the Great Post Road crossed Ring Run. The Hessian aide's description was accurate, as the stream was indeed surrounded by heavy swampy terrain. The British and Hessian soldiers would need to clear the hills to their right and left before they could continue down the road. However, the closer they came to the river, the more artillery fire they received from Proctor's Pennsylvania artillery on the hill beyond Chads's Ferry. "Under cover of a continuous cannonade," continued von Baurmeister, the 28th Regiment of Foot moved off to the right to push another body of patriot light infantry out of yet another of the ubiquitous gorges along the road.[23]

The lead elements of Knyphausen's column arrived at this position about 8:00 a.m. after having marched and fought Maxwell's men for nearly three hours. While the fighting up to this point had occasionally been sharp, the combat was about to significantly intensify. "Heretofore the enemy had been

---

22 Ibid. Ferguson may have inflated the strength of his opposition in an effort to portray his own efforts in an even more effective light. On the issue of Ferguson's contempt for American tactics, one may well argue that his own rifle allowed his men to reload while kneeling or lying down, of which Ferguson was justifiably proud. Ferguson's men were not fighting with much eighteenth-century "honor," either.

23 Von Baurmeister, "Letters of Baurmeister," 405.

repulsed by our vanguard alone," observed von Baurmeister, "but now the engagement became more serious."[24]

One of the Queen's Rangers remembered their arrival at the new American position. "[We drove the] Rebels till within a half mile of the [Brandywine] Creek," he reported, "where they made a stand behind a breast work of some logs they had made." The strung-out column began deploying to reduce the American strongpoint. Ferguson moved behind a house to the right of the road on the far edge of the lowland, supported by about 100 men under Capt. Le Long from the Hessian Brigade.[25]

Knyphausen, meanwhile, ordered some dragoons and a battalion of the 71st Highlanders deeper into the woods on the right to find and get behind the American log works. Eventually, British artillerists moved forward four guns and deployed them on a hill opposite Maxwell's position across from the road junction. Since the Queen's Rangers had suffered significant casualties and exhaustion pushing down the road, Knyphausen ordered Maj. Gen. James Grant's First British Brigade forward to take its place. Grant's command was comprised of the 4th, 23rd, 28th, and 49th Regiments of Foot, about 1,400 men. Sergeant Thomas Sullivan, who served in the latter regiment, recalled that the "much disabled" condition of the Queen's Rangers "occasioned our Brigade, i.e., 1 st. to advance to the front, being separated (when we formed upon a little hill) by a small Creek, which ran between that & the opposite hill on which the Enemy took post." The 28th and 49th Regiments of Foot were positioned to directly support the advanced artillery.[26]

With his right secure, the experienced Knyphausen ordered Grant to march the 4th Regiment of Foot to the left to cover the Brinton's Ford Road and bolster what would otherwise have been an exposed flank. The regiment's advance to a position directly overlooking the ford caught the attention of American division commander John Sullivan, who responded by dispatching a small force down to the ford to better cover its approaches. The pieces were in place for a sharp combat at Brinton's Ford.[27]

---

24 McGuire, *Philadelphia Campaign*, vol. 1, 176; Von Baurmeister, "Letters of Baurmeister," 405.

25 James Parker, journal entry for September 11, Parker Family Papers; Von Baurmeister, "Letters of Baurmeister," 405.

26 Sullivan, *From Redcoat to Rebel*, 130.

27 Smith, *Brandywine*, 21.

Captain-Lieutenant Francis Downman of the Royal Artillery remembered that the "heavy artillery was ordered to make haste, and we galloped our horses some time, but were prevented from continuing [on] the road by reason of trees being cut down and laid across." While the British infantry skirmished with their American counterparts, Downman and his gunners turned north off the road into the woods and, after some difficulty, reached a position "with[in] shot of the rebel batteries on the other side of the creek. We immediately began to fire upon them from our 12 pounders and howitzers, and they returned it very smartly. This continued for some time, likewise a heavy fire of infantry and artillery to our right." The firing "on our right" referenced by Downman was the sharp fighting between Maxwell's light infantrymen and Gen. Grant's regiments. The maneuvering and reinforcement there triggered nothing but light skirmishing. Sometime early in the artillery action, one of the two American guns on the east side of Brinton's ford ceased firing when British counter-battery fire exploded an ammunition wagon.[28]

As the fighting at Brinton's Ford petered out, Knyphausen turned his attention south of the Great Post Road to deal with Maxwell's reinforced position. His Second Brigade, also led by James Grant and comprised of the 4th, 10th, 27th, 40th, and 55th Regiments of Foot, moved up and took a position just south of the road. By this time Maxwell had been reinforced from the east side of the Brandywine, likely by elements of Nathanael Greene's division. Knyphausen opened fire on the breastworks with his artillery to soften up the position, and then ordered the 28th Regiment of the First Brigade, which had been supporting the guns, to move forward. The infantry marched down the slope, crossed the small valley between the high ground, and deployed on a hill to Maxwell's left and somewhat behind him. The tactical thrust was expertly executed and threatened to turn and crush the American position.[29]

With his left flank compromised, Maxwell had little choice but to withdraw from his advanced position. Some of the British battalion guns imparted a sense of urgency to the retrograde movement by lobbing shells into the retreating Americans. The Royal Artillery, recalled the 49th Regiment of Foot's Sergeant Sullivan, "played upon them with two 6 Pounders for half an hour, and drove

28 Whinyates, ed., *Services of Downman*, 33.

29 General James Grant, the commander of the First Brigade, led both his own and the Second British Brigade at Brandywine. Exactly why he did so, and who if anyone was or had been in command of the Second British Brigade during the campaign, remains a mystery.

them out of the breastworks which was made of loose wood, upon the declivity of the hill. The 2nd Brigade British formed on another hill upon our left and played their two six pounders also upon the Enemy's Battery at Chad's ford. As we crossed the brook [Ring Run] they formed behind another fence at a field's distance, from whence we soon drove 'em, and a Battalion of Hessians which formed at the left of our Brigade, fell in with them as they retreated, taking them upon their Right flank."[30]

Maxwell's men fell back to a previously prepared breastwork—their final position west of the Brandywine. They were close to the ford now, on a low ridge running between the two roads leading down to the ford and the ferry. By this time Ferguson and the Queen's Rangers had pushed across Ring Run, moved beyond the road fork leading to Chads's Ford and Chads's Ferry, and were on Maxwell's exposed left flank. The 23rd, 28th, 40th, and 55th Regiments of Foot, along with the Leib and von Mirbach Hessian regiments, were in line of battle on the height beyond the lowland on the road to Chads's Ford. The Combined Hessian Battalion and von Donop's Regiment remained in column along the road. Likewise, the 5th, 27th, and 49th Regiments of Foot remained in reserve on the heights west of the lowland. The Royal Artillery units covered Knyphausen's column as it unfolded itself, "the various pieces being mounted with all possible haste in strategic places and on high ground," explained a British staff officer. While the Americans continued to pour fire in from across the river, and "though the balls and grapeshot were well aimed and fell right among us, this cannonoade had but little effect—partly because the battery was placed too low."[31]

Believing that Maxwell had been neutralized and was perhaps falling back, the Queen's Rangers, Ferguson's riflemen, the 23rd Regiment of Foot, and a battalion of the 71st Highlanders moved forward toward Chads's Ferry. The detachment of dragoons remained behind to cover the rear. Simultaneously, Maj. Gen. Johann Daniel Stirn's Hessian Brigade, about 2,000 strong, stepped forward, picked up the detached group of 100 men at the road junction, and proceeded toward the ford. As the Hessians advanced down the road, however, Maxwell's men opened fire from the wooded ridge to the south. The flying lead balls coursing through their ranks brought the Hessians up short. After orders were shouted, the professionals performed a wheel under fire and moved

30 Sullivan, *From Redcoat to Rebel*, 130.

31 Von Baurmeister, "Letters of Baurmeister," 405-406.

smartly off the road and up the ridge in an effort to flank the American position. While the Germans engaged, the bloodied Queen's Rangers, with the support of the Royal Welsh Fusiliers (23rd of Foot), moved off the road and against the left front of Maxwell's reinforced position.[32]

Captain Wemys and the Queen's Rangers attacked with bayonets locked. Despite their earlier exhaustion and losses, the Rangers pitched into the fight with a ferocious intensity that further thinned their ranks. This part of the fight, recalled a staff officer, "after a short but very rapid musketry-fire . . . quickly drove the rebels out of their woods and straight across the lowland." James Parker remembered the Americans "formd on the declivity of a hill on clear ground & stood till Majr. Grymes Attackd them with ye Bayonets, when they broke fled to the Woods & heid. . . . At this time Capt. Robt. Murdon fell, & many more Wounded, but they drove them over the Creek. While this passed on our Right . . . [Captain] Weems with part of the Regt. drove them through the woods on the left till they crossed the Creek also, when their Canon began from a battry in our front, & I took Stations on high Commanding ground on our left." Captain Murden's wound proved mortal. Sergeant Stephen Jarvis remembered the attack for another reason: "My pantaloons received a wound, and I don't hesitate to say that I should be very well pleased to have seen a little blood also." Almost as an afterthought he added, "The enemy stood until we came near to bayonet points, then gave us a volley."[33] The successful assault pleased Knyphausen, who later reported that the Rangers attacked "with a Spirit & Steadiness I can not too highly commend – Notwithstanding the strong Fire to oppose them, they rush'd upon the Ennemy with Charged Bajonets."[34]

Although successful, and while accounts made the assault sound almost a fait accompli, Ferguson remembered the difficult nature of the fighting and added additional details, including pursuit. At the head of 30 men, Ferguson struck farther to the right than did the Queen's Rangers. His thrust hit "a breast work 100 yards in extant well lined with men whose fire they received at twelve

---

32 The fighting east of the Brandywine has proven difficult to interpret. Soldiers in battle are heavily focused on the fighting in front of them, and their letters, diaries, and journals reflect that. Piecing the story together and reconciling the various eighteenth-century sources has been difficult. What follows is the author's best interpretation; Von Baurmeister, "Letters of Baurmeister," 405.

33 Von Baurmeister, "Letters of Baurmeister," 405; James Parker, journal entry, September 11, Parker Papers; Jarvis, *Stephen Jarvis*, 97-98.

34 Von Knyphausen to Germain, October 21, 1777.

yards and when every body thought they were all destroy'd they Scrambled into the breast work and the Dogs ran away." However, Ferguson's attempt to pursue the fleeing Americans was brought to a quick halt. "Stop'd from following them by a heavy flanking fire from a very extensive breast work at 80 yards distance," he explained. "I threw my party immediately on the ground."[35] After waiting a short while listening to the Rangers fight their way over the breastworks farther to the left, Ferguson gave the order to continue advancing. "This fire continued for some minutes very heavy until we Sicken'd [of] it, after which upon the Signal to rise my Lads like Bay's dead men Sprung up and not one hurt." Ferguson remained unimpressed with Maxwell's ability. The Patriot general, sneered the Loyalist officer, should start his "prencticeship as a corporall, and that their Light troops . . . have learnt to rely upon their heels."[36]

With his right turned by the Hessians and his left collapsing, Maxwell withdrew the last of his command safely across the Brandywine. It was about 10:00 a.m. According to Knyphausen, "the Enemy were driven back over the Creek evacuating their very advantageous posts on this side. The most obstinate resistance they gave was on the road to Brandywine Creek's Bridge [Chads's Ford], but the gallant and Spirited Behavior of the 4th and 5th Regiment forced them to leave their Ground." A sergeant in the 49th Regiment of Foot wrote, "After we pursued the Rebels as close as we could without being in danger of their cannon above the Ford, all the men lay upon their arms in a close valley with wood."[37]

With Maxwell finally shoved back across the river, Knyphausen pushed his outposts closer to the Brandywine, spent about 30 minutes straightening his lines of battle, and presented a strong front. Once all was in good order, he sent forward a battalion of the 71st Highlanders and positioned a detachment of the 16th Light Dragoons on the height on their right flank. The baggage train with the other two battalions of the 71st remained on the heights west of the lowland, where the heavy fighting near the ford had initially erupted. It was now about 10:30 a.m. Knyphausen had thus far played his diversionary role perfectly. In keeping with Gen. Howe's overall plan of battle, he kept up a threatening front but remained on the west side of the Brandywine awaiting

35 Bailey, *Flintlock Rifles*, 49.

36 Ibid.; Rankin, "Correspondence of Ferguson," 299-300.

37 Smith, *Brandywine*, 11; Von Knyphausen to Germain, October 21, 1777; Sullivan, *From Redcoat to Rebel*, 131.

word from Gen. Cornwallis's flanking column. "[T]he musketry, he explained, "ceased entirely."[38]

As the fighting fell into silence, Knyphausen's force remained positioned essentially where it had stopped fighting. Opposite Chads's Ferry were the First British Brigade (minus the 4th Regiment of Foot), the Queen's Rangers, Ferguson's Riflemen, and a battalion of the 71st Highlanders. General Stirn's Hessian Brigade was positioned a short distance west of Chads's Ford. The front between that ford and Brinton's Ford farther north was held by the Second British Brigade. The 4th Regiment of Foot remained watching Brinton's Ford. Knyphausen kept in reserve the dragoons, the army's baggage, and the other battalions of the 71st Highlanders. Two heavy and two light 12-pounders sat atop a hill across the river from Proctor's American guns, and two 6-pounders were positioned farther south below the Great Post Road where the 27th Regiment of Foot provided support. The 28th Regiment of Foot held the far right flank on yet another piece of high ground.[39]

While no one faulted Knyphausen's performance, that was not the case with Maxwell. The officer Lafayette had labeled "the most inept brigadier general in the army" guided his riflemen in an hours-long harassment that slowed down a strong column of professional enemy soldiers. Ferguson's contempt notwithstanding, the defensive effort inflicted significant casualties. "[O]ur loss in the above action," boasted Lt. Col. William Heth of the 3rd Virginia Regiment, "was very inconsiderable in comparison with the Enemys." Indeed, one of Gen. Greene's brigade commanders, George Weedon, proudly recalled that his command was "spectators of the gallantry of this little Corps."[40]

Maxwell's force had arguably done well, especially for an organization in its infancy, but once all was said and done Heth strenuously argued otherwise in language that left no room for misunderstanding. "We had opportunities," he complained, "and any body but an old-woman, would have availd themselves of them." Maxwell had not seized such opportunities, continued Heth, because he was "a Damnd bitch of a General." Ferguson would have agreed with Heth's

---

38 Von Baurmeister, "Letters of Baurmeister,"406.

39 Von Knyphausen to Germain, October 21, 1777. The British guns were located where the modern Chadds Ford Elementary School now sits.

40 Idzerda, et. al., eds., *Lafayette Selected Letters and Papers*, vol. 1, 94; Weedon to Page, September 11, 1777.

conclusion. The terrain, argued the Loyalist, was very favorable to the Americans, and they should have had "no difficulty in interrupting our march had they shewn firmness equal to the ingenuity of their dispositions." Ferguson continued his unfavorable judgment by concluding that Maxwell's men were only capable of two things: "discharging their pieces in the air and running in a direct line behind them."[41]

Many in the Queen's Rangers, which had been particularly hard hit, may well have disagreed with Ferguson's assessment. One of Maxwell's officers, William Heth, was correct when he wrote that "a great proportion of British Officers fell." Howe would later report that the Queen's Rangers suffered 14 killed and 57 wounded, and that Ferguson's Riflemen suffered 10 casualties— two killed and eight wounded. Ferguson explained why his casualties were relatively light: "Such is the great advantage of an arm that will admit of being loaded and fired on the ground without exposing my men that I threw my people on the ground without exposing my men under pretty Smart firing six times that morning without losing a man, although I had ¼ part of those afterward kill'd or wounded." As for the loss to Maxwell's unit, Washington reported to Congress that "it does not exceed fifty in the whole."[42]

Whether he had fought well or otherwise, because Maxwell's men were now on the east side of the Brandywine, the British and Hessian infantry could finally rest. "[A]fter the most advanced troops captured one height after another with great difficulty and heavy losses," Carl Rueffer, a Hessian ensign, recalled, "we received orders not to advance any farther and we lay on the heights at Chads Ford."[43]

41 Heth, "Diary," 33; Rankin, "Correspondence of Ferguson," 299.

42 In addition to Capt. Murden being killed, the following officers were wounded: Capt. Job Williams (he would later die of his wounds), Capt. Saunders, Capt. John McKay, Capt. Robert McCrea, Capt. Burns, Lt. Kerr, Lt. Agnew, Lt. Smith, Lt. Toel, and Lt. Close. Heth, "Diary," 33; *Remembrancer; or, Impartial Repository of Public Events for the Year 1777* (London, 1778), 416; George Inman, ed., "List of Officers Killed Since the Commencement of the War 19th April 1775, Regiments Etc. and Officers of Marines Serving on Shore," in *Pennsylvania Magazine of History & Biography* (Philadelphia, 1903), vol. 27, 176-205; Bailey, *Flintlock Rifles*, 49; Fitzpatrick, ed. *Writings of Washington*, vol. 9, 206.

43 Burgoyne, ed., *Enemy Views*, 175.

An Artillery Duel, With Skirmishing

The action during the remainder of the morning and during the early afternoon around Chads's Ford consisted of fitful skirmishing by light infantry elements, punctuated with bouts of artillery fire. According to Joseph Clark, Adam Stephen's adjutant, "The valley was filled with smoke. . . . [T]here was nothing for the men on either side to do but to find as much cover as possible until the heavy cannonade ceased." Knyphausen's artillery was situated almost directly opposite the American batteries. James Parker of the Queen's Rangers recalled that "the hill on which our artillery was commanded a Very fine prospect of the Rebels ground, to this place the Genls. Kniphausen & Grant came."[44]

The long range counter-battery fire did little damage, but Knyphausen had another purpose in mind. "Our cannon fired from time to time," explained his staffer, Carl von Baurmeister, "each shot being answered by the enemy; but the purpose of our gunfire was only to advise the second column [Cornwallis] of our position." Knyphausen's quartermaster, Johann Ludwig von Cochenhausen, remembered the Royal Artillery giving the Americans "a fairly fresh cannonade, which was only answered occasionally to save powder, since it was of no particular effect." James Parker of the Queen's Rangers also recalled and wrote about the gunfire: "a Cannonade Continued for Some time, I believe without doing much damage on either side."[45]

Several area inhabitants opted to stay in their homes that morning instead of fleeing for safer locales. William Harvey's stone home on the west side of the Brandywine was directly in the line of fire of Proctor's guns. Built early in the century, the modest dwelling housed William's worldly belongings, and he intended to protect them. Neighbor Jacob Way pleaded with William to leave, to no avail. According to a postwar account, the men were exchanging words when "a twelve-pound cannon-ball came from Proctor's battery directly for the house, passed through both walls of the kitchen and plunged along the piazza floor, tearing up the boards and barely avoiding William's legs, until, a little

---

44 Clark, "Diary, 99. James Parker, journal entry, September 11, Parker Papers.

45 Von Baurmeister, "Letters of Baurmeister," 406; Johann Ludwig von Cochenhausen to Gen. Friedrich von Jungkenn, October 9, 1777, *Journal of the Johannes Schwalm Historical Association*, eds. Henry Retzer and Donald Londahlsmidt, no. 2. (1998), vol. 6, 2; James Parker, journal entry, September 11, Parker Papers.

farther on, it buried itself six feet deep in the earth." Proctor's battery did not contain a 12-pounder, but the civilian may have exaggerated or misjudged the size of the ball. After that close call, Harvey wisely opted to leave. His home was later ransacked by the British.[46]

Jacob Nagle was an American soldier serving with Proctor's Pennsylvania artillery. Like so many others that day, the 15-year-old was hungry that morning and looking forward to a late breakfast. "The provision wagons being sent a way, we ware three day without provisions excepting what the farmers brought in to sell in their wagons and what the soldiers could plunder from the farmers," he scribbled into his journal. "I went to my father, his rigment being on our right, and received a neats tounge from him. . . . Mr. Hosner bought some potatoes and butter the evening before the British arrived, and we concluded to have a glorious mess from breakfast. Mr. Hosner gave it to one of the soldiers wives that remained with the army to cook for us in the morning." Fondly anticipating his meal, Nagle and other American soldiers were marking time on the east bank of the Brandywine when enemy artillery rounds began landing on their side of the river. "Early in the morning, she had the camp kittle on a small fire about 100 yards in the rear of the Grand Artilery, with all our delicious meal, which we expected to enjoy," the teenager continued. "The Brittish at this time hoisted the red flag on the top of the farm house on the rige of the hill abreast of us, and their artillery advancing towards us down the ploughed field, we then begin a cannonading." What followed was one of the worst things that could happen to any hungry soldier throughout history: "Unfortunately one of the enemies shot dismounted the poor camp kettle with the fire and all its contents away with it. The woman informed Mr. Folkner. He replied, 'Never mind, we have no time to eat now.' Therefore we made another fast day."[47]

---

46 Howard M. Jenkins, "Brandywine, 1777" in *Lippincott's Magazine of Popular Literature and Science* (London, September 1877), vol. 20, 334. The story of William Harvey's brush with death was written a century after the battle, and there is no contemporary source that documents the event. However, the Harvey home was behind Knyphausen's artillery positions and thus in the line of fire, and was indeed constructed many years prior to the battle. William Harvey inherited the property when his father died in 1754, and was living there in 1777. Following the battle, many local residents filed damage claims—including William Harvey. Documentation for the claim can be found in Futhey and Cope, *History of Chester County*, 107. Based upon these corrabborating details, I decided to include the story as factually accurate.

47 Nagle, *Journal*, 6-7. Nagle lived a remarkable life. He served with Washington at Valley Forge, resigned in 1778, and joined the Continental Navy. Nagle was captured by the British in 1781, freed by the French the following year, arrested by the British immediately thereafter, and

Infantrymen also exchanged shots across the river. The adjutant of Proctor's artillery, added Nagle, "rode down to the ford to water his horse. . . . [A] Hessian laying in the brush fired at him and missed him but wounded the horse in the right shoulder. The horse staggered, the adjutant jumped off with his pistols in hand and run up to the spot, which was not more than 15 yards from him, and several of the artillery run down to him, but the Hessian could not be found." Nagle mistook Ferguson's green-uniformed men as jaegers. This was the first of many recorded instances of mistaken identity that day.[48]

Nagle also remembered one of Maxwell's riflemen lying on his back to load before rolling over to assume a firing position and squeeze his trigger in the direction of Ferguson's men on the far bank. "I took notice of one in a white frock laying on his back to lead his gun. . . . On the edge of the wood next to the road was some trees cut down, and the Hessions got amongst them; this riffelman fired 7 or 8 shots at them as fast as they came there. The buckwheat being in bloom, they could not see him, but we ware on the highth over him. At length finding no more coming, he crawled on his hands and knees to the fence where he fell in with six more. They all rise and crossed the ford and went to the place he had been firing at them, as we supposed to overhall them."[49]

Although Ferguson had nothing but contempt for his opponents, he let slip a few words that confirmed the abilities of the American riflemen. "Whilst Knyphausen was forming the Line within a Mile of the Rebell Camp to wait for G. Howe's attack," reported the British officer, "their Rifle men were picking off our men very fast by random shots from a wood some hundred yards in front as it is easy execution upon such large objects." He continued: "I had only 28 men with me (a few having been disabled by the Enemy the rest from Fatigue) who however proved Sufficient, for my Lads first dislodged them from the skirts of the Wood, then Drove them from a breast work within it, after which our purpose being answered we lay down at the furthest skirt of the wood—not necessarily to provock an attack, being so few without Support."[50]

---

spent many years in the British navy and with the merchant marine. After being shipwrecked on an island for a year, he sailed to England, married, had seven children, and went to sea again under Lord Nelson during the Napoleonic Wars. Nagle left the sea for good in 1824 after his wife and all of his children died of yellow fever. His own grand adventure ended in 1841.

48 Ibid., 8.

49 Ibid.

50 Rankin, "Correspondence of Ferguson," 299-301.

At times, the skirmishing along the river escalated into more substantial fighting that sucked in more than just a few troops, as future jurist John Marshall recorded:

> A skirt of woods, with the river, divided him [Knyphausen] from Maxwell's corps, small parties of whom occasionally crossed over, and kept up a scattering fire, by which not much execution was done. At length one of these parties, led by Captain [Andrew] Waggoner [12th Virginia Regiment] and Porterfield, engaged the British flank guard very closely, killed a captain with ten or fifteen privates, drove them out of the wood, and were on the point of taking a field piece. The sharpness of the skirmish soon drew a large body of the British to that quarter, and the Americans were again driven over the Brandywine.[51]

The body of troops the British sent across to deal with the threat included the 10th and 40th Regiments of Foot. Sergeant Thomas Sullivan, the reliable scribe of the 49th Regiment of Foot, also described the escalating fire fight. "A Company of the 28th and a Company of our Regiment advanced upon the Hill to the right of the ford, and in front of the Enemy's left flank, in order to divert them, who were posted at 100 Yards distance in their front, behind trees, to the amount of 500, all chosen marksmen," recalled the sergeant. "A smart fire was maintained by both sides for two hours, without either party's quitting their Posts. Out of the two Companies there were about 20 men killed and wounded during that time."[52]

"[T]wo 6 Pounders [commanded by Lt. George Wilson of the Royal Artillery] were ordered up the hill to dislodge the Enemy if possible and assist the part engaged," Sgt. Sullivan continued. "Those guns played upon them for some time, but they were so concealed under the cover of the Trees, that it was to no purpose to endeavor to bring the Cannon to do any execution: In the mean time, by our Guns being in an open field, there was one man killed, and a horse wounded." Lieutenant Colonel Robert Donkin of the 44th Regiment of Foot remembered that Lt. Wilson "was ordered with two Guns to support a Party of the 49th Regt & that he silenced the Enemy's fire for some time & behaved extremely well in general." Wilson was initially hesitant to move his

---

51 John Marshall, *The Life of George Washington, Commander in Chief of the American Forces, During the War Which Established the Independence of his Country, and First President of the United States* (Fredericksburg, VA, 1926), vol. 2, 299-300.

52 McGuire, *Philadelphia Campaign*, vol. 1, 181; Sullivan, *From Redcoat to Rebel*, 131.

guns up. "Lt. Wilson was attached to the 40th Regt. with two 3 pounders. . . . [U]pon the Brigade being ordered to form, there was a Wood thro' which he thought it might be difficult for the Guns to pass, he therefore ordered them to wait, but Lt. Wilson soon after brought them up, before he [Lt. Col. Thomas Musgrave] sent for them." Captain James Wilson of the 49th Regiment of Foot also left an account of the two British guns. "Lt. Wilson was ordered with two Guns to support his Company which was then engaged, and was the principal means of first driving back the Enemy, & that he did not see any appearance of fear in Lt. Wilson's behavior that day; that one of his Men were killed, and another wounded, & a horse in the Ammunition Waggon also wounded."[53]

These British artillery pieces annoyed the Americans to no end. "About this time General Washington came riding up to Col Procter with his Life Guards with him and enquired how we came on," recalled teenage gunner Nagle. "He informed the general that there was two field pieces on our left wing behind the wood which annoyed us very much and could not be seen except by the flash of the guns." Washington ordered Proctor to turn four field pieces against the enemy guns. "Accordingly they aimed for the flash of the guns, so direct, though they could not see the guns, that in 15 or 20 minutes we received no more shot from that quarter," confirmed Nagle. "Their guns were either dismounted, or otherwise it was two hot to remain there any longer."[54]

Actually Nagle was wrong on both counts. Proctor's guns had not dismounted or driven away their crews. They were withdrawn for a particular purpose. "The Guns were ordered back and also the two Companies," explained Sergeant Sullivan, "in order to draw the Enemy after them from the trees, which scheme had the desired effect, for they quitted their post and advanced to the top of the hill, where they were attacked by four Companies of the 10th Battalion, in front, while the 40th made a charge upon their left flank, by going round the hill, and put them to an immediate rout."[55]

Sometime during this phase of the fighting, one of the most famous (and potentially momentous) events of the entire battle of Brandywine transpired:

53 Sullivan, *From Redcoat to Rebel*, 131; Judge Advocate General Office: Court Martial Proceedings and Board of General Officers' Minutes, Great Britain, War Office, March 31, 1778, Court Martial Testimony, WO71/86/66-8, microfilm copy at the David Library of the American Revolution, Washington Crossing, PA, film 675, reel 10.

54 Nagle, *Journal*, 8.

55 Sullivan, *From Redcoat to Rebel*, 131-132.

Ferguson locked Gen. Washington in his gun sights—but did not pull the trigger. "[A] Rebell Officer remarkable by a Huzzar [Hussar] Dress passed towards our army within 100 yards of my right flank, not perceiving us—he was followed by another dressed in Dark Green or blue mounted on a very good bay horse with a remarkable large high cocked hat," wrote Ferguson following the battle. "I ordered three good shots to steal near them and fire at them but the idea disgusted me and I recalled them." The two American riders, however, did not leave the area. "The Huzzar in returning made a circuit but the other passed within 100 yards of us upon which I advanced from the wood towards him, upon my calling he stopd but after looking at me proceeded. I again drew his attention, and made signs to him to stop leveling my piece at him, but he slowly continued his way. As I was within that distance at which in the quickest firing I have seldom missed a sheet of paper and could have lodged a half dozen of balls in or about him before he was out of my reach I had only to determine but it was not pleasant to fire at the back of an unoffending individual who was acquitting himself very coolly of his duty so I let him alone."[56]

Not long after this remarkable incident, a bullet shattered Ferguson's right elbow. It would take more than a year for the painful wound to heal. Ferguson was lying in a hospital the day after the battle, beginning what would be a long recovery, when a surgeon told him that "Genl. Washington was all the morning with the Light Troops generally in their front and only attended by a French Officer in a huzzar Dress he himself mounted and dressed as above described," wrote the wounded officer. It was "the oddness of their dress [that] had puzzled me and made me take notice of it." Now having learned the likely identity of the man he could have easily killed, Ferguson claimed he was not "sorry that I did not know all the time who it was."[57]

The surgeon was right: Washington was at the front that morning, riding the length of his lines to observe the enemy and encourage his men. "General Washington walked the length of his two lines, and was received with acclamations that should have promised victory," wrote Lafayette. Ferguson believed the man accompanying Washington was a French officer. While he could have been one of the officers in Lafayette's entourage, the man in Hussar

---

56 Hussars were a form of light cavalry originating in central Europe known for wearing a highly ornamented, Hungarian-style uniform with ostentatious riding boots. McGuire, *Philadelphia Campaign*, vol. 1, 180; Rankin, "Correspondence of Ferguson," 299-301.

57 Rankin, "Correspondence of Ferguson," 299-301.

dress was more likely Casimir Pulaski, who wore such a uniform at this point of the war and was serving, unattached, on Washington's staff during the battle.

As the hours passed, the fighting along this portion of the Brandywine fell away into an infrequent artillery duel accented with occasional sharpshooter activity. "The Brittish being in the open ploughed field, we could perceive when they saw the flash of our guns they would leave the gun 2 or 3 yards till the shot struck and then close," recorded Nagle. "We then ceased about an hour, excepting a few shot at different times."[58]

While the artillery exchanged rounds across the Brandywine, Knyphausen did his best to convince Washington that he was opposing Howe's entire army. The Hessian general could not risk bringing on a general engagement, however, because Washington outnumbered his division about two to one. To accomplish his diversionary mission, Knyphausen marched his various units one way and then back again, using the hills and swales to show them or hide them as he saw fit, all in an effort to artificially swell his numbers. Knyphausen, reported Howe, "kept the enemy amused in the course of the day with cannon, and the appearance of forcing the ford, without intending to pass it, until the attack upon the enemy's right should take place."[59]

The next several hours would determine the effectiveness of Knyphausen's ruse and thus the fate of both armies. On the east side of the river, Washington sorted through verbal reports in an effort to determine who, exactly, Maxwell had spent the morning fighting. Did his light infantry harass and fall back in the face of Howe's entire army? If not, then a large portion of Howe's command was no longer in his front.[60]

---

58 Idzerda, et al, eds., *Lafayette Selected Letters and Papers*, vol. 1, 94; Nagle, *Journal*, 7.

59 Reed, *Campaign to Valley Forge*, 121; Stockdale, ed., *The Parliamentary Register*, vol. 10, 427.

60 Mowday, *September 11, 1777*, 99.

Chapter 12

Mid-Day Lull:
September 11, 1777

The intelligence Washington received "remaining a long time surprisingly
uncertain, it was late before a disposition was made to receive
the enemy on that quarter."[1]

— Timothy Pickering, September 11, 1777

The Flanking Column: Cornwallis's March

At the same time General Knyphausen's division began its march
eastward toward Welch's Tavern and its rendezvous with
General Maxwell's light infantry, Gens. Howe and Cornwallis led the rest of the
army out of Kennett Square in search of General Washington's right flank. The
previous day, Cornwallis's men had marched through the village and the head
of the column camped near Marlborough Meetinghouse. On the morning of
the battle, Cornwallis's column tramped north before bearing left onto the Red
Lion Road heading toward the Red Lion Inn.[2]

---

1 Pickering, *Life of Pickering*, vol. 1, 155.

2 Marlborough Meetinghouse was close to the present Unionville High School. The road
north taken by Cornwallis is the present-day Unionville-Lenape Road. In that era, the road
probably continued on to Trimble's Ford. Today, in order to get to the ford one must turn left
at the T-intersection onto Unionville-Wawaset Road for a short distance before turning right
on to Northbrook Road, which leads down to the ford.

Cornwallis's men had a long march ahead of them—the head of his strike force would have to march about four miles just to reach one of two crossings they would need to make that day. Just above Buffington's Ford, where a battalion of Moses Hazen's Canadian regiment was posted, the river splits into two smaller streams known as the east and west branches of the Brandywine. Howe's intended route to Washington's exposed right flank was designed to carry the column well west and then north of Buffington's Ford, which required crossing both branches.

One of the generals, Howe or Cornwallis, created a select detachment of 250 troops to scout ahead of the British column. This advance force consisted of 60 dismounted Hessian jaegers, Lt. Wilhelm von Hagen with 15 mounted Hessian jaegers, the light company of the 42nd Highlanders under Capt. James McPherson, and the light company of the 17th Regiment of Foot under Capt. William Scott. All the jaegers were under the capable command of Capt. Johann Ewald, with the entire advance detachment under McPherson.

Confused Intelligence Reports

As the Queen's Rangers and Ferguson's Riflemen were being routinely ambushed by Maxwell's light infantry during their slow slog east along the Great Post Road, the first of many conflicting reports concerning Howe's activities reached Washington's headquarters. About 8:00 a.m., a vague report arrived concerning the existence of a flanking column. Washington dispatched Maj. John Jamison of Col. Theodorick Bland's Continental Light Dragoons to investigate. At that early hour, Howe's column was still en route to Trimble's Ford and had not yet reached the west branch of the Brandywine.

Around 9:30 a.m., while the action at Brinton's Ford was unfolding and Knyphausen was doing his best to appear more powerful than in fact his column was, another scouting report reached Washington. The army leader was observing Proctor's artillery duel with the British guns when news arrived from Maj. Gen. John Sullivan. "Maj. Jamison came to me . . . at nine o'clock [and said that he had] come from the right of the army, and I might depend there was no enemy there." Charles Cotesworth Pinckney, a South Carolinian who seems to have attached himself to Washington's entourage during the battle, recalled that "[s]ome Light Horse were dispatched above the Forks of the Brandywine to see if they actually had there crossed; & they, when they returned, brought information that there was no appearance of the Enemy in that quarter." Jamison's report was undoubtedly accurate because at that time Howe's flanking column had not yet crossed the west branch of the Brandywine. The news likely relieved Washington, who took no known further action on the rumor of a flanking effort. The fighting around Chads's Ford continued.[3]

When Maxwell's men pulled back across the Brandywine, the fighting died down near Chads's Ford. As the opposing artillery and skirmishers fired at one another, confusion began to settle in among the Americans. Colonel John Stone of the 1st Maryland Regiment, part of a brigade of Marylanders fighting in Sullivan's division, watched Knyphausen's men on the west side of the river "intrench themselves, by which we readily concluded their main body was taking another route. To be certain of this, light horse was dispatched to scour the country." Timothy Pickering, Washington's adjutant general, observed that Knyphausen's artillery was only taking occasional shots at the Americans while his battalions deployed on the distant hills. The conclusion chilled him. "Thus when sitting on my horse, at the side of General Washington," reported Pickering, "I said to him, 'This firing of field artillery by the enemy is merely to amuse. The main body must be marching to cross at some other place. If the serious main attack were intended at this place, they would . . . cross the ford at once.'" Pickering continued his post-battle account by explaining that Washington had received some intelligence on the move, "but it was contradicted by others; and, the information remaining a long time surprisingly uncertain, it was late before a disposition was made to receive the enemy on that quarter."[4]

For several hours conflicting reports arrived concerning the presence of an enemy flanking column off to the north beyond the American right flank. About 10:00 a.m., just as Maxwell was pulling the last of his men eastward across the Brandywine, Gen. Sullivan forwarded an aide with a report from Col. Moses Hazen at Buffington's Ford that indeed the British were making a flanking movement. Jeffries's Ford, about a mile and one-half north of

---

3   Chase and Lengel, eds., *Papers of Washington*, vol. 11, 601; Charles Cotesworth Pinckney to Henry Johnson, November 14, 1820, in *The Historical Magazine, Notes and Queries, Concerning the Antiquities, History and Biography of America*, ed. Henry B. Dawson (Morrisania, NY, 1866), vol. 10, 202-3.

4   John Stone to William Paca, September 23, 1777, in *The Chronicles of Baltimore; Being a Complete History of "Baltimore Town" and Baltimore City From the Earliest Period to the Present Time*, ed. J. Thomas Scharf (Baltimore, 1874), 166; Timothy Pickering, Pickering Papers, Massachusetts Historical Society, Boston, MA, microfilm copies at the David Library of the American Revolution, Washington Crossing, PA, film 220, reel 52, 184-186; Octavius Pickering, *Life of Pickering*, vol. 1, 155.

Buffington's Ford, was where Cornwallis's flanking column would cross the east branch of the Brandywine. The only troops Washington had above Buffington's Ford were some of Bland's light dragoon patrols. There were additional American patrols, both on foot and on horseback, searching the area between the east and west branches of the Brandywine during the morning hours. When the initial confusing reports arrived at headquarters that morning, Washington had ordered all the light horse that had been sitting in reserve near his headquarters to make for the right to patrol the network of roads there.

The muddled intelligence situation did not sit well with John Sullivan, who was responsible for protecting the American right flank. He had little to no intelligence about the ground to his north and Washington was doing precious little to keep him informed. "I had no Orders, or even Hints to look at any other places, but those mentioned," Sullivan wrote after the battle, "nor had I Light troops, or Light Horsemen furnished for the purpose. . . . I had but four Light Horsemen, two of which I kept at the upper Fords, to bring me Intelligence, the others I kept to send Intelligence to Head Quarters." According to Sullivan, "It was ever my opinion that the enemy wou'd come round on our Right flank. This opinion I often gave the general. I wrote him that morning that it was clearly my opinion: I sent him two messages to the same purpose in the forenoon."[5]

General James Grant, whose command was attached to Knyphausen's division, had his own low opinion of Washington's intelligence-gathering abilities. "Washington in his Accounts to the Congress," explained Grant, "owns He did not look for an Enemy in force [on his right and makes] an excuse for not having prepared for & complains of his want of intelligence, which in fact it was impossible for Him to procure unless Lord Cornwallis or I had sent it to Him."[6]

Given the conflicting reports, Washington decided to wait for confirmation from Col. Bland's horsemen before deciding upon a course of action. It was a curious decision. Moses Hazen was a veteran officer and in command of the northernmost American detachment (at Buffington's Ford). He was in the best position to know what was taking place north and west of Washington's lines that morning.

5 Hammond, ed., *Papers of Sullivan*, vol. 1, 475-476, 549. There is an oft-repeated story of Washington and Knox laughing at Sullivan's aide when he reported Sullivan's opinion to headquarters. However, no available contemporary document corroborates the claim.

6 James Grant to Harvey, October 20, 1777, James Grant of Papers.

There are a number of reasons why Washington and his key subordinates were confused about the location of the British flanking column. First, the early morning fog, dust, and heat combined to make it difficult for American patrols to spot the column at a distance. Second, Cornwallis marched north out of Kennett Square on the Great Valley Road, which was not one of the roads Washington's scouts had examined. Third, locals kept Howe very well informed, but the same cannot be said for Washington. As noted earlier, the British column was guided by the three Chester County loyalists (Curtis Lewis, a blacksmith and large landowner from West Bradford Township; John Jackson, a clockmaker from East Marlborough; and Joseph Galloway, who was in overall control of the guides). The knowledge provided by the locals astounded Hessian officer Ewald. One guide, he observed, was a "real geographical chart. I often spoke with him regarding the area which was beyond the horizon. He constantly judged so correctly that I always found the enemy there where he presumed him to be. His description was so good that I was often amazed at the knowledge this man possessed of the country." Ewald's orders were to move as "slowly as possible, and to use all caution in order not fall into an ambuscade, as the area was traversed by hills, woodlands, marshes, and the steepest defiles."[7]

Around the same time Maxwell was pulling the last of his men to the east side of the Brandywine, Capt. Mountjoy Bayly with a detachment of the 7th Maryland Regiment (Sullivan's division) rode onto a farm owned by Joel Bailey, a wealthy Quaker farmer who owned 250 acres and a gristmill. His property overlooked Trimble's Ford on the west branch of the Brandywine, across from James Trimble's mill and farm. This was about two miles above the forks of the Brandywine (Buffington's Ford) and about four miles northwest of Brinton's Ford. Next to Galloway, Bailey was one of the better-known civilians on the battlefield that day. He made clocks, furniture, and guns, and was also a surveyor and astronomer. Bailey had assisted Mason and Dixon with their famous survey a decade earlier, and in 1769 was part of a team that observed the transit of Venus at Cape Henlopen, for which he was elected to the American Philosophical Society. Bailey was also an acquaintance of botanist Humphrey Marshall, whose home, botanical garden, and observatory were one mile north of Bailey's place on the Strasburg Road near Martin's Tavern.[8]

---

7 McGuire, *Philadelphia Campaign*, vol. 1, 184; Ewald, *Diary*, 83-84.

8 McGuire, *Philadelphia Campaign*, vol. 1, 185. The original road to Trimble's Ford is now partially private and is called Bragg's Hill Road.

Captain Bayly's men from the 7th Maryland may have been dressed that morning in old red Maryland militia coats. According to a local history, "The hospitable old farmer mistook the Maryland company for British, and greeted them with a hearty welcome." Joel Bailey was a loyalist, so he invited the supposed British soldiers in for a meal, "of which they freely partook, and Mountjoy kept his aged host in pleasant conversation, without in any way correcting his misapprehensions." While they were eating with Bailey, the Marylanders spotted the head of Cornwallis's column approaching the ford. "The advance of the British column was seen approaching when Capt. Bayly concluded it was about time for his Marylanders to be moving. He so stated to the hospitable old farmer, who thereupon urged him to remain, assuring him that the approaching troops were certainly good friends." The quick-thinking scout settled upon a believable lie: "Capt. Bayly, however, excused himself by alleging that the duty of his company was to keep some distance ahead of the column; and so he speedily made his escape from a rather critical position."[9]

The head of Cornwallis's flanking column reached Trimble's Ford around 10:30 a.m. The crossing point on the west branch of the Brandywine was about five and one-half miles from Kennett Square. It had taken Cornwallis about five and one-half hours to cover that distance. Cornwallis's rate of march was unimpressive—especially considering that Knyphausen made much faster progress along the Great Post Road in a fitful advance while under fire. Knyphausen's artillery duel at Chads's Ford was 30 minutes old by the time Cornwallis's advance spotted Trimble's Ford.[10]

Once across the west branch of the Brandywine, Cornwallis's division entered West Bradford Township. Howe's German aide, Capt. Friedrich von Muenchhausen, remembered that the pace of the column picked up and

---

9 Futhey and Cope, *History of Chester County*, 80. The story is believable, but the source is questionable. Dr. William Darlington was one of the earliest historians of Chester County and an occasional member of Congress in the early 1800s. In 1822, the former Capt. Mountjoy Bayly was serving as the sergeant-at-arms in the U.S. Senate. Darlington spent an evening at Bayly's home that year, during which the latter told the war story to his guests. Darlington, therefore, is the source of the story, and not Bayly himself. Two facts support this version. First, Bayly was indeed a captain in the 7th Maryland in 1777, and second, he died in 1836—after the supposed dinner party in 1822. See also, Francis B. Heitman, *Historical Register of Officers of the Continental Army During the War of the Revolution* (Baltimore, 2003), 81. Despite Joel Bailey's loyalism, the passing British troops plundered his farm. Although two British officers gave him £45, he lost household items and clothing valued at nearly £140—including four horses with harnesses, five sheep, and 300 pounds of cheese. Futhey and Cope, *History of Chester County*, 80.

10 McGuire, *Philadelphia Campaign*, vol. 1, 186.

"moved forward quickly in spite of the great heat." The fog had now burned off, and the soldiers discovered they were surrounded by a lush rolling terrain dotted with farm buildings and mills, rich fields surrounded by rail fences, plump orchards, and soon-to-be harvested fields of corn.[11]

Just more than one mile up the ridge from Trimble's Ford was Martin's Tavern, operated by a 60-year-old former Quaker. The tavern was located at an important crossroads and was also known as the Center House because of its location at what was then the geographic center of the county. Militia and various county officials used the large stone building as a gathering place. Three militia officers slept there the night before the battle. Colonel John Hannum, whose farm sat along the eastern branch of the Brandywine, was commander of the 1st Battalion of the Chester County Militia. Another officer, Maj. Joseph Spear of the 8th Battalion of the Chester County Militia, accompanied Hannum. The last of the three was Thomas Cheyney, a large landowner from nearby Thornbury Township to whom many historians would assign a legendary role in the upcoming battle. He had served for years in a variety of county government positions, and had recently been named a sub-lieutenant with the job of organizing the newly created militia.[12]

By this time Washington was beginning to suspect that something was indeed amiss to the north. "I earnestly entreat a continuance of your vigilant attention to the movements of the enemy," he wrote Col. Bland of the Continental Light Dragoons, "and the earliest report not only of their movements, but of their numbers and the course they are pursuing." Washington also wanted the horseman to gather information about "a body confidently reported to have gone up to a ford seven or eight miles above this [Chads's Ford]. It is said the fact is certain. . . . [B]e particular on these matters." It was Washington's deep distrust of militia officers that prompted his dispatch to Bland with orders to investigate the possibilities of an enemy flanking column—even though Bland was a Virginian with no knowledge of the area. One of the many prescribed roles of dragoons was reconnaissance work, and Washington was counting on them to do their job.[13] As late as 11 or 12 o'clock, Washington bitterly lamented "that Col. Bland had not sent him any

11 Von Muenchhausen, *At General Howe's Side*, 31.

12 McGuire, *Philadelphia Campaign*, vol. 1, 186-187.

13 Charles Campbell, ed., *The Bland Papers: Being a Selection from the Manuscripts of Colonel Theodorick Bland, Jr.* (Petersburg, VA, 1840), vol. 1, 67.

information at all, & that the accounts, he had received from others were of a very contradictory nature."[14]

According to Brig. Gen. George Weedon, Washington surmised the British were heading for Jones's Ford (the crossing north of Brinton's Ford), so he ordered Lord Stirling's and Maj.. Gen. Adam Stephen's divisions to shift north to protect what was now a very vulnerable right flank. The divisions headed out by different routes and had gone about "1 ½ Mile when the General had Intelligence that the Enemy had not gone up & ordered the advanced Divisions to halt which they did for two Hours."[15] These divisions did not return to the main army, halting instead just under half way to Birmingham Hill.

Lieutenant Colonel James Ross of the 1st Pennsylvania Regiment was riding north of Washington's main positions during the early morning hours. Although records are incomplete, Ross and the 70 men with him were likely assigned to Maxwell's infantry and sent to scout and guard his exposed right flank while west of the Brandywine. If Maxwell was at Kennett Meetinghouse, his right flank would have been in the vicinity of the Great Valley Road— exactly the route upon which Cornwallis's column was marching north.

It was about noon when Washington received the following report from Ross: "A large body of the enemy from every account 5000, with 16 or 18 field pieces, marched along this road just now. This road leads to Taylor's [Trimble's] and Jeffries ferries on the Brandywine. . . . There is also a road from Brandywine to Chester by Dilworth's Tavern." Ross informed Washington that he was close on the British column's rear "with about 70 men. Capt. [Michael] Simpson lay in ambush with 20 men, and gave them three rounds within a small distance, in which two of his men were wounded, one mortally." Ross's report went on to state, "Genl. Howe is with this party as Joseph Galloway is here known by the inhabitants with many of whom he spoke, and told them that Genl. Howe is with him." Ross also mentioned skirmishing with the column, and Ewald confirmed this in his diary when he wrote about running into a "warning post of the enemy, five to six hundred men strong, who withdrew from one favorable position to another under constant skirmishing until around noontime." Where this first skirmish between Ewald and Ross took place remains unclear.[16]

14 Pinckney to Johnson, November 14, 1820, 202-203.

15 Weedon to Page, September 11, 1777.

16 Ewald, *Diary*, 83; Chase and Lengel, eds., *Papers of Washington*, vol. 11, 196.

Ross had recently served as an officer of the day to Washington, was the son of a signer of the Declaration of Independence, and was someone who could be trusted. However, Ross's information was also a bit erroneous because the Great Valley Road did not lead to Jeffries Ford. After crossing Trimble's Ford, the main road continued north to Martin's Tavern—away from the American right flank—while a branch road curved eastward to Jeffries Ford. Although Howe's column took this branch to the ford, Washington could have reasonably inferred that either Howe was marching more northerly than he was, or that he was dividing his army a second time. Washington concluded from this report that Howe had already crossed the west branch of the Brandywine and that he was going after Washington's supply depots at Reading, Pennsylvania.

Ross's message reached Washington while he was near the Chads House attempting to discern what was transpiring on the west side of the river. Amos House, a nephew to Mrs. Chads, remembered the scene and left the following description (including himself in the third person):

> Gen. Washington, with a few attendants, rode up into the field above Mrs. Chads's dwelling, and was engaged, with the aid of glasses, in reconnoitering and endeavouring to ascertain the character and position of the hostile forces on the hills west of the stream. While they were thus engaged, Amos House and two or three others were led by curiosity to approach and observe what was going on. Pretty soon, said Mr. House, some cannon-balls from the enemy's artillery began to drop in the field quite near to the company thus collected, when Gen. Washington remarked to the visitors, 'Gentlemen, you perceive that we are attracting the notice of the enemy. I think you had better retire.'"[17]

James Parker of the Queen's Rangers confirmed the story. "About 12 I saw Washington Come out of A farm house. I pointed him out to the Generals; he had Some of his Officers about him with two White flags. . . . I was afterwards told by a Rebel, it was just at that time he got intelligence that Genl. Howe was crossing the B. Wine above him." Parker, a bitter loyalist who had lost everything in Virginia, managed to get some artillery to fire at the distant group. "I had in short enough to get a Canon fired at the Group. . . . [M]y prayers went with the ball that it might finish Washington & the Rebelion together." For the

---

17 Futhey and Cope, *History of Chester County*, 80.

second time that day, the most important man in America barely escaped severe injury or death.[18]

The Abortive Attack at Brinton's Ford

Ross's message convinced Washington there was no longer an imminent threat against his right flank, and that Howe with a large portion of his army was still absent from his front. Was there an opportunity to seize the initiative by assaulting the enemy opposing him at Chads's Ford? A divided enemy offered an aggressive general the opportunity to attack and defeat his opponent in detail. The effort would have to be organized and launched quickly, however, before the returning column could threaten the assaulting American army.[19] His decision made, Washington ordered Sullivan to attack with his division across Brinton's Ford against Knyphausen's left flank while the division and brigade under Gens. Nathanael Greene and William Maxwell crossed at Chads's Ford to attack Knyphausen's right and center. It was a bold strategy.

According to Sullivan, he was ordered "to cross the Brandewine with my Division & attack the enemy's left while the army crossed below me to attack their Right." The army's adjutant general, Timothy Pickering, outlined the plan. "It was satisfactorily concluded that only a part of the enemy's army was on the other side at Chads' Ford; and in consequence, preparations were made for attacking it," he explained. "Sullivan as well as Greene, was to cross over & attack, with the whole Army in two columns." It was a critical decision that would have changed the course of the battle. In fact, Washington was planning to launch the first offensive by the Continental Army against a significant portion of the British Army during the American Revolution.[20]

As ordered, Maxwell pushed his way west across the Brandywine, shoving aside Knyphausen's pickets in front of him as he moved. Simultaneously, Sullivan's advance troops under Col. Nathaniel Ramsey of the 3rd Maryland Regiment crossed the Brandywine at Brinton's Ford and skirmished with the British 4th Regiment of Foot and some of Ferguson's riflemen. The thrust quickly escalated into a lively fight, with light infantry and artillery opening up

18 James Parker, journal entry, September 11, Parker Family Papers.

19 Reed, *Campaign to Valley Forge*, 124.

20 Hammond, ed., *Papers of Sullivan*, vol. 1, 475-476; Pickering Papers, Film 220, Reel 52, 184-186; McGuire, *Philadelphia Campaign*, vol. 1, 191.

on both sides. Lieutenant Colonel Samuel Smith of the 4th Maryland Regiment remembered that Ramsey crossed the river, and "skirmished with and drove the Yagers."[21] Smith once again mistook the green uniforms of the Queen's Rangers and Ferguson's riflemen for Hessian jaegers.

Just as the fighting was heating up, Washington "gave orders for the greatest part of the army to cross the several fords, but before this order was put in execution it was countermanded." Lieutenant Colonel Smith recalled that every regiment had been prepared to pass over the river before the orders were reversed. A Hessian officer remembered the beginning of the troop movement before Washington ground it to a halt when he wrote, "Meanwhile the enemy caused a number of their troops belonging to the right wing to cross the river at Edwardsmill and advance." A member of the 4th Regiment of Foot also recalled the American move. "They [the Americans] immediately detached from the Opposite Height, a Column with a Field Piece, and some Light Horse down to the Ferry [Brinton's Ford], and advanced some of their Rifle Men to cover their Working Party, while they fell'd trees &c." Sergeant Major Francis Thorne of the 4th Regiment of Foot picked up the action, adding, "A pretty hot fire of Musquetry continued for about a quarter of an hour." After the American infantry withdrew from the area, Proctor's artillery zeroed in on the 4th Regiment's position. The heavy and accurate fire forced the battalion guns of the British regiment to be moved "into the Road, [whereupon] they [Sullivan's men] retired to their former ground."[22]

General Greene's division, recorded a Hessian scribe, "showed signs of occupying the hills on this side of the river behind the morass with more troops," and Maxwell's men "reinforced their outposts, who were standing in the woods that extended to the foot of these heights, so as to dispute the passage of the morass." Therefore, "General Knyphausen ordered the Queen's Rangers to cross the same, and attack the enemy in the wood on the other side of it." Repeating what had taken place all morning, the light troops of both

---

21 McGuire, *Philadelphia Campaign*, vol. 1, 191; Samuel Smith, "The Papers of General Samuel Smith," in *The Historical Magazine and Notes and Queries, Concerning the Antiquities, History and Biography of America*, 2nd series, no. 2 (Morrisania, NY, February 1870), vol. 7, 85.

22 Stone to Paca, September 23, 1777, 166; Smith, "Papers of Smith," 85; Journal of the Hessian Corps in America under General von Heister, 1776-June 1777, Hessian Documents of the American Revolution, Morristown National Historical Park, Morristown, New Jersey, copy in the David Library of the American Revolution, Washington Crossing, PA, microfiche 326-327, letter Z, 84; Francis Thorne to Lord Percy, September 29, 1777, in Percy Papers, Alnwick Castle, Alnwick, England, vol. 52.

armies engaged once more. Maxwell's men, "who consisted of nothing but sharpshooters, killed and wounded many of our men, but withdrew to the woods in the direction of Chatsesfort [Chads's' Ford] on this side of the Brandewyn when these advanced with levelled gun and the English Jagers [Ferguson's riflemen] approached their left flank." Additional English regiments were fed into the combat. "The 4th and 5th Regiments had to march towards the passage across the Brandewyn river, so as to dislodge the enemy who were posted on this side of same and chase them across the water." Artillery from both sides quickly engaged to keep the soldiers from both armies away from the river banks.[23]

The reason for Washington's reversal was yet another contradictory report. Just as the operation was commencing, a new piece of intelligence arrived that convinced the American army commander to order Sullivan to stop his movement west across the Brandywine. About 12:30 p.m., Maj. Joseph Spear of the 8th Battalion of the Chester County Militia rode in to report that he had just been in the upper country, had come in by the road which the enemy must pass to attack the American right, and not a single British soldier was to be found there. According to Sullivan, Washington had sent Spear "out for the purpose of discovering whether the enemy were in that Quarter." Spear was one of the three men who had spent the previous night at Martin's Tavern. The major rose before sunrise that morning and headed south on the Great Valley Road in the direction of Welch's Tavern, about five miles distant. Spear filed his reconnaissance report with Sullivan, who in turn forwarded Spear with the information and a light horseman on to Washington's headquarters. "Since I sent you the message by Major [Lewis] Morris [Sullivan's aide] I saw Major Joseph Spear of the Militia who came this morning from a Tavern called Martins in the Forks of the Brandywine—he came from thence to Welches Tavern & heard nothing of the Enemy about the Forks of the Brandywine & is confident they are not in that Quarter," Sullivan wrote Washington. "So that Colonel Hazen's information must be wrong. I have sent to that Quarter to know whether there is any foundation for the Report and shall give Yr. Excy. the earliest information."[24]

23 Journal of the Hessian Corps, Letter Z, 84.

24 Hammond, ed., *Papers of Sullivan*, vol. 1, 451, 476; Chase and Lengel, eds., *Papers of Washington*, vol. 11, 197-198.

But what neither Washington nor Sullivan knew at that time was that Moses Hazen was not wrong: the British were indeed aiming a massive blow for the American right flank. Because Sullivan remained suspicious, he dispatched Sgt. William Tucker of the dragoons to confirm Spears's report. Tucker returned and substantiated Spears: there was no enemy in that quarter. Sullivan dutifully forwarded the new information on to Washington. Even though he did not trust its reliability, Sullivan felt duty-bound to report what Spears had seen. "Had the General crossed over . . . & found the whole British army well posted in his front & his Army put to the rout having a river unfordable in rear, except in one or two places & most of his troops pushed into it . . . & he had afterwards found out that I had received & withheld the intelligence, which might have prevented this misfortune & demanded my reasons I believe I never shou'd have been able to give one which wou'd be Satisfactory to him to congress or to the world."[25]

Nevertheless, Sullivan later claimed that he remained convinced Howe was conducting a flanking march: "This intelligence did by no means alter my opinion . . . upon an apprehension that Genl. Howe would take that advantage which any good officer in his situation would have done." If Sullivan believed this during the early stage of the battle, there was precedent for his supposition, for he had been captured the previous year on Long Island after a similar Howe move. As a result, Sullivan was justifiably wary of flank attacks. Still, observes one historian, if Sullivan expected Howe to launch one, "he failed to take proper initiative to check on possible crossing places."[26]

Washington put his trust and faith in the incorrect scouting report. He would indeed be outflanked later that afternoon, but never blamed Sullivan for it. "I ascribed the misfortune . . . principally to the information of Major Spear, transmitted to me by you; yet I never blamed you for conveying the intelligence," explained the army commander. "On the contrary . . . I should have thought you culpable in concealing it. The Major's rank, reputation and knowledge of the Country, gave him a full claim to credit and attention. His intelligence was no doubt a most unfortunate circumstance. . . . But it was not your fault that the intelligence was eventually found to be erroneous."[27]

---

25 Hammond, ed., *Papers of Sullivan*, vol. 1, 476-477.

26 Ibid.; Billias, ed., *George Washington's Generals and Opponents*, vol.1, 149.

27 Fitzpatrick, ed., *Writings of Washington*, vol. 9, 425-426.

Washington's confusion over the conflicting intelligence reports is understandable. But what was not clear was why he would put faith in a low-level militia officer's report. Washington believed a militia soldier, explains one historian, who "knew nothing of the tactical situation or the troop dispositions and refused to believe the reports of two experienced Continental officers, one of whom had actually skirmished with the British column."[28]

The reality is that the news convinced Washington that Howe was trying to trick him—again. "It was possible," explains a historian of the campaign, that Howe was setting a trap similar to the one a few months earlier at Short Hills: lure him out of his position in the high ground, then turn and catch him in a pincher movement."[29]

In the end Washington concluded Howe's "flanking" movement was a feint, and that the column was returning to Knyphausen. Once he reached that decision his next step was obvious, and he called off the attack across the Brandywine. He ordered Sullivan to pull back, confirm the reports, and wait for intelligence from Col. Bland. Maxwell, too, was directed to withdraw his troops to the east side of the river. Greene had not yet crossed, and so remained on the west side.

How was it that Spear missed Cornwallis's large column marching north? Although we will never know with certainty, it is probable that he examined the roads prior to Cornwallis's departure from Kennett Square. That is the only reasonable explanation why he did not encounter any of Cornwallis's troops. What duty Spear performed between that early hour and the middle of the day, however, remains a complete mystery. "He must have been very slow, dallying somewhere, or thorough to a fault, investigating byways and side paths," opines one historian. "The area he passed through has numerous lanes, woods, parallel roads, and abrupt hills; this was the terrain that Cornwallis used to screen his march, and it was well chosen."[30] The Spear incident simply reinforced Washington's long and existing mistrust of all things militia, who wanted to wait for confirmation from Col. Bland before deciding his next move.

Sullivan's and Maxwell's infantrymen were only lightly engaged before the order to retire reached them. When they withdrew, behind them were "thirty

---

28 Pancake, *1777*, 172.

29 McGuire, *Philadelphia Campaign*, vol. 1, 193.

30 Ibid.

Men left dead on the Spot, among them a Captn' of the 49th, and a number of Intrenching Tools with which they were throwing up a Battery."[31] Once Washington disengaged, Knyphausen let the Americans fall back without following up closely with an attack of his own. Knyphausen's objective was to divert attention and hold Washington's main army in place until he heard from Howe.

Cornwallis's Column

While Washington weighed the various scouting reports and marked time around Chads's Ford, Cornwallis marched. The head of his column arrived at Jeffries's Ford around 1:00 p.m. The distance along the roads between Trimble's Ford and Jeffries's Ford is about three miles,[32] and it took Cornwallis about two hours to cover it. Jeffries's Ford was very deep, with the water as high as a man's middle.[33] According to Howe's staffer, Capt. von Muenchhausen, "we crossed the Brandywine seven miles up from Chads Ford, where the river is divided into two branches; the bridges were destroyed. The men had to cross these two branches in up to three feet of water. We then continued our march a short distance straight ahead."[34] Once across, the men fell out of marching order to take a rest from the midday heat as the elements stacked on the western side of the branch waited for their turn to cross.

31 Fitzpatrick, ed., *Writings of Washington*, vol. 9, 207; Inman, ed., "List of Officers Killed," 184. The only officer matching this description was Capt. John Stewart of the British 49th Regiment of Foot, who fell wounded, but survived.

32 The eighteenth-century road from Trimble's Ford to Jeffries Ford no longer exists. Following the general route today, once across Trimble's Ford, Cornwallis's column moved north on modern Northbrook Road and turned right onto Camp Linden Road, made a left onto Wawaset Road, and a right onto a modern private farm lane. Traces of the eighteenth-century road can still be seen crossing modern farm fields toward Jeffries's Ford. This trace ties back in with modern Lucky Hill Road on the opposite side of the present farm fields before continuing down to the east branch of the Brandywine at Jeffries's Ford.

33 One of the many local legends about the battle involves liquor being stored at the Jeffries house. The home stood just on the west side of the ford of the same name. Legend has it that Wilmington, Delaware, merchants had shipped large quantities of wine and liquor to Chester County for safekeeping. Supposedly, all this liquor was stored in the Jeffries home and was found by Howe's men as they marched down to the ford. The story seems to have originated in Jenkins, "Brandywine, 1777," 335. No eighteenth-century source mentions the liquor, so I omitted the unconfirmed tale from the main body of the text.

34 Von Muenchhausen, *At Howe's Side: 1776-1778*, 31.

Just to the east of Jeffries's Ford, the road to Birmingham intersects the road coming from Jeffries's Ford at right angles, cutting through a sharp defile. The Birmingham Road ran southwest like a giant arrow roughly parallel to, and about one mile from, the Brandywine. It was the perfect avenue to march troops behind Washington's Army, and was the route Cornwallis would take to do so. "My guide," recalled Captain Ewald, "asserted that if we did not meet with the enemy here [intersection], he must have been defeated by General Knyphausen, whose fire we had heard during the whole day." Ewald sent his jaegers into the defile by twos, with specific orders to fall back if they encountered the enemy. The Hessian "was astonished when I had reached the end of this terrible defile, which was over a thousand paces long, and could discover nothing of the enemy a good half hour away. Lord Cornwallis, who had followed me, was surprised himself and could not understand why the warning post with which I had fought from morning until around noon was not stationed here. The pass had been left wide open for us," he concluded, "where a hundred men could have held up either army the whole day."[35]

At least in this experienced officer's opinion, this was a spot Washington should have defended. It was the second time in less than a week that the Americans had left undefended a defile Ewald found frightening in its defensive capabilities. Jeffries's Ford was just over one-half mile from Sconneltown—a crossroads hamlet consisting of little more than a wheelwright shop and a few houses—and about three miles from Birmingham Meetinghouse. At Sconneltown, one road ran to Birmingham, the other led to Turk's Head Tavern (modern-day West Chester) a few miles farther east. About 1:00 p.m., a mounted American officer with a handful of others was positioned east of the Birmingham Road looking westward in search of a potential enemy advance. Information as to Howe's intentions in that quarter had been contradictory and muddled all morning. The true state of affairs, however, was about to crystallize for the American scout and his commanding officer.

At 1:15 p.m., Bland forwarded the following note to Sullivan: "I have discovered a party of the enemy on the heights, just on the right of the two widow Davises', who live close together on the road called the Fork Road, about a half mile to the right of the meeting-house." The "party of the enemy"

---

35 Ewald, *Diary*, 83. "The warning post with which I had fought from morning until around noon" was another reference by Ewald to the 1st Pennsylvania's Lt. Col. James Ross and his 70 men, who had reported his skirmishing to Washington.

was almost certainly Ewald's advance (including Ewald himself). Of the houses Bland mentioned, one was located at the intersection of the Birmingham Road and Street Road, and the other along Radley Run just east of the road intersection. Finally, "the heights" was Osborn's Hill north of Radley Run.[36]

Sullivan forwarded Bland's report to Washington at 2:00 p.m. with the following note scribbled upon it: "Colonel Bland has at this moment sent me word, that the enemy are in the rear of my right, about two miles, coming down. There are, he says, about two brigades of them. He also says he saw a dust back in the country for above an hour." When he was later defending his actions, Sullivan declared, "[T]he very first intelligence I received, that they were actually coming that way, I instantly communicated to him [Washington]."[37]

While Bland and his cavalrymen were counting enemy troops beyond the American right flank about 1:00 p.m., Washington and his staff were returning to headquarters at the Ring House for dinner. It was there, sometime shortly after 2:00 p.m., that the general received Bland's message forwarded on by Sullivan. The bad news surely chilled Washington, who was not only caught off guard but also badly out of position to influence the course of events. Was there time to salvage his Brandywine position? He decided in the affirmative and within minutes riders galloped out of the Ring yard with orders for troops to immediately march northward to confront the enemy column. As the army commander's adjutant, Timothy Pickering, remembered it, their small party had "just dined at Head Quarters, & briskly started from thence."[38] The divisions of Lord Stirling and Adam Stephen would indeed continue their march, begun earlier and halted, toward the threatened sector.

The Role of Thomas Cheyney

A fascinating and nearly ubiquitous story that appears in every history of the battle concerns a man named Thomas Cheyney and his role along the Brandywine. According to this story, Cheyney is credited with warning Washington about the flanking column and thus saving the American Army from possible destruction.

---

36 Chase and Lengel, eds., *Papers of Washington*, vol. 11, 198; Smith, *Brandywine*, 15.

37 Hammond, ed., *Papers of Sullivan*, vol. 1, 453, 475.

38 McGuire, *Philadelphia Campaign*, vol. 1, 197; Pickering Papers, film 220, reel 52, 184-186.

John Reed's 1965 study of the campaign included the Cheyney tale and added supposed dialogue spoken by him: "No sooner had Bland's message been dispatched to the Commander-in-Chief than Squire Thomas Cheyney, a patriot of local repute, rode hastily in to Sullivan and verbally confirmed Bland's report. . . . Sullivan, however, was little inclined to take the word of a civilian against that of a soldier," explained Reed. "Cheyney, taken aback by Sullivan's disbelief, demanded permission to proceed in person to Washington. Sullivan, somewhat grudgingly, granted this demand, and Cheyney rode to Chad's Ford. There Washington, perhaps a little petulant at the conflicting reports, told Cheyney with no uncertainty his own doubtful opinion of the extent of the British maneuver." Reed went so far as to include what Cheyney supposedly told Washington: "'If you doubt my word,' Cheyney said heatedly, 'put me under guard until you can ask Anthony Wayne or Persie Frazer if I am a man to be believed.' Then, turning to the assembled staff, he observed, 'I would have you know that I have this day's work as much at heart as e'er a blood of you.'"[39]

A bicentennial-era history of 1777 included this description of Cheyney warning the American army leader: "About 2:00 in the afternoon an excited man named Thomas Cheyney arrived at headquarters. The big, black-eyed farmer shouldered Washington's aides aside and insisted on seeing the commander in chief. The army, he told Washington, was nearly surrounded. He himself had seen a huge column on the eastern side of the Brandywine. Washington refused to believe him, but he seems to have been doubtful enough to start off to see for himself."[40]

Gregory Edgar's 1998 version opens with a description of Cheyney: "Just before two o'clock, a very large, dark complexioned man named Thomas Cheyney came riding hard into headquarters, shouting that the army must retreat or they will all be cut off. Though aides tried to quiet him, he kept shouting, demanding to speak to the commander in chief. Hearing the ruckus, the tall Virginian came out of the house and faced the man. He told Washington that he was a patriot, lived in the area, and had been out on his own doing some scouting all morning." According to Edgar, Cheyney described what he had seen, and recounted how the British "fired at him, but he'd got away." When

39 Reed, *Campaign*, 127.

40 Pancake, *1777*, 172. Pancake's citation for this portion of his book includes eight sources in a single endnote. However, not one of these eight sources provides an eighteenth-century source confirming any of the Cheyney story.

Washington doubted the civilian's account, "Cheyney got down off his horse and quickly drew a rough map in the dirt, to illustrate where he had seen the enemy column, where they would cross, and the steep defile near it, where they could be ambushed. But the general still looked doubtful." Edgar went on to repeat the same dialogue from Reed's study. Mowday's 2002 study included a lengthy retelling of the Cheyney story full of secondary quotations. Later in the work, the author adds, "[B]y 2 p.m. Squire Thomas Cheyney made his impassioned plea to Washington concerning Howe's advance."[41]

Thomas McGuire's 2006 history of the campaign nearly eliminated the Cheyney story, though he did include the possibility that the first direct warning originated with Cheyney: "Several hours after Spear left the Center House, Colonel Hannum and Squire Cheyney saddled up and headed south on the Great Valley Road. Passing down the long ridge through the woods, the sight that met their eyes as they approached Trimble's Mill would have brought them up short. There across the Brandywine on the hill above Trimble's Ford, was . . . Cornwallis's troops. . . . At this point," continued McGuire, "as local tradition maintains, Cheyney rode off in a hell-for-leather dash to warn Washington of the flank march."[42]

As is readily obvious, all of these secondary sources simply repeat and enhance the Cheyney story, one building off the other. Thomas Cheyney did in fact exist, and he had served the Chester County government before the battle. Unfortunately, not a single eighteenth-century primary source has surfaced to corroborate the story. No officers at Washington's headquarters that day, including Washington himself, make any mention of Cheyney. Washington wrote that he wanted to wait for confirmation from Col. Theodorick Bland of an enemy flanking move. John Sullivan, who had been forwarding reports to Washington's headquarters all morning, did not send Cheyney to Washington, nor did he forward any reports from him. In addition, if the Cheyney story was accurate, he would have ridden into the vicinity of Trimble's Ford just as Mountjoy Bayly's men were withdrawing from the area. The sources are silent on this aspect of Cheyney's involvement as well. Bayley made no mention of an

---

41 Edgar, *The Philadelphia Campaign*, 24; Mowday, *September 11, 1777*, 107. Mowday's sources for the Cheyney tale are Cheyney family stories supposedly passed down through the generations. Unless an eighteenth-century source becomes available to substantiate the story, it is difficult to accept the family's version of the tale.

42 McGuire, *Philadelphia Campaign*, vol. 1, 187-188.

encounter with any other Americans near the ford. Lastly, no account by Cheyney and the important role he supposedly played has come to light.

What are we to conclude from this? In all likelihood, the Cheyney story is a local legend passed on without primary substantiation—but given credence by historians and writers who have simply reiterated and embellished the tale with each passing stroke of the pen. The report that shifted American divisions northward came from Col. Bland through Sullivan—not from Cheyney.

The Armies Arrive Near Birmingham Hill

While Washingon was digesting Bland's report, Cornwallis's main flanking column was pressing through the defile and Sconneltown. It was about 2:00 p.m. Like the British and German troops tramping around the American flank, the ranks of the Continental Army had a sizeable number of sick men. "A considerable number of the soldiers were sick, in consequence of their long marches through the excessive heat of the season of the year," recalled Quaker Joseph Townsend. Since Washington's Army was using the Birmingham Meetinghouse as a hospital for these ill men, the Quakers of Birmingham were holding their mid-week meeting in Phillip Crist's wheelwright shop in Sconneltown. The commotion of a passing army sent several Quakers outside to see what was happening. When they did not return, "suspicions arose that something serious had taken place." The meeting was quickly called to an end and the remaining Quakers moved outside as well. As Townsend put it, "They found it to be an alarm amongst some of our neighboring women that the English Army was coming and they murdered all before them—young and old."[43]

Townsend watched as the British poured across the Brandywine: "Our eyes were caught on a sudden by the appearance of the army coming out of the woods into the fields belonging to Emmor Jefferis, on the west side of the creek above the fording place. In a few minutes the fields were literally covered with them, and they were hastening towards us. Their arms and bayonets being raised, shone as bright as silver, there being a clear sky and the day exceedingly warm." The scene was indeed impressive. Most locals had never seen more than

---

43 Townsend, *Some Account*, 20, 21. Later in the day, fighting would rage around the Birmingham Meetinghouse. The fate of the sick Americans inside is unclear. No known account mentions them in conjunction with the fighting.

a few score of people gathered in one place at a time. Now, before them in bright uniforms and armed to the teeth, were thousands of soldiers pouring across their farm fields "in an extraordinary spectacle of martial pomp and arrogance, the very antithesis of Quaker culture."[44]

The sight of the advancing enemy army sent Townsend rushing home to check on his family. Their safety confirmed, his curiosity got the better of him. Returning to the scene, he received permission from a British officer to ride through the army. Once the British turned up the Birmingham Road and began moving through Sconneltown, Townsend found himself in . . .

> the midst of a crowd of military characters, rank and file: little to be discovered but staff officers and a continued march of soldiers and occasionally a troop of horse passing; great numbers of baggage wagons began to make their appearance, well-guarded by proper officers and soldiery. We [Townsend and some friends] passed through them until we reached one of the most eligible houses in the town (Sconneltown). Soon after the principle officers came in, who manifested an uncommon social disposition. They were full of inquiries respecting the rebels, where they were to be met with, and where Mr. Washington was to be found, etc. The officers were replied to by brother William Townsend, who modestly and spiritedly told them that if they would have patience a short time, he expected they would meet with General Washington and his forces, who were not far distant.[45]

Townsend continued his description of the army before adding, "It may be observed that most or all of the officers who conversed with us, were of first rank, and were rather short, portly men, were well dressed and of genteel appearance and did not look as if they had ever been exposed to any hardship; their skins being as white and delicate as is customary for females who were brought up in large cities or towns."[46]

With his column strung out after crossing the ford, Cornwallis ordered Captain Ewald to halt his advance just beyond Sconneltown in the vicinity of the stone grist mill owned by the Strode family. The mill sat in a small valley just less than one mile from Sconneltown and about half of that distance short of Osborn's Hill, which was one of the highest points in the area. The regiments

---

44 McGuire, *Philadelphia Campaign*, vol. 1, 195.

45 Townsend, *Some Account*, 22.

46 Ibid., 23.

stacked up one behind the other and the division rested for about thirty minutes.[47]

Cornwallis used this respite to reorganize his division into three columns before continuing the advance. The center column, which continued to follow the Birmingham Road, consisted of the jaegers, the British light infantry, and the British and Hessian grenadiers. The second column shifted 400 yards west of the road and included the Brigade of Guards and the 16th Light Dragoons, while the third column consisting of the 4th British Brigade moved east of the road a similar distance. Cornwallis positioned the 3rd British Brigade in reserve on the main road behind his center. Once so deployed, the formation, including the flankers, was more than a mile wide. Aside from this reorganization, Townsend "discovered . . . the halt that had been made was only to refresh their horses, to enable them to perform the several duties prescribed them."[48]

While the British rested, Washington concluded that Stirling's and Stephens's divisions would not be sufficient to check the flanking column. Judging that Gen. Knyphausen's diversionary column was now the lesser of two evils, he directed Sullivan to also pull his infantry out of line and shift his division north to link up with Stirling and Stephen. Reinforcing the American right flank to confront Howe and Cornwallis necessitated significantly weakening the front along Chads's Ford. The stripping of this part of the American line did not go unnoticed by keen observers across the river. According to Gen. Knyphausen, "four Battalions with Artillery from their Right filed off, to where the Attack to the left of our Army was to be made, & the Road to Chester was covered with Waggons going this Way & that Way." Knyphausen's aide von Baurmeister also noted the changes in American dispositions: "We saw several battalions, some artillery, and some troops of dragoons file to the right to reinforce their right wing and other changes in the line being made to give the necessary defensive strength to their left wing, which had been weakened by the removal of some of these troops."[49]

---

47 Joseph Strode purchased the mill complex from an earlier family in 1737. In addition to the grist mill (for grinding grain), it also included a sawmill and cider mill. It used Plum Run as its water source. This mill provided grain to Washington's Army. It ceased operations sometime in the early twentieth century; Ewald, *Diary*, 84.

48 Archibald Robertson, text accompanying his manuscript map, "The Battle of Brandywine," RCIN 734026.A., King's Map Collection, Windsor Castle; Townsend, *Some Account*, 23.

49 Von Knyphausen to Germain, October 21, 1777; Von Baurmeister, "Letters of Major Baurmeister," 406.

The terrain in the area immediately north and east of Chads's Ford is craggy and convoluted, riddled with steep thickly wooded hills and deep ravines, and the few roads there were narrow and torturous. Indeed, there was no direct route north close to the Brandywine, nor was there any direct route between Sullivan and the other two marching divisions. In order to approach Birmingham Hill, Stirling had to march his division on a roundabout route through Dilworth, a small community about two miles east of the river, and from there northwest toward the Birmingham Meetinghouse. Stephen's division, recalled one officer, followed Stirling "in a trott." Artillery and ammunition wagons followed them, all kicking up thick clouds of dust that made the muggy afternoon that much more unbearable for the men and animals involved. Coordination between the three divisions was going to be difficult, at best.[50]

Cornwallis, meanwhile, was fanning part of his force out on Osborn's Hill, about a mile and a quarter from Sconneltown and two miles from Birmingham Meetinghouse and Birmingham Hill. His flanking column had been on the road more than nine hours. One of the impediments to a faster march (and there were several, including the nature of the roads, the fords, and early morning fog followed by excessive heat) was the artillery's difficulty traversing the numerous hills along the way. Now essentially halted, the soldiers dropped their knapsacks and rested, littering the fields with heaps of blankets and other equipment of all varieties.

Cornwallis's division had earned the rest. Its march had covered about a dozen winding miles that included fording two streams. Each crossing had taken two or more hours to complete. According to engineer Capt. John Montresor, the troops were "both sultry and dusty and rather fatigued, many remaining along the road on that account." British Lt. Loftus Cliffe wrote to his brother, "some of our best men were obliged to yield, one of the 33rd [Regiment of Foot] droped dead." William Hale of the British grenadiers was among those marchers not feeling well that day. "Our rum too failed some days before the action and the quality of the different waters we were obliged to drink gave me the bloody flux," complained Hale, "by which I was so weakened as to faint twice in the morning of the affair. However I recovered strength sufficient to go through the fatigue of the afternoon, Col. Monckton supplied me with claret, in which I mixed Ipecacuanha and Rhubarb, a never failing medicine."[51]

Generals Howe and Cornwallis had a commanding view from their position on Osborn's Hill that included distant views of the Americans changing front to meet their advance. Colonel Moses Hazen's regiment, posted to protect Wistar's Ford, was now behind (north and west of) the British right flank. A mile or so farther south ran Street Road, a direct route to Jones's Ford where Col. David Hall's Delaware regiment was posted. According to Montresor, they "observed the Gros[s] of the rebel army forming upon an opposite height [Birmingham Hill]. . . . This position of the Enemy was remarkably strong." Montresor believed he was witnessing the entire American Army forming to their front. The Americans, he reported, had "a large body advanced, small bodies still further advanced and their Rear covered by a wood wherein their main body was posted with a natural glacis for ¾ of a mile." Archibald Robertson, the other engineering officer accompanying Howe and Cornwallis that day, also remembered seeing the enemy at "Birmingham Meeting, but moving and unsettled."[52]

Lieutenant Frederick Augustus Wetherall, who was with the advance guard, also took note of the American movement: "sev'ral Rebel Officers came to Reconnoitre, & from the Columns of Dust their Army was perceiv'd to be at no great Distance but from the Woods & the uneaveness of Ground in the Front it was not easy to conjecture of their Intentions." The British lieutenant also left a helpful and instructive description of Howe. The general, he wrote, "with the most Cheerful Countenance convers'd with his Officers & envited sev'ral to a slight refreshment provided on the Grass. The pleasing Behavior of that great Man on this Occasion had a great Effect on the Minds of all who beheld him. Evry One that remembers the anxious Moments before an Engagement may conceive how animating the sight of the Commander in Chief in whose Looks nothing but Serenity & Confidence in his Troops is painted. In

51 Montresor, "The Montresor Journals," 449; Cliffe to brother Jack, October 24, 1777, Loftus Cliffe Papers; Wilkin, *Some British Soldiers*, 246-247. Carapichea ipecacuanha is a flowering plant in the Rubiaceaae family native to Brazil. Its common name, as Hale noted in his recollection, ipecacuanha, can be translated from Portuguese to "duck penis." The root has been touted by various botanists over the centuries for a variety of ailments, including as a powerful emetic.

52 Robertson map key.

This modern view looks south from Osborne's Hill toward Birmingham Hill, the tree line on the far horizon. Street Road runs through the low ground between the two heights. *Author*

short," concluded Wetherall, "the Army resum'd their March in full assurance of Success & Victory."[53]

Stirling's and Stephen's divisions, in that order, were first to arrive on Birmingham Hill one-half mile south of Birmingham Meetinghouse. After passing through Dilworth, the divisions swung to the left and followed the Birmingham Road over rolling terrain dotted with thick stands of woods and farm fields until they arrived on the high ground. Stirling aligned his division southwest from the Wylie Road-Birmingham Road intersection about 800 yards along a partially wooded ridge. Accompanying Stirling was future president James Monroe, who was serving as an aide to the general. Stephen, meanwhile, formed his infantry on Stirling's right along the Birmingham Road, extending back through the woods above an area known as Sandy Hollow. Five light field pieces (3- and 4-pounders) were positioned on an open knoll in the center of the two divisions about 200 yards south of the road intersection aimed toward the meetinghouse. "They formed two lines in good order along their heights," confirmed Howe's Hessian aide von Muenchhausen. "[W]e could see this because there were some barren places here and there on the hills, which they occupied."[54]

These two American divisions arrived well ahead of Sullivan's men because of their partial march toward the area earlier in the day. Sullivan's sparse directions were to rendezvous with them. "At half-past two, I received orders to march with my division, to join with, and take command of . . . [Stirling's and Stephen's divisions] to oppose the enemy," reported Sullivan, "who were coming down on the right flank of our army. I neither knew where the Enemy were or what Rout the other Two Divisions were to take . . . & of course could not Determine where I should form a Junction with them." Traversing difficult hills, woods and thickets, marshy streams, farm fields, and dusty farmland was going to make locating Stirling and Stephens difficult and time-consuming.[55]

In order to get his division north, Sullivan was forced to use an old road that was mostly a couple of hundred feet upland, weaving in and out through the small ravines leading down to the Brandywine. Sullivan's original position at Brinton's Ford was only about eight-tenths of a mile from Birmingham Hill, but

53 Frederick Augustus Wetherall, *Journal of Officer B* in the Sol Feinstone Collection of the David Library of the American Revolution, Washington Crossing, PA, item no. 409.

54 Von Muenchhausen, *At Howe's Side: 1776-1778*, 31.

55 McGuire, *Philadelphia Campaign*, vol. 1, 199.

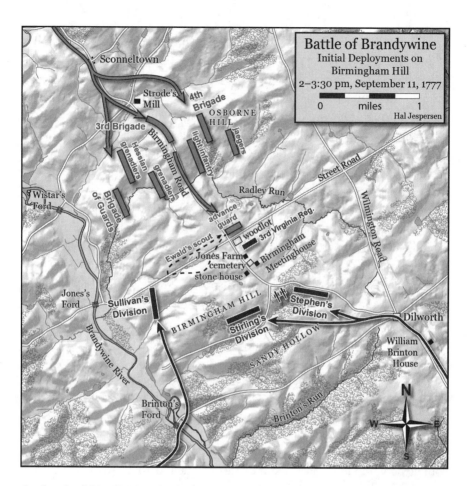

the head of his division had not marched more than a mile before Sullivan spotted the enemy. Along the way Sullivan met Col. Hazen, who had vacated Wistar's Ford and now added his withdrawing regiment to the marching column. Sullivan would later write to John Hancock that he "had not marched a mile when I met Colo. Hazen with his Regiment which had been Stationed at a Ford three miles above me who Informed that the Enemy were Close upon his Heels & that I might Depend that the principal part of the British army were there."[56]

The previous day, Brig. Gen. Phillipe Hubert de Preudhomme de Borre had complained that more than half of his brigade had been detached to guard

---

56 Hammond, ed., *Papers of Sullivan*, vol. 1, 463.

the upper fords (de Borre was referring to Hazen's regiment). The 60-year-old French general who barely spoke English led one of the Maryland brigades in Sullivan's division. When he learned Hazen had once again returned to the division, the French general requested the regiment's return to his brigade. "In our way I met the Congress regiment and Sent So Soon my brigade major to general Sullivan to have ordered for that regiment to join my brigade," wrote the French officer. "The general has refused." Because of his rank, Sullivan assumed overall command on Birmingham Hill, which for the same reason left de Borre in command of his division.[57]

The Continentals appeared through British and German eyes to be forming a formidable line of battle. "The enemy had a body of about 1000 men standing on the hill on the other side of the Meetinghouse," wrote one Hessian. "A numerous body of Light cavalry appeared on their left, and soon after that a body of infantry consisting of about 2000 men with 5 guns, who joined the men on the hill; several battalions were also observed, who marched to the woods on the right and left, and uniting themselves with the above 3000 men presented a formidable front."[58] Cornwallis, meanwhile, watched the hasty deployment of his enemy while aligning his own division for attack. Given the terrain and from what he could discern of the American alignment, the British general decided the British assault formation would be about one half-mile wide. When all was said and done, nearly 5,300 American troops would be available to oppose roughly 9,000 British troops with their allies at this location.

Howe's flanking maneuver had achieved his first goal. The majority of his army was now positioned beyond and behind the original American right flank, facing only a portion of Washington's Army. Howe must surely have hoped there would be no repeat of the bloody assaults on Breed's Hill.

* * *

Once, again, Washington had been deceived by a Howe-instituted flanking movement. Despite having faced this same tactic on more than one occasion during the past year, he was somehow unprepared for it at the Brandywine.

57 Preudhomme De Borre to Congress, September 17, 1777, Washington Papers online, Library of Congress, series 4, General Correspondence, September 1777, images 341-42, accessed March 12, 2012.

58 Journal of the Hessian Corps, Letter Z, 87-88.

Washington, wrote Gen. James Grant, part of Knyphausen's diversionary division, was convinced that "our whole force was opposite to Him & was confirmed in that opinion, by Detachments which I made in the course of the Day of the 4th, 5th, & 27th regts. with Artillery to keep possession of the Heights upon our Left & to prevent the Rebells from passing the River. . . . Those Regts. He [Washington] consider'd as so many Brigades detached in order to pass the River in different Columns & was so much convinced of it, that He took no Care of his Right & only sent detached Corps to defend the Fords in my Front."[59]

Perhaps Douglas Southall Freeman, the author of a Pulitzer Prize-winning multi-volume biography of Washington, summed up best what had just transpired: "Washington conducted the Brandywine operation as if he had been in a daze. . . . The general who always had stressed the necessity of procuring the fullest intelligence and of analyzing it correctly had failed to do either or to employ his Light Horse adequately when the price of error might be the loss of Philadelphia."[60]

---

59   Grant to Harvey, October 20, 1777, Grant Papers.

60   Douglas Southall Freeman, *George Washington: A Biography*, 7 vols. (New York, 1951), vol. 4, *Leader of the Revolution*, 488-489.

Chapter 13

The British Assault Birmingham Hill:
Afternoon, September 11, 1777

"The line moving on exhibited the most grand and noble sight imaginable.
The grenadiers beating their march as they advanced contributed
greatly to the dignity of the approach."[1]

— Lt. Frederick Augustus Wetherall, September 11, 1777

The British Advance Guard

By the middle of the afternoon on September 11, Gen. Howe's veteran troops under the steady hand of Gen. Cornwallis were poised to deliver the crowning blow of Howe's flanking strategy.

Sometime after 3:00 p.m., Capt. Johann Ewald "caught sight of some infantry and horsemen behind a village on a hill in the distance, which was formed like an amphitheatre." A short time later, Capt. Alexander Ross, General Cornwallis's aide-de-camp, delivered an order to Ewald to take the advance guard and attack the American infantry and cavalry spotted up ahead. The capable Hessian captain organized the advance guard with the 17th Regiment of Foot's light company deployed on the left, the light company of the 42nd Highlanders deployed on the right, and the mounted jaegers

---

1   Wetherall, *Journal of Officer B.*

positioned on the road in the center. The foot jaegers moved out front in skirmish order while the main line formed.[2]

The Americans spotted by Ewald and targeted for attack were not, as the Hessian believed, "behind a village," but near the Samuel Jones farm buildings and Birmingham Meetinghouse, which the captain mistook for a small community. The patriots were elements of Col. Thomas Marshall's 3rd Virginia Regiment, part of Brig. Gen. William Woodford's brigade of Maj. Gen. Adam Stephen's division, together with some of Col. Theodorick Bland's light dragoons. The Virginians had deployed on the Jones property south of the Street Road - Birmingham Road intersection east of the latter road about one mile below Osborn's Hill. Southeast of the intersection was the Jones woodlot. His brick farmhouse (which Ewald had also spotted) was another 150 yards farther south along Birmingham Road, and just south of the house was the family orchard. The Americans, first positioned in the woodlot and later in the orchard, enjoyed a slight advantage in elevation over the light troops immediately confronting them.

The British advance guard extended its line eastward as it advanced toward the American position in an effort to outflank Colonel Marshall's 3rd Virginia Regiment. The regiment, explained one American officer in his memoirs, "having been much reduced by previous service, did not amount to more than a battalion; but one field officer, the colonel, and four captains were with it."[3] The Virginians opened a long-range small arms fire. Captain William Scott of the 17th Regiment of Foot's light company recalled the effort to get around the American right. His company, he wrote, "received a fire from about 200 men in the orchard, which did no execution."[4]

After watching Cornwallis's men march through Sconneltown and returning home to check on his family, young Quaker Joseph Townsend passed through the moving British Army as he walked south down the Birmingham Road to Osborn Hill and down its southern slope toward Street Road. "We reached the advanced guard, who were of the German troops," recalled Townsend. "Many of them wore their beard on their upper lips." The youth,

---

2   Ewald, *Diary*, 84; McGuire, *Philadelphia Campaign*, vol. 1, 200.

3   Lee, *Memoirs*, vol. 1, 16.

4   William Scott, *Memoranda on the Battle of Brandywine and The Battle of Germantown*, in the Sol Feinstone Collection of the David Library of the American Revolution, Washington Crossing, PA, item no. 111.

who was unaware that British troops also comprised the advance guard, recalled the opening moments of the battle after the Virginians had fired upon Ewald's command: "The attack was immediately returned by the Hessians, by their stepping up the bank of the road alongside the orchard, making the fence as a breast work through which they fired upon the company who made the attack."[5] If Townsend's recollections are accurate, some of the jaegers pushed far enough beyond Street Road to use the eastern embankment of the Birmingham Road as protection to fire into the Jones orchard.

Townsend continued, "From the distance we were from them (though in full view until the smoke of the firing covered them from our sight) I was under no apprehension of danger [from the American fire] especially when there was such a tremendous force coming on [Cornwallis's division] and ready to engage in action." Townsend observed the approaching British and German formations with deep interest: "[W]e had a grand view of the army as they advanced over and down the south side of Osborne's Hill and the lands of James Carter, scarce a vacant place left. . . . [A]lmost the whole face of the country around appeared to be covered and alive with these objects." By this time the novelty of examining the British Army had worn off and it dawned on the youngster that he had walked directly into the middle of a growing battle: "I concluded it best to retire, finding that my inconsiderate curiosity had prompted me to exceed the bounds of prudence." The Quaker turned northward, and walked back alongside the Birmingham Road.[6]

The opening and wildly inaccurate American fire hit but two of his men, which in turn allowed Ewald to push ahead and reach one of the buildings on the Jones property with both his foot and mounted jaegers. At that point the firing intensified. "Unfortunately for us," explained Ewald, "the time this took favored the enemy and I received extremely heavy small-arms fire from the gardens and houses." The sharp fire and firm stand offered by the Virginians, who may have been more numerous than Ewald originally believed, convinced the captain to pull his jaegers and the two British light companies back to the fence line along Street Road. The Americans let them fall back without advancing in return.[7]

5 Townsend, *Some Account*, 24.

6 Ibid., 24-25.

7 Ewald, *Diary*, 85.

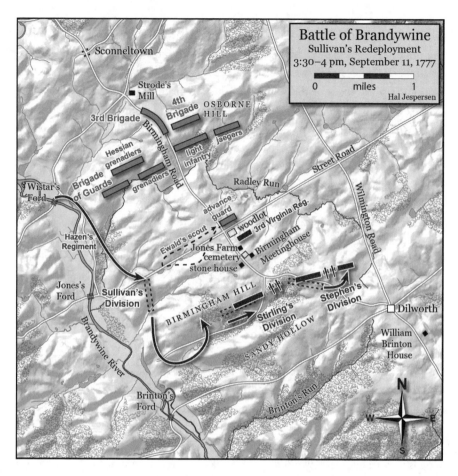

It was at this time that Ewald realized his advance guard was more than living up to its name. Indeed, it was now much too far in advance of the balance of Cornwallis's division. "They [the other members of the advance guard] shouted to me that the army was far behind, and I became not a little embarrassed to find myself quite alone with the advanced guard," reported the Hessian. "But now that the business had begun, I still wanted to obtain information about these people who had let me go so easily."[8]

Once he was satisfied with his new fallback position, Ewald took three men and rode well to the right (west) in an effort to better scout the American position. His initial route carried him to the top of a small hill southwest of the

8 Ewald, *Diary*, 85.

Street Road-Birmingham Road intersection. What he beheld stunned the veteran officer: "I gazed in astonishment when I got up the hill, for I found behind it—three to four hundred paces away—an entire line deployed in the best order, several of whom waved to me with their hats but did not shoot. I kept composed, examined them closely, rode back, and reported it at once to Lord Cornwallis" via a mounted jaeger named Hoffman. Ewald's reconnaissance discovered Lord Stirling's division in line less than one-half mile farther south on Birmingham Hill. Lieutenant William Keugh of the 44th Regiment of Foot, who was far behind Ewald at this time, would recall the strength of this American position and describe the terrain as "Hills which Nature Unassisted, had abundantly fortified." Lieutenant Colonel Ludwig von Wurmb remembered Cornwallis receiving Ewald's report back on Osborn's Hill: "Captain Ewald of the advance guard reported the enemy was approaching and they were forming up on a hilltop and that another column was approaching on the right." Captain Scott, whose company of the 17th Regiment of Foot was part of the advance guard that afternoon, took note of additional American troops when he observed, "it was evident tho' the enemy fell back they were well supported."[9] The "additional" troops were the now very visible divisions of Stephen and Stirling forming farther south along Birmingham Hill.

Ewald was one of the first to see and realize the formidable nature of the American position, and that the Virginians on the Jones farm were not a small picket or advance force, but part of much larger command. It is likely that both Howe and Cornwallis believed the Americans were by this time retreating from their former position east of the Brandywine, their exposed flank turned and a strong force under Gen. Wilhelm von Knyphausen pressing their rear. Now they learned the truth: the Americans had simply maneuvered northward with a strong force to blunt Howe's flanking effort. The British would not be dropping into Washington's rear area without a fight.

After sending his report to Cornwallis, Ewald continued his reconnaissance by riding down the hill and then west along Street Road toward Jones's Ford. He spotted more American troops as he approached the crossing—"a whole enemy column with guns marching through the valley in which Lord Cornwallis's column had been marching for some time, a quarter or half an hour away to the right." The "enemy column" was Moses Hazen's regiment

---

9   Ibid.; Von Wurmb to von Jungkenn, October 14, 1777, 10; McGuire, *The Philadelphia Campaign*, vol. 2, 280, reproduces the entire letter; Scott, *Memoranda*.

marching south to link back up with the rest of Maj. Gen. John Sullivan's division, which was approaching Street Road on its march from Brinton's Ford. Hazen would fall in with the division and continue the march to unite with the divisions on Birmingham Hill. "[T]he Enemy headed us in the Road about forty Rods from our advance Guard," reported Sullivan. "I then found it necessary to turn off to the Right to form & to get nearer to the other two Divisions [Stirling's and Stephen's] which I that moment Discovered Drawn up on an Eminence both in the Rear & to the Right of the place I was then at."[10]

Sullivan's change of direction moved his division onto the same hill Ewald had used just minutes earlier to observe Stirling's position. The other two American divisions were deployed on Birmingham Hill about one-half mile to Sullivan's right and rear. His division was the last major piece of the American blocking force, which was now aligned, by division, from left to right as follows: Sullivan, Stirling, and Stephen, with Sullivan in command of all three. Although most of three divisions had succeeded in shifting north at the last moment to meet Howe's substantial flanking column, argues one historian, "these hurried alterations were liable to dent inexperienced troops' confidence."[11]

Ewald, meanwhile, returned to the advance guard still pinned down along the fence line near the Street Road-Birmingham Road intersection. His hurried ride had discovered Stirling's division to his right front, and the arrival of more enemy troops in that quarter. Cornwallis had been duly informed. Now back with his men, the Hessian oversaw the fitful skirmish fire for which his men were famous, and awaited orders. He would not have long to wait. With the information from Ewald's reconnaissance in hand, Howe directed Cornwallis to "to form the line." Within minutes the columns of soldiers redeployed into crisp, heavy lines of battle. It was time to brush aside the incompetent Americans and drive into the rear of Washington's imperiled army.[12]

The Main Body Advances

Cornwallis's division (excluding elements of the 16th Light Dragoons and the 3rd British Brigade, which initially remained on Osborn's Hill with Gen.

---

10 Ewald, *Diary*, 85-86; Hammond, ed., *Papers of Sullivan*, vol. 1, 463.

11 Spring, *With Zeal*, 64.

12 Von Wurmb to von Jungkenn, October 14, 1777, 10.

Howe), moved in column down the southern slope of Osborn's Hill in preparation for its attack. It was about 4:00 p.m., and Howe's Hessian aide, Friedrich von Muenchhausen, was there to witness it: "Our two battalions of light infantry and the Hessian Jagers marched down the hill. They marched first in a column, but later, when they approached the enemy, in line formation, deploying to the left." To the right of the light infantry, von Muenchhausen continued, "the English grenadiers did the same in the center, almost at the same time." Joseph Townsend, who had earlier approached Street Road and watched the opening of the fighting between the Virginians and Ewald's advance guard, was walking back through the British formations at this time. Among the troops, he wrote, "the hurry was great, and so many rushing forward under arms."[13]

Once Cornwallis's advancing columns reached the farm fields at the bottom of the slope, commands rang out to form lines of battle on both sides of the Birmingham Road. The general's plan of attack called for two lines of battle supported by a strong reserve. The front line included his elite troops. The Hessian and Ansbach Jaegers commanded by Lt. Col. Ludwig von Wurmb anchored his far left east of the road. The British light infantry brigade formed next to the Germans on their right, with Maj. John Maitland's 2nd Battalion on the left and Col. Robert Abercromby's 1st Battalion on the right. Maitland's 14 companies deployed in fields sprinkled with light stands of timber. His remaining company, detached from the 42nd Royal Highlanders, was still in front skirmishing with Capt. Johann Ewald's advance guard. Abercromby's 1st Battalion, meanwhile, formed in the fenced fields immediately along the Birmingham Road with its right resting on the road itself. Behind this first line of the left wing was a second line of battle, or a reserve for the front line troops, comprised of Brig. Gen. James Agnew's 4th British Brigade. This left wing, roughly 3,000 troops, would advance directly south against Adam Stephen's well-placed division of 2,100 men on Birmingham Hill about one mile distant. Cornwallis's right front deployed west of the Birmingham Road. Extending the front line in that direction were two battalions of British grenadiers. The 16 companies of Lt. Col. William Medows's 1st Battalion formed in front, while the 2nd Battalion's 15 companies led by Col. Henry Monckton formed behind them. The left flank of the grenadiers abutted the road. Cornwallis anchored his right with Brig. Gen. Edward Mathew's British Brigade of Guards, with the 1st

---

13 Von Muenchhausen, *At General Howe's Side*, 31; Townsend, *Some Account*, 25.

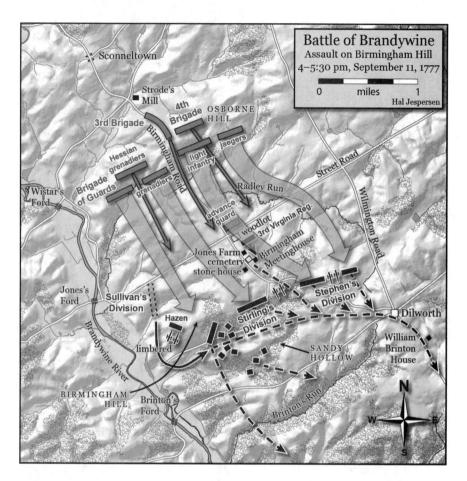

Battalion on the far right and the 2nd Battalion on the left next to the grenadiers. The Guards light company spread in front of the two battalions, with the Guards grenadier company holding the position of honor on the right of the line. The British light infantry and the Guards were about 200 yards farther advanced than the British grenadiers.[14]

Behind this first line of the right wing was a second line of battle (or reserve) comprised of the Hessian grenadiers under the overall command of 45-year-old Col. Carl von Donop, the son of a noble family and distinguished veteran of the Seven Years' War. The von Minnigerode Battalion tramped behind the Brigade of Guards, with the von Lengerke Battalion and the von

Linsing Battalion stretching the line eastward behind the British grenadiers (with the von Linsing on the left closest to the road). Cornwallis's right wing, about 3,700 veteran troops, would attack south about one mile and strike Lord Stirling's and John Sullivan's divisions, some 3,200 strong, deployed atop Birmingham Hill.[15]

Behind these lines marched the deep reserve comprised of the 3rd British Brigade under Maj. Gen. Charles Grey, the 42nd Regiment of Foot under Lt. Col. Thomas Stirling, and the pair of squadrons of the 16th Light Dragoons. Although the historical record is unclear, it is reasonable to assume that these commands remained in column on the road for ready movement and rapid deployment, as circumstances dictated. The squadrons of the 16th Light Dragoons would later be ordered to assume a reserve position behind the Brigade of Guards.

One of the most impressive scenes to ever play out on the North American continent was unfolding on these Chester County farm fields. "Put on your caps," yelled Lt. Col. William Medows to his grenadiers west of the Birmingham Road, "for damned fighting and drinking I'll match you against the world!" The grenadiers took off their cloth forage caps, pulled their bearskin caps from their packs, brushed the fur, and placed them atop their heads. The imposing headgear added more than a foot to the already physically imposing men. Buttressed between the two battalions of British grenadiers were 62 drummers and British fifers. Drums, trumpets, whistles, and small brass hunting horns sounded the advance from both ends of the British lines. One historian painted the scene thusly: "Drumsticks dropped in one crisp motion, and a visceral thunder of drums rumbled out as 1,200 grenadiers stepped off together in a mesmerizing, glittering mass." After a few steps, the impressive array of drummers and fifers began playing "The British Grenadiers," which "shrilled across the once peaceful Quaker landscape, above the relentless, reverberating throb of drums." Lieutenant William Hale of the British 45th's grenadier company long remembered the impressive scene and would live through the day to write about it: "Nothing could be more dreadfully pleasing than the line moving on to the attack; the Grenadiers put on their Caps and struck up their march, believe me I would not exchange those three minutes of rapture to avoid ten thousand times the danger." Yet another British officer recalled that the

---

15 Ibid., 204. At this time, Sullivan's division was moving back to take a position on Birmingham Hill.

"line moving on exhibited the most grand and noble sight imaginable. The grenadiers beating their march as they advanced contributed greatly to the dignity of the approach."[16]

As the light infantry battalions advanced steadily south, their line of battle perpendicular to the Birmingham Road, the majority of Lieutenant Colonel Wurmb's jaegers shifted farther west and moved ahead through heavier, broken wooded terrain on the far left of Cornwallis's advancing division. Royal artillery pieces moved ahead with the German troops—a pair of small 3-pounders supported by Lt. Balthasar Mertz and 30 grenadiers—as did two amusettes, described as "large, heavy muskets capable of lobbing 1-inch balls several hundred yards."[17]

The early part of the advance proceeded smoothly except for a number of fences cutting across the front. Each of these barriers had to be climbed or torn down, which slowed the advance and required the realignment of the lines of battle before pressing ahead. The grenadiers confronted eight stout Pennsylvania fences between Osborn's Hill and the American lines on Birmingham Hill.

A thankful if anxious Capt. Ewald watched the advance of Cornwallis's division with deep interest. It was approaching 4:30 p.m., and his men had been holding their forward position, trading skirmish fire with the Virginians, for the better part of a very long hour. When the British and German front lines stepped within 300 or 400 paces of Street Road, Ewald ordered his advance guard to renew its assault against the American position on the Jones property. According to Ewald, "[f]rom this time on, I did not see one general. Where they were reconnoitering I don't know."[18] Using the embankment and fences lining the east side of Birmingham Road, Ewald and his jaegers outflanked the Virginians holding the orchard and forced them to retire to the meetinghouse proper.

---

16 Martin Hunter, *The Journal of Gen. Sir Martin Hunter and Some Letters of his Wife, Lady Hunter*, ed. A. Hunter (Edinburgh, 1894), 29. Two companies from the 52nd Regiment of Foot—its light and grenadier companies—fought at the Brandywine. Martin Hunter was a lieutenant in the light infantry company, which was attached during the battle to the 2nd Light Infantry Battalion; McGuire, *Philadelphia Campaign*, vol. 1, 210-211; Wilkin, *Some British Soldiers*, 231; Wetherall, *Journal of Officer B.*

17 McGuire, *Philadelphia Campaign*, vol. 1, 204.

18 Ewald, *Diary*, 86.

Townsend and his companions, meanwhile, were on their way back to Osborn's Hill. They were walking along the fence line separating the Birmingham Road from the fields east of it when a German officer ordered Townsend to take the fence down. "As I was near the spot I had to be subject to his orders," recalled Townsend, "as he flourished a drawn sword over my head with others who stood nearby." It wasn't until the youth was removing the rails that it occurred to him he might be violating his pacifist Quaker tenets. "As the hurry was great, and so many rushing forward under arms, I found no difficulty in retiring undiscovered and was soon out of reach of those called immediately into action," he explained.[19]

Once Cornwallis's front lines reached a point about halfway between Osborn's Hill and Birmingham Hill (approximately where Street Road crossed their path), American artillery rounds began to find their range. The extreme range of the American 3- and 4-pounders firing solid shot was only about 1,200 yards, but late that afternoon that was enough, and the exploding shells wounded many British troops, some mortally. "Some skirmishing began in the valley in which the enemy was drove," reported Capt. John Montresor, "upon gaining something further of the ascent the enemy began to amuse us with 2 guns." The valley mentioned by Montresor was Carter's open farm field between Osborn's Hill and Birmingham Hill, and the Americans were using more than just a pair of artillery pieces on the British formations. Five American artillery pieces were firing from the knoll separating Stirling's division from Stephen's position. The gunfire was not enough to seriously disrupt the advancing professionals, who continued apace southward toward Birmingham Hill. When they stepped within 500 yards, however, the Americans switched to grape and canister rounds, which were more effective as anti-personnel weapons.[20]

In an effort to silence the American guns and soften the enemy infantry positions, the British rushed forward guns from the 4th Battalion of the Royal Artillery, 6- and 12-pounders that probably deployed along Street Road.[21] The

19 Townsend, *Some Account*, 24-25.

20 Montresor, "Montresor Journals," 450.

21 McGuire, *Philadelphia Campaign*, vol. 1, 212. Exactly where these guns deployed is unknown, but they were likely down near Street Road, and therefore would have been at an elevation disadvantage. Just as there is a lack of source material specifics for the American artillery, the same problem exists for the British long arm. The only unit sent to North America was the 4th

small arms fire combined with heavy bluish-white clouds of artillery gun smoke to limit visibility and obscure formations. Artillery rounds arced through the muggy Pennsylvania air before dropping among the Continentals, shearing off tree branches and sending splinters large and small of both iron and wood flying in every direction. Whizzing hot chunks of iron dismembered some, and crushed and killed others. Grapeshot belched from the smaller battalion guns ripped through the American ranks of both Lord Stirling's and Adam Stephen's divisions and wreaked similar havoc. Private John Francis, "a negro" in the 3rd Pennsylvania Regiment, wrote one eyewitness, "had both legs much shattered by grape shot," and another member of the same regiment, Ensign William Russell, lost a leg from a cannonball. Both belonged to Thomas Conway's brigade (Stirling's division). Stacey Williams, "a negro private" in the 6th Pennsylvania Regiment, also part of Conway's command, fell with a wound in the right thigh, as did a sergeant from the same regiment. The day after the battle, American artilleryman Elisha Stevens took a few minutes to write a description of the gruesome scene he had witnessed the previous day. "Cannons roaring, muskets cracking, Drums Beating Bombs Flying all Round, men a dying & wounded Horred Grones which would Greave the Hardest of Hearts to see," he lamented. "[S]uch a Dreadful Sight as this to see our Fellow Creators [creatures] slain in such a manner as this."[22] The American artillerymen, however, weathered the deadly storm of iron and stuck to their pieces. Their steady firing found the range and opened gaps in the advancing British line of grenadiers.

The Assault on Sullivan's Division

While Cornwallis's division was slow-stepping its way down Osborn's Hill in all its sublime grandeur, John Sullivan's division was moving south to get into

---

Battalion of Royal Artillery. How this unit was divided and allocated amongst the various British commands in North America is not always clear, and we do not know which specific batteries participated on the flanking march with Howe and Cornwallis. Circumstantial evidence suggests the entire battalion may have been with Howe's army during this campaign, but how it was divided remains to be determined.

22 Elisha Stevens, *Fragments of Memoranda Written by him in the War of the Revolution* (Meriden, CT, 1893), September 12, 1777 entry. Private John Francis account, see Montgomery, ed. *Pennsylvania Archives*, Series 5, vol. 4, 508; Ensign William Russell account, see Heitman, *Historical Register of Officers*, 478. Stacey Williams account, see Montgomery, ed. *Pennsylvania Archives*, Series 5, vol. 3, 187; Trussell, *Pennsylvania Line*, 275.

a line of battle on Birmingham Hill. Part of the problem bedeviling the command that day was its lack of senior leadership. When Sullivan was temporarily elevated to command the right wing of the American army (he was to assume command of all three divisions once he arrived upon Birmingham Hill), the commander of the 2nd Maryland Brigade, Brig. Gen. Phillipe Hubert de Preudhomme de Borre stepped into Sullivan's boots to lead the division. The brigade's senior colonel was Moses Hazen, but it is unclear whether Hazen's regiment (which had been on detached duty watching Wistar's Ford and would be tasked with protecting the artillery at the tail end of the division) ever rejoined the brigade or instead fought the battle independently. The commander of the 1st Maryland Brigade, Brig. Gen. William Smallwood, was on detached duty in Maryland raising militia (as was his senior colonel, Mordecai Gist). The record is unclear who commanded the brigade in their absence. Presumably it was John Stone, the colonel of the 1st Maryland Regiment, who had only been a colonel since that February. The result of this command shuffling put the division under a disliked French officer few Americans could understand, and both brigades in the hands of less capable junior colonels.[23]

Once Sullivan reached the area and formed his division into line east of Jones's Ford and south of Street Road, he realized he had taken up a position well in front and west of the other two American divisions. This left his command exposed to being turned on either flank and crushed, too far away to lend ready help to the remaining divisions on his right, and too far removed for either Lord Stirling or Stephen to assist him. Sullivan had no choice but to reposition his division. It was probably at this point that he turned command of the division over to Gen. de Borre with orders to move the division south to Birmingham Hill. Once arranged, Sullivan rode southwest to inform Stirling and Stephen that he was in command of all three divisions, and discuss how best to align the front once his own division arrived. From the information they shared, together with a view of the field, Sullivan realized the British, in the form of the jaeger corps, were in a position that could outflank the right side of the American line. The entire line, urged Sullivan, including his own division,

---

23 The next two senior colonels in the 2nd Maryland Brigade were Thomas Price and Josias Hall, both of whom were commissioned on the same day, December 10, 1776. Who led de Borre's brigade into battle that day remains something of a mystery. Heitman, *Historical Register of Officers*.

"[s]hould Incline further to the Right to prevent our being out flanked."[24] Sullivan was correct, but the difficult movement would have to take place during the British advance toward Birmingham Hill.

What might look easy drawn on a map or scratched into the dirt with a stick rarely was in practice. The American soldiers were not yet veterans, and accomplishing such a maneuver under enemy fire was sure to be difficult. Nevertheless, Stirling and Stephen managed to shift their divisions several hundred yards to the right without substantial difficulty. Howe and Cornwallis spotted the maneuver and countered the patriot move by ordering the 4th British Brigade to leave its reserve position and form on the left flank of the jaegers, extending the line a significant distance in the same direction. The 3rd British Brigade was also called up from its reserve position on the road and deployed into a direct supporting position behind the light infantry west of the road. What was relatively uneventful for Stirling's and Stephen's divisions, however, proved to be nearly disastrous for Sullivan's division under de Borre.[25]

After his consultation with Stirling and Stephen, Sullivan rode back in search of his division, which he found moving south but still some distance from Birmingham Hill. Sullivan, as he later explained, "ordered Colo. Hazens Regiment to pass a Hollow way, File off to the Right & face to Cover the Artillery while it was passing the Same Hollow way, the Rest of the Troops followed in the Rear to assist in Covering the Artillery the Enemy Seeing this did not press on but gave me [Sullivan] time to form my Division on an advantageous Height in a Line with the other Divisions but almost half a mile to the Left."[26] Hazen's regiment covered the division's artillery and thus constituted the tail end of the division.

Once his division was on Birmingham Hill, however, Sullivan realized yet again he was out of position because a large gap existed between his right and Lord Stirling's left. Once again, Sullivan sought out Stirling and Stephen, leaving de Borre to shift the division to the right (eastward) to better align it with Stirling's command. Several histories of the battle insist Sullivan demanded his division be placed on the far right of the line in what was considered the

---

24 Hammond, ed., *Papers of Sullivan*, vol. 1, 464.

25 McGuire, *Philadelphia Campaign*, vol. 1, 221.

26 Hammond, ed., *Papers of Sullivan*, vol. 1, 463-464.

This modern view looks south toward Birmingham Hill. The British Brigade of Guards assaulted across this ground toward the tree line on the horizon, where John Sullivan's American division was struggling to get into position. (Compare this modern view with the 1777 watercolor on the back cover of the book.) *Author*

position of honor. Contemporary accounts, however, agree that Sullivan ordered his division onto the left flank of the American line as a matter of military necessity.[27]

While Sullivan's division was struggling to get into its new position, lethal danger was approaching in the form of the British Brigade of Guards. Thus far unaffected by American artillery fire, the Guards (holding the far right front of Cornwallis's division) continued moving directly toward the American left. Unfortunately for the Americans, Sullivan's division was not smoothly or quickly shifting right, and the delay and confusion experienced during the change of position can be laid firmly at de Borre's feet. Rather than simply sliding to the right to align with Stirling's men, de Borre instead attempted a complicated maneuver. The French officer marched the division down the south slope of the hill, turned east for some distance, and then attempted to

---

27 McGuire, *Philadelphia Campaign*, vol. 1, 220-221. Throughout the rest of the day, Sullivan remained near the gap between Stirling's and Stephen's divisions except for a short time when he tried to rally his own broken division.

wheel the large command back up the hill into precisely the correct position. Curiously, he settled upon this series of movements about the same time British artillery rounds began pounding Birmingham Hill.[28]

Colonel John Stone's 1st Maryland Regiment led Sullivan's column away from its position and down the slope of the hill. The enemy, recalled Stone, who was almost certainly in command of Smallwood's 1st Maryland Brigade, "had begun to cannonade the ground allotted for us, which was very bad, and the enemy within musket shot of it, before we were ordered to form the line of battle." The Americans were marching up a narrow lane to reach their new position and just cresting Birmingham Hill when, to their surprise, a strong line of enemy troops appeared directly in front of them, leveled their muskets, and fired a deadly volley directly into their faces at nearly pointblank range. The line was composed of the Brigade of Guards, whose advance was supported by two medium 12-pounders.[29]

Sullivan's men were attempting to form when the Guards fired their single volley and charged into the quickly demoralized Marylanders. The immediate confusion within the American ranks collapsed effective resistance, and the Guards suffered only one killed, five wounded, and one missing. Sir George Osborn described the assault in a letter to his brother: "We attacked the left flank of the rebel army, and raining upon the brigades of Sullivan . . . with an impetuosity really that it would have been scarcely possible for them to resist . . . we saved much loss we might otherwise have sustained, and certainly made the enemy first give way. . . . I had but one Grenadier wounded, the Light Company who were with me had only three."[30]

The same cannot be said for Sullivan's men, who within a few short minutes lost 26 men of the 1st Maryland dead or wounded, including an injured Col. Stone. The sudden assault threw the entire 1st Maryland Brigade into wild confusion and sent its members running in several directions. Lieutenant Colonel Samuel Smith, the son of a wealthy Baltimore merchant and now second in command of the 4th Maryland Regiment, confirmed the desperate

28 Ibid., 222.

29 Stone to Paca, September 23, 1777, 166-167.

30 *Remembrancer for 1777*, 416; McGuire, *Philadelphia Campaign*, vol. 1, 222, 225. The Osborn letters are in a private family collection in England and are inaccessible. The Osborn quotes rely on the accuracy of McGuire's transcriptions. According to a return in the National Archives, the Guards fired an average of only six or seven shots per man for the entire battle, including their engagement later in the day near Chads's Ford.

plight of the brigade. It "counter-marched through a gateway, to the top of a hill, under a galling fire from the enemy—thus bringing the rear to the front. Pressed by the enemy, they had no time to form, and gave way at all points."[31]

Captain Enoch Anderson of Col. David Hall's 1st Delaware Regiment, part of the 1st Maryland (Smallwood's) brigade, wrote a series of letters in 1819 to his nephew, Alexander Anderson, describing his wartime experiences. The captain, who was "in the centre of our Regiment," recalled marching about half a mile (likely from the position south of Street Road to Birmingham Hill and then again as part of de Borre's grand wheeling movement), "when Lord Stirling rode up. 'Officer,' says he, 'General Washington is in the rear. Face about!' I did so, as the British were firing on us. I looked about for my Lord, to obey his [further] commands, but saw his Lordship whipping and spurring down the road at full gallop!" The sight of most of Sullivan's men pouring down the southern slope of Birmingham Hill in abject rout shocked the young officer. "Some of our soldiers were wounded. I thought, 'well, I have no business here fighting in this place . . . [I can do no] good,'—the British aimed to surround [us . . .] and with a quick marching, I [fell back . . . and with the] rest of the Regiment."[32]

Other important officers also made for the scene of the unfolding disaster, including Marquis de Lafayette. The French general recalled that "Sullivan's corps' had scarcely had time to form one line in front of a thinly wooded forest" when the enemy struck. Colonel Stone confirmed as much after the battle. "I received orders . . . to wheel to the left and take possession of a rising ground about 100 yards in our front, to which the enemy were marching rapidly," recalled the regimental commander. "I wheeled off, but had not reached the ground, before we were attacked on all quarters, which prevented our forming regularly, and by wheeling to the left it doubled our division on the brigade immediately in the rear of the other. Thus we were in confusion," admitted Stone, "and no person to undue [undo] us to order, when the enemy pushed on and soon made us all run off." Only two of the Maryland regiments had time to form, "and as soon as they began to fire, those who were in our rear could not

---

31 Smith, *Brandywine*, 17; Smith, "Papers of Smith," 85.

32 Anderson, *Personal Recollections*, 36-37. Some of what Captain Anderson wrote decades after the event is clearly out of order, but the vibrancy of what he recalled about the combat, coupled with the fact that he was at the Brandywine battle, makes it worthwhile to piece his memory together wherever possible.

be prevented from firing also. In a few minutes we were attacked in front and flank, and by our people in the rear," he continued. "Our men ran off in confusion, and were very hard to be rallied." Despite these disastrous results, Stone understood the dire circumstances into which the Marylanders had been thrust. "Although my men did not behave so well as I expected, yet I can scarcely blame them, when I consider their situation; nor are they censured by any part of the army. My horse threw [me] in the time of action, but I did not receive any great injury from it."[33]

While the 1st Maryland Brigade was being thrown into confusion, the 2nd Maryland Brigade was behind its sister organization, forming in the valley south of Birmingham Hill. When the leading brigade was routed, the men of the 2nd assumed a retreat had been ordered and many of its members took to their heels. "It was said a retreat had been ordered," reported Col. Smith, writing in the third person, "but Colonel Smith not knowing it, found himself, to his surprise—being on the left of the Regiment—with only Lieutenant [Thomas] Cromwell and about thirty men. Seeing no enemy, he retired deliberately." Nearly to a man, the two Maryland brigades—effectively Sullivan's entire division—took to the cornfields. The only unit that was not thrown into confusion was Moses Hazen's regiment, which was farther to the rear covering the division's artillery. "While my Division was marching out & before it was possible for them to form to advantage," admitted Sullivan, "the Enemy pressed on with Rapidity & attacked them, which threw them into Some kind of Confusion." The sudden appearance and assault of the Brigade of Guards had, with the exception of Hazen's command, completely dispersed Sullivan's two-brigade division before it could even take up a defensive position. Lieutenant Colonel Smith confirmed, "Colonel Hazen's Regiment retreated in perfect order."[34]

Lieutenant Colonel Smith and his handful of steadfast survivors of the 4th Maryland Regiment had little choice but to follow those who had fled. Eventually Smith reached the top of a small hill, where he formed nearly 1,000 men into a rough line of battle. When Gen. de Borre arrived, Smith offered him command of the new line, but the Frenchman "declined the offer." Smith assumed command and "remained until near sunset." According to Smith, de

---

33 Idzerda, et al., eds., *Lafayette Selected Letters and Papers*, vol. 1, 94; Stone to Paca, September 23, 1777, 167.

34 Smith, "Papers of Smith,", 85-86; Hammond, ed., *Papers of Sullivan*, vol. 1, 464.

Borre "showed some scratches on his cheek, which he said had been done by the English firing fish-hooks, but more probably by the briars."[35]

De Borre later claimed in a letter to Congress that he could not hold the division together because American troops would not stand and fight: "I done my Duty to go and fetch them to bring again against the enemy. It is not my fault if the americanes troops run away to first fire of enemy. . . . [N]obody of them is killed or wounded. I alone received a light wound in the cheek by a bal." Despite his poor grasp of English, de Borre went on to claim that the ability of the officers and men to understand him was not a concern. "I did not know your Language in my arrival in this country," he admitted, "I believed prudently I must Learn it. . . . [N]ow know enough your Language to Weild my orders & to understand that I read." General de Borre was mistaken or being deliberately untruthful. Some of the Maryland regiments did attempt to form a line and withstand the British onslaught, and their casualties (and other eyewitness sources) attest to that fact. According to the 4th Maryland's Lt. Col. Smith, de Borre made no effort to reform the division; de Borre resigned from the army three days later.[36]

The same allegation could not be leveled against John Sullivan, who did all he could to reassemble his command. "I sent off four aides-de-camp for the purpose & went myself but all in vain," he later reported. "No sooner did I form one party, that which I had before formed would Run off & even at times when I, though on horseback and in front of them, apprehended no danger. I then left them to be rallied if possible by their own officers & my aides-de-camp." Sullivan, who was in command of all three divisions on the army's right, returned to Birmingham Hill, "where our artillery was which by this time began to feel the effects of the enemy's fire." Although Moses Hazen's regiment avoided the ignoble fate suffered by the rest of Sullivan's division of being routed without much if any opportunity to form and fight, it suffered significant losses nonetheless. Hazen's command, Sullivan later claimed, "Still Stood firm on our Left," where it fought and was badly mauled. Captain Matthew McConnell's leg was struck and broken, Pvt. Francis Tiscount was wounded in the left arm, and during Hazen's retreat, Pvt. John Sweeney was captured. In all, Hazen's command lost four officers and 73 enlisted men killed, wounded, and

35 Smith, "Papers of Smith," 86.

36 Preudhomme De Borre to Congress, September 17, 1777; McGuire, *Philadelphia Campaign*, vol. 1, 284.

taken prisoner in just a handful of minutes.[37] A recent study of Brandywine claims Hazen's regiment was driven off Birmingham Hill "by the charge of the Hessian grenadiers" ordered into the front line by Gen. Howe "to fill the gap between the British Guards and Grenadiers." This claim perpetuates one of the longstanding myths of the battle that Hessian grenadiers played a prominent, and in some ways decisive, role at Brandywine. In fact, primary sources prove otherwise.[38]

At the time of the American Revolution (and for a long while thereafter), Americans were genuinely angry that King George III hired German troops to fight in North America. In many ways, this mindset induced histories of the war to emphasize the role the Hessians played—real or imagined. The legend seems to have originated with George Bancroft, an American diplomat and secretary of the navy who established the United States Naval Academy at Annapolis in 1845. He was also a historian who studied extensively in Germany and wrote *History of the United States, From the Discovery of the American Continent* (1854-78) in 10 volumes. The American position on Birmingham Hill, wrote Bancroft, broke under "the vigorous charge of the Hessian and British grenadiers, who vied with each other in fury as they ran forward with the bayonet." Samuel Smith's 1976 study of the battle led readers to believe that Sullivan's division was attempting to align itself with Lord Stirling's division "when the Hessian grenadiers struck." Gregory Edgar's history of the campaign noted that Sullivan's division was "hard pressed by a regiment of Hessian grenadiers that Howe had thrown in to close up his lines when his right wing had gone too far toward the river." Finally, Mowday's 2002 book on the battle witnessed Hazen's regiment driven off the high ground "by the charge of the Hessian

---

37 Hammond, ed., *Papers of Sullivan*, vol. 1, 464; John Hawkins, "Battle of Brandywine Described," in *Pennsylvania Magazine of History and Biography* (Philadelphia, 1896), vol. 20, 421. Montgomery, ed., *Pennsylvania Archives*, Series 5, vol. 4, 576; Linn and Egle, eds., *Pennsylvania Archives*, Series 2, vol. 11, 100, 107. Sweeney was later confined at the Academy in Wilmington, Delaware, with a number of other prisoners. Samuel Hazard, et al, eds., *Pennsylvania Archives*, Series 1 (Harrisburg & Philadelphia, 1853), vol. 6, 58. Hazen's final engagement position remains something of a mystery. Sullivan's observation that he "Still Stood firm on our Left" could have meant he assumed a position on the left side of Lord Stirling's division. However, Hazen was at the tail end of Sullivan's division a short while earlier watching the divisional artillery. It is doubtful his command could have remained intact and moved so far east so quickly to Stirling's position with the Brigade of Guards at the top of the hill and the balance of Sullivan's troops in chaos in between. Until additional documentation is discovered, the position from which he engaged the British remains open to reasonable speculation.

38 Mowday, *September 11, 1777*, 120, 125.

grenadiers" who, as noted earlier, Howe supposedly ordered to move into the front line "to fill the gap between the British Guards and Grenadiers."[39]

A careful examination of available primary sources, however, paints a very different picture of the Hessian role that September day. The Hessians began the assault that afternoon on the right side of the Birmingham Road behind the Brigade of Guards and British Grenadiers. The Hessians' march was so methodical and painfully slow that the British troops to their front quickly outdistanced them. "[W]hen the first line formed, the Hessian Grenadiers were close in our rear, and began beating their march at the same time with us," recalled Lt. Hale of the British grenadiers. "[F]rom that minute we saw them no more till the action was over, and only one man of them was wounded by a random shot which came over us." Hale was mistaken on this last point. According to Hessian records, two officers were wounded (Lts. DeBuy and von Baumbach), with the grenadiers as a whole losing one killed and five wounded.[40]

"I believe them steady," continued Hale, "but their slowness is of the greatest disadvantage in a country almost covered with woods, and against an Enemy whose chief qualification is agility in running from fence to fence and thence keeping up an irregular but galling fire on troops who advance at the same pace as at their exercise." Hale knew that British light infantry was accustomed to fighting "from tree to tree, or charg[ing] even in the woods; and Grenadiers who after the first fire lose no time in loading again, but rush on, trusting entirely to that most decisive of weapons the bayonet." British troops commonly began their assaults at about 120 paces per minute, moving approximately 100 yards in that timeframe. The Hessians, concluded Hale, "make no scruple of owning our superiority over them, but palliate so mortifying a confession by saying 'Englishmen be the Divel for going on, but Hesse men be soldier.'" Hessian records, which should be the definitive primary source on the matter, report their "loss is very small, as *no battalion or regiment actually took part in an engagement* [emphasis added]."[41]

39 Bancroft, *History of the United States*, vol. 9, 337. This set is available in both 8 and 10 volume editions; Smith, *Brandywine*, 17; Edgar, *The Philadelphia Campaign*, 30; Mowday, *September 11, 1777*, 120, 125.

40 Wilkin, *Some British Soldiers*, 245; *Remembrancer*, 415-417; Lowell, *The Hessians*, 301.

41 Wilkin, *Some British Soldiers*, 245; Journal of the Hessian Corps in America under General von Heister, letter Z, 90.

The role of the Hessian grenadiers that afternoon is fairly easy to reconstruct. The Hessians quickly fell behind in the assault; the British Brigade of Guards on Cornwallis's far right struck at a fortuitous moment, just as the head of Sullivan's division was arriving, and collapsed the entire division; on the Guards's left, the British grenadiers stopped briefly to deliver a volley and then immediately assaulted Lord Stirling's division with leveled bayonets. The proud Hessian grenadiers were well trained capable professionals who somehow managed to allow a large distance to develop between themselves and the front line of British troops. They suffered lightly from over-shots, and by the time they reached the front the Americans had been driven back and the high ground of Birmingham Hill was in the hands of General Howe. As a result, the Hessian grenadiers never fired a shot that September afternoon because they could not keep pace with the rapidly moving British bayonets in front of them.[42]

It is likely that not a single Hessian grenadier set eyes on Moses Hazen or his regiment at the Brandywine. Most certainly they did not drive any American troops off Birmingham Hill.

Later Judgments

"I never yet have pretended that my Disposition in the Late Battle was perfect," wrote General Sullivan to the president of Congress, John Hancock. "I know it was very far from it but this I will venture to affirm . . . it was the best that time would allow me to make." Thomas Burke, a North Carolina delegate to Congress who was with the Continental Army at the Brandywine, disagreed and leveled serious accusations against Sullivan. His demands led to a Congressional investigation that would have resulted in Sullivan's recall had Washington not put a stop to it. Burke's primary accusation claimed Sullivan made "a circuit of two Miles when one quarter in the direct road would have brought him to his ground."[43] In other words, Sullivan should have marched his division on the same route to Birmingham Hill that Stirling and Stephen had taken to reach that high ground. Doing so, however, would have further clogged that narrow road and perhaps prevented Sullivan from finding the two

---

42 McGuire, *Philadelphia Campaign*, vol. 1, 208.

43 Hammond, ed., *Papers of Sullivan*, vol. 1, 462-463; Smith, et al., eds., *Letters of Delegates*, vol. 7, 680.

regiments of his division watching the three fords north of his original position along the Brandywine.[44]

Nearly every history of the battle misinterprets Sullivan's movement. One recent account places all the blame on the back of General de Borre. "Brigadier General Preudhomme de Borre insisted his troops should be given the honor of holding the extreme right of the line," asserts one modern author. "De Borre pulled his men from their positions and marched them to the right, forcing a quick reorganization of the whole American line." This statement is not based on any known eighteenth-century documents, and de Borre never advanced such a claim. In addition, de Borre was in command of Sullivan's division. He was not the senior division commander of the three divisions present that afternoon on Birmingham Hill. Therefore, he had no claim to the honor of holding the right of the line. De Borre did, however, execute the unusual maneuver that pulled Sullivan's division out of line in an attempt to move it into position farther to the right and in the face of the British assault that led to so much carnage.[45]

At least one senior officer who was on Birmingham Hill that afternoon argued that Sullivan was not to blame for the division's debacle. Brigadier General Thomas Conway, who commanded Lord Stirling's Pennsylvania brigade, believed that "[i]f part of the Division was not formed completely before the Engagement, The fault can not be imputed to Genl Sullivan, who although he had a right to take the right of the Line, took the Left, in Order to save time, a proof that the Division of the Right, had full time to form," argued Conway. "[T]he short time left to his troops in order to Form, was hardly sufficient, for well disciplined troops, and well exercised, and by no means sufficient for the troops of this Army, who appear to me to maneavre upon false Principles, and where I cannot discover as yet, The least notion of displaying Columns, and forming briskly upon all Emergencies."[46]

---

44 McGuire, *Philadelphia Campaign*, vol. 1, 219. Burke seems to be describing the entire movement of Sullivan's division, from the initial move from Brinton's Ford to near Street Road, back south and east to Birmingham Hill, and then the botched attempt to shift farther east near Stirling's left flank. That distance would have been more than two miles. The essence of his argument is that if the division had made a beeline for where it ultimately ended up, the march would have been just under one mile instead of double that distance. Burke, of course, ignores the reality of operating in real time without hindsight under battlefield conditions.

45 Mowday, *September 11, 1777*, 118.

46 Hammond, ed., *Papers of Sullivan*, vol. 1, 555-556.

Some, like Lord Stirling's aide William Willcox, attributed the rout of Sullivan's division to bad luck. "[The] enemy by good luck, or perhaps policy, made their attack before the intended disposition of your division . . . could be carried into execution," Willcox posited. "It was therefore rather to be considered as unfortunate, as ill-judged, and not to be laid at the door of any particular officer." Others attributed the disaster to a lack of training, good leadership, and morale—all of which would dramatically improve during the transformation of the Continental Army at Valley Forge. In September of 1777, however, the fighting at the Brandywine required complex marches and maneuvers the American troops simply could not perform as a matter of routine. Rather than conducting an ill-conceived march, as Congressman Burke believed, Sullivan's Marylanders failed on Birmingham Hill, argued one historian, because of "bad timing and poor training, compounded by low morale resulting from a lack of inspirational brigade-level leadership."[47]

Sullivan answered Congressman Burke's accusations by issuing the following statement:

> Sullivans division did not take too Large a Circuit as he Suggests but went on to meet the Enemy agreeable to their orders & were obliged to fall back, upon finding that the other Divisions which proceeded by Different Routs had taken ground & formed half a mile to the Rear of where that Division had advanced. They were under a necessity of falling back & Filing off to the Right in order to form a Junction with the other Troops & before this could be completed They were attacked & Thrown into Confusion from which they never fully Recovered.[48]

The fighting on Birmingham Hill had barely begun in earnest, and about one-third of the defenders were already in full retreat. As far as Howe and Cornwallis were concerned, the battle was unfolding much as expected.

---

47 "Papers Related to the Battle of Brandywine," in *Proceedings of the Historical Society of Pennsylvania* (Philadelphia, 1846), vol. 1, No. 8, 53; McGuire, *Philadelphia Campaign*, vol. 1, 219.

48 Hammond, ed., *Papers of Sullivan*, vol. 1, 472-473.

Chapter 14

The British Assault Stirling and Stephen:
Afternoon, September 11, 1777

"[T]he whole Rebel Line presented itself to View & so close that those who
compos'd this spirited Attack had nothing to Expect but Slaughter."[1]

— Lt. Frederick Augustus Wetherall, September 1777

The Assault on Stirling's Division

Once the main British line reached Street Road, Capt. Johann Ewald's
original advance guard was absorbed into the main body of Cornwallis's
division. The 17th Regiment of Foot's light company formed on the right of
Col. Abercromby's 1st Light Infantry Battalion, and the 42nd Highlanders' light
company formed on the left of the battalion. Ewald's jaegers dispersed in front
of the entire line, traded shots with the Americans, and continued moving
forward.

Members of the 3rd Virginia, meanwhile, fired from the Jones orchard at
the powerful lines of professionals tramping steadily toward them. When the
pressure became too great, the Virginians fell back to the three-foot stone wall
surrounding the one-acre cemetery abutting the Birmingham Meetinghouse
some 300 yards south of the Street Road-Birmingham Road intersection.
Because the Quakers believed gravestones to be nothing short of "monuments

1 Wetherall, *Journal.*

A modern view of the cemetery wall at Birmingham Meetinghouse. After retiring from the Jones orchard, the 3rd Virginia Regiment defended this position as the British approached from the right side of the photograph. *Author*

to vanity," other than scattered mounds and depressions from recent burials, the cemetery constituted unencumbered ground. Once behind the rock wall, the 3rd Virginia began picking off members of Abercromby's battalion. Lord Stirling, who was watching the action unfold to his front from his post on Birmingham Hill, ordered his artillery to open fire as the British light infantrymen ascended the small hill upon which sat the meetinghouse.[2]

With a wall in their front and a hedge running parallel to Birmingham Road, Abercromby's men found themselves in a dangerous position and under a heavy fire from the well-postioned Virginians. The men of the 17th Regiment's light company decided attacking the wall was out of the question, and instead moved to their right and pushed through a hedge lining the Birmingham Road. When artillery shells found them there, they ran south along the road to the base of Birmingham Hill in an effort to get under the fire of the American guns, losing several men in the process. As one light infantry officer tried to explain it

2   McGuire, *Philadelphia Campaign*, vol. 1, 201.

A modern view of the Birmingham Meetinghouse. The cemetery with its surrounding wall sits to the left rear of the building, which was used as a hospital in the bloody battle's aftermath. *Author*

later, "a High Stone Wall prevented their keeping up with the Battalion, those companies leap'd over the Fence into the high Road which divided them from the British Grenadiers & in order the sooner to avoid the danger of the Shot ran down the Road & shelter'd themselves at the foot of the Hill." The pelting artillery fire under which the light infantry bolted left "the hedge on the left side of the road much cut with the grape shot." The light infantrymen sprinted down Birmingham Road between the Quaker meetinghouse on one side and a stone house on the other. While the 17th Regiment's light company moved into the road, other elements of Abercromby's battalion shifted east to slip around the opposite side of the meetinghouse in an effort to avoid the steady enemy fire and bypass the enemy stronghold.[3]

The 3rd Virginia, boasted one American officer, "bravely sustained itself against superior numbers." Indeed it had, but its men were now almost surrounded, with British light infantrymen sweeping around both sides of the

---

3   Wetherall, *Journal*; Scott, *Memoranda*. The dash of the light infantry along the road passed a stone house (1735) on the western side that is still in existence, though it has been considerably enlarged.

A modern view from the northern slope of Birmingham Hill looking north. The Quaker sanctuary (Birmingham meetinghouse) is located behind the trees on the right edge of the image. The dominant structure in the center is the enlarged 1735 house that sits west of the meetinghouse. The hollow in which the detached companies of British light infantry took shelter is in the left foreground near the partially visible barn. *Author*

cemetery. What was left of the regiment fell back up the slope at the last possible moment, where it probably reformed and assumed a position with Woodford's brigade on the far right of Stephen's division. The small Virginia command was in shambles. Its commander, Col. Thomas Marshall, was on foot after his horse was shot. Marshall carried 150 men into the fight that afternoon and left eight officers, 13 noncommissioned officers, and 60 privates on the field killed, wounded, and captured. The regiment's stand so far in advance of the rest of the army deeply impressed Capt. Henry Lee of the dragoons: "[N]ever yielding one inch of ground, and expending thirty rounds a man, in forty-five minutes [the regiment] was now ordered to fall back upon Woodford's right, which was handsomely accomplished by Colonel Marshall, although deprived of half his officers, where he renewed the sanguinary contest."[4]

4   Lee, *Memoirs*, vol. 1, 16; McGuire, *Philadelphia Campaign*, vol. 1, 215. Of the regiment's four captains in the fight, Capt. John Chilton was killed, Capt. Philip Lee was mortally wounded, and

Within a relatively short time, the 17th's company was joined by those of the 38th, 33rd, and 4th Regiments of Foot at the base of Birmingham Hill. Once there, the four separated companies proceeded to crawl up the slope of Birmingham Hill, where they "caught a glimpse of the enemy as far as the eye could reach to the right and left." The enterprising British infantrymen were soon discovered, however, and as one recalled it, "compelled to throw ourselves on our knees and bellies, and keep up a fire from the slope of the hill." The new arrivals were far removed from immediate support on either flank and faced immediate overwhelming odds. "The Inspiration & Courage of both Officers & Men inducing them to ascend the Height, the whole Rebel Line presented itself to View & so close that those who compos'd this spirited Attack had nothing to Expect but Slaughter," was how one soldier put it.[5]

Although they were not slaughtered, they did take substantial casualties. Captain William Scott of the 17th Regiment of Foot's light company remembered that "the enemy repeatedly attempted to come on, but were always drove back by our fire. At this time a most tremendous fire of musketry opened from both lines." Captain Charles Cochrane's light company of the 4th Regiment of Foot suffered heavily while pinned down, losing an officer and 11 men. Captain William Dansey of the 33rd's light company was fighting his men when a bullet struck him in the joint of his right thumb. It would be nearly a month before Dansey could pick up a pen and let his mother know about his injury. "I write to you . . . as soon as I was able to handle a Pen which I do now in Pain and can not bear to write long at a time, owing to a slight Wound I received," he explained. "I was shot thro' the joint of my right Thumb, which did not make me quit the Field or my Duty afterwards. . . . Thank God it is no worse. . . . I wou'd have given half a Dozen Thumbs to have been assured Life and Limb at the Time."[6]

The remaining 12 companies of the 1st Light Infantry Battalion (including the attached company of the 42nd Royal Highlanders), meanwhile, remained

---

Capt. John Peyton was wounded but remained with his men. Several junior officers in the regiment also fell. Lieutenants Apollos Cooper and Robert Peyton, and Ens. George Peyton were killed. Lieutenant William White was mortally wounded. Lieutenants John Mercer and John Blackwell were wounded. Heitman, Historical Register, multiple pages of alphabetic listings.

5   Scott, Memoranda; Wetherall, Journal.

6   William Dansey to Mrs. Dansey, October 9, 1777, original in the William Dansey Letters.

pinned down behind a fence running perpendicular to the Birmingham Road about 100 yards behind and to the left of the four advanced companies. The heavy fire and steady accumulation of losses prompted the officers of the detached light companies on Birmingham Hill to cast their eyes about for assistance. The grenadiers, in their rear, had still not moved south of the fence lining Street Road. "Looking back to see how far the grenadier line was off from which alone we could receive immediate support, to my surprise I saw close to me Major Stuart of the 43rd whose regt. Being at Rhode island attended the army as a spectator," recalled the 17th's Capt. Scott. "[R]ecollecting the 43rd grenadier company was the left of their line, we persuaded Major Stuart to run down the hill and prevail on that company to hasten to our support." The 24-year-old Maj. Stuart was dispatched earlier in 1777 to Rhode Island to command a grenadier battalion. General Howe recalled the unit to New York—without Stuart. This very public action humiliated the young ambitious officer, who believed Howe's action was based solely upon political, rather than military, reasons. Anxious to remain in the field, Stuart accompanied the army to the Brandywine as an observer, joined in the assault, and now found himself in the thick of the fighting. Stuart's journey back in the direction of his fellow grenadiers was not without danger, for "a ball gave me a pretty severe scratch in the cheek, and another went through the crown of my hat at the Brandy-Wine, or else I have escaped full well from all the dangers we have been in."[7]

From atop Birmingham Hill, Gen. Sullivan, who remained in overall command of Stirling's and Stephen's divisions (as well as his own routed outfit), realized the importance of holding the high ground. "This Hill Commanded both the Right & Left of our Line & if carried by the Enemy I knew would Instantly bring on a Total Rout & make a Retreat very Difficult," explained the American general. "I therefore Determined to hold it as Long as possible to give Lord Sterlings & General Stephens Divisions which yet stood firm as much assistance from the artillery as possible & to give Colo Hazens . . . Regiment which Still Stood firm on our Left the Same advantage & to Cover the Broken

---

7   Scott, *Memoranda*. Although Scott used the word "run," as a major, Stuart almost certainly would have been mounted; Wortley, ed., *A Prime Minister and His Son*, 116-117. Major Charles Stuart was the son of the influential and much hated Tory minister John Stuart Lord Bute. After Howe's effective dismissal, Stuart exchanged several sharp letters with the general and sought permission to return to England, a request Howe denied. Stuart returned to New York in the spring of 1777 and went into the field with the army without a command. McGuire, *Philadelphia Campaign*, vol. 1, 39.

This modern view looks south through the eyes of the British advance toward the American line on Birmingham Hill. Lord Stirling's Continental division was in position where the modern fence line visible in the distance stands today. *Author*

Troops of my Division & give them an opportunity to Rally & come to our assistance which Some of them did & others could not by their officers be brought to do any thing but fly."[8] The sudden rout of Sullivan's division on the

8 Hammond, ed., *Papers of Sullivan*, vol. 1, 464. Another story involving this part of the battle involves Capt. Joseph McClellan of the 9th Pennsylvania Regiment (Thomas Conway's brigade, Lord Stirling's division). Captain McClellan commanded a company opposite the grenadier company of the 42nd Highlanders. He later wrote in the third-person about an episode involving one of the Scots: "A stout man whom he took to be a Scotchman, and who was evidently under the influence of liquor advanced recklessly and placed himself behind a little mound, made by the root of a tree which had been blown down. From this position, which was within pistol- shot of McClellan's company, the British soldier fired, and killed the sergeant, who was standing by Capt. McClellan's side. . . . Capt. McClellan, seeing his sergeant fall, and observing whence the fatal missile came, perceived that the man was reloading his piece as he lay crouched behind the mound, and partially protected by it, and determined to anticipate him. He discharged his carbine with deliberate aim, and said he saw the soldier roll over, evidently disabled, if not killed." Futhey and Cope, *History of Chester County*, 79. No contemporary account corroborates this story. McClellan was a captain in the 9th Pennsylvania, but no sergeant in that regiment was killed (known losses do not include a sergeant). Captain William Mackey was wounded and captured when a musket ball passed through his lungs and Pvt. Peter Eager was also wounded. A ball entered Pvt. Adam Koch's head below his right eye and passed out below his right ear, Ensign Benjamin Morris and Pvt. Daniel Mullen were both killed. Trussell, *Pennsylvania Line*, 277; Montgomery, ed., *Pennsylvania Archives*, Series 5, vol. 4,

western side of the American defensive line left the Brigade of Guards on the hill top and four companies of light infantry advancing up the hill farther east. The British grenadiers were still advancing, concentrating on Stirling's division. When the Brigade of Guards shifted to the right earlier to assault Sullivan's men, the 1st British Grenadier Battalion also slid to the right to fill the gap between the Guards and the 2nd British Grenadier Battalion. However, when the grenadiers stepped within 40 paces of the patriot position, Stirling's men, wrote Howe's staff officer, gave them "a whole volley and [they] sustained a very heavy fire." The grenadiers had already been subject to artillery shells and grapeshot while negotiating fence lines and other obstacles. Now, within direct small arms killing range, the Americans poured a heavy musket fire into them. This was, observed an eyewitness who mananged to survive the carnage, "the heaviest firing I ever heard . . . continuing a long time, every inch of ground being disputed."[9]

Confusion erupted in both armies when heavy black powder smoke billowed along the lines and the cacophony of discharging muskets made it difficult and in many cases impossible for the enlisted men to hear their officers shouting orders. As a New Jersey surgeon named Ebenezer Elmer from Lord Stirling's division later recalled, "A large Column Came on in front playing ye Granediers March & Now the Battle began wh[ich] proved Excessive severe the Enemy Came on with fury our men stood firing upon them most amazingly." The grenadiers dropped to the ground under the flying lead, temporarily halting their advance while they fixed bayonets into place. Once all was in order, the grenadiers stood and continued their attack. From this point forward the grenadiers quickened their pace to reduce the time spent under fire. As Lt. William Hale so eloquently observed, the method grenadiers typically

---

537, 560; John Blair Linn and William H. Egle, eds., *Pennsylvania Archives*, Series 2 (Harrisburg, PA, 1880), vol. 10, 693-709; Montgomery, ed., *Pennsylvania Archives*, Series 5, vol. 3, 456.

9 Von Muenchhausen, *At Howe's Side*, 31; "A Biographical Sketch of Governor Richard Howell, of New Jersey," ed. Daniel Agnew, in *The Pennsylvania Magazine of History and Biography* (Philadelphia, 1898), Vol. 22, 224. There is some evidence that women were present at this time at the front even though they had been ordered to remain with the baggage train. An account by Capt. John Markland claimed women of the 6th Pennsylvania Regiment took "the empty canteens of their husbands and friends and returned with them filled with water, which they persisted in delivering to the owners during the hottest part of the engagement, although frequently cautioned as to the danger of coming into the line of fire." "Revolutionary Services of Captain John Markland," *Pennsylvania Magazine of History and Biography* (Philadelphia, 1885), vol. 9, 105.

This modern view looks west across the northern slope of Birmingham Hill. The British grenadiers advanced from the right side of this image and advanced across the rolling terrain toward Birmingham Hill off to the left. *Author*

employed with such success was to level their weapons and fire, not waste any time reloading, and instead "rush on, trusting entirely to that most decisive of weapons the bayonet; will ever be superior to any troops the Rebels can ever bring against them."[10]

Howe's aide von Muenchhausen verified that this preferred method was indeed employed against Lord Stirling's men at the Brandywine when he observed that the grenadiers "fired a volley, and then ran furiously at the rebels with fixed bayonets." A British grenadier officer who history has yet to identify confirmed the intense action and the use of cold steel to drive away the Americans. "At the battle of Brandywine," he penned in a letter home that winter, "we had the most dreadful fire for one hour I ever saw. I heard nothing equal to it all last war in Germany. At last we gave the rebels the bayonet, which soon dispersed them." The conclusion scribbled in the diary of Joseph Clark, a member of Stephen's staff, agreed with the anonymous British officer's observation: "The Fireing while the action lasted was the warmest I believe that has been in America since the War began."[11]

Once the final attack was underway, it did not take long for the British to close the distance and bring on the final act of the Birmingham Hill drama. The momentum of the advancing 1st Light Infantry Battalion, together with the 2nd Grenadier Battalion, carried them up the slope and into Brig. Gen. Thomas Conway's brigade of Stirling's division. About the same time, the 1st Grenadier Battalion lapped around the flank of the New Jersey Brigade on Stirling's left.

It was about this time in the battle that Major General Lafayette reached this part of the line. As he later explained, "as [a] volunteer, [I] had always accompanied the general [Washington]. The left wing [opposite Chads's Ford] remaining in a state of tranquility, and the right wing appearing fated to receive all the heavy blows, he obtained permission to join Sullivan." His arrival, thought Lafayette, "seemed to inspirit the troops." The Chevalier Dubuysson, who accompanied Lafayette, vividly recalled the fighting. "The English left attacked very rapidly and in good order, and threw back every American until they met," wrote Dubuysson in reference to the overall attack that would wrest

---

10 Wilkin, *Some British Soldiers*, 245; Ebenezer Elmer, "Extracts from the Journal of Surgeon Ebenezer Elmer of the New Jersey Continental Line, September 11-19, 1777," ed. John Nixon Brooks, *The Pennsylvania Magazine of History and Biography* (Philadelphia, 1911), vol. 35, 105.

11 Von Muenchhausen, *At Howe's Side*, 31; "London, December 18: Extract of a letter from an Officer at Philadelphia to his friend at Edinburgh, dated Oct. 27," *Felix Farley's Bristol Journal 26*, no. 1400 (December 26, 1777); Clark, "Diary," 98-99.

This modern view depicts the Lafayette memorial shaft that was erected in 1895 on the crest of Birmingham Hill. The monument was intended to mark the location of Lafayette's wounding. Given our understanding of the battle today, however, the shaft is almost certainly in the wrong location. *Author*

control of Birmingham Hill from the Continentals. "Only the divisions of . . . Stirling and Conway [Stephen] held out for any length of time." The French aide continued, recalling how "The Marquis de Lafayette joined the latter [Conway's brigade], where there were some Frenchmen. He dismounted and did his utmost to make the men charge with fixed bayonets." The Frenchmen [Lafayette and his several aides] personally grabbed bayonets and locked them onto the ends of American muskets, after which, continued Chevalier Dubuysson, Lafayette "pushed them in the back to make them charge." But it was no use, continued the French eyewitness, for "the Americans are not suited for this type of combat, and never wanted to take it up."[12]

Lafayette recalled the "confusion became extreme." Some of Conway's men began slipping away from the front and down the southern slope of the hill. The French general was working to rally the troops when a musket ball "passed through his leg." It was at that moment, he later wrote, "the remaining forces gave way, and [I] was fortunate to be able to mount a horse, thanks to Gimat, [my] aide-de-camp." Conway's now completely broken brigade streamed southeast for Dilworth.[13]

Captain-Lieutenant John Peebles of the 42nd Grenadiers also remembered the fighting, though from the opposite perspective: "after giving them a few rounds charged . . . with such spirit that they immediately fled in confusion." Lieutenant Henry Stirke of the 10th Regiment of Foot's light company was attacking farther east that day against Stirling's right flank. "Our men," he remembered, advanced "under a heavy fire both of Cannon and small arms, notwithstanding which, and the difficulty of the ground we had to march over, we push'd the Rebels from ye heights, in about 15 minutes, with great loss." Captain Archibald Robertson, a member of the Royal Engineers, would spend several days after the Brandywine fighting preparing a map and narrative key for

---

12 Lafayette, *Memoirs*, vol. 1, 23; Idzerda, ed., *Letters and Papers*, vol. 1, 84, 95.

13 Idzerda, ed., *Letters and Papers*, vol. 1, 95; Montgomery, ed., *Pennsylvania Archives*, Series 5, vol. 3, 673, 684. Gimat was Jean-Joseph Sourbader de Gimat, a volunteer French officer who served in the Continental Army during the Revolution. A memorial shaft, installed in 1895 to mark the location of Lafayette's wounding, is almost certainly misplaced. Some of the several witness sources who agree on this claim to have been with Lafayette during his 1825 visit to the battlefield. According to a Nathan Jester of Dilworthtown, Lafayette pointed the spot out from his carriage, and a temporary marker was placed along the road between Birmingham Meetinghouse and Dilworth, approximately 275 yards beyond Sandy Hollow. "It was proposed to place the memorial shaft at that point, and the inscription was framed to suit that location. It is however equally adapted to its present location." *Lafayette at Brandywine: Containing the Proceedings at the Dedication of the Memorial Shaft to Mark the Place Where Lafayette Was Wounded at the Battle of Brandywine* (West Chester, PA), 73. As with almost all Victorian-era battlefield monuments, the permanent Lafayette monument's present location was chosen for visibility, not accuracy. "The place selected for the shaft is a triangular piece of ground on the north side of the public road leading from Dilworthtown to Birmingham meetinghouse. . . . This is one of the highest points of what is known as "Battle Hill," is in full view of the meetinghouse, and the hills to the north, over which the British approached, and is a short distance from where Lafayette was wounded." Ibid., 10-11. Many monuments of this period, like those on Civil War battlefields, were placed along main roads for visibility, often several hundred yards from where a unit actually fought. Lafayette was almost certainly wounded west of the location of the monument, somewhere near where Conway's brigade fought near the intersection of Birmingham Road and Wylie Road.

Gen. Howe. "The Rebels were Drawn up upon very Strong ground and seem'd determin'd to stand," he observed, "but the impetuosity of our Troops was irresistable." Another engineering officer, Capt. John Montresor, described the final moments of the assault that cracked open the American line: "The British Grenadiers and Guards at the same time labouring under a smart and incessant fire from the Rebels out of a wood and above them, most nobly charged them without firing a shot and drove them before them."[14]

Despite their best efforts and favorable ground, Stirling's men were unable to survive the rout of Sullivan's division on the left, withstand the heavy firing in front, and repulse the grenadiers' bayonet charge. After a defensive effort perhaps best described as stout and short, Stirling's men fell back down the southern slope of Birmingham Hill. Somehow, despite the proximity of the enemy, his regiments retreated in better order than did Sullivan's.[15]

As Stirling's men began melting away, and the American gunners abandoned their pieces that had inflicted substantial carnage, the four light infantry companies pinned down near the crest, together with the rest of the 1st Light Infantry Battalion farther to the east, rose up and added their weight to the charge. Captain William Scott of the 17th Regiment of Foot recalled the moment of victory, as he lay pinned down with the advanced light infantry companies. "[I] saw Captain Cochrane of the 4th company on my left throw up

14 Peebles, *Peebles' American War*, 133; Henry Stirke, "A British Officer's Revolutionary War Journal, 1776-1778," S. Sydney Bradford, ed., *Maryland Historical Magazine* (1961), vol. 56, 170; Robertson, *His Diaries and Sketches*, 146; Montresor, "Montresor Journals," 450. An account of the battle by Lt. John Shreve of the 2nd New Jersey Regiment includes his father's wounding. However, the 2nd New Jersey was not at the Brandywine, and no available account documents Shreve's attachment to any other unit. As the story is questionable, it is omitted from the main narrative. John Shreve, "Personal Narrative of the Services of Lieut. John Shreve," *The Magazine of American History with Notes and Queries* (New York, 1879), vol. 3, 567-568.

15 John Hawkins, "Battle of Brandywine Described," in *Pennsylvania Magazine of History and Biography* (Philadelphia, 1896), vol. 20, 421. Montgomery, ed., *Pennsylvania Archives*, Series 5, vol. 4, 576; Linn and Egle, eds., *Pennsylvania Archives*, Series 2, vol. 11, 100, 107. Sweeney was later confined at the Academy in Wilmington, Delaware, with a number of other prisoners. Samuel Hazard, et al, eds., *Pennsylvania Archives*, Series 1 (Harrisburg & Philadelphia, 1853), vol. 6, 58. Hazen's final engagement position remains something of a mystery. Sullivan's observation that he "Still Stood firm on our Left" could have meant he assumed a position on the left side of Lord Stirling's division. However, Hazen was at the tail end of Sullivan's division a short while earlier watching the divisional artillery. It is doubtful his command could have remained intact and moved so far east so quickly to Stirling's position with the Brigade of Guards at the top of the hill and the balance of Sullivan's troops in chaos in between. Until additional documentation is discovered, the position from which he engaged the British remains open to reasonable speculation.

his cap and cry "Victory!"; and, looking round," reported the officer, "saw the 43rd [grenadier] company hastening to our relief." When orders to advance rang out, the isolated companies "dashed forward, passed the five pieces of cannon which the enemy had abandoned, and made some few prisoners, the enemy running away from us, with too much speed to be overtaken." Ensign George Ewing of the 3rd New Jersey Regiment, part of Stirling's command, recalled "being over-powered, we were obliged to retire and leave them [the British] master of the field." Surgeon Richard Howell, also of New Jersey, barely escaped. "After having been among them, with the loss of my mare, saddle and bridle, and great coat and hat," he wrote, "with all my misfortunes I think myself happy, not to be taken prisoner." Not everyone was so fortunate. In addition to the five artillery pieces that had formed the main patriot battery, the British captured a sizeable number of prisoners.[16]

Lieutenant George Duke of the 33rd's grenadier company believed the British went into the fight with "more spirit and determined resolution than [the Americans] did, to drive them out of the field where the rebels were posted on the most advantageous ground that they could wish." Had the Americans behaved like soldiers, Duke added, nothing could have pushed them off the hill, "but they showed themselves just what they are, nothing but a rebel banditti."[17]

In the days and weeks following the battle, some participants came to believe they had in fact emerged from the fighting having inflicted a more damaging blow to the British than they had themselves suffered. "When we found the right and left oppressed by numbers and giving way on all quarters, we were obliged to abandon the hill we had so long contended for," Gen. Sullivan explained in a report to Congress, "but not till we had almost covered the ground between that and Birmingham meetinghouse with the dead bodies

---

16 Scott, *Memoranda*; George Ewing, "Journal of George Ewing, a Revolutionary Soldier, of Greenwich, New Jersey," in *American Monthly Magazine*, vol. 38 (1911), 6; "Biographical Sketch of Howell," 224; William Henry Egle, ed., *Pennsylvania Archives*, Series 3, vol. 23 (Harrisburg, PA, 1897), 816. One of the captured was John Portman of the 6th Pennsylvania Regiment. He was later confined on James Island, South Carolina, but escaped the evening before the British evacuated Charleston. John Portman, pension application. Captain-Lieutenant Gibbs Jones led an independent Pennsylvania battery during the battle, but it is unclear where the unit fought. Jones later reported the loss of his papers at the Brandywine, including the unit's muster rolls. Gibbs Jones to Joseph Howell, December 20, 1786, National Archives and Records Administration, Manuscript File RG93, accessible at www.wardepepartmentpapers.org.

17 Lieutenant George Duke, Grenadier Company, 33rd Regiment of Foot, to unknown correspondent, October 13, 1777, ed. Thomas McGuire, original posted online to be auctioned in May 2008, edited copy in author's collection.

This modern view looks north from Adam Stephen's position on the edge of Sandy Hollow. The British light infantry and Hessian jaegers assaulted Stephen's division from the tree line visible in the distance. *Author*

of the enemy." There were not enough British casualties to "cover the ground," but there is a reasonable explanation why Sullivan left that description: Gen. Howe had trained his soldiers to drop to the ground when the rebels fired upon them. He instilled some light infantry tactics in all of his troops prior to the 1776 New York campaign, and many of the army's regiments were still following this practice. In the smoke and confusion of battle, men deliberately lying on the ground were easily confused with casualties.[18]

Sullivan also went on to claim, "Five times did the enemy drive our troops from the hill, and as often was it regained, and the summit often disputed muzzle to muzzle. The general fire of the line lasted an hour and forty minutes, fifty-one of which the hill was disputed almost muzzle to muzzle, in such a manner, that General Conway, who has seen much service, says he never saw so close and severe a fire." When Sullivan wrote these words he was defending himself against a series of accusations, and exaggerated some of the details of the fighting. No one disputes, however, that the combat was intense while it lasted, and that the British who made the attack in this quarter suffered as a result.[19]

According to official British casualty returns, the grenadier battalions suffered 24 killed and 126 wounded, including 14 officers. One of these officers was Lt. Col. William Medows, the commander of the 1st British Grenadier Battalion. According to Capt. George Harris of the 5th Regiment of Foot's grenadier company, "He [Medows] received a shot, in the act of waving his sword-arm just above the elbow, that went out at the back, knocking him off his horse, and the fall breaking his opposite collar-bone." Captain Harris, who was wounded at Iron Hill about a week before the battle and would later rise to the rank of general, was advancing behind the attack in a carriage. He jumped a horse without a saddle and, claimed his biographer, "had the honour to share in the glory of that day, but attended with the drawback of finding his gallant commander and friend most literally in the hands of the surgeon, having lost the use of both his own." Knocked senseless by the painful wound and subsequent fall, Colonel Medows had not yet "recovered his senses when Captain Harris came to him, but looking at him some time, and knowing his voice, he

18 McGuire, *Philadelphia Campaign*, vol. 1, 209.

19 Hammond, ed., *Papers of Sullivan*, vol. 1, 465.

attempted to put out his hand, and not being able to use either, [said] 'Its hard.'"[20]

Assault on Stephen's Division

While Sullivan's division was routing and Lord Stirling's division was being hard-pressed and beginning to fall back, Adam Stephen's division on the far right of the American line remained in place atop Birmingham Hill. Stephen's two brigades, the 3rd Virginia under Brig. Gen. William Woodford and the 4th Virginia under Brig. Gen. Charles Scott, were formed on the military crest of the high ground directly above and north of Sandy Hollow, with Woodford on the right side of the division front and Scott on the left. A cloud of skirmishers fanned out well forward of the main line of battle, with the 3rd Virginia Regiment, part of Woodford's brigade, fighting to hold the cemetery near the Birmingham Meetinghouse.

Advancing against Stephen were, right to left, the British 1st Light Infantry Battalion, stalled on both sides of the Birmingham Road; 15 companies of the 2nd Light Infantry Battalion; and on the far left, elements of the Hessian and Anspach jaegers. The Germans had swung well east of Birmingham Meetinghouse but were now bogged down in the low ground between Street Road and Birmingham Hill. Brigadier General James Agnew's 4th British Brigade was well behind this advancing line supporting the attack. The British had engulfed the cemetery, threatened the capture of the advanced Virginia outfit (as described above), and forced the regiment to retire.

Lieutenant Colonel Ludwig von Wurmb, the jaeger commander, oversaw the advance and described the initial encounter with the American skirmishers a short time earlier. "I saw that the enemy wanted to form for us on a bare hill, so I had them greeted by our two amusettes and this was the beginning of General

---

20 *Remembrancer for 1777*, 415-417; Inman, ed., "List of Officers Killed," 176-205. The following grenadier officers were killed: Capt. Edward Drury (63rd Regiment of Foot), Lt. William Faulkner (15th Regiment of Foot), Lt. Minchin (27th Regiment of Foot), Lt. Richard Barber (40th Regiment of Foot), Lt. Hadley Doyle (52nd Regiment of Foot), and Lts. John Harris and Adam Drummond (33rd Regiment of Foot). In addition to those killed, the following were wounded: Capt. Andrew Cathcart (15th Regiment of Foot), Capt. John Simcoe in the arm (40th Regiment of Foot), Capt. Fish (44th Regiment of Foot), Lts. Ligonier Chapman and Stephen Cooke (37th Regiment of Foot), and Lt. Thomas Peters (64th Regiment of Foot). S. R. Lushington, *The Life and Services of General Lord Harris, G.C.B. During His Campaigns in America, The West Indies, and India* (London, 1840), 88.

Howe's column's [arrival]." The bare hill described by von Wurmb was the eastern extension of the rise that Birmingham Meetinghouse sits upon. The jaegers encountered American skirmishers on the end of this rise about 1,500 feet east of Birmingham Road.[21]

Although the Germans could not effectively use their smaller guns to support their advance, the Americans had no such problem. Situated on good terrain with a commanding view, the battalion guns attached to Stephen's division did outstanding work defending the position with shell and grapeshot, as did the patriot muskets, which were loaded and fired as fast as humanly possible. The inherent strength of Stephen's position was undeniable. According to the *Jaeger Corps Journal*, the Americans were "advantageously posted on a not especially steep height in front of a woods, with the right wing resting on a steep and deep ravine." The stout defense put up by the Americans likely surprised Lt. Richard St. George of the 52nd Foot's light company, who remembered "a most infernal fire of cannon and musket—smoak—incessant shouting—incline to the right! Incline to the Left!—halt!—charge! . . . the balls ploughing up the ground. The Trees cracking over ones head, The branches riven by the artillery—The leaves falling as in autumn by grapeshot." Lieutenant Martin Hunter, another officer in St. George's light company, agreed with his fellow officer and also took note of the imposing defensive nature of the terrain: "The position the enemy had taken was very strong indeed—very commanding ground, a wood on their rear and flanks, a ravine and strong paling in front. The fields in America are all fenced in by paling."[22]

One of the jaeger officers fighting on the left wing, Lt. Heinrich von Feilitzsch, recalled the "counter-fire from the enemy, especially against us, was the most concentrated. . . . The enemy had made a good disposition with one height after the other to his rear. He stood fast," he added, perhaps with grudging respect. Lieutenant Colonel von Wurmb agreed: "We drove the enemy [Stephen's skirmish line] from this [bare] hill and they positioned themselves in a woods from which we dislodged them and then a second woods where we found ourselves 150 paces from their line which was on a height in a

---

21 Von Wurmb to von Jungkenn, October 14, 1777, 10.

22 Burgoyne and Burgoyne, eds., *Journal of the Hesse-Cassel Jaeger Corps*, 14; Richard St. George, "The Actions at Brandywine and Paoli Described by a British Officer," *The Pennsylvania Magazine of History and Biography* (Philadelphia, 1905), vol. 29, 368; Hunter, *Journal of Hunter*, 29-30.

woods and we were at the bottom also in a woods, between us was an open field. Here they [Stephen's main line] fired on us with two cannon with canister and," continued the German commander, "because of the terrible terrain and the woods, our cannon could not get close enough, and had to remain to the right." The German light infantrymen, reported one participant, "were engaged for over half an hour, with grape shot and small arms, with a battalion of light infantry. We could not see the 2nd Battalion of Light Infantry because of the terrain, and while we received only a few orders, each commander had to act according to his own best judgment."[23]

Despite the tactical flexibility of light infantry, the wooded, swampy, and sloping terrain in this area, coupled with the heavy American fire, stalled the elite British and German units. The swampy lowlands and thickets had also forced the 4th British Brigade, part of Cornwallis's reserve, to swing well west of the Birmingham Road, which in turn denied the light troops their promised support. Unless the jaegers could turn the American right flank, it would be difficult to reach, let alone carry, Stephen's position.

Stirling's retreat into Sandy Hollow exposed Stephen's left flank to the surging British troops. Stephen attempted to maintain his position rather than retreat, perhaps to provide as much time as possible for Stirling and Sullivan to withdraw their shattered commands to a safe distance and form elsewhere. General Scott's brigade, holding the left side of Stephen's division, was but a short distance from the American artillery position that had just been overrun by the British light infantry and grenadiers, some of whom were still pressing against his front. Woodford's brigade on Scott's right, meanwhile, was facing a fresh threat from the advancing jaegers and newly placed enemy artillery. After encountering significant obstacles in the form of woods, fences, and swampy terrain, the British and Germans finally managed to wheel three guns into an ideal position to enfilade Woodford's brigade with grapeshot. Two of the guns, 3-pounders that were probably attached to the 2nd Battalion of Light Infantry, unlimbered along the 2nd Light Infantry Battalion front, with nine companies on their left and another five companies advancing on their right. The third

23 Burgoyne, trans. and ed., *Diaries of Two Jaegers*, 18; Von Wurmb to von Jungkenn, October 14, 1777, 10; Burgoyne and Burgoyne, eds., *Journal of the Hesse-Cassel Jaeger Corps*, 14. The woods, combined with a slight elevation change, blocked the Germans' view of the British light infantry advancing and fighting on their right. The cannon referenced by von Wurmb were the two 3-pounders assigned to support the advancing jaegers that had been left behind due to the difficulties of terrain.

piece, a 12-pounder, set up between the battalions, with the 1st Light Infantry Battalion advancing on its right. From this advantageous position the British gunners rammed grapeshot down the hot tubes and fired, spraying deadly iron rounds at an oblique angle into Woodford's line. Whether these metal balls were responsible for taking out the horses of Stephen's pair of field pieces is unknown, but the animals fell and when the infantry eventually retreated there was no way to take the invaluable field pieces with them. Woodford was also struck in the hand and retired down the southern slope to dress his injury.

While the British guns roared, the 2nd Light Infantry Battalion and jaegers, supported by an advancing Brig. Gen. James Agnew's 4th British Brigade, pressed Stephen's front. Five companies from the 2nd battalion had finally managed to cross the marshy bottomland in front of Birmingham Hill and assault Scott's brigade on Stephen's left. "The fire of Musquetry all this time was as Incessant & Tremendous, as ever had been Remember'd," wrote Lt. Frederick Augustus Wetherall of the 17th Regiment of Foot's light company, "But the Ardour & Intrepidity of the Troops overcoming every Opposition & pressing on with an Impetuosity not to be resisted." Ultimately, he continued, "the Rebel Line incapable of further Resistance gave way in every part & fled with the utmost disorder." Montresor, Howe's engineer who watched the fighting from Osborne's Hill and later rode the ground to study the terrain, described the difficult attack made by the British light infantry: "the ground on the left being the most difficult the rebels disputed it with the Light Infantry with great spirit, particularly their officers, this spot was a ploughed hill and they covered by its summit and flanked by a wood; however unfavourable the circumstances [the light infantry's] ardour was such that they pushed in upon [the Americans] under a very heavy fire."[24]

Scott's men held as long as possible, but Stirling's withdrawal exposed their left, which was turned and engulfed by surging British troops. When the patriot guns on the hill ceased firing, the 1st Light Infantry Battalion closed the distance and overwhelmed the front and engulfed the flank of Scott's line, which collapsed and retreated down the back of Birmingham Hill into Sandy Hollow and beyond.[25]

---

24 Wetherall, *Journal*; Montresor, "Montresor Journals," 450.

25 Revolutionary War Pension and Bounty-Land-Warrant Application Files (M804) [RWPF], file S37758. William Beale of the 12th Virginia Regiment was wounded in the forehead during the defensive effort by Scott's brigade.

While Scott's brigade was in the process of being driven back, as late as 6:00 p.m. Woodford's embattled brigade was still standing firm against the oncoming jaegers and blasts of grapeshot. His men, however, were falling with uncomfortable regularity. Sergeants Noah Taylor and Banks Dudley, both from the 7th Virginia Regiment, were taken out by flying metal. Colonel John Patton's Additional Continental Regiment lost Pvt. John Stewart with a wound in his left arm and Pvt. Jacob Cook with a shot to his right leg. Captain James Calderwood, whose independent company was attached to the 11th Virginia Regiment, was wounded and died two days after the battle. Eleven years later, his widow would apply to the War Department for half-pay.[26]

When the fighting intensified on his right, Col. von Wurmb "had the call to attack sounded on the half moon [hunting horn], and the Jaegers, with the [Second] battalion of light infantry, stormed up the height." Despite Woodford's best efforts, once Scott's brigade on his left was swept away, it was simply impossible to remain in place for long. The final straw, however, arrived on the opposite flank when Col. von Wurmb's jaegers struck Woodford's right flank when a sergeant and six men worked around the American right to pick off men from the rear. Captain Ewald recorded this tactic in his diary: "During the action Colonel Wurmb fell on the flank of the enemy, and Sergeant [Alexander Wilhelm] Bickell with six jagers moved to his rear, whereupon the entire right wing of the enemy fled to Dilworthtown." According to another account, Bickell's movement around Stephen's right flank put the German troops in a good position to "inaccomodat[e] the enemy for a half hour." Von Wurmb later wrote with pride that his jaegers "attacked them in God's Name and drove them from their post."[27]

---

26 Revolutionary War Pension and Bounty-Land-Warrant Application Files, file S6085; Linn and Egle, eds., *Pennsylvania Archives*, Series 2, vol. 10, 810-811. Jonathan Nicholson to Joseph Howell, September 17, 1788, National Archives and Records Administration, Ltrs sent J. Howell, Comm. Accounts RG93, accessible at www.wardepartmentpapers.org. Lieutenant Philip Slaughter of the 11th Virginia Regiment remembered the bloody day of combat for the remainder of his life. After the end of the Revolutionary War, he returned to central Virginia and named his farm "Brandywine." Slaughter lived a long life and did not die until 1849. Ironically, his farm was the scene of heavy fighting during the American Civil War at the battle of Cedar Mountain on August 9, 1862. Robert K. Krick, *Stonewall Jackson at Cedar Mountain* (Chapel Hill, NC, 1990), 50.

27 Burgoyne and Burgoyne, eds., *Journal of the Jaeger Corps*, 14; Ewald, *Diary*, 86. "Dilworthtown" was Dilworth, about one-half mile southeast of Stephen's position on Birmingham Hill; Von Wurmb to von Jungkenn, October 14, 1777, 10. Two of the jaeger officers were later recognized for their service at the Brandywine: Capts. Johann Ewald and

"They allowed us to advance till within one hundred and fifty yards of their line," remembered Lt. Martin Hunter of the 52nd Regiment of Foot's light company, "when they gave us a volley, which we returned, and then immediately charged. They stood the charge till we came to the last paling. Their line then began to break, and a general retreat took place soon after." An unidentified officer with the 2nd Light Infantry Battalion described the assault from his perspective. "Our army Still gained ground, although they had great Advantig of Ground and ther Canon keep a Constant fire on us. Yet We Ne'er Wass daunted they all gave way." According to the *Jaeger Corps Journal*, "the enemy retreated in confusion, abandoning two cannons and an ammunition cassion, which the Light Infantry, because they had attacked on the less steep slope of the height, took possession of."[28]

Stephen's division ended up as scattered and difficult to organize as Sullivan's broken command. Unlike Sullivan's men, however, Stephen's troops were in position and prepared when the British attacked, and acquitted themselves well. This was amply demonstrated when the jaegers reached the summit of the hill and realized that "many dead [Americans] lay to our front." The 52nd's Lt. Hunter admitted the Americans had "defended [their guns] to the last; indeed, several officers were cut down at the guns. The Americans never fought so well before, and they fought to great advantage." Although eventually driven from the hill, the Continentals had fought so hard and well against the veteran British units that Gen. Howe believed Sullivan had defended the position with 10,000 troops.[29]

Many of Cornwallis's units suffered heavily in their victory, not only the grenadier battalions but the light infantry as well. Fifteen light infantry officers fell, and the battalions reported losses of 16 killed and 103 wounded. The jaegers suffered another eight killed, including two officers, and 38 wounded.[30]

Carl von Wreden received the Hessian order *pour la vertu militaire*. They were the first officers of that rank to be thus honored. Lowell, *The Hessians*, 199.

28 Hunter, *Journal of Hunter*, 29-30; *Captured British Officer's Accounts Ledger, 1769-1771, and Diary*, Washington Papers online, Library of Congress, series 6: Military Papers, 1755-1798: Subseries C, accessed March 28, 2013; Burgoyne and Burgoyne, eds., *Journal of the Jaeger Corps*, 14.

29 Von Wurmb to von Jungkenn, October 14, 1777, 10; Hunter, *Journal of Hunter*, 29-30; *Narrative of Howe*, 98.

30 American losses are reported later in this study, as we do not have them broken out separately as we have for the British and German units. Jaeger casualties are from Burgoyne and Burgoyne, eds., *Journal of the Jaeger Corps*, 15; *Remembrancer for 1777*, 415-417; Inman, ed., "List of

A Note on Generalship

Generals Howe and Cornwallis watched the assault from Osborn's Hill. "A cherished tradition, one fostered by admiring biographers and some generals," explains historian John Luzader, "represented general officers as personally leading their armies into battle in the heroic mode of Alexander the Great and Henry V." While there were times when a commanding general believed his presence on the front line was needed to resolve a crisis, it was far more common for him to exercise command from a central position in the rear where he could be located, receive intelligence, and issue orders through his aides. General Washington had been doing just that all day at Chads's Ford, where he remained near his headquarters at the Ring House so scouts and aides could find him. "The advent of firearms and field artillery wrought a tactical revolution that changed the way officers, especially generals, functioned," continues Luzader. Massed formations of men stacked eight to ten ranks deep at the beginning of the seventeenth century had faded into formations of two or three ranks by the end of the eighteenth century. "That thinning and attendant extension of the front rendered impossible the personal control of large units." While it was not uncommon during the American Revolution for a general officer to ride along the front lines, doing so substantially increased the risk of losing overall control of the battle. A general commanding from the front "ceased to be able to influence events occurring outside his severely limited field of view." Commanding generals had to direct the various divisions of their army, and violating that tenet "was so risky as to limit doing so to moments when extreme conditions demanded extreme measures."[31]

Officers Killed," 176-205. Among the light infantry officers who fell, Lt. Francis Johnson (38th Regiment of Foot's light company) was killed. In addition to those mentioned earlier, the following light infantry officers were wounded: Capt. Thomas Mecan (23rd Regiment of Foot), Capt. James Douglas (15th Regiment of Foot), Capt. Nicholas Wade (49th Regiment of Foot), Capt. Henry Downing (55th Regiment of Foot), Capt. James Murray in the ankle (57th Regiment of Foot), Capt. James DeCourcy (40th Regiment of Foot), Lt. John Birch (27th Regiment of Foot), Lt. Thomas Nicholl (33rd Regiment of Foot), Lt. Charles Leigh (15th Regiment of Foot), Lt. Samuel Ruxton (45th Regiment of Foot), Lt. Thomas Armstrong (49th Regiment of Foot), and Lt. Bent Ball (63rd Regiment of Foot). Over a month and half later, Captain Murray was still recovering from his wounded ankle. That day he wrote, "[N]ow that my fever has left me I shall be perfectly recovered in a few days." Eric Robson, ed., *Letters from America, 1773 to 1780: Being the letters of a Scots officer, Sir James Murray, to his home during the War of American Independence* (New York, 1950), 49.

31 Luzader, *Saratoga*, 227.

As the American line collapsed on Birmingham Hill, Gens. Howe and Cornwallis spurred their mounts ahead to direct the pursuit of the fleeing Continentals. "As usual, the General [Howe] exposed himself fearlessly on this occasion," recalled staffer von Muenchhausen. "He quickly rushed to each spot where he heard the strongest fire. Cannon balls and bullets passed close to him in numbers today. We all fear that, since he is so daring on any and all occasions, we are going to lose our best friend, and that England will lose America."[32]

*   *   *

After having retired through the fields past the advancing British and Hessian columns, Joseph Townsend found himself back on Osborn's Hill near General Howe and his entourage watching the final push on Birmingham Hill. There, he wrote, "we heard a tremendous roaring of cannon, and saw the volume of smoke arising therefrom at Chadd's ford. General Knyphausen having discovered that the engagement was on . . . immediately forced the troops under his command across the Brandywine."[33]

The next phase of the battle was underway, just as Howe has scripted it.

---

32 Von Muenchhausen, *At Howe's Side*, 32. A local tale claims Howe forced farmer Emmor Jefferis to guide the army to Birmingham Meetinghouse, with Howe telling him, "Don't be afraid Mr. Jefferis, they won't hurt you." The army already had guides directing the flanking column to Osborn's Hill, with the meetinghouse immediately beyond. No source has been found to corroborate the claim. "Papers Related to Brandywine," 53.

33 Townsend, *Some Account*, 25.

Chapter 15

Knyphausen Assaults Chads's Ford:
Evening, September 11, 1777

"But nothing could stand before our lads, they routed them from the Meadow, & all afterwards was a mere Chace, so far I saw."[1]

— James Parker, September 11, 1777

The Second Front Opens

The many hours of waiting in position west of Chads's Ford along the Brandywine had taken a toll on Wilhelm von Knyphausen and some of his high ranking officers. General James Grant "expected the Action to begin about two o'clock. I had made my mind up to that, but from two to four I became anxious. The minutes were Hours, I was uneasy & impatient."[2]

Indeed, Grant and his fellow officers had spent much of the day facing the bulk of the American army, hoping all the while that General Washington would not figure out that Howe had divided his command in the face of a unified enemy. If the Continentals assaulted across the various Brandywine fords before Howe completed his flanking maneuver, Washington could crush and disperse Knyphausen's diversionary wing. Once the middle afternoon

---

1 Parker, journal entry for September 11, Parker Family Papers.

2 James Grant to Harvey, October 20, 1777, James Grant Papers.

arrived, however, and the Continentals could be seen moving rapidly north, their concern shifted to Howe and his flanking column. "We began to be uneasy about General Howe," wrote Royal Artilleryman Francis Downman, "for a great force of the rebels [Sullivan's, Stirling's, and Stephen's divisions] marched from the hills and woods before us towards him. . . . [O]ur doubts were eased, for we heard a firing on our left, at first gentle, but in a little very heavy indeed both of cannon and musketry."[3]

The firing referenced by Downman was Gen. Cornwallis's move off Osborn Hill and the early stages of the attack against Birmingham Hill. The distant rattle of musketry and booming artillery was exactly what General Knyphausen had been waiting to hear. "[A]t 4 o'clock by uninterrupted firing of Musketry . . . we discovered the commander in chief's approach," reported the Hessian general, "whereupon I immediately formed my attack." The time to push across Chads's Ford had arrived. Some members of Knyphausen's wing not only heard Cornwallis's assault, but also saw portions of it (probably elements of the Brigade of Guards) through breaks in the otherwise heavy woods. Downman recalled watching "our brave fellows under Howe push out of the wood after the rebels. We renew our fire from the artillery to scour the woods."[4]

The British plan was bold but simple: Howe would engage first, and when Knyphausen heard the fighting to the north (off his left), he would attack across Chads's Ford. He moved as fast as possible, but forming the attack column took time. After the conclusion of the morning fighting, Knyphausen spread out his division along the west bank of the Brandywine to cover crossing points and protect his flanks, and to better shift units in and out of Washington's view across a wide front to create the illusion Howe's entire army was present. As a result, he was unable to launch his attack until after 5:00 p.m.—about one hour after Cornwallis opened his attack.

While Knyphausen organized his men, the Americans were busy on the east side of the river. It was around 5:00 p.m. when Washington dispatched Nathanael Greene's division to march north to reinforce that sector as the three divisions under Sullivan were being driven from Birmingham Hill. Departing with Greene was the North Carolina brigade of Francis Nash. Greene's departure left the Chads's Ford front lightly defended. The only troops

---

3   Whinyates, ed., *Services of Downman*, 33.

4   Von Knyphausen to Germain, October 21, 1777; Whinyates, ed., *Services of Downman*, 33.

remaining to oppose Knyphausen's division were the Pennsylvanians of Brig. Gen. Anthony Wayne's division and Brig. Gen. William Maxwell's light infantry. Colonel Thomas Proctor's American artillery remained where it had been deployed since that morning, on the heights above the John Chads house overlooking the ferry crossing. A park of American reserve artillery was stationed farther east in reserve. The only other Americans in the area after 5:00 p.m. belonged to Maj. Gen. John Armstrong's Pennsylvania Militia Division, positioned about mile south watching Pyle's Ford. Knyphausen had nearly 6,700 British, Hessian, and loyalist troops to assault a force of nearly 6,000 Americans, but nearly half of the defenders were unreliable militia.[5]

Two considerations convinced Knyphausen to make his main push across the Brandywine at Chads's Ferry instead of Chads's Ford. The first was a matter of trees. The Americans had felled many and blocked Chads's Ford, which would have made the crossing much more difficult to navigate. The second discovery that afternoon was that the American battery had a much better command of Chads's Ford than it did of the ferry crossing because Proctor's view of the latter was partially blocked by a tree line.[6]

The 4th and 5th Regiments of Foot were given the honor of leading the crossing at the ferry. When the orders arrived, the 4th Regiment was at Brinton's Ford and had to move three-quarters of a mile south. The 5th Regiment was already opposite the ferry and had to await the arrival of the 4th Regiment before moving. The order of assault after the 4th and 5th Regiments crossed consisted of the 2nd battalion of the 71st Highlanders, Ferguson's Riflemen, the Queen's Rangers, and the 23rd Regiment of Foot, followed by the remainder of the regiments from the British brigades, and the light dragoon detachment, with the Hessian brigade bringing up the rear. Brigadier General Samuel Cleaveland placed two 12-pounders and two 6-pounders near the Brandywine to clear the way and cover the crossing during the advance.[7]

Washington was just about to leave the Ring House and ride north to see the state of affairs there firsthand when the British artillery unleashed its fire against the Americans opposite Chads's Ferry. "At half after four O'Clock, the Enemy attacked Genl Sullivan . . . and the Action has been very violent ever

5   This estimate of the number of troops available to Knyphausen at this point in the day takes into account casualties from the morning action.

6   Smith, *Brandywine*, 22.

7   Von Knyphausen to Germain, October 21, 1777.

since," he dictated in a message to Congress. "It still continues. . . . [A] very severe Cannonade has begun here too and I suppose we shall have a very hot Evening."[8]

When the British assault column was spotted ready to cross at the ferry, Proctor's guns, supported by some of Maxwell's men, deployed closer to the water to offset the enemy artillery, raked the crossing with grapeshot. "The Rebels fired grape & exploding shells. . . . [O]ur battery kept a warm fire for near a half hour," recalled a British officer. Artillery rounds pounded the eastern bank of the Brandywine. Adam Stephen's adjutant, Joseph Clark, who for reasons unknown did not accompany his division north, witnessed the heavy barrage. "The batteries at the middle ford opened upon each other with such fury as if the elements had been in convulsions," explained the staff officer. "[T]he valley was filled with smoke, and now I grew seriously anxious for the event: for an hour and a half, this horrid sport continued." Sergeant Thomas Sullivan of the British 49th Regiment of Foot recalled the Americans "being posted upon a Hill on the other side of the Road, [and] plaid upon us with four Pieces of Cannon during that attack."[9]

Across the River

The river was 50 paces wide and half a man deep at Chads's Ferry. The men had no choice but to carry their muskets in one hand and their ammunition in the other to keep them dry. Colonel Proctor's gunners engaged the enemy from directly in front with deadly grape shot, while elements of Gen. Wayne's divisional artillery fired into the right flank of the British advance. The patriot guns could not prevent a crossing, but they did exact a toll for the privilege. Sergeant Stephen Jarvis of the Queen's Rangers remembered the artillery "playing upon us with grape shot, which did much execution. The water took us up to our breasts, and was much stained with blood." Jarvis added, "Many poor fellows fell in the river and were swept away with the current."[10]

Although bloodied in the effort, Gen. Grant personally led his 4th and 5th Regiments through the water and up the opposite bank. Once across the

8 Fitzpatrick, ed., *Writings of Washington*, vol. 9, 206.

9 Jarvis, *Stephen Jarvis*, 16; Parker, journal entry for September 11, Parker Family Papers; Clark, "Diary," 99; Sullivan, *From Redcoat to Rebel*, 134.

10 Ewald, *Diary*, 82; Jarvis, *Stephen Jarvis*, 98-99.

Brandywine, the British troops were faced with a swampy morass some 200 yards wide. Reaching the enemy line would not be easy. Royal Engineer Archibald Robertson recalled that the troops "were obliged to advance in Column along the Road on Account of the Morass on their Flanks, they were galled by Musketry from the Woods on their right and by round and grape Shot from two Pieces of Cannon and an 8 inch Howitzer from the Battery in their Front." "The Battery in front" mentioned by the engineer was a reference to Proctor's command, whose gunners were ensconced in an earthwork servicing their pieces as fast as possible.[11]

The foot soldiers advanced as fast as possible, stacked up as they were on a causeway-like road until the land was dry enough on both sides for the officers to fan out their commands in proper lines of battle. It was a long slog, recalled one soldier, who thought they were "half mile in front of the trenches" once they reached the east bank of the river. The trenches that seemed so distant were a reference to a fortified line erected by Wayne's division beyond the swampy morass.[12]

While the infantrymen struggled to get across the Brandywine River, advance along the road, and then organize themselves again on dry land, the British artillery rained shells on Proctor's position. Fortunately for the Americans, most or all of them failed to explode. "The Brittish shells that they hove from their howetors never busted, which saved a good many men," recalled 15-year-old gunner Jacob Nagle. "One shell, while the fuse was burning, a soldier run and nocked out the tube which prevented it from bursting."[13]

When he realized his artillery was not having the desired effect of silencing the enemy or driving them away, Knyphausen ordered his guns to cease fire so the infantry could storm the battery and finish the job. Once beyond the swampy terrain, the leading 4th and 5th Regiments left the road and formed into lines of battle. Proctor's guns were to their left front on a small hill. With their orders in hand, the regiments moved at a run around the west side of the hill upon which John Chads house sat to assault the battery from the river side. Nagle, who left a graphic account of the fight at the redoubt, watched the

11 Smith, *Brandywine*, 23; Robertson map and accompanying text.

12 Burgoyne, ed., *Enemy Views*, 177.

13 Nagle, *The Nagle Journal*, 8.

British close the distance to the earthwork, "though our artillery made a clear lane through them as they mounted the works, but they filled up the ranks again." One British officer mounted the works and yelled, "'Come on my Brittons, the day is our own!'" Just then, wrote Nagle in a clever turn of phrase, an American 9-pounder discharged and "he was no more, with a number more."[14]

At this point in the fighting, it became obvious to both sides that there was no effective way to stop the charging enemy. According to Col. James Chambers of the 1st Pennsylvania Regiment, British artillery fire allowed the 4th and 5th regiments to advance "under the thick smoke" and take "possession of the redoubt. . . . As there were no troops to cover the artillery in the redoubt, the enemy was within thirty yards before being discovered; our men were forced to fly, and to leave three pieces behind." The absence of American infantry to help defend the battery all but guaranteed its capture, and the embattled artillerymen carried only a limited number of small arms for defensive purposes.[15]

One British sergeant recalled the final moments in the embattled American redoubt: "The Enemy's Cannon missing fire in the Battery as they crossed, and before the Gunners could fire them off, the men of that Battalion [4th of Foot] put them to the Bayonets, and forced the Enemy from the Entrenchment." Several of Proctor's men fell defending the stronghold. Henry Conkle, a matross (gunner's mate), collapsed when a howitzer round struck him in the leg. John Conrad, another matross, was shot through the left knee by a musket ball before being run over by a gun carriage. A private named David Chambers also went down during this stage of the battle with a wound. Higher ranks were not immune to the flying enemy metal. Artillery quartermaster James Livingston was killed about this time, and an enemy round killed Proctor's mount, which the American artillery commander later described as his "best horse." When he realized there was no hope of saving the position, Proctor ordered his men to move quickly and save themselves. The surviving gunners fled on foot, abandoning their pieces and equipment. The 4th Regiment of Foot captured

---

14 Ibid. None of the known British officers killed in the battle were in this area. However, Capt. John Rawdon of the 4th Regiment of Foot was severely wounded in the knee and could be the officer Nagle described.

15 Account reproduced in Thomas Lynch Montgomery, ed., *Pennsylvania Archives*, Series 5 (Harrisburg, PA, 1906), vol. 2, 621.

three brass field pieces and a 5.5-inch howitzer at the cost of two killed and 21 wounded.[16]

The reason Proctor was left without infantry was because the divisions under Lord Stirling and Adam Stephen that had been protecting the artillery were pulled out of line and marched north, and were now confronting Cornwallis on Birmingham Hill. Some of Wayne's men, probably the 1st Pennsylvania Regiment, were repositioned to protect the American artillery park, which was about one mile east of Chads's Ford behind the hills (near the modern-day Brandywine Battlefield State Historic Site). When the British successfully crossed the river and attacked inland, Proctor ordered the reserve artillery withdrawn to avoid capture. By the time the orders arrived and the guns were beginning to roll, British troops were just west of the position and rapidly advancing toward the guns. The enemy, reported Colonel Chambers of the 1st Pennsylvania, "advanced on the hill, where our park was, and came within fifty yards of the hill above me." Chambers shouted to his men to fire: "Two or three rounds made the lads clear the ground."[17]

In their haste to escape, the withdrawing artillerymen left several pieces behind. When the Pennsylvania volleys halted the enemy advance, Chambers sent men to retrieve them. "Two field pieces went up the road protected by about sixty of my men, who had very warm work, but brought them safe," he proudly related. "I then ordered another party to fly to the howitzer and bring it off. Captain [Thomas] Buchanan, Lt. [Michael] Simpson and Lt. [Thomas] Douglass [one of Proctor's artillery officers] went immediately to the gun, and

16 Sullivan, *Journal*, 134. Proctor later informed Congress that he lost "my best horse and my Portmanteau Horse taken by the Enemy, together with my Baggage of a considerable Value." Thomas Proctor to the Continental Congress, April 10, 1778, Papers of the Continental Congress, available online at www.fold3.com, accessed March 25, 2013. Many years later in his pension application, Jacob Strembeck claimed a lieutenant named Thomas Bowde was killed during this action. Revolutionary War Pension and Bounty-Land-Warrant Application Files (M804) [RWPF], file S4896. No Thomas Bowde, however, appears in the Continental Army Officer List. For information on Henry Conkle and John Conrad, see Montgomery, ed., Pennsylvania Archives, Series 5, vol. 4, 558. For information on David Chambers, see Linn and Egle, eds., Pennsylvania Archives, Series 2, vol. 11, 181. For information on artillery quartermaster James Livingston, see Egle, ed., Pennsylvania Archives, Series 3, vol. 23, 817; Thorne to Percy, September 29, 1777.

17 There are a series of hills (or rises and swales) as you move east from Chads's Ford. Proctor's redoubt artillery position had been on the hill closest to the river. The artillery reserve was positioned on one of the hills, likely within the grounds of the current park. This was where Chambers's 1st Pennsylvania Regiment was deployed to protect the guns, to buy enough time to get the artillery out of harm's way.

the men followed their example, and I covered them with the few I had remaining."[18] The opposing British troops, continued the Pennsylvania colonel with some exaggeration, "kept up the most terrible fire I suppose ever heard in America, though with very little loss on our side. I brought all the brigade artillery safely off, and I hope to see them again fired at the scoundrels."[19]

While the 4th and 5th Regiments assaulted the redoubt near the Chads House, the battalion of 71st Highlanders and the Queen's Rangers passed between the battery and the river to advance upon the American guns placed at Brinton's Ford. The men tending them were also part of Proctor's command. By this time, however, only one gun was still in operation and there were few gunners left to defend it. The approaching enemy troops convinced the artillerymen to flee toward a nearby buckwheat field, where they were pinned against a fence line and bayoneted. Sergeant Sullivan of the British 49th Regiment of Foot may not have witnessed the attack, but he certainly heard about it. The enemy, he recorded in his meticulous journal, "being attacked by the Rangers and 71st in a Buck Wheat field was totally scivered with the Bayonets before they could clear the fence round it."[20]

By now, all of the American batteries and their gunners had either withdrawn out of harm's way or were desperately attempting to save the guns. Continental artilleryman Jacob Nagle, who had barely escaped from the captured redoubt, remembered some of Wayne's men (likely Chambers's regiment) overseeing their retreat, and how they had "marsh or swampy ground to cross with the artillery to get into the road, and the horses being shot, the men could not drag the pieces out." Three of the guns had to be spiked and abandoned. During the confused withdrawal, Nagle recalled coming across "a

---

18 Montgomery, ed., *Pennsylvania Archives*, Series 5, vol. 2, 621-622. Flying over Chambers's men of the 1st Pennsylvania was one of the few Continental flags that survive today. "The flag was a large square of green silk with a small, red square in the center, on which was depicted a hunter holding a spear against a netted, rampant tiger. Below this was a scroll with the motto Domari Nolo." McGuire, *Philadelphia Campaign*, vol. 1, 249.

19 Montgomery, ed., *Pennsylvania Archives*, Series 5, vol. 2, 622. One of the artillery officers who had abandoned the guns was Capt. Hercules Courtney, who was later court-martialed for "[l]eaving his howitzer in the field . . . in a cowardly unofficerlike manner." Courtney was found guilty and ordered "to be reprimanded by Gen. Knox in the presence of all the Artillery officers." Luckily for Courtney, Washington reprieved the captain and had him released from arrest. Courtney was dismissed from the service in February 1778 for neglect of duty. "Orderly Book of General Edward Hand, Valley Forge, January 1778," *The Pennsylvania Magazine of History and Biography* (Philadelphia, 1917), vol. 41, 202

20 Smith, *Brandywine*, 23; Sullivan, *Journal*, 134.

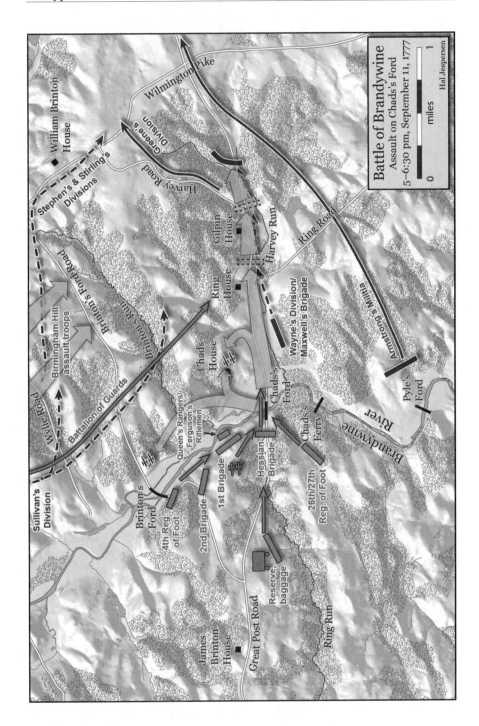

Battle of Brandywine
Assault on Chads's Ford
5–6:30 pm, September 11, 1777

Hal Jespersen

miles

0   1

beautiful charger, all white, in a field next to the road with an elegant sadlle and holsters, and gold lace housing, and his bridle broke off, and his rider gone." The teenager "made an attempt to ketch him, but he was skared, and the enemy keeping up a constant fire, I thought it best to leave him." The well-appointed mount may have been Proctor's reported "Portmanteau Horse taken by the Enemy."[21]

The artillerymen spilled out of the redoubt and the reserve gunners withdrew above the Chads house. Many attempted to rally in an orchard on the Ring farm, where Washington's headquarters had recently been located, and the fighting there was often "Bayonet to Bayonet." The presence of Chambers's 1st Pennsylvania did little to stem the tide of advancing enemy troops. The fighting, especially in and around the orchard, was hard, brutal, and short. "Many of them Ran to an Orchard to the right of the fort, from which they were Drove to a Meadow, where they made a Stand for some time in a ditch," recalled British soldier James Parker. "But nothing could stand before our lads, they routed them from the Meadow, & all afterwards was a mere Chace, so far I saw." General Knyphausen's aide, von Baurmeister, agreed. After crossing the Brandywine, some of the "troops attacked them furiously, partly with the bayonet." From the captured artillery position, Queen's Ranger Stephen Jarvis watched "our brave comrades cutting them up in great style." More British troops had crossed the river, formed, and were now driving inland, explained one observer, so the Americans "were obliged to retreat in the greatest confusion, leaving their Artillery & Ammunition in the Field."[22]

Knyphausen summarized the fighting that swirled around Proctor's position in his report nearly six weeks later to Lord Germain. Once across the ford, explained the Hessian general, the 4th and 5th Regiments of Foot, the battalion of the 71st Highlanders, Ferguson's men, and the Queen's Rangers assaulted the batteries "in such a manner as forced them to quit [them] notwithstanding the uninterrupted Fire of round & Grape Shot which

---

21 Nagle, *Journal*, 8-9. Spiking an artillery piece involved jamming a file or other metal object into the vent hole and snapping it off to render the piece incapable of being fired until the vent hole was cleared again. Two of these guns had been captured from the Hessians at Trenton.

22 Parker, journal entry for September 11. The ditch to which Parker referred was probably the lane leading to the Ring farm; Von Baurmeister, "Letters of Major Baurmeister," 407; Jarvis, *Stephen Jarvis*, 99; Sullivan, *Journal*, 134. Following the battle, British engineer officer Archibald Robertson created a detailed map of the battlefield. He placed only a few trees near Proctor's artillery position, but included two fenced tree lots or orchards on the Ring property just east of the position.

continued ever [since] the Troops pass'd the Creek, & was supported by the Musketry of the [enemy] Battalions." As more and more of his men poured across the river, the Americans retired from one hill after another, "driven by the gallant Behaviour of the Troops."[23]

In the midst of the confusion and retreat, the ubiquitous Jacob Nagle experienced yet another traumatic moment. "In the heat of the action close to the orchard," he later wrote, "I see some men burien an officer who wore the same dress that my father wore, which was green turned up with read fasings and gold lace. I was ready to faint. I run up to the officer and enquired what rigment he belonged to," continued the teenager. "He informed me he was a colo belonging to the Virginia Line, which gave me comfort but sorrowful."[24]

The fighting withdrawal of Proctor's artillery sets the scene for yet another long-running Brandywine battle story, this one having to do with a wagon driver named Edward Hector. One version of the story has Hector, "a Negro artillerist from Pennsylvania [Proctor's regiment]. . . [saving] a few wagonloads of ammunition and arms as the army withdrew." Another version of the tale claims "Hector was a wagoneer and refused to abandon his horses and wagon. He gathered up some abandoned arms and made good his escape from the British." The most complete and sourced account is found in Thomas McGuire's history of the campaign, which relied upon Hector's 1834 obituary notice, "A colored man had charge of an ammunition wagon attached to Col. Proctor's regiment," reported McGuire. According to the obituary, when the British overran the battery, "an order was given by the proper officers to those having charge of the wagons, to abandon them to the enemy, and save themselves by flight." Hector replied, "The enemy shall not have my team; I will save my horses and myself. . . . [A]mid the confusion of the surrounding scene, he calmly gathered up a few stands of arms which had been left on the field by the retreating soldiers, and safely retired with his wagon, team and all, in face of the victorious foe."[25]

23 Von Knyphausen to Germain, October 21, 1777.

24 Nagle, *Journal,* 9. If Nagle's memory is accurate, the fallen officer has not been identified.

25 Edgar, *The Philadelphia Campaign,* 35. Edgar provides no citation for his version of the story; Mowday, *September 11, 1777,* 149. Mowday's source for the story is a secondary source, not an eighteenth-century one; McGuire, *Philadelphia Campaign,* vol. 1, 247; William Summers, "Obituary Notices of Pennsylvania Soldiers of the Revolution," in *Pennsylvania Magazine of History and Biography* (Philadelphia, 1914), vol. 38, 444. Historians must be careful when relying on sources such as this obituary notice written 57 years after the war. To date, no contemporary

Wayne Attempts a Defense

The bulk of his command across the river and the threat of enemy artillery fire neutralized, Knyphausen shoved the majority of his division eastward on both sides of the Great Post Road. Wayne's division, comprised of the brigades of Cols. Thomas Hartley and Richard Humpton, were aligned along a slight ridge facing north by northwest on the south side of the Great Post Road, with Humpton on the left and Hartley on the right. Four pieces of divisional artillery bolstered his line. The alignment of Gen. Maxwell's light infantry remains problematic, but they were likely positioned north of the road on Wayne's right flank in a hollow.

For a short while, Wayne's men were in a position to offer some long distance enfilade fire while the enemy negotiated patches of swampy terrain on their drive eastward. Within a few minutes, however, Knyphausen's advancing lines leveled their muskets and opened fire, the balls rattling through the American ranks and whizzing above their heads. Lieutenant Colonel Adam Hubley, of the 10th Pennsylvania Regiment of Hartley's brigade, recalled the "Brittish Troops came on with the Greatest boldness & bravery, and began a most heavy fire on us," but [we] "returned it a heavy."[26]

Humpton's brigade, on Wayne's left, began taking casualties. The 8th Pennsylvania's Sgt. Thomas Wyatt went down with a broken shoulder bone. Lieutenant Gabriel Peterson was near "[Major] Bayard . . . when he was struck down by a cannon ball, that broke a rifle gun of Sergt. Wyatt and his shoulder, and then struck Bayard on the head and shoulder, and tumbled him over on the ground for near two rods." Peterson "helped him up on his feet—he was frantic, and seemed much hurt, but being much engaged at that time [he] could not render him any assistance."[27]

Captain John Mears and Pvt. Patrick Martin, both of the 4th Pennsylvania, fell wounded. Colonel Francis Johnston's men of the 5th Pennsylvania were

---

account has surfaced to confirm Hector's war story. However, there was an Edward Hector carried on the muster rolls who served as a bombardier in the Pennsylvania regiment. Montgomery, ed., *Pennsylvania Archives*, Series 5, vol. 3, 1056.

26 Adam Hubley to John Hubley, September 15, 1777, Peter Force Papers, series 9, conts. 21-24, microfilm reel 104, David Library of the American Revolution, Washington Crossing, PA. The road along which Maxwell formed his men was probably where the Ring Road runs today, near the modern entrance to Brandywine Battlefield State Historic Site.

27 Account reproduced in Montgomery, ed., *Pennsylvania Archives*, Series 5, vol. 3, 312.

much harder hit. A musket ball tore through Pvt. Thomas Owen's right thigh while another round struck Cpl. Arthur Parterson in the back. Lieutenant Colonel Thomas Robinson fell wounded and Capt. Joseph Potts was shot through the thigh and shoulder and captured. Corporal Christian Cowpland was hit in the left arm, Pvt. Christopher Still received an especially painful injury when a bullet shattered his right elbow joint, and Pvt. Daniel Davis was shot in the wrist and captured. Sergeant Hugh Brandley was wounded and believed to have died until he escaped from the British following the American victory at Stony Point. Continuing the 5th regiment's losses, John Byrne watched Lt. Alexander McClintock go down with a wound (he would linger several days before dying), and Ens. Matthew Langwell killed. Byrne found himself in the thick of the fighting and "received a bayonet wound in the right side," though somehow lived to tell the tale.[28]

The 11th Pennsylvania, also of Humpton's brigade, had three men killed, nine wounded (Capt. James Calderwood mortally), and another two captured. All three of the men killed (Thomas Lucas, Peter Martin, and Alexander Carmichael) were lieutenants. The wounded included Lt. John Stotesbury, Pvt. Jacob Hartman (struck above the knee), Pvt. John Pursell (shot through the shoulder), Pvt. Samuel Smith (lost his left leg, cause unknown), Pvt. Jacob Cook (wounded in the right leg by a musket ball), Pvt. James Cain (shot in the back), and Pvt. Joseph Vanlovring (injury unknown). James Dougherty was especially unlucky when a bullet took out one of his eyes. Others, like Lt. Nathaniel Martin and Capt. William Mackay, were unwounded but not fleet of foot and captured.[29]

Just as Humpton's men suffered on the left of the line, Hartley's brigade likewise experienced heavy losses on the right. Captain Robert Hopes from Hartley's Additional Continental Regiment was killed, as were Lts. James Lemmon and James Dill. A private, Philip Graham, was wounded. During this "most heavy fire," Maj. Lewis Bush of Hartley's Additional Continental Regiment had his horse killed from under him. He was in the process of remounting a different horse when he was shot, and, as Lt. Col. Hubley recalled,

28 Revolutionary War Pension and Bounty-Land-Warrant Application Files (M804), file S2408.

29 The severe casualties the 11th Pennsylvania suffered at the Brandywine and later at Paoli and Germantown in the campaign forced the proud remnants of the unit to fold into the 10th Pennsylvania Regiment in the spring of 1778.

"fell in my Arms." Bush's injury proved mortal, and would earn him the unlucky distinction of being the highest-ranking American to die along the Brandywine.[30]

The 7th Pennsylvania, also of Humpton's brigade, also had a number of men go down with wounds. A musket ball ripped through both of Pvt. John Brown's legs and while he lived, Pvts. Walter Denny, John Neil, and John Wilson did not. The 10th Pennsylvania's Lt. Peter Shiles collapsed from a wound and died on November 5; Pvts. John Groff and Leonard Weyer fell wounded, and later that evening Pvt. Samuel Lasley was injured during the retreat. The 2nd Pennsylvania, perhaps aligned on the far right side of Wayne's front and thus less exposed, suffered lighter losses, with Pvt. Jacob Holder going down with a wound and Pvt. John Davis hit in the left leg and captured.[31]

Despite the heavy close-quarter fighting and losses, Wayne's men stood tall and temporarily checked Knyphausen's advance. Even the generals aide von Baurmeister offered grudging admiration when recalling how "[t]hey withstood one more rather severe attack behind some houses and ditches." By this time the sun was beginning to wane, and the shadows lengthened on the field.[32]

Sergeant Major Francis Thorne of the 4th Regiment of Foot recalled some momentary confusion in the gathering darkness among the hills east of the Brandywine. Having decisively dealt with Proctor, the 4th and 5th Regiments of Foot were approaching Wayne's soldiers when some of the British mistook them for Hessians and were "sure of it. It being almost dark—the color of their cloths, blue with red & white, it was too readily believed and the regiments inclin'd to their left." In the confusion of battle, with darkness descending and the smoke heavy, the blue coats with red facings worn by some Pennsylvanians

---

30 Hubley to Hubley, September 15, 1777.

31 Lieutenant John Bush suffered the misfortune of losing his personal chest with all his papers. Nine years later, he was still trying to settle his accounts with the army due to those missing documents. Heitman, *Register of Officers of the Continental Army*, 300. The Pennsylvania casualties are documented in the following sources: Linn & Egle, eds., *Pennsylvania Archives*, Series 2, vol. 10, 428, 433, 545-572, 646-654, 720-757, 764-772 & 799-800; Montgomery, ed., *Pennsylvania Archives*, Series 5, vol. 4, 513-515, 557-558, 571, 596; Montgomery, ed., *Pennsylvania Archives*, Series 5, vol. 3, 75, 374, 663; Montgomery, ed., *Pennsylvania Archives*, Series 5, Vols. 2, 1032, 1085; Jonathan Nicholson to Joseph Howell, February 15, 1788; John Bush to Joseph Howell, November 31, 1786; Richard Humpton to Joseph Howell, May 1787, National Archives and Records Administration: Ltrs Sent, J Howell, Comm. Accounts, RG93, available at www.wardepartmentpapers.org.

32 Von Baurmeister, "Letters of Baurmeister," 407.

passed for Hessian uniforms. Whether Sgt. Maj. Thorne realized it at the time or not, or was simply reiterating what others around him were advocating, it would have been impossible for Hessian troops to have gotten in front of his regiment. Thorne continued: "[O]n our moving to the left for this Purpose, the Division [Wayne's] threw in their whole fire, on the two regiments, which fortunately being directed too high, did little execution, however this sufficiently discovered the Error, and it [musket fire] was so hotly Return'd" that Wayne's and Maxwell's men retreated "through the Swamp in [their] rear, and their loss was considerable."[33]

By this time, the 1st Battalion of the Brigade of Guards from General Cornwallis's flanking division had dispersed Sullivan's unlucky division atop Birmingham Hill farther north. This body of elite British troops continued marching nearly straight south along the heights on the east side of the Brandywine, though each step widened the growing gap between their left and the right flank of their sister battalion and the British grenadiers. The Hessian grenadiers were apparently called upon to fill this growing gap, but their slow rate of march and inability to keep up with the front ranks made it impossible to accomplish that or offer any meaningful support. The Guards did receive some assistance from the squadrons of 16th Light Dragoons attached to Cornwallis's division.

The terrain the Guards crossed was difficult to negotiate, with one high rocky climb and descent after another through woods and soggy creek bottoms emptying into the Brandywine flood plain. This was the same terrain Sullivan had crossed when heading north earlier in the day. The battalion's move south carried them from their victorious Birmingham Hill fight into the combat swirling east of Chads's Ford. Knyphausen referenced this in his battle report to Lord George Germain.[34]

While Wayne was temporarily holding Knyphausen's heavy assault in check, the British redirected the captured, unspiked American guns to fire on his position. The abandoned artillery pieces proved a gift for Knyphausen, who could not bring his own artillery train across the river fast enough to employ.

---

33 Thorne to Percy, September 29, 1777. If "the regiments inclin'd to their left," perhaps he and others thought some of the Hessian grenadiers from Howe's flanking column had moved to their right after the Birmingham Hill fight. In fact, a battalion from the Brigade of Guards from that very column soon joined them.

34 Von Knyphausen to Germain, October 21, 1777.

Indeed, remarked Sullivan of the 49th Foot, we "had no Cannon to play upon the Enemy's line, except one of the Pieces left in the Battery, which we turned upon them." It was about at this point in the fighting, when American guns were unleashing fire against Wayne's embattled line and musket balls and bayonet thrusts were taking their toll, that the Guards battalion appeared on the hill to Wayne's right front. The Guards' march carried them behind Proctor's abandoned artillery lunette.[35]

Worried that his avenue of retreat was rapidly closing, and during an apparent lull in the fighting, Wayne skillfully disengaged his division and moved his men eastward toward Ring Road. Wayne may have also sent orders for Maj. Gen. John Armstrong to withdraw his Pennsylvania Militia Division from its position farther south along the Brandywine protecting Pyle's Ford. Wayne's disengagement was not without cost. Once his troops entered the Great Post Road, the British followed up as professionals would, pressing hard and inflicting more casualties.

Colonel James Chambers's 1st Pennsylvania Regiment suffered serious losses, although like most of the other men who fell that day, the stage of the fighting during which they were shot down is not known. Chambers was among the wounded, hit by a musket ball in his right side. Although he would survive, the wound would bother him for the rest of his life. Eleven other members of the 1st Pennsylvania also fell. Sergeant John Maloney was wounded when a cannon ball struck a fence rail that flew through the air, struck his right thigh, and dislocated his knee. Private Archibald McClane was wounded in the left arm and right thigh, Pvt. Isaiah McCord was hit in the right shoulder and arm, and Capt. Charles Craig and Pvt. John Malone also went down, as did Sgt. Alexander Simonton. An enemy bullet struck Nicholas Nail in the right hand and clipped off the tips of two of his fingers. Ensign James Holliday was killed, Sgt. Benjamin Carson was hit in the right thigh, and Cpl. John Cavanagh took a bullet in the left shoulder. Private James Dougherty left the field with but one eye.[36]

If Wayne was hoping for substantial assistance from Armstrong's militia, he was sorely disappointed. In fact, if Wayne had time to even think about it, it

---

35 Sullivan, *Journal*, 134.

36 Trussell, *Pennsylvania Line*, 271; Montgomery, ed., *Pennsylvania Archives*, Series 5, vol. 4, 537, 566-570; Linn and Egle, eds., *Pennsylvania Archives*, Series 2, vol. 10, 337; Montgomery, ed., *Pennsylvania Archives*, Series 5, vol. 3, 643-737.

must have appeared to the general as if the militia division had simply vanished. The exact role played by Armstrong's Pennsylvania militia that late September afternoon and early evening remains yet another mystery of the complex Brandywine battle. At some point Armstrong pulled his militia back from Pyle's Ford. Perhaps the heavy firing farther north at Chads's Ford, coupled with the initial British thrust across the river, unnerved the part-time soldiers and their leaders.

A surprising number of the militiamen, however, remained on the field in an effort to do their duty. Most of these men participated in the fighting during the closing stages of the battle (though the role of the militia commanders is unclear). One member named James Johnston claimed militia brigade leader Brig. Gen. James Potter "had no active part in the conflict of that day." Whether he did or not remains open to question, but after the war many former militiamen left vivid recollections about their own experiences at the Brandywine. Numerous accounts describe the wholesale retreating of entire militia units. After it fell back from Pyle's Ford, Jacob Ritter's battalion was ordered forward "over the dead and dying, and I saw many bodies crushed to pieces beneath the wagons, and we were bespattered with blood. But no orders were given to use our small arms. . . . As we marched directly under the English cannon which kept up a continual fire, the destruction of our men was very great."[37]

John Kuntz, another member of the Pennsylvania militia, claimed in his pension application that he was wounded in the breast by a musket ball. Alexander Beggs's day started off well enough before he was caught up in Knyphausen's attack. Beggs "& some others were sent, in the morning before the battle, to fell trees in the road for the purpose of obstructing the march of the enemy." That afternoon, however, Beggs was captured when Knyphausen's division overran the American left flank. He managed to escape that night and make his way back to the army.[38]

While some of these militiamen stood firm, the vast majority vacated the battlefield when they got the chance. Borick Bechtel recollected "on this day,

---

37 John C. Dann, *The Revolution Remembered: Eyewitness Accounts of the War for Independence* (Chicago, 1980), 404; Joseph Ritter, *Memoirs of Jacob Ritter, A Faithful Minister in the Society of Friends*, ed. Joseph Foulke (Philadelphia, 1844), 15-16.

38 Revolutionary War Pension and Bounty-Land-Warrant Application Files (M804), files S2713, S32114.

they were once fired upon by the British artillery, when he is very positive the whole regiment ran." Neal McKay recalled that "when the British troops came up about one half of our Brigade retreated. . . . Genl Potter," he added, contradicting James Johnston's recollection of the same officer, "was much agitated and became almost furious at the desertion of his men." Disgusted by the actions of the militia, Samuel Hay, a major in the 7th Pennsylvania Regiment, part of Col. Hartley's brigade, scoffed that "they may as well stay at home for not one fourth of them are of any use—about three fourths of them run off at the first fire, their officers foremost. . . . There is no more regulation amongst what I have seen of them, than there is amongst a flock of Bullocks." Washington's well-known distrust of militia was borne out once more. Unfortunately, it was Wayne and Maxwell who suffered the most because of it.[39]

Fortunately for the Americans, darkness effectively ended the fighting in this sector of the field. Colonel Chambers recalled the final position his men assumed before Knyphausen's men halted their attack and the sunlight vanished altogether that September day. "We retreated to the next height in good order, in the midst of a very heavy fire of cannon and small arms. Not thirty yards distant, we formed to receive them," he reported, "but they did not choose to follow." While darkness played perhaps a deciding factor in ending the fighting, there was just enough light for the British to determine that Wayne's final position was formidable. "Finally, we saw the entire enemy line and four guns," recorded von Baurmeister, "which fired frequently, drawn up on another height in front of a dense forest, their right wing resting on the Chester road."[40]

Although it is difficult and at this date likely impossible to precisely determine when the fighting ended east of Chads's Ford, it was probably about 6:30 p.m.—about the same time the serious combat to the northeast was winding down. According to the 10th Pennsylvania's Lt. Col. Adam Hubley, "The Action Lasted Nearly to Night when the Genl. thought proper to retire . . . [to] an Eminence opposite the Enemy, leaving the Enemy to bemoan the Loss

---

39 Ibid., files S23542, S22899; Samuel Hay to William Irvine, November 14, 1777, Irvine Papers within the Draper Manuscripts, the David Library of the American Revolution, Washington Crossing, PA, Series AA, vol. 1, film 60, reel 70.

40 Montgomery, ed., *Pennsylvania Archives*, Series 5, vol. 2, 622; Von Baurmeister, "Letters of Baurmeister," 407.

of Considerable Numbers of their Vatren Soldiers, slain on the field of Battle."[41]

Ironically, General Knyphausen's attacking troops suffered heavier losses during their fitful morning fighting while advancing along the Great Post Road against Maxwell's light infantry than they suffered during the late afternoon and early evening attack into the hills east of Chads's Ford. The unbrigaded 71st Highlanders, for example, lost but three men wounded east of the river. The pair of British brigades under Maj. Gen. James Grant suffered 12 killed and 69 wounded. Among that number, three soldiers were killed and another ten wounded in the 49th Regiment of Foot, and just one fell injured in the 40th Regiment of Foot. Major General Johann Daniel Stirn's Hessian brigade probably lost only one killed and nine wounded, including two wounded from the von Mirbach Regiment. Several officers fell during Knyphausen's assault across the Brandywine, including Capt. John Rawdon of the 4th Regiment of Foot, Lt. James Edwards of the 28th Regiment of Foot, a "Captain Stuart" of the 49th Regiment of Foot, and Ens. William Andrew of the 5th Regiment of Foot.[42]

General Wayne and his infantrymen gave a good account of themselves that late afternoon, even though heavily outnumbered and often out of position because of the flanking surprise on the right side of the army and the speed with which Knyphausen drove his legions across the Brandywine. Although finally pushed off the field, Wayne and his soldiers managed to protect much of the artillery and wagons during what was a chaotic mess of an engagement. Lieutenant Colonel Hubley relayed his thoughts on the battle a few days after the firing stopped, and seemed to believe many officers failed to do their duty. "Nothing but misconduct lost us the field, the men behav'd like Vetrans, and Fought with the Greatest bravery," explained the lieutenant colonel. "Aboutt half an hour after knight we Moov'd off the Eminence to which we had returnd & Marchd that Knight to Chester."[43]

Darkness prevented a more severe American loss on this part of the field. Knyphausen's aide von Baurmeister bemoaned exactly that when he wrote about the fighting. "[H]ad not darkness favored their retreat," he explained,

41 Hubley to Hubley, September 15, 1777.

42 *Remembrancer*, 415-417; Inman, ed., "List of Officers Killed," 176-205.

43 Hubley to Hubley, September 15, 1777.

"we might have come into possession of much artillery, munitions and horses." Hessian brigade commander Johann Daniel Stirn agreed with von Baurmeister's assessment. "The approach of the night," penned the German leader, "made it impossible to pursue the enemy further."[44]

44   Von Baurmeister, "Letters of Baurmeister," 407; Johann Daniel Stirn, "Diary Installment from Major General Johann Daniel Stirn," ed. Henry Retzer and Donald Londahlsmidt, in *Journal of the Johannes Schwalm Historical Association*, vol. 6, no. 2. (1998), 6.

Chapter 16

Nathanael Greene Makes a Stand
Evening, September 11, 1777

"Gave the enemy such a check as produced the desired effect."[1]

— George Weedon, September 11, 1777

The Stand According to the Map

While General Knyphausen's troops were crossing the river at Chads's Ford, assaulting Proctor's artillery redoubt, and breaking apart Washington's left wing, what would be the final act of the Brandywine drama was playing out in the fields about one mile south of the little village of Dilworth. There, Gen. Nathanael Greene set up a defensive line to stop the advancing victorious British and Hessian troops and protect the fleeing survivors of the Birmingham Hill disaster.

Prior to Thomas McGuire's 2005 discovery of Archibald Robertson's invaluable manuscript map in the Windsor Castle collection, most authors and students of the American Revolution believed Greene waged his defensive stand somewhere along the road between Birmingham Hill and Dilworth. A brief overview of the historiography on this point is instructive. "As the American line broke to the rear, Greene's division arrived and set up a hasty line

1 Weedon to Page, September 11, 1777.

in the woods on the swell of ground to the rear of Sandy Hollow, forming across the road to Dilworth," argued John Reed. Gregory Edgar described Greene's stand in similar terms: "Opening their ranks, Greene's reserves let their exhausted comrades through to safety, then they closed ranks to oppose the oncoming regulars. . . . Here on Sandy Hill, a half mile from Dilworth, a New Jersey soldier was proud to see the retreat come to a halt." John Pancake had Greene marching almost to Birmingham Meetinghouse before engaging the oncoming British and Hessian troops. "As Greene's van . . . neared the Meeting House they met Sullivan's men retreating in disorder. Weedon's men calmly opened ranks to let the fugitives through, then closed and threw a hard check into the British advance." Bruce Mowday's history of the battle claimed Greene conducted a fighting withdrawal before reaching Harvey Road, "where it was decided that Weedon's brigade would halt and take the British in flank as they came down the road." Samuel Smith's version claimed Greene's two brigades advanced north of Harvey Road to assault the oncoming British lines. Robertson's official map, however, produced immediately following the battle, confirms that Greene's division fought south of both Dilworth and Harvey Road on both sides of the Wilmington Road—nowhere near Sandy Hollow or Birmingham Meetinghouse.[2]

Cross-Country Pursuit

Once John Sullivan's temporary wing command of three divisions (his own, and those of Lord Stirling and Adam Stephen) was driven off Birmingham Hill, the British and Hessian grenadiers pushed on and down the southern slope. The 1st British Grenadier Battalion and the Hessian grenadiers pushed on straight south, but came up against something of a dead end (at the present Brinton's Bridge Road). Joining them on their right was the 2nd Guards Battalion, which had become separated from the 1st Guards Battalion that was about that time sweeping behind Proctor's abandoned lunette east of Chads's Ford. The grenadiers and 2nd Guards battalion attempted to push on, but maneuvering lines of battle through the swampy ground around Brinton's Run proved difficult, wrote royal engineer Archibald Robertson, "having in their

---

2 Reed, *Campaign to Valley Forge*, 135; Edgar, *Philadelphia Campaign*, 34-35; Pancake, *1777*, 173; Mowday, *September 11, 1777*, 132-133; Smith, *Brandywine*, 21; Robertson, text accompanying his manuscript map.

Front a Ravine, and a woody rocky Hill almost impassable." The 2nd British Grenadier Battalion changed its course southeast toward Dilworth, about seven-tenths of a mile from Sandy Hollow and about a mile from Birmingham Hill.[3]

The terrain played a large role in slowing down this aspect of what was a formidable British advance, but the role of exhaustion should not be overlooked. These men were up before dawn that morning and spent long hours on the road to get into position beyond the American right. Once there, they had advanced against a strong American position and broken through it. Now they were toiling south, likely hungry and thirsty, moving through unscouted wet and rocky terrain. The day's exertions had simply worn them down. An officer of the 17th Regiment of Foot's light company admitted as much when he wrote, "The men being blown, we halted and formed to a fence, and were immediately joined by the 2nd grenadiers to our right."[4]

Farther right, meanwhile, the mopping up and pursuit of most of the three broken American divisions consumed additional British and Hessian energy and time. Sergeant Major John Hawkins of Congress's Own Regiment (2nd Canadian Regiment) under Col. Moses Hazen evaded his pursuers as he fled away from Birmingham Hill. "The weather was very warm and though my knapsack was very light, [it] was very cumbersome, as it swung about when walking or running and in crossing fences was in the way, so I cast it away from me, and had I not done so would have been grabbed by one of the ill-looking Highlanders, a number of whom were firing and advancing very brisk towards our rear," recalled Hawkins after the war. "The smoke was so very thick and about the close of the day I lost sight of our regiment." Hawkins's experience was likely duplicated hundreds of times through the routing American ranks.[5]

The pursuers also left descriptions of this running engagement that help us better understand the course of events. Howe's Hessian aide-de-camp, Capt. Friedrich von Muenchhausen, reported (with some exaggeration as to the distance involved) that the redcoats "drove them back three miles with their bayonets without firing a shot, in spite of the fact that the rebel fire was heavy." Hessian captain Johann Ewald of the jaegers wrote that the American line was

3 Robertson, text accompanying his manuscript map.

4 Scott, *Memoranda*. The jaegers remained on the far left of the army and did not rejoin the column until after dark.

5 Hawkins, "Battle of Brandywine Described," 420.

driven back as far as Dilworth "after a steady, stubborn fight from hill to hill and from wall to wall." Lieutenants John Peebles and William Hale, both with the 2nd Battalion of Grenadiers, recorded that they and their comrades "pursued the fugitives through woods and over fences for about three miles," driving them "from six successive railings under an exceeding heavy fire. . . . [T]he battle continued for three miles." Captain John Montresor, another of Howe's engineers, recalled how the Americans "cover[ed] their retreat with their Light Troops from one patch of woodland to another firing upon us, as we advanced into the cleared intervals until our Cannon surmounted the summits from one to another which effectually drove them beyond its Posts." In the end, darkness and exhaustion halted this drive as well. Lieutenant Frederick Augustus Wetherall of the 17th Foot remembered pursuing the Americans "closely but the fatigue of the day having been very great & the Men encumber'd with their blankets, & C: it soon became necessary to halt & form."[6]

Washington to the Front

Once he realized the critical point on the battlefield was his right flank, Washington left the Chads's Ford area to supervise what, to his dismay, would be Gen. Sullivan's collapsing command. He did so about the time Knyphausen was moving to assault across the Brandywine. While we know Washington reached his endangered right flank, how he got there triggers yet another tale surrounding the Brandywine battle.

This story involves a local man named Joseph Brown who was supposedly forced by Washington to guide him to the point of danger. Reed, in his *Campaign to Valley Forge*, claims, "Brown had demurred from assuming the office, but an officer's pistol had altered his mind. The horses thundered cross-country over the fields, hurdling the fences as though no obstructions were there. Brown could hear his eminent companion repeat over and over, 'Push on, old man, push on!'"[7]

---

6   Von Muenchhausen, *At General Howe's Side*, 31; Ewald, *Diary*, 86; Peebles, *Peebles' American War*, 133; Wilkin, *Some British Soldiers*, 230-231; Montresor, "The Montresor Journals," 450; Wetherall, *Journal of Officer B.*

7   Reed, *Campaign to Valley Forge*, 135. Unfortunately, Reed does not provide a citation for his version of the story.

Gregory Edgar, in his *The Philadelphia Campaign*, includes a lengthier version of the story worth quoting for its interesting, if fanciful, details. Washington, Edgar began,

> was anxious to proceed thither by the shortest route. He found a resident of the neighborhood named Joseph Brown and asked him to go as a guide. Brown was an elderly man and extremely loth to undertake the duty. He made many excuses, but the occasion was too urgent for ceremony. One of Washington's suite dismounted from a fine charger and told Brown if he did not instantly get on his horse and conduct the General by the nearest and best route to the place of action, he would run him through on the spot. Brown thereupon mounted and steered his course towards Birmingham Meetinghouse with all speed—the General and his attendants being close at his heels. He said the horse leapt all the fences without difficulty, and was followed in like manner by the others. The head of General Washington's horse, he said, was constantly at the flank of the one on which he was mounted. . . . When they reached the road, Brown said the bullets were flying so thick that he felt uncomfortable; and as Washington now no longer required nor paid attention to his guide, the latter embraced the first opportunity to dismount and make his escape.[8]

Many issues of Edgar's version should raise eyebrows, including his claim that Brown was guiding Washington to Birmingham Meetinghouse. By this time the meetinghouse was well behind British lines and anyone familiar with its location would have known that just from the sound of the fight. It would have made little sense to lead Washington there.

Thomas McGuire described the story for what it was: "Local tradition maintains that an elderly man named Joseph Brown was pressed into service to guide the commander in chief up the quickest route." Bruce Mowday's recent history of the battle also discounted the story: "In seeking out the fastest route he enlisted an elderly farmer, Joseph Brown, to lead him to the battle. Brown declined but was forced into service. Legends, one printed more than 70 years after the battle, have an aide threatening Brown with death by the sword if he didn't lead the way to Birmingham. . . . This version is discounted by a number of historians, as Washington's actions don't match the future president's

---

8 Edgar, *The Philadelphia Campaign*, 33-34. While Edgar provided no citation for the story, he noted in his narrative that local resident William Darlington told the tale. Darlington was not living at the time of the battle, but later became an amateur historian of Chester County. Darlington's telling constitutes questionable history.

documented demeanor." If Joseph Brown did exist, it is likely he was nowhere near Continental headquarters and neither Washington nor anyone on his staff recalled what would have been a rather interesting and important incident in their accounts of the battle.[9]

Regardless of how he found his way to the right of the army, Washington arrived on the field only to see the remnants of Sullivan's three-division command streaming south and east. When Sullivan was later being accused of incompetence by members of Congress, Washington admitted to the embattled general, "I saw nothing of the disposition you had made, not getting up till the action was, in a manner over; & then, employed in hurrying on a reinforcement, and looking out a fresh ground to form the Troops on, which, by this time, were beginning to give way."[10]

The army commander set his spurs and galloped toward the point of danger with Henry Knox, Alexander Hamilton, John Laurens, Charles Cotesworth Pinckney, and the unattached Polish Count Casimir Pulaski thundering along with him. The group of officers, all brave to a fault, did so in a manner that exposed them to personal injury. Expressing the recklessness of the younger Laurens, Lafayette wrote to the aide's father Henry, "It was not his fault that he was not killed or wounded he did every thing that was necessary to procure one or t'other."[11]

Shortly afterward, Timothy Pickering, Washington's senior staff officer, arrived to find Washington in an open field across from the William Brinton House, a two-story stone structure built in 1704. It was nearly dark. "[T]he sun shone," Pickering recalled, "and was perhaps 15 or 20 minutes above the horizon." The army's artillerist, Gen. Knox, spotted a small hill in front of the group of officers. "General Knox asked—'Will your Excellency have the artillery drawn up here?' I heard no answer," reported Pickering, "nor did I see any body of infantry to support it." The capable Knox, however, supervised the positioning of his pair of artillery pieces on the knoll and began shelling the

9 McGuire, *Philadelphia Campaign*, vol. 1, 252. McGuire cites Futhey and Cope's *History of Chester County* as the source of the story; Mowday, *September 11, 1777*, 131.

10 Hammond, ed., *Papers of Sullivan*, vol. 1, 454. Exactly what Lord Stirling and Adam Stephen did after their commands collapsed atop Birmingham Hill is unknown. Neither officer is mentioned in the various primary accounts, and no report or letter discussing their participation has been found. Almost certainly they worked like Gen. Sullivan to organize their men into a defensive front, and participated in the final repulse of the British.

11 Smith, *Brandywine*, 20-21; Chesnutt and Taylor, eds., *Papers of Henry Laurens*, vol. 11, 547.

A modern view of the 1704 William Brinton house. General Washington rode into the yard of this house with several members of his staff at a critical moment during the early evening fighting on the northern portion of the battlefield. *Author*

advancing British lines. The relentless British, meanwhile, continued advancing across the fields. Pickering sat his horse and watched rather helplessly as "[a] shot from their [British] artillery . . . cut down a file of those [American] troops."[12]

Among those withdrawing within the remnants of Sullivan's own division was Col. John Stone of the 1st Maryland Regiment, who remembered the arrival of patriot reinforcements and what would be the forming of a final line of resistance. "[We] retreated about a quarter of a mile and rallied all the men we could," reported the colonel, "when we were reinforced by Greene's and Nash's corps, who had not till that time got up. Greene had his men posted on a

---

12 Charles F. Hobson, ed., *The Papers of John Marshall*, vol. 10, January 1824-March 1827 (Chapel Hill, NC, 2000), 340. The sun set that night at 6:15 p.m. The pair of artillery pieces placed by Knox were almost certainly from the artillery reserve park, although their exact identity has not been determined.

good piece of ground." The final stage of the Brandywine battle was about to begin.[13]

Pickering, Washington, and other members of the staff (probably in the vicinity of the William Brinton House) were well in front of where Nathanael Greene would eventually form, watching the disorganized retreat of the divisions coming from Birmingham Hill while Knox put up a brave show of resistance with a pair of artillery pieces. It was at this time, as Pickering would note, that the decision was made to form Greene's men, who were arriving to protect the avenue of retreat. "We retreated farther," Pickering recalled. "Col. R. K. Mead[e], one of the General's aids, rode up to him about this time, and asked 'if Weedon's brigade [one of Greene's two Virginia brigades], which had not yet been engaged, should be ordered up?'" At this critical moment, one of Washington's officers saw him "within 200 yards of the enemy, with but a small party about with him & they drawing off from their station."[14]

A Charge?

"Count Pulaski, a veteran of the Polish Army and another recently arrived volunteer in the cause, proposed that George Washington give him 'command of his body guard, consisting of about 30 horsemen.' Pulaski led them to the charge." Or so popular histories of the battle recount. Did Pulaski perform this daring feat to buy time for Greene's division to get into position? Another version credits Pulaski with both making the charge and helping "to rally some of Sullivan's men and oppose the British under General James Agnew."[15]

Two other popular accounts, one by Samuel Smith and the other by Thomas McGuire, outline the same event in some detail, and both rely upon the 1824 book *Pulaski Vindicated from an Unsupported Charge, Inconsiderately or Malignantly*, by Louis Hue Girardin and Paul Bentalou:

13 Stone to Paca, September 23, 1777, 167.

14 Hobson, ed., *Papers of Marshall*, vol. 10, 340-341; Clark, "Diary," 99.

15 Edgar, *Philadelphia Campaign*, 35. Edgar provided no citation for the story of the Pulaski charge. Mowday, *September 11, 1777*, 133, also includes a lengthy narrative supposedly written by one of the horsemen who participated in the charge. The story was published in 1839—more than six decades after the battle—in the *Portland Transcript* of Maine, which in itself makes it unreliable. In addition, the article is unclear as to which battle the man was referring. It is just as likely the fighting took place somewhere other than at the Brandywine. Therefore, this account cannot be relied upon.

Count Pulaski proposed to Gen. Washington to give him command of his body guard, consisting of about thirty horsemen. This was readily granted, and Pulaski with his usual intrepidity and judgment, led them to the charge and succeeded in retarding the advance of the enemy—a delay which was of the highest importance of our retreating army. Moreover . . . Pulaski soon perceived that the enemy were maneuvering to take possession of the road leading to Chester, with the view of cutting off our retreat, or, at least, the column of our baggage. He hastened to General Washington, to communicate the information, and was immediately authorized by the commander in chief to collect as many of the scattered troops as he could find at hand, and make the best of them. This was most fortunately executed by Pulaski, who, by an oblique advance upon the enemy's front and right flank, defeated their object, and effectually protected our baggage, and the retreat of our army."[16]

This source is especially interesting because Bentalou was a lieutenant in the German Regiment, part of Gen. de Borre's brigade (Sullivan's division). Bentalou fought at the Brandywine, and thus could have witnessed the scene. His regiment was among those scattered when the British Guards attacked Sullivan's division, so he was on that part of the field. Whether he was in a position to witness Pulaski's supposed act is unknown. It should also be taken into account that Girardin and Bentalou published their book five decades after the battle, which makes its reliability suspect. Neither Washington nor anyone who was present on that part of the battlefield during the closing phase mentioned Pulaski's heroics at the time or thereafter, and no British or Hessian source mentions any type of cavalry charge by the Americans during any point in the battle. Unless a contemporary source corroborating Pulaski's deed surfaces, the story of his heroic charge is open to reasonable doubt.

Greene to the Rescue

The last elements of Lord Stirling's and Adam Stephen's commands were being driven from Birmingham Hill (about 5:00 p.m.) when Washington ordered Nathanael Greene's division of two brigades to leave its position east of Chads's Ferry and march northeast about two and one-half miles to reinforce the embattled flank. Greene's division set off with Brig. Gen. George Weedon's

16 Louis Hue Girardin and Paul Bentalou, *Pulaski Vindicated from an Unsupported Charge, Inconsiderately or Malignantly* (Baltimore, 1824), 23-24; McGuire, *Philadelphia Campaign*, vol. 1, 254-255; Smith, *Brandywine*, 21.

brigade in advance, followed by another under Brig. Gen. John Peter Muhlenberg, entered the Great Post Road and marched east, turned northeast on Harvey Road toward Dilworth, and arrived near the intersection with the Wilmington Road (modern-day Oakland Road) about 6:00 p.m. According to Greene, he "marched one brigade of my division . . . between three and four miles in forty-five minutes. When I came upon the ground I found the whole of the troops routed and retreating precipately, and in the most broken and confused manner. I was ordered to cover the retreat, which I effected in such a manner as to save hundred[s] of our people from falling into the hands of the enemy."[17]

South Carolinian Charles Cotesworth Pinckney, a colonel on leave from his unit in Charleston, was attached to Washington's staff that day. Long after the battle he recalled seeing Greene's division arrive on the northern end of the battlefield. "Sullivan proposed to the General [Washington] to halt it there & to display & take the Enemy in flank as they came down," recalled Pinckney. "This Genl Washington acceded to, & I was directed to carry the orders." Sullivan, Pinckney continued, "turning to me, requested I would ride up to General Weedon, and desire him to halt Colonel [Alexander] Spottswood's [Spotswood] and Colo [Edward] Stephens's [Steven's] Regiments in the plough'd Field, on our right, & form there."[18]

Pinckney set his spurs and delivered his instructions to Greene, who in turn ordered Gen. Weedon to move east of the Wilmington Road and align his men accordingly. While Greene was moving into position, the British continued advancing on Dilworth (on a line parallel to modern-day Brinton's Bridge Road). The 4th British Brigade under Brig. Gen. James Agnew, which earlier had been ordered to fill the gap on the left of the 2nd British Light Infantry Battalion, took the place of the light infantry on the left of the British line east of the road. The brigade of about 1,400 men presented a grand and imposing front aligned right to left as follows: 37th, 64th, 46th, and 33rd Regiments of Foot.

---

17 Smith, *Brandywine*, 20; Showman, McCarthy, and Cobb, eds., *Papers of Greene*, vol. 2, 471. Dilworth was a small village of a dozen mostly stone buildings, located at a five-point crossroads. The most substantial structure was Charles Dilworth's brick tavern. Dilworth was a Quaker who served on the county committee and as a county sheriff. Due to his politics, the Friends Meeting disowned him, and the British Army stripped his tavern bare in the aftermath of the battle. A British raiding party burned the tavern the following winter.

18 Pinckney to Johnson, November 14, 1820, 203; Hammond, ed., *Papers of Sullivan*, vol. 1, 557. Colonel Alexander Spottswood commanded the 2nd Virginia Regiment, and Col. Edward Stevens's led the 10th Virginia Regiment.

Just as Agnew's men passed Dilworth, Hessian Capt. Johann Ewald reported the advancing lines "received intense grapeshot and musketry fire which threw the grenadiers into disorder." The grenadiers thrown into "disorder" belonged to the 2nd British Grenadier Battalion. The advancing British angled to their left (east) to avoid the raking fire from Knox's pair of guns, and eventually halted to realign their front and await artillery support. Within a few minutes, the Royal Artillery rolled forward with three 12-pounders, unlimbered, and opened fire upon Knox's pair of advanced artillery pieces. The American artillerist withdrew his pair of light guns a short distance south, unlimbered a second time, and continued the action.[19]

General Sullivan, meanwhile, was riding to and fro reforming knots of retreating soldiers along a fence behind Knox's guns, where they remained but a short while before falling back farther south. He was aligning his survivors when an enemy round struck and killed his horse from under him. Some of his men streamed through and temporarily disrupted Greene's arriving men, while others shook out a rough though weak line of battle on a cleared piece of rising ground southwest of the Wilmington Road-Harvey Road intersection. Captain Francois Fleury, one of Sullivan's brigade majors, later wrote that some of these survivors formed "near the Road, behind a House, to the left of General Green's Division." Other survivors from the Birmingham Hill disaster had streamed east of the road and were then forming on what would be Gen. Weedon's right flank in a thick stretch of woods.[20]

While Knox worked his guns and Sullivan attempted to salvage something from his shattered command, American officers shouted out orders to their men to form a line on the reverse slope of a rise about one mile southeast of Dilworth. Despite the tight window of time he had to march his command northeast into a blocking position and then effectively deploy his men, Nathanael Greene succeeded on both counts. His division numbered about 2,500 men, but the exact composition of his final line of battle, and how many made it into that line in time to engage the approaching British, remains a subject of historical debate. According to Col. Pinckney, it was Gen. Sullivan

19 Ewald, *Diary*, 86-87. While it is not known with certainty, it is likely it was the artillery at this stage of the fighting that forced Knox to fall back while he was fighting for extra time to allow the infantry to form behind him.

20 Hammond, ed., *State of New Hampshire*, vol. 4, 200. The house to which Captain Fleury refers was a farmhouse and its outbuildings at the intersection of the Wilmington Road and Harvey Road.

who suggested the general location of Greene's final line, and that Weedon move east of the road (the American right) and form there. Sullivan was on this part of the field (and thus enjoyed some familiarity with it) before either Washington or Greene arrived. He knew the axis of the British advance (south) from Dilworth. The rising terrain, coupled with heavy woods on the right, would make the proposed line all but invisible to the approaching enemy. The location of the final line made good tactical sense. Pinckney's detailed account has verisimilitude.[21]

The Wilmington Road bisected the final line of battle. General Weedon's brigade, with survivors from the Birmingham Hill disaster, formed Greene's right wing east of the road. In its final form, this part of the front settled into an L-shaped formation with both ends anchored in woods. The long stem of this L-shaped formation faced generally west and was likely comprised of Weedon's Virginia regiments and the Pennsylvania State Regiment. The shorter leg was probably comprised of remnants from Stirling's and Stephen's divisions. This shorter front was ensconced along a line of woods nearly perpendicular to Weedon's front and faced south. Each end of the L-shaped line was refused, with the far right running deep into the stand of woods, and the other end running for a short distance along a fenceline bordering the Wilmington Road.[22]

The composition of Greene's left wing west of the road is much more problematic. Archibald Robertson's invaluable manuscript map depicts a heavy line of battle west of the road, which faced and blunted the advance of the 2nd Grenadier Battalion. But who fought in this line? Both Gens. Sullivan and Greene later wrote that only Brig. Gen. George Weedon's brigade (from Greene's division) was engaged that evening on this part of the field. Greene, who did not leave a report or extended account of his actions at Brandywine, mentioned in a letter that he marched north with only one (Weedon) of his two (Weedon and Muhlenberg) brigades. There are no primary accounts from Gen. Muhlenberg or anyone from his brigade regarding this issue. It is unlikely, however, that Muhlenberg remained on the southern part of the field, and indeed must have marched northeast behind Weedon's regiments. If he did so, it is equally likely that, with Weedon formed (or already fighting) east of the road as Greene's right wing, as the trailing organization Muhlenberg would

---

21 Hammond, ed., *Papers of Sullivan*, vol. 1, 557.

22 Robertson map, with accompanying text.

have deployed his command west of the road with Sullivan's survivors gathered into line from the three divisions driven from Birmingham Hill.[23]

This line that formed west of the Wilmington Road sketched a wide concave tree-lined front facing generally northwest. This line was also a short distance farther west than Greene's right (Weedon), and a gap of perhaps 100 yards, together with the road itself, separated the two wings. Both wings enjoyed wide-open fields of fire against their approaching enemy. The terrain, woods, fences, and growing shadows guaranteed the advancing British troops in general, and Agnew's 4th Brigade in particular, would move into a crossfire before seeing or realizing the full extent of the Continental line. The result, which could not have been by accident, was a giant killing box.[24]

Washington did not intend for Greene to make his stand alone. Soon after leaving the Chads's Ford area, Washington concluded his right was in more danger than he originally believed, and decided to call up Brig. Gen. Francis Nash's North Carolina brigade for more support. He sent the army's adjutant general, Timothy Pickering, to deliver the order. Once he did so, Pickering "fell in with Col. Fitzgerald, one of the Generals' [Washington's] aids, and we galloped to the right where the action had commenced, and as we proceeded, we heard heavy and uninterrupted discharges of musketry (and doubtless of artillery) but the peals of musketry were most stricking."[25]

Agnew's 4th British Brigade, meanwhile, remained stalled outside Dilworth just west of the road and facing generally south while the 2nd British Grenadier

---

23 Ibid. A careful cartographer, Royal engineer Archibald Robertson confirmed two separate extensive lines of American troops separated by a gap and the Wilmington Road. Although strengths and names are not present, a comparison with other depictions of troops (like Stephen's division atop Birmingham Hill, or the 2nd Grenadier Battalion), is instructive. No primary accounts of this part of the fighting from Muhlenberg's or Francis Nash's commands have been located. Based upon this map, my study of the sources, and personal familiarity with the terrain, I believe Muhlenberg reached the field and formed west of the road in time to assist in throwing back the grenadiers. Showman, McCarthy, and Cobb, eds., *Papers of Greene*, vol. 2, 471; Hammond, ed., *Papers of Sullivan*, vol. 1, 473; Robertson Map and accompanying text. Colonel Moses Hazen's regiment (2nd Canadian, or Congress's Own), which appears to have escaped the catastrophe of Birmingham Hill, may well have formed the core of this line around which Sullivan's survivors formed before Muhlenberg arrived.

24 McGuire, *Philadelphia Campaign*, vol. 1, 256; Robertson map, with accompanying text. Every source that says Muhlenberg fought on this part of the Brandywine field is a secondary source.

25 Pickering, Pickering Papers, film 220, reel 52, 184-186. Douglas Southall Freeman, in *Washington*, vol. 4, 482n, does not believe Nash reached the northern part of the field in time to participate in the fighting. The unlucky "promising young" officer, was struck in the leg by a cannonball at the battle of Germantown on October 4 and died three days later.

Battalion advanced alone toward the American position. Captain Ewald gathered together his surviving jaegers from his advance guard and attached himself to the tramping grenadiers. Captain-Lieutenant John Peebles, a member of the Scottish 42nd (Royal Highland) Regiment of Foot's grenadier company, recalled their advance and came up against a "second & more extensive line of the Enemys best Troops drawn up & posted to great advantage, here they sustain'd a warm attack for some time & pour'd a heavy fire on the British Troops as they came up."[26]

The discovery of a strong and perhaps unexpected line of American resistance sent Ewald riding rearward in search of reinforcements. When the intrepid Hessian found Gen. Agnew and the 4th British Brigade at a standstill well to the rear, he "requested him to support the grenadiers, and pointed out a hill which, if he gained it, the enemy could not take the grenadiers in the flank." Agnew, whose command was near Dilworth on the western side of the Wilmington Road, agreed and ordered his troops to move out. His brigade marched from right to left as follows: 37th, 64th, 46th, and 33rd Regiments of Foot, with the left flank of the 33rd aligned along the edge of the Wilmington Road. His troops moved rapidly south past the William Brinton house in an effort to come up with the 2nd Grenadier Battalion's left flank. The brigade continued its steady tramp until clear of a large point of woods, south of which the road continued on for some distance before carving its way east toward the American position. With the grenadiers advancing ahead and well to his south and right, Agnew swung his line in a large left wheel until it faced generally east. Five companies of 2nd Light Infantry Battalion joined Agnew's line by squeezing into position between the 33rd and 46th regiments. When all was as he wanted it, Agnew ordered his regiments across the Wilmington Road, and pushed them up the slope to come up on the left flank of the grenadiers. "[W]e had no sooner reached the hill," explained Ewald, "than we ran into several American regiments."[27]

---

26 Peebles, *Peebles' War*, 133. Peebles's company was attached to the 2nd Grenadier Battalion.

27 Ewald, *Diary*, 86-87; Robertson map, with accompanying text. When the five companies of 2nd Light Infantry Battalion joined Agnew's line, why they did so, and who led them is unclear. Their presence with the 4th Brigade during this stage of the fighting was unknown until the 2005 discovery of the Robertson map, which meticulously notes their presence. The parent battalion is depicted on the map just southeast of Dilworth with the jaegers. Major John Maitland's 2nd Light Infantry Battalion originally formed between the jaegers and 1st Light Battalion east of the Birmingham Road and helped drive Stephen's division off Birmingham

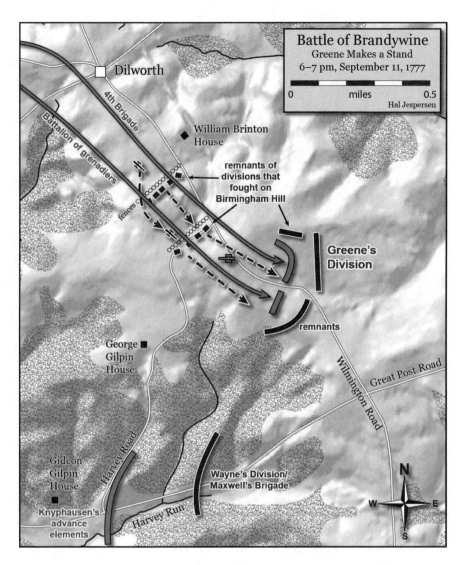

Battle of Brandywine
Greene Makes a Stand
6–7 pm, September 11, 1777

0   miles   0.5
Hal Jespersen

Dilworth

4th Brigade

Battalion of grenadiers

William Brinton
House

remnants of
divisions that
fought on
Birmingham Hill

fences

Greene's
Division

remnants

George
Gilpin
House

Wilmington Road

Great Post Road

Gideon
Gilpin
House

Harvey Road

Wayne's Division/
Maxwell's Brigade

Knyphausen's
advance
elements

Harvey Run

N
W   E
S

Most of the roughly 2,000 British and Hessian troops advancing into the interlocking fields of fire across Greene's expansive front were thoroughly

Hill. During that action, five companies became separated, but appear to link back up with the rest of the battalion northwest of Dilworth. The next thing the map shows is the 2nd Light battalion southeast of Dilworth (but not how it got there) and Agnew's 4th Brigade advancing southwest of the Wilmington Road. It seems likely that the same five companies separated in the fight on Birmingham Hill were absorbed into Agnew's advancing brigade line below Dilworth, even though Robertson's map doesn't show them until the final position facing Greene's line.

This modern view (on both pages) looks north across the fields toward Dilworth from present-day Harvey Road. The British lines advanced across these fields toward Greene's hidden position. *Author*

exhausted after their hard marching and bloody fight for Birmingham Hill. The sudden discovery of Greene's troops formed on both sides of the road in good order and in strong lines took them by surprise, and gives further meaning and context to grenadier Peebles's recollection of meeting a "second & more extensive line of the Enemys best Troops drawn up & posted to great advantage."[28]

On Greene's right, Weedon's Continentals held their fire until the left front and flank of the Agnew's line were almost directly in front of them. When they opened fire, his four Virginia regiments, together with 21-year-old Col. Walter Stewart's Pennsylvania State Regiment, caught Agnew's British regiments in an

---

28 Peebles, *Peebles' War*, 133. This strength assigned to the British force takes into account the casualties the 2nd British Grenadier Battalion suffered assaulting Stirling's division.

open field. It was obvious almost immediately that Agnew's command was in trouble. When the lead began flying through the ranks of his left regiment, the 33rd Foot stopped advancing, wheeled to the left to face the enemy hidden in the woods, and returned fire. The five companies of the light infantry on the 33rd's right seem to have followed suit. The 46th and 64th, however, continued tramping deeper into a heavy fire that was at this stage primarily still coming from their front. The 37th Foot on the far right of the line kept marching west, its front bisected by the Wilmington Road. Although the brigade elements seem to have maintained a relatively cohesive line, the center of Agnew's front bowed toward Greene's line, mimicking the patriot front though on a smaller scale. Agnew's advance, however, had captured—at least temporarily—part of the higher elevation Ewald had pointed out, and in so doing protected the 2nd Grenadier Battalion's exposed flank. And Greene's men were about to extract a high price for doing so.[29]

29 Robertson map, with accompanying text.

This modern view spread (see both pages) looks toward Nathanael Greene's American line from the present-day Harvey Road. The British advanced south across these fields toward the distant tree line, which marks Greene's final line of battle. The British Battalion of Grenadiers would advance on the right side (opposite page), and Agnew's 4th Brigade on the left (above). *Author*

"[T]his day for a severe and successive engagement exceeded all I ever saw," recorded Lt. James McMichael of the Pennsylvania State Regiment. "Our regiment fought at one stand about an hour under incessant fire, and yet the loss was less than at Long Island; neither were we so near each other as at Princeton, our common distance being about 50 yards." Washington's adjutant, Timothy Pickering, remembered seeing the Pennsylvania State Regiment "close up to the edge of a thick wood in its front, and firing briskly; [Colonel] Stewart on foot, in its rear, animating his men." The woods, darkness, and inaccuracy of the enemy's small arms fire worked to their advantage. "[A]lthough I was within 30 or 40 yards of this regiment," continued Pickering, "I could not see any troops of the enemy at whom they were firing." The raplidly descending darkness and

powder smoke effectively hid large swaths of the opposing lines from one another.[30]

West of the Wilmington Road, meanwhile, the 2nd Grenadier Battalion had faced and marched southeast toward the concave line of Americans arrayed against them. The grenadiers appear to have stopped advancing about the same time as Agnew's men, leveled their muskets, and traded fire with the better protected patriots. The positions of the two commands left a yawning gap between the 4th Brigade's right and the 2nd Battalion's left. Because the space was so far in advance of the Americans, and Agnew's men were now in possession of the rising ground east of the road, the once-exposed grenadier flank was now firmly protected. Not all of Agnew's regiments, however, enjoyed that advantage.[31]

---

30 McMichael, "Diary," vol. 16, 150; Hobson, ed., *Papers of Marshall*, vol. 10, 340.

31 Robertson map, with accompanying text. Unfortunately, we know very little about the fighting west of the Wilmington Road between the 2nd Battalion of Grenadiers and the American troops arrayed as Greene's left wing other than that the grenadiers advanced within a

The convex front assumed by Agnew's 4th Brigade exposed Maj. Robert McLeroth's 64th Regiment of Foot (the 2nd Staffordshire Regiment) on the right center of the line to both a frontal and enfilading fire, and left the regiment with but little ability to effectively return the favor.[32] Once the enemy moved within effective killing distance, explained Gen. Weedon, his men opened a sustained fire: "[We] gave the enemy such a check as produced the desired effect." If the "desired effect" was the near-destruction of the officer corps, the patriots succeeded. "There was a terrible firing," reported Ewald, "and . . . nearly all of the officers of these two regiments the [46th] and 64th were slain." An American bullet knocked Maj. McLeroth out of the fight while leading the regiment, and 20-year veteran Capt. Henry Nairne was killed. Four lieutenants were struck and wounded to varying degrees, as was an ensign. The 4th Brigade reported seven killed and 75 wounded. The 64th Regiment marched into battle with 420 bayonets that evening, and suffered 47 dead and injured.[33]

During the approach to Greene's killing field, James Agnew, who spent much of the action fighting with the embattled 64th Regiment, barely escaped with his life when one of Henry Knox's gun rounds came within inches of killing him. "The general had the misfortune to be grazed by a cannon-ball, but continued to head his brigade," wrote Agnew's personal servant, Pvt. Alexander Andrew of the 44th Regiment of Foot. "It happened to be the last engaged that night, and, though he was very much indisposed, yet he commanded his gallant troops. . . . During the action the general remained at the head of the 64th, which regiment suffered more than any of the brigade."[34]

---

couple hundred yards of the patriot line, exchanged fire for an indeterminate amount of time, and the fighting ended about the same time, and for the same reason, as it did on Agnew's front.

32 McGuire, *Philadelphia Campaign*, vol. 1, 259.

33 Weedon to Page, September 11, 1777; Ewald, *Diary*, 86. The officer corps of the 64th Regiment of Foot was particularly hard hit. In addition to those named, the four lieutenants included Michael Jacobs, George Torriano, William Wynyrd, and Thomas Freeman; the ensign was Alexander Grant. In the 46th Regiment, Ensign Skeffing Bristow was wounded. *Remembrancer*, 415-417; Inman, ed., "List of Officers Killed," 176-205. The Craig Farm, located along Harvey Road, may still contain graves from the battle. In the mid-nineteenth century, remains from the 64th Regiment of Foot were found, and in the late 1970s another grave was found on the property containing a member of the 17th Regiment of Foot (Grey's 3rd Brigade).

34 Hagist, *British Soldiers*, 229. General Agnew's luck ran out a few weeks later outside Philadelphia at Germantown, where he was killed by a civilian sharpshooter named Hans Boyer during the American attack. He was carried back to his headquarters in John Wister's Big House (now called Grumblethorpe) on Germantown Avenue, where he died. His blood stains

Lieutenant Loftus Cliffe of the 46th Regiment of Foot, which fought on the left of the hard-hit 64th Regiment, was proud of the service Agnew's 4th Brigade turned in that evening. The "2d Grenadier Battn were out flanked and must [have] give[n] way if not immediately supported. [W]e had the Honour & with our fire closed the Day," boasted the lieutenant, who concluded, "The fatigues of this Day were excessive."[35]

Pennsylvania State Regiment member James McMichael, part of Weedon's brigade that fired into both the 64th and 46th regiments, remembered the fighting continued "without giving way on either side until dark. Our ammunition almost expended, firing ceased on both sides." Before the shooting stopped, however, several men in the regiment fell. What was described as "Grapeshot" struck Sgt. Joshua Peeling in the left hand and head, while a musketball pierced Sgt. Adam Christ's chest. Private Frederick Paul was hit in the left side by a musketball, and his comrade George Chapman also fell wounded. Ensign Alexander Huston from the same regiment was less fortunate and died on the field.[36]

The killing and maiming was much heavier on the other side of the field where Howe's troops would have suffered even more, thought Capt. Ewald, if Royal Artillery had not rolled up and shelled the patriot line. The "affair would have turned out to be an even more dirty one if an English artillery officer had not hurried up with two light 6-pounders and fired on the enemy's flank with grapeshot," wrote Ewald, "whereupon the enemy retreated." The guns mentioned by the Hessian deployed west of the Wilmington Road behind Agnew's left and shelled the extreme right of Greene's line. In reality, it was the onset of darkness, British fatigue, and a firm American line, and not the arrival of a pair of light artillery pieces, that brought an end to the Brandywine fighting.[37]

---

are still visible on the parlor floor. Agnew is buried at the De Benneville Family Burial Grounds in Philadelphia.

35 Cliffe to brother Jack, October 24, 1777, Loftus Cliffe Papers.

36 McMichael, "Diary," 150; Montgomery, ed., Pennsylvania *Archives*, Series 5, vol. 2, 499, vol. 4, 514-571. The British rolled up two light field pieces on the other side of the line, from which a distant shot may have struck Sgt. Peeling. It is also possible his wound was not caused by grapeshot. Trussell, *Pennsylvania Line*, 280, claims the regiment lost just one killed and two wounded, but archival records show otherwise.

37 Ewald, *Diary*, 87.

Regardless of how it ended, nearly everyone on the British side of the field understood what had just taken place: the outflanked and beaten Americans had rallied, assumed an outstanding defensive position, and fought them to a standstill. The reality of that conclusion did not sit well with the European professionals, some of whom argued that the successful American stand was as much the result of confusion as patriot competence.[38] Earlier in the fighting, the uniforms worn by some of Wayne's men had confused Knyphausen's troops near Chads's Ford. According to Lt. George Duke of the 33rd Regiment of Foot's grenadier company, something similar happened during the fighting with Greene's division, which accounted for the embarrassing losses. The 64th Regiment of Foot, explained Duke, "mistook a party of the rebels for Hessians, as did we and the 46th, but their heavy fire fell on the 64th. . . . The Grenadiers had at that time a very heavy fire and was rather at a stand, upon which the General ordered the 33rd to support them." Duke thought it "was the best stand they ever made."[39]

The outfit the British mistook for Hessians was almost certainly the Pennsylvania State Regiment, one of the few American commands wearing new blue uniforms. The Pennsylvania command was not a militia battalion, but rather a unit of state regulars that had not yet been fully integrated into the Continental Army. Organized from the remnants of several Pennsylvania battalions that had been decimated during the New York campaign, the regiment numbered around 500 men during the fighting along the Brandywine. The Pennsylvanians sported blue coats faced with red, and pewter buttons stamped with the letters "P.S.R." The regiment's young Irish-born commander, explained one veteran, had the reputation of being "the handsomest man in the army," and one "the Philadelphia ladies styled [as] the Irish beauty." In the smoke and dusk of the evening, the new uniforms sported by these Pennsylvanians could have easily been mistaken for blue Hessian uniforms.[40]

---

38 Another legend regarding the battle has some of the Anspach jaegers recognizing Peter Muhlenberg, with whom they had fought in a previous war, and shouting out "Here comes Devil Pete." While a stirring story, no available primary source confirms the legend.

39 Duke, Brandywine British officer's letter. Whether Agnew ordered the 33rd to pull away from the left to support the embattled 64th is unknown.

40 McGuire, *Philadelphia Campaign*, vol. 1, 102; Joseph Plumb Martin, *Private Yankee Doodle: Being a Narrative of Some of the Adventures, Dangers and Sufferings of a Revolutionary Soldier*, George E. Scheer, ed. (Eastern National, 1962), 187; Ewald, *Diary*, 86.

Greene, who was justifiably proud of how his men performed that evening, later opined that his stand saved hundreds of men from falling into enemy hands. "We were engaged an hour and a quarter, and lost upwards of an hundred men killed and wounded," he wrote in a letter after the battle. "I maintained the ground until dark, and then drew off the troops in good order. We had the whole British force to contend with, that had just before routed our whole right wing."[41]

Retreat With No Pursuit

"[I]t being by this time almost Dark, unacquainted with the Ground, and the Troops very much fatigued, it was impossible to pursue further the Advantage they had gained," was how British engineer Archibald Robertson described the cessation of hostilities. When Greene and others pulled back southeastward, Howe halted pursuit and the exhausted British and Hessian troops dropped where they stood. Ensign George Inman of the 17th Regiment of Foot's light company recalled being able to "sitt down and refresh ourselves with some cold Pork and Grogg, on the Ground the Enemy had first posted themselves, which we enjoyed much, as our march before the attack was better than 18 miles."[42]

It was unfortunate for Howe that he was unable to conduct an effective pursuit and deliver the final blow against Washington's fleeing Continental Army. Captain John Andre, who served as aide to Gen. Grey at Brandywine, blamed exhaustion: "Night and the fatigue the soldiers had undergone prevented any pursuit." "It was now near dark, and our army so very much fatigued that we could not follow up our victory," concluded Martin Hunter of the light infantry. "[I]ndeed, it could not have been attended with much success, in a country so much intersected with rivers and woods, and it is always very difficult to come up with a retreating army with infantry." Howe had plenty of footsoldiers, tired though they were. What he needed was cavalry, but there were not enough mounted troops available to conduct an effective pursuit.

---

41 Showman, McCarthy, and Cobb, eds., *Papers of Greene*, vol. 2, 471.

42 Robertson map, with accompanying text; George Inman, "George Inman's Narrative of the American Revolution," in *The Pennsylvania Magazine of History and Biography*, vol. 7 (Philadelphia, 1883), 241.

General Cornwallis's flanking division only had two squadrons of mounted troops, at most 100 dragoons.[43]

Even if Howe had had sufficient horsemen, a successful pursuit of an enemy army—even a beaten one in retreat—was always difficult and usually impossible. Brandywine was a pitched battle, and in most such affairs, both sides emerged wounded and exhausted. A generation later at the end of the Napoleonic Wars, the Duke of Wellington, Gen. Arthur Wellesley, would famously observe, "The only thing worse than a battle lost is a battle won." Even without those words ringing in his head, Gen. Howe would have understood their meaning. His army was disorganized, tired, and had suffered significant losses. Still, Howe had two fresh brigades of regular troops on the field. The 3rd Brigade under Charles Grey, part of the flanking column, had remained in reserve all day and had yet to fire a shot, while Johann von Stirn's Hessian brigade had been but lightly engaged with Gen. Knyphausen near Chads's Ford. Neither brigade, however, was in a position to follow up on Greene's heels, and Howe wisely decided against even the attempt.[44]

As Howe likely surmised, Washington's Army was in full retreat toward Chester. There was little panic, however, and certainly no repeat of the mob-like flight after the flanking disaster at Long Island or surprise landing at Kip's Bay the previous year. This did not mean, however, that the Continental Army was organized or even intact. In fact, it was neither. Only Gens. Greene, Maxwell, Nash, and Wayne managed to leave the battlefield with their commands relatively well in hand. Otherwise, the battle had scattered the army, jamming the roads and fields with exhausted troops from various commands, many of whom stumbled on without the guidance of officers. It would take the better part of that night and more for the men to find their units.[45]

Timothy Pickering rode his horse next to Washington that disappointing night. "The sun had for some time disappeared: it began to grow dusky," recalled the aide, "and as we proceeded, in retiring, the General said to me—'Why 'tis a perfect rout.'" Pickering thought it was "fortunate for us that the night came on, for under its cover the fatigued stragglers and some wounded made their escape." Like so many others that night, the wounded Marquis de

---

43 Andre, *Journal*, 46-47; Hunter, *Journal*, 30; Spring, *With Zeal*, 270-271.

44 Spring, *With Zeal*, 9.

45 Pancake, *1777*, 174.

Lafayette was caught up in the surging rout of the army. "Fugitives, cannon, and baggage crowded in complete disorder on the road to Chester," was how the Frenchman described the journey.[46]

Sergeant Major John Hawkins of Congress's Own Regiment (2nd Canadian Regiment) under Col. Moses Hazen evaded pursuers and "fell in with the North Carolina troops [Nash's brigade] and about two o'clock in the morning arrived at Chester." Stephen's aide Joseph Clark saw "night coming on adding . . . gloom to our misfortunes, amidst the noise of cannon, the hurry of people, and wagons driving in confusion from the field. I came off with a heart full of distress. In painful anxiety, I took with hasty step the gloomy path from the field, and traveled 15 miles to Chester, where I slept two hours upon a couple of chairs." James McMichael of the Pennsylvania State Regiment walked "all night until we neared the town [Chester] when we halted, but not to sleep."[47]

The exertions of the day left thousands of parched throats. Teenage artilleryman Jacob Nagle worked his way toward Chester from the southern portion of the field after he and his comrades were driven away by General Knyphausen's division. "It coming on night, I was famishing with drouth," he wrote. "Coming to a well, but could not get near it for the mob of soldiers, but falling in with one of the artillerymen, he worked his way through them and brought me water in his canteen. Otherwise I should of fell on the road."[48]

After surviving the horror of participating in the rout of Sullivan's division by the British Guards, Col. Samuel Smith of the 4th Maryland Regiment, part of Gen. de Borre's brigade, had to deal with a pious Quaker during the night retreat to Chester. The exhausted and likely none-too-patient colonel "applied to a Quaker Farmer, to guide him to the road leading to Chester, which he refused; but a pistol having been pointed at his breast, he complied. On being thanked he replied, 'I want no thanks, thee forced me.'" Smith assured him "he was a dead man if he did not get his horse instantly and show the way to Chester. The Friend was alarmed, and, exclaiming, 'What a dreadful man thou art!' went and saddled his horse and prepared to set out." Smith was not in a trusting mood, and told him as much. "I have not entire confidence in your

46 Hobson, ed., *Papers of Marshall*, vol. 10, 341; Pickering, *Life of Pickering*, vol. 1, 155; Lafayette, *Memoirs*, vol. 1, 24.

47 Hawkins, "Battle of Brandywine Described," 420; Clark, "Diary," 99; McMichael, "Diary," 150.

48 Nagle, *The Nagle Journal*, 9.

fidelity," cautioned the colonel, "but I tell you explicitly, that if you do not conduct me clear of the enemy, the moment I discover your treachery, I will blow your brains out.' The terrified farmer exclaimed, 'Why, thou art the most desperate man I ever did see!'"[49]

A Quaker girl never forgot what occurred in her yard along the road to Chester that September night. "In the evening a great company of American soldiers came flocking into the yard, and sat down on the cider press, troughs and benches, and every place they could find, they seemed so tired," she wrote. "Father said, 'Bring bread and cheese and cut for them.' They were so hungry. As it happened . . . [we] had baked that day, and we cut up all the bread and cheese we had. I know, I got no supper."[50]

The Human Toll

The Battle of Brandywine was one of the bloodiest of the war. Although the official records are woefully incomplete, the generally accepted casualties for Washington's Continental Army are about 300 men killed, 600 wounded, and another 400 captured, for a total of 1,300. With a command strength that morning of about 17,000, Washington lost roughly eight percent of his army. Many of the American prisoners were also wounded men who had been left on the field during the retreat. The Americans also lost 11 invaluable artillery pieces, which at this stage of the war were harder to replace than men.[51]

General Howe's casualties vary widely depending upon the source, but no one disputes that his losses were substantial. The official casualty list detailed 93 men killed, 488 wounded, and six missing for a total of 587 out of about 15,800, or nearly four percent.[52] Two other officers straddled this number, with jaeger Lt. Heinrich Carl Philipp von Feilitzsch setting the army's casualties at about 500, and General Knyphausen reporting 622.[53] Captain Ewald, however, thought Howe's losses were substantially higher and put the number at 900 men

---

49 Smith, "Papers of Smith"; Futhey and Cope, *History of Chester County*, 80.

50 McGuire, *Philadelphia Campaign*, vol. 1, 263-264. The website McGuire cited as his source for the story is no longer accessible.

51 Montresor, "Journals," 451.

52 *Remembrancer for 1777*, 415-417.

53 Burgoyne, trans. and ed., *Diaries of Two Jaegers*, 18; Von Knyphausen to Germain, October 21, 1777.

(killed, wounded, and captured). A Philadelphia civilian named Christopher Marshall put British losses as "near two thousand killed and wounded, nine hundred of which were killed in action."[54] That appears sheer hyperbole until one considers an official British memorandum found by an American officer during the October 4, 1777, battle of Germantown that records Cornwallis's flanking column lost 1,032 killed and wounded, and Knyphausen's diversionary column lost 944 killed and wounded, for a total of 1,976 casualties.[55]

*   *   *

Regardless of the precise numbers lost along the Brandywine, one thing was certain: both armies suffered severely in the fighting, and dead and wounded men lay scattered across miles of Pennsylvania countryside. The injured needed medical attention, and everyone still alive needed food, drink, rest, and reorganization. These priorities would consume both armies for the next several days.

54 Ewald, *Diary*, 87; Christopher Marshall, *Extracts from the Diary of Christopher Marshall, Kept in Philadelphia and Lancaster, during the American Revolution 1774-1781*, ed. William Duane (Albany, NY, 1877), 127.

55 "Notes and Queries: Loss of the British Army at Brandywine," *The Pennsylvania Magazine of History and Biography* (Philadelphia, 1880), vol. 4, 121. Regardless of the various estimates, the officially reported 587 casualties remain the generally accepted figure for Howe's losses.

Chapter 17

The Aftermath of Battle:
September 12-16, 1777

"[M]any of the dead . . . lay exposed to the open air, having been washed bare,
and some few of them had never been interred."[1]

— Joseph Townsend, account compiled later in life

It was about midnight when George Washington and his aides reached Chester. Some of the army reached the town before him, but much of his beaten command was still spread out on a variety of roads and byways stretching all the way back to the battlefield.

While no one knows what passed through Washington's mind during his ride away from the scene of his latest battlefield defeat, the exhausted general certainly must have looked forward to a few hours of much-needed sleep. Before he could close his eyes, however, Washington picked up his pen and did his duty; John Hancock, the president of Congress, had to be informed of what had just transpired. "I am sorry to inform you, that in this day's engagement, we have been obliged to leave the enemy masters of the field," began Washington. "Unfortunately the intelligence received of the enemy's advancing up the Brandywine, and crossing at a ford about six miles above us, was uncertain and contradictory, notwithstanding all my pains to get the best. . . . [Y]et our loss of

---

1 Townsend, *Some Account*, 28-29.

men is not, I am persuaded, very considerable, I believe much less than the enemy's."[2]

Other Accounts

Washington's report to Hancock was not the first notice that politicians and other civilians received that a major battle had been waged. The fighting was audible at least 30 miles away, and everyone who heard the deep-throated thunder of artillery and small arms fire knew what it meant. The Reverend Henry Muhlenberg was at his home in Trappe, Pennsylvania, north of the Schuylkill River on September 11 when the fighting opened. "This morning," he wrote, "we heard heavy and long continuing cannonading some thirty miles away on Brandywine Creek, where the two armies were engaged in a hard struggle."[3]

Margaret Stedman left us a vivid account of what she witnessed in Philadelphia:

> This very moment we have accounts that both armies are, and have been since 7 o'clock in the morning in close engagement. . . . Mr. Stedman with numbers of others is just returned from a walk to the Bettering House, where the firing is very distinctly to be heard, so that it is no vague report. I really tremble for the event, and am so agitated that I must lay down my pen. . . . [A] Man at this very instant is parading through the City ringing a Bell and ordering all Houses to be immediately shut up, alarming the inhabitants that General Howe is advancing and that every man who can carry a Gun must appear on the Commons. The morning had been chiefly employed in pressing Carts, Horses and Wagons, a great number of Boats and Cannon are sent down to Schuylkill. We are now so closely shut up that I can scarcely tell what is going on in the busy scene, nor have I yet heard whether any express is came in with an account of the Battle."[4]

A week after the battle, Congressman Elbridge Gerry recalled how the country was rocked by "a Cannonade, which We distinctly heard at this place [Philadelphia] & which was returned by our Army." The battle, he continued

---

2 Fitzpatrick, ed. *Writings of Washington*, vol. 9, 207-208.

3 Muhlenberg, *Journals*, vol. 3, 74.

4 Margaret Stedman to Mrs. E. Fergusson, September 11, 1777, in *Pennsylvania Magazine of History and Biography* (Philadelphia, 1890), vol. 14, 64-65.

was a "warm" one, "in which as heavy a Fire from the Musketry as perhaps has been known this war in America."[5]

Other civilians also wrote about hearing the distant combat. Henry Marchant was in Philadelphia when General Howe arrived at the Brandywine. The state attorney general of Rhode Island and member of the Continental Congress remembered the battle beginning "a little before Nine in the Morning with a heavy Cannonade, which was very distinctly heard in Our State House [Independence Hall] yard about 30 miles from the Place of Action . . . it lasted till dusk." William Williams, a member of Congress from Connecticut and a signer of the Declaration of Independence, remembered and described much the same thing: "a very heavy & tremendous Fire took place for considerable time; old officers & all I have seen say beyond what they conceived possible from Musquetry."[6]

Sarah Frazer was the daughter of Persifor Frazer, who owned a large farm near the Brandywine and would one day become the head of one of Philadelphia's leading families. On September 11, 1777, Persifor was fighting with Gen. Wayne's division. Eight-year-old Sarah was at school with her brother and sister when the battle started. "The teacher went out and listened some time and returned saying there is a battle not far off, children you may go home," she later recalled. After returning home, Sarah continued, "[we] heard musketry with an occasional discharge of heavy artillery through the day, but particularly towards evening. There was a continual discharge of small arms heard at our house." She was asleep by the time her father slipped quietly into the house after helping a wounded man onto a wagon at Seven Stars Tavern in Aston Township. When she woke the next morning, Sarah continued, "I got up and seeing my fathers Regimental coat all stained and daubed with blood I set up the murder shout as I thought he must have been killed." The frightened little girl turned around to see her father standing behind her; his daughter's screams had awakened him.[7]

Thomas Cope would grow up to be a prominent Philadelphia merchant, but in 1777 he was "a small boy at the time, having with my brother Israel been placed at school in the neighbourhood. We were within hearing of the battle,

5   Smith et al., eds., *Letters of Delegates*, vol. 7, 683-684.

6   Ibid., 657, 689.

7   Frazer, *General Persifor Frazer*, 155.

even to the small arms. Our teacher was sadly alarmed & the scholars but little at ease." Thomas was sleeping at his uncle's home on the night of the battle when a small group of American soldiers roused them from their slumber demanding food and shelter. One of them, recalled the youngster, was in a "sad plight, being destitute of hat & coat & his hands & face besmeared with gunpowder." The man in a "sad plight" was Lt. Col. James Ross—the same Ross who, with a mixed group of Continentals and dragons, skirmished with Howe's column earlier in the day.[8]

Young Phebe Mendenhall's family experienced a harrowing night and morning at their farm along the cluttered road to Chester. "A captain came on his horse. . . . He was wounded and had his servant and a Doctor," she recalled. "He wanted to stay all night. Father didn't want him to stay, for he told him he expected the English would be along in the morning, and would tear us all to pieces, but they didn't mind that. They took him off his horse, brought him in and they staid. The girls brought him a bed, and he laid there in the common house and the Doctor staid with him. The servant slept in the barn. They all got their suppers too." The next morning, the captain found it impossible to mount a horse because of a serious wound in the thigh. Phebe wrote about the incident: "They got the horse there, and the girls helped to lift him, but he couldn't get on. Father didn't want him there when the English came. As the wounded man was laying there, Adam came running in and said 'The Red-Coats are coming! The Red-Coats are coming!' The poor sick man raised up and called for mercy. The Doctor hid under the porch, but it was only one of the neighbors that had a reddish-brown coat."

Like nearly everyone in the region, the Mendenhalls had heard all the horror stories about British and German depredations and worried the same thing would happen to them if they were found harboring a wounded American. "Finding that the Captain couldn't ride," continued Phebe, "Father geared up a great black horse we had, a noble fellow, to the carriage, and they took him to the Black Horse [Tavern near Chester]. . . . Oh! How glad I was to see father come home. . . . He had just put the horse away, when the English came, sure enough, but they didn't come to the house. We were so afraid while Father was away, but he wasn't gone long. I remember when I saw him coming

---

8   Thomas P. Cope, *Philadelphia Merchant: The Diary of Thomas P. Cope, 1800-1851*, Eliza Cope Harrison, ed. (South Bend, IN, 1978), 401-402.

I couldn't think what made the gears all white, but it was the foam" from the overheated horse.[9]

The Armies in the Aftermath

While the civilian population dealt with the fallout of the battle and the politicians attempted to wrap their heads around what had just occurred and whether Philadelphia had been lost, Washington set about regrouping his army. Within a few days nearly 11,000 soldiers were once again present in camp for duty. Few of them were militia, however, for once the battle was over most of them had taken to their heels and deserted en masse.

The performance of the militia from the beginning of the campaign through the battle disgusted Timothy Pickering. "How amazing, that Howe should march from the Head of Elk to the Schuylkill, a space of sixty miles, without opposition from the people of the country, except a small band of militia just around Elk!" wrote Washington's adjutant general. "Such events would not have happened in New England." John Armstrong, who commanded Washington's militia at the battle of the Brandywine, generally agreed with Pickering's assessment: "[M]any, too many" of the militia were a "Scandle to the military profession, a nuisance in service & a dead weight on the publick." However, Armstrong also believed the general condemnation of the militia was in some ways unfair. He argued against what he called the "disagreeable doctrine of comparison" with the Continental Line, which to Armstrong was a patently unfair measure of competence. He also claimed that many people judged the militia "from a single action, [and] still worse . . . brand the whole with the infamous conduct of only a part."[10]

Despite the sweeping extent of his victory, Geneal Howe did little in its immediate aftermath to complicate Washington's task of withdrawal and reorganization. Instead of launching a vigorous pursuit, Howe kept his army on or near the battlefield outside Dilworth until September 15, using the George Gilpin homestead as his headquarters. The Brigade of Guards camped in the vicinity of the Ring house (Washington's former headquarters) on the night of

9   McGuire, *Philadelphia Campaign*, vol. 1, 265-266. The website McGuire cited as the source of the story was no longer available.

10   Pickering, *Life of Pickering*, vol. 1, 164; Hazard, et al, eds., *Pennsylvania Archives*, Series 1, vol. 6, 100-101.

the battle, and the next day marched the short distance east to the vicinity of Dilworth.[11]

Given the nature of the marching that preceded the combat, followed by the fighting and extent of his casualties, Howe's army was exhausted, unorganized, and needed rest. "The fatigues of this Day were excessive," confirmed Lt. Loftus Cliffe of the 46th Regiment of Foot. "If you knew the weight a poor soldier carries, the length of time he is obliged to be on foot for a train of Artillery to move 17 Miles, the Duties he goes thro when near an Enemy & that the whole night of the 9th we were marching, you would say we had done our duty on the 11th."[12]

Howe also had other matters of import to address, including attending to the wounded and burying the dead. A bridgehead had to be established at Wilmington, Delaware, in order to evacuate the injured, seriously ill, and the gathered provisions. Because he did not have enough wagons to do it all simultaneously, he spent five days evacuating his wounded to Wilmington, where the men were taken aboard Admiral Howe's waiting ships. The dearth of sufficient wagons, coupled with a paucity of healthy horses, hampered his operational ability.[13]

The Impact on Local Civilians

This prolonged British occupation of the region had a devastating effect on the civilian population. The troops took whatever they wanted, and most of them did so with reckless abandon. Food and livestock were stolen, as were bed linens and all other types of cloth for bandages. Crops the families needed to survive the oncoming winter months were destroyed, consumed, or confiscated. Fences were used as firewood and furniture was broken up for kindling. The men also took personal items like watches, books, jewelry, and guns. Even the vegetation had suffered: just three years later, the Marquis de Chastellux visited the battlefield with Lafayette and noted that "the fire must

---

11 This is not the same Gideon Gilpin House at which Lafayette supposedly stayed. This Gilpin home belonged to a relative of Gideon's. George Gilpin built the two-story brick home in 1754 on the original Gilpin family tract, which was located near where the fighting ended. Robertson, Manuscript Map.

12 Cliffe to brother Jack, October 24, 1777, Loftus Cliffe Papers.

13 Spring, *With Zeal*, 269.

have been very severe, for most of the trees bear the mark of bullets or cannon shot."[14]

Quaker Joseph Townsend left a detailed description of the destruction suffered by many farms in the area:

> We had a full opportunity of beholding the destruction and wanton waste committed on the property of the peaceable inhabitants of the neighborhood, and on the ground of encampment. Those who were obliged to remain had their stock of cattle destroyed for the use of the army—their houses taken away, and their household furniture, bedding, etc., wantonly wasted and burned. It was not uncommon to see heaps of feathers lying about the farms, the ticks having been stripped off and made use of, and the remains or small pieces of valuable furniture which lay about their fire places in the fields unconsumed, when there was no want of timber and fence rails that might have been used for their cooking. Being in an enemy's country, inhabited by rebels, there was no restraint on the soldiery or rabble who accompanied them.[15]

Sarah Frazer's homestead suffered a similar fate the day after the battle when the British discovered it belonged to her father Persifor, an American officer who had fought in the battle. A British foraging party, recalled Sarah's older sister Sally, "had got at the liquor and were drunk—the officers were obliged to drive them off with their swords." The British officer in charge "had understood the house was full of arms and ammunition [and] asked me to open the door leading up stairs." When Sally's mother denied knowing about any ammunition being in the house, the officer "opened up the case of the clock hoping to find money; he found an old musket with the lock broken off, this he jammed up into the works and broke them to pieces. . . . He then told me to show him every thing that belonged to me and that it should not be touched,

---

14 Years later, 379 farmers and other citizens of Chester County filed damage claims for reparations. Smith, Brandywine, 23. Some of the claims filed read as follows: Joseph Dilworth of Birmingham Township: 100 bushels of wheat, 18 sheep, 800 pounds of cheese, 25 yards linen, 1 beaver hatt, and 2 gallons of peach brandy; William Harvey of Birmingham Township: 2 Milch Cows, 6 Yearling Cattle, 22 Sheep, 130 Bushels of wheat, 1 copper coffee pot, and 16 tons of hay; Charles Dilworth of Birmingham Township: 2 beef cattle, 2 heifers, 2 horse colts, 24 large fat hogs, 45 pigs, 10 sheep, wheat, hay. Accounts of property taken and destroyed by the British Army under the command of General Howe, located in the Chester County Historical Society, West Chester, PA; Marquis de Chastellux, *Travels in North America in the Years 1780, 1781 and 1782 by the Marquis de Chastellux*, ed. Howard C. Rice (Chapel Hill, NC, 1963), vol. 1, 152.

15 Townsend, *Some Account*, 28-29.

which I did. . . . When he saw the [Continental Army] baggage which was packed in chests and ammunition boxes, turning to me, he said, 'you told me there was no ammunition,' and breaking them open found only the soldiers clothes. Now it became a scene of pillage and confusion—they plundered the house—what they could not carry away they destroyed: took the beautiful swords worn by officers on parade, carried off the clothes, one man put on five shirts."[16]

Howe tried to curtail the plundering when it got out of hand. According to Capt.-Lt. John Peebles of the British grenadiers, "A Light Infantry man of the 5th & a Grenadier of the 28th were executed today at 11 o'clock in front of the 1st Grenadiers for mauroding, The 1st. Examples made, tho often threaten'd, & many deserved it." The German troops were as bad or worse than their British allies. General Knyphausen complained that from the time the new Hessian recruits arrived that spring, pilfering within the regiments and plundering outside of them was essentially impossible to restrain. The effect of the fighting was bad enough, but it took years for the locals to recover from the occupation.[17]

After the British moved on, the locals were left with a host of gruesome responsibilities. "The ground which they had lately occupied at Birmingham exhibited a scene of destruction and waste," recorded Joseph Townsend. "Some few of the inhabitants who remained, and some others who were returning to their places of abode, found it necessary to call in the assistance of their neighbors, to re-bury many of the dead who lay exposed to the open air, having been washed bare, and some few of them had never been interred."[18]

The Fate of the Wounded

Despite being driven from the battlefield, the Americans somehow managed to carry off many of their wounded. The suffering men were dispersed to every point of the compass. Many were sent to Trenton, but several towns received the injured including Reading, Philadelphia, Northampton, Burlington, Easton, Allentown, Ephrata, and Bethlehem. Others ended up in

16 Frazer, *Memoir*, 159.

17 Peebles, *Peebles' American War*, 134; Lowell, *The Hessians*, 38.

18 Townsend, *Some Account*, 28-29.

smaller local settlements, such as Trappe, Hanover, Skippack, Evansburgh, Lancaster, Falkner's Swamp, and Pennypackers' Mill, and still more in Yellow Springs, the site of a mineral springs Pennsylvanians had been visiting for years. General Lafayette was initially conveyed by barge from Chester to Philadelphia, where he rested at the Indian Queen Tavern before being taken in a carriage to Bethlehem where his lengthy recovery began. Dr. John Cochran opened a small hospital at his home, Hope Lodge, in an effort to treat the large numbers of wounded.[19]

Handling battlefield casualties quickly and in an organized manner is a modern achievement still being improved upon. In the late eighteenth century, finding treatment was as much a matter of luck as anything else. Prompt medical care eluded Maj. Joseph Bloomfield of the 3rd New Jersey Regiment, who was forced to ride unescorted for two miles with a musket ball lodged in his arm. Luckily for him, he encountered "a stranger who dressed my wound . . . and wrapped my arm in a handkerchief." With his limb swelling and painful, Bloomfield continued another seven painful miles to Chester, in search of a doctor. It was not until he reached Trenton on September 13 ("53 hours after I was wounded. 20 hours of which it bled") that he found an army surgeon who could treat his injury.[20]

The many hundreds of American, British, and Hessian wounded who lay scattered across several miles of Pennsylvania countryside also needed medical attention. Quaker Joseph Townsend left an invaluable description of the medical scene he witnessed at Birmingham Meetinghouse on the night of the battle:

When the engagement appeared to be nearly over and the day being on the decline, I proposed to some of my companions that we should go over to the field of battle and take a view of the dead and wounded, as we might never have such another opportunity. We hastened thither and awful was the scene to behold—such a number of fellow beings lying together severely wounded, and some mortally a few dead, but a small proportion of them considering the immense quantity of powder and ball that had been discharged. Some of the doors of the meeting house were torn off and the wounded carried thereon into the house to be occupied for an hospital. After assisting

19 Richard L. Blanco, *Physician of the American Revolution: Jonathan Potts* (New York, 1979), 163; Chadwick, *Washington's War*, 234-235; Reed, *Campaign to Valley Forge*, 144.

20 Blanco, *Physician of the Revolution*, 163.

in carrying two of them into the house I was disposed to see an operation performed by one of the surgeons, who was preparing to amputate a limb by having a brass clamp or screw fitted thereon, a little above the knee joint, he had his knife in his hand, the blade of which was of a circular form, and was about to make an incision when he recollected that it might be necessary for the wounded man to take something to support him during the operation. The man then informed the surgeon, 'No doctor, it is not necessary, my spirits are up enough without it'. . . . As I was listening to the conversation one of my companions caught me by the arm and mentioned that it was necessary to go out immediately, as they were fixing the picquet guards, and if we did not get away in a few minutes we should have to remain within the lines during the night. I instantly complied.[21]

Outside, Townsend saw "fields in front of us containing great heaps of blankets . . . baggage and provision wagons, arms and ammunition, together with a host of plunderers and rabble that accompanied the army. Almost the whole face of the country around appeared to be covered and alive with those objects."[22]

No stranger to overseeing sizeable battles, Howe knew that faster care for his wounded increased the likelihood of their recovery. The logistics behind their collection was key. "A small party," he ordered on the night of the Brandywine combat, "with a Surgeon's Mate and Waggon from each Corps, to be sent off by day-break in the morning, to Pick up their Wounded in the Woods and bring them to the General Hospital at Dilworth." The "General Hospital" was the inn at Dilworth, which was transformed into a medical facility. Howe also ordered four women from each British brigade be sent to the Dilworth hospital to tend the wounded, and for the surgeons there to use them accordingly. According to British Capt. John Andre, "Parties were sent from the different Regiments to find their wounded in the woods and bury their dead." Another British officer wrote much the same thing, if in less eloquent language, on the day after the fighting: "Orders wuss given for to Revew the ground to Berrie the dead and the surgeons to attend the Wounded."[23]

Because so many American wounded remained on the battlefield, the day after the battle Howe requested assistance from Washington's surgeons. "The

---

21 Townsend, *Some Account*, 26.

22 Ibid., 25.

23 Kemble, *Journals*, 492, 493; Andre, *Journal*, 47; Captured British Officer's Accounts Ledger.

Number of wounded Officers and Men of your Army in this Neighbourhood, to whom every possible Attention has been paid," explained the British commander, "will nevertheless require your immediate Care, as I shall not be so situated as to give them the necessary Relief. Any Surgeons you may chuse to send to their Assistance upon Application to me, in consequence of your Orders, shall be permitted to attend them." Washington replied on September 13: "Agreeable to the permission you offer, I have directed the following Gentn—Doctrs Rush, Leiper & Latimer, and Mr. Willet, a Mate in the Hospital with their Attendants, to wait upon you, and to take them under their care. . . . I have thought proper to add Doctrs Way & Coats to the Surgeons above mentioned, that the Wounded may have the earliest relief." Captain Andre confirmed the consummation of the arrangement when he noted that "surgeons . . . from the rebel army" were allowed into British lines "to attend their wounded."[24]

One of the doctors Howe received personally at the George Gilpin house was Benjamin Rush, whose presence within the British lines raises interesting questions. As a signer of the Declaration of Independence, Howe could have hanged him as a traitor. Ironically, Rush was nearly taken prisoner on the night of the battle while caring for American wounded "in the rear at the battle of Brandywine." It was his "delay in helping off the wounded" that nearly resulted in his capture. A few days after the battle, Rush described his experience behind enemy lines to help the American wounded:

> Here I saw and was introduced to a number of British officers. Several of them treated me with great politeness. I saw likewise within the British lines and conversed for some time with Jos. Galloway and several other American citizens who had joined the British army. While I was at my quarters, I was waited upon by Col. Mawhood, who said that he was deputed to convey to me the thanks of the officers of the 17th Regiment for my care of Capt. McPherson after the battle of Princeton. I was much struck in observing the difference between the discipline and order of the British and Americans. I lamented this upon my return. It gave offense and was ascribed to fear and to lack of attachment to the cause of my country.[25]

24 Chase and Lengel, eds., *Papers of Washington*, vol. 11, 208, 215; Andre, *Journal*, 47.

25 Benjamin Rush, *The Autobiography of Benjamin Rush: His "Travels Through Life" Together with His Commonplace Book for 1789-1813*, George W. Corner, ed. (Westport, CT, 1948), 132-133.

A modern view of the memorial stone to the battle dead buried at Birmingham Meetinghouse. *Author*

Rush also spoke with a British subaltern who, somewhat surprisingly, did not think very highly of his own comrades. This British soldier "observed to me that his soldiers were infants that required constant attendance, and said as a proof of it that although they had blankets tied to their backs, yet such was their laziness that they would sleep in the dew and cold without them rather than have the trouble of untying and opening them. He said his business every night before he slept was to see that no soldier in his company laid down without a blanket."[26]

Four days after the battle, on September 15, the American wounded were moved to what is today West Chester, where Rush and the other American surgeons continued to care for them. Many wounds turned out to be mortal. Gilbert Purdy, an officer serving with the British Corps of Pioneers, remembered receiving orders to assist in the burial of the dead and recalled burying 55, "[b]esides was Buryed By the rest of the Army." Within two short days of the fighting the corpses on the field were putrefying, and locals were hired (or in some cases, likely impressed) to dig the graves. "The peasants about

26 L. H. Butterfield, ed., *Letters of Benjamin Rush* (Princeton, NJ, 1951), vol. 1, 154-155.

A modern view of the memorial stone dedicated to the battle dead who are buried at Kennett Meetinghouse. *Author*

employed in burying the dead Rebels without our Centries," wrote Captain Montresor, "who have now become very offensive."[27]

Transitional Considerations

The day following the battle, Washington began issuing orders in Chester to begin the reassembling of his army. Among other things, he ordered: "The commanding officer of each brigade is immediately to send off as many officers as he shall think necessary on the roads leading to the places of action yesterday, and on any other roads where stragglers may be found; particularly to Wilmington, where 'tis said, many have retired, to pick up all the stragglers from the army, and bring them on. In doing this, they will proceed as far, towards the enemy, as shall be consistent with their own safety, and examine every house." In addition to sending all the wounded who could be moved, together with the sick, to Trenton, Washington also ordered up a gill of rum or whiskey to every

27 Smith, *Brandywine*, 24; Gilbert Purdy diary, original located in the Canadian Archives, Item MG23-B14, vol. 1; Montresor, "Journals," 451.

man in the ranks. Washington also needed to know the extent of his losses, and make sure his commands were ready to fight again, and quickly. To that end, he directed each "Brigadier, or officer commanding a brigade will immediately make the most exact returns of their killed, wounded and missing. The officers are, without loss of time to see that their men are completed with ammunition; that their arms are in the best order, the inside of them washed clean and well dried; the touch-holes picked, and a good flint in each gun. . . . The commanding officer of each regiment is to endeavour to procure such necessaries, as are wanting, for his men."[28]

After dispatching these orders, Washington put the American army back on the road. He needed to find fresh defensive ground to meet Howe. The Continentals fell back from Chester through Darby, and marched on to the floating bridge at the Middle Ferry on the Schuylkill River (modern-day Chestnut Street), where it crossed. The marchers bypassed Philadelphia and moved to the Falls of the Schuylkill at East Falls, about five miles from the Middle Ferry in the vicinity of Germantown. He completed the entire move in a single day.

From Darby, Washington wrote to Brig. Gen. William Smallwood, who was gathering the Maryland militia around Oxford Meeting in southern Chester County. "It appears to me, that the Forces under your command, cannot be employed to so much advantage in any way, as by falling on the Enemy's Rear and attacking them as often as possible. I am persuaded many advantages will result from this measure," explained Washington. "It will greatly retard their march and give us time, and will also oblige them, either to keep a string guard with their Sick and Wounded, with which they must now be much incumbered, or to send them back to their Shipping under a escort, which you will have an opportunity of attacking with a good prospect of Success." The set piece battle at Brandywine excepted, Washington's strategy of harassing Howe's army continued.[29]

Washington's primary concern, and one that led him to risk his army along the Brandywine, was protecting Philadelphia. There was now just one natural barrier, the Schuylkill River, remaining between the city and Howe's victorious army. Although swift-flowing, the Schuylkill was fairly shallow in the eighteenth

---

28 Fitzpatrick, ed. *Writings of Washington*, vol. 9, 209-210.

29 Ibid., 210.

century. The Falls of the Schuylkill were comprised of rapids that passed through large boulders where the river dropped some 30 feet. Except for a floating bridge, there were no permanent bridges spanning the river. However, Philadelphia was accessible at the Upper, Middle, and Lower ferries, and several fords were present farther upriver.[30]

Most of the fords on the Schuylkill were winding, narrow affairs that snaked across a gravelly river bottom and used islands or mud flats to span the river. Those fords would play a role in the future campaign included Levering's, Matson's, Swedes', and Fatland's. High hills surround the Schuylkill along much of its course, and many of the ford roads meandered down steep inclines. Any army crossing the river in this manner would find itself vulnerable against a well-positioned and alert opponent. The hills around Swedes Ford, however, were more gradual and the ford itself was located in a wide and shallow valley where the river bottom was hard and stony—all of which in turn provided more space for a large force to maneuver and better protect itself. Much as it was along the Brandywine River, all of the fords and ferries along the Schuylkill River would need to be defended if Philadelphia was to remain in American hands.[31]

Washington faced a difficult decision as he moved his army into the Germantown area. Philadelphia sits at the tip of a peninsula bordered on the east by the Delaware River and on the west by the Schuylkill River. Washington needed to defend the capital, but he could not afford to leave his supply depots at Reading and other places to the west unprotected. A move northwest to protect Reading would expose the city, while positioning his army to fight for the capital exposed his supply depots. Washington knew Philadelphia was difficult to defend, and once he lost at the Brandywine it was nearly impossible.

---

30 McGuire, *Philadelphia Campaign*, vol. 1, 273-274. The rapids no longer exist because dams were built that raised the water level. The Lower Ferry, also known as Gray's Ferry, was located where Gray's Ferry Avenue Bridge crosses the river today, between South Philadelphia and Southwest Philadelphia. The Middle Ferry was located between the modern Market Street and Chestnut Street Bridges, near 30th Street. The Upper Ferry was located within the bounds of modern-day Fairmount Park, near the Philadelphia Art Museum and the Spring Garden Street Bridge.

31 Ibid., 274. Levering's Ford is in modern-day Manayunk, just below the big concrete arch bridge. Matson's Ford is in modern-day Conshohocken, just north of the Fayette Street Bridge. Fatland Ford is in modern-day Valley Forge National Historic Park, behind where the chapel stands today. Swedes Ford is in what is Norristown today, just below the Route 202 bridge.

He may have already made the decision to protect his storehouses to the detriment of the American capital.[32]

Panic, meanwhile, gripped Philadelphia. Many of its citizens had already fled, while others prepared for the worse (or, if their loyalties were elsewhere, rejoiced quietly as Howe's army approached). When General Sullivan supposedly found documents in northern New Jersey claiming Quakers were plotting to aid the British, a number of that sect were arrested earlier in the month and confined in the city's Masonic Lodge. With the combat at Brandywine concluded, they were released and sent away. Even though no formal charges were filed, Congress decided to remove these prominent Quakers from the capital.[33]

While Washington continued retreating on September 12 toward Germantown, parts of Howe's army crept after him. General James Grant with the 1st and 2nd British Brigades, a squadron of dragoons, and the Queen's Rangers led a reinforced scouting expedition two miles east of the battlefield to Concord Meeting to search for Washington's army and round up stragglers. British horseflesh was still in deplorable condition. Phebe Mendenhall watched the British approach her family farm near Concord and later recalled that Grant's troops "had the poorest little horses to pull their big guns, they couldn't pull them up the big hill by the barn."[34]

Other troops dispersed to find food or continued helping the wounded. Carl von Baurmeister remembered burying the dead that day and moving wounded to Dilworth, "where we found a flour magazine, from which the army was provisioned for two days." Later in the afternoon, elements of the light dragoons and the fresh and relatively unbloodied 71st Highlanders were sent 10 miles beyond Dilworth to Wilmington to secure the town to help establish a rendezvous with the fleet. A general hospital was also established in Wilmington, where many troops injured along the Brandywine were eventually dispatched.[35]

Members of the 71st Highlanders promptly arrested John McKinley, the president of Delaware, upon entering Wilmington. According to McKinley, he

32 Pancake, *1777*, 174.

33 Muhlenberg, *Journals*, vol. 3, 74; McGuire, *Philadelphia Campaign*, vol. 1, 272-273.

34 McGuire, *Philadelphia Campaign*, vol. 1, 264-265.

35 Von Baurmeister, "Letters of Baurmeister," 409.

remained behind because he was "more solicitous to perform my Duty, than for my own personal Safety." The few American militia still in Wilmington's defensive works fled when they spotted the approaching Highlanders. In addition to the capture of McKinley, they also seized seven artillery pieces. With Wilmington secured as a base of operations for the Royal Navy, Admiral Howe assured his brother "that he would have several ships at Wilmington on September 15th at the latest."[36]

Other than these movements, Howe's army remained idle on September 12. If the British general had aggressively pursued Washington's beaten army, he may have been able to maintain the initiative, forced additional fighting on his terms, and crushed or otherwise further dispersed the Americans. He could also have crossed the Schuylkill River's upper fords, as he would later do, and by doing so cut off Washington's troops from their critical Reading depot. The last issue was especially important to Howe, who had earlier stated that capturing the patriot storehouses was one of the goals of his 1777 campaign. Thomas Paine, the author of *Common Sense*, wrote to Benjamin Franklin that "the enemy's not moving must be attributed to the disability they sustained, and the burthen of their wounded. They move exceedingly cautious on new ground," he continued, "and are exceedingly suspicious of villages and towns, and are more perplexed at seemingly little things which they cannot clearly understand than at great ones which they are fully acquainted with." What Paine leaves unwritten was that Howe had a record of unenthusiastic follow-through in the aftermath of planning and waging successful battles. His army was also much more badly injured than many understood at the time, something Howe would only fully discover in the days immediately following the September 11 combat.[37]

With immediate matters in hand and having withdrawn far enough beyond Howe's immediate range, Washington congratulated his army for its performance along the Brandywine two days after the battle. "The General, with peculiar satisfaction," announced Washington in a set of general orders, "thanks those gallant officers and soldiers, who, on the 11th. instant, bravely fought in their country and its cause." Although the battle, "from some

---

36 Delaware Archives: *Revolutionary War* (Wilmington, DE, 1919), vol. 3, 1,416; Reed, *Campaign to Valley Forge*, 145; Von Baurmeister, "Letters," 409.

37 Reed, *Campaign to Valley Forge*, 143; "Military Operations near Philadelphia in the Campaign of 1777-8," *The Pennsylvania Magazine of History and Biography* (Philadelphia, 1878), vol. 2, 283.

unfortunate circumstances, was not so favorable as could be wished," he continued, "the General has the satisfaction of assuring the troops, that from every account he has been able to obtain, the enemy's loss greatly exceeded ours; and he has full confidence that in another Appeal to Heaven (with the blessing of providence, which it becomes every officer and soldier humbly to supplicate), we shall prove successful." Once the orders were read to the troops, the more practical business at hand resumed, with militia elements constructing redoubts above the Schuylkill River fords and other units drilling and reorganizing their ranks.[38]

Howe, meanwhile, continued shifting his army about the vicinity of the Brandywine battlefield. Lord Cornwallis took the British light infantry and British grenadiers and joined Grant in the vicinity of Concord before marching to the heights at Aston within five miles of Chester. A few patrols probed to the outskirts of Chester without opposition. According to an unidentified officer serving in the 2nd Light Infantry Battalion, his unit spent September 13 marching "to Chester and on the Roade fell in With Several Out houses and Barns full of Wounded men Who tould us that If We keep on that Night We Should have put a total End to the Rebelion." Howe also dealt with his sharpshooters. With Patrick Ferguson disabled, he ordered his riflemen to rejoin their respective light companies.[39]

The Next Campaign Begins

On September 14, most of Washington's army left the Germantown area, marched down Ridge Road, crossed the Schuylkill at Levering's Ford, and moved to the Old Lancaster or Conestoga Road (modern-day U.S. Route 30). The army camped across a wide area from near modern Radnor at the Widow Miller's Tavern to Merion Meeting. Washington established his headquarters at the Buck Tavern.

Timothy Pickering was not happy with the manner in which the army crossed the Schuylkill into Chester County. "We lost here much time, by reason of men's stripping off their stockings and shoes, and some of them their breeches," complained Washington's aide. "It was a pleasant day, and, had the

38 Fitzpatrick, ed. *Writings of Washington*, vol. 9, 211.

39 McGuire, *Philadelphia Campaign*, vol. 1, 279; Captured British Officer's Accounts Ledger; Bailey, *British Military Rifles*, 51. See Appendix E regarding the Rifles' future disposition.

men marched directly over by platoons without stripping, no harm could have ensued, their cloaths would have dried by night on their march, and the bottom would not have hurt their feet. The officers, too, discovered a delicacy quite unbecoming soldiers; quitting their platoons, & some getting horses of their acquaintances to ride over, and others getting over in a canoe. They would have better done their duty had they kept to their platoons and led in their men." The delay, believed Pickering, potentially imperiled the army.[40]

Washington was not ready for another battle, but Anthony Wayne certainly was. The ever-combative commander worried that Howe's army would recover from the blow it had suffered at the Brandywine because Washington was leaving him to lick his wounds rather than inflicting new ones. To Thomas Mifflin, the army's quartermaster general, Wayne argued that Howe might "steal a March and pass the fords in the Vicinity of the Falls, unless we Immediately March down and Give them Battle." In search of a satisfactory answer, Wayne figuratively urged Howe, "[C]ome then and push the Matter and take your fate."[41]

In an effort to better defend Philadelphia, Washington ordered the Middle Bridge removed and sent French engineer Col. Louis Le Begue de Presle du Portail to Gen. Armstrong of the Pennsylvania militia with orders to fortify Swedes' Ford with a redoubt and heavy cannon. "As it is not expected that these Works will have occasion to stand a long defence," explained Washington, "they should be as such as can with the least labour & in the shortest time be completed, only that part of them which is opposed to cannon, need be of any considerable thickness & the whole of them should be rather calculated for Dispatch than any unnecessary Decorations or Regularity which Engineers are frequently too fond of." The redoubt eventually constructed was the only earthwork built west of Philadelphia for defense.[42]

Desperate for reinforcements, the American commander ordered Alexander McDougall's Connecticut brigade down from the Hudson Highlands. William Smallwood was with the Maryland militia at Oxford Meeting in southern Chester County, which meant he had 1,400 half-armed poorly trained men with no artillery, little ammunition, and almost no supplies.

---

40 Pickering, *Life of Pickering*, vol. 1, 158-159.

41 Anthony Wayne to Thomas Mifflin, September 15, 1777, Anthony Wayne Papers, vol. 4.

42 Chase and Lengel, eds., *Papers of Washington*, vol. 11, 224.

Although Smallwood's men were in Howe's rear, they were unreliable and would be of little use. "The Condition of my Troops, their Number, the State of their Arms, Discipline and Military Stores," Smallwood wrote Washington, "I am Apprehensive will not enable me to render that essential Service." Howe may "detach a Body of Infantry with their light Horse to Attack and disperse the Militia. . . . Your Excelly. is too well acquainted with Militia to place much Dependence in them when opposed to regular and veteran Troops, without Regular Forces to support them." Harassing the British, one of Washington's favorite tactics, was simply beyond the capabilities of the Maryland militia.[43]

The American army suffered another blow on September 14 when Congress voted to recall General Sullivan pending an inquiry into his actions on Staten Island and Brandywine. French General de Borre resigned that same day. Washington's entreaties delayed Sullivan's recall. "Our Situation at this time is critical and delicate," he pleaded with the politicians. "[T]o derange the Army by withdrawing so many General Officers from it, may and must be attended with many disagreeable, if not ruinous, Consequences." Washington's optimism returned when he penned a letter to General Heath that same day: "Our troops have not lost their spirits, and I am in hopes we shall soon have an opportunity of compensating for the disaster we have sustained."[44]

While Washington was attempting to keep his generals together and defend Philadelphia, Hessian troops under Col. Johann von Loos, which included the combined Hessian battalion, escorted the sick and wounded from the Brandywine to Wilmington. The shuffling column included 350 American prisoners. According to James Parker, they "consisted of 134 Irish immigrants, 65 English immigrants, 16 German immigrants, 9 Scots, 3 Italians, 1 Swiss, 1 Russian, 1 Gernsey, 3 French, and 82 'Americans.'"[45]

On September 15, Washington moved his army down the Lancaster Road another 12 miles (to what is today modern Malvern and Frazer). Washington made his headquarters in the Malin House at the intersection of the Swedes Ford Road and Lancaster Road. Advance parties of the army were situated three miles farther west in the vicinity of the White Horse Tavern (modern Malvern). With its rear stretching back to the General Paoli Tavern in

43 Reed, *Campaign to Valley Forge*, 148; Chase and Lengel, eds., *Papers of Washington*, vol. 11, 241.

44 Fitzpatrick, ed., *Writings of Washington*, vol. 9, 227-278; Chase and Lengel, eds., *Papers of Washington*, vol. 11, 227.

45 James Parker, journal, no date but entered at end of October 1777, Parker Family Papers.

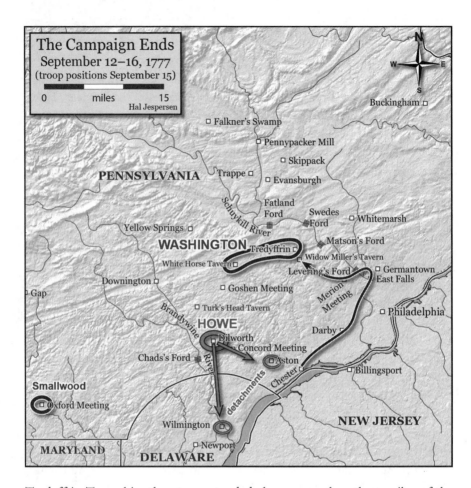

The Campaign Ends
September 12–16, 1777
(troop positions September 15)

0   miles   15
Hal Jespersen

Tredyffrin Township, the army extended along more than three miles of the Lancaster Road. With this move, Washington was now in a position to block an enemy advance toward the Schuylkill in the Great Valley. This new location, however, did not protect Philadelphia along the Delaware River. Captain Alexander of the Continental frigate *Delaware*, anchored off Billingsport, believed 100 men could capture the place, which highlighted the river's continued vulnerability to British warships. Washington, however, thought otherwise. He wanted to improve the defenses along the Delaware, but believed that "if we should be able to oppose Genl Howe with success in the Feild, the Works will be unnecessary."[46]

46 Jackson, *Pennsylvania Navy*, 121; Chase and Lengel, eds., *Papers of Washington*, vol. 11, 213.

That same evening of September 15, Howe issued orders that would send his army marching the next morning into the Great Valley. The next day, Cornwallis would leave the vicinity of Chester for a rendezvous with the main army while the Hessian von Mirbach battalion moved to Wilmington. Cornwallis marched up the Edgemont Road to Goshen Meeting to rejoin Howe, who then proceeded in the direction of the White Horse Tavern. That same morning, Washington's men began marching down the Lancaster Road to ascend the South Valley Hill and block Howe from the Schuylkill River.[47]

Once again the two armies were on a collision course, and only five days after what would be the largest battle of the Revolutionary War. The Brandywine campaign had ended. The final phase of the 1777 campaign to seize the American capital of Philadelphia was underway.

---

47 Reed, *Campaign to Valley Forge*, 145.

Epilogue

Brandywine Considered

"Certainly no General ever planned his battles more judiciously [than Washington].
But if deranged during the course of the action, if any member of his plan
was dislocated by sudden circumstances, he was slow in readjustment.
The consequence was, that he often failed in the field."[1]

— Thomas Jefferson, January 2, 1814

George Washington's retreat from the battlefield did not end
the fighting for the city of Philadelphia, but the battle
along the Brandywine would prove to be the major engagement of the 1777
Philadelphia Campaign.

Fifteen days after the September 11 engagement, Lt. Gen. Sir William
Howe marched his large and victorious army into the colonial capital. His
triumphant arrival, which was greeted with glee by Loyalists and dread by
independence-seekers, began an occupation that would end nine long months
later. A series of complicated maneuvers, skirmishes, and engagements would
mark the final months of 1777, and end with the armies going into winter
quarters.

What did the fighting and bloodshed waged in the rolling hills of the
Brandywine River valley mean to the cause of American independence?

---

1 Thomas Jefferson, *Writings*, ed. Merrill D. Peterson (New York, 1984), 1318.

Contemporary Views

The men who participated in the battle and those who simply lived during that time left a variety of opinions in the immediate aftermath of the fighting. Despite losing the battle, many American officers remained optimistic. Lieutenant Henry Livingston of Washington's Life Guard thought the battle was "the most unlucky affair that general Howe has ever encountered on this continent. . . . I was myself a witness to the havock which general Maxwell made among them in the morning, being directly on the opposite side of the Brandywine. Had it not been for the incongruous information which general Washington received concerning the movement of the enemy's main body to our right; had we been apprized of it in time to bring up our whole army, and form," he concluded, "I believe, in my soul, that day would have put an end to the British army in America."[2]

"Notwithstanding we gave the Enemy the ground," wrote Gen. Nathanael Greene, "the purchase has been at much blood, this being by far the greatest loss they have met with since the commencement of the War. From the circumstances and from several accounts of people that has seen the field of action," Greene continued, "there must have been a terrible carnage among his [Howe's] troops. I expect the next action to ruin Mr. How totally." General Weedon agreed with Greene's assessment when he penned, "Such another victory would establish the Rights of America and I wish them the honor of the Field again on the same terms."[3]

Major William Willcox, an aide to Lord Stirling, believed that "the victory was ours, and the ground the enemy's." "Our people behaved well," Henry Knox wrote to his wife, "but Heaven frowned upon us in a degree. We were obliged to retire after a very considerable slaughter of the enemy; they dared not pursue a single step." Lieutenant Samuel Shaw of Proctor's Artillery also remained positive, especially considering the pounding sustained by his unit. "Our troops, far from being discouraged, wish for nothing more ardently than another chance with the enemy," asserted the lieutenant. "It is now four o'clock in the afternoon, two days after the action, and no account of Howe's pursuing,

---

2 Letter reproduced in William S. Stryker, ed., *Documents Relating to the Revolutionary History of the State of New Jersey*, Vol. 1, *Extracts from American Newspapers 1776-1777* (Trenton, NJ, 1901), 483.

3 Showman, McCarthy, and Cobb, eds., *Papers of Greene*, vol. 2, 162; Weedon to Page, September 11, 1777.

or attempting to pursue, his advantage. It is not at all impossible that he received a severe blow, and that the victory he gained may be of that kind, of which it has been said, 'Another such, and I am ruined.'"[4]

A Delaware officer wrote just as optimistically: "Here then we experienced another drubbing. . . . But our army . . . wanting many things, also having a number of raw recruits, did, I think, as well as could be expected. . . . We had our solacing words always ready for each other—'Come boys, we shall do better another time.' . . . Had any man suggested, merely hinted the idea of giving up—of relinquishing further opposition—he would have been knocked down, and if killed it would have been no murder!"[5]

"The 11th of September last I was preparing dispatches for you when the report of cannon at Brandywine interrupted my proceedings," essayist Thomas Paine wrote in a letter to Benjamin Franklin. "The event of that day you have doubtless been informed of, which, excepting the enemy keeping the ground, may be deemed a drawn battle." Franklin would later pen one of the best-known (and prescient) conclusions of the campaign when he wrote, "Instead of Howe taking Philadelphia, Philadelphia has taken Howe."[6]

While a number of officers remained hopeful that overall strategic conditions would improve, several realized that tactical mistakes had been made on the 11th of September. Washington knew almost immediately what had gone wrong. "Unfortunately the intelligence received of the enemy's advancing up the Brandywine, and crossing at a ford about six miles above us, was uncertain and contradictory," he wrote Hancock, "notwithstanding all my pains to get the best." About a month after the battle, he expressed his sentiments again: "If the uncommon fogginess of the morning and the smoke had not hindered us from seeing our advantage, I am convinced it would have ended in a complete Victory . . . but we . . . [should] rejoice . . . that our Ranks are as full or rather fuller than they were before."[7]

4   "Papers Related to the Battle of Brandywine, 53; Noah Brooks, *Henry Knox: A Soldier of the Revolution* (New York, 1900), 104; Samuel Shaw, *The Journals of Major Samuel Shaw: The First American Consul at Canton*, ed. Josiah Quincy (Boston, 1847), 36.

5   Anderson, *Personal Recollections*, 37-8.

6   "Military Operations near Philadelphia," 283 ; Walter Isaacson, *Benjamin Franklin: An American Life* (New York, 2003), 342

7   Fitzpatrick, ed., *Writings of Washington*, Vol. 9, 207-8; Chase and Lengel, eds., *Papers of Washington*, Vol. 11, 479.

Congressman Thomas Burke, who was with the army that day, criticized the generals six days later: "I had an Opportunity of observing that our Troops and Inferior Officers are exceedingly good, but that our Major Generals (one only excepted) are totally inadequate. They were so disconcerted by the unexpected attack of the Enemy that they knew not what to do but to permit (some say to order), a precipitate retreat."[8]

One of the harshest critics of the army's performance was Timothy Pickering, Washington's own adjutant general. "I observed no original orders from the General [Washington]," Pickering claimed, "but that whatever orders were given, they appeared to be in answer to leading questions." Pickering later detailed three lessons from the battle. First, the ground should have been thoroughly scouted. The army was in place in plenty of time to have learned of all the fords and roads to the north. Next, quality maps of the potential battlefield should have been prepared. Lastly, men well acquainted with the region should have been procured ahead of time and "not be sought for just at the critical moment when you want them." Each of his conclusions can be read as a criticism of the army's commander.[9]

Baron Johann de Kalb, who had arrived in America with Lafayette, leveled this critique against Washington: "He is the most amiable, obliging, and civil man but, as a general, he is too slow, even indolent, much too weak, and is not without his portion of vanity and presumption." Perhaps Col. Aaron Ogden of the New Jersey Line offered the best summation of the general understanding of how the September 11 combat evolved as it did: "This battle, in all probability was lost and won by th[e] contrary intelligence."[10]

Any positive feelings Nathanael Greene had about the battle evaporated less than a year later in the summer of 1778 when he had an opportunity to read Washington's reports of the battle. "In the action of Brandywine last campaign, where I think both the general and the public were as much indebted to me for saving the army from ruin as they have ever been to any one officer in the course of the war," observed Greene, "but I was never mentioned upon the occasion." Greene offered a theory on why his name was so conspicuously absent: he had saved the army with a brigade that "happened to be all

8   Smith, et al., eds., *Letters of Delegates*, vol. 7, 680.

9   Hobson, ed., *Papers of Marshall*, vol. 10, 341; Pickering, *Life of Pickering*, Vol. 1, 160.

10 Chernow, *Washington*, 305-6; Aaron Ogden, *Autobiography of Col. Aaron Ogden, of Elizabethtown* (Paterson, NJ, 1893), 7.

Virginians. They being the general's countrymen, and I thought to be one of his favorites, prevented his ever mentioning a single circumstance of the affair."[11]

As the months and years slipped past, others waded into the controversy and passed judgment on Washington's military abilities. "Certainly no General ever planned his battles more judiciously," wrote Thomas Jefferson not long before his own death but many years after Washington had died. "But if deranged during the course of the action, if any member of his plan was dislocated by sudden circumstances, he was slow in readjustment. The consequence was that he often failed in the field."[12]

*   *   *

Many British and Hessian officers expressed praise for the Continental effort and Washington's management of the battle. Engineer John Montresor acknowledged the significance of the battle (but not that it was a grand British victory) when he stated, "[N]ow was [the Americans'] time for their utmost exertions as their liberties and the fate of America depended upon one general action." American disposition and use of terrain impressed grenadier John Peebles. The Continentals, he observed, were "drawn out & posted to the greatest advantage, on all the high grounds from the North side Shades's ford to the westwd. of Dilworth Village (a space of 4 miles)." British soldier Gilbert Purdy felt "the Rebels stood considerable a Smart Battle more than usual." Even William Howe's aide, Capt. von Muenchhausen, praised the American effort: "As far as I can tell, Washington executed a masterpiece of strategy today by sending columns from his right to his left wing in the beginning. . . . Soon after this Washington withdrew from his left wing. . . . All this was done with great speed and especially good order."[13]

An entry in the *Journal of the Hessian Grenadier Battalion von Minnigerode* gloated that General Washington had withdrawan out of the frying pan and into the fire: "They say that General Washington has retreated to Chester on the Delaware, and that when he reached there he was received in a very unfriendly

---

11 Showman, McCarthy, and Cobb, eds., *Papers of Greene*, Vol. 2, 471.

12 Jefferson, *Writings*, 1318.

13 Montresor, "Journals," 451; Peebles, *Peebles' American War*, 133-4; Purdy diary, original located in the Canadian Archives; Von Muenchhausen, *At General Howe's Side*, 31.

and grumpy manner by 7 frigates which had come from New York, that he was now placed in the greatest difficulties and did not know what to do next."[14]

Regardless of their impressions of the Continental Army and Washington, many British officers were impressed with Howe's strategy that day. Von Muenchhausen had nothing but praise for his commanding officer: "We all admire the strong and unexpected march of General Howe, and the special bravery, which the English showed in the battle, and I am convinced that everyone in Europe would admire General Howe if they were as familiar with all of the obstacles he faces, as we are."[15]

When the House of Commons was investigating Howe's conduct during his tenure in North America, a member posed this question to Gen. Charles Cornwallis: "Did your Lordship concur with Sir William Howe in the propriety of dividing the army, to bring the enemy to action at Brandywine?" Cornwallis's reply was unequivocal: "The manoeuvre that brought on the action of Brandywine certainly reflects the highest honour on the General." General Charles Grey was also questioned by Parliament and also defended Howe. When asked whether the division of the army before the enemy "was judicious and expedient?" Grey responded, "I think the division of the army before the battle of Brandywine was a masterly movement, deceived the enemy, and brought on the action with almost certainty of success." When Grey was asked, "Did you observe, that any advantage was lost, that might have been taken, in consequence of the battle?" Grey replied, "I know of none." General James Grant agreed with Cornwallis and Grey: "Genl. Howe surely deserves great Credit for the Move, his Disposition was masterly, & He executed his Plan with ability."[16]

However, some British officers believed Howe let an opportunity slip through his grasp. "Had General Howe set out two hours earlier, or marched faster," asserted Hessian officer Capt. Johann Ewald, "Washington's army would have been caught between two fires." Ewald continued: "[S]everal good friends from headquarters assured me that this mistake was caused by the guides, who had declared the route shorter than we found it to be." Ewald,

14 Journal of the Hessian Grenadier Battalion von Minnigerode, Microfiche 232, Hessian Documents of the American Revolution, Morristown National Historical Park, Morristown, NJ, copies from the David Library of the American Revolution, Washington Crossing, PA.

15 Von Muenchhausen, *At Howe's Side*, 32.

16 *Narrative of Howe*, 95-96; James Grant to Harvey, October 20, 1777, James Grant Papers.

however, thought otherwise: "I conclude that the slow march of the left column took place with all deliberation, so that the American army would not be destroyed to pay a fresh compliment to the Opposition Party, and to bring forth a new proposal." Ewald was referring to the Howe brothers' peace proposal to the Americans earlier in the war. The frustrated jaeger captain described the British army that night as "perfectly quiet, without a single man sent after the enemy and without any outposts—so quiet, in fact, that if Washington had been such a great man as they proclaimed him to be on the other side, and had returned during the night," he could have recovered everything lost that day.[17]

British officer George Duke agreed with Ewald that the long march earlier in the day prevented a proper pursuit. "We only wanted a few more hours of daylight; if we had, it's the general opinion the rebellion must have been over, for they were all dispersed, some run one way and some another."[18]

Howe's aide von Muenchhausen summed up the day. The complex flanking maneuver, he explained, "could not be carried out quickly enough to prevent our left wing from suffering somewhat initially, and for this reason the battle lasted longer than it should have." The aide concluded this "delay benefited Washington, who . . . could not be pursued by us because of darkness, and . . . his still fresh men, who knew the terrain very well, could have the same advantage they would have in daylight." The aide also complained that the British failed to use their artillery to proper advantage: "[W]e had 62 cannon . . . of which we used not even 20, nor were more than half our troops under fire."[19]

Reports in the British Press

On October 28, 1777, the *London Chronicle* published this brief initial report of the battle: "Accounts received yesterday by the way of France say, that there has been a general engagement between Washington and Gen. Howe, near Philadelphia. On the approach of the British army Gen. Washington called a council of war, whether they should defend their magazines, which was agreed to, the consequence of which was total defeat, with the loss of 2000 men killed and wounded, and all their magazines. About seven or eight hundred of the

17 Ewald, 87.

18 Duke, Brandywine British officer's letter.

19 Von Muenchhausen, *At Howe's Side*, 31-2.

British troops fell in the action. Policies were opened at Lloyd's to receive fifteen guineas to pay a hundred if the above is not true."[20] The account was generally, but not entirely, accurate: Washington did not lose his supply depots.

On November 15, 1777, the *London Chronicle* published an updated version of the battle: "11th of September, about five o'clock in the afternoon, having had several skirmishes with the enemy's out-posts in the course of the day, and the rebels were at last brought to a general action, which lasted till dark, when Washington, taking the advantage of the night, made a precipitate retreat, leaving behind all his cannon, baggage, and 1800 of their dead on the field." Washington, of course, did not lose his army's baggage or all his artillery.[21]

Thomas Paine's Take

At various times during the Revolution, an essay by the author of *Common Sense*, Thomas Paine, would appear in newspapers warning the public that despite the grave difficulties, the cause of liberty would prevail. Perhaps his most famous essay along these lines is the one he wrote when the Continental Army was disintegrating during its retreat across northern New Jersey in late 1776 just before Washington led it to victory at Trenton and Princeton. Now, in the aftermath of the battle of the Brandywine, Paine published his thoughts in *Crisis #4*. Excerpts are reproduced here at some length to provide the full intent and flavor of Paine's nose-thumbing:

> Those who expect to reap the blessings of freedom, must, like men, undergo the fatigues of supporting it. The event of yesterday was one of those kind of alarms which is just sufficient to rouse us to duty, without being of consequence enough to depress our fortitude. It is not a field of a few acres of ground, but a cause, that we are defending, and whether we defeat the enemy in one battle, or by degrees, the consequences will be the same. . . . Howe has been once on the banks of the Delaware, and from thence driven back with loss and disgrace: and why not be again driven from the Schuylkill? . . . Shall a band of ten or twelve thousand robbers, who are this day fifteen hundred or two thousand men less in strength than they were yesterday, conquer America, or subdue even a single state? The thing cannot be, unless we sit down and suffer them to do it. . . .

20 Reproduced in Todd Andrlik, *Reporting the Revolutionary War: Before it was History, it was News* (Naperville, IL, 2012), 224.

21 Reproduced in Ibid., 225.

It is distressing to see an enemy advancing into a country, but it is the only place in which we can beat them, and in which we have always beaten them, whenever they made the attempt. The nearer any disease approached to a crisis, the nearer it is to a cure. Danger and deliverance make their advances together, and it is only the last push, in which one or the other takes the lead.... Our army, though fatigued, is yet entire.... Our strength is yet reserved; and it is evident Howe does not think himself a gainer by the affair, or he would this morning have moved and attacked General Washington....

Our army must undoubtedly feel fatigue, and want a reinforcement of rest though not of valour. Our own interest and happiness call upon us to give them every support . . .

I close . . . with a short address to General Howe. You, sir, are only lingering out the period that shall bring with it your defeat. You have yet scarce began upon the war, and the further you enter, the faster will your troubles thicken. What you now enjoy is only a respite from ruin; an invitation to destruction; something that will lead on to our deliverance at your expense. We know the cause which we are engaged in, and though a passionate fondness for it may make us grieve at every injury which threatens it, yet, when the moment of concern is over, the determination to duty returns. We are not moved by the gloomy smile of a worthless king, but by the ardent glow of generous patriotism. We fight not to enslave, but to set a country free, and to make room upon the earth for honest men to live in. In such a case we are sure that we are right; and we leave to you the despairing reflection of being the tool of a miserable tyrant.[22]

Paine certainly had a talent for interpretation, and he put the best one possible on the outcome of the battle of the Brandywine.

The View of Historians

Historians have treated the battle of the Brandywine with a mixture of reverence, myth, and fact. Jacob Neff's 1845 history of the American military included this simplistic summary of the battle: "With . . . great disadvantage on the part of the Americans (who were also much inferior in numbers and in arms), the armies rushed together in fierce and desperate conflict."[23]

John Fiske's 1891 history of the American Revolution was a tip of the hat toward the Americans. "The poor organization of the American army was of

---

22 Thomas Paine, *Crisis #4,* available at www.thefederalistpapers.org/founders/paine/the-american-crisis-part-4-by-thomas-paine, accessed April 1, 2013.

23 Neff, *Army and Navy of America,* 336.

course well known to the British commanders, and they took advantage of the fact," claimed Fiske. "Had they been dealing with an organization as efficient as their own, their course would have been foolhardy. On the other hand, when we consider the relative strength of the two armies, it is clear that the bold move of Cornwallis ought not simply to have won the field of battle. It ought to have annihilated the American army, had not its worst consequences been averted by Washington's promptness, aided by Sullivan's obstinate bravery and Greene's masterly conduct of the retreat upon Dilworth."[24]

Smith Burnham took a bold patriot stance when he announced in 1918 that "The eleven thousand ragged farmers who tried to hold this field against the flower of the British army were the men who made this republic possible." The 150th anniversary of the battle in 1927 produced another light summary: "Although a defeat for the Americans it showed courage when one considers the Americans lacked arms and equipment and discipline."[25]

Troyer Steele Anderson's 1939 conclusion excuses Howe's generalship style and lack of pursuit: "His plan required the conservation of his army at all costs. If a safe opportunity to shatter Washington's army in battle did not appear, he felt he could cause its disintegration by the steady pressure of the campaign. Hence it was unnecessary to assume unusual risks in battle and, by contemporary standards, a continuation of the action at Brandywine after dark was certainly an unusual risk."[26]

Christopher Ward's 1952 history claims the British "came on with the arrogant assurance that marked the disciplined troops of that period of formal, dress-parade warfare." The Americans "had been as badly beaten as any army could be without being entirely destroyed, there had been no panic."[27]

More recent historians, all of whom have been frequently cited throughout this book, reached their own conclusions worthy of inclusion. John Reed summed up the battle of the Brandywine thusly: "Though Brandywine was admittedly an American defeat, it had stunned Howe by its fierceness, and gave the Americans spirit. Despite Charles Lee's often repeated conviction to the

---

24 John Fiske, *The American Revolution*, Vol. 1, 316.

25 Burnham, "Story of Brandywine," 42; MacElree, Heathcote, & Sanderson, "Battle of Brandywine," n.p.

26 Anderson, *Command of the Howe Brothers*, 288.

27 Ward, *War of the Revolution,* Vol. 1, 350-4.

contrary, American troops had proved that they could stand against British regulars in open fight."[28]

The Americans, argued John Pancake, had not suffered a major defeat: "Perhaps the best proof was the fact that within two days the army had pulled itself together, crossed the Schuylkill to Germantown, and stood once more between Howe and the capital, its commander ready for a fight." Gregory Edgar referenced Long Island in his battle summary: "The Battle of Brandywine had been reminiscent of the Battle of Long Island in that, once again, the lack of a mobile communications force had resulted in the Americans being surprised by a British flanking column. But, this time, they proved that they could stand and fight on open ground against European regulars. Though outflanked and outnumbered, the Continental Army resisted the urge to panic." Howe, Edgar added, "had won the battle, but the rebel army had survived to fight another day. He had not captured Philadelphia yet. A battle-tested, more confident army would oppose him in his next battle for the rebel capital."[29]

Finally, there is the summary offered by Bruce Mowday in his recent book. "Both the British and the Americans had their disappointments at Brandywine," he concluded. "Howe allowed the American army to escape and fight another day. Howe failed to rally the civilian population to the side of the British and his presence in Pennsylvania meant he couldn't aid Burgoyne's forces in New York. For Washington, he failed to secure credible information concerning the fords of the Brandywine and allowed Howe to flank his army and drive it from the field." Mowday went on to conclude that the "most important reason the Battle of Brandywine was crucial to the American cause for freedom was the confidence the American army received from standing up to the British army, one of the most professional in the world."[30]

Final Analysis

Everyone agrees Washington suffered a tactical defeat along the Brandywine. Despite having been defeated and outmaneuvered by Howe at least five times prior to September 1777 (Long Island, White Plains, Short Hills,

---

28 Reed, *Campaign to Valley Forge*, 140.

29 Pancake, *1777*, 174; Edgar, *The Philadelphia Campaign*, 39-40.

30 Mowday, *September 11, 1777*, 201-202.

Cooch's Bridge, and along Red Clay Creek), Washington was somehow unprepared for its use at the Brandywine. Howe's tactical success was more the result of Washington's failure to learn from his mistakes than his brilliance.

The young Continental Army that would mature that winter at Valley Forge fought remarkably well. Maxwell's newly formed light infantry brigade conducted the difficult delaying action during the morning as Washington requested. The three divisions that shifted to the right flank (Stephen, Lord Stirling, and Sullivan) quickly found good defensive ground on Birmingham Hill. They defended it well until Sullivan's command on the left under de Borre was caught by the British out of position (more by luck than design) and broken. Outmanned and then outflanked, the remaining defenders were driven away. That evening, Nathanael Greene's division outside Dilworth and Anthony Wayne's command on the American left stood against heavy numbers and held the roads to Chester open for the army. Given the circumstances, the Continentals did their job about as well as anyone could have expected.

The most obvious failure experienced by the American army was its intelligence-gathering operation by the light dragoons and militiamen, the lack of local scouts, and the interpretation of intelligence once it was received. Washington's inability to gather reliable information about the region in which he was operating haunted him all day. Knowledge of the fords and other terrain features could have made the difference. In this regard Washington failed the army; the army did not fail Washington. By contrast, despite operating in hostile territory, Howe's army succeeded in getting all the information it needed to achieve it main goal of flanking the American army and driving into its rear.

The veteran British and Hessian soldiers under Howe's command performed brilliantly—they did all that was asked of them. General Knyphausen's column created the diversion that confused Washington into thinking he was facing the entire British army opposite Chads's Ford. The men comprising Cornwallis's division not only completed a grueling flank march, but went on to fight and crush an American line holding a formidable position.

Any mistakes by Howe's men resulted from a lack of mounted troops. Effective mounted scouting at the end of the day, for example, would have prevented the 2nd Grenadier Battalion and Agnew's 4th British Brigade from marching into the metal cul-de-sac Greene had waiting for them outside Dilworth. The lack of light dragoons prevented Knyphausen from effectively pursuing the routed Continentals when darkness fell. Finally, the overall lack of pursuit that allowed Washington's army to escape virtually intact was the direct result of a lack of fast-moving cavalry.

*   *   *

The next several months would witness several actions large and small. After the aborted affair known as the Battle of the Clouds on September 16 and the small but bloody massacre at Paoli four days later, Howe marched his army into Philadelphia on September 26. Washington launched a daring attack at Germantown on October 4, but was beaten back. A series of engagements around Forts Mifflin and Mercer were initiated to open the Delaware River to British shipping. Washington lost the capital city, but his entire strategy that year was to block and defeat Howe if possible, but make sure the Continental Army lived to fight another day. In this he was successful. And in doing so, he further battle-tested his army and preserved it. That army, with the addition of French infantry and naval forces, would ultimately go on to win the war.

The war took what many consider a decisive turn that October when General Burgoyne's army marching south into New York from Canada was trapped and surrendered at Saratoga. The news convinced the French the American cause was indeed viable and they entered an alliance with the colonists. As far as Howe was concerned, the justification for not supporting Burgoyne was the importance and psychological impact of capturing Philadelphia. The inordinate amount of time it took to seize the city, and the circuitous route chosen to accomplish that feat, guaranteed there would be no support for Burgoyne. The important American supply centers at Reading, Lancaster, and York were never captured. Worst of all for the British, the promised uprising by Pennsylvania Loyalists never came to fruition.

After all that effort and bloodshed, Howe concluded the war could not be won as it was currently being waged and tendered his resignation that October with the explanation that his policies had not been sufficiently supported to warrant remaining in command. London accepted it the following April. Howe was replaced by Lt. Gen. Sir Henry Clinton, and returned to England. The focus of British policy shifted to the Southern colonies, which in turn required the abandonment of Philadelphia in the spring of 1778. Clinton marched his army across New Jersey back to New York City, fighting along the way the bitterly contested, but ultimately inconclusive, combat at Monmouth on June 28.

With the victory at Saratoga, the promise of economic and military support from France, and the failure of the British to win the war when they could (and should) have, American independence was well on the way to becoming reality.

ORDER OF BATTLE
The Battle of the Brandywine

Continental Forces

Gen. George Washington, Commander in Chief

1st Division: Maj. Gen. Nathanael Greene

1st Virginia Brigade: Brig. Gen. Peter Muhlenberg
1st Virginia Regiment: Col. James Hendricks
5th Virginia Regiment: Col. Josiah Parker
9th Virginia Regiment: Col. George Matthews
13th Virginia Regiment: Col. William Russell

2nd Virginia Brigade: Brig. Gen. George Weedon
2nd Virginia Regiment: Col. Alexander Spottswood
6th Virginia Regiment: Col. Thomas Elliot
10th Virginia Regiment: Col. Edward Stevens
14th Virginia Regiment: Col. Charles Lewis
Pennsylvania State Regiment: Col. Walter Stewart

2nd Division: Maj. Gen. Adam Stephen

3rd Virginia Brigade: Brig. Gen. William Woodford
3rd Virginia Regiment: Col. Thomas Marshall
7th Virginia Regiment: Col. Alexander McClanachan
11th Virginia Regiment: Lt. Col. Christian Febiger
15th Virginia Regiment: Col. David Mason
4th Virginia Brigade: Brig. Gen. Charles Scott
4th Virginia Regiment: Col. Robert Lawson
8th Virginia Regiment: Col. Abraham Bowman
12th Virginia Regiment: Col. James Wood
Grayson's Regiment: Col. William Grayson
Patton's Regiment: Col. John Patton

3rd Division: Maj. Gen. John Sullivan

1st Maryland Brigade[1]
1st Maryland Regiment: Col. John Stone
3rd Maryland Regiment: Lt. Col. Nathaniel Ramsey
6th Maryland Regiment: Lt. Col. Benjamin Ford
Delaware Regiment: Col. David Hall
5th Maryland Regiment (2 companies): Capt. Jesse Cosden

2nd Maryland Brigade: Brig. Gen. Preudhomme de Borre
2nd Maryland Regiment: Col. Thomas Price
4th Maryland Regiment: Col. Josias Hall
7th Maryland Regiment: Col. John Gunby
German Regiment: Col. Henry Arendt
Congress's Own Regiment (2 battalions): Col. Moses Hazen

4th Division: Brig. Gen. Anthony Wayne

1st Pennsylvania Brigade: Col. Thomas Hartley
1st Pennsylvania Regiment: Col. James Chambers
2nd Pennsylvania Regiment: Maj. William Williams
7th Pennsylvania Regiment: Lt. Col. David Grier
10th Pennsylvania Regiment: Col. George Nagel
Hartley's Regiment: Lt. Col. Morgan Connor

2nd Pennsylvania Brigade: Col. Richard Humpton
4th Pennsylvania Regiment: Lt. Col. William Butler
5th Pennsylvania Regiment: Col. Francis Johnston
8th Pennsylvania Regiment: Col. Daniel Brodhead
11th Pennsylvania Regiment: Maj. Francis Mentges

5th Division: Maj. Gen. William Alexander (Lord Stirling)

3rd Pennsylvania Brigade: Brig. Gen. Thomas Conway
3rd Pennsylvania Regiment: Col. Thomas Craig
6th Pennsylvania Regiment: Lt. Col. Josiah Harmar
9th Pennsylvania Regiment: Maj. Francis Nichols
12th Pennsylvania Regiment: Col. William Cooke
Spencer's New Jersey Regiment: Col. Oliver Spencer

New Jersey Brigade: Col. Elias Dayton[2]
1st New Jersey Regiment: Col. Mathias Ogden
3rd New Jersey Regiment: Col. Elias Dayton

---

1   The brigade's regular commander, Brig. Gen. William Smallwood, was on detached duty raising Maryland militia. Senior colonel John Stone probably led the brigade at Brandywine.

2   William Maxwell, the brigade's commander, was detached to command the light infantry.

Light Infantry Brigade: Brig. Gen. William Maxwell[3]

North Carolina Brigade: Brig. Gen. Francis Nash
1st North Carolina Regiment: Col. Thomas Clark
2nd North Carolina Regiment: Col. Alexander Martin
3rd North Carolina Regiment: Col. Jethro Summer
4th North Carolina Regiment: Lt. Col. James Thackston
5th North Carolina Regiment: unknown commander
6th North Carolina Regiment: Lt. Col. William Taylor
7th North Carolina Regiment: Col. James Hogan
8th North Carolina Regiment: Lt. Col. Samuel Lockhart
9th North Carolina Regiment: unknown commander

Light Dragoons Brigade[4]
Bland's Continental Dragoons: Col. Theodorick Bland
Sheldon's Continental Dragoons: Col. Elisha Sheldon
Byrd's Continental Dragoons: Lt. Col. Francis Byrd
White's Continental Dragoons: Lt. Col. Anthony White

Artillery Brigade: Brig. Gen. Henry Knox
Pennsylvania Regiment: Col. Thomas Proctor
New Jersey Company: Capt. Thomas Clark
New Jersey Company: Capt. Randall
New York Company: Capt. Sebastian Bauman
New York Company: Capt. John Dougherty
Continental Regiment: Col. John Lamb
Massachusetts Regiment: Col. John Crane
Artillery Company: Capt. James Lee
Artillery Company: Capt. Andrew Porter
Pennsylvania Company: Capt.-Lt. Gibbs Jones

Pennsylvania Militia Division: Maj. Gen. John Armstrong

1st Pennsylvania Brigade: Brig. Gen. James Potter
Philadelphia County Regiment: Moor
Philadelphia County Regiment: Col. Benjamin McVaugh
Bucks County Regiment: Maj. John Folwell
Lancaster County Regiment: Col. James Watson
Berks County Regiment: Col. Daniel Hunter
York County Regiment: Col. James Thomson
Cumberland County Regiment: Col. James Dunlap

2nd Pennsylvania Brigade: Brig. Gen. James Irvine
Philadelphia County Regiment: Lt. Col. Jonathan Smith

---

3 The Light Infantry Brigade under William Maxwell included detachments from the entire army including Col. Patterson Bell's 8th Battalion of Chester County Militia.

4 No brigade commander was assigned to the light dragoons at Brandywine. Each regiment reported directly to Washington.

Chester County Regiment: Col. William Evans
Lancaster County Regiment: Col. Philip Greenwalt
Lancaster County Regiment: Col. Alexander Lowry
Northampton County Regiment: Ballat
Berks County Regiment: Col. David Udree

Crown Forces

Gen. William Howe, Commander in Chief

Headquarter's Guard
42nd Regiment of Foot (Royal Highlanders):[5] Lt. Col. Thomas Stirling

Left Division: Maj. Gen. Charles Cornwallis

3rd British Brigade: Maj. Gen. Charles Grey
15th Regiment of Foot: Lt. Col. John Bird
17th Regiment of Foot: Lt. Col. Charles Mawhood
44th Regiment of Foot: Lt. Col. Robert Donkin

4th Brigade: Brig. Gen. James Agnew
33rd Regiment of Foot: Lt. Col. James Webster
37th Regiment of Foot: unknown commander
46th Regiment of Foot: Lt. Col. Enoch Markham
64th Regiment of Foot: Maj. Robert McLeroth

Guards: Brig. Gen. Edward Mathew
1st Battalion: Lt. Col. Henry Trelawny
2nd Battalion: Lt. Col. James Ogilvie

Light Infantry Brigade[6]
1st Battalion: Col. Robert Abercromby
2nd Battalion: Maj. John Maitland

---

5   This regiment was detached from the 3rd British Brigade to serve as headquarters guard.

6   The 1st Light Infantry Battalion was composed of the light companies of the following Regiments of Foot: 4th, 5th, 7th, 10th, 15th, 17th, 22nd, 23rd, 26th, 27th, 28th, 33rd, 35th, 37th, and 38th. The 2nd Light Infantry Battalion was composed of the light companies of the following Regiments of Foot: 40th, 42nd, 43rd, 44th, 45th, 46th, 49th, 52nd, 54th, 55th, 57th, 63rd, 64th, and two companies from the 71st. The Orderly Book of Capt. Thomas Armstrong, 64th Light Company (in the George Washington Papers, available online at the Library of Congress site), dates September 15 - October 3, 1777, confirms the composition of the 2nd Light Infantry Battalion. Ensign William Lord Canteloupe of the Guards painted a chart into the flyleaf of his copy of the list of British officers (Philadelphia, February 1778) detailing the composition of the light infantry battalions. These charts are largely accurate. Reconstruction of the composition of these battalions was possible through the research of Thomas McGuire.

British Grenadier Brigade[7]
1st Battalion: Lt. Col. William Meadows
2nd Battalion: Col. Henry Monckton

Hessian Grenadier Brigade: Col. Carl von Donop
Von Linsingen Battalion: Lt. Col. Christian von Linsingen
Von Minnigerode Battalion: Lt. Col. Ludwig von Minnigerode
Lengerke Battalion: Lt. Col. George Lengerke

Hessian Jaegers:[8] Lt. Col. Ludwig von Wurmb
Mounted Jaegers
16th Light Dragoons (Queen's Own), 2 squadrons

Royal Artillery

Right Division: Lt. Gen. Wilhelm von Knyphausen

1st Brigade
4th Regiment of Foot (King's Own): Lt. Col. James Ogilvie
23rd Regiment of Foot (Royal Welsh Fusiliers): Lt. Col. Benjamin Bernard
28th Regiment of Foot: Lt. Col. Robert Prescott
49th Regiment of Foot: Lt. Col. Henry Calder

2nd Brigade: Maj. Gen. James Grant
5th Regiment of Foot: Lt. Col. William Walcott
10th Regiment of Foot: Maj. John Vatass
27th Regiment of Foot (Enniskillings): Lt. Col. John Maxwell
40th Regiment of Foot: Lt. Col. Thomas Musgrave
55th Regiment of Foot: unknown commander

Independent detachment
71st Highlanders:[9] Lt. Col. Archibald Campbell

Hessian Brigade: Maj. Gen. Johann von Stirn
Leib Regiment: Col. Friedrich von Wurmb
Von Mirbach Regiment: Lt. Col. Justus von Schieck
Von Donop Regiment: Lt. Col. Philip Heymell

---

7   The 1st British Grenadier Battalion was composed of the grenadier companies of the following Regiments of Foot: 4th, 5th, 7th, 10th, 15th, 17th, 22nd, 23rd, 26th, 27th, 28th, 33rd, 35th, 37th, 38th, and 40th. The 2nd Grenadier Battalion consisted of the following grenadier companies: two Royal Marine companies, and the following Regiments of Foot: 42nd, 43rd, 44th, 45th, 46th, 49th, 52nd, 54th, 55th, 57th, 63rd, 64th, and 71st. The composition of the grenadier battalions is based primarily on research conducted by historian Thomas McGuire.

8   Includes the Anspach-Bayreuth jaegers.

9   Composed of three battalions.

Combined Regiment von Loos:[10] Col. Johann von Loos
16th Light Dragoons (Queen's Own), 1 squadron

Queen's Rangers: Maj. James Wemys

Riflemen: Capt. Patrick Ferguson

New Jersey Volunteers: commander unknown[11]

Royal Artillery: Brig. Gen. Samuel Cleaveland

10 Composed of the remnants of the regiments decimated at Trenton.

11 These men were attached to the baggage train.

Was the Earliest American Flag Carried into Battle at Cooch's Bridge and/or the Brandywine?

Was the earliest flag of the United States (commonly referred to as the "Betsy Ross flag") first used in battle at either Cooch's Bridge or the Brandywine? Some writers argue in the affirmative, but their evidence is slim at best.

In *September 11, 1777: Washington's Defeat at Brandywine Dooms Philadelphia*, Bruce Mowday argued in the affirmative and based his findings on an address given by John P. Nields in 1927 at Cooch's Bridge. Nields supposedly cited several factors supporting his contention that the flag flew during the engagement there on September 3, 1777. "Those facts included the resolution by Congress creating the flag, that Washington had the flag when his army marched through Philadelphia, that Maxwell's corps was formed before the battle of Cooch's Bridge, that Maxwell was ordered to engage the enemy and, finally, 'that in such an engagement it was appropriate that a standard with colors be carried.'" Ergo, if the flag flew during the engagement at Cooch's Bridge, it had to be at the Brandywine. Let's examine each of these "facts" on its own.

Congress passed a resolution in June 1777 creating an American flag. This does not mean flags were created or distributed to the army—a major logistical undertaking for which there is no primary evidence. Second, no primary source mentions Continental troops carrying the stars and stripes as they passed through Philadelphia. That would have been a proud and important event, but no account by a soldier or civilian mentions it. Third, Maxwell's brigade was created before the battle, and ordered to engage the enemy, but that does not mean his organization did so carrying American flags.

Mowday concludes: "Nields's five facts don't prove the flag appeared at Cooch's Bridge. All of the facts listed by Nields applied to Brandywine. The crucial difference was that Washington, himself, was at Brandywine and not present at the Cooch's Bridge skirmish. Also, the Reverend Jacob Trout made reference to the flag at Brandywine in the sermon he preached to troops on the night before the battle."

Washington is known to have carried a headquarters flag of a completely different design than the American or Betsy Ross flag, but his presence does not offer any support for or against the Betsy Ross flag being at the Brandywine. In addition, Trout may or may not have preached a sermon prior to the battle (see discussion in Chapter 10). Relying upon a sermon that was probably never made to prove a particular flag's presence perpetuates two myths at the same time. Nevertheless, Mowday claimes "the first documented firing on the Betsy Ross American flag was at Brandywine."[1]

A 2011 analysis of the question of the flag at Cooch's Bridge went far toward dispelling the myth. The legend of the "Betsy Ross" flag being present at Cooch's Bridge "appears to have its beginning during the Colonial Revival period. In 1901, the first monument erected at the battlefield stated the flag was present during the engagement. However, the monument was modified in 1932 to be less definitive." In 1940, Edward Cooch stated there was circumstantial evidence the flag had been present there. However, recent research has found it unlikely that the flag was at Cooch's Bridge. According to archeologist and historian Wade Catts, "The American formation fought as an ad hoc light infantry corps composed of picked men and volunteers from throughout the army and only existed for a month. The whole purpose of the infantry was stealth and secrecy so it is highly unlikely they would have carried a flag into battle." Charles Fithian, Curator of Archeology for the Delaware Division of Historical and Cultural Affairs, agrees: "The Stars and Stripes started as a Naval Flag so it is unlikely a light infantry unit that had just been formed would have had the flag. And they tended not to carry flags which would announce their presence." Most importantly, no eighteenth-century source has been found proving the flag was at Cooch's Bridge.[2]

As for the Brandywine, the reasons Catts and Fithian note for the flag not being at Cooch's Bridge also apply to the Brandywine. What we now think of as the "American" flag was initially used by naval ships and at some fortifications. A version of the flag may have been present at Fort Stanwix in August of 1777 or Fort Mifflin in November of that year. However, the "American" flag did not function as a symbol of the country, carried by infantry and cavalry regiments into battle, until after the Federal period. Flags carried by Continental regiments at the Brandywine came in a wide variety of colors and patterns. In September 1777, American regiments did not carry a standard flag.

To date, no primary source has been discovered proving the flag was carried during the battle. Beth-Ann Ryan states: "When and where the American Flag was first flown in battle has not been definitely determined by scholars. . . . It was certainly flown during the Mexican War (1846-1848) and the American Civil War (1861-1865)."[3]

---

1 Mowday, *September 11, 1777*, 73, 202.

2 Beth-Ann Ryan, "Where was the American Flag first flown in battle? Was it Cooch's Bridge?" http://library.blogs.delaware.gov/2011/06/14/american-flag-first-flown-in-battle/.

3 Ibid.

Appendix C

Where did Lafayette Sleep?

The Commonwealth of Pennsylvania has owned the Benjamin Ring and Gideon Gilpin houses for many years. The latter house (Gilpin's) has been, and continues to be, interpreted as Lafayette's headquarters during the Battle of Brandywine. Eyewitness accounts, however, call this conclusion into question.[1]

In 1780, just three years after the Brandywine, Lafayette visited the battlefield on his way to take up a command in Virginia. His traveling party reached the area late at night with the intention of touring the field the next morning. One of his companions, the Marquis de Chastellux, left this account of that night: "It was already late when we came within reach of the field of battle, and as we could see nothing until next morning and were too numerous to remain together, we had to separate into two divisions. Messrs. de Gimat, de Mauduit, and my two aides-de-camp, stayed with me at an inn three miles this side of Brandywine; and M. de La Fayette, attended by the other travelers, went further on to ask for hospitality from a Quaker named Benjamin Ring, *at whose house he had lodged with General Washington the night before the battle* [emphasis added]." The next morning, Chastellux rejoined Lafayette and "found him in great friendship with his host who, Quaker though he was, seemed delighted to entertain 'the Marquis.'"[2] According to this reliable account penned just three years after the battle, Lafayette lodged with the Ring family just as he had done prior to the battle with General Washington.

The contention that Lafayette slept in the Gilpin home the night before the Brandywine battle seems to have derived from an account penned long after the war by

---

1 It should also be noted at the outset that, as an unattached general, Lafayette did not hold a formal command at Brandywine. He was not entitled to occupy a "headquarters."

2 De Chastellux, *Travels in North America*, vol. 1, 148.

Lafayette's secretary August Levasseur. On July 26, 1825, during his lengthy visit to the United States, Lafayette and his son George Washington Lafayette toured the Brandywine battlefield. According to Levasseur, "At Chads-Ford the general learned that one of his companions in arms, Gideon Gilpin, under whose roof he had passed the night before the battle, was now confined to bed by age and infirmity, and despaired of being able to join his fellow citizens in their testimony of respect to the general; he went to visit the aged soldier, whom he found surrounded by his family. Gideon Gilpin, notwithstanding his extreme weakness, recognized him on his entrance," continued Levasseur, "and proved by tears of grateful and tender recollection how much this visit tended to the comfort and soothing of his last moments."[3]

There are several problems with this account. First, Levasseur penned it nearly 50 years after the battle, long after memory becomes unreliable. Second, if Lafayette had stayed with Ring in 1777, he could not have visited him in 1825 because Ring died in 1804. The account also refers to Gilpin as a "comrade in arms." If by this Lafayette's secretary meant that Gilpin fought with the French general at the Brandywine, he is mistaken. Gilpin served in the militia *after* the battle; he did not fight on September 11, 1777, and it is unlikely he ever served under Lafayette's command at any time during the war.

It is my contention that Lafayette stayed with Washington either in the Ring house or in a tent in the Ring yard prior to the battle of September 11. The 1780 account is consistent with this interpretation. Any confusion on where he spent that night arises from the account of his 1825 visit, during which he made a point of visiting Gilpin. Unfortunately, Lafayette did not leave a personal account of the subject. It seems more likely than not that in 1825 he wanted to see a man (Gilpin) he likely met long ago and one of the few still alive nearly half a century after the battle—but with whom he probably did not stay with in 1777. Unless a new source becomes available to substantiate that Lafayette lodged with Gilpin in 1777, it is more likely he slept on the Ring property on September 10, 1777.

---

3 Auguste Levasseur, *Lafayette in America in 1824 and 1825; or, Journal of a Voyage to the United States*, trans. John D. Goodman (Philadelphia, 1829), vol. 2, 237.

Thomas Burke's Attack Against John Sullivan's Battlefield Performance, and Sullivan's Defense

Who was at fault for the defeat along the Brandywine? Although George Washington as army commander was responsible (and deserved much of the personal blame for the loss) some politicians and civilians pointed the finger of blame at John Sullivan. Congress, which was already scrutinizing Sullivan for the manner in which he conducted his August 22, 1777, Staten Island raid, recalled Sullivan on September 14 pending an investigation. The move angered Washington, who was in the midst of a campaign and needed all of his officers. He delayed the recall the following day. Sullivan requested a court of inquiry to clear his name and Washington agreed, but told him the matter would have to wait until the campaign ended.

Congressman Thomas Burke of North Carolina led the attack against Sullivan and demanded he be dismissed from the army. On October 12, 1777, Burke penned a long letter to Sullivan outlining his discontent with the general's actions at the Brandywine:

Sir: I was present at the action at Brandiwine and saw and heard enough to convince me that the Fortune of the day was injured by Miscarriages where you Commanded. I understood you were several days posted with the Command on the Right Wing, that you were Cautioned by the Commander in chief early in the day to be particularly attentive to the Enemys' Motions who he supposed would attempt to cross higher up the Creek and attack your Flank, that you were furnished with proper Troops for reconnotring, and yet you were so ill informed of the Enemy's motions that they came up at a time and by a rout which you did not expect. That you Convey'd Intelligence to the Commander in Chief which occasioned his Countermanding the Dispositions he had made for encountering them on the rout by which it afterwards appeared they were actually advancing. That when at length the mistake was discovered you brought up your own Division by an unnecessary Circuit of two Miles, and in the greatest disorder, from which they never recovered, but fled from the fire of the Enemy without resistance. That the miscarriages on the Wing made it Necessary to draw off a great part of the Strength from the Center which exposed General Wayne to the Superiority of the Enemy.—

I heard Officers on the Field lamenting in the bitterest Terms that they were cursed with such a Commandr and I overheard Numbers during the Retreat Complain of you as an Officer whose evil Conduct was forever productive of Misfortunes . . .

From these Facts I concluded that your Duty as a General was not well performed. Otherwise the Enemy's motions on the Wing where you particularly Commanded would not have been unknown to you during great part of the day of action, nor could they have advanced by an unknown and unexpected rout, for you ought to have made yourself well acquainted with the Ground. Nor would you have brought up your Troops by an unnecessary Circuit and in disorder, which exposed them to be Surprised and broken.

I also concluded that the Troops under your Command had no Confidence in your Conduct, and from the many Accounts I had Officially received of your miscarriages, I conceived, and am still possessed of an Opinion that you have not sufficient Tallents for your rank and office, tho I believe you have Strong dispositions to discharge your Duty well—

I consider it as one Essential part of my Duty to Attend to the Appointments of the Army, and where I perceive that any person so unqualified as I deem you to be has got into a Command, where Incompetence may be productive of disasters and disgrace, it is my Duty to Endeavour at removing him. In discharge of this I gave to Congress all the Information I was able, carefully distinguishing what I saw, what I heard, and from whom, as far as I was acquainted with persons. I urged your recall with all the force I could, and thought it, and still do think it necessary for the public good because, in all your Enterprises and in every part of your Conduct, even as represented by yourself, you Seem to be void of Judgement and foresight in concerting, of deliberate Vigor in Executing, and of presence of mind under Accidents and Emergencies—and from these defects Seem to me to arise your repeated ill Success. These Seem to me to form the great Essentials of a Military Character—nor do I think you the only Officer in our army who is deficient in them—Nor were my Endeavours to free the army from Insufficient Officers intended to be Confined to you. I scarcely know your person, and was not conscious of any Injury from you.—for a particular Reason I should have had great pleasure in Justly forming a better Opinion of you, but no reason can induce me to overlook the defects of Officers on whom so much depends. Nor will any thing deter me from pursuing the measures Suggested to my own Judgement.

I have not related every thing which I acted with relation to you in Congress together with my motives—I have Set down every Intelligence, and the Opinion I gave concerning you. What Hills you struggled for what fires you Sustained, I neither saw or heard of. Your personal Courage I meddled not with. I had no knowledge of it, and I was Cautious to Say nothing unjust or unnecessary. My objection to you is want of Sufficient Tallents, and I consider it as your misfortune, not fault. It is my Duty, as far as I can, to prevent its being the Misfortune of my Country.

The purpose of this Information is that you may Indubitably know I gave Congress all the Intelligence and Opinions Concerning you here set down, and then to ask you in direct Terms if you meant the disrespectful Expressions in your later Letter to Congress on the Subject of your Conduct at Brandiwine to be applied to me? If you did Sir I must inform you, you are mistaken in the matter Contained in those Expressions. My demeanor was entirely void of parade and Ostentation, and entirely Simple and attentive. I did not Gallop my Horse at all but when I attempted to rally some of your flying Troops. The manner of those Expressions which I suppose you meant for Wit and Sarcasm are as unbecoming the Soldier as the Gentleman, and Inconsistant with that plain and dignified Simplicity which ought to be the Stile of persons in either rank.[1]

In addition to some of its factual inaccuracies, Burke's letter interfered with Washington's management of the army and unfairly accused Sullivan of matters outside his personal command and control. An incensed Sullivan replied in kind, triggering a heated exchange between Sullivan, Congress, and various officers of the army.

Sullivan methodically gathered evidence on his behalf from fellow officers and wrote a letter to John Hancock, the president of Congress, in reply to Burke's charges. "I never yet have pretended that my Disposition in the Late Battle was perfect," explained the general on September 27, 1777, who went on at length:

I know it was very far from it but this I will venture to affirm & appeal for proof to the Inclosed Testimonies it was the best that time would allow me to make—at half past Two I Received orders to march with my Division to Join & take Command of that & Two others to oppose the Enemy who were coming Down on the Right flank of our army. I neither knew where the Enemy were or what Rout the other Two Division were to take & of course could not Determine where I Should form a Junction with them. I began my march in five minutes after I Received my orders & had not marched a mile when I met Colo Hazen with his Regiment which had been Stationed at a Ford three miles above me who Informed that the Enemy were Close upon his Heels & that I might Depend that the principal part of the British army were there: although I knew the Reports Sent to head Quarters made them but two Brigades

---

1 Hammond, ed., *Papers of Sullivan*, vol. 1, 534-537.

as I knew Colo Hazen & our Troops Still upon their march the Enemy headed us in the Road about forty Rods from our advance Guard. I then found it necessary to turn off to the Right to form & to get nearer to the other two Divisions which I that moment Discovered Drawn up on an Eminence both in the Rear & to the Right of the place I then was at.

I ordered Colo Hazens Regiment to pass a Hollow way File off to the Right & face to Cover the artillery while it was passing the Same Hollow way, the Rest of the Troops followed in the Rear to assist in Covering the Artillery the Enemy Seeing this did not press on but gave me time to form my Division on an advantageous Height in a Line with the other Divisions but almost half a mile to the Left. I then rode up to Consult the other General officers who upon receiving Information that the Enemy were Endeavouring to out Flank us on the Right were unanimously of opinion that my Division should be brought in to Join the others & that the whole Should Incline further to the Right to prevent our being out flanked but while my Division was marching out & before it was possible for them to form to advantage The Enemy pressed on with Rapidity & attacked them which threw them into Some kind of Confusion. I had taken post myself in the Centre with the artillery & ordered it to play briskly to Stop the progress of the Enemy & give the Broken Troops time to Rally & form in the Rear of where I was with the artillery. I sent off four Aid De Camps for this purpose & went myself But all in vain no Sooner did I form one party but that which I had before formed would Run off & Even at times when I though on Horseback and in front of them apprehended no Danger.

I then left them to be Rallied if possible by their own officers & my aid De Camp & Repaired to the Hill where our artillery was which by this time began to feel the Effects of the Enemy's fire. This Hill Commanded both the Right & Left of our Line & if carried by the Enemy I knew would Instantly bring on a Total Rout & make a Retreat very Difficult. I therefore Determined to hold it as Long as possible to give Lord Sterlings & General Stephens Divisions which yet Stood firm as much assistance from the artillery as possible & to give Colo Hazens Daytons & Ogdens Regiments which Still Stood firm on our Left the Same advantage & to Cover the Broken Troops of my Division & give them an opportunity to Rally & come to our assistance which Some of them did & others could not by their officers be brought to do any thing but fly: The Enemy Soon began to bend their principal force against the Hill & the fire was Close & heavy for a Long time & Soon became General. Lord Sterling & General Conway with their Aid De Camps were with me on the Hill & Exerted themselves beyond Description to keep up the Troops: five times did the Enemy drive our Troops from the Hill & as often was it Regained & the Summit often Disputed muzzle to muzzle how far I had a hand in this & whether I Endured the Hottest of the Enemys Fire I Chearfully Submit to the Gentlemen who were with me—The General fire of the Line Lasted an hour & forty minutes Fifty one minutes of which the Hill was Disputed almost Muzzle to Muzzle in Such a manner that General Conway who has

Seen much Service Says he never Saw So Close & Severe a fire—on the Right where General Stephen was it was Long & Severe & on the Left Considerable—when we found the Right & Left oppressed by Numbers & giving way in all Quarters we were obliged to Abandon the Hill we had So Long contended for but not till we had almost Covered the Ground between that & Bremingham meeting House with The Dead Bodies of the Enemy—when I found that victory was on the Side of the Enemy I thought it my Duty to prevent as much as possible the Injurious Consequences of a Defeat for which purpose I rallied my Troops on Every advantageous piece of Ground to Retard their pursuit & give them Fresh opposition how far I Exerted myself in this Congress will readily See by Consulting the Inclosed Testimonies: The Last partys that I assisted to Rally & post against them was between Sunset & Dark by this means the Enemy were So much Fatigued that they Suffered our whole army with their artillery Baggage &c to pass off without Molestation & without attempting to pursue us a step—I wish Congress to Consider the many Disadvantages I Laboured under on that Day—It is necessary in Every action that the Commanding officer Should have a perfect knowledge of the number & Situation of the Enemy the Rout they are pursueing The Ground he is to Draw up his Troops on as well as that where the Enemy are formed & that he have Sufficient time to view & Examine the Position of the Enemy & to Draw up his Troops in Such a manner as to Counteract their Designs: all of which were wanting we had Intelligence only of Two Brigades against us when in fact it was the whole Strength of the British Army Commanded by General Howe & Lord Cornwallis.

They met us unexpectedly & in order of Battle & Attacked us before we had time to form & upon Ground we had never before Seen under these Disadvantages & against Those unequal numbers we maintained our Ground an hour & forty minutes & by giving fresh opposition on Every Ground that would admit we kept them at Bay from Three of Clock till after Sunset; what more could be Expected from between three & four Thousd Troops against the Chief part of the British Army—I would now beg Leave to ask this warlike Son of Achilles who has Censured my Conduct whether it is proper for the Best officer in the world to make a perfect Disposition of Three Divisions of Troops to Receive an Enemy vastly Superior in numbers already formed and advancing . . . when he has not time upon the Swiftest Horse to Ride from the Right to the Left of the Line before he is attacked—But I need not Dwell upon this matter till Some future period may furnish me with a more proper opportunity.

I now beg Congress to Consider whether my Services in Political & military Life have Deserved So ill as to Render me Liable upon vague Reports & private opinions to have my Character Stigmatized by Resolves against me—Though I have never yet wrote or Said any thing in favor of myself I am Compelled for once to alter my

Conduct. My Political Character is well known in most parts of America & the part I have taken in the present Dispute—I am Exceeding happy that in the Military Line I have witnesses of all my Conduct.[2]

A little over a week later, Sullivan sent another letter to Hancock explaining how he had warned Washington of the flanking movement:

Dear Sir: Since writing the letter which accompanies this, I have had no opportunity of forwarding my papers to congress & beg Leave to trouble Congress with Some remarks upon the severe & I think very unjust censure cast upon me respecting the intelligence sent by me to Genl Washington the day of the Battle on Brandywine: I wish only to acquaint Congress with the facts: It was ever my opinion that the enemy wou'd come round on our Right flank. This opinion I often gave the general. I wrote him that morning that it was clearly my opinion: I sent him that morning that it was clearly my opinion: I sent him two messages to the same purpose in the forenoon & the very first intelligence I received, that they were actually coming that way, I instantly communicated to him: After which the Genl sent me word to cross the Brandewine with my Division & attack the enemy's left while the army crossed below me to attack their Right; this I was preparing to do, when Major Spear came to me & inform'd that he was from the upper country, that he has come in the Road, where the enemy must have passed to attack our right & that there was not the least appearance of them in that Qr & added that Genl Washington had sent him out for the purpose of discovering whether the enemy were in that Qr.

The account was confirmed by a Serjeant Tucker of the L. Horse, sent by me on purpose to make discoveries & had passed on as he said to Lancaster road. This intelligence did by no means alter my opinion wch was founded not upon any knowledge I had of the facts but upon apprehension that Genl Howe would take that advantage which any good officer in his situation would have done. I considered however that if my opinion or the intelligence I had sent the Genl had brought him into a plan of attacking the enemy on the advantageous heights, they were posses'd of & a defeat shou'd follow, that I shou'd be justly censur'd for withholding from him part of the intelligence I had receiv'd & therby brought on the defeat of our army; I therefore set down & wrote Major Spear's account, from his own mouth & forwarded it to his Excy by a Light Horseman & order'd the major to follow himself. I never made a comment or gave my opinion the matter. Col. Harrison member from Virginia is posses'd of a copy of the letter as the Generals Aid-de-Camps inform me.

---

2 Hammond, ed., *Papers of Sullivan*, vol. 1, 462-467.

I beg Congress to see it & then judge whether I cou'd have been excused for withholding that intelligence merely because my opinion did not coincide with the declaration. Had the General crossed over; left his own advantageous post (where I considered to oppose an enemy in front) & found the whole british army well posted in his front & his Army put to the rout having a river unfordable in rear, except in one or two places & most of his troops pushed into it, which must inevitably have been the case if he was defeated: I say if this had all hap'ne'd (w'ch was at least possible & he had afterwards found out that I had received & withheld the intelligence, which might have prevented this misfortune & demanded my reasons I believe I never shou'd have been able to give on[e] which wou'd be Satisfactory to him to congress or to the world.

I know it to be part of my duty to give him every intelligence I received without withholding any part of it, because it does not coincide with my own opinion, and I as well know it is exceeding hard to be censured for doing my duty, which has been too much the case with me since I have been in the Army.[3]

Washington did not blame Sullivan for the defeat, and was in fact pleased he did not withhold any of the conflicting intelligence he received during the day of the battle:

Dear Sir: It ever has been, and I hope ever will be, a ruling principle with me, to endeavor to do impartial justice to every officer over whom I have the honor to preside. I shall therefore, in answer to the queries, contained in your letter of this date, readily declare.

That although I ascribed the misfortune which happened to us on the 11th. of Septr., principally to the information of Major Spear, transmitted to me by you; yet I never blamed you for conveying the intelligence. On the contrary, considering from whom, and in what manner it came to you, I should have thought you culpable in concealing it. The Major's rank, reputation and knowledge of the Country, gave him a full claim to credit and attention.

His intelligence was no doubt a most unfortunate circumstance, as it served to derange the disposition that had been determined on, in consequence of prior information of the enemy's attempt to turn and attack our right flank, which ultimately proving true, too little time was left us, after discovering its certainty, to form a new plan, and make adequate arrangements to prevent its success. Hence arose that hurry and consequently confusion which afterwards ensued. But it was not your fault, that the intelligence was eventually found to be erroneous!

With respect to your other quaere, whether your being posted on the right was to guard that flank, and if you had neglected it? I can only observe, that the obvious, if not

3   Hammond, ed., *Papers of Sullivan*, vol. 1, 475-477.

declared purpose of your being there, implied every necessary precaution for the security of that flank. But it is at the same time to be remarked, that all the fords above Chads, which we were taught to apprehend danger from, were guarded by detachments from your division; and that we were led to believe, by those whom we had reason to think well acquainted with the Country, that no ford above our picquets could be passed, without making a very circuitous march.

Upon the whole then, no part of your conduct, preceding the action, was, in my judgment, reprehensible. What happened on your march to the field of battle, your disposition there, and your behavior during the action, I can say nothing about, no part 'till the retreat commenced having come under my immediate observation. I can only add therefore, that the whole tenor of your conduct, so far as I have had opportunities of judging, has been spirited and active.[4]

On October 25, 1777, Sullivan once again addressed a letter to Hancock detailing the specific charges Thomas Burke had leveled against him:

In a Letter from Mr. Burk, Member from No. Carolina dated the 12th Inst: he informs me that he has represented to Congress that I was posted with the Command on the Right Wing of our Army previous to the Battle of Brandywine—

2nd. That I was early in the day cautioned by the Commander in Chief to be particularly attentive to the Enemy's motions, who he supposed would attempt to cross higher up the Creek: And that I was furnish'd with Light Troops for that purpose which I neglected, & suffered them to come upon me by a Rout I never expected—

3rd. That I conveyed false Intelligence to the General, which caused him to Alter his dispositions, and brought on a defeat.

4th. That when the mistake was at length discover'd, I brought up my Troops by a Circuitous March, and in a disorder from which they never recover'd—

5th. That He heard my Officers lamenting in the bitterest terms, that they were cursed with such a Commander, whose evil Conduct was ever productive of misfortunes to the Army—

6th. That my Troops, had no confidence in my Conduct.—

7th. That I had not sufficient Talents for my Rank and Office, that I am void of Judgment & foresight in concerting of Deliberate vigor in Executing, and of presence of mind under Accidents & Emergencies—from which has arisen my repeated ill Success—

As the Gentleman has been generous enough to acknowledge the several points he has urged against me, it becomes my duty to remove ev'ry impression from the

4   Fitzpatrick, ed., *Writings of Washington*, vol. 9, 425-426.

minds of Congress which those assertions might have made, and I doubt not Congress will indulge me in it while I treat with Decency the Gentleman who informs me that as a Member of that Respectable Body he made the representatives, as I wish freedom of speeches ever to be maintain'd in that August Assembly. I have the most sanguine hopes that the Person whose Conduct has been by mistake of a member misrepresented, may have every opportunity of removing the prejudice which those representatives may have made—

As to the first of those, it was so far from being true, that I was never sent to the Lower Ford, 'til the Ev'ning before the Action, this was called Brenton's Ford. I was ordered to take Post there, with my Main Body, to send a Guard to the next Ford, about a mile & half above me, another to Jones's Ford, One & half miles still higher up, and another to Buffenton's Ford, a mile above that, immediately upon my Arrival, I detached the Delaware Regiment to the first Ford, one Battallion of Hazens to Jones, & another to Buffentons—when I received those Orders, as I ever had been of opinion that the Enemy would endeavour to turn our Right, I enquired of His Excellency whether there were no Fords still higher up, to which, the persons who were then giving him information of the Country, replied there is none within twelve miles, the Roads leading to, & from which, are almost inaccesable—His Excellency also Observed, that all the Light Horse of the Army were Ordered on the right Wing to give Information, and of course I had no Orders, or even Hints to look at any other places, but those before mentioned, nor had I Light troops, or Light Horsemen furnished for the purpose, nor will any Person attempt to say it who knows the Facts. I had but four Light Horsemen, two of which I kept at the upper Fords, to bring me Intelligence, the others I kept to send Intelligence to Head Quarters—But to this Charge, as also to the Second & third, which the Gentleman has been pleased to Exhibit against me, I offer in opposition, His Excellencys Declaration Copy of which I enclose, and Congress must soon see how void of foundation they are—

The fourth Article of Charge I have fully answered in my State of the Affair of Brandywine—

As to the fifth & Sixth Articles of Charge I can only say, that I think the Gentleman much mistaken, as all the officers present in my division have sign'd the Contrary, except part of the officers in Hazen's Regiment, the reason of which may easily be conceived. I take the opportunity of Inclosing a Copy of one from the third Maryland Regiment, but have not time to copy the Others, to forward them by this opportunity—I think the Gentleman had better taken more pains to inform himself before he made the representation, as I am confident he cannot find three in my Division that would to be from under my Command, not even the Writer of the Letter against me, who is every day expressing his sorrow for being the author of it.

As to the seventh Article, I can only Observe that the Gentleman's Judgement is so far superior to all the Generals, & other Officers, with whom I have served, and his opportunities of forming an opinion respecting my Abilities so much greater, that I dare not attempt to contradict him, but leave him to enjoy what opinion of me He thinks proper.[5]

One of the officers offering testimony in defense of Sullivan was Thomas Conway, the commander of a brigade in Lord Stirling's division:

> I do hereby Certify, that on the 11th Septr Major Genl Sullivan, shewed all the Bravery, and Coolness, that can be expected, from a man of Honour, during the Action, and all the possible Activity after the rout to rally the Troops. Genl Sullivan having come up with his division, when the Enemy was within half a mile of our front, the short time left to his troops in order to Form, was hardly sufficient, for well disciplined troops, and well exercised, and by no means sufficient for the troops of the Army, who appear to me to maneavre upon false Principles, and where I cannot discover as yet, The least notion of displaying Columns, and forming briskly upon all Emergencies. The Division of the Right had full time to form, the Ground upon which said Division was to draw up, was exceedingly favourable, and if part of the Division was not formed completely before the Engagement, The fault can not be imputed to Genl Sullivan, who altho: he had a right to take the right of the Line, took the Left, in Order to save time, a proof that the Division of the Right, had full time to form. That Lord Sterlings Division, which was next to it, was completely formed, when the Enemy appeared. This is my sincere Opinion, the true cause of the loss of the Battle cannot be known to all those who are acquainted with what passed that day, and two days before the Action.[6]

Lord Stirling's aide, William Willcox, composed the following letter to Sullivan:

Sir: Your letter of the 24th instant has deprived me of the pleasure of doing an unsolicited favour, for antecedent to the reception of it, I had determined, so far as my influence, and knowledge of facts enabled me, to rescue your reputation from the undeserved calumny thrown upon you by the captious and ungenerous multitude. And to convince you, that my declarations are entirely uninfluenced by any thing which has passed between us, since the day of action, I have the further satisfaction to assure you, that in retiring from the field, I more than once expressed the highest sense of your personal bravery, and great activity in rallying the troops.

   With respect to the arrangement of the army, you must be sensible, it was out of my province to know by whom it was commanded, and, of course, on whose

5   Hammond, ed., *Papers of Sullivan*, vol. 1, 547-550.

6   Ibid., vol. 1, 555-556.

shoulders the censure, if any was incurred, ought to fall. But this circumstance may undoubtedly be ascertained from Lord Sterling, and other General officers in the field. As your division took its place in the line, after you had seen them, I always supposed it to be the result of council.

The enemy by good luck, or perhaps policy, made their attack before the intended disposition of your division, which in my opinion was remarkably advantageous, could be carried into execution. It was therefore rather to be considered as unfortunate, as ill-judged, and not to be laid at the door of any particular officer. But sir, whatever turns the scale of victory (by the by, let me digress to observe, that the victory was ours, and the ground the enemy's) whether accident or design—like the ancient usuage of the Jews—some sacrifice must be made to the people, and it is not less frequent than to be lamented, that in the Military Department, the man who may have embarked every thing in the common bottom, and bravely, but without success, defended in person his country's cause, is more liable to become the victim than the fortunate coward or the clamorous pretender.

The place which I have the honour to hold in the army, naturally gave me the best opportunity of observing the behavior of every general officer, in the centre of the line, and to my great concern, I saw you and Lord Sterling, with General Conway, from the commencement of the action, until you was deserted almost by every man, ride from right to left, encouraging and driving the soldiers to their duty, till the enemy were pouring a severe fire on both flanks, and pressing on with charged bayonets in front. Sometime before this, I thought you had exceeded the bounds, both of prudence and courage.

Be assured, sir, that I claim little merit in the above narration, for I defy any man who was a witness of your conduct, to gainsay it. Whatever others may say, must be the effect of caprice, or ungenerous prepossessions.[7]

Alexander Hamilton and John Laurens wrote a joint letter on Sullivan's behalf:

We have just received your favour of Yesterday, desiring from us a Testimony of your Conduct, so far as it fell under our Observation, the day of the Battle . . .

As we had not the pleasure of seeing you in the fore part of that Action, when the Line at large was Engaged, We are unable from our own Knowledge, to say any thing of your Conduct at that time;—But we can cheerfully testify in justice to your Reputation, that when we had an opportunity of seeing you, it was in circumstances which did you Honour.—This was from the time you rode up, and joined Genl Weedon's Brigade 'till your Horse was wounded.—You were employed in animating

---

7 "Papers related to the Battle of Brandywine," 53-54.

and encourageing the Men, to their duty, both by your Words and example; and in every Respect behaved, with becoming bravery, and Activity.[8]

Charles C. Pinckney (South Carolina) also submitted evidence supporting Sullivan:

> In Compliance with the Request of General Sullivan, that I would mention what I saw of his behavior at the action of Brandywine on the 11th of this month, I declare when I saw him in the Engagement (which was in the Evening, about the time that General Weedon's Brigade, was brought up to the Right) He appeared to me to behave with the greatest Calmness, and Bravery: And at that time I had Occasion to Observe his Behaviour, as I was then with General Washington, and heard General Sullivan, tell him that all the Superior Officers of his Division had behaved exceedingly well, after some other conversation with the General, General Sullivan turning to me, requested I would ride up to General Weedon, and desire him to halt Colonel Spottswoods & Colo Stephens's Regiments in the Plough'd Field, on our right, & form them there; which I did, & on my return I was informed that General Sullivan while I was delivering his Orders, had his Horse shot under him.[9]

Major Edwards, an aide to Lord Stirling, documented Sullivan's conduct:

> Since the Battle of Brandywine, I have been sorry to hear very Illiberal Complaints thrown out, against the Conduct of Major General Sullivan—As I was present during the Whole Action, and being Obliged from my Situation, with Lord Sterling, to be near Genl Sullivan, of Course I had an opportunity of Discovering such Specimens of Courage as could not escape the attention of any one. 'Tis with great Pleasure as well as Justice to His Character I can declare that his uniform bravery, Coolness, & Intrepidity, both in the Heat of Battle, rallying & forming the Troops when broke from their Ranks, appeared to me to be truly consistent with, or rather exceeding any Idea I had ever of the greatest Soldier.[10]

Finally, the Marquis de Lafayette testified to Sullivan's courage:

> Tho' very far from thinking that Major Genl Sullivan cou'd ever want a certificate however it is with the greatest pleasure, that according to his own desire, I repeat here how sensible I have been of his bravery at the affair of Brandywine the 11th Septemr. I

---

8 Hammond, ed., *Papers of Sullivan*, vol. 1, 556-557.

9 Ibid., vol. 1, 557.

10 Ibid., vol. 1, 563-564.

can assure him, that such courage as he show'd that day will always deserve the praises of every one.[11]

While Sullivan continued complaining to friends and colleagues about the charges leveled against him, he fired off one last letter to Thomas Burke:

> I received your polite favor . . . in consequence of which have enclosed in a letter to Congress certificates from the commander in Chief & the officers of my division; which totally contradict those points you have urged to congress & upon which you have formed so strenuous an opinion: If you are that candid person you intimate in some parts of yr letter & wish to be convinced of yr error, you may call on one of yr colleagues for a copy of my last letter & the papers inclosed & you will have nothing left to support yr opinion but that prejudice which I think yr letter too plainly discovers—
>
> As to yr opinion of my Military abilities, it can give me no uneasiness until you give me better evidence of yr Capacity to judge in matters of this nature. If you have sett yrself upon clearing the army of officers, who are unequal to the Task: I have only to lament that some of the Judges furnished by my country are so competent.
>
> Your peremptory demand of an explanation of my letter to congress, must be as peremptorily denied; so far as you are conscious the Germent suits I have no objection to your wearing it; that part which does not fit, you need not meddle with; but give me leave to assure you, it is not the Last thing I shall say against those who have meddled with my character: As to my being within yr reach; the fault must be your own, If I am not, perhaps no man in America is more easily found than myself & I can assure you with truth that when you appear in the character you Promise, no man will be more rejoic'd to see you than yr Hum Servt.[12]

The court of inquiry Sullivan desired never took place, although why it did not remains unknown. There are three possible reasons: Washington interceded and put a stop to the process; the testimony Sullivan amassed was too overwhelming in his defense, or; Thomas Burke's fellow congressmen decided to ignore his accusations against Sullivan.[13]

---

11 Ibid., vol. 1, 565.

12 Ibid., vol. 1, 565-566.

13 See Appendix F for a brief summary of Sullivan's life after Brandywine.

Appendix E

The Ferguson Rifles
after the Battle of the Brandywine

There is a commonly held belief among historians that the Ferguson rifles known to have been used at the Brandywine were placed in storage, never to be used again after General Howe disbanded the rifle company following Patrick Ferguson's wounding. However, there is a good deal of circumstantial evidence that the rifles were used after the battle, most notably at Kings Mountain, South Carolina, in October 1780.

After Ferguson was wounded and the special rifle corps was deprived of his personal leadership, Howe believed it could not operate efficiently without him. (There is some evidence Howe disliked Ferguson and his "experiment" and was looking for any opportunity to rid himself of the organization.) Adam Ferguson (no relation), who came to North America in 1778 as secretary to the Carlisle Peace Commission, stated: "It was well known in the army that the Commander-in-Chief, Sir William Howe, had taken umbrage at the rifle corps having been formed without his being consulted. It was therefore perhaps not to be expected that he would exert himself to support it." Howe ordered Patrick Ferguson's men reincorporated into their home units. "For the present," explained J. Paterson, the adjutant general of the army, "he [Howe] has thought proper to incorporate the rifle corps into the light companies of the respective regiments."[1]

This order indicates the special company was disbanded, but it does not say anything about the rifles being placed in storage. Indeed it is reasonable to assume the men took the Ferguson rifles with them. Nine days after the Brandywine, the British

---

1 Bailey, *British Military Rifles*, 51-52.

conducted a raid on Anthony Wayne's division near the Paoli Tavern. Xavier della Gatta's painting of the battle, which was commissioned by two British participants, includes five men wearing green coats and carrying weapons with longer-than-usual bayonets. This indicates that some of Ferguson's men may have been using their Ferguson rifles while operating with British light infantry battalions. Also, one of the British light infantry officers referred to some of the Americans being "instantly dispatched by the Riflemens Swords," which is yet another reference to the long bayonets of the Ferguson rifles.[2] While there is no primary documentation to prove it, the rifles were likely present in the hands of some of the light infantrymen at the Battle of Monmouth in 1778, as well.

Many believe the use of the rifles ended in July 1778 when the rifles, bayonets, and flasks of the Fergusons were ordered to be turned in to the Ordnance Office for repairs.[3] However, considerable research in recent years indicates the possibility that Ferguson reacquired his rifles and used them in his 1778 operation at Egg Harbor, New Jersey, and again when he moved south to command a Loyalist force. A great deal of the evidence is circumstantial, but it seems that at least some of the original 100 Ferguson rifles were used later in the war and especially at Kings Mountain.

While in Charleston, Ferguson ordered the "British standard carbine ball (.615) and Double Glazed Rifle powder for his troops." Since there is no record of Ferguson acquiring the British short rifles (Tower Rifles) for his command, what use would he have for this small ammunition? In addition, note two historians, "the counts from the inspection returns indicate captured French muskets for the militia and rifles for part of his Loyal Americans Volunteers Company, also known as Ferguson's Corps."[4] The French muskets took a larger ball and did not require the special gunpowder that the Ferguson required.

Arent de Peyster, who fought with Ferguson at Kings Mountain, reported that after repelling the Americans from the mountaintop for the third time, Ferguson's Corps was 'reduced to twenty rifles [fighting men]."[5] Since Ferguson's men were not issued the British short rifle, to what other rifles would de Peyster be referring?

Both William Campbell and Isaac Shelby reported rifles among the 1,500 weapons captured at Kings Mountain by the American militia.[6]

---

2   Ibid., 52.

3   Ibid., 54.

4   Ricky Roberts and Bryan Brown, *Every Insult & Indignity: The Life, Genius and Legacy of Major Patrick Ferguson* (Lexington, KY, 2011), 95.

5   Ibid.

6   Ibid., 96.

Lastly, there are only two known Ferguson rifles still in existence from the original 100. The Milwaukee Museum of Fine Arts owns one, and the other is in the collection at Morristown National Park. Both of these rifles were brought north by Union Civil War veterans returning home from the Deep South. If all the rifles were put into storage in New York in 1778, Roberts and Brown inquire, "how were they captured somewhere in the Southern United States and taken back to the North in the 1860s?"[7]

While there is no hard direct evidence to indicate the continued use of the Ferguson rifles after 1777, there is enough circumstantial evidence to question the traditional interpretation and believe they were used later in the war, especially at Kings Mountain.

7 Ibid.

Appendix F

The Main Characters, Thereafter

Philadelphia was finally captured by the British after **George Washington** was defeated at the Brandywine. He fought and lost Germantown the following month, which ensured the Howe and his legions would hold the city as long as they liked. When British strategy changed, the British withdrew and Washington attacked them at Monmouth in June of 1778. The long and hard-fought battle made it clear Washington had finally crafted a Continental Army that could stand toe-to-toe in a fight with European professionals. Monmouth was the last major battle he would fight in the Northern theater.

With the help of French land and naval forces, Washington trapped General Cornwallis at Yorktown in 1781 in a decisive victory in a long war that would not officially end until 1783. Washington presided over the Constitutional Convention in 1787 and was unanimously elected president in 1788 and re-elected in 1792. He retired in 1797 (setting a precedent for two terms and a peaceful transition of power) and died at the age of 67 on December 14, 1799.

Anthony Wayne was surprised by Howe at Paoli on September 21, 1777, and his men suffered as a result. He took part in the actions at Germantown, Monmouth, and Stony Point, and helped resolve a mutiny of the Pennsylvania Line in 1781. He and his troops participated in the Yorktown operations in Virginia. Wayne served as a member of the Pennsylvania Assembly in 1784 and was elected to Congress from Georgia in 1791 (but lost his seat because of residency qualifications). He won a decisive victory at Fallen Timbers (modern-day Ohio) in 1794 against a confederacy of Indian tribes, and died in 1796 during a journey to Pennsylvania from Detroit. In 1809 his son disinterred his remains, boiled them to remove remaining soft tissue, packed most of his bones into a pair of saddlebags, and buried them in the family plot in Radnor, Pennsylvania.

Despite the competency cloud hanging over his head, **John Sullivan** led his division at Germantown the following month and during the summer of 1778 commanded the American forces in the aborted effort to capture Newport, Rhode

Island, and thereafter headed up an expedition into Indian country in New York. In 1781, Sullivan returned to New Hampshire, rose to political prominence, and led the drive in the state to ratify the U.S. Constitution in 1788. He helped put down Shays's Rebellion. Washington appointed him to the Federal bench. He died in 1795 at 54.

After the Philadelphia Campaign, **Nathanael Greene** acquiesced to Washington's pleas in March 1778 and accepted the thankless post of quartermaster general of the army. He did so insisting that he retain a command position, and so led troops at Monmouth that June. He resigned as quartermaster general in 1780, presided over the military court that convicted British Maj. John Andre of espionage for his involvement in Benedict Arnold's treasonous plot, and was in command of West Point when Washington elevated him to command in the Southern colonies. His skillful handling of affairs in that difficult theater climaxed with his tactical loss but strategic victory over Cornwallis at Guilford Courthouse in March 1781. After the war, Greene was given grants and land, which he sold to meet obligations he had incurred in an effort to feed his troops. He finally settled on an estate near Savannah but died at the young age of 43, probably of sunstroke, in 1786.

John Armstrong's militia division did not perform well at the Brandywine or Germantown. Armstrong retired from the army and served in the Continental Congress after the campaign. Later in life, he served on the first Board of Trustees for Dickinson College. He died in 1795.

William Maxwell served at Germantown, Valley Forge, and Monmouth. In 1779, he took part in Sullivan's New York expedition against the Indians. The hard-drinking Maxwell was too often drunk as a soldier, and resigned in 1780. He died 18 years later.

Adam Stephen's intemperate habits at the Battle of Germantown on October 4, 1777, resulted in his dismissal from the army later that year. After his return to Virginia, he served on the state's constitutional convention, and died in 1791 in Martinsburg.

Following his solid showing at Brandywine, **William Alexander (Lord Stirling)** fought well at Germantown and Monmouth. When Washington moved south into Virginia in 1781, he left Stirling in command of the northern army. The heavy drinker, who suffered from arthritis, died two years later just before the formal end of the war.

The unfortunate **Francis Nash** was leading a delaying action at Germantown when a musket ball struck him in the head and a British cannon round struck him in the hip and killed his horse. (The same artillery round killed Maj. James Witherspoon, whose father John was a signer of the Declaration of Independence.) Thomas Paine, the author of the influential pamphlet *Common Sense*, was present at the time and wrote that after his injuries the North Carolinian was no longer recognizable. Nash lingered for three days (while bleeding profusely) before succumbing. He was 35.

Washington's gunner, **Henry Knox** served at Germantown, Valley Forge, and Monmouth. His magnificent handling of the siege artillery at Yorktown resulted in his elevation to major general. After the war, Knox served as secretary of war both under the Articles of Confederation and during Washington's presidency under the Federal Constitution. He resigned in 1794, settled in Maine, and dabbled in numerous business ventures. He died in 1806 at 56 after swallowing a chicken bone, which become lodged in his throat and infected.

Thomas Mifflin resigned his position on October 10, 1777. Later in the year, he became part of Congress's Board of War. In this position, he was one of the organizers of the movement to have Horatio Gates replace Washington as commander in chief. In 1783, Mifflin became president of Congress and was a signer of the Federal Constitution. He went on to serve as speaker of the Pennsylvania General Assembly and in 1788, held the equivalent of governor of Pennsylvania. He died in 1800 and was buried in Lancaster. Fort Mifflin in Pennsylvania is named in his honor.

Benjamin Rush served at Brandywine, and played a role in the Conway Cabal that winter, a plot by army officers to have Washington removed as commander in chief. In 1783, Rush became a part of the staff at Pennsylvania Hospital and a decade later played a leading role fighting the 1793 yellow fever outbreak in Philadelphia. After the war, he came to recognize Washington's greatness and wrote a letter to John Adams requesting his former letters criticizing the general be removed from the historical record. "Washington has so much martial dignity in his deportment," explained Rush, "that you would distinguish him to be a general and a soldier from among 10,000 people. There is not a king in Europe that would not look like a *valet de chambre* (a manservant) by his side." Rush died in 1813 and is buried at Christ Church Cemetery in Philadelphia.[1]

Four days after the battle of the Brandywine, **Casimir Pulaski** was made a brigadier general and the chief of cavalry. In early 1778 he resigned to form a cavalry-infantry legion in Baltimore, and later that year took the legion in an expedition around Little Egg Harbor, New Jersey, during which his men were surprised in a night attack near modern-day Tuckerton. In 1779, his legion was transferred to the Southern theater of operations. He led troops in the defense of Charleston in 1779, and may have been instrumental in saving the city from capture at that time. Pulaski was mortally wounded by grapeshot near the groin during the battle of Savannah on October 9, 1779. He never regained consciousness and died aboard a ship two days later. His final resting place is within the Pulaski Monument in Savannah. Ironically, the grapeshot that killed him is on display at the Georgia Historical Society in the same city.

Many of Washington's staff officers rose to positions of prominence in the future United States government. Later in the Philadelphia campaign, **Timothy Pickering**, always a wise man, urged bypassing the stone Chew house during the battle of Germantown, the siege of which some say may have cost Washington the battle. Pickering succeeded Nathanael Greene as the army's quartermaster general in 1780. He ran a business after the war, and was appointed postmaster general in 1791 and secretary of war four years later. In August of that year, he took over as secretary of state, and served as a U.S. senator from 1803 until 1811. He died in 1829 at 84.

---

1 Butterfield, ed., *Letters of Rush*, 92.

Alexander Hamilton commanded a light infantry battalion during the Yorktown siege. After the war, he served in the Continental Congress, opened a law practice, and took part in the Constitutional Convention. Under Washington, he served as the first secretary of the treasury and helped shape the future economic direction of the United States. During his life, Hamilton was variously a soldier, lawyer, congressman, leading proponent of the Constitution, secretary of the treasury, general in the army during the undeclared war with France (1798-1800), and leader of the Federalist party. He died fighting a duel with Aaron Burr in 1804.

In 1780, **Tench Tilghman** was made an official aide-de-camp. When Cornwallis surrendered at Yorktown, Tilghman delivered the surrender news to Congress. Tilghman was Washington's longest-serving aide. After the war, he ran a mercantile business in Baltimore that imported European goods and exported tobacco. He died in 1786, probably from hepatitis, leaving behind a pregnant wife and daughter. He was 41.

After Brandywine, Lafayette is said to have remarked of young **John Laurens**, "It was not his fault that he was not killed or wounded . . . he did everything that was necessary to procure one or the other."[2] If so, Laurens had "better" luck a few weeks later at Germantown, where he was wounded in the shoulder in a bold attempt to set fire to Cliveden (a stone mansion manned by British soldiers). His horse was shot out from under him at Monmouth in 1778, the same year he wounded Gen. Charles Lee in a pistol duel. Laurens served as Washington's liaison with French Admiral d'Estaing, fought at Charleston in 1779, was wounded in the right arm at Coosawhatchie, and elected to the South Carolina House of Representatives but continued to serve in the field. Laurens pushed to enlist blacks into American service, and although authorized to raise a command his idea was rejected by many prominent leaders in and out of the army. He was captured in the siege of Charleston and exchanged. In 1781, Congress sent him to France to help Benjamin Franklin negotiate for supplies and hard currency, and he arrived back in America in time to play a prominent role at Yorktown. Laurens was just 27 when he was killed in August 1782 at Combahee River in South Carolina. When he learned of his death, Washington wrote, "In a word, he had not a fault that I ever could discover, unless intrepidity bordering upon rashness could come under that denomination; and to this he was excited by the purest motives."[3]

Besides Washington, the most famous man to fight at the Brandywine was the **Marquis de Lafayette**. After he recuperated from his leg wound Lafayette was given command of a division of Virginia troops. That winter he was placed in command of a planned re-invasion of Canada that never took place. After negotiating a peace treaty with the Six Nations he led the May 1778 operation to Barren Hill, Pennsylvania, from

2   Chesnutt and Taylor, eds., *Papers of Henry Laurens*, vol. 11, 547.

3   *The Writings of George Washington: Being His Correspondence, Addresses, Messages, and Other Papers, Official and Private*, Jared Sparks, ed, 12 vols. (Boston, 1834-1837), vol. 9, 100.

the Valley Forge encampment, fought that June at Monmouth, participated in the August expedition to Rhode Island, and returned to France in February 1779 where his son George Washington was born that December. He returned in April 1780 with the news that General Rochambeau's French troops would be sent to America. He led his division into Virginia in early 1781 and commanded one-third of the army later that year at Yorktown.

In 1784, he returned to the United States and saw Washington for the last time. Louis XVI appointed Lafayette a member of the Assembly of Notables to advise him on the financial crisis in 1787. During the French Revolution in 1792, Jacobins under Robespierre attacked both the monarchy and Lafayette as a tool of the king. Lafayette fled France, was captured by the Austrians, and imprisoned in Olmutz, Moravia. His wife was arrested in France, released in 1795, and joined her husband in Olmutz with their two daughters. Their son, George Washington Lafayette, was sent to America to live with General Washington.

Napoleon arranged for Lafayette's release in September 1797 after being imprisoned more than five years. He voted against life consulship for Napoleon in 1802, and in 1815 was elected to the Chamber of Deputies during the Hundred Days War. After Waterloo, he proposed Napoleon's abdication. Following the return of royal rule, he was elected to the National Assembly in 1818.

Lafayette's final trip to the United States was in 1824, during which he visited all 24 states over a 13-month period. Lafayette returned to France, continued public service, and died on May 20, 1834. He is buried at the Picpus Cemetery in Paris alongside his wife. Lafayette's grave is forever honored by the presence of an American flag.

* * *

Despite his capture of Philadelphia, **William Howe** sent London a resignation letter in October of 1777 complaining, among other things, of a lack of support for his policies. He learned of its acceptance the following April, and Henry Clinton relieved him in May. Ironically, Howe's brother, Admiral Richard Howe, also resigned in 1778. Some argue this allowed them to defend their actions before Parliament before strong opposing views could take root. In 1779, both Howes demanded a parliamentary inquiry into their American policies and actions, which ended with inconclusive findings. This did not stop oral and published attacks against General Howe. One of his most bitter critics was loyalist Joseph Galloway.

He was promoted to lieutenant general in 1782. It was eleven years, however, before Howe saw action in the French Revolutionary Wars. He was promoted to full general in 1793. His health was deteriorating in 1805 when he was appointed governor of Plymouth, and died at Twickenham in 1814 after a long illness at the age of 85.

After the fall of Philadelphia, **Admiral Richard Howe** spent the next several months reducing and capturing various American forts and strongholds controlling the Delaware River so that British shipping could safely reach Philadelphia. Howe, who longed to negotiate a peace with the Americans, grew annoyed with the appointment of a new peace commission in 1778 and resigned. French entry into the war kept the admiral on station. Although outnumbered, Howe performed well off Sandy Hook and blocked Admiral d'Estaing's combined effort with American land forces to take Newport, Rhode Island. Howe left America in September 1778. As noted in his brother's entry, a 1779 Parliamentary inquiry into his conduct ended inconclusively, and the admiral spent years castigating what he believed was his government's mismanagement of the war at sea. He accepted command of the Channel Fleet in 1782, managed several actions well, and served as First Lord of the Admiralty from 1783-1788. Now in his late 60s, Howe turned in the best performance of his long career in 1794 in the mid-Atlantic at the Third Battle of Ushant (also called The Glorious First of June). He died in 1799.

Wilhelm von Knyphausen continued fighting during the balance of the Philadelphia campaign and fought at Monmouth the following summer. He temporarily commanded British forces in New York between 1779 and 1780. During the latter year, he led British forces at Connecticut Farms and Springfield. He returned to Europe in 1782 and became the military governor of Kassel. He died in 1800.

Charles Cornwallis fought at Germantown, took a short leave, and returned in time to fight in June 1778 at Monmouth the following summer. As second in command in America (Howe having been replaced by General Clinton), Cornwallis was given command in the Southern colonies. He decisively defeated Horatio Gates (the hero of Saratoga) at Camden, but his strategic blunders in North Carolina led to a costly tactical victory against Nathanael Greene in March 1781 at Guilford Courthouse. With his army critically weakened, Cornwallis grew disillusioned about victory in the South and believed Virginia was the key to success. Without permission he moved his army northward, where Washington and the French trapped him at Yorktown and forced his surrender. He was exchanged for Henry Laurens, a former president of the Continental Congress and John's father.

Cornwallis was appointed governor-general of India in 1786, where his administrative skills and field victories over a sultan helped redeem his reputation. As the viceroy of Ireland he quelled an insurrection in 1798, and four years later was plenipotentiary to France and helped negotiate the end to one of the Napoleonic wars. He returned to India in 1805 but died soon afterward and is buried there.

James Grant continued to command troops during the war. He led the unsuccessful attempt to surround Lafayette at Barren Hill in May 1778, and captured a French garrison on St. Lucia in the West Indies. Grant returned to England in 1779, was promoted to lieutenant general in 1782, and elevated to command of the army of Scotland in 1789. He retired in 1805 and died the next year at 86.

The indefatigable jaeger officer whose observations have helped us better understand Brandywine, **Johann Ewald,** was captured at Yorktown. Following the war he entered the service of Denmark and was promoted to colonel in 1795, major general in 1802, and eventually lieutenant general. In 1809, he was made commanding general of the duchy of Holstein. Ewald retired in 1813 after 53 years of military service and died that same year at age 70. Unfortunately, Ewald's gravesite was obliterated by Allied bombing during World War II.

Following **Patrick Ferguson's** wounding at the Brandywine, Howe ordered the rifle corps dispersed—supposedly because he believed the rifles' rapid rate of fire wasted ammunition. Like many lessons that should have been learned in North America, this elite corps was an innovation the British military tossed aside (see Appendix E for more details). Despite his disabled arm, Ferguson formed a small corps known as The American Volunteers, a group of 122 New York and New Jersey loyalists drawn from several existing loyalist regiments to carry out raids and reconnoiter. In October 1778, Ferguson commanded a 400-man expedition to Little Egg Harbor, New Jersey, where he led a successful surprise night attack on Pulaski's Legion. The following summer he helped prepare the defensive works at Stony Point, New York, and in early 1780 served around Savannah. During an incident of "friendly" fire in March, he was bayoneted in his good arm. He and his men were involved in raids across Georgia and South Carolina, and in April 1780 he was made a permanent major in the 71st Highlanders. Ferguson was killed on October 7, 1780, while commanding a loyalist force at Kings Mountain, South Carolina.

After aiding the British column at the Brandywine and helping the British achieve a victory there, infamous loyalist **Joseph Galloway** was present a couple of weeks later when the British captured Philadelphia and began their occupation. As Superintendent General of Philadelphia, Galloway ran its civil government. Galloway suppressed trade with Americans, the city flourished, foreign trade resumed, and many loyalists returned. Unhappy with Howe's management, Galloway organized an intelligence network, established a civilian commissary as well as a new sanitation department, and involved himself in a host of civil matters neglected by Howe.

After Howe's resignation during the winter of 1777-78, British policy in the colonies changed and Philadelphia was evacuated. Galloway argued against the move, and accompanied the British back to New York. He left his wife behind to attend to his estate, but since many viewed him as a traitor his property was confiscated. Late in 1778, Galloway journeyed to London, where he argued unsuccessfully on behalf of the loyalist cause for many years. Parliament eventually awarded Galloway a pension for his losses, and he retired abroad, writes one author, "to near obscurity."[4]

Like many powerful men in the mid-1770s, Galloway had to make a decision whether to support the independence movement or the loyalist opposition. Next to Benjamin Franklin, no one was more prominent in Pennsylvania in 1775. It was Galloway who, with Franklin, had created the political party that opposed the

---

4   Benjamin H. Newcomb, *Franklin & Galloway: A Political Partnership* (New Haven, CT, 1972), 287-8.

proprietary family of Pennsylvania. When push came to shove, his colleague Franklin turned toward the patriot cause, and eventually transcended life itself to become an American icon. Galloway, however, could not bring himself to swing with the political winds, so he continued his adamant support for King George. His ego and political aspirations led him to a life of ruin. He never returned to the United States and died in England at age 72 in 1803.

* * *

What of the Americans who lived in the Brandywine area? Today, the Commonwealth of Pennsylvania continues to preserve the homes of **Benjamin Ring** and **Gideon Gilpin**. Despite their property being plundered during the British occupation, the Quaker Ring family rebuilt its fortunes. Unfortunately, the Rings' eight-year-old daughter Lydia died in October 1777, perhaps from a disease contracted when the armies moved through and fought in the area. Their daughter Elizabeth was born early in 1778, and they eventually had another daughter, Hannah. According to George Washington's expense account, the general paid Benjamin Ring 22£ 10s for the use of his property during the battle. Benjamin was disowned from the Society of Friends for his involvement with the war effort, but later apologized and was readmitted to the Society. Both Benjamin (75) and his wife Rachael (66) died in 1804 and are buried at Concord Meetinghouse. At the time of Benjamin's death, his estate was valued at $10,000.

After the battle, Gideon Gilpin filed a damage claim amounting to 502£, 6s in Pennsylvania currency, which was never paid. In an effort to rebuild his fortunes, Gilpin established a tavern on his property about one mile from Chads's Ford. He was banned from the Society in 1779 after supposedly selling liquor and, so the allegation went, of taking an oath of allegiance to the revolutionary government. For almost nine years Gideon lived apart from his religious association until he acknowledged his transgression. He was readmitted to membership in 1788, but also continued his interest in the tavern operation, petitioning for a license again in 1789. His wife Sarah passed away in Philadelphia in 1801 and is buried at Concord Meetinghouse. Gideon married Susanna Hoopes in 1807, who died in 1823 at 75. Gideon died two years later at age 87.

A History of the Battlefield:
Commemoration and Preservation

The battlefield was visited twice by the Marquis de Lafayette, first in 1780 as he was passing through the area on the way to Virgina (with the Marquis de Chastellux and other French officers), and again in 1825 during his 15-month tour of America. During the latter visit, Lafayette pointed out where he was wounded, and visited the elderly Gideon Gilpin (see Appendix C). In 1847, 70 years after the battle, the Historical Society of Pennsylvania published an unpretentious but valuable monograph on the battle, thereby preserving personal accounts and "reliable" traditions that otherwise might have been lost or obscured. However, it was not until after the American Civil War that markers started to appear on Brandywine farm fields.

During the 1877 centennial, artillery pieces were placed to mark the fighting near Sandy Hollow, and the inscription on one of these guns claims to be the spot where Lafayette was wounded. On September 11, 1895, the schoolchildren of Chester County dedicated a marble column monument along Birmingham Road to commemorate Lafayette's wounding. Five thousand people attended the ceremony.

Efforts to preserve and commemorate the battlefield began in earnest at the beginning of the twentieth century. It was not an easy task, however, because the sprawling battlefield covered some 10 square miles of often difficult terrain. In 1900, the local post of the Grand Army of the Republic acquired two Civil War-era cannon to place on the battlefield, one at the corner of Wylie and Birmingham roads, the other along Birmingham Road near the edge of Sandy Hollow.

In early 1915, the Commonwealth of Pennsylvania placed 16 bronze tablets in the area to guide visitors. Eight of these tablets remain today: (1) at the Old Kennett Meeting House; (2) Trimble's Ford; (3) Sconnelltown; (4) Osborne's Hill; (5) John

Chads's house; (6) Birmingham Meetinghouse; (7) Dilworthtown, and; (8) Howe's headquarters. The missing tablets that had once been in place had been erected at: (1) the bridge that crosses at Chads's Ford proper; (2) about one mile east of Kennett Square at U.S. Route 1 and the intersection with Schoolhouse Road; (3) along Route 1 near the Chadds Ford Elementary School, honoring the American light infantry; (4) Jeffries's Ford; (5) the intersection of Street Road and Birmingham Road; (6) near the intersection of Birmingham Road and Wylie Road; (7) and Sandy Hollow. The last tablet that went missing marked the site of Lafayette's wounding.

On September 10, 1927, a pageant was held near Dilworth marking the 150th anniversary of the battle. In December 1946, the Colonial Society of Pennsylvania created a committee to look into preserving the Brandywine battlefield. On July 5, 1947, Governor James Duff created (and very modestly funded) The Brandywine Battlefield Park Commission. The Commission made an initial purchase of property in June of 1949 along U.S. Route 1 and is known today as the Brandywine Battlefield State Historic Site. Unfortunately, no master plan of either the landscape or the architecture was created by the Commission, and administrative decisions concerning the park did not appear to require approval in the state's capital at Harrisburg.

The initial 1949 purchase consisted of five parcels (50 acres). The buildings included the Gilpin House, with the smokehouse and the shop/garage on the Gilpin property, and the ruins of the Ring House, with the springhouse and the icehouse on the Ring property. The Commission applied that same year to the Pennsylvania Department of General Services for funds to rebuild the Ring House and restore the Gilpin House. The Commission used the funds to eventually complete these projects.

Around the time of the 175th anniversary of the battle, volunteers planted a row of pin oaks interspersed with sugar maples. For the 200th anniversary, a row of dogwoods was planted near the visitor center. Around the time of the bicentennial, the National Park Service considered taking over the management of Valley Forge, Washington's Crossing, and the Brandywine battlefield from the Commonwealth of Pennsylvania. Valley Forge was turned over to the Federal government, but Brandywine and Washington's Crossing remained under the Commonwealth's management.

Brandywine Battlefield was designated a National Historic Landmark on January 20, 1961. According to National Register standards, it has historical archaeological value, regardless of the value of existing structures or buildings. In 1997, the park was the first site in Pennsylvania to be named a Commonwealth Treasure. Unfortunately, the economic collapse of 2008 brought about severe budget cuts and the entire professional and interpretive staff was furloughed in 2009. Currently, the park operates on a volunteer basis and consists of just 52 acres. Very little if any direct fighting occurred within the modern park boundaries. Despite its recognition as a National Historic Landmark, the area around the Brandywine Battlefield State Historic Site has been heavily developed. Most of the property within the boundaries is privately owned. Consequently, the viewshed of several parts of the site have been impaired, and other areas are actively threatened by development pressure.

Local concern over this historically significant ground being compromised by modern land-use practices led to the creation of the Brandywine Battlefield Task Force in 1993. The Task Force is a volunteer group representing local governments, nonprofit organizations, historical groups, regional planning agencies, and concerned residents of the area. Its mission is "the implementation of public and private partnerships to preserve the ten square-mile Brandywine Battlefield Landmark, to educate the community about its cultural resources, and to develop interpretation of the Battle and its historical and physical setting."

Visitors today can experience the scenes of fighting in a variety of ways. Unfortunately, many portions of the battlefield have been obliterated by development, but large portions remain undeveloped. The Brandywine Battlefield State Historic Site preserves Gideon Gilpin's home and the reconstructed Benjamin Ring house. A drive along U.S. Route 1 offers visits to the Barns-Brinton House (preserved by the Chadds Ford Historical Society) and the still-active Kennett Meetinghouse. Enthusiasts can pull into the parking lot at the Brandywine River Museum and walk a trail along the Brandywine to see where Chads's Ford and Chads's Ferry were once located. Other preserved sites include the John Chads House (Chadds Ford Historical Society) and the still-active Birmingham Meetinghouse.

Over the years, large monuments were erected in the cemetery adjacent to Birmingham Meetinghouse. These three monuments honor Lafayette, Pulaski, a local colonel by the name of Taylor, and local Joseph McClellan. Much of Dilworth maintains its eighteenth-century character and is worth a visit.

Two recent preservation successes are worthy of note. Birmingham Township maintains Sandy Hollow Park, which includes a walking trail over a portion of the battlefield where Adam Stephen's men fought against Cornwallis's flanking column. The township has also recently built a walking trail along Birmingham Road. The trail parallels the road and allows hikers to retrace part of the path the British grenadiers followed on the day of the battle.

Despite all these efforts, most of the battlefield remains, unfortunately, in private hands, and is under constant threat from additional development.

The Ring House

After Benjamin Ring died in 1804, the Harvey family owned the home for the next 59 years. Eli Harvey purchased the farm at a public sale on September 5, 1805. It consisted of 170 acres, 19 perches (an almost obsolete term for area measurement) at $51.50 per acre, for a total of $9,123.38. It is this connection that gives Harvey's Run its name. Ring's son Joshua continued to live on the property for a few years after the sale. By 1808, Eli Harvey's son Joseph was operating the grist and saw mills, and by 1825 Joseph was paying the taxes on the entire property. In 1863, Eli died and his daughter Anna Mary took over the house with her husband, Gideon Speakman. In 1864, the

A modern view of the monument honoring the Marquis de Lafayette and Casimir Pulaski. Erected in 1900, the memorial is located in Lafayette Cemetery adjacent to Birmingham Meetinghouse. *Author*

house and 200 acres were sold at public sale to Gideon Speakman for $115 per acre, for a total cost of $22,056.87.

In 1866, the house and 150 acres were sold to Joseph Turner at $150 per acre. Turner's Mill, which is across the street (the current township building), is named after

A modern view of the monument to Joseph McClellan in Lafayette Cemetery adjacent to Birmingham Meetinghouse. At the time of the battle, McClellan was a captain in the 9th Pennsylvania Regiment. Despite the claim of the monument, McClellan fought under Lord Stirling on Birmingham Hill, and not under Anthony Wayne. The monument was erected by his descendants in 1895. *Author*

him. In 1892, the title of the property was transferred to Turner's wife, Eliza. In 1906, Chris Sanderson and his mother moved into the eastern half of the house. The other half was occupied by the Guss sisters, who were Quaker women. Sometime after 1913, the property was owned by Richard M. Atwater and Arthur H. Cleveland, Sr. The Sandersons moved out in 1922. The Pennsylvania Historical & Museum Commission purchased the property with a small amount of acreage in 1949 from the Richard M. Atwater Estate, Arthur Cleveland, Jr., and Ethelwyn Cleveland Rice.

The house was severely damaged by fire on September 16, 1931. In 1949, the Brandywine Battlefield Park Commission applied to the Pennsylvania Department of General Services for funds to reconstruct the building. G. Edwin Brumbaugh performed the reconstruction in the early 1950s. However, no documentation has been found for Brumbaugh's design, so it is not known how closely the current structure

A modern view of the monument to Isaac Taylor in Lafayette Cemetery adjacent to Birmingham Meetinghouse. Despite the monument's claim, there is no evidence that Taylor fought with Anthony Wayne's division at Brandywine. Taylor served in John Armstrong's Militia Division. The monument was built by his grandson in 1898. *Author*

reflects the home's 1777 appearance. Although the home was left to deteriorate for two decades after it burned, Brumbaugh did have the original foundation to work from, as well as photographs and other visual evidence from before and after the fire. Those photographs, however, were taken long after 1777, and may have shown the home with later additions. Brumbaugh's reconstruction was dedicated on September 11, 1952. Approximately half of the stones are from the original building.

The Gilpin House

After Gideon Gilpin's death in 1825, the 231-acre property was sold to William Painter in 1828. Painter used it as a tenant property, and converted it into an extensive dairy operation. One of the barns burned down and the business ceased in 1929 when the herd was struck with bovine tuberculosis.

The house was inherited by William's son, Samuel Painter, in 1845. He sold it in 1870 to Joseph C. Turner, to whose widow, Eliza, the house passed in 1902. During Turner's ownership, the farm operation had eight black workers and one head farmer who lived in the house known today as Painter's Folly, just east of the Gilpin home. Around 1900, the Gilpin house was used by Howard Pyle, a well-known illustrator, when he conducted a summer art school. Pyle was the Director of the School of Illustration of the Drexel Institute of Art, Science, and Industry in Philadelphia. The building was used as a dormitory during the summer schools and as a setting for many paintings. Some of these images can be found in Paul Leicester Ford's two-volume novel Janice Meredith—A Story of the American Revolution. The house was used as background in paintings by both Howard Pyle and N. C. Wyeth.

When the widow Eliza died in 1903, the property was sold to Dr. Arthur H. Cleveland and passed to his son Arthur H. Cleveland, Jr., in 1940. However, Richard Atwater had received a one-half interest in the property in 1908. Atwater deeded part of his interest to H. P. Dorman, who immediately transferred it to Arthur H. Cleveland. Ultimately, Arthur H. Cleveland, Jr., and his wife obtained full control of the property and were living there prior to 1949.

In 1949, the Commonwealth of Pennsylvania purchased the house from Cleveland, but the family remained in the house during the early development of the park. The existing form of the house was created in the 1950s under the direction of architect G. Edwin Brumbaugh.

During the course of the property's history, numerous outbuildings have come and gone. This is not unusual, considering the property's long farm history. In Turner's time, an earlier three-bay, stone-banked barn north of the house was enlarged. In the 1930s and 1940s, the structure was used as a garage and workshop. In 1946, the dilapidated barn was pulled down. The current stone barn is a 1950s construction that does not rest upon historic foundation walls. Sometime after 1986, a privy was removed from the property. At this time, the property also contained a corn crib. There is a foundation for some former structure slightly south and west of the current blacksmith shop. There used to be a carriage shed along the eastern edge of the property. A well located slightly west of the house was removed in 1975.

The Use of Cavalry and Artillery at the Battle of the Brandywine

What can be said of the manner in which the battle of the Brandywine was fought? From a tactical standpoint, was it a "good" fight? A useful lens through which to view this question is an analysis in terms of linear warfare.

Henri de Jomini was a French (and later Russian) general who wrote extensively on the art of war in the Napoleonic era. His writings were a staple at military academies for many decades and are still widely studied around the world. Prussian officer Carl von Clausewitz stressed the political aspects of warfare (war is "the expression of politics by other means") Unlike Jomini, he argued that war could not be quantified, i.e., made a matter of mapwork and geometry. Jomini's and Clausewitz's military principles were laid down in the century following the American Revolution, but their principles of linear warfare and the proper use of arms are directly applicable to the style of warfare waged outside Philadelphia in 1777.

Use of Cavalry

Screening friendly forces and conducting reconnaissances were functions usually assigned to cavalry. Because horse units were capable of faster movement, they were also used to pursue defeated enemy organizations. In the days leading up to the battle of the Brandywine, during the battle itself, and during Washington's retreat, neither the American nor the British effectively used their cavalry units to perform these roles.

Jomini, a disciple of Napoleon, wrote throughout much of the nineteenth century on linear tactics. His discussions also covered the tactical use of horse units. "As a general rule," explained Jomini, "it may be stated that an army in an open country should contain cavalry to the amount of one-sixth its whole strength."[1]

Jomini believed that the great value of cavalry was its speed and versatility. Such attributes could make a victory complete by breaking up and trapping retreating enemy formations. "An army deficient in cavalry rarely obtains a great victory," he continued, "and finds its retreats difficult." When on the defensive, Jomini felt that cavalry could be used to advantage by causing destruction to an enemy elated and disorganized by victory. In contrast to prevailing theory that cavalry's primary purpose was to screen an army's flanks, Jomini believed "it may not be regarded as a fundamental rule to post the cavalry on the wings." As noted earlier, Washington did not post any of his four dragoon regiments on his flanks, and on the morning of the battle held them in reserve near his headquarters.[2]

A contemporary of Jomini, Carl von Clausewitz wrote on cavalry tactics from the Prussian point of view. Clausewitz argued (and Jomini agreed) that "a serious lack of cavalry impairs the mobility of an army." In Clausewitz's eyes, one of its key roles was the pursuit of a beaten enemy. "A body of cavalry or horse artillery with the task of pursuing a retreating enemy or cutting off his escape," explained Clausewitz, "will find infantry completely useless." He elaborated his point: "Cavalry increases the mobility of the army. Where there is not enough of it the rapid course of war is weakened, since everything proceeds more slowly (on foot) and has to be organized more carefully. The rich harvest of victory has to be reaped not with a scythe but with a sickle."[3]

As far as Clausewitz was concerned, there could never be too much cavalry, nor could it ever be considered a hindrance to the army. However, horse units required significant maintenance, such as the need for proper fodder and blacksmiths to shoe the horses; without healthy horses, cavalry units were next to useless. Because of these factors, the cost of maintaining cavalry in the field made that branch "the most easily dispensable arm."[4]

Johann Ewald, one of Howe's and Washington's Brandywine contemporaries, wrote about the use of horse units. Ewald entered the German military at the age of 16 during the Seven Years' War. After the American Revolution, he wrote *Treatise on Partisan Warfare* in which he discussed reconnaissance: "If an officer is sent into an open terrain for these purposes, the detachment assigned has to consist of cavalry."[5]

---

1   Baron de Jomini, *The Art of War* (Philadelphia, 1862; reprint, Westport, CT, 1974), 278.

2   Ibid., 264, 278, 279.

3   Carl Von Clausewitz, *"On War,"* in *On War*, eds. Michael Howard and Pater Paret (Princeton, 1976), 286-88.

4   Ibid., 286.

5   Ewald, *Treatise*, 97.

This understanding of the prevailing thoughts on cavalry tactics in linear warfare makes possible an analysis of how Washington and Howe utilized their available horse units. Washington's previous limited military experience did not prepare him for what he faced during the Revolution. As historians Allan Millett and Peter Maslowski put it, the American general's "frontier service had given him no opportunity to become acquainted with cavalry tactics, massed artillery, or the deployment of large forces."[6]

In addition to the Continental light dragoon regiments, elements of the Pennsylvania militia mobilized to meet Howe's invasion were also likely mounted. The only other mounted element in Washington's army was his personal bodyguard of about 30 horsemen. Taking all these elements into account, Washington probably had between 700 and 800 mounted personnel with him at the Brandywine. (Unfortunately, a more precise number of mounted troops cannot be determined.) His entire army numbered approximately 17,000 troops, which means his mounted element constituted under five percent of his total force—far below Jomini's recommended level. His deficiency in cavalry (at least according to Jomini's standard) and its improper use affected the outcome of the battle; Washington did not have enough mounted troops to scout all the roads in the area or properly screen his exposed right flank.

Only two dragoon regiments (the 16th and 17th Light Dragons) were authorized for service in the colonies with the British army during the Revolution. One of those, the 17th Light Dragoons, remained in New York during most of the Philadelphia Campaign and so was not available for Howe's use at the Brandywine. Three squadrons of the 16th Light were present at the Brandywine. Technically, dragoons were mounted infantry, but they were commonly used as cavalry in North America. These mounted units were used for outpost duty, scouting and reconnaissance, and pursuing a retreating enemy. According to General Howe's aide-de-camp, Capt. Friedrich von Muenchhausen, the strength of these three squadrons when the army embarked at New York was 300 men. "The two main factors responsible for this paucity of mounted troops," wrote Matthew Spring, "were the difficulty of procuring suitable horses and the problems of feeding them."[7]

Howe's army also included Hessian jaegers, about 100 of whom were mounted. The Queen's Rangers, a loyalist regiment, was also attached to Howe's command. Elements of this regiment were mounted later in the war, but there is no available evidence of them being mounted at the Brandywine in September 1777. Therefore, approximately 400 mounted troops accompanied Howe to the Brandywine. Since his army numbered about 15,200 troops at the Brandywine, the mounted element numbered just two and one-half percent of his force—also well below Jomini's recommended level.

6   Millett and Maslowski, *For the Common Defense*, 59.

7   Pancake, *1777*, 69; Von Muenchhausen, *At General Howe's Side*, 22; Spring, *With Zeal*, 271.

How did Howe utilize his mounted troops? The three squadrons of the 16th Light Dragoons were divided between the two divisions of the army and thus did not fight as a united force. As one recent historian notes, "Particularly during the campaigns in the middle colonies, what little horse was available was usually parceled out between the different divisions or columns." The result of this decision was predictable: "general officers often had negligible mounted forces with which to improve an advantage."[8]

The available evidence indicates that the dragoons were used to protect moving baggage trains and did not engage in combat roles in the northern theatre. The lack of healthy mounts following the voyage could account for this circumstance. Rarely were they used for scouting or screening moving columns. The mounted jaegers, however, were usually found leading columns of attack, like those at Brandywine attached to Cornwallis's division. Placed in advance of the main column, they acted as an early warning system.

However, the lack of mounted men affected the outcome of the battle. Once he flanked Washington's divisions and drove them from the field, Howe lacked the mounted element necessary to conduct an effective pursuit of his routed adversary.

Use of Artillery

According to Jomini, artillery could be formidable on both the offensive and the defensive. Offensively, a battery could throw an enemy line into confusion, break it up, and by doing so prepare the way for an infantry assault. As he saw it, artillery's primary value was to shatter an enemy line before attacking it with infantry and/or cavalry. Defensively, artillery doubles a position's strength by damaging an approaching enemy, raising the morale of the troops around it, and "greatly increasing the peril of approaching near, and specially within the range of grape." Jomini believed that three pieces of artillery for every 1,000 combatants was the proper proportion for an army.[9]

Clausewitz argued that artillery intensifies firepower and considered it the most destructive of the combat arms. When an army lacks sufficient artillery, he asserted, the "total power of the army is significantly weakened." The long arm, however, had several disadvantages. First, it was the least mobile of the branches of the army and thus slowed it down and made it less flexible. Second, artillery required infantry protection because it was incapable of effective hand-to-hand combat. Finally, artillery could be used by the enemy if captured.[10]

---

8   Ibid.

9   Jomini, *Art of War*, 288-289, 290-291.

10   Von Clausewitz, "*On War*," 287.

No definitive statistics exist regarding the number of artillery pieces Washington's army possessed at the Brandywine. According to Jomini, Washington's 17,000 men should have had 51 guns to assist them. According to one historian, after the Trenton campaign Washington attached two to four artillery pieces to each of his brigades. If this is correct, Washington's 11 Continental brigades could have had as many 44 pieces with them in September 1777. Without factoring in any artillery that may have been attached to the Pennsylvania Militia Division and any that was held in reserve, Washington would have been only seven guns shy of nineteenth-century standards. Thus, it is entirely possible he met or came very close to Jomini's standard. However, without definitive primary evidence of the number of guns with the Continental Army, any such finding is somewhat speculative.[11]

Washington's artillery performed well during the battle. Proctor's guns conducted an effective artillery duel at Chads's Ford. They were overrun due to a lack of infantry support, though not through any fault of their own. The guns attached to Lord Stirling's and Adam Stephen's divisions also performed by "greatly increasing the peril of approaching near, and specially within the range of grape." That remained the case until their infantry support abandoned them and they were overrun. Henry Knox's pair of small guns performed similar service on a much smaller scale farther south later that evening as Nathanael Greene's division was taking up its final defensive position.

According to Jomini's standards, Howe's army should have had three guns for every 1,000 combatants, or 45 artillery pieces. Much as with the Continental Army, no definitive primary source confirms the number of guns with the British army. Howe had 25 regiments or 35 battalions when counting the grenadiers, light infantry, jaegers, and Guards. Just those regiments should have had 70 guns with them, not counting any reserve artillery. Friedrich von Muenchhausen thought the army had 62 artillery pieces.[12] It is highly probable that Howe's army exceeded Jomini's expectations for artillery.

The Royal Artillery performed as admirably as Washington's long arm during the battle. It conducted the artillery duel in the morning well, and provided fire support for Cornwallis's legions in the afternoon that helped soften up the American line on Birmingham Hill for the attacking infantry. The difficulty of moving the guns, which slowed Cornwallis's flanking column throughout the day, is the only legitimate criticism of Howe's long arm.

11 Bobrick, *Angel in Whirlwind*, 312.

12 Von Muenchhausen, *At Howe's Side*, 32.

Bibliography

Manuscripts

Alnwick Castle, Alnwick, England

　Percy Papers

Author's Collection

　Brandywine British officer's letter written by Lieutenant George
　Duke, Grenadier Company, 33rd Regiment of Foot. Ed. Thomas
　McGuire. Original posted online to be auctioned in May 2008

Canadian Archives, Ottawa, Canada

　Gilbert Purdy diary, Item MG23-B14.

Chester County Historical Society, West Chester, PA

　Accounts of property taken and destroyed by the British Army under
　the command of General Howe

Chicago Historical Society, Chicago, IL

　George Weedon to John Page, letter dated September 11, 1777.

William L. Clements Library, University of Michigan, Ann Arbor, MI

　Loftus Cliffe Papers

Germain Papers

David Library of the American Revolution, Washington Crossing, PA

Sol Feinstone Collection

Horatio Gates Papers

Peter Force Papers

William Irvine Papers within the Draper Manuscripts

Parker Family Papers (originals in Liverpool, England. Microfilm copies)

Delaware Historical Society, Wilmington, DE

William Dansey letters

Durham University, England

Grey Papers, Lord Cantelupe Diary

Historical Society of Pennsylvania, Philadelphia, PA

Christopher Marshall Papers

Dreer Collection

Anthony Wayne Papers

Library of Congress, Washington, D.C.

Washington Papers online

Massachusetts Historical Society, Boston, MA

Timothy Pickering Papers

Morristown National Historical Park, Morristown, NJ

Hessian Documents of the American Revolution

National Archives and Records Administration, Washington, D.C.

Ltrs Sent, J Howell, Comm. Accounts, RG93 (also available
at www.wardepartmentpapers.org

Papers of the Continental Congress (available online at www.fold3.com)

Revolutionary War Pension and Bounty-Land-Warrant Application
Files (M804) [RWPF], Record Group 15, Records of the
Veterans Administration. Accessible at www.fold3.com

National Archives of Scotland, Edinburgh

James Grant Papers

Princeton University Library, Princeton, NJ

Thomas Glyn, Journal of American Campaign: 1776-1777

Public Records Office, London

Judge Advocate General Office: Court Martial Proceedings and Board of
General Officers' Minutes, War Office. WO71/86/66-8

Records of the American Loyalist Claims Commission 1776-1831.
Audit Officer. AO 12/40/52

Wilhelm Von Knyphausen to George Germain, letter dated
October 21, 1777, CO 5/94

Windsor Castle, England

Archibald Robertson, manuscript map and accompanying text
of "The Battle of Brandywine." RCIN 734026.A. King's Map Collection

Printed Original Sources

Anderson, Enoch. "Personal Recollections of Captain Enoch Anderson, an officer of the Delaware Regiments in the Revolutionary War." Henry Hobart, ed. *Historical and Biographical Papers of the Historical Society of Delaware*, vol. 2, No.16 (1896): 3-61.

Andre, John. *Major Andre's Journal: Operations of the British Under Lieutenant Generals Sir William Howe and Sir Henry Clinton. June 1777 to November, 1778. Recorded by Major John Andre, Adjutant General*. Tarrytown, NY: William Abbatt, 1930.

The Annual Register, or a View of the History, Politics, and Literature for the Year 1776. London: J. Dodsley, 1788.

The Annual Register: or, a View of the History, Politics, and Literature, for the year 1777, 4th ed. London: J, Dodsley, 1777.

Asbury, Francis. *Journal of Rev. Francis Asbury, Bishop of the Methodist Episcopal Church, Vol. 1, From August 7, 1771, to December 31, 1786*. New York: Lane & Scott, 1852.

Beatty, William. "Journal of Capt. William Beatty, 1776-1781." *Maryland Historical Magazine*, vol. 3 (1906): 104-119.

"A Biographical Sketch of Governor Richard Howell, of New Jersey." Daniel Agnew, ed. *The Pennsylvania Magazine of History and Biography*, vol. 22 (Philadelphia: The Historical Society of Pennsylvania, 1898): 221-230.

Browne, William H. *Archives of Maryland, Vol. 16, Journal and Correspondence of Safety/State Council 1777-1778*. Baltimore: Maryland Historical Society, 1897.

Burgoyne, Bruce E., trans. and ed. *Diaries of Two Ansbach Jaegers*. Westminster, MD, 2007.

——. *Enemy Views: The American Revolutionary War as Recorded by the Hessian Participants*. Bowie, MD: Heritage Books, Inc,, 1996.

Burgoyne, John. *State of the Expedition from Canada as laid before the House of Commons, by Lieutenant-General Burgoyne, and Verified by Evidence; with a Collection of Authentic Documents, and An Addition of Many Circumstances Which were Prevented from appearing Before the House by the Prorogation of Parliament*. London: J. Almon, 1780.

Burgoyne, Marie E., and Bruce E. Burgoyne, eds. *Journal of the Hesse-Cassel Jaeger Corps and Hans Konze's List of Jaeger Officers*. Westminster, MD: Heritage Books, Inc., 2008.

Butterfield, L. H., ed. *Letters of Benjamin Rush*. Princeton, NJ: Princeton University Press, 1951.

Campbell, Charles, ed. *The Bland Papers: Being a Selection from the Manuscripts of Colonel Theodorick Bland, Jr*. Petersburg, VA: Edmund & Julian C. Ruffin, 1840.

Chase, Philander D., and Frank E. Grizzard, Jr., eds. *The Papers of George Washington*, Revolutionary War Series. Charlottesville and London: University Press of Virginia, 1994, 2000.

Chastellux, Marquis de. *Travels in North America in the Years 1780, 1781 and 1782 by the Marquis de Chastellux*. Trans. Howard C. Rice. Chapel Hill, NC: The University of North Carolina Press, 1963.

Chesnutt, David R., and C. James Taylor, eds. *The Papers of Henry Laurens*. Columbia: University of South Carolina Press, 1988-90.

Clark, Joseph. "Diary of Joseph Clark." *Proceedings of the New Jersey Historical Society* (1855): 93-116.

Clinton, Henry. *The American Rebellion: Sir Henry Clinton's Narrative of His Campaigns, 1775-1782, With an Appendix of Original Documents*. William B. Willcox, ed. Hamden, CT: Archon Books, 1971.

Commager, Henry Steele, and Richard B. Morris, eds. *The Spirit of Seventy-six: The Story of the American Revolution as Told by its Participants*. Edison, NJ: Castle Books, 1967.

Cope, Thomas P. Philadelphia Merchant: *The Diary of Thomas P. Cope, 1800-1851*. Eliza Cope Harrison, ed. South Bend, IN: Gateway Editions, 1978.

Cresswell, Nicholas. *The Journal of Nicholas Cresswell, 1774-1777*. New York: The Dial Press, 1928.

Dann, John C., ed. *The Revolution Remembered: Eyewitness Accounts of the War for Independence*. Chicago: The University of Chicago Press, 1980.

Delaware Archives: Revolutionary War. Wilmington, DE: Charles Story Co., 1919.

Drinker, Elizabeth. *The Diary of Elizabeth Drinker, vol. 1: 1758-1795*. Elaine Forman Crane, ed. Boston: Northeastern University Press, 1991.

Duncan, Henry. "The Journals of Henry Duncan." *Publications of the Navy Records Society*. John Knox Laughton, ed. London: Navy Records Society, 1902.

Egle, William Henry, ed. *Pennsylvania Archives, Series 3, vol. 23*. Harrisburg, PA, 1897.

Elmer, Ebenezer. "Extracts from the Journal of Surgeon Ebenezer Elmer of the New Jersey Continental Line, September 11-19, 1777." John Nixon Brooks, ed. *The Pennsylvania Magazine of History and Biography*, vol. 35 (Philadelphia: The Historical Society of Pennsylvania, 1911): 103-107.

Ewald, Johann. *Diary of the American War: A Hessian Journal: Captain Johann Ewald*. Joseph P. Tustin, ed. and trans. New Haven, CT: Yale University Press, 1979.

———. *Treatise on Partisan Warfare*. Westport, CT: Greenwood Press, 1991.

The Examination of Joseph Galloway, Esq; Late Speaker of the House of Assembly of Pennsylvania. Before the House of Commons, In a Committee on the American Papers. With Explanatory Notes. London: J. Wilkie, 1779.

Ewing, George. "Journal of George Ewing, a Revolutionary Soldier, of Greenwich, New Jersey." *American Monthly Magazine*, vol. 38 (1911): 5-8, 50-53.

Fisher, Sarah Logan. "A Diary of Trifling Occurrences." Ed. Nicholas B. Wainwright. In Pennsylvania Magazine of History and Biography, Vol. 82 (Philadelphia: The Historical Society of Pennsylvania, 1958): 411-65.

Fitzpatrick, Capt. Richard. "Fitzpatrick to the Countess of Ossory, September 1, 1777." *Pennsylvania Magazine of History and Biography*, vol. 1 (Philadelphia: The Historical Society of Pennsylvania, 1877): 289n.

Fitzpatrick, John C., ed. *The Writings of George Washington from the Original Manuscript Sources 1745-1799*. Washington, D.C.: Government Printing Office, 1931-3.

Fortescue, John, ed. *The Correspondence of King George The Third: From 1760 to December 1783: Printed from the Original Papers in the Royal Archives at Windsor Castle*. London: Macmillan and Co., 1928.

Frazer, Persifor. *General Persifor Frazer: A Memoir Compiled Principally from His Own Papers by His Great-Grandson*. Philadelphia, n.p., 1907.

Galloway, Joseph. *Letters to a Nobleman on the Conduct of the War in the Middle Colonies*. London: J. Wilkie, 1779.

———. "Mr. Joseph Galloway on the American War." *Scots Magazine*, 41 (October 1779): 526.

Graydon, Alexander. *Memoirs of a Life, Chiefly Passed in Pennsylvania, within the Last Sixty Years*. Edinburgh: William Blackwood, 1822.

Grizzard, Frank E., ed. *The Papers of George Washington, Revolutionary War Series*. Charlottesville and London: University Press of Virginia, 1998.

Hagist, Don N., comp. *British Soldiers American War: Voices of the American Revolution*. Yardley, PA: Westholme Publishing, 2012.

Hammond, Isaac W., ed. *State of New Hampshire, Part I, Rolls and Documents Relating to Soldiers in the Revolutionary War*. Manchester, NH: John B. Clarke, 1889.

Hammond, Otis G., ed. *Letters and Papers of Major-General John Sullivan: Continental Army*. Concord, NH: New Hampshire Historical Society, 1930.

Hawkins, John. "Battle of Brandywine Described." *The Pennsylvania Magazine of History and Biography*, vol. 20 (Philadelphia: The Historical Society of Pennsylvania, 1896): 420-1.

Hazard, Samuel, et. al., eds. *Pennsylvania Archives: Selected and Arranged from Original Documents in the Office of the Secretary of the Commonwealth, Series 1*. Harrisburg and Philadelphia, 1853.

Heitman, Francis B. *Historical Register of Officers of the Continental Army During the War of the Revolution*. Baltimore: Clearfield Company, Inc., 2003.

Heth, William. "The Diary of Lieutenant William Heth while a Prisoner in Quebec." B. Floyd Flickinger, ed. *Annual Papers of Winchester Virginia Historical Society*, vol. 1 (1931): 31-33.

Hill, Baylor. *A Gentleman of Fortune: The Diary of Baylor Hill, First Continental Light Dragoons, 1777-1781*. John T. Hayes, ed. Ft. Lauderdale, FL: Saddlebag Press, 1995.

Historical Anecdotes, Civil and Military: in a Series of Letters, Written from America, in the Years 1777 and 1778, to Different Persons in England; Containing Observations on the General

Management of the War, and on the Conduct of our Principal Commanders, in the Revolted Colonies, During that Period. London: Printed for J. Bew, 1779.

Hobson, Charles F., ed. *The Papers of John Marshall,* vol. 10, January 1824-March 1827. Chapel Hill, NC: University of North Carolina Press, 2000.

Hoffman, Ronald, Sally D. Mason, and Eleanor S. Darcy, eds. *Dear Papa, Dear Charley: The Papers of Charles Carroll of Carrollton, 1748-1782.* Chapel Hill, NC: University of North Carolina Press, 2001.

Hunter, Martin. *The Journal of Gen. Sir Martin Hunter and Some Letters of his Wife, Lady Hunter.* A. Hunter, ed. Edinburgh: Edinburgh Press, 1894.

Idzerda, Stanley J., et. al., eds. *Lafayette in the Age of the American Revolution: Selected Letters and Papers.* Ithaca, NY: Cornell University Press, 1977.

Inman, George. "George Inman's Narrative of the American Revolution." *The Pennsylvania Magazine of History and Biography*, vol. 7 (Philadelphia: The Historical Society of Pennsylvania, 1883): 237-248.

———, ed. "List of Officers Killed Since the Commencement of the War 19th April 1775, Regiments Etc. and Officers of Marines Serving on Shore." *The Pennsylvania Magazine of History and Biography*, vol. 27 (Philadelphia: The Historical Society of Pennsylvania, 1903): 176-205.

Jarvis, Stephen. *Stephen Jarvis: The King's Loyal Horseman, His Narrative 1775-1783.* John T. Hayes, ed. Fort Lauderdale, FL: The Saddlebag Press, 1996.

Jefferson, Thomas. *Writings.* Merrill D. Peterson, ed. New York: Library of America, 1984.

Kemble, Stephen. *Journals of Lieut.-Col. Stephen Kemble, 1773-1789.* New York: New York Historical Society, 1883.

Lafayette, Marquis de. *Memoirs, Correspondence and Manuscripts of General Lafayette: Published by his Family.* New York: Saunders and Otley Ann Street, 1837.

Lamb, Martha J., ed. *Magazine of American History with Notes and Queries,* vol. 13 (January-June 1885). New York: Historical Publication Co., 1885: 281.

Lee, Henry. *Memoirs of the War in the Southern Department of the United States.* Philadelphia: Bradford and Inskeep, 1812.

Lesser, Charles H., ed. *The Sinews of Independence: Monthly Strength Reports of the Continental Army.* Chicago: The University of Chicago Press, 1976.

Levasseur, Auguste. *Lafayette in America in 1824 and 1825; or, Journal of a Voyage to the United States.* Trans. John D. Goodman. Philadelphia: Carey and Lea, 1829.

Linn, John Blair, and William H. Egle, eds. *Pennsylvania Archives, Series 2.* Harrisburg, PA, 1880.

"London, December 18: Extract of a letter from an Officer at Philadelphia to his friend at Edinburgh, dated Oct. 27." *Felix Farley's Bristol Journal,* 26, no. 1400. December 26, 1777. [Officer is unidentified.]

Lushington, S. R. *The Life and Services of General Lord Harris, G.C.B. During His Campaigns in America, The West Indies, and India*. London: John W. Parker, 1840.

McMichael, James. "Diary of Lieutenant James McMichael, of the Pennsylvania Line, 1776-1778." William P. McMichael, ed. *The Pennsylvania Magazine of History and Biography* (Philadelphia: The Historical Society of Pennsylvania, 1892): 129-159.

The Manuscripts of the Earl of Carlisle, Preserved at Castle Howard. *Historical Manuscripts Commission, 15th Report*, Appendix, Part 6. London: Her Majesty's Stationery Office, 1897.

Marshall, Christopher. *Extracts from the Diary of Christopher Marshall, Kept in Philadelphia and Lancaster, during the American Revolution, 1774-1781*. William Duane, ed. Albany, NY: Joel Munsell, 1877.

Marshall, John. *The Life of George Washington, Commander in Chief of the American Forces, During the War Which Established the Independence of His Country, and First President of the United States*. Fredericksburg: The Citizens' Guild of Washington's Boyhood Home, 1926.

Martin, Joseph Plumb. *Private Yankee Doodle: Being a Narrative of Some of the Adventures, Dangers and Sufferings of a Revolutionary Soldier*. George E. Scheer, ed. Eastern National, 1962.

Miller, Lillian B., Sidney Hart, and Toby A. Appel, eds. *The Selected Papers of Charles Willson Peale and His Family*, vol. 1, *Charles Willson Peale: Artist in Revolutionary America, 1735-1791*. New Haven, CT: Yale University Press, 1983.

Montgomery, Thomas Lynch, ed. *Pennsylvania Archives, Series 5*. Harrisburg, PA, 1906.

Montresor, John. "The Montresor Journals." G. D. Delaplaine, ed. *Collections of the New York Historical Society for the Year 1881* (1882).

Mordecai, Jacob. "Addenda to Watson's Annals of Philadelphia." *Pennsylvania Magazine of History and Biography*, vol. 98 (Philadelphia: The Historical Society of Pennsylvania, 1974): 131-70.

Morgan, William James, ed. *Naval Documents of the American Revolution*. Washington, D.C.: Naval History Division, Department of the Navy, 1986.

Muhlenberg, Henry Melchior. *The Journals of Henry Melchior Muhlenberg*. Trans. by Theodore G. Tappert and John W. Doberstein. Philadelphia: The Muhlenberg Press, 1958.

Murray, James. *Letters from America, 1773 to 1780: Being the letters of a Scots officer, Sir James Murray, to his home during the War of American Independence*. Eric Robson, ed. New York: Barnes & Noble, Inc., 1950.

Nagle, Jacob. *The Nagle Journal: A Diary of the Life of Jacob Nagle, Sailor, from the year 1775 to 1841*. John C. Dann, ed. New York: Weidenfeld and Nicolson, 1988.

The Narrative of Lieut. Gen. Sir William Howe, in a Committee of the House of Commons, on the 29th of April, 1779, Relative to His Conduct, During His Late Command of the King's Troops in North America: to Which are Added, Some Observations Upon a Pamphlet, Entitled, Letters to a Nobleman. London: H. Baldwin, 1780.

"Notes and Queries: Loss of the British Army at Brandywine." *The Pennsylvania Magazine of History and Biography*, vol. 4 (Philadelphia: The Historical Society of Pennsylvania, 1880): 121.

Ogden, Aaron. *Autobiography of Col. Aaron Ogden, of Elizabethtown.* Paterson, NJ: The Press Printing and Publishing Co., 1893.

"Orderly Book of General Edward Hand, Valley Forge, January 1778." *The Pennsylvania Magazine of History and Biography*, vol. 41 (Philadelphia: The Historical Society of Pennsylvania, 1917): 198-223.

Paine, Thomas. Crisis #4. Available at www.thefederalistpapers.org/founders/

———. Paine/the-american-crisis-part-4-by-thomas-paine. Accessed April 1, 2013.

———. "Military Operations near Philadelphia in the Campaign of 1777-8." *The Pennsylvania Magazine of History and Biography*, vol. 2. (Philadelphia: The Historical Society of Pennsylvania, 1878): 283-296.

"Papers Related to the Battle of Brandywine." *Proceedings of the Historical Society of Pennsylvania*, vol. 1, No. 8 (Philadelphia: The Historical Society of Pennsylvania, 1846): 40-63.

Peebles, John. *John Peebles' American War: The Diary of a Scottish Grenadier, 1776-1782.* Ira D. Gruber, ed. Mechanicsburg, PA: Stackpole Books, 1998.

Pennsylvania Packet, July 8, 1777. [No author, no editor.]

"Pinckney, Charles Cotesworth, to Henry Johnson, November 14, 1820." *The Historical Magazine, Notes and Queries, Concerning the Antiquities, History and Biography of America*, vol. 10 (Morrisania, NY, 1866): 202-4.

Rankin, Edward S., ed. *Proceedings of the New Jersey Historical Society*, vol. 51, no. 3 (Newark, NJ, July 1933).

Rankin, Hugh F., ed. "An Officer Out of his Time: Correspondence of Major Patrick Ferguson, 1779-1780." *Sources of American Independence: Selected Manuscripts from the Collections of the William L. Clements Library.* Howard H. Peckham, ed. Chicago: The University of Chicago Press, 1978. 287-360.

Remembrancer; or, Impartial Repository of Public Events for the Year 1777. London: J. Almon, 1778.

Report on the Manuscripts of Mrs. Stopford-Sackville, of Drayton House, Northhampshire. Hereford: Historical Manuscripts Commission, 1910.

"Revolutionary Services of Captain John Markland." *The Pennsylvania Magazine of History and Biography*, vol. 9 (Philadelphia: The Historical Society of Pennsylvania, 1885): 102-111.

Ritter, Jacob. *Memoirs of Jacob Ritter, A Faithful Minister in the Society of Friends.* Joseph Foulke, ed. Philadelphia: T. E. Chapman, 1844.

Robertson, Archibald. *Archibald Robertson, Lieutenant General Royal Engineers: His Diaries and Sketches in America, 1762-1780.* Harry Miller Lydenberg. ed. New York: New York Public Library, 1930.

Rodney, Caesar. *Letters to and from Caesar Rodney, 1756-1784.* George Herbert Ryden ed. New York: University of Pennsylvania Press, 1970.

Rush, Benjamin. *The Autobiography of Benjamin Rush: His "Travels Through Life" Together with His Commonplace Book for 1789-1813.* George W. Corner, ed. Westport, CT: Greenwood Press, 1948.

Ryan, Dennis P., ed. A Salute to Courage: The American Revolution as Seen Through Wartime Writings of Officers of the Continental Army and Navy. New York: Columbia University Press, 1979.

St. George, Richard. "The Actions at Brandywine and Paoli Described by a British Officer." *The Pennsylvania Magazine of History and Biography*, vol. 29 (Philadelphia: The Historical Society of Pennsylvania, 1905): 368-9.

Serle, Ambrose. The *American Journal of Ambrose Serle, Secretary to Lord Howe, 1776-1778.* Edward H. Tatum, Jr., ed. San Marino, CA: The Huntington Library, 1940.

Shaw, Samuel. *The Journals of Major Samuel Shaw: The First American Consul at Canton.* Josiah Quincy, ed. Boston: William Crosby & H. P. Nichols, 1847.

Showman, Richard K., Robert M. McCarthy, and Margaret Cobb, eds. *The Papers of General Nathaniel Greene*, vol. 2, 1 January 1777 - 16 October 1778. Chapel Hill, NC: University of North Carolina Press, 1980.

Shreve, John. "Personal Narrative of the Services of Lieut. John Shreve." *The Magazine of American History with Notes and Queries*, vol. 3 (New York, 1879): 564-79.

Simes, T. *A Military Course for the Government and Conduct of a Battalion, Designed for Their Regulations in Quarter, Camp, or Garrison; with . . . Observations and Instructions for Their Manner of Attack and Defense.* London: n.p., 1777.

Smith, George. *A Universal Military Dictionary.* London: J. Millan, 1779.

Smith, Paul H., et, al., eds. *Letters of Delegates to Congress.* Washington, D.C.: Library of Congress, 1981.

Smith, Samuel. "The Papers of General Samuel Smith." *The Historical Magazine and Notes and Queries, Concerning the Antiquities, History and Biography of America*, vol. 7, 2nd series, no. 2 (Morrisania, NY, February 1870): 81-92.

Sparks, Jared, ed. *The Writings of George Washington: Being His Correspondence, Addresses, Messages, Official and Private*, vol. 9. Boston, 1834-1837.

"Stedman, Margaret, to Mrs. E. Ferguson, September 11, 1777." *The Pennsylvania Magazine of History and Biography*, vol. 14 (Philadelphia: The Historical Society of Pennsylvania, 1890): 64-7.

Stevens, Elisha. *Fragments of Memoranda Written by him in the War of the Revolution.* Meriden, CT: H. W. Lines, 1893.

Stirke, Henry. "A British Officer's Revolutionary War Journal, 1776-1778." S. Sydney Bradford, ed. *Maryland Historical Magazine*, vol. 56 (1961): 150-175.

Stirn, Johann Daniel. "Diary Installment from Major General Johann Daniel Stirn." Henry Retzer and Donald Londahlsmidt. eds. *Journal of the Johannes Schwalm Historical Association*, vol. 6, no. 2 (1998): 6-7.

Stockdale, John, ed. *The Parliamentary Register; or, History of the Proceedings and Debates of the House of Commons: Containing an Account of the most interesting Speeches and Motions; accurate Copies of the most remarkable Letters and Papers; of the most material Evidence, Petitions, &c laid before and offered to the House, During the Fifth Session of the Fourteenth Parliament of Great Britain*, Vol. 10 (London: Wilson and Co., 1802): 20-415.

"Stone, John, to William Paca, September 23, 1777." *The Chronicles of Baltimore; Being a Complete History of "Baltimore Town" and Baltimore City From the Earliest Period to the Present Time*. J. Thomas Scharf, ed. Baltimore: Turnbull Brothers, 1874. 166-8.

Stryker, William S., ed. *Documents Relating to the Revolutionary History of the State of New Jersey*, vol. 1, *Extracts from American Newspapers, 1776-1777*. Trenton, NJ: John L. Murphy Publishing Co., 1901.

Sullivan, Thomas. *From Redcoat to Rebel: The Thomas Sullivan Journal*. Joseph Lee Boyle, ed. Bowie, MD: Heritage Books, Inc., 1997.

Syrett, Harold C., ed. *The Papers of Alexander Hamilton*. New York: Columbia Univeristy Press, 1961.

Townsend, Joseph. *Some Account of the British Army, Under the Command of General Howe, and of The Battle of Brandywine, on The Memorable September 11th, 1777, And the Adventure of that Day, Which Came to the Knowledge and Observation of Joseph Townsend*. Philadelphia: Press of the Historical Society of Pennsylvania, 1846.

Twohig, Dorothy, and Philander D. Chase, eds. *The Papers of George Washington, Revolutionary War Series*. Charlottesville and London: University Press of Virginia, 1999.

Von Baurmeister, Carl. "Letters of Major Baurmeister During the Philadelphia Campaign, 1777-1778." *The Pennsylvania Magazine of History and Biography*, vol. 59 (Philadelphia: The Historical Society of Pennsylvania, 1935): 392-409.

"Von Cochenhausen, Johann Ludwig, to Gen. Friedrich von Jungkenn, letter dated October 9, 1777." Henry Retzer and Donald Londahlsmidt, eds. *Journal of the Johannes Schwalm Historical Association*, Vol. 6, no. 2 (1998): 1-6.

Von Donop, Carl. "Letters from a Hessian Mercenary (Colonel von Donop to the Prince of Prussia)." Hans Huth, ed. *Pennsylvania Magazine of History and Biography*, vol. 62 (Philadelphia: The Historical Society of Pennsylvania, 1938): 488-501.

Von Muenchhausen, Friedrich. *At General Howe's Side: 1776-1778: The Diary of General William Howe's aide de camp, Captain Friedrich von Muenchhausen*. Ernst Kipping, trans., and Samuel Steele Smith, ed. Monmouth Beach, NJ: Philip Freneau Press, 1974.

"Von Wurmb, Ludwig, to Gen. Friedrich von Jungkenn, letter dated October 14, 1777." *Journal of the Johannes Schwalm Historical Association*, vol. 6, no. 2 (1998): 7-12.

Watson, Winslow C., ed. *Men and Times of the Revolution; or, Memoirs of Elkannah Watson, Including Journals of Travels in Europe and America, From 1777 to 1842, with his Correspondence with Public Men and Reminiscences and Incidents of the Revolution.* New York: Dana and Company, 1856.

Whinyates, F. A., ed. *The Services of Lieut.-Colonel Francis Downman, R.A. in France, North America, and the West Indies, Between the Years 1758 and 1784.* Woolwich: Royal Artillery Institution, 1898.

Wilkin, Walter Harold. *Some British Soldiers in America.* London: Hugh Rees, Ltd., 1914.

Wortley, Mrs. E. Stuart, ed. *A Prime Minister and His Son: From the Correspondence of the Third Earl of Bute and Lt. General The Honourable Sir Charles Stuart, K.B.* London: John Murray, 1925.

Secondary Sources

Anderson, Fred. *Crucible of War: The Seven Years' War and the Fate of Empire in British North America, 1754-1766.* New York: Vintage Books, 2000.

Anderson, Troyer Steele. *The Command of the Howe Brothers During the American Revolution.* New York and London: Oxford University Press, 1936.

Andrlik, Todd. *Reporting the Revolutionary War: Before it was History, it was News.* Naperville, IL: Sourcebooks, Inc., 2012.

Bailey, DeWitt. *British Military Flintlock Rifles: 1740-1840.* Lincoln, RI: Andrew Mowbray Publishers, 2002.

Bancroft, George. *History of the United States, From the Discovery of the American Continent.* Boston: Little, Brown, & Co., 1866.

Beattie, Daniel J. "The Adaptation of the British Army to Wilderness Warfare, 1755-1763." *Adapting to Conditions: War and Society in the Eighteenth Century.* Maarten Ultee, ed. Birmingham, AL: University of Alabama Press, 1986.

Benninghoff II, Herman O. *Valley Forge: A Genesis for Command and Control, Continental Army Style.* Gettysburg, PA: Thomas Publications, 2001.

Billias, George Athan, ed. *George Washington's Generals and Opponents: Their Exploits and Leadership.* New York: Da Capo Press, 1994.

Blanco, Richard L. *Physician of the American Revolution: Jonathan Potts.* New York: Garland STPM Press, 1979.

Boatner, Mark M. *Encyclopedia of the American Revolution.* New York: David McKay Company, 1966.

Bobrick, Benson. *Angel in Whirlwind.* New York: Penguin Books, 1997.

Bowler, R. Arthur. *Logistics and the Failure of the British Army in America 1775-1783.* Princeton: Princeton University Press, 1975.

Breisach, Ernst. *Historiography: Ancient, Medieval and Modern*. Chicago: The University of Chicago Press, 2007.

Brooks, Noah. *Henry Knox: A Soldier of the Revolution*. New York: G. P. Putnam's Sons, 1900.

Bruce, Robert. *Brandywine: The Battle at Chadds Ford and Birmingham Meeting House, in Adjoining Parts of Chester and Delaware Counties, Pennsylvania, September 11, 1777*. Clinton, NY: Robert Bruce, 1922.

Burnham, Smith. "The Story of the Battle of Brandywine." *Second Report of the Pennsylvania Historical Commission*. Harrisburg, PA: General Assembly, 1918.

Carp, E. Wayne. *To Starve the Army at Pleasure: Continental Army Administrations and American Political Culture, 1775-1783*. Chapel Hill, NC: University of North Carolina Press, 1984.

Chadwick, Bruce. *The First American Army: The Untold Story of George Washington and the Men Behind America's First Fight for Freedom*. Naperville, IL: Sourcebooks, Inc., 2005.

———. *George Washington's War*. Naperville, IL: Sourcebooks, Inc., 2004.

Chernow, Ron. *Washington: A Life*. New York: The Penguin Press, 2010.

Cook, Don. *The Long Fuse: How England Lost the American Colonies, 1760-1785*. New York: The Atlantic Monthly Press, 1995.

Cotter, John L., Daniel G. Roberts, and Michael Parrington. *The Buried Past: An Archaeological History of Philadelphia*. Philadelphia: University of Pennsylvania Press, 1993.

Cox, Caroline. *A Proper Sense of Honor: Service and Sacrifice in George Washington's Army*. Chapel Hill, NC: The University of North Carolina Press, 2004.

Curtis, Edward E. *The British Army in the American Revolution*. Gansevoort, NY: Corner House Historical Publications, 1998.

Drake, Francis S. *Life and Correspondence of Henry Knox, Major-General in the American Revolutionary Army*. Boston: Samuel G. Drake, 1873.

Eastby, Allen G. "Battle of Brandywine: Setback for the Continental Army." *Military History*, December 1998.

Edgar, Gregory T. *The Philadelphia Campaign*. Bowie, MD: Heritage Books, Inc., 1998.

Ferling, John A. *Leap in the Dark: The Struggle to Create the American Republic*. Oxford: Oxford University Press, 2003.

———. *Struggle for a Continent: The Wars of Early America*. Arlington Heights, IL: Harlan Davidson, Inc., 1993.

Fischer, David Hackett. *Washington's Crossing*. Oxford: Oxford University Press, 2004.

Fisher, Sydney George. *The Struggle for American Independence*. Philadelphia: J. B. Lippincott Company, 1908.

Fiske, John. *The American Revolution*. Boston: Houghton Mifflin Company, 1891.

Flexner, James Thomas. *Washington: The Indispensable Man.* Boston: Little, Brown and Company, 1969.

Ford, Worthington Chauncey. *British Officers Serving in the American Revolution, 1774-1783.* Brooklyn: Historical Print Club, 1897.

Frantz, John B., and William Pencak, eds. *Beyond Philadelphia: The American Revolution in the Pennsylvania Hinterland.* University Park, PA: The Pennsylvania State University Press, 1998.

Freeman, Douglas Southall. *George Washington: A Biography: Leader of theRevolution.*, Vol. 4. New York: Scribners, 1951.

Futhey, J. Smith, and Gilbert Cope. *History of Chester County Pennsylvania.* Philadelphia: Louis H. Everts, 1881.

Gilchrist, M. M. *Patrick Ferguson: A Man of Some Genius.* Glasgow: NMS Enterprises Limited, 2003.

Girardin, Louis Hue, and Paul Bentalou. *Pulaski Vindicated from an Unsupported Charge, Inconsiderately or Malignantly.* Baltimore: John Toy, 1824.

Gordon, William. *The History of the Rise, Progress, and Establishment of the Independence of the United States of America: Including an Account of the Late War, and of the Thirteen Colonies, from Their Origin to that Period.* New York: Samuel Campbell, 1801.

Gruber, Ira D. *The Howe Brothers & the American Revolution.* New York: Atheneum, 1972.

Haller, Stephen E. *William Washington: Cavalryman of the Revolution.* Bowie, MD: Heritage Books, Inc., 2001.

Hay, Denys. "The Denouement of General Howe's Campaign of 1777." *English Historical Review*, vol. 74 (1964): 498-512.

Hibbert, Christopher. *Redcoats and Rebels.* New York: W. W. Norton & Company, 1990.

Isaacson, Walter. Benjamin Franklin: An American Life. New York, 2003.

Jackson, John W. *The Pennsylvania Navy, 1775-1781: The Defense of the Delaware.* New Brunswick, NJ: Rutgers University Press, 1974.

———. *With the British Army in Philadelphia.* San Rafael, CA: Presidio Press, 1979.

Jenkins, Howard M. "Brandywine, 1777." *Lippincott's Magazine of Popular Literature and Science*, vol. 20 (London, September 1877): 329-39.

Jomini, Baron de. *The Art of War.* Philadelphia, 1862; reprint, Westport, CT: Greenwood Press, 1974.

Katcher, Philip R. N. *Encyclopedia of British, Provincial, and German Army Units 1775-1783.* Harrisburg, PA: Stackpole Books, 1973.

Ketchum, Richard M. *Saratoga: Turning Point of America's Revolutionary War.* New York: Henry Holt and Company, 1997.

Knouff, Gregory T. *The Soldiers' Revolution: Pennsylvanians in Arms and the Forging of Early American Identity.* University Park, PA: Pennsylvania State University Press, 2004.

Krick, Robert K. *Stonewall Jackson at Cedar Mountain*. Chapel Hill, NC: The University of North Carolina Press, 1990.

Lewis, Charlton T., ed. *Lafayette at Brandywine: Containing the Proceedings at the Dedication of the Memorial to Mark the Place Where Lafayette Was Wounded at the Battle of Brandywine*. West Chester, PA: Chester County Historical Society, 1896.

Leach, Douglas Edward. *Roots of Conflict: British Armed Forces and Colonial Americans, 1677-1763*. Chapel Hill, NC: The University of North Carolina Press, 1986.

Lefkowitz, Arthur S. *George Washington's Indispensable Men: The 32 Aides-de-Camp Who Helped Win American Independence*. Mechanicsburg, PA: Stackpole Books, 2003.

——. *The Long Retreat: The Calamitous American Defense of New Jersey 1776*. New Brunswick: Rutgers University Press, 1999.

Lemon, James T. *The Best Poor Man's Country: Early Southeastern Pennsylvania*. Baltimore: The Johns Hopkins University Press, 1972.

Lengel, Edward. *General George Washington: A Military Life*. New York: Random House, 2005.

Lossing, Benson J. *The Pictorial Field-Book of the American Revolution*. New York: Harper and Brothers, 1852.

Lowell, Edward J. *The Hessians and the Other German Auxiliaries of Great Britain in the Revolutionary War*. Gansevoort, NY: Corner House Historical Publications, 1997.

Luzader, John F. *Saratoga: A Military History of the Decisive Campaign of the American Revolution*. New York: Savas Beatie, 2008.

MacElree, Wilmer W., Charles W. Heathcote, and Christian C. Sanderson. "Battle of Brandywine." 150th Anniversary of the Battle of Brandywine. Brandywine Memorial Association, 1927.

Mackesy, Piers. *The War for America: 1775-1783*. Lincoln, NE: University of Nebraska Press, 1964.

Mahon, John K. "Anglo-American Methods of Indian Warfare, 1676-1794." LW524: Student Reading Package, APUS Faculty, Fall 2009. Charles Town, WV: National Archive Publishing Company, 2009.

Martin, David G. *The Philadelphia Campaign: June 1777-July 1778*. Conshohocken, PA: Combined Books, Inc., 1993.

Mayer, Holly A. *Belonging to the Army: Camp Followers and Community during the American Revolution*. Columbia, SC: University of South Carolina Press, 1996.

McGuire, Thomas J. *The Philadelphia Campaign: Brandywine and the Fall of Philadelphia*. Mechanicsburg, PA: Stackpole Books, 2006.

——. *The Philadelphia Campaign: Germantown and the Roads to Valley Forge*. Mechanicsburg, PA: Stackpole Books, 2007.

Millett, Allan R., and Peter Maslowski. *For the Common Defense: A Military History of the United States of America*. New York: The Free Press, 1994.

Mowday, Bruce E. *September 11, 1777: Washington's Defeat at Brandywine Dooms Philadelphia*. Shippensburg, PA: White Mane Books, 2002.

Neff, Jacob. *The Army and Navy of America: Containing a View of the Heroic Adventures, Battles, Naval Engagements, Remarkable Incidents, and Glorious Achievements in the Cause of Freedom*. Philadelphia: J.H. Pearsol & Co., 1845.

Newcomb, Benjamin H. *Franklin and Galloway: A Political Partnership*. New Haven, CT: Yale University Press, 1972.

Newland, Samuel J. *The Pennsylvania Militia: The Early Years, 1669-1792*. Annville, PA: Commonwealth of Pennsylvania, The Department of Military and Veterans Affairs, 1997.

Pancake, John S. *1777: The Year of the Hangman*. Tuscaloosa, AL: The University of Alabama Press, 1977.

Patterson, Benton Rain. *Washington and Cornwallis: The Battle for America, 1775-1783*. Lanham, MD: Taylor Trade Publishing, 2004.

Pearson, Michael. *Those Damned Rebels: The American Revolution as Seen Through British Eyes*. Cambridge, MA: Da Capo Press, 2000.

Peckham, Howard H. *The Colonial Wars: 1689-1762*. Chicago: The University of Chicago Press, 1964.

Pickering, Octavius. *The Life of Timothy Pickering*. Boston: Little, Brown and Company, 1867.

Pierce, Arthur D. *Smugglers' Woods: Jaunts and Journeys in Colonial and Revolutionary New Jersey*. New Brunswick, NJ: Rutgers University Press, 1960.

Reed, John F. *Campaign to Valley Forge: July 1, 1777-December 19, 1777*. Philadelphia: Pioneer Press, 1965.

Resch, John, and Walter Sargent, eds. *War & Society in the American Revolution: Mobilization and Home Fronts*. DeKalb, IL: Northern Illinois University Press, 2007.

Roberts, Ricky, and Bryan Brown. *Every Insult & Indignity: The Life, Genius and Legacy of Major Patrick Ferguson*. Lexington, KY: self published, 2011.

Rosswurm, Steven. *Arms, Country, and Class: The Philadelphia Militia and the "Lower Sort" during the American Revolution*. New Brunswick, NJ: Rutgers University Press, 1989.

Royster, Charles. *A Revolutionary People at War: The Continental Army & American Character, 1775-1783*. Chapel Hill: The University of North Carolina Press, 1979.

Russell, Peter E. "Redcoats in the Wilderness: British Officers and Irregular Warfare in Europe and America, 1740-1760." LW524: Student Reading Package, APUS Faculty, Fall 2009. Charles Town, WV: National Archive Publishing Company, 2009.

Ryan, Beth-Ann. "Where was the American Flag first flown in battle? Was it Cooch's Bridge?" http://library.blogs.delaware.gov/2011/06/14/american-flag-first-flown-in-blattle/. Accessed April 2, 2013.

Scheer, George F., and Hugh F. Rankin. *Rebels & Redcoats: The American Revolution Through the Eyes of Those Who Fought and Lived It*. New York: Da Capo Press, 1957.

Smith, Samuel S. *The Battle of Brandywine*. Monmouth Beach, NJ: Philip Freneau Press, 1976.

Spring, Matthew H. *With Zeal and With Bayonets Only: The British Army on Campaign in North America, 1775-1783*. Norman, OK: University of Oklahoma Press, 2008.

Steele, Ian K. *Warpaths: Invasions of North America*. New York: Oxford University Press, 1994.

Stember, Sol. *The Bicentennial Guide to the American Revolution: The Middle Colonies* , vol. 2. New York: E. P. Dutton, 1974.

Stille, Charles J. *Major-General Anthony Wayne and the Pennsylvania Line in the Continental Army*. Philadelphia: J.B. Lippincott, 1893.

Summers, William. "Obituary Notices of Pennsylvania Soldiers of the Revolution." *The Pennsylvania Magazine of History and Biography*, vol. 38 (Philadelphia: The Historical Society of Pennsylvania, 1914): 443-60.

Trussell, John B. B. *The Pennsylvania Line*. Harrisburg, PA: Commonwealth of Pennsylvania, Historical and Museum Commission, 1993.

Unger, Harlow Giles. *Lafayette*. Hoboken, NJ: John Wiley & Sons, Inc., 2002.

Urban, Mark. *Fusiliers: The Saga of a British Redcoat Regiment in the American Revolution*. New York: Walker and Company, 2007.

Van Buskirk, Judith L. *Generous Enemies: Patriots and Loyalists in Revolutionary New York*. Philadelphia: University of Pennsylvania Press, 2002.

Von Clausewitz, Carl. *On War*. Michael Howard and Pater Paret, eds. Princeton: Princeton Univeristy Press, 1976. 61-637.

Ward, Christopher. *The War of the Revolution*. 2 vols. New York: Macmillan Company, 1952.

Wood, W. J. *Battles of the Revolutionary War: 1775-1781*. Cambridge, MA: Da Capo Press, 1990.

Index

About the Author

Michael C. Harris is a graduate of the University of Mary Washington and the American Military University. He has worked for the National Park Service in Fredericksburg, Virginia, Fort Mott State Park in New Jersey, and the Pennsylvania Historical and Museum Commission at Brandywine Battlefield. He has conducted tours and staff rides of many east coast battlefields and enjoys speaking with audiences about all things military, and especially the American Revolution and Civil War.

Michael is certified in secondary education and currently teaches in the Philadelphia region. He lives in Pennsylvania with his wife Michelle and son Nathanael. *Brandywine: A Military History of the Battle that Lost Philadelphia but Saved America, September 11, 1777* is his first book.